Income-Tested Transfer Programs
THE CASE FOR AND AGAINST

Income-Tested Transfer Programs
THE CASE FOR AND AGAINST

A 1979 Conference

FUNDED BY
> *The Ford Foundation*
> *The Social Security Administration*

SPONSORED BY
> *The Institute for Research on Poverty*
> *The Ford Foundation*
> *The Social Security Administration*

This is a volume in the

INSTITUTE FOR RESEARCH ON POVERTY
MONOGRAPH SERIES

A complete list of titles in this series appears at the end of this volume.

Income-Tested Transfer Programs

THE CASE FOR AND AGAINST

Edited by

IRWIN GARFINKEL

Institute for Research on Poverty
University of Wisconsin–Madison

ACADEMIC PRESS
A Subsidiary of Harcourt Brace Jovanovich, Publishers
New York   London
Paris   San Diego   San Francisco   São Paulo   Sydney   Tokyo   Toronto

This book is one of a series sponsored by the Institute for Research on Poverty
of the University of Wisconsin pursuant to the provisions of the
Economic Opportunity Act of 1964.

ACADEMIC PRESS, INC.
111 Fifth Avenue, New York, New York 10003

United Kingdom Edition published by
ACADEMIC PRESS, INC. (LONDON) LTD.
24/28 Oval Road, London NW1 7DX

Library of Congress Cataloging in Publication Data
Main entry under title:

Income-tested transfer programs.

(Institute for Research on Poverty monograph series)
Proceedings of a 1979 conference sponsored by the
Institute for Research on Poverty, the Ford Foundation,
and the Social Security Administration.
Includes bibliographical references and index.
1. Income maintenance programs--Congresses.
2. Public welfare--Congresses. I. Garfinkel, Irwin.
II. University of Wisconsin--Madison. Institute for
Research on Poverty. III. Ford Foundation. IV. United
States. Social Security Administration. V. Series.
HC79.I5I49 1982   362.5'82   82-8697
ISBN 0-12-275880-3   AACR2

PRINTED IN THE UNITED STATES OF AMERICA

82 83 84 85   9 8 7 6 5 4 3 2 1

Contents

1

Introduction   1

    IRWIN GARFINKEL

2

Stigma in Income-Tested Programs   19

    LEE RAINWATER

3

Income Testing and Social Cohesion   67

JAMES COLEMAN

4

Income Testing and Politics: A Theoretical Model   97

GORDON TULLOCK

5

Social Policy Development in Europe and America: A Longer View on Selectivity and Income Testing   141

ARNOLD J. HEIDENHEIMER with JOHN LAYSON

6

A Simulation Analysis of the Economic Efficiency and Distributional Effects of Alternative Program Structures: The Negative Income Tax versus the Credit Income Tax   175

DAVID BETSON, DAVID GREENBERG, and RICHARD KASTEN

7

Taxpayer Behavior and the Design of a Credit Income Tax   215

JONATHAN R. KESSELMAN

8

Income Testing and Social Welfare: An Optimal Tax–Transfer Model   291

EFRAIM SADKA, IRWIN GARFINKEL, and KEMPER MORELAND

9

Income Testing of In-Kind Transfers   325

BRIAN ABEL-SMITH

13
Conclusion   495
IRWIN GARFINKEL

List of Figures and Tables

Contributors

Numbers in parentheses indicate the pages on which the authors' contributions begin.

HENRY AARON (212), Senior Fellow, The Brookings Institution, Washington, D.C. 20036, and Professor of Economics, University of Maryland, College Park, Maryland 20742

BRIAN ABEL-SMITH (325), Professor of Social Administration, University of London, London, England WC2A 2AE

VERNON L. ALLEN (47), Professor of Psychology, University of Wisconsin–Madison, Madison, Wisconsin 53706

KENNETH J. ARROW (319), Joan Kenney Professor of Economics and Professor of Operations Research, Stanford University, Stanford, California 94305

DAVID BERRY (449), Graduate Student, Department of Economics, University of Wisconsin–Madison, Madison, Wisconsin 53706

DAVID BETSON (175), Research Affiliate, Institute for Research on Poverty, University of Wisconsin–Madison, Madison, Wisconsin 53706

JOHN BISHOP (59), Research Affiliate, Institute for Research on Poverty, University of Wisconsin–Madison, Madison, Wisconsin, and Associate Director, Research Division, National Center for Research in Vocational Education, Columbus, Ohio 43210

EVELINE M. BURNS (344), Professor Emeritus, Columbia University School of Social Work, New York, New York 10027

JUDITH H. CASSETTY (432), Assistant Professor of Social Work, University of Texas at Austin, Austin, Texas 78712

JAMES COLEMAN (67), Professor of Sociology, University of Chicago, Chicago, Illinois 60637

PETER DIAMOND (314), Professor of Economics, Massachusetts Institute of Technology, Cambridge, Massachusetts 02139

ANTHONY DOWNS (117), Senior Fellow, The Brookings Institution, Washington, D.C. 20036

IRWIN GARFINKEL (1, 291, 449, 495), Professor of Social Work, and Research Affiliate, Institute for Research on Poverty, University of Wisconsin–Madison, Madison, Wisconsin 53706

EDWARD M. GRAMLICH (204), Professor of Economics, University of Michigan, Ann Arbor, Michigan 48104

DAVID GREENBERG (175), Economist, SRI International, Menlo Park, California 94305

ARNOLD J. HEIDENHEIMER (141), Professor of Political Science, Washington University, St. Louis, Missouri 63130

GEORGE JAKUBSON (405), Graduate Student, Institute for Research on Poverty, University of Wisconsin–Madison, Madison, Wisconsin 53706

CHRISTOPHER JENCKS (89), Professor of Sociology, Northwestern University, Evanston, Illinois 60201

RICHARD KASTEN (175), Staff Economist, Office of Income Security Policy, Department of Health and Human Services, Washington, D.C. 20036

JONATHAN R. KESSELMAN (215), Associate Professor of Economics, University of British Columbia, Vancouver, British Columbia V6T 1Y2, Canada

ROBERT J. LAMPMAN (164), Professor of Economics, and Research Affiliate, Institute for Research on Poverty, University of Wisconsin–Madison, Madison, Wisconsin 53706

JOHN LAYSON (141), Graduate Student, Department of Political Science, Washington University, St. Louis, Missouri 63130

ROBERT I. LERMAN (444), Senior Research Associate and Adjunct Lecturer, Florence Heller Graduate School for Advanced Studies in Social Welfare, Brandeis University, Waltham, Massachusetts 02254

STEPHEN H. LONG (367), Assistant Professor of Economics, The Maxwell School, Syracuse University, Syracuse, New York 13210

KEMPER MORELAND (291), Assistant Professor of Economics, Eastern Michigan University, Ypsilanti, Michigan 48197

ALICIA H. MUNNELL (481), Vice President and Economist, Federal Reserve Bank of Boston, Boston, Massachusetts 02210

RAYMOND MUNTS (449), Professor of Social Work, University of Wisconsin–Madison, Madison, Wisconsin 53706

LARRY ORR (129), Director, Office of Technical Analysis, Office of the Assistant Secretary for Policy, Evaluation, and Research, Department of Labor, Washington, D.C. 20210

BENJAMIN I. PAGE (136), Associate Professor of Political Science, University of Chicago, Chicago, Illinois 60637

JOHN L. PALMER (367), Senior Fellow, Urban Institute, Washington, D.C. 20037 (on leave from the federal government)

JOSEPH A. PECHMAN (282), Director, Economic Studies Program, The Brookings Institution, Washington, D.C. 20036

LEE RAINWATER (19), Professor of Sociology, Harvard University, Cambridge, Massachusetts 02138

MARTIN REIN (351), Professor of Urban Studies, Massachusetts Institute of Technology, Cambridge, Massachusetts 02139

EARL R. ROLPH (285), Professor of Economics, University of California, Berkeley, Berkeley, California 94720

EFRAIM SADKA (291), Senior Lecturer in Economics, Tel Aviv University, and Research Affiliate, Institute for Research on Poverty, University of Wisconsin–Madison, Madison, Wisconsin 53706

ALVIN L. SCHORR (55), Professor of Family and Child Welfare, School of Applied Social Sciences, Case Western Reserve University, Cleveland, Ohio 44106

FELICITY SKIDMORE (405), Editorial Consultant and Director of Special Projects, Institute for Research on Poverty, University of Wisconsin–Madison, Madison, Wisconsin 53706

LAWRENCE H. THOMPSON (487), Director, Office of Research and Statistics, Social Security Administration, Washington, D.C. 20009

GORDON TULLOCK (97), University Distinguished Professor, Virginia Polytechnic Institute, Blacksburg, Virginia 24601

HAROLD W. WATTS (405), Professor of Economics and Director of the Center for the Social Sciences, Columbia University, New York, New York 10027

HAROLD L. WILENSKY (166), Professor of Sociology, University of California, Berkeley, Berkeley, California 94720

BARBARA L. WOLFE (400), Associate Professor of Preventive Medicine and Economics, and Research Affiliate, Institute for Research on Poverty, University of Wisconsin–Madison, Madison, Wisconsin 53706

Foreword

A new era of radical experimentation with the income-transfer system may be on the horizon. The "New Federalism" proposes to give to the states wide latitude to restructure two of this nation's largest income-tested programs: Aid to Families with Dependent Children (AFDC) and the Food Stamp program. We have in prospect, then, fifty very different programs. One option will be to design entirely new programs intended to achieve the same general objectives as AFDC and Food Stamps but without any income-testing provisions. For example, a universal child allowance, available to all, but taxable, might replace AFDC. A refundable credit income tax at the state level could make Food Stamps unnecessary. There is ample evidence that such options are practical, since they are in place in various Western European countries or in Canada. It can happen here. It is therefore most fortuitous that this volume should appear at this time, for these papers weigh the advantages and disadvantages of income testing in the administration of transfers.

The complexity of the problem was evident at the outset, as the participants struggled to determine the salient distinction between income-tested and non-income-tested transfer programs. The criterion that emerged—income-tested programs are those with a higher marginal tax rate on the poor than is experienced by those who are not poor—

illustrates the maze that must be threaded. The distinction is hardly intuitively appealing. Indeed, to the nonspecialist it undoubtedly seems to fasten onto an irrelevancy. Not so, of course, which is ample evidence of the need for this set of papers.

The authors represent an international and interdisciplinary sampling from among the best of policy analysts. They thought hard, argued fiercely, and wrote and rewrote tenaciously. The result is focused discussion, with breadth and depth on an emerging area of great significance. The Institute is proud to put this book before the public.

EUGENE SMOLENSKY
Director, Institute for Research on Poverty

1

Introduction

IRWIN GARFINKEL

Most Americans now believe that it is the responsibility of government to assure a certain minimum level of living to American citizens. No disagreement exists between the Democratic and Republican parties on this score. Of course there is now and always will be disagreement concerning just what the minimum level of living is that we should assure to our citizens. For example, whereas former President Carter proposed some expansions in programs assuring minimums, President Reagan proposes to take away welfare support from those who are near-poor and even from some who are poor. But he has not proposed that such benefits be eliminated entirely.

There is also disagreement about how the government should assure this minimum. Should the government assure the minimum by providing cash or by providing goods and services? Should the government provide minima to everyone or only to certain groups? This book is addressed to a particular aspect of the last question: namely, should the government provide minima only to the poor, or to all regardless of income?

At least since the enactment of universal elementary and secondary public education in the early nineteenth century, government(s) in the United States have done both. Welfare programs, that is, those designed to aid only the poor, date back to the prerevolutionary colonial governments. The Social Security Act in 1935, an outgrowth of the Depression, brought the federal government into the area with some programs, like Old Age Insurance and Unemployment Insurance, open to all regardless of income, and others, like Aid to Dependent Children, Aid to the Aged, and Aid to the Blind, open to only the destitute. Costs of programs for all obviously dominated welfare expenditures.

The Civil Rights Movement, the War on Poverty and the Great Society led to a new outburst of social legislation in the 1960s and early 1970s. Medicaid, Food Stamps, and Supplemental Security Income were new programs for only the poor, while Medicare was open to all the aged regardless of income. During this period of expansion, expenditures on welfare programs grew more rapidly than those on nonwelfare programs. Indeed by the end of the 1960s a consensus had developed in both the academic and policy worlds that welfare or, to use the more technical term, income-tested programs were somehow superior to non-income-tested programs.

To address the question of whether social science knowledge justified the consensus in favor of income testing, a conference of leading social scientists was convened. The papers in this book were first presented at that two-day conference (March 15 and 16, 1979) sponsored by the Institute for Research on Poverty.

Aside from the question of how high the minimum level of support should be, the degree to which benefits should be income-tested may now be the critical issue in income maintenance policy. It is the principal source of disagreement between advocates of alternative methods of integrating the Supplemental Security Income and the Old Age Insurance programs. It plays a key role in determining alternative positions on the national health insurance issue. It crops up in the debate over what kind of public financing should be provided for day care and higher education. It is the primary source of difference between the credit income tax and the negative income tax. Finally, it underlies differences in approach to increasing the well-being and/or work effort of female-headed families with children. More broadly, the income-testing issue devolves into the issue of what kind of a society and economy we wish to have.

A second reason for the conference and this volume is that income maintenance policy since World War II has been characterized by piecemeal changes to one part of the system, then another, without any serious, general consideration being given to the kind of system that over the long run we really want to achieve. Systematic thought about the long-run direction that reform should take is long overdue.

Eleven papers were commissioned for the conference. These, along with comments of the formal discussants, are reproduced in this vol-

ume. Each author was assigned the task of asking what socia
knowledge and analysis could contribute to settling the argun
the current debate about the merits of income testing in transf
grams. Social scientists qua scientists cannot, of course, provide answers
to such broad questions as what kind of society we want to live in or
even to more narrow questions, such as whether we should have an
income-tested or a non-income-tested program. For, as in all social policy choices, the choice depends upon values as well as facts; upon what
people value as well as upon how the world works. (Because of this,
participation of social scientists from all parts of the political spectrum
was solicited.) But given their knowledge about how the world works,
social scientists can help us to understand what the consequences of
alternative policy choices are. Conference participants—77 in all, including authors and discussants and others drawn both from the academic
community and from the public policy arena—struggled with the issue
for two days. Not surprisingly, given the basic nature of the topic, the
sessions stimulated lively discussion and elicited strongly held views.
This introductory chapter sets the stage for the conference papers and
the formal comments of the discussants. The next four sections (*a*) define more precisely the terms "income-tested" and "non-income-
tested"; (*b*) discuss the historical importance of the income-testing issue
and briefly trace the development of both income-tested and non-
income-tested programs in the United States; (*c*) present a brief overview of our current income support system; and (*d*) discuss the issues in
the income-testing debate and relate the conference papers to them.
Chapters 2–12 consist of the conference papers plus the comments of the
formal discussants. In the concluding chapter I draw upon these papers,
the comments, and the informal discussion at the conference itself to
summarize what the conference has taught us. I argue that on
balance—given values held by myself and, I believe, most Americans—
the evidence indicates we have too much income testing in our overall
income maintenance system. Consequently, I conclude the chapter with
a reform agenda designed to reduce the role of income testing.

Terms and Concepts

In non-income-tested programs rich and poor alike participate. Eligibility does not depend on income. Nor are gross (before-tax) benefits
related to income per se. The net (after-tax) benefit, of course, depends
on the amount of taxes paid and will vary with income to the extent that
the tax system does. In this sense public education, Social Security, and

Medicare are not income tested. In income-tested or welfare programs, only those with low incomes (and usually low assets as well) are eligible to participate. Gross as well as net benefits explicitly decline with income. Aid to Families with Dependent Children, Food Stamps, and Medicaid are income tested.

In order to confine benefits to low-income people, income-tested programs reduce benefits as income rises. A 50% benefit-reduction rate is equivalent to a 50% tax rate. Consequently, income-tested programs impose higher marginal tax rates on their beneficiaries than is imposed on the rest of the population to finance the program.[1] That is, by their nature, income-tested programs, which confine benefits to the poor, result in tax–transfer regimes with regressive marginal tax-rate schedules. By contrast non-income-tested tax–transfer regimes may be, but need not be, regressive; they may or may not lead to regressive marginal tax rates. The retirement (or earnings) test in Old Age Insurance, for example, places a higher tax rate on low than on high earnings. The work test in Unemployment Insurance has the same economic properties. Thus, it is possible for programs that are non-income-tested in administrative terms to have economic attributes of income testing. (See Arrow's and Aaron's discussions of Chapters 6 and 8, respectively.) Despite this possibility, in this chapter, an income-tested tax–transfer regime is defined as one in which marginal tax rates faced by the poor exceed those faced by the nonpoor, while a non-income-tested regime is defined as one in which marginal tax rates on the poor are equal to or less than tax rates on the nonpoor.

Income testing is not the only characteristic by which to distinguish among income maintenance programs. There are categorical and non-categorical programs, social insurance and non-social-insurance programs, and cash and in-kind programs. None of these other distinctions relate in any unique way to income testing. A categorical program is one in which eligibility is limited to certain groups in the population—such as the aged or children. Old Age Insurance and children's allowances are categorical non-income-tested programs as the terms are used here; Supplemental Security Income is a categorical income-tested program; a program for which eligibility depends *only* on income, such as the negative income tax (NIT), is a noncategorical income-tested program; a pro-

---

[1]Marginal tax rates refer to the tax rate on either an additional dollar of earnings or the last dollar of earnings. Average tax rates are measured by total taxes paid divided by total income. If benefits in a transfer program are reduced by 50 cents for each dollar earned, the marginal tax rate is 50%. Yet a transfer program pays out benefits rather than collecting taxes. Thus the average tax rate can be said to be negative, hence the term "negative tax." Income-tested transfer programs which pay out benefits to more than half the population need not result in a regressive marginal tax rate structure.

gram in which gross benefits are paid to everyone in society, such as a credit income tax (CIT), is a noncategorical, non-income-tested program. The term "universal" is reserved in this essay to describe programs that are noncategorical and non-income-tested. However, several authors use the term as a synonym for a non-income-tested program. (In my original correspondence with authors I also used the term that way.)

The benefits of social insurance programs do not depend upon income directly but rather upon some event which in practice is closely related to income, at least in the short run. In the United States social insurance programs are non-income-tested. Yet the first old-age insurance program, which was instituted in Germany, was confined to low-income workers. Moreover, not all non-income-tested programs are social insurance programs. Social insurance programs like Unemployment Insurance, Workers' Compensation, Old Age, Disability, and Survivors' Insurance provide cash benefits that are positively related to previous income. This is not the case for in-kind social insurance programs nor for all non-income-tested cash programs. Public education, the British national health service, and, in most countries, programs that provide allowances for children are examples of non-income-tested programs that are not of the social insurance type. A national health insurance program is an example of an insurance program in which eligibility and benefits do not depend upon previous income, although in some countries eligibility may depend upon having been in covered employment. (See Table 1.1 for a categorization of the major programs in the United States today.)

Historical Importance of the Income-Testing Issue

The debate over the merits of income testing is not new. In this country it goes back to at least the 1820s, when the issue arose in connection with the provision of free public education.[2] Many had favored subsidizing

[2]In Great Britain, the debate goes back to the 1905 Royal Commission on the Poor Laws. Beatrice Webb, who wrote the minority report, which was to become the income maintenance reform agenda for democratic socialists in Western Europe and liberals in the United States throughout most of the twentieth century, argued for breaking up the old Poor Law, a noncategorical income-tested program, by enacting a set of non-income-tested, mostly social insurance, programs (see Great Britain, Royal Commission on the Poor Laws, 1909). Unfortunately, as a consequence, the income-testing issue has often been posed as noncategorical income-tested programs versus categorical social insurance programs.

the education of only the poor. By about 1850, however, the issue had been settled in favor of universal free public education, a non-income-tested system.

The 1935 Social Security Act, which established the basic framework of our current income support system, contained both income-tested and non-income-tested programs. Two were social insurance: Old Age Insurance (OAI) and Unemployment Insurance (UI). Three were welfare: Aid to the Blind (AB), Old Age Assistance (OAA), and Aid to Dependent Children (ADC). The architects of the act considered the non-income-tested programs a more appropriate and a more important way of aiding both the typical workers and the less fortunate members of our society (Witte, 1973). The rationale for the Old Age Assistance program was to provide aid to the current aged poor who had not contributed to and were therefore not eligible for the Old Age Insurance program. As the Old Age Insurance program matured, it was fully expected that the number of beneficiaries of Old Age Assistance would dwindle. (Ironically, during the debate prior to the passage of the landmark Social Security Act, the OAA program was the most controversial of the welfare programs.) The welfare programs for both the blind and dependent children were also expected to remain small. The latter was viewed as a program for aiding widows. The architects of the Social Security Act expected future amendments to create a survivors' insurance program.

During the period between 1935 and the War on Poverty, social insurance programs were expanded with a view to reducing the role of welfare. But new welfare programs were also created and existing ones changed in ways that increased the role of welfare. Most important, the growth in the frequency of divorce, desertion, and out-of-wedlock births converted Aid to Dependent Children from a minor, relatively uncontroversial welfare program into the focal point of the welfare reform debate in the 1960s, 1970s, and 1980s.

The first major reform of the Social Security Act came in 1938, when Old Age Insurance was modified to reduce poverty and the reliance of the aged on welfare. Social security benefits were extended to survivors (the Survivors' Insurance program) and dependents of covered workers. Retirement benefits were tied to earnings over a minimum covered period rather than to lifetime earnings. And a minimum benefit unrelated to covered lifetime earnings was also introduced into the system. These reforms permitted benefits to be paid which were far in excess of the value of the taxes of the retirees: their contributions to the system. It was hoped that the Survivors' Insurance program would in time reduce the need for Aid to Dependent Children and that making Old Age Insurance more effective in reducing poverty would reduce the need for Old Age Assistance. In 1950, the Social Security Act was again amended to add a new categorical welfare program—Aid to the Permanently and Totally Disabled (APTD). In 1956 a further amendment created the Disability Insurance program.

In the 1960 presidential election the income-testing issue arose in the context of what kind of health insurance coverage to provide for the aged. Kennedy favored an insurance approach; Nixon, a welfare or income-tested approach. In 1965 Congress compromised and gave us both Medicare, which is not income tested, and Medicaid, which is.

As the 1960s progressed, the many proponents who agreed on the need for more generous and more widely spread income support again split on the issue of income testing. This time the debate took the form of whether to favor a children's allowance or a negative income tax (NIT) proposal.[3] The principal focus was on how to aid the so-called working poor. Since the middle of the 1960s, one of the most important criticisms of our income-tested transfer system was that it did not cover the working poor. The "working poor" are families headed by able-bodied adults expected to work, whose incomes, despite full-time or near full-time work, are below what is considered an acceptable minimum level. It used to be that only nonaged males were expected to work. As of the early 1970s, 40% of all poor people still lived in such families; in half of these families, the male head worked *full time* all year round. (Now, many expect single mothers to work. If they are counted, in 1980 well over half of all poor people must be counted among the working poor.)

Failure to cover the working poor had been criticized on three grounds. First, it was argued that because the working poor constitute

[3]Most income maintenance experts from the economics profession favored a negative income tax, while most from the social work profession favored a children's allowance. Milton Friedman, Robert Lampman, and James Tobin were the most important advocates in the economics profession. See Friedman (1962); Tobin (1966); and Green and Lampman (1967). There were, however, notable exceptions on both sides. Perhaps the best-known exchange in the 1960s on this issue is the James Tobin–Alvin Schorr debate in the Summer and Fall 1966 issues of the *Public Interest*. Edward Schwartz and Alan Wade, both faculty members at the University of Chicago School of Social Service Administration, favored a negative income tax. James Vadakin and Harvey Brazer were the principal advocates in the economics profession of a children's allowance (see Vadakin, 1968, and Brazer, 1969). Brazer's proposal was actually a cleverly designed compromise between income testing and non-income-testing designed to achieve the major benefits of non-income-tested programs and the apparent small budget costs of income testing. The foremost American economist who advocated children's allowances, was of course, Paul Douglas (1927). Eveline Burns, though an economist, was identified with the social welfare profession (she taught at the Columbia School of Social Work during the 1960s) and was the foremost advocate of children's allowances in that profession (Burns, 1965b).

such a large proportion of the total number of poor people, transfer programs that do not cover the working poor obviously cannot eliminate poverty. Second, providing aid to one group of poor persons (such as female-headed families) but not to another equally poor group is inequitable. Third, the existence of this horizontal inequity between male-headed and female-headed families creates an incentive for the breakup of families. Given these strong arguments for coverage of the working poor, why had they not been covered by cash transfer programs?

At least two reasons seem to explain the omission of the working poor from the system. The first reason is the public's fear that, if aided, large numbers of male heads of families would either reduce their work effort substantially or quit work entirely. Most of the empirical evidence suggests that reductions in the work effort of male heads would be quite small. Nevertheless, concern about work effort still persists.

A second reason for noncoverage of the working poor was that reducing poverty had only recently become an explicit objective of public policy. Prior to the 1960s the principal objective of our income transfer system was to reduce economic insecurity. The idea was to replace a *normal* flow of earnings that, for some unavoidable reason, had been interrupted. If earnings were reduced because of retirement, there was Old Age Insurance; if because of disability, Disability Insurance; if because of the death of the breadwinner, Survivors' Insurance; if because of unemployment, Unemployment Insurance. As noted above, the three federal income-tested transfer programs that were established by the 1935 Social Security Act—Aid to the Aged, Aid to Dependent Children, and Aid to the Blind—were supposed to be small programs that would wither away as the social insurance system matured. It was as if poverty was viewed as just a special case of economic insecurity.

In the 1960s, however, it began to be emphasized that income insecurity was only one cause of economic hardship. Many poor people have not suffered a significant, sudden reduction in their normal earnings. They are poor because the family head does not have capacity to earn enough income to provide what, in society's judgment, is a minimally acceptable standard of living. This emphasis upon the working poor was due, at least in part, to the adoption of poverty elimination as an explicit object of public policy in the 1964 Economic Opportunity Act, and, perhaps even more important, to the development and acceptance of an official government definition of poverty. Once poverty was defined and measured, it was possible to identify the large proportion of the poor who were "working poor." The data made clear that poverty is neither identical with nor simply a special case of economic insecurity. Many who suffer a sudden reduction in their customary income flow are not poor; many who are poor are *at* their normal income level. If reducing income poverty is a social objective, even the elimination of income insecurity will not achieve it.

Moreover, if poverty is defined not in absolute terms but in relation to the income of others—that is, when it is based on a relative standard, as it has been over the long run in the past—poverty, including that among families with able-bodied male heads, will continue to exist. Even with economic growth and greater general prosperity, the need for income-transfer programs would not be likely to vanish. By the late 1960s, analysts had reached a consensus that the working poor should be aided. Moreover, income testing appeared to have won the day in academic and policy analytic circles.

President Johnson's Income Maintenance Commission recommended a negative income tax. President Nixon's proposal for a Family Assistance Program (FAP) was essentially a cash negative income tax for families with children. Two subsequent studies of the welfare system by the Department of Health, Education, and Welfare in 1972 and Congress in 1974 also recommended enactment of NITs. But FAP never passed Congress, in part because of reluctance to aid families headed by able-bodied males through welfare and in part because of the high tax rates that FAP would have imposed on beneficiary families.

Although FAP was never enacted, income testing grew dramatically between the advent of the War on Poverty and the mid-1970s. New programs were added and old ones expanded. Particularly notable was the expansion of in-kind aid. Medicaid has already been mentioned. In addition, Congress enacted the Food Stamp program in 1964 and amended it in 1971 and 1973 to turn it into the country's first noncategorical welfare program, entitling all Americans to a uniform nationwide minimum-income guarantee in food purchasing power. Title IV of the 1965 Higher Education Act created a new program of educational opportunity grants, which provided federal scholarships to needy students. Amendments in 1972 changed the name of the program to the Basic Educational Opportunity Grants (BEOG) program and liberalized it somewhat. The Supplemental Security Income (SSI) program, enacted in 1972 to take effect in 1974, established for the first time a federal minimum cash income for the aged, blind, and disabled ($1752 per adult and $2628 per couple). This amounted to about 75% of the poverty level for a single individual and almost 90% for a couple. Also for the first time, benefits in a welfare program were indexed to the cost of living.

The Earned Income Tax Credit, which, like SSI, emerged out of the debate over President Nixon's proposal for a Family Assistance Program, was enacted in 1974 and reflected a desire to give assistance to the working poor without taking them through the welfare system. As such it may be viewed as an expression of a desire to seek a middle road between income-tested and non-income-tested programs. Indeed it does not fit the dichotomy very well. Benefits are clearly related to income, but the benefit-reduction (tax) rate is low and the program is administered by the Internal Revenue Service, which deals with all Americans.

Existing income-tested programs were also changed in a number of ways which made them more like non-income-tested programs. Until a decade ago welfare programs reduced benefits by a dollar for each dollar of income that a beneficiary received. Indeed, prior to 1960, welfare mothers were actually worse off if they worked, because benefits were not only reduced by one dollar for each dollar earned, but no allowance was made for work-related expenses. Since then, until the Reagan administration, there has been a continuing trend in the direction of lower tax rates. In 1962, at the urging of President Kennedy, Congress allowed welfare mothers to deduct work-related expenses from earnings before benefits were reduced. In 1967 Congress reduced the benefit-reduction rate in AFDC to zero for the first $30 per month and reduced benefits by only 67 cents for each additional dollar earned. In 1972, Congress set the tax rate on earnings in the newly created SSI program at only 50%. The Food Stamp program has only about a 25% tax rate on earnings. Lower tax rates mean not only less disincentive to work for existing beneficiaries, but also an increase in the number of people eligible for benefits. In addition they increase the budget costs of these programs. Similar though more sweeping effects would be achieved by shifting entirely from welfare to non-income-tested programs.

Welfare benefits are based increasingly on average or presumptive need, as determined principally by family size and income rather than a detailed investigation of each family's particular circumstances and needs. Assets tests, a feature of most welfare programs, have also been liberalized. The value of an aged person's home, for instance, is no longer counted at all in determining eligibility for SSI. Moreover, both the name of the new Supplemental Security Income program and the choice of the Social Security Administration to administer it demonstrate a desire to reduce the stigma associated with this welfare program.

The War on Poverty also led to dramatic increases in social insurance. Medicare has already been mentioned. Congress also created the Black Lung program and substantially liberalized the Unemployment Insurance program. But the biggest increases came in the Old Age Insurance program. In 1965 Congress provided a 7% across-the-board increase in

OASDI benefits. In 1967 President Johnson requested a 15% across-the-board increase in order to lift 1.4 million of the aged out of poverty and remove 200,000 aged from the welfare rolls. Congress enacted a 13% increase in that year and went on to increase benefits by 15% in 1969, 10% in 1971, and 20% in 1972. The 1972 amendment also tied future social security benefits to the cost of living.

So policymakers since the Great Depression have had a split personality with regard to the form of income support—opting for income testing on some occasions, non-income-testing on others.

Our Current Income Support System

Currently, there are over 40 separate programs which together constitute the income maintenance system in the United States. About one of every two American families receives benefits from at least one of these programs. Table 1.1 presents the estimated expenditures of the most important ones for fiscal year 1981.

Total expenditures for fiscal 1981 are estimated to be $294.8 billion, equalling about 10% of GNP and about 48% of the total federal budget. This is a substantial sum, although by comparison with other Western industrialized countries not excessive. Average expenditures for income maintenance in the European Economic Community countries in 1972 equalled about 11% of GNP (Organisation for Economic Co-operation and Development, 1977b).

Several other characteristics of the current system stand out in Table 1.1. First, the system is clearly a categorical one. There are separate programs for single parents of families, veterans, the aged, blind, and disabled, students from poor families, and the working poor. Most, though not all, of this categorization is a response to the work issue—an attempt to separate (and treat differently) those who are expected to work from those who are not. All the social insurance programs are closely tied to previous labor force attachment. Of these, only the UI program aids those expected to work, and even in this case the aid provided is normally short term (though during the 1974–1976 recession, Congress extended the maximum period of coverage to well over a year). The tax credit for earned income and several of the recently enacted welfare programs—most notably Food Stamps and housing assistance—also provide aid to those expected to work. Whereas the President's Commission on Income Maintenance found in 1969 that the working poor were systematically excluded from our categorical welfare

TABLE 1.1

Estimated Benefit Expenditures for Major Income Support Programs, Fiscal Year 1981
(*$ billions*)

Program	Federal	State and Local	Total
Total	267.1	27.7	294.8
Social insurance—non-income-tested	209.8	7.2	217.0
Cash benefits			
Old Age and Survivors and Disability Insurance and Railroad Retirement	143.6	0	143.6
Special compensation for disabled coal miners	1.0	0	1.0
Unemployment Insurance	18.8	0	18.8
Veterans' and survivors' service-connected compensation	7.5	0	7.5
Workers' Compensation	1.5	7.2	8.7
Total	172.4	7.2	179.6
In-kind benefits			
Medicare	37.4	0	37.4
Refundable tax credits			
Earned Income Tax Credit	1.9	0	1.9
Welfare—income-tested	55.4	20.5	75.9
Cash benefits			
Aid to Families with Dependent Children	6.9	5.8	12.7
Supplemental Security Income	6.9	1.6	8.5
Veterans' and survivors' non-service-connected pensions	4.0	0	4.0
General Assistance	0	1.3	1.3
Total	17.8	8.7	26.5
In-kind benefits			
Food Stamps	9.7	0	9.7
Child nutrition and other Department of Agriculture food assistance	4.2	0	4.2
Medicaid	15.8	11.8	27.6
Housing Assistance	5.5	0	5.5
Basic Educational Opportunity Grants	2.4	0	2.4
Total	37.6	11.8	49.4

SOURCES: "The Budget of the United States, Fiscal Year 1981," from *Statistical Abstract of the United States: 1979* (1979). Data on Workers' Compensation and General Assistance are for 1977 and come from U.S. Department of Commerce (1979).

system, this is no longer the case. The system remains categorical, but the working poor are currently eligible for aid.

Second, expenditures for the social insurance programs are substantially larger than those for welfare programs—$217 billion as compared to $75.9 billion. In all, social insurance expenditures account for nearly three-quarters of total income support expenditures. As a consequence, social insurance programs lift more people out of poverty than do welfare programs (see Table 1.2), even though a larger *proportion* of the benefits from welfare go to the poor.

Third, the hybrid Earned Income Tax Credit is small in comparison to both social insurance and welfare programs. The federal income tax does, however, provide substantial subsidies to nonpoor families for housing, medical care, and child care, which amounted to over $40 billion in 1980.

Fourth, cash benefits account for a larger share of total expenditures than in-kind benefits—$206.1 billion versus $86.8 billion. But, note that welfare benefits that are in kind exceed both cash welfare benefits and in-kind social insurance benefits.

Fifth, although many people identify the Aid to Families with Dependent Children (AFDC) program with welfare, it actually accounts for only 17% of total welfare expenditures and not much more than 4% of total expenditures on income support. By far the largest welfare program is Medicaid.

Sixth, the bulk of income support expenditures are financed by the federal government—$267.1 billion out of a total of $294.8 billion. Just as in-kind benefits play a bigger role in welfare than in social insurance programs, state and local financing also plays a bigger role in welfare

TABLE 1.2
Persons in Poverty in Fiscal Year 1980 under Alternative Income Definitions

Persons in Poverty	Pre-Transfer Income	Pre-Tax Post-Social-Insurance Income	Pre-Tax Post-Money-Transfer Income	Pre-Tax Post-In-kind-Transfer Income		Post-Tax Post-Total-Transfer Income	
				No Med[a]	Med[b]	No Med[a]	Med[b]
Number (thousands)	41,096	22,811	18,793	12,957	8,496	13,455	8,951
% of total population	18.8%	10.4%	8.6%	5.9%	3.9%	6.2%	4.1%

Source: Hoagland (1980).
[a] Excludes medical-care transfers.
[b] Includes medical-care transfers.

programs than in social insurance. Twenty-seven percent of total welfare expenditures are borne by state and local governments. In contrast, less than 4% of total social insurance expenditures are borne by state and local governments.

It is worth noting that this overview of the income maintenance system would differ if public elementary and secondary education were included as part of the system. Most analysts of income maintenance programs do not think of free public education as an income maintenance program, because elementary and secondary education have been provided for so long in this country on a universal basis that free public education is taken as an essential feature of our social landscape. The argument can be made that it should be so included, however, because if primary and secondary education were predominantly privately financed, with income-tested subsidies for the poor (as many advocated in the early nineteenth century), the income-tested educational subsidy program(s) would clearly be counted as part of our income support system (just as the Basic Educational Opportunity Grants program now is). If education is included, total expenditures on income support rise by $97 billion and the difference between expenditures on non-income-tested and welfare programs becomes correspondingly larger—$314 billion (rather than $217 billion) on non-income-tested programs compared to $75.9 on welfare programs. The share of non-income-tested programs accounted for by in-kind benefits would increase from 17% to 43% of the total, and the share of state and local expenditures would increase from 9% to 30% of the total.

The Issues and the Papers

In earlier debates on the income-testing issue, advocates of non-income-tested programs argued that income-tested programs (a) stigmatize the poor; (b) reduce social cohesion; and (c) provide less aid to the poor. Advocates of income-tested programs on the other hand argued that (a) income-tested programs can be administered to treat beneficiaries with dignity and not result in a loss of self-respect; (b) the alleged social cohesion costs of income-tested programs are small or nonexistent; (c) non-income-tested programs are a costly and inefficient way of aiding the poor; and (d) non-income-tested programs provide less aid to the poor because of the existence of fiscal budget constraints.[4]

---

[4]See the references in footnote 3.

Advocates of non-income-tested programs argued that one of the costs of participating in a welfare program is a loss of self-esteem. To receive benefits, persons must declare themselves poor. In our country, where so much stress is put on economic success and where the dominant ideology is that "with hard work, anyone can make it," to declare oneself poor is almost synonymous with declaring oneself to be a failure. Yet it is frequently asserted that veterans' programs and income-tested scholarship programs entail little or no stigma. Moreover, it is estimated that nearly 100% of those who are eligible for AFDC now receive benefits.[5] Advocates of income-tested programs argued that it is possible to design and administer these programs so that stigma is minimized. The Rainwater paper examines the theoretical and empirical evidence on whether income-tested programs reduce the self-respect of beneficiaries and subject them to treatment that they would not be subject to in non-income-tested programs.

Income-tested programs create a sharp distinction between beneficiaries and nonbeneficiaries. This accentuates class divisions and thereby reduces social cohesion, according to advocates of non-income-tested programs. The same logic argues that non-income-tested programs mute such divisions and thereby reinforce social cohesion. Advocates of income-tested programs questioned the evidence for this effect. The Coleman paper evaluates the theoretical and empirical evidence on the effects of income testing on class cleavages and also considers the effects of income testing on cleavages between bureaucrats and beneficiaries.

Advocates of non-income-tested programs argued that such programs gain more political support than income-tested programs because they provide net benefits to so many more of the population. As a consequence, they argued, non-income-tested programs would provide more aid to the poor. Yet, perhaps the strongest argument of those who advocated income-tested programs is that they are more pro-poor in that they provide more aid to the poor out of a given budget. If budgets are fixed, it is obvious that income-tested programs will reduce poverty more than universal programs. It is equally obvious that if budgets for non-income-tested programs are larger than those for income-tested programs, the poor might be better off under the former. A small share of a big pie can be bigger than a large share of a tiny pie. Are budgets fixed?

In view of these diametrically opposed views about the politics of the

[5]See Bolland (1973). More recent estimates suggest participation rates are only less than 90% (see Michel, 1980).

income-testing issue, it is worth while to examine both (a) the political scientific basis underlying various assumptions about political feasibility of different-sized budget cuts, and (b) the effects of income testing on the economic well-being of the poor under a variety of assumptions about political feasibility. The papers by Tullock and Heidenheimer address from theoretical and empirical perspectives respectively, the first issue, while the Berry, Garfinkel, and Munts paper and the Betson, Greenberg, and Kasten paper address the second.

A big part of the explanation for why income-tested programs were judged to be superior is that economists were asserting that income-tested programs were more "efficient" than non-income-tested programs. For example, the 1972 annual Brookings assessment of the U.S. budget (Schultze et al., 1972) stated:

> universal payment systems are a very inefficient means for helping those with low incomes, since the benefits are not concentrated where the need is greatest. Large numbers of families would receive allowances and at the same time have their taxes increased to pay for the allowance. Tax rates would have to be raised simply to channel money from the family to the government and back to the family again [p. 200].

The belief that income-tested programs were more efficient rested on the concept of target efficiency. "Target efficiency" is defined as the proportion of total benefits of a program that goes to the poor. By definition, programs which confine benefits to the poor are quite a bit more target-efficient than those that do not. By the late 1960s, this measure had become a widely used criterion by which alternative income maintenance programs were judged.[6] Yet target efficiency is not a good measure of economic efficiency. (Neither, as will become apparent below, is it a good measure of how pro-poor programs are, which is what it originally was designed to measure. See further discussion in Chapter 13).

Most people think of economic efficiency (as opposed to target efficiency) in terms of maximizing the total output of the economy as measured by, for example, the gross national product (GNP). Economists, however, have a more precise definition. An efficient allocation of resources is one in which it is impossible to make anyone better off with-

[6]For early work on target efficiency, see Klein (1966); Green (1967, especially chapters 5 and 6); Green and Lampman (1967); Tobin et al. (1967); and Weisbrod (1969).

Target efficiency has been used by some of the most prominent economists in the field of income maintenance to evaluate alternative transfer programs. See Musgrave, Heller, and Peterson (1970); Haveman (1973); Barth, Carcagno, and Palmer (1974); and Rea (1974).

out making at least one person worse off. These two definitions of efficiency frequently coincide.

The relationship of target efficiency to economic efficiency is suggested by the quote above. To finance a non-income-tested program which benefits the poor as much as an income-tested program requires higher tax rates. Higher tax rates sometimes lead to lower GNP, and if they are unnecessary, they are always inefficient.[7]

If it were true, as the Brookings quote implies, that tax rates on everybody are higher in non-income-tested programs, it would also be true that these programs are inefficient. For unnecessarily raising tax rates will reduce productivity and efficiency. But it is not true that tax rates on everybody are higher in non-income-tested programs. For, in order to confine benefits to the poor, income-tested programs reduce benefits as income increases. And, reducing benefits as income increases is perfectly equivalent to putting a tax on income. On this all economists agree. Consequently, compared to the tax rates they face in welfare programs, the tax rates which the poor must pay to finance programs that provide benefits to everyone are lower. So whether income-tested or non-income-tested programs are more efficient depends upon whether it is more efficient to place higher tax rates on the rich or the poor. The papers by Sadka, Garfinkel, and Moreland, and by Betson, Greenberg, and Kasten address this issue. In addition, the Kesselman paper examines the effects of income testing on administrative and other aspects of efficiency not covered by the first two papers.

Whereas each of the foregoing papers addresses a particular issue in the income-testing debate, the paper by Abel-Smith cuts across all the issues. He was asked how to decide which in-kind subsidies should be income tested. The Long, Palmer paper places the U.S. debate over national health insurance in the context of the income-testing issue. Finally the papers by Watts, Jakubson, and Skidmore, and by Berry, Garfinkel, and Munts examine the effects of income testing on two groups who receive special attention in our current categorical income maintenance system: single parents and the aged.

[7]Higher tax rates can lead to more work effort and therefore greater output of goods and services. Raising tax rates makes working less worth while. This reduces work. On the other hand, higher tax rates also reduce income. This has the effect of increasing work. Which effect dominates is an empirical question. Studies show, for example, that in response to increased tax rates most married men work more while married women work less (see Cain and Watts, 1973; Masters and Garfinkel, 1976).

2

Stigma in Income-Tested Programs

LEE RAINWATER

The rubric "stigma" refers to the possible negative social-psychological consequences for recipients produced by income-tested government transfer programs.* Assertions that income-tested programs carry stigmatizing effects generally point to four facts:

1. Nonrecipients have negative attitudes toward participants in income-tested programs. Recipients are characterized in a variety of negative ways.
2. As a consequence of these negative attitudes, recipients are treated differently from nonrecipients. Officials, caretakers dealing with recipients, and the general public treat recipients in particular ways on the basis of assumptions about them.
3. Recipients themselves make negative self-characterizations based on the fact that they are recipients of "charity." They share in society's negative evaluation of people such as themselves.

*I am indebted to a number of people for information, bibliographical suggestions, and critical discussions of the ideas presented in this paper—in particular Hans Berglind, Richard Coleman, Cherl Connor, David Donnison, Robert Erickson, Sten Johansson, Walter Korpi, Jan Nascenius, Thomas Pettigrew, Annika Puide, Martin Rein. I also want to thank Vernon Allen, John Bishop, Irwin Garfinkel, Alvin Schorr, Eric Wright, and other reviewers at the Institute for Research on Poverty for helpful comments and criticisms.

19

4. Because of differences in attitudes and treatment on the part of the larger society and because of their own negative self-conceptions, recipients of income-tested programs are believed to engage in behavior which in one way or another is responsive to the fact of their being in a derogated status.

To be sure, some social policy analysts have argued that stigma should not be an important concern in evaluating universal versus selective benefits. One English writer, in the process of reviewing concerns involved in the selectivity debate, suggests:

> Lurking behind much of the selectivity debate, sometimes explicitly acknowledged by the proponents of selective strategies and frequently wheeled out by universalists as if it were the ultimate counterargument to selectivity, is the issue of stigma. Perhaps because there is much dispute about the nature or the very existence of the beast—it tends to have been badly handled by both sides. If anything the selectivist has felt obliged to minimise its presence or to seek sub-strategies which minimise its likelihood. Meanwhile the universalist has perhaps over-stressed its presence at least in association with means-tests. . . .
>
> However, too much credit should not be given to the notion of stigma—its presence has certainly not been proved beyond reasonable doubt. There is little conclusive empirical evidence to ratify the various interpretations [Reddin, 1978, pp. 64–66].

In this paper I argue instead that the bulk of the existing evidence suggests that all four assertions have a considerable amount of truth to them. The evidence that can be brought to bear does not, however, tell one much about the extent or intensity of these various effects in even the most widely studied American income-tested program—the AFDC program—let alone other income-tested programs. Nevertheless, the evidence does suggest that at least in terms of attitudes toward recipients and self-conceptions by recipients, a participant in an income-tested program does elicit considerable negative feelings.

One important fact is that income-tested programs can have other effects besides those involving stigma. Stigmatizing effects represent a cost to welfare recipients. Although they would suffer more if they had to live without the money that they received, they receive less net benefit under the effects of stigma than is apparent if one pays attention only to the money that they receive. Not only are there minor transaction costs involved in applying for and receiving benefits, but there are also social–psychological costs in becoming a "charity" case.

In some discussions, stigmatization is thought of as merely a "prejudice" on the part of members of society, including recipients, that does not seem to have any particular function. More likely, howeve is an expression of much broader philosophies of equity, fairn incentive.

The balance of the paper will first address the theoretical perspectives in sociology and social psychology that bear most directly on the issue of stigmatization and, then, evidence concerning the extent of stigmatization of the poor, particularly those who avail themselves of income-tested benefits, or "charity." Then the paper will analyze the more complex issue of the social–psychological effects of the stigma of welfare, briefly discuss means-tested programs other than welfare, and set the issue of the means-test stigma in the context of different welfare state strategies. Finally, the paper will consider the question of the research needed to increase understanding of the effects of the stigmatizing process that may operate in connection with transfer programs.

Stigmatization Processes

In some discussions of stigma, the fact of stigmatization is thought of merely as a "prejudice" on the part of members of society, including recipients. This prejudice is not seen as having any particular function. It seems much more likely, however, that stigma is an expression of much broader philosophies of equity, fairness, and incentive, and there is much evidence, some of which is noted in the next section, that the differential evaluation of classes of which stigma forms a part is deeply ingrained in the world views of members of modern industrial society, not just superficial attitudes subject to ready change by better public relations on behalf of those groups—"the poor"—that are stigmatized.

Erving Goffman, who has characterized stigmatization processes as basic and pervasive in all societies, defines stigma in this way:

> While a stranger is present before us, evidence can arise of his possessing an attribute that makes him different from others in the category of persons available for him to be, and of a less desirable kind—in the extreme, a person who is quite thoroughly bad, or dangerous, or weak. He is thus reduced in our minds from a whole and usual person to a tainted, discounted one. Such an attribute is a stigma, especially when its discrediting effect is very extensive; sometimes it is also called a failing, a shortcoming, a handicap. . . .
>
> The term stigma, then, will be used to refer to an attribute that is deeply discrediting, but it should be seen that a language of relationships, not attributes, is really needed. . . . A stigma, then, is really a special kind of relationship between attribute and stereotype [Goffman, 1963, p. 9].

There are those who argue that the violation of our normative expectations that leads to stigmatization may be at the very core of our social systems, at least insofar as pure differences in power are elaborated to include differences in the presumed worth of individuals. Thus, Ralf Dahrendorf (1968) finds in the primitive categories of those who succeed in conforming to society's norms versus those who do not the building blocks of social stratification.

The theoretical arguments concerning stigmatization developed by sociologists have been extensively confirmed in socio-psychological experiments. These studies routinely show that persons stigmatized because of physical or mental handicaps and disabilities are treated differently from "normals." Usually they are derogated in one way or another; under certain circumstances they may be treated more positively than "normals," but in the experimental situation it is not possible to know how long such "charitable" responses persist. (See Gergen and Jones, 1963; Farina et al., 1965, 1966, 1968; Kleck, 1966, 1969; Kleck, Ono, and Hastorf, 1966; and Doob and Ecker, 1970.)

All of this suggests that there are ample grounds in sociological and social–psychological theory for expecting stigmatization of those who are not able to support themselves by their own resources, at least in modern Western society. Much of this theory has been generated inductively in an effort to understand, explain, and place in a context known attitudes and behavior toward the economically weak.

The Stigma of Poverty

The social scientist should treat the issue of stigmatization in income-tested programs in the broader context of stigmatization of the poor, whether or not they participate in such programs. As Thomas Pettigrew (1980) observed in an exhaustive review of social-psychological perspectives on poverty, "Being poor in the United States in many significant ways constitutes social deviance in the eyes of many Americans, poor and non-poor alike." He noted that the tendency for social stigmatization is greatest "for the visibly poor who are held responsible for their condition [pp. 198–199]."

Not only have the poor or, in class terms, "the lower class," historically suffered heavy stigmatization, but the poor as a special group, distinct from the "ordinary" working class, has been a special focus of American social politics and policy. Part of this tradition comes from England, but it has been intensified in the American context. Concern with the dangerous classes, the criminal classes, paupers, vagrants, and the like has dominated much of American social policy discussion.

This is not canonical, as has often been observed by European social commentators, most recently Walter Korpi (1978). In some European countries, particularly in Scandinavia, politics and policy in the social area have tended to focus on the working class as a whole, with little specific attention paid to the special character of the most deprived. The political choice in this context emphasizes working-class solidarity and avoids any semblance of a break in that solidarity which might be caused by paying attention to working-class segments such as the "labor aristocracy" or the "lumpen proletariat."

Still the historical focus on the "charity class" as a special problem is deeply ingrained in the social welfare perspectives of Americans. It is a bias held in common by elites, middle-class Americans, and even the poor themselves. The vocabulary for characterizing the people at the bottom may change from time to time, but the meaning of the characterization changes very little.

Most Americans are concerned first with making ends meet and then perhaps with enjoying something of the rewards of the good life with the surplus. They believe that they themselves make ends meet and enjoy whatever surplus they have by virture of their own hard work. They believe that effort (and the accretion of effort over time that we call merit) is what principally accounts for how well people do in life. This ideology serves as a guide to striving and as an explanation for one's success. Such considerations lead to a perception of the world as a basically just one.

However, that people perceive the world as just does not necessarily mean that they perceive it as accommodating or nurturing. In fact, people often see the world as a harsh and demanding although just place where those who do not strive, though not necessarily bad persons, do much less well. This is the context in which one should understand the survey results summarized below, which indicate that most people believe that the poor have only themselves to blame for their poverty. Not that they really believe that the poor in some sense "ought" to be poor. Rather they believe that those who are poor simply haven't tried hard enough, have not been quite circumspect enough (Rainwater, 1974).

The most systematic investigation of American conceptions of the poor (Feagin, 1972a) demonstrates quite forcefully that persons are believed to be poor primarily as a result of their own failings, though other, nonmotivational factors may also contribute to their plight. Table 2.1 shows the distribution of candidates for the causes of poverty.

TABLE 2.1
Respondents Rating the Importance of Various Causes of Poverty

Reasons for Poverty Selected by Americans in National Survey	Percentages of Americans Feeling Reason		
	Very Important	Somewhat Important	Not Important
1. Lack of thrift and proper money management by poor people.	58	30	11
2. Lack of effort by the poor themselves.	55	33	9
3. Lack of ability and talent among poor people.	52	33	12
4. Loose morals and drunkenness.	48	31	17
5. Sickness and physical handicaps.	46	39	14
6. Low wages in some businesses and industries.	42	35	20
7. Failure of society to provide good schools for many Americans.	36	25	34
8. Prejudice and discrimination against Negroes.	33	37	26
9. Failure of private industry to provide enough jobs.	27	36	31
10. Being taken advantage of by rich people.	18	30	45
11. Just bad luck.	8	27	60

SOURCE: Feagin, 1972a, p. 104. Reprinted from *Psychology Today Magazine,* copyright © 1972, Ziff–Davis Publishing Company.

We see from Feagin's results that most people regard lack of thrift, effort, ability, or downright moral failing (as in "loose morals and drunkenness") as the cause of poverty. To be poor is to expose oneself to such labels.

A similar study, carried out by the Commission of the European Communities, suggests that similar negative views of the poor exist in most of Europe. However, there are important differences among the countries. The United Kingdom and Ireland are most similar to the United States in seeing moral blemishes as the cause of poverty. Thus British and Irish respondents chose "laziness and lack of will power" most often (see Table 2.2) as the chief cause of poverty. Sixty-five percent of the Irish respondents and 40% of the British respondents who had had personal contact with people in poverty (36% and 27% of the

TABLE 2.2
The Causes of Poverty by Country (*percentages*)

	Belgium	Denmark	Germany	France	Ireland	Italy	Luxembourg	Netherlands	United Kingdom	Total[a]
Because there is much injustice in our society.	17	14	23	35	19	40	16	11	16	26
Because of laziness and lack of willpower.	22	11	23	16	30	20	31	12	43	25
Because they have been unlucky.	21	17	18	18	25	14	20	20	10	16
It's an inevitable part of progress in the modern world.	15	28	10	18	16	10	6	16	17	14
None of these.	9	8	8	7	4	4	6	11	4	6
Don't know.	16	22	18	6	6	12	21	30	10	13
Total	100	100	100	100	100	100	100	100	100	100

SOURCE: Commission of the European Communities (1977).
[a]Weighted average.

respective samples) listed drink as a principal cause. In Britain the most popular candidate was laziness (45%).

As in the United States, respondents in the lower-status groups held negative views more often: "The poor income groups, the less well educated and the nonleaders tend to suggest that the victims themselves are to blame [Commission of the European Communities, 1977, p. 72]."

A British analysis of the reasons why families did not take advantage of free school meals found that the most common explanation for poverty in some families was that they were mainly at fault (Davies, 1976). These views were common among the poor as well (Table 2.3).

Not that the people who offer these extremely negative views of the poor cannot or do not conceive of some people being poor through no fault of their own. Mainly they have difficulty accepting the notion that because of the way it operates, society causes poverty. However, one

TABLE 2.3
The Factors to Which Respondents Attribute the Blame for Poverty
(*percentages of respondents*)

	Nonpayers		Payers		Receivers of Free Meals	
	U	O	U	O	U	O
If people are in poverty it's mainly						
1. Their own fault.	44	47	48	42	38	35[a]
2. The government's fault.	3	3	8	3	2	12
3. The fault of their education.	4	5	1	4	4	4
4. The fault of industry (for) not paying better wages.	3	8	3	4	12	6
5. A combination of some of these.	34	36	30	43	43	48
6. None of these.	4	0	5	0	0	0
7. Anything else.	4	0	1	1	0	3
8. Don't know.	5	15	4	4	2	4
Number of respondents replying	77	66	79	79	68	80

SOURCE AND NOTES: Bleddyn Davies, *Universality, Selectivity and Effectiveness in Social Policy* (London: Heinemann, 1976). Reprinted with permission from Heinemann. U and O are two different communities; nonpayers are a sample of persons whose children do not take meals at school; payers are a sample of persons whose incomes are too high for their children to receive free meals, though the children lunch at school; receivers of free meals are a sample of persons whose children receive free meals.

[a] There is an error of unknown origin in this column.

can easily elicit from a sample of Americans the view that "something ought to be done" to help these weak-willed people work their way out of poverty and thus overcome their shortcomings (Rainwater, 1974).

It is important to understand that the differential evaluation of classes which these views reflect is deeply ingrained in the world views of members of modern industrial society. These are not just superficial attitudes that are subject to ready change by better public relations on behalf of the poor. One particularly trenchant experiment in this regard was carried out in London (Open University, 1971). Actors impersonating middle-class and working-class (not even poor) men approached commuters in Paddington Station in London to ask for directions. Their interactions were photographed, and later the researchers counted such simple patterns as the length of time the commuter was willing to talk with the person asking for help and the amount of time he smiled or otherwise expressed positive affect. Both middle-class and working-class commuters (as judged by their dress) interacted for a longer period of time with the middle-class actors and smiled more often than with the working-class actors. The commuters are not unlikely to have left the working-class actors with the feeling that the people they dealt with were stigmatized. Nevertheless, their behavior clearly reflects the typical lower evaluation of those persons.

The Intensified Stigma of Charity

In the context of these extremely widespread views concerning the moral character of the poor, income-tested programs cannot help but serve as further symbolization of that lowly status. If the plea of poverty is a necessary basis for asking government for support, then that claim must carry with it all the negative meanings associated with poverty. If, on the other hand, a claim for support can be based on other grounds, such as disability or widowhood, then perhaps one can escape those meanings. The social symbolic dynamics of defining persons as deserving support or not, or more important, as being "essentially" poor or not, has not escaped lobbyists for groups claiming public support. It is a common observation that lobbyists, such as those for the disabled, do not want their (morally clean) constituents to be confused with the poor who are "merely" poor.

Holding a low opinion of people who are poor and receive charity must be understood as part of the social control mechanism of society, both ideologically and on the basis of the relationships between recipients and the rest of society. Many find it sensible that charity carry with it a cost to the recipient. People should be encouraged to work and discouraged from depending on charity.

One way to discourage people is to make it very clear that they lower their esteem when they ask for charity. The same psychology can be used to encourage recipients to leave the relief rolls as fast as they can.

More broadly, stigmatization of those who must rely on others for their livelihood serves as a symbolic expression of everyone's determination to pull his own weight, to work for what he gets. Kai Erikson (1966), following Durkheim, observes that norms (such as those involved in the "work ethic" complex) cannot be maintained in society without recurrent punishment of violators. Punishment serves to dramatize the validity of the norm and to help people define themselves by contrast as proper, law-abiding members of society. Conversations and interactions in which stigmatizing goes on thus have the important function of maintaining the dominant norms (ideology) of the society.

In his classic paper on "the social division of welfare," Titmuss recognized the vital connection for conservatives between the "test of need" and the preservation of middle-class advantage.

> The Beveridge "revolution" did not, it is argued, imply an equalitarian approach to the solution of social problems. The error of welfare state policies since 1948 has been, according to this diagnosis, to confuse ends and means, and to pursue equalitarian aims with the result that the "burden" of redistribution from rich to poor has been pushed too far and is now excessive. Thus the upper and middle classes have been impoverished, in part a consequence of providing benefits for those workers who do not really need them. "Why," ask Macleod and Powell, "should any social service be provided *without* [their italics] test of need?" [Macleod and Powell also observed] "The social services only exist for a portion of the population," namely that portion that takes out more than it puts in [1959, pp. 35–36].

Titmuss observes that these conservative analyses of welfare state social services have:

> helped . . . to produce in the public eye something akin to a stereotype or image of an all pervasive Welfare State for the Working Classes. . . . As Gerth and Mills have pointed out, ". . . if the upper classes monopolize the means of communication and fill the several mass media with the idea that all those at the bottom are there because they are lazy, unintelligent, and in general inferior, then these appraisals may be taken over by the poor themselves and used in the building of an image of themselves." That is one danger in the spread of the "Welfare State" stereotype. A second emanates from the vague but often powerful fears that calamity will follow the relaxation of discipline and the mitigation of hardship which, in the

eyes of the beholders, seem implicit in this notion of collective benevo-
lence. Such fears inevitably conjure up a demand for punishment and
reprisals; the history of public opinion in recent years on the subject of
juvenile delinquency (to take one example) is suggestive. . . . The corollary
for any society which invests more of its values and virtues in the promo-
tion of the individual is individual failure and individual consciousness of
failure [pp. 37–38, 55].

There is every reason to believe (although marshaling evidence that
comes close to any standard of proof is difficult) that stigmatization
functions quite effectively to reduce the use of income-tested programs.
In other words, it works. An argument sometimes used with respect
to the AFDC program is that stigma cannot be really important because just about all the families that are eligible are, in fact, receiving the
benefits (Boland, 1973). However, the effort to estimate the extent to
which families who are eligible are on AFDC is a futile exercise, since
female-headed families with children have considerable control over
their eligibility for welfare. Most mothers do not have the kinds of assets
that would disqualify them from welfare if they did not work. The well-
known fact that a great many who do work and are therefore not eligible
to go on welfare are no better off than recipient families suggests that
women have considerations other than economic benefits when they
decide whether or not to work. Given the changes in welfare regulations
over the last 10–15 years, the work/welfare decision is not an either/or
matter, but a question of whether or not a woman applies for welfare
before going to work. In most states in the 60s and 70s, if a woman went
on welfare first, she could then take a job and still retain her welfare
status. In this way she increased her family's well-being. That more
women did not do this probably has much to do with widely shared
conceptions of what it means to go on welfare.

In the United States the growth of welfare programs seems to have
been accompanied by the growing salience of welfare recipients for images of the lowest class in society. Thus, Coleman, Rainwater, and
McClelland (1978) found in interviews in Boston and Kansas City that a
very common response to questions about "the lowest class" in society
involved a reference to those on welfare:

> The word used most often by our sample members to characterize the
> life style and income source of people at the bottom was welfare. For a
> great share of the Bostonians and Kansas Citians we interviewed, the
> answer to our question, "Who is at the very bottom of the ladder?" was
> quite simple: "It's the welfare person. . . . The lowest class is people on
> welfare." The phraseology for this condition varied somewhat—"they are
> receiving public assistance," "That's the public aid group," "people on
> government handouts," "the person on relief," "those on the dole of some

sort," "charity cases"—but the concept did not vary. The principle enunciated in any case was that the welfare class and people at the bottom are nearly synonymous terms, that any American for whom welfare has become a way of life is thereby to be accounted among the nation's lowest-class citizens [p. 195].

As welfare has grown steadily in the public's consciousness over the past two decades, the sharpness of the image of welfare mothers, fathers, and families as representing the dregs of society has increased apace. The conflict between the ideology of a just world and the understanding that jobs are not necessarily easier to find even when people want to work (at least if they have few skills) is easier to avoid if one can believe that those who should work but don't have jobs are simply people who have learned to be welfare chiselers. Feagin's survey, referred to earlier, shows a similar perspective on welfare (Table 2.4).

One would be hard put to find really significant differences in the imagery surrounding welfare recipients in Britain and the United States. In Britain the role of stigma in reducing the consumption of benefits has been discussed extensively. British researchers believe that the stigma

TABLE 2.4
Americans Agreeing with Attitudes toward Welfare

American Attitudes toward Welfare and Welfare Recipients	Percentage of Americans		
	Agreeing	Disagreeing	Uncertain
1. There are too many people receiving welfare money.	84	11	5
2. Many people getting welfare are not honest about their needs.	71	17	12
3. Many women getting welfare money are having illegitimate babies to increase the money they get.	61	23	16
4. Generally speaking, we are spending too little money on welfare programs in this country.	34	54	13
5. Most people on welfare who can work try to find jobs so they can support themselves.	43	49	8
6. One of the main troubles with welfare is that it doesn't give people enough money to get along on.	45	43	12
7. A lot of people are moving to this state from other states just to get welfare money here.	41	31	28

SOURCE: Feagin, 1972a, p. 107. Reprinted from *Psychology Today Magazine*, copyright © 1972, Ziff–Davis Publishing Company.

associated with supplementary benefits reduces the number of eligible families who apply for the benefits to which they are entitled. One study concerned with the use of free school meals, an income-tested program, found that a high proportion of individuals interviewed in two areas of the country (under- and overachieving authorities—a distinction not relevant to this discussion) believed that stigma was the principal reason why eligible families did not apply for free school meals—stigma defined as parents' pride or shame and dislike of the invasion of privacy. A substantial proportion of the respondents also believed that other children stigmatized those receiving benefits, and a smaller proportion believed that teachers stigmatized the children who received free school meals (Table 2.5).

TABLE 2.5

Explanations Given by Respondents of Why Eligible Families Did Not Apply for Free School Meals (*percentages of respondents*)

	Nonpayers		Payers		Receivers of Free Meals	
	U	O	U	O	U	O
1. Stigma (including parents' pride or shame, or the dislike of the invasion of privacy involved).	39	43	48	55	40	39
2. Ignorance (including not realizing that they are eligible, not knowing about free meals, not understanding the system).	35	24	40	22	18	20
3. Dislike of food.	12	18	5	7	19	17
4. Parents can afford to pay.	6	0	2	7	2	1
5. Parents apathetic.	0	4	7	6	12	10
6. Prefer to eat at home.	4	11	0	3	5	10
7. Other.	6	2	2	0	4	1
Total number of persons giving codable explanation (%)	100	100	100	100	100	100
N	66	56	61	71	67	69
Total number of respondents to the survey N	77	68	79	79	68	81

SOURCE AND NOTES: Bleddyn Davies, *Universality, Selectivity and Effectiveness in Social Policy* (London: Heinemann, 1976). Reprinted with permission from Heinemann. U and O are two different communities; nonpayers are a sample of persons whose children do not take meals at school; payers are a sample of persons whose incomes are too high for their children to receive free meals, though the children lunch at school; receivers of free meals are a sample of persons whose children receive free meals.

Although there were some differences, these views were generally shared among the three groups interviewed in the study, which included families with children who received free meals and those who did not (Davies, 1976; Table 2.6).

The evidence given by the Supplementary Benefits Commission to the Royal Commission on the Distribution of Income and Wealth eloquently summarizes the problem of stigma in income-tested and discretionary programs in Britain:

> The most obvious characteristic of supplementary benefit which distinguishes it from most income from other sources is that it is subject to a means test of a searching and detailed kind. . . . The process of assessing entitlement can too easily reinforce the feelings of stigma that may accompany the initial claim. Questions about the claimant's private affairs—not only his income but what savings he has, who else lives in the house and on what terms, whether he has "exceptional" needs of various kinds, and so on—are necessary and in most cases inoffensive; but such questioning is not involved in a claim for a national insurance benefit, "earned" by contributions. Enquiries of a still more personal nature may be necessary before a discretionary payment for exceptional needs is made. It must be degrading for a mother to have to show an official her worn-down shoes or the frayed and stained bedding of her children, or for an elderly gentleman to have to discuss with strangers his growing problems of incontinence and the laundry bills it entails. . . . The waiting rooms, interviewing environment and counters of those sections of local Social Security office which deal with supplementary benefit claimants are often distinctly bleak and less inviting than those which greet the claimant seeking contribution benefits. . . .
>
> Similarly, the fact that the actual rent payable by the claimant is included in the calculation of his benefit places an additional onus on him to keep his rent payments up to date, even if in other circumstances he might think it right to defer paying the rent in order to meet a more pressing commitment. In some cases, benefit may be paid partly in kind or to a third party, for instance where rent is paid direct to the landlord. In others, a deduction is made from the weekly benefit payments, for example to build up a fund to meet fuel bills. These practices are adopted in the interests of the claimant and his dependents, and often at the claimant's request; but they nevertheless help to emphasise the fact that supplementary benefit is different from other forms of income and involves an element of supervision of the claimant's private life, however justifiable.
>
> Similarly, the tendency to make receipt of supplementary benefit a "passport" to entitlement to other benefits, ranging from butter tokens and free prescriptions to electricity discounts and free school meals, reinforces the impression that supplementary benefit claimants are a class apart. At the same time, these "fringe benefits" encourage the view that supplementary benefit claimants are treated too generously compared with those who work for their living and have to manage without such extras.

TABLE 2.6

Respondents Agreeing with Propositions as Important Explanations of Why Eligible Children Did Not Receive Free School Meals

	Nonpayers		Payers		Receivers of Free Meals	
	%	N	%	N	%	N
1. Do not need them.	32	76	27	79	53	68
2. Other children stigmatize receivers.	58	77	61	79	56	68
3. Teachers pick on receivers.	30	77	15	79	10	68
4. Thought to be charity.	70	76	70	79	78	68
5. Application too complicated.	51	76	56	79	34	68
6. Don't like stating incomes.	44	77	70	79	76	68
7. Don't like employer to know that applying.	57	77	54	79	50	68
8. Don't know about the service.	74	77	70	79	60	68
1. Do not need them.	40	67	27	78	19	81
2. Other children stigmatize receivers.	68	68	65	79	62	81
3. Teachers pick on receivers.	12	68	15	79	12	81
4. Thought to be charity.	82	68	75	79	78	81
5. Application too complicated.	43	68	52	79	25	81
6. Don't like stating incomes.	65	68	63	79	74	81
7. Don't like employer to know that applying.	57	68	52	79	63	81
8. Don't know about the service.	63	68	47	79	46	81

SOURCE AND NOTES: Bleddyn Davies, *Universality, Selectivity and Effectiveness in Social Policy* (London: Heinemann, 1976). Reprinted with permission from Heinemann. U and O are two different communities; nonpayers are a sample of persons whose children do not take meals at school; payers are a sample of persons whose incomes are too high for their children to receive free meals, though the children lunch at school; receivers of free meals are a sample of persons whose children receive free meals.

N = the number of persons giving an answer referring to the proposition. The percentages are proportions of this number.

For all these reasons, we believe that it is important not only to tackle the problem of poverty by raising the lowest levels of money incomes to a more adequate level, but also to ensure that income is distributed in ways which are not damaging to the self-respect of those who receive it. In carrying out our functions in relation to the supplementary benefits and FIS schemes, we constantly pursue this aim to the best of our ability, but in the knowledge that we cannot fully achieve it without changes both in legislation and in public attitudes [Great Britain, Supplementary Benefits Commission, 1977, pp. 29–31].

In Sweden, also, recipients of "social help" tend to be highly stigmatized in public imagery, and there is evidence that, just as in the United States, persons in great need still try to avoid availing themselves of this program of last resort:

> In spite of efforts by the authorities to establish social assistance as a citizen's right, the stigma which by tradition is attached to "welfare clients" still remains strong in Sweden. . . . Persons more or less permanently on social assistance were by law denied the right to vote up to 1945. The prohibition for them to have certain elected offices in the communes was removed a few years later. Scattered public opinion questions and various incidents indicate rather wide-spread suspicions with regard to assistance recipients in Sweden [Korpi, 1978, p. 121].

The person who is unemployed and has no unemployment insurance benefits (because participation in the unemployment insurance program in Sweden is voluntary) must throw himself on the mercy of his commune and thus lies vulnerable to the same accusations of laziness and shiftlessness applied to an American in similar circumstances (Berglind et al., 1975; Puide, 1977). Although in Sweden there is less cultural weight behind these accusations, the stigma nevertheless remains. In Sweden the popular imagery of welfare chiselers applies more to men than to women, reflecting Sweden's preoccupation with problems of male alcoholism. In America, the imagery applies more to women because of the preoccupation with the superfecund mother who doesn't want to work. It is perhaps significant of the intimate connection between the derogation of the very poor and the stigmatization of welfare recipients that these images exist in Sweden despite the fact that only a small proportion of welfare recipients in Sweden receive benefits for more than a few months.

Annika Puide has studied attitudes toward social help in a large Swedish town and a rural area. She interviewed samples of politicians, social workers, clients, and the general public in each area on whether they would grant assistance to persons having different combinations of work ethic (wants to work/does not want to work), levels of need (great or lesser need), and availability of jobs for the applicants (job available or not). All of the cases judged by the respondents were legally entitled to public assistance and the social workers so judged all the case examples.

The general public placed by far the heaviest emphasis on the work ethic in judging whether a family was entitled to assistance (37% and 40% of the variance in the large town and rural areas, respectively). The clients, although placing some emphasis on this factor, placed the greatest emphasis (46% and 44% of the variance, respectively) on level of need. Overall, clients and the general public judged that slightly over half of the cases were deserving of assistance. The following table shows the effects of the three different factors (Table 2.7).

There are perhaps two basic images of those who use income-tested programs—at least the most common ones such as welfare and food

TABLE 2.7
Respondents in Storrestad (Large Town) Who Granted Assistance to Cases with Specific Lack Combination (Factors Two by Two: Third Factor at a Constant Level) (*Percentages of Respondents*)

	Wants to Work	Doesn't Want to Work
Need held constant		
Politicians ($N = 36$)		
Jobs available	100	94
Jobs not available	84	83
Clients ($N = 202$)		
Jobs available	98	68
Jobs not available	90	53
General public ($N = 254$)		
Jobs available	98	59
Jobs not available	88	44
Work availability held constant		
Politicians ($N = 36$)		
Great need	100	94
Less need	90	40
Clients ($N = 202$)		
Great need	98	68
Less need	39	18
General public ($N = 254$)		
Great need	98	59
Less need	70	25

Source and note: Puide (1977). See text for explanation of categories.

stamps. One is the set of labels already noted, which in general describe those on welfare as in some sense weak—either lazy, shiftless, or (more eloquently) with little motivation to work, or with little skill to offer on the labor market, willing to work but with little human capital. Another type of weakness is moral weakness, as for example the stereotypic male alcoholic or promiscuous woman on welfare. To accept charity, then, is to accept an identity of weakness, in some sense impotent and unable to manage one's own life.

The second, but less common, conception of welfare recipients is of persons who are potent but in a morally reprehensible way. These are the welfare chiselers, who aggressively seek out unearned rewards and whose use of welfare partakes more of the positively criminal than of the dependent.

Thus the dominant stereotypes of those who make use of income-tested benefits, as of the poor in general, can involve conceptions of those people as either pitiable or frightening. In either case, such people are not to be indulged, and one clearly would wish to avoid being labeled by society or by oneself as a member of either of these categories.

Thus it is crucial to understand that most of the research that touches in some way on the self-identification of welfare recipients suggests that they largely share the conceptions that the dominant society has of charity cases. However, they often work very hard to explain to themselves and others why these stereotypes do not apply to their particular case.

Issues of welfare equity according to public conceptions of distributive justice are very complex. Because we do not know exactly how the public and welfare recipients think about the deserts of persons in need of welfare, social–psychological equity theory is not particularly useful. For example, in a study designed to investigate evaluations of just incomes, Alves and Rossi (1978) find that a fair income for a single person on welfare would be $2538 compared with an income for the lowest-status worker (garbage collector for males or laundry worker for females) of $11,348. On the other hand, we find fair income for those families on welfare is given as $7211 compared with that for the lowest-status working husband of $13,655. Obviously, these imply very complex calculations of distributive justice. One is struck with how generous the sample seems to be with couples, and how stingy with the single heads.

Although the richly developed models of equity theory cannot offer much to be learned deductively, they can serve as a very useful guide to new research to investigate stigma (as discussed in the final section of the paper).

Responses to Stigmatization

Recipients seem to recognize their stigmatization in at least three different ways. First, they superficially recognize the status of being stigmatized. Most of the relevant research shows that welfare recipients are aware that others tend to stigmatize them, and they throw up various defenses to protect themselves. They often maintain to themselves and to others that their dependence on welfare is merely temporary, and they hold out the hope of getting off welfare to ward off some of the negative self-definitions that they might otherwise have to accept.

There seems to be good reason to believe, however, that the effects of stigmatization are not simply superficial ones. Women on welfare are likely to explain their welfare experiences along the following lines (and perhaps it's easier to talk this way after the fact than during the experience): "Being on welfare hurt me because I felt as if I were irresponsible. If I were working and bringing home $60.00 a week, I would know it was my money, and I would feel better about myself. On welfare I began feeling as if I was asking them to give me something I didn't deserve [Coles, 1978, p. 28]."

Such negative self-perceptions are extremely painful. Individuals ordinarily strive very hard to ward off or encapsulate such feelings. But it is difficult to do so in a world where one is aware of the highly negative views surrounding persons in the same circumstances (Weiss, 1979).

Indeed, for the typical American welfare recipient, a solo mother, other women who are in exactly the same situation but have chosen not to go on welfare are likely to hold the most negative views. After all, they have confronted the choice between welfare and work and have rejected the first (Burlage, 1978). Welfare is not a particularly visible status to the general public, but individuals know that they are on welfare, and the people close to them are likely to know. Therefore, recipients show a great preoccupation with their special situation of being unable to support themselves.

Very little research has been done on the Food Stamp program. But one would expect the experience of stigmatizing interactions to be more common because in order to use food stamps, one has to display them in public. Thus, Pettigrew (1980) reports an observation:

Bright, large stamps are handed over the checkout counter while the non-poor in line eye the shopper's food cart for suspicious items. "Look!" exclaimed one woman in a loud voice, pointing at a six-pack of beer in a food stamp shopper's cart in front of us, "and paid for by *my* taxes!" That the beer in question was properly paid for in cash and that the rest of the cart contained relatively nutritious items and that the irate shopper had three six-packs of the same beer in her cart did not deter her anger in detecting another "welfare chiseler." Some markets make the program even more salient by having specially marked check-out lines for those with food stamps.... Little wonder that some users of food stamps report that each week's trip to the market is a tense, traumatic occasion [p. 222].

A methodological observation is perhaps important here. The typical approach in empirical policy research involving sample surveys using highly structured questions is unlikely to capture the kind of reality reflected in the above observations. Persons would rather avoid reflecting on unpleasant experiences and therefore will often pass off survey questions with answers that do not require them to experience their negative feelings a second time. Given our existing methodologies, there is an almost inevitable conflict between collecting data on representative samples and probing fully the actual experiences of those samples.

For a great many families the negative experiences of being on welfare are intensified by the knowledge that one is deriving all or a good portion of one's livelihood from a derogated source. Women on welfare typically show a considerable amount of enterprise in getting off welfare—working their way out and striving to reduce their dependency bit by bit until they no longer need welfare at all (Anderson-Khleif, 1978). Although one very full case study of a long-term welfare mother suggests that she was not affected by, indeed not even aware of, stigma directed toward her kind (Sheehan, 1977), most qualitative research suggests that women on welfare take very much to heart the social significance of their situation.

One study sought to measure the psychological effects of being on welfare. Goodban (1977) found, using the Panel Study of Income Dynamics (PSID) data, that women who go on welfare change their world view in a decidedly negative direction. They tend to become less trustful of people and more concerned about what others think of them. They tend to become more uncertain about their futures, and they report getting angry more easily. Much social-psychological research confirms that people retreat into learned helplessness when faced with the accusation that they are undeserving (Adams, 1965; Pettigrew, 1979).

I do not mean to suggest that people who depend on income-tested programs like AFDC (or for whom income-tested programs such as Food Stamps are an important, though not crucial, source of support) remain passive in the face of the stigmatizing influences of the rest of society and their own world view. Instead, in line with the labeling paradigm, they often are quite energetic in warding off the stereotype. But, to return to our concern with stigma as a cost, it should be obvious that the cost of warding off stigmatization is lower with some kinds of programs, such as universal payments, than with others.

One common argument, supported by very little evidence, is that the cost from stigmatization is lower for the person who lives in a world where many people are on welfare. This argument, however, ignores the fact that if a person's opinion of those around him on welfare is fairly negative, the cost may, in fact, be higher, since he must constantly work to reject the notion that he is as bad as those others.

Long-term welfare mothers commonly react to this notion by redefining their economic dependency as an occupation. They argue that they deserve support because they are good mothers and are doing society's work in raising their children in a responsible way. Depression is another defense mechanism that is common among the poor, particularly the long-term welfare poor. They simply come not to care about their situation. Denial is equally common—a refusal to introspect, a preference not to think about themselves, their situation, their feelings (Rainwater, 1970).

There is also the possibility that people who depend on welfare over a long period of time creatively reinterpret the societal message that there is something wrong with them and define themselves as sick or disabled in some way. They seek professional confirmation of those definitions. The very common nervous complaints—nervous stomachs, nerves, tension, and high blood pressure—among long-term welfare recipients can be understood, in part, as a psychological response to derogated dependence (Rainwater, 1970).

The most common defenses are actually more constructive. The woman accepts, because she cannot avoid it, the social status into which she has fallen, but she demonstrates her basic commitment to mainstream values by moving as rapidly as she can to dig out of her situation of dependency and to "get back on her own feet."

We have been discussing the issue of cost to the recipient: whether stigmatization associated with programs such as welfare or food stamps in fact represents a cost. On this question such evidence as exists is overwhelmingly confirmatory. The other issue of concern is whether stigmatization has deeper consequences that affect not only feelings and the subjective sense of net value derived from the program but also the person's future life course. The evidence for this is much more fragmentary. There is reason to believe, however, that at least for some significant minority of "charity cases," long-term effects can be quite negative in shaping a self-definition that suggests they are in some way permanently impaired and failed. (It would be hard to distinguish the negative personality and physical health effects of a stigmatizing income-tested program from the absence of meaningful work roles that may come from more or less exclusive dependence on transfers. The effects apparently associated with long-term welfare dependency may be really those of constrained idleness.)

Stigma in Other Income-Tested Programs

Unfortunately, there is little research dealing with public conceptions of other relevant income-tested programs such as unemployment insurance, Headstart, or veterans' benefits. Veterans' benefits are not likely to be stigmatizing in any broad sense because they affect a group of the population that is presumably meritorious. Benefits for veterans that are means-tested are mixed with benefits that all veterans enjoy so that the formers' capacity to symbolize derogated status is not large.

Some impressions of the Headstart programs suggest that to some extent potential beneficiaries worry that enrolling their children will bring stigma both to themselves and to the children, who will be set off from the normal, average, American kid. Stigma thus has affected the program's enrollment.

Unemployment insurance is an interesting case for analyzing stigma because it is earnings-tested: A person without a job has no earnings and, therefore, is unemployed and entitled to benefits. However, anyone can become unemployed—everyone knows that even highly trained professionals can lose their jobs if there is a shift in the demand for their services. Therefore making use of the program is in itself unlikely to be stigmatizing. Particular systems for administering the program, of course, could be highly stigmatizing; but whether in fact they are does not seem to have been studied.

Being unemployed for a long time, however, is stigmatizing exactly as is being poor. The person whose unemployment turns out not to be purely temporary exposes himself to all of the dynamics of "explaining" failure reviewed above.

Although there do not seem to be studies of social-psychological effects of participating in income-tested programs such as college loans or the work–study program, one has the impression that these programs are not stigmatizing—primarily because the beneficiaries can present a prima facie case that they are meritorious; and although they may need a little help at the moment, they will turn out to be not just ordinary, but above average in social standing. Besides, the whole question of support for college students is tied to issues of dependence on and autonomy from one's family. Given at least the relatively high income levels associated with college-loan programs, for a student to avail himself of support programs is to demonstrate a high degree of commitment to the "work ethic" by refusing to be dependent on his parents.

Conclusion: Income Testing as an Intensifier of the Poverty Stigma

This review of research bearing on stigma in relation to income-tested programs suggests that programs stigmatize both by symbolizing a person's poverty and by marking recipients as "special" even among the poor. Typically, welfare recipients in the United States, at least at the time they apply for welfare, look to welfare as almost the sole means of support. Their needful situation thus challenges in a most forceful way the dominant ideology. While, in Beck's (1966) terms, people with slight income deficits, who need a little help, have no great problems of "rolelessness," those who have no visible means of support have enormous problems of rolelessness. This latter group, with no earnings and no family to help out, is the core population that suffers the symbolism surrounding welfare in American society. This group is also very much at the core of the symbolism surrounding public assistance in Britain and, despite its heavy commitment to welfare-state values, Sweden.

One Swedish income-tested program, however, is interesting because it apparently suffers very little stigmatization. Sweden's housing allowance program by 1978 benefited almost half of all the country's families. Eligibility is determined by income and housing costs together. A family of four earning a median income receives housing-allowance benefits if its housing costs amount to somewhat over 10% of its income.

A number of factors probably account for the very low level of stigmatization in Sweden, at least for housing-allowance recipients. First is the difference in the general context of government transfer benefits between the two countries. In the United States, fewer than one-fifth of families in the middle portion of the life cycle receive any kind of government transfer. In Sweden, slightly over 80% of such families receive transfers. Most common, of course, are those who receive family allowances (62%), but the proportion includes a very high number of beneficiaries from one or another social insurance program (38%). Thus, almost as many Swedes receive cash from the government as pay taxes to the government (Rainwater, Rein, and Schwartz, forthcoming).

The broad coverage of universal programs in Sweden (family allowances, sickness benefits, basic pensions) may well set a context in which even some kinds of income-tested programs are not stigmatized. After all, some of the universal programs are also income tested in a positive way—sickness benefits and pensions, for example, increase with earnings. Benefit income testing is therefore highly routinized and a matter of more or less confidential routine between the applicant and the responsible government agency. The shift from positive to negative income testing, so long as the program benefits a very broad section of the population, is unlikely to set in motion stigmatizing effects such as those examined above.

Furthermore income-tested programs are possibly less stigmatizing when they principally supplement the family income and on a regular basis over time instead of as the sole source of support even for a few months or so. Though the Swedish income-tested housing-allowance program is large in terms of budget, even the poorest recipients are not likely to depend very much on it. It would be a rare family, indeed, that received as much as 30% of its income over the course of a year from the housing allowance.

That there is nothing to be ashamed of in the receipt of housing allowances and that quite ordinary people do receive the allowances is emphasized forcefully for all Swedes by receipt of annual computer printouts that state on the basis of their last year's income tax whether they could be eligible for a housing allowance. The government publishes full and attractive broadsides explaining housing-allowance benefits and how one qualifies for them. Public communication suggests most emphatically that there is nothing to be ashamed of.

As this example and much of the research reviewed above suggests, analyzing the social-psychological effects of particular income-tested programs independent of the social context provided by the system of class relations in a society would be a mistake.

To the extent that programs are sharply targeted to the poor and to the extent that poverty is itself highly stigmatized in a society (and this latter is probably inevitable in any society), those programs are likely to end up being stigmatizing. In short, there is a great deal of truth in the slogan "programs for the poor become poor programs." This is inevitable because society's derogation of the poor is the obverse of the value it necessarily places on personal responsibility, and on "incentives" as a way of symbolizing the value placed on personal responsibility for one's own welfare. (A great deal of the research and policy discussion concerned with incentives and disincentives in the design of programs has

quite likely been misplaced. People may not respond in their own behavior as strongly as economic theory suggests to such incentives, but
they certainly do judge the justness and fairness of programs in terms of
whether they seem to preserve incentives for recipients to better themselves through hard work.)

As a consequence income-tested programs will always be vulnerable
to definitions that are stigmatizing to beneficiaries. They therefore involve a cost that reduces the value of the money benefit. The main
factors involved in whether individuals are stigmatized have to do with
their labor market position. If people who "should" work had full-time
jobs and it was understood that all beneficiaries of transfer programs
were full-time workers who, nevertheless, needed a little additional
help, stigmatization probably would not operate with the same
virulence. However, it certainly would still be present due to the man-
ifest "weakness" of individuals who work full time but still cannot fully
earn their own way.

We have no studies of the social–psychological meanings associated
with being the beneficiary of universal programs such as the family
allowance. Such benefits are likely to be defined by both recipients and
others as justified assistance to hard-working citizens. One is deserving
of transfer payments without proof of special needs (which signify special shortcomings) if one does his part by playing some valued role in
society, has either a first- or second-hand connection with the labor
market (via a husband or parent, for example), works hard at socially
valued tasks (labor market jobs or family responsibilities or school), or
pays for social insurance through contributions. With universal programs as a backdrop and with the positive income tax a broadly understood and, albeit reluctantly, accepted transfer system, having a stigma-
free, income-tested program is possible. (But note that in Sweden less
than 10% of the government transfers going to persons in the mid-years
of the life cycle are income tested compared with well over 40% of
government transfers in the United States.)

Probably no society can do without a residual income-tested program
for some families who are not able to make their way by a principal
reliance on the labor market and a secondary reliance on broadly based
universal programs and semi-universal income-tested programs. But
the dynamics of stigmatization argue very strongly that such programs
should be last resorts for families whose economic needs are not
adequately served by the maintenance of a full-employment economy
and a transfer system that recognizes the need everyone has to be not
totally dependent on a day-in, day-out paying job. One test, then, for

universal transfer programs is how much they contribute to reducing the size of the class that in the end must avail itself of charity and pay the price that goes with it.

Needed Research

Because the stigmatizing effects of means-tested programs are fairly subtle and not easy to get at in ordinary questionnaire self-reports, a research program concerned with the social–psychological effects of income-tested versus universal benefits should concentrate on observational studies and qualitative interview surveys. Several different kinds of studies would be useful.

INTERVIEW STUDIES OF PROGRAM RECIPIENTS AND POTENTIAL RECIPIENTS

One useful study would be of benefit recipients, persons who qualify but are not recipients, and former recipients of food stamps, AFDC, and unemployment, disability, and social security widows' benefits. Interviews should probe respondents' own conceptions of their entitlement to benefits and experiences dealing with functionaries and caretakers. The interviews should determine reactions beneficiaries have experienced from those close to them, experiences with strangers, and the attitudes they perceive others to have.

I would recommend that the samples include former but recent beneficiaries because people may find it less painful to report negative experiences associated with stigmatizing treatment once they have left a program. Those who qualify for benefits, but have not claimed them, should be interviewed systematically about what they know about their eligibility and (to the extent that they are aware of their eligibility) why they have not applied for benefits and how they feel those in their social world would respond if they did apply. Interviewing a sample of solo mothers who have not received AFDC about how they have thought about issues of "going on welfare versus working" would be particularly useful.

Small replications in other countries would be particularly illuminating. I would recommend comparative studies in such countries as Canada, Britain, and Sweden. (An exploration of stigma related to the Swedish housing-allowance program might be useful.)

OBSERVATIONAL STUDIES

As a companion to the interview studies, small observational studies of interactions between recipients and functionaries would be useful.

Such studies should combine observation of interaction with analysis of administrative records of applicants and beneficiaries. Such observational studies would be useful not only in welfare departments but in a variety of other settings as well, such as those relevant to disability benefits, offices where Unemployment Compensation is dispensed, and offices and stores associated with the Food Stamp program.

COHORT STUDIES

Another group of studies might test the long-term effects of receipt of income-tested benefits. One such study could proceed with an interview of a sample of long-term recipients along the lines indicated for the interview study above. Systematic use should be made of Welfare Department and other records. In addition, the caretakers with whom recipients deal should be questioned on their understanding of the beneficiaries' situations and their conception of such persons..

Longitudinal studies in which more control could be exercised over the variables that may affect the physical/mental status of long-term beneficiaries would also be useful. Such studies should be designed to test in a reasonable, rigorous way the effects of long-term receipt of welfare compared with social security benefits. Despite the fact that the groups eligible for the two kinds of benefits may be different, one ought to be able to control for the most important differences between them by careful selection of the sample.

STUDIES OF UNIVERSAL BENEFITS

Finally, as best I can determine, there has been no research on the meaning attached by recipients to universal categorical benefits. The first study suggested above includes the one common category of such recipients in the United States—widows on social security. It would be useful to explore in other countries the meanings attached to family allowances and health insurance benefits, the two largest programs affecting the nonelderly. Such comparative studies could be carried out using the same interviewing instrument in Canada, Britain, and Sweden.

TRANSFERS AND DISTRIBUTIVE JUSTICE

Jasso's (1978) reformulation of the justice evaluation function can serve as a starting place for very useful studies of distributive justice in means-tested and universal benefits. Using methods developed by Rossi and his coworkers (Alves and Rossi, 1978), it should be possible to investigate the conceptions that the general public, recipients, and likely recipients of various kinds of transfer benefits have of fair levels of

benefits and the relationship between characteristics of the family receiving the benefits and the fairness of those benefits. The various payment
schedules developed by experts for such programs as public assistance,
proposed negative income taxes, proposed universal programs, and
proposed modifications of social insurance, have implicit normative
elements concerning distributive justice. (One might add policymakers
to surveys using the Rossi method.)

I would propose that a survey be designed to investigate justice
evaluation functions of the general public and recipients for the range of
income-transfer benefits currently in existence. The justice evaluation
functions derived from such a survey can be tested for degree of consensus (indexed roughly by the proportions of the variance in ratings of
profiles accounted for by stimulus items) and variations around that
consensus as a function of the characteristics of persons making the
judgment.

Discussion

VERNON L. ALLEN

In the short space available I shall, first, attempt to summarize briefly the salient points made in Rainwater's interesting paper, and then offer a few of my own comments about the issues that are raised.

Basic Points of Rainwater's Paper

The purpose of Rainwater's paper is to examine data concerning the possible negative social–psychological consequences accruing to recipients of income-tested programs. He subsumes all the negative psychological effects under the general term "stigma." Such negative effects can be considered to be psychological "costs" that are borne by participants of these programs. It is asserted that support for the claim that stigma is associated with income-tested programs can be found in the evidence indicating that other people express negative attitudes toward recipients; that recipients are treated differently from other persons; that recipients share society's negative definition by likewise holding negative views of self; and that recipients behave in ways consistent with, or responsive to, their derogated self-image. Rainwater argues that these general statements possess a "considerable" degree of truth. I shall organize my summary of the paper by focusing upon the four basic issues that Rainwater addresses.

THEORETICAL BASIS FOR THE STIGMATIZATION OF PARTICIPANTS IN INCOME-TESTED PROGRAMS

At the theoretical level, stigma derives from societal ideology and values concerning fairness and incentives. Derogating those persons who receive help can be viewed as a social control mechanism which discourages others from engaging in such behavior. The process of stigmatization is interpreted within the framework of labeling theory. According to theory, when social norms have been violated the attaching of negative labels to deviants helps reinforce the norms and also provides a causal explanation in terms of personal attributes of the deviant for the discrepancy between the ideal and reality in society. Both from the broad functionalist theoretical framework and from the perspective of labeling theory, it would be predicted that the poor in general, and the "welfare poor" especially, will be stigmatized.

ATTITUDES OF THE PUBLIC TOWARD WELFARE RECIPIENTS

Does the public hold negative stereotypes about the poor, and in particular about the welfare poor? Apparently so, according to literature cited in the paper. The prevalent stereotype seems to be that the poor are "lazy, stupid, dishonest, and ambitionless." Accepting the ideology of the just world (i.e., that effort and hard work account for one's position in life), most Americans believe that the poor deserve their lot because of their own personal failings. Data indicate that other people attribute lack of thrift, effort, and ability to the poor. Rainwater suggests that means-tested programs can only further emphasize the "lowly status" of the poor in the eyes of others. He concludes that we hold two basic images of participants in the most common income-tested programs, viz., welfare and food stamps. The principal perception is that those on welfare are weak: lazy, shiftless, and lacking in work motivation. A secondary image is of a type that is more powerful but morally reprehensible—the chiseler. Thus, the dominant stereotypes of welfare recipients are of persons who are mostly "pitiable" and somewhat "to be feared."

SELF-ATTITUDES OF WELFARE RECIPIENTS

What are the conceptions and attitudes that welfare recipients hold about themselves? Rainwater argues that recipients share the negative stereotypes of themselves held by others. Data are cited suggesting that those on welfare may change their world view: They become less truthful, more uncertain about the future, and express anger more often. Depression and physical symptoms are reputed to be common occurrences. All of the evidence leads to the conclusion that long-term effects of being on welfare produce (for many) a definition of self as a failure or impaired in some way.

COMPARISON AMONG TYPES OF PROGRAMS

The evidence for stigmatization discussed by Rainwater deals exclusively with one type of income-tested program—welfare. He states that there is little evidence available relevant to the question of the social-psychological effects of other income-tested programs, such as veterans' benefits, Headstart, and college loans. On the basis of impressionistic evidence, however, he does not believe that benefits from these programs would be stigmatizing (perhaps with the exception of Headstart). Other factors seem to prevent derogation from occurring: veterans are presumably meritorious, and attending college demonstrates commitment to the work ethic. The interesting suggestion is offered that perhaps it is not the income-tested programs, per se, that are stigmatizing, but rather being in need of them as the sole source of support. For example, the Swedish housing allowance is used as an income supplement; it is an income-tested program but appears to produce little stigmatization. Unfortunately, adequate data do not seem to be available for examining the social–psychological impact of universal programs. Though recognizing the probable necessity of income-tested programs for some families, Rainwater argues in conclusion that the psychic cost of stigmatization for recipients of such programs justifies the recommendation that they be used only as a last resort.

Critique of the Paper

In this paper Rainwater has presented an interesting, useful, and thought-provoking excursion into the area of the psychological impact of economic and social policy, an area fraught with difficult methodological and conceptual problems. In addition to numerous problems of internal validity, sampling, and control groups with specific studies, comparing the psychological effects of income-tested programs in the United States with universal programs in other countries is a very precarious undertaking. Many cultural and other differences between the countries might readily explain results of this type of comparison. The overriding impression that I gained from this paper is that, on the basis of evidence presented, the empirical data do not appear to be sufficient in terms of quantity or quality to contribute significantly toward a policy decision concerning income-tested versus universal programs. The argument and the data are based entirely upon welfare programs (typi-

cally, AFDC and Food Stamps); these programs can certainly be characterized as having many exotic and idiosyncratic features relative to the
full gamut of potential income-tested programs.

Attitudes toward Welfare Recipients

The basic thrust of the argument advanced by Rainwater is that
income-tested programs of the welfare type tend to produce negative
social-psychological effects—psychic costs—for recipients. The argument has two complementary parts: one, that the public holds negative
attitudes toward recipients; and, two, that recipients agree with these
negative attitudes. Data are presented to buttress both portions of the
argument. Let us first discuss the attitudes of the public toward welfare
recipients. If we rely completely on the empirical evidence presented in
the paper, the argument would not seem to be strongly supported. It
goes without saying that one must be highly skeptical of the many
anecdotal and journalistic reports in this area. More systematic data are
presented from a study by Feagin (1972b) which indicate that people do
attribute the cause of poverty to the shortcomings of the poor themselves. The data do indeed show that 80% of the respondents choose as
"somewhat" or "very important" the lack of effort by the poor themselves as a cause of poverty. But note that data in the same table from
Feagin's article reveal that other causes also received high endorsements
from respondents: low wages in some businesses (77%), prejudice and
discrimination against blacks (70%), and sickness and physical handicaps (85%). Thus, the respondents appear to hold a multiple-causation
view of poverty; they do not assign its cause exclusively to any single
factor.

Several studies have been conducted concerning the attitudes of
other people toward the poor and toward welfare recipients. Results
often seem to suggest that such attitudes are ambivalent. Several studies
have reported negative attitudes, of course. Yet one survey (Potter,
Coudy, and Larson, 1968) reported that 80% of respondents agree that
"most people on public assistance are needy, not greedy." In general,
the available data suggest that it would be wise to avoid drawing conclusions too broadly; rather, it is worth recognizing that there are wide
differences in the attitudes manifested by persons from different segments of the population (e.g., social class, education, geographic area);
and that attitudes vary about different sorts of welfare programs and
about different types of recipients. The assumption of a strong consensus would thus seem not to be warranted (Alston and Dean, 1972). In
addition, attitudes may vary depending upon the image of the particular

type of welfare recipient that is evoked by an interview question. For instance, a study conducted in Chicago (Greenleigh Associates, 1960) which asked about attitudes toward AFDC families found that "respondents quickly transformed the question to one of attitudes toward blacks in general and lower-class blacks in particular." (The lack of control for the specific attitudinal object evoked by the diffuse stimulus "welfare recipient" is an important methodological problem.) In short, it would appear that data support the position that the public's attitudes toward welfare recipients are quite differentiated among segments of the respondent population, and likewise are differentiated according to the categories of recipients who are objects of the attitudinal response.

Negative attitudes expressed by members of the public toward income-tested programs are important if they have serious consequences: if they are translated into lack of political support for a valuable social policy; if they prevent needy persons from availing themselves of available resources; or if they result in undesirable behavior toward recipients. But a word of caution is in order in any discussion of attitudes. It must be remembered that there is a substantial body of empirical evidence indicating a complete lack of consistency between one's attitudes and behavior, and that other studies have obtained consistency between attitudes and behavior only under certain conditions and in certain social contexts (Wicker, 1969).

Psychological Effects on Recipients

Perhaps the most critical issue raised by Rainwater is the possible negative psychological impact of income-tested programs on the recipients themselves. Negative consequences would certainly be predicted from the theoretical perspective advanced by Rainwater. There are also psychological theories that can be applied to the problem, such as social exchange (Homans, 1958) or reciprocity (Gouldner, 1960), attribution (Kelley, 1967), reactance (Brehm, 1966), and ingroup–outgroup categorization (Tajfel, 1969). These theories also lead to the prediction that a recipient of help is likely to respond negatively both to the helper and to self. However, these psychological theories focus on a relationship consisting of face-to-face contact between individuals, and the help that one receives from another person is relatively direct and immediate. By contrast, aid to the poor typically consists of institutional rather than interpersonal help. Thus, caution is advised in applying these psychological theories to transfer programs that operate in a rather indirect and often impersonal way.

Some data are presented in Rainwater's paper consistent with the expectation of negative effects on participants of welfare programs. Nevertheless, it must be stressed that the data are not quite so clearcut and consistent as one might expect. Most of the information obtained from anecdotal, literary, journalistic, and self-report sources has strongly emphasized the negative consequences of public assistance on the recipient. On the other hand, survey studies often have discovered that recipients' attitudes are less negative than expected. For example, on the basis of data collected from a large sample of AFDC recipients (N = 766), Handler and Hollingsworth (1968) concluded, "There seems to be far less negative feelings on the part of welfare recipients than one would have expected from reading the literature [p. 31]." As for feelings about the stigma of being on welfare, in their study half the respondents reported they never felt embarrassed or uncomfortable when with others who were not on welfare, and only 12% characterized the attitudes of others as negative. Feelings of stigma did affect the use of social services, but in a way contrary to what might be expected from Rainwater's analysis. Recipients who experienced stigma actually used the program more, and were "far more aggressive in asserting what they think they are entitled to under the program." Finally, the measure of stigma did not differentiate between recipients who left welfare and those who remained in the program. I do not take the position that participants in welfare programs never experience negative psychological conse-quences; at the same time, however, we should beware of making an overly simple and sweeping conclusion in the face of conflicting data.

In addition to the existence of inconsistent empirical evidence, two further points should be taken into consideration in discussing the ef-fects of welfare programs on participants. First, research in this area is replete with methodological pitfalls. Because of the respondents' fear of adverse consequences, self-report data in this area must be viewed with extreme caution. It is possible, Rainwater suggests, that recipients may erect self-defenses against feeling stigmatized, and thereby deny having a negative self-concept or feelings of shame. Such self-defensive strategies might account for the results of studies that failed to find strong negative consequences. But a similar interpretation can be of-fered for opposite results as well. Thus, self-reports of negative psychological effects may be due to giving socially desirable responses, that is, giving the responses that one believes the investigator wants to hear.

A second point concerns alternative interpretations of results even if the conclusion were accepted that participants do experience strong negative psychological effects. Results pointing to negative conse-quences experienced by participants may be spurious, in the sense that they can be attributed to variables other than the income-tested aspects of the program. That is, variables that are confounded with participation in the program may be the principal determinants of the behavioral impact. That this is a very real possibility is suggested by the absence of negative psychological effects at several levels of income support in the New Jersey negative income tax study (Middleton and Allen, 1977). This study—an income-tested program—was subjected to a much more rigorous experimental design and statistical analysis than is found in most of the studies reviewed earlier. Are there plausible alternative interpretations for any negative results of welfare programs on participants? Two suggestions can be offered. The first possibility is that frustration associated with the administrative aspects of the program (a condition that may exist, of course, in either income-tested or universal programs) is one of the major sources of negative affect. Thus, it may well be that factors associated with the discretionary aspects of the program are the source of much of the dissatisfaction, frustration, and negative affect reported by participants. A second very likely alternative interpretation of any negative psychological effects (e.g., low image of self, fatigue, depression, etc.) is that such responses are prior characteristics of the type of persons who choose to seek help, rather than the consequence of participating in the program. Consistent with this second suggestion, one study found that recipients needed a substantial amount of psychological as well as financial assistance as a result of their having experienced emotional, social, and economic deprivation in early childhood (Greenleigh Associates, 1960). In addition to the need for financial aid, multiple emotional and physical problems were commonly found among applicants for assistance. Rainwater appears to recognize the possibility of a similar interpretation of negative psychological effects by noting that "rolelessness" or "enforced idleness" may contribute to the negative psychological effects.

One of the basic assumptions underlying Rainwater's theoretical analysis is that the Protestant work ethic is widely accepted. Since the poor presumably share this ideology, they feel responsible for their condition and hence attribute causality for their poverty to dispositional (personal) causes. Some evidence is available that calls into question this assumption, at least for certain subgroups of the poor. Relevant data are available from a study by Barr (1968), in which over 200 interviews were conducted with poor persons in New York City, almost all of whom were receiving welfare. One conclusion of this study was that "poor persons see themselves as victimized by society and do not see themselves to blame for the variety of financial difficulties in which they find themselves [p. 575]."

Taking a broad historical perspective, Segalman (1968) traces the development of social welfare in the context of the Protestant ethic. He concludes that as a result of social programs since the Depression, "the Protestant Ethic went out of 'style' as an American belief... and the *right* to public assistance arrived [p. 137]." Whether or not one accepts this sweeping conclusion, evidence does suggest that there may have been an increase in the tendency to attribute responsibility to the social system as opposed to self for one's economic situation in life. Gurin et al. (1969) obtained data from black youth that seem to support this position. Other developments also point to the possibility of an increasing tendency to blame the social system for one's plight, and thus to view financial assistance as being a right—as equity rather than "charity." As cases in point, note the growth of welfare rights organizations and the demand from racial minorities for increased assistance expressed in terms of equity or compensation for past wrongs by society. To the extent that attribution about the causes of poverty may have shifted from the self to the external system, then the basic foundation upon which Rainwater builds his analysis of stigma associated with income-tested programs would seem to be in jeopardy.

Conclusion

I am sorry to conclude by repeating the ambidextrous behavior so characteristic of social scientists: "On the one hand . . . but on the other hand." It does seem, however, that the empirical data are at present insufficient in terms of quantity, quality, and consistency across studies to justify drawing a strong and simple conclusion concerning the relative psychological effect of income-tested versus universal programs. An important contribution could be made by attempting to isolate the variables or components in any income-tested and universal programs that might be responsible for important effects (positive or negative) at the psychological level. Interesting questions can also be raised about potential threshold effects. If a person participates in some sort of mixture of income-tested and universal programs, is there a point at which the nature of the psychological impact changes? Rainwater offers the stimulating suggestion that income-tested programs may produce negative psychological effects only if they constitute one's sole source of support.

Considering all the unanswered questions in this area leads me to finish by saying that even though the omnipresent concluding statement is as trite as ever, it is also still as true as ever: More research is needed!

Discussion

ALVIN L. SCHORR

I find Dr. Rainwater's paper a useful and persuasive summary of social and psychological evidence on the effects of stigma. I have nothing of substance to add and only details to quarrel with. For example, I would not have called Unemployment Insurance income tested. If Dr. Rainwater is correct in the way he justifies that, retirement and disability insurance would also have to be called income tested. That is, those circumstances also cause low income. But cloudy definition hangs over the issues we address these couple of days and a common nomenclature would represent an unexpected and uncommon contribution. Rather than spend my ten minutes on casuistry, I will outline a possibly modern problem brought on by income testing.

I ask you to think about the social compact between citizens and government in the United States. The social compact is an understanding about the way each conducts itself with respect to the other, including honest reporting and the responsibility to deliver legal benefits. Without a general understanding, adhered to by most citizens and officials, no amount of enforcement is adequate to produce reasonable government functioning. Citizens have always manipulated their property and affairs for maximum personal benefit. Advantage and disadvantage are weighed with respect to family members, business associates, and competitors. With the growth of government programming in the last forty years, however, the government has become the main player across the table. And it is faceless—with respect to individuals—not pained if it loses, not aggrieved if one gets the better of it.

In all transfer programs, knowledgeable citizens play the rules for best advantage. They perceive that "disability insurance is not a bad alternative to a lousy, low-paying job with intermittent employment [Levitan, 1977]." Youths declare legal emancipation from their parents earlier than otherwise in order to qualify for college aid (*New York Times*, 1978). Among the aged who have assets, some dispose of or sequester them in order to qualify for SSI or Medicaid (Moon, 1977b, p. 21; U.S. Department of Health, Education, and Welfare, 1978b). Such activity carries with it a penumbra of illegal manipulation, the extent naturally difficult to ascertain. Legal and illegal manipulation are connected in that both are rooted in at least a degree of covert social approval. "Where ceilings on assets are not high," for example, "lax enforcement of asset rules spares potential beneficiaries from rapid consumption of their capital (Hausman, 1977, p. 113). In other words administrators, themselves dubious of the merits of the rules, are willing to be inattentive to evasion.

It is not as if only citizens manipulate and, at a margin, overstep legal bounds; so too does government. Before SSI eliminated relative responsibility, many welfare departments required children's contributions on a scale they knew courts would not support (Schorr, 1960). That is certainly now the case with respect to child support enforcement. For reasons that are well understood, few appeal to the courts for their rights. Although HEW (now HHS) has continuously audited public assistance for overpayments to recipients, auditing for funds *withheld* in error was discontinued for many years and only recently reinstated. Whereas overpayment imposes a financial penalty on states, the finding that recipients have been cheated does not. As a third example, the Federal Council on Aging, speculating in print about the reason for poor participation in a number of federal programs, names among the possibilities "outright denial of benefits through discriminatory practises [1975, p. 34]."

The government reaction to the citizens' end of the problem is increasing activity concerned with auditing and enforcement. But concurrent developments make the problem worse while government tries to regulate it. Difficulties occasioned by large, carelessly developed, overlapping programs have now widely been noted (U.S. Congress, 1972–1974; Federal Council on Aging, 1975, p. 2). Therefore more is at stake in getting into a particular program and staying in. The logic of program interrelationships resists understanding and so invites evasion. And citizens accurately perceive that those who are program-wise can attain benefits while others cannot; that invites emulation. And so study groups are appointed to address these problems. They tend to have a rich mix of experts and professionals and perhaps naturally find themselves recommending eligibility and review mechanisms staffed by experts and professionals. But the spread of professional, individualized access to benefits builds delay and complexity and polarizes the citizen–government relationship.

Added to all this, and of most relevance here, is that the last decade has seen a marked growth of income-tested programs relative to social insurance.[1] Yet it is precisely income-tested programs that present acute problems of interrelationship—one program providing entitlement to another and, irrationally different definitions of income, assets, and household. It is income-tested programs in which questions about manipulation and improper receipt most usually arise. And it is income-tested programs that widely suffer from problems of take-up. In Cleveland, according to a Government Accounting Office study, "89 percent of those eligible were not using public housing; 77 percent were not using food stamps, 52 percent were not using SSI; and 29 percent were not using Medicaid [U.S. Government Accounting Office, 1978, p. iii]."

Because stigma is involved, income-tested programs tend to be laden with the necessity to demonstrate a variety of circumstances or statuses somewhat marginal to financial need—whether children are in school, where a father is, capacity to work, and so forth. The day-by-day monitoring of these qualities turns income-tested benefits into *discretionary* benefits, whether or not the law intended that. Under the pressure of increased regulation, civil servants learn that improper denial is better than improper entitlement. In a four-month search in East Harlem, for example, a special project found 78 families that said they had been turned down for welfare but thought they were really eligible. Of the 78, 63 turned out really to be eligible. Indeed, when the project took up their cases, they were granted assistance (D. Reich, 1977a, 1977b).

The relationship of improper denial to failure of take-up should not be overlooked. Of course, the improperly denied are not counted among recipients but, more important, multiples of that number read the message and do not apply. All these difficulties that can be documented—manipulation and fraud and failure of take-up—are especially characteristic of income-tested programs. And they are particulars of an erosion of trust between citizens and government.

[1]Dr. Heidenheimer has noted how much more income testing the United States has, relatively, than West Germany. (See his paper, Chapter 5 in this volume.)

One understands that these broad developments are mutually reinforcing and lead to trouble. The revolutionary significance to citizens of government programs, combined with difficulty in understanding their broad outlines, uncertainty about ultimate entitlement, complexity, delay, and income testing lead to a grasping attitude on one side of the desk and withholding on the other. Hostility evidences itself on one side with a sense of grievance, if not belligerence, and a determination to get benefits, no matter how; and on the government side with boredom, callousness, and evident alienation from work. Citizen and government distrust of each other are a single problem.

We have tended to treat the crisis of the social compact as a moral issue, which means it is no one's problem, or perhaps the churches'. That is a cop-out. The structure of government programming is at least partially at fault, and those who are assembled here at least in part responsible. If we are to maintain or restore the social compact, we must move carefully and thoughtfully towards programming that is legible. ("Legible" is a word I borrow from urban planners, who mean that one sees evident logic in a complex design, that a neighborhood or town has landmarks with which one orients himself.) In outline, at least, citizens must be able to understand their compact with the government and count on it. The growth of income testing is inimical to such design.

Discussion: Modeling the Decision to Apply for Welfare

JOHN BISHOP

In the United States income-tested welfare programs have surprisingly low take-up rates. The Social Security Administration (U.S. Department of Health, Education, and Welfare, 1974) has estimated that half of the aged poor that were eligible for SSI failed to apply. Maurice MacDonald (1977) and Richard Coe (1977) both found that participation rates by eligible two-parent families in the Food Stamp program in the early 1970s were under 40%. Estimates of participation rates by eligible two-parent families in the AFDC Unemployed Parent program are also low. Barbara Boland (1973) estimated the participation rate to be 23% in 1967 and 29% in 1970. Mildred Rein's (1972) and Russell Lidman's (1975) estimates for 1969 are, respectively, 20.6% and 15%. Kevin Hollenbeck's (1975) estimate of the 1973 participation rate is 21%. In 1974 roughly half of the poor families headed by a nonaged male reported that they had received no transfers of any kind that year (Danziger and Plotnick, 1979). The only income-tested transfer program with high participation rates during the early seventies seems to be the basic AFDC program. Boland estimates that in 1967, 58%, and in 1970, 81% of eligible single-parent families participated in AFDC. Using data from the Denver Income Maintenance Experiment, Arden Hall (1976) calculates that in June 1970, 87% of legally eligible families were receiving AFDC payments.

The low rates at which eligible families participate in income mainte-nance programs needs an explanation. The two most common expla-nations proposed for the seeming irrationality of not applying for money that is your right are (*a*) the high costs of applying (including obtaining information on whether you are eligible); and (*b*) stigma costs of apply-ing and/or being a recipient of charity. When these costs are incorpo-rated into a model of participation, not applying for welfare, even when the odds of being eligible are very high, is found to have a rational explanation.

I shall explore how these costs enter the decision by formally model-ing an individual's decision to apply for welfare. I shall begin by treating as exogenous the information the individual has about the generosity and rules of eligibility of the program. Later I shall relax this assumption.

A utility-maximizing individual who is eligible for welfare will apply for welfare if the expected money benefits are greater than the sum of the time costs of application and the stigma costs of application and recipiency.

Welfare participation = 1 if net benefits of applying > 0
= 0 if net benefits of applying ≤ 0
$$\text{Net benefits} = NB_a = \hat{P}(\hat{B} - S) - (A + S_a), \tag{1}$$

where

$\hat{P}$ = the probability of being eligible as perceived by the individual;
$\hat{B}$ = the expected cash payment if one is eligible discounted over the time one expects to remain on welfare;
S = the psychological costs (continuing stigma costs) of being a welfare recipient;
A = time costs of applying = (wage rate) · (hours spent filling out form);
S_a = stigma costs that result from the application process or from the redefinition of self as being an applicant for welfare.

Since it seldom takes more than a few hours to fill out an application form, and wage rates of the potentially eligible population are low, time costs of applying would seem to have an upper bound of $20.00. Even if the stay on welfare is just a few months, these costs are a small fraction of the cash payments that will be received. If stigma costs were zero, the perceived probability of being eligible would have to be substantially less than 10% before the expected net benefit of applying would fall to zero. Consequently, time costs (A) cannot by themselves explain why application rates are so low.

The psychological factors (stigma costs) that discourage participation include (*a*) fear of embarrassment or humiliation, whether while applying for aid, or at the check-out counter of the supermarket, or during home visits by social workers; (b) distaste for the loss of privacy that applying for and receiving welfare entails; and (c) the loss of self-respect that may occur if one admits that he/she is incapable of supporting his/her family and in need of charity.

In studies conducted during the thirties, this last motive was found to be extremely important, despite the fact that extended periods of unemployment were by no means unusual.

> Every goal he seeks to reach as a normal worker recedes further from realization when he turns to relief. Until that moment he could in a measure realize that even without current earnings the efforts he made in the past in the role of a "producer," a "good provider," a "good father" were still contributing to the support of his family. But now he has made a public declaration of his failure, and no rationalization can quite cover up the fact that a "reliefer" is not among the roles his associates respect [Bakke, 1940, p. 255].

Stigma costs are potentially much larger than the time costs of application and, therefore, may be the source of the low rates of participation that are typical of U.S. income-tested cash assistance programs.

The final elements of the net benefit calculation are the subjective probability of being eligible for welfare ($\hat{P}$) and the expected amount of the benefit ($\hat{B}$). Expectations about the level of benefits and the probability of being eligible depend upon the level and quality of the individual's knowledge of welfare programs. Well-informed people would have subjective $\hat{B}$s and $\hat{P}$s that would closely correspond to their true eligibility status. Poorly informed people can be expected to have $\hat{B}$s and $\hat{P}$s that correlate weakly with their true eligibility status and that may systematically understate or overstate the true probability of being eligible and the true levels of benefits.

An assertion that ignorance is responsible for the low participation rates of eligible two-parent families amounts to saying that a large proportion of eligible families underestimate their true probability of being eligible ($\hat{P}$) and/or the benefits for which they are eligible ($\hat{B}$). Such an assertion begs a very important question, however. Why are potential eligibles ignorant and why are they ignorant in this particular way?

To answer these questions one must drop the assumption that the individual's knowledge about welfare programs is exogenous. A poorly informed individual becomes well informed by investing in the gathering and processing of information. This investment may involve nothing more than a passive act of listening and remembering when someone else brings up the subject of welfare benefits. More actively, it may involve asking a friend who is on welfare, calling up the welfare office or a community-based organization, or picking up and reading explanatory literature. When will an individual who has not applied for welfare and does not currently intend to apply for welfare choose to invest in gathering information about whether he/she is likely to be eligible for welfare? The investment will produce one of three outcomes:

1. $\hat{P}$ and/or $\hat{B}$ rise sufficiently to induce the individual to apply and the application is successful. (The probability of this outcome is P_1.)
2. $\hat{P}$ and/or $\hat{B}$ rise sufficiently to induce the individual to apply and the application is unsuccessful. (The probability of this outcome is P_2.)
3. $\hat{P}$ and/or $\hat{B}$ do not rise enough to induce an application. The cost of this investment in knowledge is C so the net benefit of the investment in more knowledge about welfare (NB_k) is

$$(NB_k) = P_1(\hat{B} - S - A - S_a) + P_2(-A - S_a) + (1 - P_1 - P_2)(0) - C \tag{2}$$

There is a payoff to learning more only if the new knowledge causes one to initiate an application and the application is successful. If the application is turned down one loses the time spent applying and suffers whatever stigma is attached to having applied for welfare and having been turned down. The size of the net benefit is the welfare payment minus all stigma and application-time costs. Thus, the incentive to invest in knowledge about whether one is eligible for welfare is a negative function of the perceived stigma of applying for and being on welfare. This means that stigma is an important determinant of how well informed one becomes about welfare as well as whether one applies for welfare given the state of one's knowledge. People who expect to be stigmatized by applying for or being on welfare will avoid investing in knowledge about their eligibility.

In fact, some people may feel there are psychological costs to even contemplating the possibility of going on welfare. An effort to learn whether one is eligible makes sense only if there is a possibility of utilizing welfare, so gathering the information incurs psychological as well as time costs. The individual who chooses to eschew learning more can say, "I might be eligible for handouts, but I would never as a matter of principle apply for them." The person that has actively tried to learn more takes the risk of having to say, "I checked it out, found I was not eligible. Even if I were, however, I would never apply as a matter of principle." The time and money costs of getting adequate information about one's eligibility are so small and the monetary benefits of a successful application so large that even if widespread ignorance were the proximate cause of low participation rates among eligibles, one would still have to posit stigma as an important cause of the ignorance.

More evidence for the importance of stigma can be found in the pattern of participation rates across different groups of eligibles. We hypothesize that the likelihood that an eligible family participates in an income-tested transfer program depends upon (a) the size of the transfer the family would receive if it applied; (b) information-gathering abilities and the time costs of applying; and (c) stigma.

If stigma is an important cause of nonparticipation, we would expect that, *controlling for the size of the welfare payment*, the family's likelihood of participation will

1. Fall with a rise in the family's income and assets (in other words, distaste for stigma is a normal good).
2. Fall with the number of adults in the family (because the number of people experiencing the stigma has risen).
3. Be lower when the family head is a male.
4. Be higher when a female head has children to care for.
5. Be lower for the Food Stamp program and in rural areas (because stigma is greater when one's neighbors know that one is receiving welfare).
6. Be higher when other people in one's neighborhood are having financial difficulties or are on welfare (i.e., when unemployment rates are high). Association with others who are on welfare will not only reduce stigma; it will also lower the costs of obtaining information about welfare. Both of these factors predict a positive association with local unemployment rates.
7. Fall with the individual's and/or the community's belief in the Protestant ethic and the justness of the economic system.

This last prediction is the hardest to test. Regionally, the bastions of the Protestant ethic and belief in the system would seem to be the Rocky Mountain states, the Plains states, and the South. There is likely to be a debate about the correlates of the Protestant ethic and belief in the system at the individual level. Let me suggest the following: education, IQ, having sources of information accessible, and membership in an older cohort.

If ignorance of the availability of welfare is the major reason for the nonparticipation of eligibles, and stigma is not the primary cause of this ignorance, one would expect that—holding constant the size of the welfare benefit—participation would have a positive partial correlation with such indicators of information-processing ability as IQ and education. One would also expect a negative partial correlation with indicators of the time and money cost of applying for welfare, such as the wage rate, distance from the welfare office, and the accessibility of potential sources of information.

Three multivariate studies of welfare participation contain variables that address some of these hypotheses. All of the studies control for size of the welfare benefit. Two studies examine the Food Stamp program. MacDonald's (1977) study of 1971 Food Stamp participation found that most of the hypothesized indicators of stigma were negatively associated with participation. Families with higher previous incomes and with greater current assets were considerably less likely to participate. Coe's (1977) study of 1974 Food Stamp participation rates did not contain measures of assets or family income. Contrary to expectations, both studies found no tendency for rural areas to have higher participation rates than large cities and no tendency for the South to have a lower participation rate. The stigma hypotheses that families with children were considerably more likely to be on food stamps is supported. Families that are or have recently been on welfare are more likely to participate. This finding can be interpreted either as related to stigma or to information cost. Female-headed families are more likely to participate than two-parent families, but much of the difference seems to be due to their greater propensity to be on welfare. The older cohorts, who presumably have a more internalized Protestant ethic, do have lower Food Stamp participation rates in both the Coe and MacDonald studies.

The tests of the hypothesis that the cost of applying is the most important variable do not fare as well. Coe finds that people with no access to private transportation have higher rather than lower participation rates; people living more than 50 miles away from a city of 50,000 have the same participation rates as those living less than 5 miles away. MacDonald finds that the ready availability of potential sources of help was associated with lower participation rates. The hypothesis that being a more capable information gatherer improves one's knowledge about welfare and thereby increases participation rates is not supported. MacDonald finds no tendency for better educated eligibles and those with higher IQs to have higher participation rates.

The third study to be examined is Jennifer Warlick's (1979) study of participation in Supplemental Security Income by eligible individuals over the age of 65. The SSI benefits for which aged individuals are eligible do not depend upon the income of their children, even when they are living in the same household. Nevertheless, Warlick found that controlling for benefit size, the probability these SSI eligibles will be participating in SSI is negatively and significantly related to their children's income. Another stigma hypothesis—that single individuals and single-parent families will have higher participation rates—also received support. Those eligible for $600 in SSI benefits have predicted participation rates of 41% when they are individuals living in their own homes, of 36% if they are a couple, and of 32% when they are living in their children's home. Warlick's study also found that schooling had a negative impact on SSI participation. This result tends to support the hypothesis that the Protestant ethic—presumably correlated with schooling—will increase a sense of stigma. It tends to count against the assumption that ignorance explains the low participation rate.

3

Income Testing and Social Cohesion

JAMES COLEMAN

As governments in liberal democracies have assumed an increasingly broad range of responsibilities for the welfare of their citizens, major questions have arisen about how these responsibilities should be met. One important question is whether a program should be universally available or available only to those persons or households with income below a certain level.

One issue that arises in resolving this question is the possibility that income-tested programs will bifurcate the society by creating two classes above and below the income-transfer line. Will a welfare program, available to the poor alone, pit the taxed against the recipients, benefactors against beneficiaries? If so, this could replace the multiple lines of crosscutting political cleavage by a single line that fractionates society. In this case government would be an instrument of one side—or a mediator between the two. If this scenario were realized, the cohesion of society would be sharply reduced, and the potential for exacerbated political conflict would rise.

In certain cases, like education, redistribution has characteristically taken the form of benefits provided to all, while in income support programs benefits are means tested. But if the range of government responsibilities were to increase, as is the trend throughout the world, the question arises whether society might not function with less internal conflict if most benefits were not means tested, but provided to all.

The answer is not at all clear. There are arguments and evidence on both sides. In order to better assess the nature of these arguments and the weight of evidence on both sides, I will first present the case against income-tested and for universal programs, and then present the case on the opposite side. The discussion will not address the general question of the overall merits of the two approaches, but rather the considerably narrower question of their impact on social cohesion.

What Is Social Cohesion?

Before presenting the arguments, however, I want to be more precise about what I mean to include under the rubric "social cohesion." Cohesion implies strong positive bonds. The lack of social cohesion, whether brought about by government policies or by other factors, may arise in either of two ways: the presence of conflict, hostility, and other antagonisms, or the absence of any kind of relationship.[1]

Second, cohesion may imply strong positive bonds between different members and groups in the society, or between the government on the one hand, and the society on the other. That is, just as social cohesion can be lacking either because of conflict or because of mutual indifference, it also can be lacking either because of the absence of cohesion among members and groups or between the government and the governed. I will demonstrate that policies may not affect both of those kinds of threats to cohesion in the same way.

Argument 1: Universal Programs Are Less Likely to Reduce Social Cohesion Than Are Income-Tested Programs

In the movement to the welfare state in the presence of a market economy, there arises a division between two classes in society that is as fully grounded in the structure of the economy as was the division that Marx pointed to in the nineteenth century.

Whatever might be said of other aspects of Marx's historical materialism, or of the accuracy of his predictions, the conceptual distinction between those who own the means of production and those who must alienate their labor is very important. The line of cleavage it defines has been the major basis of political conflict in Europe and the United States.

[1] I am grateful to Christopher Jencks for pointing out the necessity for such a distinction. This distinction was made long ago by Georg Simmel, as a point in social theory; its relevance to effects of government policies will become apparent in later discussion.

In more advanced capitalism, with ownership dispersed (labor having large holdings through pension fund investment) and the function of management no longer held by owners but by employees, the simple distinction cannot be maintained intact; but this does not reduce the importance of Marx's grounding political conflict in the differential relations of different groups to the economic structure.

But in the welfare state, the corresponding functional division is the division between those who earn an income and are financially independent versus those who are dependent recipients of support. Or to state it differently, viewing government as an institution of redistribution through income transfers, there become two parts of the population, or two types of households: Those *from* whom income is taken to be transferred, and those *to* whom income is transferred.[2] It is possible, and indeed easy, for these two classes to be distinguished when government payments or subsidies are income tested. Those with incomes above the point at which payments are received are the contributors; those with incomes below that point, to whom payments go, are the recipients. This division is as apparent to both groups as the functional division between the capitalist and working classes was in Marx's time.

These two groups, the contributors and the recipients, have sharply divided interests on many political issues. Although in the early stages of the welfare state they are not fully aware of these interests, they will gain such awareness as the welfare state matures—partly through increased class-consciousness, and partly through an increase in the frequency of divisive political issues. For example, there has already been class organization on specific issues: One class has organized to bring about "tax revolts," and the other has organized around "welfare rights." Thus income-tested programs bring a threat to cohesion through their potential for creating conflict among classes.

Interests of the contributors lead them to evaluate social programs on a very different basis than the recipients. They look primarily to the costs, since they experience no benefits. They come to demean, disdain, and dislike the recipients, and act in various ways on national, local, and individual levels to separate themselves from them by supporting federal regulations to restrict the rights of recipients (e.g., the "man-in-the-house" rule for AFDC); by confining public housing to lower-class areas; and by showing personal disdain toward and moving away from areas with many recipients. They clearly attach a stigma to the receipt of public funds.

[2]One legal theorist has in fact described the government-distributed benefits as "the new property" (C. Reich, 1966). Obviously, in a society with private property, there will come to be fundamental conflicts between holders of the "old property" and the "new property."

Thus when there is a sharp distinction between contributors and recipients, the former will attempt to reduce the objective benefits of the latter through the use of political power, and will reduce their subjective quality of life through individual actions directed toward them, and made possible by their high visibility. The contributors, who see their interests as sharply opposed to those of the recipients, will, in their pursuit of those interests, fractionate society.

On the other side of this functional division of society, the recipients gain consciousness as well. The demeaning character of an income-tested program generates resentment among those who find it necessary to subject themselves to it. Following a general psychological principle, they come to despise those on whom they are dependent. Their rights are restricted through the political actions intended to do just that. These restrictions further distinguish them, and reinforce the resentment created by their dependence itself. All the preconditions for class solidarity are present: Recipients come to see those on the other side of the income-transfer boundary as their oppressors, and react to them as such.

From both sides, then, the conditions for class conflict are ripe. Whether overt class conflict will result in the mature stage of a welfare state is, of course, dependent on other conditions; but the fabric of society is weakened by this cleavage, and a more fragile political system results. Government is likely to become the instrument of one of these two classes, either temporarily or for a long period of time. This will decrease for the other class the legitimacy of government.

When government programs are universal, as they are with public education (elementary, secondary, and university), national health insurance, food subsidies, and child allowances, there is not the sharp functional division between the two classes. Although it may be possible in principle to determine whether a household experiences net gains or losses from government redistribution, it is difficult to do in practice. Since all experience the benefits of a program, the program is evaluated on the benefits it provides. The "public good" of a program, and not merely the costs and benefits to oneself, enters into political considerations that surround a redistribution program. This not only softens the political debate but has the desirable quality that the issue will not be decided by whether the contributors or recipients are the majority. For example, this is apparent in the factors that affect support of funds for public education. Tax increases and bond issues for education are generally supported or opposed on the basis of how satisfied people are with the functioning of the schools, not on the basis of which side of a redistributive line the voter is on.

Democratic political systems work least well on issues which internally divide the electorate into a group which gains and one which loses. They work best when the issue concerns a public good which creates costs and benefits for each member of the electorate. Social welfare programs (whether providing education, health care, housing, food, or income supplements) that contain a redistributive or income-transfer component are most divisive when they are income tested and most cohesive when they are universal.

There are, of course, other arguments against income-tested programs. A major contention is that such programs foster and encourage cheating. If recipients of government transfers are not seen as passive (as program planners are often likely to do), but as rational and self-interested, then it becomes clear that they will use various elements in the law to their benefit. Cheating is one strategy which reduces social cohesion by increasing the hostility of nonrecipients to recipients.

Although the evidence presented in a later section to support these arguments is selected to bear upon precisely those points that are raised by the pro-universal argument (and not on different points which will be raised by the pro-income-testing argument), it has not been selected to show only results favorable to this argument. Consequently, the evidence should shed some light on just how fully the assertions that income testing is divisive are borne out in fact.

There is, however, a difficulty in doing this. For some of the assertions in this argument do not refer to the present situation in the United States and other Western states in the process of evolving into welfare states, but to mature and fully developed welfare states. It is only then that government policy will cover a sufficiently wide range of social welfare programs (or if they consist primarily of income supplements, a sufficiently large segment of the population) to create the full recognition of class interests and their full entry into political conflict. Thus if current or recent evidence fails to show as much political conflict as is asserted in the argument, the question of whether that conflict will occur in a mature welfare state with income-tested welfare programs is still not settled.

Argument 2: Universal Programs Are No Less Likely, Perhaps Even More Likely, to Reduce Social Cohesion Than Income-Tested Programs

If one accepts the argument that income testing is potentially divisive, there are several arguments to suggest why it is not, even in a mature welfare state. The principal one of these is that different social welfare programs, although income tested or in another way means tested, divide the society at many points—a multiplicity that will increase as the programs themselves increase. As the number of programs designed to assist persons economically increases, the diversity in economic level, in age, in duration of assistance needed also will increase. With such a diversity, the society hardly will be fractionated along a single line; there will not be distinct groups of contributors and recipients, for the economic interaction of all the population with government will become far more complex and varied.

The major arguments against universal programs are different ones, however. The argument against income testing assumes that the single aspect of welfare programs that can affect social cohesion is means testing. This assumption ignores many other properties of such programs that can have a far greater effect on social cohesion than their universality—for example, the level of government at which such programs function. Separate and distinct local welfare systems, such as the poor farms of years past, may have a different effect on social cohesion than a nationally administered system. There is a vastly different popular reaction to a school system that is locally financed and controlled than to one that is nationally financed and controlled.

In response to the argument that income-tested programs produce stigma, the argument for income-testing would assert that such stigma is valuable and necessary. Stigma is associated principally with redistribution programs in which the condition for which the transfer is being made is regarded as avoidable (though in fact it may not be avoidable in all cases, i.e., unemployment or low income). There is no stigma to receipt of transfers, such as veterans' benefits, which do not fall into this class. Stigma can be seen as the price that nonrecipients exact from recipients to make receipt of the benefit costly, and thus it induces avoidance of the stigma-and-benefit whenever possible.

But the property of welfare systems that has perhaps the greatest effect on social cohesion is the amount of redistribution, rather than the specific form it takes. It is the fact of the transfer itself, increasing the role of the government as the agent on which the population is dependent, and decreasing the mutual dependency among members of the society itself, that is critical. It is critical for two reasons: first, it increases the dependency of the population upon the government, and second, it decreases the direct bonds of social cohesion between different sectors of the population.[3] For both these reasons, a universal program, which makes the *whole* population dependent on the government, reduces social cohesion more than an income-tested program.

[3]As Durkheim would have said, it reduces the organic solidarity of society. Durkheim would argue that this functional interdependence among sectors of society is central to its cohesion.

Note that these two threats to social cohesion characteristic of universal programs differ in both of the dimensions discussed earlier. The first increases the potential for conflict between government and society, and the second reduces the positive bonds that maintain cohesion among members of the society. Although these are two different kinds of changes in the social fabric, both can be characterized as reductions in social cohesion.

Consider an illustration of the second effect. In an analysis of the effects of the Denver–Seattle income maintenance experiment, Hannan, Tume, and Groenveld find that the availability of income maintenance payments after divorce made women more likely to obtain a divorce and less likely to remarry.[4] Thus in this welfare experiment cohesion between husband and wife was reduced. This is not to say that the payment may not have helped improve the lot of some of these women. It does, however, accord with other evidence which shows that people use economic gains to escape from the bonds of mutual help that occur in extended families and close neighborhoods, into more isolated situations that may be less psychologically healthy.[5]

More generally, bonds of social cohesion between segments of society are broken to the extent that government becomes the intermediary that takes from some and returns to all. With the dependency of the aged upon their adult children, or wife upon husband, or children upon parents, comes a social bond, a basis for interaction that—although attended by differential power—is a bond between *persons*, not the dependence upon an impersonal bureaucracy that is characteristic of government welfare. Thus the aim should not be to create universal programs that place all persons in a dependent role, but rather to find ways to make the necessary income-transfer programs more humane.

If this argument is correct, universal programs are *more* damaging,

[4]See Hannan, Tuma, and Groenveld (1977). This effect did not exist at the higher payment levels, but was unmistakably present at the lower levels. The size of this effect is great; the proportion of unmarried women at equilibrium among the income group involved is estimated to increase from about one-third to over one-half. Note that this experiment is income tested, so that these results are not directly relevant to income testing versus universality of the program, but rather to the amount of redistribution.

This result in the effects of the negative income tax reveals a defect in the form of exposition I have chosen for this paper. The effects of transfer of personal responsibility for support to government are several, in part aiding social cohesion and in part damaging it. The use of contrasting "arguments" in different sections does not lend itself to such complexity. However, in a later section, I will reintroduce the complexity of these effects.

[5]For example, during the Depression, families doubled up by adult children moving in with parents; but as soon as it became possible, they moved out again. Or Young and Willmott (1962) show that residents of Bethnal Green in London, a close and friendly neighborhood, used their increased economic positions to move out to suburbs, where social isolation replaced neighborhood cohesion.

not less, to social cohesion than are income-tested programs. Universal programs increase the total volume of tax-and-redistribution, they make government the apparent provider for all, and thus create a line of cleavage which is even more dangerous than that between contributors and recipients. By precisely the same logic used earlier to describe contributors' reaction to recipients, the governmental functionaries will come to demean, disdain, and dislike the dependent population, will act to restrict the rights of this dependent mass by law, and will be personally offensive to the general population. If this sounds unlikely, it should not, for it can already be found in some socialist regimes, as well as some traditional totalitarian regimes in the Third World (e.g., in the Middle East and Africa). The theory and practice of socialism is precisely that of government-provided social welfare to all; there is no distinction between contributors and recipients, because there is not a market economy. In a managed economy, it becomes quite easy to separate compensation from contribution, so that income is arbitrarily determined. Government is the provider, and all are recipients. This is true not merely with regard to income, but with regard to a wide variety of social services.

It is exactly in these regimes in which most income distribution occurs through a central government rather than the market that one finds the greatest disdain for, and restriction of rights of, the general population. The restriction of rights is evident in all walks of life, ranging from freedom of expression to freedom to emigrate. This is true both in many socialist regimes and many traditional totalitarian societies. Although there are other regimes that restrict the rights of particular ethnic or racial groups, the only governments that place such constraints against the whole population are the socialist and traditional totalitarian ones.

Apart from the restriction of rights, there are other devices to distinguish the governing elite from the dependent mass in such centrally managed economies. In some socialist governments, such as in the Soviet Union and Eastern Europe, there are special stores with goods and prices available only to government officials. Living quarters and dachas are available to government officials and not to the general population. Children of government officials in the Soviet Union attend special schools—not by examination, but because of their fathers' positions. And this is a pale reflection of the governor–governed distinctions in some Third World countries with centrally managed economies.[6]

---

[6]In the past, monarchies were sometimes able to gain such power, although the existence of subsistence patterns of living gave the population a measure of economic independence. Bismarck instituted in Germany extensive social reforms—precisely *because* they would make the population more dependent upon the regime.

This oppression of the recipients by the government elite is much more harmful than in the case where a means test splits the population into contributors and recipients because the elite have both political and economic power. Therefore, it is not possible for the recipients to use the normal channels of politics to restrain governmental actions.

From the other side of this line of political cleavage, the same reactions occur as in the case of means testing, except that the consequences are even more damaging for social cohesion. The mass of the population gains a consciousness of kind vis-à-vis the ruling elite, develops resentment, and comes to despise those on whom they depend. With or without restrictions of rights by the elite, persons feel themselves deprived, for they have lost the capacity for self-determination. The preconditions for class solidarity exist, but in this case the class is the population as a whole, and the ruling regime is the opponent. This division is perhaps the most serious defect in the functioning of centrally managed economies. The everyday frictions, the mild or severe economic dislocations present in any system—inflation, depression—all those problems that are attributed to no single party in a market economy are attributed to the government. Thus social cohesion is damaged much more severely by such a cleavage between the government and the general population than by the far less fundamental cleavage brought about by explicit income transfers.

The scenario described in this argument is, of course, not one that will occur as a result of a single universal program such as child allowances or a credit income tax. Yet it is crucial that the issues be seen clearly, because redistribution through government is certain to grow in the future, and the general philosophy followed in early programs is likely to set the pattern for later ones. According to this argument, the best protection against this cleavage, and in the end the best protection for the government itself, is to hold down the fraction of the GNP which passes through government's hands. It is the long-range interests of the government to hold this fraction down, despite the short-range temptations for increased power. Because universal programs maximize this fraction for a given level of benefits provided to those who need them, they are precisely the wrong direction to go.

Yet it could well be argued that the central issue from the point of view of social cohesion is not that of universal versus income-tested programs, but rather that of how necessary welfare programs can be carried out with the minimum possible quantity of funds flowing through the central government. Programs operated by localities or nongovernmental agents would generally limit this flow of funds. One difficulty, of course, is how this can be done consistent with equality of benefits; a major reason why welfare programs have gravitated to national governments is that local programs tied benefits to local wealth and generosity. [7]

Although compatibility of equal benefits with minimal central government participation is not easy to achieve, it is not impossible. For example, among the lawsuits brought for equal educational expenditures within a state, the first and best-known of these suits, the Serrano case, contained such a plan. The designer of the Serrano plaintiff's brief, John Coons, devised a remedy to unequal expenditures that did minimize state participation and control, which he called "district power equalizing" (see Coons, Clune, and Sugarman, 1970). The plan is simple: Voters in each school district would determine their own tax rate, but the revenues they would raise by that tax rate would depend not on the wealth of the district, but upon the wealth of the state as a whole. If each district in the state voted the same tax rate, per pupil expenditures would be alike across the state. In this scheme, the role of the state would be merely to engage in "income transfers" from rich districts to poor districts. Taxes would continue to be raised by the local property tax, not by a state tax, and the voters of the local district would retain control of the rate of taxation. The state would merely take from the top of the revenues collected by wealthy districts and redistribute to poor districts.

Another difficulty of programs operated by localities or nongovernmental agents is the problem of totalitarian and oppressive local regimes. One characteristic of preindustrial localities (as exemplified in the United States by pre–World War II southern towns) is that they have often been dominated by an oligarchy of landowners or other controllers of major resources, and have often been oppressive to the "dependent" population. A decentralized nonmarket economy in which redistribution was in the hands of local elites might create the same condition. Thus decentralization of redistributive actions is not a panacea, even if the problem of equal benefits can be solved.

Finally, the issue of cheating, as it arises in income-tested programs,

---

[7] It can be argued, as Irwin Garfinkel has done in comments on an earlier draft of this paper, that the fraction of GNP going through government hands is not the crucial determinant of cleavage between governors and governed, but still another factor is. He argues rather that it may be the government provision of in-kind services (in contrast to cash or voucher programs) that generates this cleavage. The comment suggests that perhaps a prior question to that posed in this symposium is the question of what dimensions of redistribution programs are important to the various intended and unintended consequences of these effects. Certainly the dimension to which Garfinkel points is an important one.

can be addressed. The argument was that cheating in income-tested programs and perception by contributors of recipient cheating increase the dangers to social cohesion. However, there are various forms of cheating when increasingly large fractions of income pass through government hands for redistribution. One major kind is the creation of a second economy, in which some goods and services are exchanged by barter and others are exchanged for direct cash payment which avoids taxation. This secondary economy has become widespread in Western Europe as taxation comes to constitute an increasingly large fraction of income.

A second kind of cheating is that which is well known to former members of the military in the United States, and has become widespread throughout the Soviet Union: the commandeering of government goods and services for personal purposes. This is a reflection of the general division between the government and the governed that exists when a large fraction of resources are in government hands.

Neither of these types of cheating is specifically associated with universal programs. They can be expected to arise with greater frequency where there are universal programs, however, because universal programs increase the fraction of income passing through government, and tend to make all dependents of the government.

The overall point should be clear: There are serious dangers to the body politic with the gravitation of increasing fractions of national income to the national government for subsequent redistribution. These dangers are maximized by programs that in one way or another maximize this fraction of income handled by (and under the control of) the national government.

Before presenting the evidence relevant to these arguments I should note that in this case there is a difficulty similar to that which existed for the anti-income-testing argument. Although one can point to socialist regimes and other totalitarian regimes with centralized economies, and show that the sociopolitical problems envisioned do exist there, evidence which separates out the specific effects of universal benefit programs is difficult to obtain. Nearly all evidence is indirect. For example, it has been shown that when unions that have been under different employers come under a single employer, labor strife increases as different unions now begin to compare wages. In Sweden, the existence of centralized bargaining with a single employer, the state, has led to contagious strikes among middle-level government employees, military forces, and others, with the settlement of one strike inciting another. Such examples are merely illustrative, however, and offer only indirect evidence.

Evidence

The arguments in the two preceding sections rest their cases upon somewhat different kinds of claims, and thus the evidence presented address different points. The pro-universal position argues that with income-tested programs, the society fractionates into two functionally opposed classes: the contributors and the recipients. A social cleavage between contributors and recipients will result from reactions on both sides: the tendency of the contributors to demean the recipients, and the tendency of the recipients to develop a group consciousness and despise the contributors. As the volume of income-restribution activity increases, the multiple lines of cleavage found in society will reduce to a single line between contributors and recipients.

The anti-universal position argues first that the existence of a multitude of income-transfer programs with different cutting points between contributors and recipients means that no single line of cleavage will be formed. Second, it argues that the functional division between contributors and recipients in means-tested programs is smaller than the functional division between government and governed when programs are universal. Here, the argument goes, two things happen. First, the bonds of mutual dependency among persons on which social cohesion is dependent are severed by the interposition of government. Second, the governing class demeans the governed, and the governed despise the governing class. A final argument is that it is the centralized control and redistribution of programs, whether universal or income tested, that generate hostility on the part of the dependents. This argument denies that income-tested programs necessarily produce a class cleavage in society, and that universal programs must pit the governed against the government. The argument claims that centralization of redistribution is the most important factor in generating cleavage and posing potential dangers to society.

The evidence on all these points is fragmentary and will be used primarily to indicate the kinds of evidence that can be relevant to these arguments. By no means will it be sufficient to settle the issues.

How Does the Population Like Income-Tested versus Universal Programs?

A frequent type of question in public opinion polls is one which elicits the general attitude toward different kinds of income-transfer programs. What we are particularly interested in here is attitudes toward universal programs versus attitudes toward income-tested programs.

The most widespread universal program that contains an income-transfer component is national health insurance or a national health service. Attitudes toward the National Health Service (NHS) have been measured by the British Gallup organization, both before and after its enactment in Britain. The general result shows fairly widespread support for a government-controlled universal program.

In 1944, before it was enacted, 55% of the British said they favored such a plan, as against 32% saying they preferred the existing state (Gallup, 1976b, 1, 92).[8] Since its enactment, they have been asked a number of times in various ways how they liked it. In 1948, they were asked whether it was a good or bad thing, and only 13% said a bad thing (1, 170). In 1953, they were asked whether they were satisfied or dissatisfied with the treatment they get, and only 23% said dissatisfied (1, 299). In 1969 and again in 1973 they were asked whether they get good value for money from various components of NHS, and the negative responses had a low of 15% and a high of only 24% (2, 1053 and 1265). When asked in 1963 about getting rid of NHS and Old Age Pensions, only 7% wanted to do so (1, 707).

Particularly relevant for the question of universal versus means-tested programs, when asked if those who could afford it should pay extra toward NHS treatment, a majority said no, they should be free to all (2, 942). The split on this last question was the closest (55% to 40%), indicating that they were not as uniformly favorable to the idea of non-income-tested programs as to the NHS itself. Nevertheless, both the NHS as a whole, and the universal form that it takes, have a high degree of acceptance in British society. This is not to say that NHS has been free from criticism by the public, for it has not. Perhaps of more interest is that the use of private physicians outside the NHS has increased over time. This, however, is to be expected as incomes increase, if quality of medical care (not quantity) is income elastic.

In the United States, perhaps the most surprising point about attitudes toward government responsibility for medical care is that even as early as 1938, in a very early Gallup poll, 81% felt the government should take some responsibility (Gallup, 1972, 1, 106). After Social Security was enacted, Americans were asked (in 1943) about expanding Social Security to cover medical expenses, and a majority responded favorably (Gallup, 1972, 1, 400). A series of polls since 1956 (Michigan election studies 1956–1968 and CBS/New York Times in 1978) have asked a general question about the government helping people "get doctors and hospital care at low cost," using nearly the same wording. There has been majority support throughout, and a jump in support in the past

[8]The data on Great Britain from 1937 to 1975 are from Gallup (1976b).

decade (*Public Opinion*, 1978c, p. 35). Thus the data suggest that at least since the 1930s there has been reasonably strong support for some form of government medical care program.

Another program on which attitudes have been surveyed over a long period of time in several countries is government old age pensions. In Norway, citizens were asked in 1967, "What do you think is the wisest thing Norwegian politicians have done during the period since the last world war, i.e., during the last 20 years?" National old age pensions was the policy mentioned more often than any other. In France, people were asked, in 1956, 1965, and 1970 a question about their attitude toward social security, with somewhat different question wording. At all three points in time, a majority expressed positive attitudes (Gallup, 1976a, *1*, 201 and 486; *2*, 789). Although attitudes have fluctuated, there has consistently been majority approval for social security. In the United States, there has been even more widespread support for Social Security since it came into existence, and for the idea behind it before it was in existence.

Support for old age pensions, however, cannot be unequivocally regarded as support for a universal program. First, a question from 1935 on which there was very high consensus favoring old age pensions was one which described the pensions as "for needy persons" (Gallup, 1972, *1*, 9). Responses to another similar question, asked in 1938 (*1*, 118) and again in 1939 (*1*, 192), reemphasize this consensus. Only a small fraction of the population believed that pensions should be paid to all. Second, Social Security old age payments are income tested, although they are not wealth tested. That is, they are paid only to those earning below a given income, though they are paid to persons independently of wealth and nonearnings income.

However, it is in Social Security that perhaps the greatest change in attitude toward income-tested versus universal programs has occurred. Experience with Social Security over a number of years led to a complete reversal of attitudes about "neediness" as a criterion for payment by 1959. Not only had a majority come to believe that payments should be made to persons not in need, they believed that payments should be made independently of other earnings (Gallup, 1972, *2*, 1638).

Apparently over this time period acceptance of the Social Security as an ordinary pension, which was paid for during one's working life and to which one was entitled at 65, had grown. Thus what was initially support for a "welfare" program for the needy, was transformed, through the existence of the program and its design as a semi-universal program, into widespread support for a universal program. This change in attitude very likely exemplifies a general direction of change that occurs with many social programs. For example, before the 1890s in

England, there were two types of educational institutions: fee-charging schools and free schools for children of the needy run by charitable institutions. As the government took over responsibility for the free schools, they were first regarded as for the needy. Then increasingly they were regarded as schools available to all, and now the schools in the private sector serve a diminishing minority of children, and many of the formerly private schools have been incorporated into the public sector as "direct grant" schools.

A similar change has occurred in British attitudes toward government responsibility for medical care. As discussed earlier, there has been a generally increasing consensus favoring the National Health Service, from a bare majority before it began (at which time there would undoubtedly have been a large majority favoring government responsibility for health care of the needy) to somewhere around 75% in 1973. In America, the shift from support for means-tested medical care to universal care has been evident in the polls. In 1938 there was a strong consensus that the government should assume such responsibility "for people who are unable to pay for it." Since then, the consensus has grown that this responsibility should extend to all. Although there has been no universal government program to build this consensus, it may have arisen in part owing to the extensive voluntary Blue Cross–Blue Shield programs to which people have become accustomed—or possibly owing to the great increases in medical costs, which make an increasingly large fraction of the population vulnerable to high medical expenses.

One piece of evidence, however, suggests a different interpretation of these changes. In 1967 the consensus was surprisingly low that the National Health Service should be free to everyone (55% said yes, 40% said those who could afford it should pay extra—Gallup, 1976b, 2, 942). It may be that Social Security payroll deductions in the United States have generated a sense of entitlement to a pension which is not felt as strongly by the British concerning health care. What may be the case is that there are no general attitudes toward universal or income-tested programs, but only specific attitudes toward the universalism of particular kinds of programs. Attitudes toward old age pensions, education, health care, and income support may be inconsistent in regard to the income-testing issue.

What the data presented so far have shown is not that all universal programs generate widespread consensus, but that there are a number of universal programs that do show such consensus, and that this consensus appears to grow once such a policy has been in effect for a period of time. Yet this process of increasing acceptance of social programs may well be independent of the universality of the program. A case in point is unemployment insurance in Denmark. While 72% of Danes agreed that some unemployed refuse to take available work, and 34% said they personally knew someone who was cheating (employed elsewhere while receiving unemployment compensation), only 31% said that the 42-month payment period is too long, and only 43% said the payments are too high (*Public Opinion*, 1978b, p. 34). It is clear that while they may see problems in the existing unemployment relief program, there is no extensive sentiment to scrap it, or even reduce the benefits. Yet this is a means-tested program which many of the respondents will never be in a position to benefit from.

In public finance there is an old saw, "The only good tax is an old tax," implying that taxes are accepted not so much on their merits as according to habit: An old bad tax is more acceptable than a new good tax. The principle may extend to social programs supported by taxation. An existing social program, despite inequities, cheating, fraud, or mismanagement, may be more strongly supported than a new social program. In both cases, it may be a matter of adjustment: becoming accustomed to the bite of a tax or to the security or benefits provided by the social program.

Most of the attitude surveys that have been done on income-tested programs ask about welfare, about government responsibility for providing jobs, or in recent years about a guaranteed annual wage. Far less consensus has existed, however, concerning welfare programs than concerning health care or old age pensions. For example, the percentage of the American population believing that welfare expenditures are too great has ranged from 28% to 60% and has in most surveys been a majority of those holding an opinion (Yokelson, 1975, p. 89). There does, however, appear to be a slow increase in the fraction of the population favoring an increase in welfare expenditures. What is curious is that this trend exists concurrently with a clear increase in the proportion of persons believing that those on welfare are lazy or cheating or could find work if they tried (Yokelson, pp. 79, 80). It is as if in the 1930s, the American population believed that those in apparent need of welfare were truly in need, but were split about government assuming responsibility for their welfare. In the 1960s and 1970s, there has been a greater consensus that the government should assume responsibility, but fewer believe that most recipients are honestly in need.

There has been, at least since 1939, some consensus that the government should guarantee a job for all those who want to work (*Public Opinion*, 1978c, p. 35). There has been an even stronger consensus that men physically able to work should be required to work, and that relief payments should never be larger than potential earnings. Moreover, this consensus holds over income groups (Gallup, 1972, 3, 1920). Thus those most likely to be exposed to work requirements are just about as strongly favorable to them as are others. This raises doubts about the cleavage that is purported, earlier in this discussion, to arise for means-tested programs.

The belief that the responsibility of government includes finding or providing work for individuals without a job does not carry along with it the belief that this responsibility extends to providing cash. In every survey which has asked about the form of income relief, there has been a strong consensus in favor of providing jobs or job training rather than cash, whether these jobs are in the private or public sector (see Yokelson, 1975, pp. 101–108). This general consensus against cash payments manifests itself also in attitudes toward a guaranteed annual income. It seems unclear whether it is preferred to present welfare payments or not (Yokelson, 1975, pp. 106–107); but it has none of the popularity that providing and requiring work itself has (Gallup, 1972, 3, 1920; Yokelson, 1975, pp. 103, 106; *Public Opinion*, 1978c, p. 35).

None of the evidence presented up to this point goes very far toward supporting or countering the arguments presented earlier. Nevertheless, there are a few points for which the data do provide some evidence:

1. The assignment of responsibility to government in a given area (health care, old age pensions) for those in need precedes the assignment of responsibility to government for the whole population. This means that an income-tested program will generally gain wide support some time before a universal program in that area.

2. The level of support for universal or near-universal programs like national health insurance or old age pensions appears considerably higher than that for the major income-tested programs, welfare and relief. This may not be owing, however, to their universal nature, but to the type of problem they deal with. Programs in these areas were strongly supported even in their means-tested form. It may be owing instead to the fact that ill health and old age are seen as problems that cannot be avoided, whereas poverty and unemployment of the able-bodied are seen as avoidable by diligence and effort.

3. Since the 1930s, support for central government responsibility has steadily increased in a number of areas: health care, old age pensions, unemployment relief, welfare. This has meant an increased willingness to be taxed for these purposes.

4. At the same time, for welfare programs (and perhaps other income-tested programs), the belief has increased in the general population that cheating occurs and an unwillingness to work exists. This

suggests an increasing bind for income-tested programs, as people see an increasing need for such support yet simultaneously believe there is widespread cheating. This combination of beliefs itself may generate support for universal programs.

5. In at least areas concerning work requirements for those on welfare, there is little difference in attitude between the general population and those most likely to be on welfare.

6. There is, and has been since the 1930s, a belief in government responsibility in finding work for persons willing to work. That consensus does not carry over to cash payments, however, nor to a negative income tax.

7. General attitudes toward social programs and toward the recipients of the benefits of those programs do not appear to be principally a function of the universality or means testing of the program (except as the means testing encourages cheating), but rather a function of the kind of need fulfilled by the program. There does not seem to be a greater support for universal programs per se, independent of the kind of problem they address. There does, however, appear to be a tendency to view a problem as avoidable and thus not worthy of support if it afflicts only a small fraction of the population (as old-age poverty did in the rural areas where there were extended families and only a few needed to be consigned to the "old people's home"). The problem is viewed as unavoidable if it afflicts a large fraction (as old age poverty began to do when that era passed, or as unemployment did during the Depression).

Is Social Cohesion Reduced as the Fraction of Income Passing through Government Hands for Redistribution Increases?

The effects discussed earlier of the negative income tax are especially useful for seeing the complexity of governmental effects on social cohesion. The effect on divorce rates was cited earlier to illustrate the argument, not that universal programs reduced social cohesion, but that social cohesion is reduced by the volume of income transfers taking place through government (i.e., the substitution of dependence on government for dependence on other persons). Government had reduced the dependence of persons on one another by providing (in this example) an alternative source of income for the wife. Other examples, such as old age benefits under Social Security, illustrate the same effect. As stated earlier, this interdependence of members of society is central to the cohesion of the society.

But by allowing persons to free themselves from unhappy and

conflict-ridden relationships, such a transfer program removes a different threat to social cohesion, that arising from the conflict in the relationships that were held together only by economic necessity. Thus the overall effect on the social fabric contains both these components: reduced conflict and hostile relations, and greater social isolation. These effects, it should be noted, arise from other sources as well—from generally increased affluence which allows greater independence, and from multiple incomes in a household. And it is interesting to note that whatever the long-term effects on psychological health, persons use some parts of their income to buy independence and separation from others, including other members of their families, such as dependent parents.

There is, of course, in addition, a third potential effect of substituting dependence on government for dependence on other persons, an effect that cannot be detected in the income-maintenance experiments. As government assumes responsibility for dependence, the potential for hostility between different persons in society is removed and a potential for hostility between government and the governed is created.

The anti-universal position is that for a given level of benefit to those in need, universal programs maximize the dependence of all on government. This, in turn, increases alienation of all from government. If this argument is correct, it should lead to welfare strategies exactly the opposite of those proposed by the universal position: strategies designed to minimize, for a given level of benefit, the federal government's involvement and the amount of money flowing through it.

The conjecture that alienation from government is generated in this way is difficult to test directly, for obvious reasons. There are the cases of totalitarian political systems mentioned before. The alienation generated in these systems might appear to be only weak evidence for the postulated alienation, because of the harshness of the regimes toward the population, which is reason enough in itself for the alienation. Yet if one travels in Eastern Europe one is struck by the volume of private criticism leveled at the government for matters that are hardly caused by the government. Such casual observations are hardly evidence, but they do suggest looking further.[9]

But the focusing of hostility of the governed toward a government

---

[9]A recent article about farmer protest against the Polish government contains a quote which shows the focusing of hostility in a socialist society. The quote is from a young farmer involved in a protest group in the village of Zbrosza Duza: "The stores are empty. No food, no coal, no butter, no sugar, no building materials. Of course we blame the government [Spivak, 1979, p. 1]." This young farmer may certainly be right in blaming the government; but if the government were not the sole seller of goods to the consumer, the hostility would be diffused to various actors in the market.

which channels all resources through its hands is only half the point. The other half is the behavior of the government toward the governed. According to the argument made earlier, governments with dependent populations will begin to act harshly toward their populations because of their position of power. Thus the harshness of regimes with centrally managed economies is *itself* evidence that the cleavage between government and governed will be increased by the existence of universal programs. This is especially curious in the large number of socialist governments in which it exists. There is nothing in socialist theory to demand a high degree of coercion. Thus its emergence must arise from the very structure of a socialist system: Not only health and old-age programs are universal, but income maintenance as well, since government is almost the sole employer. Thus with all as its dependents, the government and its functionaries can behave coercively toward the population, as well as provide amenities for itself.[10]

It may be possible in addition to make use of some public opinion evidence. One striking change that has occurred over the past ten or fifteen years has been the rising alienation of the population from the leadership of the country (*Public Opinion*, 1978a, p. 23). This was a period during which there were massive increases in social programs, along with a considerable increase in the fraction of income passing through government hands. The universalism or income testing of these social programs is not important for the hypothesis at hand. What is important is the increasing dependence of the population upon the government, an increase that results directly from an increase in government social programs.[11]

But the concurrence of an increase in alienation from government with an increase in social programs may be no more than a coincidence. What would give this hypothesis greater weight would be an indication that during this same period, there was an increase in the perceived importance of government in persons' lives. Then the hypothesized process would be something like this:

[10]It is interesting to note that in the United States during a period in which the fraction of GNP being cycled through government hands in redistributive programs (both income tested and universal) increased greatly, that is, the last twenty years, the average income of government employees increased from *below* that for comparable jobs in the private sector to *above* that income. See Buchanan and Tullock (1977), who argue that it is the increased political power of government employees that that makes this possible.

[11]It is not claimed to increase with money taken from the population and spent elsewhere, as in foreign aid or defense. This does not increase the population's dependence on the government. What is claimed here to do so is the cycling of money through the government and back to the population through social programs.

(A)	(B)	(C)
Increased volume of government activity in redistribution $\rightarrow$	Increased perception of government respon- sibility for outcomes of events $\rightarrow$	Increased alien- ation from govern- ment

(There is also, as suggested earlier, a second arrow leading from (A) to increased perception by government officials of the population as dependent and then increased arbitrariness of government, which again, according to the hypothesis, will affect (C), increasing is still further.)

There is little poll data that allows examination of whether there was, during this period, an increase in the perceived importance of government in people's lives. However, there are a few questions that can provide clues to the answer. In 1947 two Gallup polls asked who was most to blame for high prices. In 1972, 1973, and twice in 1974, a similar question was asked (Gallup, 1978, *1*, 43; *1*, 145; *1*, 298). The responses to those very similar questions show, in the case of a problem without a specific source, where responsibility is seen to lie. The ratios of answers show a general rise, with government being named in 1974 2 or 3 times as often as business or as labor, considerably more often than in 1947. This does suggest that there is a generally increased perception of government as responsible for important events, which may lead to the increased alienation from government.

On the other hand, responses to another question, asked in 1968 and again in 1977 (covering a span not greatly different from that of the alienation series) show a *reduction* in the percentage who see big government as the greatest threat in the future (Gallup, 1972, *3*, 2154; and Gallup, 1978, *2*, 960). This result leaves the issue unresolved. Without a greater number of time points in the series, I do not know whether results for one of these years is distorted by particular events preceding the survey, such as the Vietnam War—a major source of antagonism against the government, which was at its height in 1968 and not present in 1977.

Altogether, the data addressing the major anti-universal argument are even less conclusive than those addressing the preceding issue. Nevertheless, some points can be made.

1. Illustrative evidence from countries with centrally managed economies provides some indirect and weak confirmation of the general proposition that a high fraction of income passing through government hands focuses unrest and hostility of the governed against the government.

2. Evidence from these same countries on the general treatment of the governed by those who govern and the discrimination against the governed by those who govern provides confirmation (again weak because of uncontrolled factors) of the other side of the proposition: that an increasing fraction of income passing through government hands leads those who govern to treat the governed as dependents to be treated harshly and discriminated against in various ways.

3. There is some indication of increasing alienation from government among Americans over the past twelve years, a period during which the fraction of income passing through government hands for redistribution has increased greatly.

The likelihood that this alienation arises from increased perception of government responsibility for events is suggested (though weakly) by poll data showing increased attribution of blame for inflation to government.

Conclusion

The evidence cited on the pro- and anti-universal arguments remain inconclusive. The evidence tends to confirm the pro-universal argument that universal programs are better liked and accepted than income-tested programs. There does not seem strong confirmation, on the other hand, that income-tested programs create a value split between contributors and recipients. Rather, the latter seem to evaluate programs very similarly to the former.

The evidence also tends to confirm the anti-universal argument that expanded government programs and government share of income (which are hastened by universal programs) increase the cleavage between governors and governed. This evidence, however, is especially weak.

Thus at least portions of the arguments on both sides appear to be confirmed. The issue remains unresolved. It is clear, however, that there may be problems of social cohesion not only from income-tested programs—as suggested in the initial conjecture with which this paper began—but from universal programs as well. The sources and types of cleavage are different in the two cases, but both contain dangers.

How these matters may be examined with more decisive evidence remains to be seen. The evidence presented here is perhaps most useful for the suggestions it gives of how the issue may be examined more fully: the kind of evidence that can be brought to bear. For the present, the matter must rest here.

Discussion

CHRISTOPHER JENCKS

James Coleman's paper suggests that both income-tested and universal programs are likely to have negative effects on social cohesion. Yet Coleman reads his empirical evidence as providing only limited support for these suggestions. I am skeptical about Coleman's theoretical argument, but in this discussion I want to concentrate on the empirical evidence. First, I will comment briefly on how we might measure "social cohesion." Then I will turn to the problem of assessing the effects of different kinds of transfer programs.

What Is Social Cohesion?

Social cohesion is like motherhood. We all favor it. As a result, we tend to define the term so as to subsume all the virtues we want our society to attain: liberty, equality, fraternity, and even happiness. To make social cohesion a useful concept, however, we must make it both more restrictive and more precise. Coleman's paper suggests several possibilities. At times he equates social cohesion with the presence of positive ties between individuals. At other times he equates it with the absence of conflict between either individuals or organized groups. His usage suggests that in principle social cohesion could have at least four meanings.

1. Positive ties between individuals. Under this definition a socially cohesive society would be one in which the typical individual had strong bonds with many other individuals, involving affection, responsibility, or both.

2. Low conflict between individuals. Under this definition cohesion would be the absence of conflict, envy, crime, stigmatization, and other forms of interpersonal abuse, but not necessarily the presence of love, empathy, responsibility, or the like. Even a collection of hermits could be "socially cohesive," so long as they all respected one another's privacy.

3. Positive ties between groups. Under this definition a cohesive society would be one in which organized social and political groups habitually cooperated in promoting the welfare of society as a whole. This could happen either if the groups in question valued the general welfare more than their own selfish interests, or if they believed that by promoting the general welfare even when this was not in their interest in the short term, they could induce other groups to do the same when the tables were turned.

4. Low conflict between groups. Under this definition a socially cohesive society would be one with a low level of internal political and social conflict. This could happen because there was a low level of role differentiation, so that individuals had the same interest on most issues, or because individuals identified strongly with the collectivity, so that they construed their interests in terms of what would benefit the collectivity, not just themselves. Alternatively, conflicts of interest could arise but could be resolved without inflaming political passions. Coleman argues, and I am inclined to agree, that conflict is most easily contained when individuals see themselves as having diverse interests and hence diverse allies. Such crosscutting cleavages help keep conflicts from escalating because participants know that today's opponent is likely to be tomorrow's ally.

Societies cannot maximize these four varieties of social cohesion simultaneously, either through their choice of transfer programs or through their other policies. Government-financed old-age pensions, for example, tend to reduce conflict between individuals by allowing old people to live separately from their children. But this kind of freedom also attenuates positive ties between aging parents and their children. Critics can therefore portray state pensions as either increasing or reducing social cohesion, depending on their definition of cohesion. Similarly, if a guaranteed income reduces marital stability, as the Seattle–Denver Income Maintenance Experiment results imply, it presumably attenuates the positive ties between children and at least one of their parents. But reducing marital stability also means reducing conflict between incompatible spouses. Once again, then, we can argue that income maintenance either reduces or increases social cohesion, depending on our definition.

These ambiguities are less obvious if one defines social cohesion in terms of relations between groups rather than individuals, but I believe they still exist. Cooperation between disparate groups ordinarily allows society to bring more and more matters under its collective control. But this trend also creates more situations in which organized political groups perceive themselves as having conflicting interests. Thus if one wants to minimize conflict, it is often best to limit cooperation as well.

Each of these definitions implies a different approach to measurement. If we want to know whether a given policy has increased or decreased positive bonds between individuals, for example, we presumably need to ask individuals directly about such bonds, and perhaps also observe how they interact with their families, friends, neighbors, co-workers, and strangers. Yet even establishing a cross-sectional association between a given transfer program and the strength of bonds between individuals would tell us nothing about the direction of causation. Such an association could arise because societies with weak bonds between individuals have to rely more heavily on transfer payments to support the needy, not because transfer programs weaken the bonds between individuals. Convincing evidence would therefore have to take the form of a time series.

If we are concerned about conflict between individuals we again need survey data, observational data, or both.

Conventional demographic data are not likely to tell us much about these matters. The divorce rate, for example, may tell us something about the strength of bonds between children and their parents, at least if we confine our attention to divorces involving parents. But the divorce rate tells us virtually nothing about the strength or character of the bonds between spouses, since most divorces are followed by remarriage, and we have no solid basis for assessing the quality of second marriages relative to that of the same individuals' first marriages. Whether aging parents live with their children is equally uninstructive without information on the quality of their relations both when they live together and when they live separately.

If we want to know whether a program has facilitated cooperation between political groups, we again need historical evidence. We might ask, for example, whether the expansion of various kinds of transfer programs has affected the extent to which business automatically opposes programs favored by labor and vice versa, or the extent to which spokesmen for the poor automatically oppose legislation initiated by representatives of the rich and vice versa. Tracing such trends to specific legislative antecedents would be remarkably difficult, however, unless we had data on large numbers of countries that introduced similar legislation at different times.

If we want to know whether a transfer program has led to political conflict, we again need relatively subtle data. It is certainly not enough to look at the percentage of individuals favoring or opposing the transfer program itself. A program is not necessarily divisive simply because it is unpopular. It may actually bring people together by giving them a common enemy. A program on which opinion is evenly divided may be more divisive, but everything depends on the intensity of the feelings. Even an extremely popular program may be divisive if there is controversy about *how* the program should be run. Furthermore, following Coleman's argument about crosscutting cleavages, even controversial programs are unlikely to be divisive unless the division of opinion about different programs follows consistent lines. Thus, if you want to argue that income testing threatens social cohesion, you must show that the same people favor or oppose a wide range of income-tested programs. So far as I know, no one has demonstrated a high level of consistency in attitudes of this kind, though that may only prove how crudely surveys usually measure attitudes. Even if opinions about income-tested or "universal" programs *are* polarized, this polarization may or may not spill over into other areas. If it does not, the threat to social cohesion is minimal. AFDC is the only income-tested program I know that clearly has effects of this kinds, and it is a very special case.

Distinguishing Types of Programs

In analyzing transfer programs, it seems essential to distinguish three rather than just two types of programs:[1] (*a*) income-tested categorical programs such as Medicaid, AFDC, or SSI; (*b*) universal categorical programs such as children's allowances or veterans' benefits; and (*c*) income-tested noncategorical programs such as food stamps or a guaranteed income. In comparing these three alternatives, we confront three possible choices:

[1] In principle, one can also have universal noncategorical transfers (i.e., a demogrant), but since one can design a negative income tax to accomplish the same things as a demogrant, the distinction is of no practical importance for present purposes.

1. Should we move from income-tested to "universal" categorical programs? Should we, in other words, drop the means test from programs like Medicaid, SSI, AFDC, and AFDC–UP? Such a shift clearly reduces the target efficiency of these programs. It might, however, increase their popularity. As a result, the shift might end up benefiting the poor. Affluent beneficiaries are likely to exert greater political influence than poor beneficiaries, so increasing the proportion of affluent beneficiaries should increase the average beneficiary's political influence. Other things equal, this should increase the average benefit, which would be good for the poor. But other things are not equal. Dropping the income test also increases total costs, which is likely to increase affluent nonbeneficiaries' resistance to the program. These affluent nonbeneficiaries may ignore a small program that provides benefits to especially needy individuals, since this costs them relatively little, but may try to trim a larger program that provides benefits to some more broadly defined group. Thus, we cannot assume with confidence that dropping the means test will in fact increase the average benefit.

2. Should we move from income-tested categorical programs to income-tested noncategorical programs? Should we, in other words, drop Medicaid, SSI, AFDC, and the like in favor of a guaranteed income, food stamps, and the like? Moving from income-tested categorical programs to noncategorical programs brings increased coverage of the needy but jeopardizes political legitimacy. Transfer programs are politically acceptable only insofar as their beneficiaries are believed to "deserve" as well as "need" help. Categorical programs identify groups who are generally believed to deserve help: the sick, the aged, mothers of children whose fathers have abandoned them, and so forth. Programs like SSI, Medicaid, and AFDC single out these "deserving" poor for special support. A guaranteed income for everyone is almost certain to end up offering lower benefits over the long run than a guarantee that is restricted to the "deserving." Thus, if one wants to maximize the resources available to the poor, one needs *both* a noncategorical guarantee, which will be low, *and* categorical supplements for the "deserving." Most states have long had precisely such a two-tier system, providing a minimum amount of "general relief" to almost anyone who was indigent, and then offering more generous support to those who "deserve" more. Society's norms about who deserves special help are, of course, always in flux. The idea that mothers of young children "can't" work, for example, commanded widespread support in the 1930s, when ADC first came into existence. This norm no longer commands widespread support, so the program is increasingly controversial. But we cannot

escape this controversy by providing a guaranteed income to "everyone."

3. Should we push for more "universal" categorical programs or for income-tested noncategorical programs? Should we, in other words, push for children's allowances, noncontributory old age pensions, and the like, or should we push for more food stamps or a guaranteed income? This choice involves a mix of the foregoing considerations. For most purposes a guaranteed income is simply another categorical program, the beneficiaries of which happen to be the poor rather than old, young, sick, or whatever. From this perspective the question is not whether a society should have categorical programs or income maintenance programs. The question is how large each kind of program should be. In practice, the relative size of these programs will depend partly on our collective judgment about the relative "deservingness" of the poor relative to the aged, the disabled, children abandoned by their fathers, and others with special claims on our sympathy, and partly on the relative political power of these groups. As a result, we can expect universal categorical programs to get a larger share of available resources than they would if all voters had an equal voice in the matter, since universal programs will have a larger fraction of affluent beneficiaries than income maintenance programs, and affluent beneficiaries exert disproportionate influence on the political process.

I can see no way of drawing general conclusions about the effects of these choices on social cohesion, however defined. Everything depends on the specific categorical programs under discussion and on the changing values of the electorate. A program like AFDC may initially provide benefits to individuals who "everyone" agrees need help. As attitudes toward working mothers change, this consensus may break down and the program may become controversial. There is no iron law of increasing or decreasing acceptance, though the usual trend is certainly towards increased acceptance once a program has been around for some time. Nor is there any general rule guaranteeing that programs aimed at the poor will be more or less divisive than programs aimed at other categories of beneficiaries. At some times, for example, we see the unemployed as victims of circumstances beyond their control and feel that they deserve help. At other times we see them as malingerers and view the benefits they receive as a subsidy for indolence.

This is not to say that research has no light to shed on these matters. Cross-cultural research could tell us something about the association between various kinds of transfer programs and various kinds of social cohesion. If such research were continued over a substantial period of time, the resulting time series might even allow us to make some causal inference. I do not think, however, that there is much to be learned in this respect by comparing the Soviet Union to the United States or by comparing Western Europe to Eastern Europe. There are just too many East–West differences in political tradition, current form of government, and management of the economy to isolate the contribution of transfer programs to differences in social cohesion. Much could, however, be learned from comparative studies *within* Eastern and Western Europe. There is probably as much variation in the character of the transfer programs in Eastern as in Western Europe. If these variations showed a consistent relationship to measures of social cohesion *within* both blocs of countries, one could have some confidence that there was a true causal connection. The prospect that anyone will actually be able to do systematic research on social cohesion in Eastern Europe remains depressingly small, however, so we would presumably have to settle for research on OECD countries. Even OECD comparisons would present formidable obstacles, since very few of these countries collect at all comparable data on who gets how much from different kinds of transfer programs, and virtually no data are available on the level of any kind of social cohesion in most of these countries.

4

Income Testing and Politics: A Theoretical Model

GORDON TULLOCK

Anyone examining the provision of income transfers or special services by the modern democratic state immediately realizes that a large amount of services are provided to people who are by no means poor.[1] The farm programs which in almost every democratic country exploit nonfarmers for the benefit of farmers tend to benefit these farmers in proportion to the amount of agricultural land they hold. The benefits are not confined, for example, to poor farmers. Perhaps the extreme case of a categorical aid program for a group that is not poor involves a very large bundle of services and special facilities provided by the American and indeed most other democratic governments for owners of private aircraft—surely one of our more prosperous groups. It would not be

[1]In a special sense one could say almost all welfare programs in Western countries are of this type since by any realistic bookkeeping, citizenship in the United States, France, etc. is the largest single asset held by the average such citizen, and people who do not have that asset (worth probably in excess of $100,000) are barred from these programs. Since most of the poor people in the world are poor specifically because they do not have that particular asset, i.e., citizenship in a developed country, we could say that substantially all existing aid programs in Western countries have a negative wealth test: you have to have something worth about $100,000 before you become eligible for payments.

Although this subject interests me a great deal, it is not what I had been asked to write on, and hence for the rest of this essay I will be discussing income testing only when relief or services are given to citizens.

particularly surprising if the facilities provided for them by the government would make them among the largest per capita recipients of transfers. These programs, however, are not the subject matter of this paper and they are relevant only insofar as their mere existence indicates that motivations for transfer activities in a democracy are frequently simply the desire of the recipients to receive the transfers rather than any desire to help the poor.

There are two different kinds of income-tested programs. In the first, the full service is provided below a certain income and above that point, none. Thus, for example, we might have programs under which everyone whose income is under some particular amount gets free medical attention from the state and anyone whose income is above that gets no such attention. The second could be termed a negative income tax where services are provided on a graduated scale. This sliding scale program would provide that at some fairly high income the state would assist in catastrophic illness cases and, as income fell, gradually add additional services until the very poor found even routine dentistry paid for.

Although administratively and in practical terms the decision of which of these two types of program should be selected is of great importance, I am not going to deal with that issue in this essay.

My line of reasoning will apply to both types of programs. I will devote more discussion to the type in which there is a sharp income cutoff because it is analytically a little easier. I will, however, give enough attention to the gradual cutoff type so that the phenomena discussed in this chapter appear to be equally relevant.

In the countries in which universal services are provided—education in the United States, medicine in England, etc.—there is usually also a special privately provided supplementary service for the upper-income groups. The private schools in the United States and the approximately 5% of the population in England who, though they carry health insurance, use the services of private doctors are examples. In Russia there is a government program to provide special medical facilities to upper-ranking members of the hierarchy.[2]

In this paper I will mainly ignore these supplements for upper-income groups for convenience of analysis. Our basic subject will be a

---

[2]Indeed, the special medical facilities for Brezhnev seem to be quite unprecedented. In his recent visit to Germany it was revealed that he is not only always accompanied by a crew of doctors, nurses, etc. but that they have a special van which is in essence a custom-designed intensive care room for his particular collection of illnesses. It was flown to West Germany in a special plane.

comparison of income-tested and universal programs, using medical provisions as an example.

There are three different ways in which medical provision could be distributed. First, everyone would pay for his own. In practice, no doubt, this approach would be accompanied by a good deal of private charity. However, I will not discuss this, not because I think it is unimportant but because it complicates the analysis and is not vital to our subject. The second way of providing medical treatment is to have a tax-supported system which provides medical aid only to the poorest part of the population. In the third case the state provides full medical care for everyone. It could be assumed in both the second and third cases that the state-provided aid is (at least by intent) all of the medical services that the individual will receive.

A Political Model

Let us begin with a very simple political model. I should like to emphasize strongly that the consequences we draw from this political model are very heavily affected by the detailed assumptions about things such as preference curves and number of people. Thus, no direct transfer of the conclusions from the model into the real world is possible. The model has been designed, however, to be extremely simple and straightforward and hence easy to follow. As we work our way through the model, I will discuss the modifications that would be necessary to fit it to a more realistic set of assumptions about the real world.

We consider then a very simple society in which there are three citizens: Mr. 1, who has an income of $100 a year; Mr. 2, who has an income of $200; and Mr. 3, who has an income of $300. At the beginning of our system there is no government-provided health care and Mr. 1 is paying $5, Mr. 2, $10, and Mr. 3, $15 for medical care each year. Let's suppose, however, that 2 and 3 become concerned about Mr. 1's welfare. They feel that more than $5 is needed to keep him in a reasonable state of health. They therefore propose a government program which will provide him with medical care at the expense of the taxpayer.[3]

---

[3]In the particular case of medicine there might be additional motives for being concerned with the medical treatment for Mr. 1, due to the externalities that sometimes arise in medical matters. Since, however, I am basically interested in income-tested programs in general and am only using the medical program as a special case, I will not discuss the problem further.

Here we must make an assumption about the tax structure: i.e., taxes are proportional to income. That means for every dollar spent on Mr. 1's health, Mr. 1 will pay one-sixth of $1, Mr. 2, one-third, and Mr. 3, one-half. In Figure 4.1, I show Mr. 1's demand for medical care, and the demands by Mr. 2 and Mr. 3, not for medical care for themselves, but for medical care for Mr. 1. The medical care cost is shown in constant value amounts by a horizontal line. Mr. 1 would purchase the amount 0, which is equivalent to $5 in the private market. When we switch to government provision, however, prices change. Let us begin by considering what benefit level each of the three would favor for Mr. 1 assuming that it be paid for by the taxpayer (i.e., by the three parties in proportion to their income). I have drawn in the cost to each per unit, and we observe that Mr. 1's demand curve crosses his cost at point 1, Mr. 2's at point 2 and Mr. 3's at point 3. With the particular tax scheme that I have imposed on my model, this is a simple case of single-peaked preferences, and the median preference voter Mr. 3 will prevail. Under this system Mr. 1 will receive somewhat more medical care than before, perhaps $6 worth. He will also pay much less than before, about $1.

Before we go on to compare this outcome with what we would

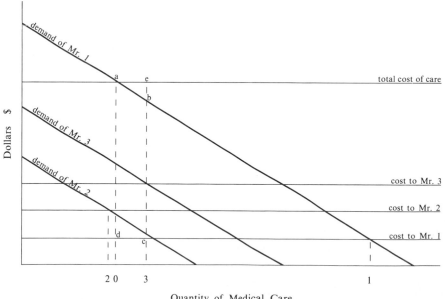

Figure 4.1. Demand for medical care for poor voter (Mr. 1) by Mr. 1, by middle-income voter (Mr. 2), and by rich voter (Mr. 3) under income-tested provision of medical care. (Figure by University of Wisconsin Cartographic Laboratory.)

expect under universal medical care, let us take a closer look at these results. First, note that wealthy Mr. 3 is median voter, not middle-class Mr. 2. This is obviously an artifact of how the diagram was drawn, but it was done this way to emphasize that this condition can and indeed is not particularly unlikely to exist. Wealthy people presumably have a greater demand for charity as well as other things than people with less money. On the other hand, they normally pay a larger share of the taxes. Whether this will lead them to want more or fewer transfers to the poor than do the middle class depends essentially on the income elasticity of demand for charity. Nothing can be said about it a priori.

The second point we notice is that this outcome does not have a great deal to commend it in strict welfare terms. It is not the social optimum which would be obtained by summing the three men's curves and observing where that sum crosses the cost line and hence is not Pareto optimal. This is a general characteristic of direct-voting outcomes. Furthermore, it is not obvious that anybody except Mr. 3 would be very happy with this particular outcome. Mr. 2 finds himself being taxed to provide more medical attention for Mr. 1 than he wants to give, and Mr. 1 is, of course, receiving far less medical attention that he would like at that price.

Note also, and this is again a general characteristic of all government-provided programs for medicine, that although if given his choice Mr. 1 would select the total quantity of medicine for himself shown by 1 on the horizontal axis when voting, if that amount has been provided, he will attempt to get from his doctor not that amount but the amount where his demand curve crosses the horizontal axis. As a voter he counts the cost of medical treatment to him as one-sixth its actual cost, as a consumer of a service on which there is no marginal charge at all, he counts it as 0.[4] Hence he will try to repeat a very general characteristic of provision of "free" services. The voters qua voters take into account the cost, the voters qua customers of the free service do not, and hence we find the amount of service provided is always less than that which is "demanded." There must be some kind of rationing system, whether that would be waiting in long lines or arbitrary decisions by doctors.

It should also be noted that Mr. 1 has another reason for being angry—he would prefer to receive the $6 in cash than in the form of medical attention. The recipient is better off if he is given cash and the

---

[4]Strictly speaking with our small group of three voters it is unlikely that Mr. 1 would make this particular calculation. With millions of voters, however, this line of reasoning applies rigorously (see Buchanan, 1972).

principal beneficiaries from making it in-kind are either upper-income groups who suspect he would just drink it up or the actual providers of the service (doctors, etc.) or both.

Let us before we move to our next model note one final characteristic of Figure 4.1. Mr. 2 may well be still consuming more medical attention than Mr. 1. To a considerable extent this reflects the fact that we have only 3 citizens in our model. Although I will not draw the diagram, consider the situation if we had not 3 but 9 citizens and that the one at the bottom (the bottom 11%) was the only one who was regarded by the others as too poor to handle his own medical expenses. This would mean that the cost to each voter of providing medical services to the poor person would be only about one-third of what it is in Figure 4.1. If the demand curves looked roughly like the ones I have drawn and the median voter was Mr. 5, it is quite probable that the medical attention provided for the poor person would be approximately the same or better than the medical attention provided for the average-income person. Most assuredly it would be higher than that Mr. 2 would provide for himself. Indeed, it would probably be higher than that available for Mr. 3 and Mr. 4.

Once again these assumptions are based on the view that in our society the demand curves have about the same shape as those shown for Mr. 2 and Mr. 3 in the diagram—that may not be true about the real world. It does seem to be true, however, that in those cases in which there is a sharp cutoff with free medical care being provided below a certain point and none above, there is always a group of voters whose incomes are just above the level at which they can get free medical attention and who will be irritated by the program. They will be paying for their own medicine and consuming less than the poor person, and at the same time paying through taxes for a sizable portion of his medical attention. The size of this group will depend on detailed assumptions, but it can very easily be quite large. Where we have graduated decline in the amount of medical service as incomes rise, much the same phenomenon occurs, but it is not quite as conspicuous. This point will be discussed at length below.

In reality in all societies, the providers of services have considerable influence on how much is provided, and the providers of the services in this case are the medical professions. They may be able to push the total provision high enough so that the indigents are receiving considerably more medical attention than is the average citizen. This is possible because the doctors, etc., are themselves likely to vote for increased provision to the poor not because they feel sympathetic towards the poor but because they want their own incomes raised. They will characteristically already have incomes well above average and the result may be that the poor, the doctors, and let us say the top 30% of the (nondoctor) population jointly make up the voting block which passes these high expenditures.

Note that in Figure 4.1 the benefit to Mr. 1 when we switch from private provision to public provision is the trapezoidal area *abcd*. If he had simply been given $6 in cash it would have been the area *ae03*, and he would have been somewhat better off. Still, he receives an unambiguous gain in the shift from providing his own service to having the government provide it. In our next step, when we move to general medical care provided by the government, the poor will still be better off than they would be if they were providing it themselves, but they may well be worse off than under the situation of Figure 4.1.

Universal Provision of Services

Consider Figure 4.2, which shows the situation under universal provision of medical care. Once again the real cost is shown by a line marked "cost, real and to Mr. 2," the cost to Mr. 1 is shown by the "cost to Mr. 1" line, and the cost to Mr. 3 by the "cost to Mr. 3" line. Note that in each of these cases the cost is three times as high as it was in Figure 4.1 simply because the medical provision instead of being provided for one person is being provided for 3 persons.

The demand curve for Mr. 1 is taken from Figure 4.1. The demand curves for Mr. 2 and Mr. 3 now represent their demand for their own medical treatment plus whatever charitable desire they may have to provide medical treatment for Mr. 1, since the only way they can do so under these circumstances is by increasing the total medical expenditure for everyone.

Let us begin our discussion by considering the effect on Mr. 1 of this change. We pointed out that his welfare gain in moving from no government provision to government provision for the poor was only the area *abcd* on Figure 4.1, which is represented on Figure 4.2 by the area *abcd*. The median voter in this case is Mr. 2 and the society will provide quantity *N* of medical attention. Mr. 1 now gets more medical care than he got in Figure 4.1 (although as mentioned earlier this is a mere artifact determined by the way the diagram has been drawn) but he has to pay more taxes. The amount in taxes he was paying on his previous medical attention is shown by the area under the dashed line near the bottom in the left-hand corner of Figure 4.2. Since the total tax burden has gone up and since he is paying one-sixth of the amount, his total taxes go up and

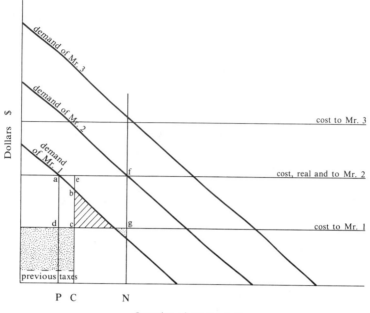

Figure 4.2. Cost of medical care for three voters—rich (Mr. 3), middle-class (Mr. 2), and poor (Mr. 1)—under universal provision of medical care. Dotted rectangle = additional taxes of Mr. 1. Dotted triangle = loss from excessive medical care to Mr. 1. Shaded triangle = gain from additional medical care for Mr. 1. (Figure by University of Wisconsin Cartographic Laboratory.)

he therefore suffers a loss through tax collection shown by the dotted rectangle. He has a further loss to the right near line *N*; the small dotted triangle is the additional medical attention which he receives which is not worth its tax cost to him. In the real world this little triangle might well not exist.

These losses, of course, are not the only effect. He also receives an unambiguous gain which is the shaded triangle. In the real world this triangle may not exist because he may already be receiving as much (or more) medical attention under the income-tested scheme as he will receive under the universal scheme. In Figure 4.2, of course, his losses exceed his gains, but again, this may be attributed to the way the diagram was drawn.

The benefits which the poor receive depend on what we might call the degree of inadequacy of the medical attention that the poor receive. In this case "inadequacy" can't be defined technically because it depends on the total resources available at a given time. The real question

is, Are the poor getting less than their per capita share of medical attention? Even that is not a fair question, because all of the empirical studies
of national health services indicate that the poor, owing to their difficulty in filling out forms, poor motivation, and sometimes their difficulty in dealing with officials, get less than their share on a per capita
basis of the medical resource of the society, even under theoretical
"universalization." Let us say they get 90% of what a middle- or upper-
class person would receive dealing with the same legal apparatus.

To clarify this issue, let us assume that some individual poor person
has an income of $1000 and was paying 1% of that or $10 as his share of
the support of the income-tested health scheme. He received under this
income-tested scheme $80 a year worth of medical attention. A govern-
ment program is then adopted which provides $100 of medical attention
for every citizen in the country. This means the total taxes used to pay
for medicine will rise say five times, and because he is still paying his
same allocated share of the cost,[5] he finds himself paying $50 in taxes.
Even if he got the full $100 worth of treatment he would be worse off
than he was before.[6] If we assume, realistically, that he actually gets
only 90% of the national standard because of bureaucratic difficulties, he
would be even worse off.

In this hypothetical case the individual would become better off only
if the increase in medical attention he received nearly doubled the
amount he had before (i.e., if the charitably provided medical care was
only a little over one-half of the national standard). Further, even this
would only be true if the marginal unit of medicine which he received
was worth more to him than the taxes he paid on that marginal unit.
Note that all of this depends on the exact numbers chosen. But I invite
the reader to experiment with realistic numbers.

No one as far as I know has figured out how much the poor actually
pay in taxes in the United States. Recent work has indicated that the tax

[5]The assumption that the tax structure is not changed at the same time is crucial here,
but necessary if I am to discuss effect of income-tested versus universal programs. There is
no doubt that by making the tax system more progressive you can benefit the poor (ignoring incentive effects). If you do that at the same time that you introduce a universal
program, the benefit which the poor received from the increase in the progressivity of the
tax could very well make the whole package much to the interest of the poor. They would,
however, still be better off if a tax were made more progressive and income testing were
retained.

[6]Some people would say this might not be true because the expenditure of the
additional $20 on medicine for him would be of more value to him than the $50 which they
would allege he would waste on something else, like drink or the numbers game. I don't
regard this as a truthful description of the behavior of the poor, but there are people who
believe this.

incidence calculations that were used in the past are suspect. But let us stick to what we might call the Musgrave generalization, which holds that the actual taxes (not the taxes in my more expanded sense) that any person in our society below the highest income brackets pays are roughly proportional to his income. If this is so, the cost to the poor of going to universal programs is apt to be very considerable.

For the poor the increasing budget drain represented by universal medical care will not only raise the taxes they pay, it will also reduce the number of other income supplements which the state can give them. Thus, their taxes will go up and the other direct payments they receive will go down. (Both of these items count as their increase in taxes.)

It is not generally realized that the expansion of one government program to aid the poor normally leads to the reduction of other such programs. There are two basic reasons. The first is simply that the government cannot spend an infinite amount of money, and thus an increase in budget on one item is likely to lead to at least some reduction in budgetary provision for other items. The second reason is that the reduction is particularly likely to occur in related items because members of Congress are likely to feel that if HHS receives generous funding for program A, it is only fair that part of the cost should come from HHS's program B.

Lindsay and Zycher's (1978) examination of distributional effects of the Canadian health plan find that "most of the cost of the Canadian National Health Insurance was borne by the economically disadvantaged [p. 3]." There are a number of statistical problems with the Lindsay and Zycher work which, though a pioneering exploration of a completely new field, needs to be replicated in other areas. Nevertheless, it is the only empirical evidence on the point at this time.

Let us consider what happens in the real world. As I mentioned earlier, in the real world we have more people and a smaller part of the population is considered to be poor than the one-third in our three-citizen society. Thus, the level of provision under income-tested health provisions is apt to be farther to the right than we show in Figure 4.2. Indeed, it can be actually to the right of the level shown by line N. Under these extreme circumstances (which apparently existed in England when the National Health Service was adopted) the poor receive a sizable welfare loss when we switch from income-tested to universal programs. Indeed, everyone except the poor and the wealthy gain from this shift and the poor are hurt. The people who gain most, however, are the near-poor (i.e., the people whose incomes are slightly above the income test level); they now find that medicine is "free" and they can consume more of it.

Other aspects of the real world should also be mentioned here. One of them is that the transfer from an income-tested to a universal system does not increase the number of hospitals or doctors in society in the short run. Thus, at best it will lead to a rearrangement of the current medical resources with some people getting more and some people getting less. In the case of the British National Health Service for example, there was a very pronounced reduction in the resources available to the poor, with the result that during the period in which medicine was being revolutionized by introduction of antibiotics, the death rate of the poorest part of the English population actually rose (Tullock, 1971).

A Gradual Form of Income Testing

Let us now consider the situation where the income testing takes a gradual rather than abrupt form. In illustration let us assume that the state pays 100% of the medical care of people who are literally penniless and then reduces this percentage payment for medical care gradually until, let us say, the individuals had an income of $5000, at which point the subsidy fell to 0. If this were converted to a universal program paid for by taxes, then the net effect would be to make the people at the bottom of the distribution worse off, because they now would pay at least some taxes that they didn't pay before and receive the same or fewer services.[7] It seems likely as shown in Figure 4.3 that the increase in medical services will begin to offset the rise in taxes at some fairly low income (I have arbitrarily chosen $2500) and then remain above taxes to reach a maximum improvement at $5000, with a gradual fall as the increase in the taxes comes closer to and eventually passes the benefits from free medical attention. The wealthy suffer most, and part of the group that we may arbitrarily refer to as poor (but the upper end of the poor group), and part of the group that I call middle class gain.

Universalization of programs often is urged on the grounds that income-tested programs in fact do not reach all of the poor. It is implied, although as far as I can see there is no evidence, that making the program available for the upper-income brackets will increase the number of poor people who avail themselves of it. Even if it were true, it would

[7]People who actually had zero income before, if they were to stay alive must at any event have consumed food. Presumably this would be slightly more expensive because of the tax increase. But they are also, as we have noted above, likely to have their other government payments reduced or not increased as much as they otherwise would have been. Note here, that I have assumed that the net effect of the change does not involve an improvement in medical service.

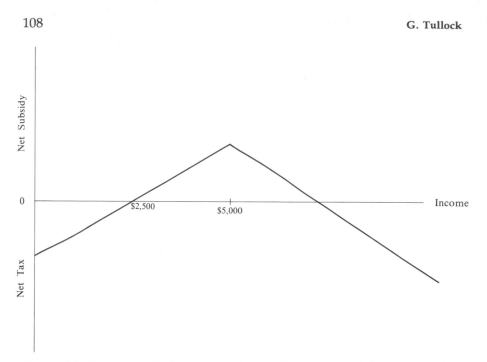

Figure 4.3. Costs of medical services as income increases in switch from a gradual income-tested program to a universal provision of medical care. (Figure by University of Wisconsin Cartographic Laboratory.)

be an extraordinarily expensive way of increasing the number of poor people in the program. The poor people who do not participate in the program do not presumably because partly they really don't like the program, partly they have difficulty with the bureaucracy, and partly through mere ignorance. The first is not a problem since people who voluntarily and with full knowledge choose not to enter the program are presumably better off outside it. The second would not in any way be affected by universalizing the program since the red tape would probably be worse in a large program than a small program. The third calls for an advertising campaign and such a campaign would surely be immensely cheaper than extending the program to the whole population.

So far I have used an extremely restricted model. Not only does it have only 3 citizens, but I arranged the possible choice patterns so the system always has a simple straightforward equilibrium. In the real world we do observe that political activity tends to reach a stopping point and so there must be an equilbrium of some sort; however, there is not necessarily an equilibrium in the simple direct sense that we have discussed so far.

Empirical Evidence

Before turning to complicating our model by taking these matters into account, however, we briefly discuss some empirical evidence which indicates that the basic conclusions drawn so far are correct. This empirical evidence is unfortunately not very sophisticated, indeed it was drawn from ordinary observation and reading the newspapers, but I think the reader will be able to confirm it from his own experience.

The specific empirical evidence seems to show that the pressure for universalizing the medical program does not come from the poor but from the lower-middle class. Indeed, there is a very high correlation between pressure groups for universal medical care and pressure groups for raising the minimum wage. Since the minimum wage clearly hurts the poor, one has to deduce that these groups do not have the interest of the poor very strongly at heart. This does not mean, however, that no one else is in favor of a minimum wage. In the upper income groups, a number of people favor it partly through miscalculation of its effects on them and partly through genuinely charitable motives. There are also those among the poor who favor it. The real push, however, comes from organizations like the AFL/CIO, whose members might well benefit.

Better empirical evidence is needed, however, because all this empirical evidence indicates is that the principal beneficiaries of universalizing medical treatment will be the people who are just above the cutout line on income-tested medical provision for the poor. It does not prove that the poor do not in fact still gain.

Consumer Preference

So far we have simply calculated what the outcome would be under both an income-tested and a universal program. Let us now permit the three citizens to vote on the issue of which alternative they want, granting that they have already been told what these outcomes will be.

Wealthy Mr. 3 will clearly be in favor of the income-tested scheme. For the other two, Mr. 1 and Mr. 2, however, their choice depends on the exact details of the income-tested scheme. In the example from Figures 4.1 and 4.2, Mr. 2 would be in favor of the income-tested scheme but Mr. 1 would not. The result, however, is heavily dependent on our specific assumptions.

From our current assumptions about taxes (i.e., that taxes are roughly proportional to income), it is clear that the exact location of the net payoff line in Figure 4.3 depends, in part, on whether, in net, the program transfers funds from the poor. If it transfers funds from the poor, the payoff line will be higher than if the switch to universal medical attention leads to more resources being spent on the poor. When this line is shifted then, of course, the dividing line between the wealthy and the middle class also shifts. If we assume that the people vote in accordance with their interest, this shift changes the number of people voting for the universalization.

In general, if universalization actually transfers funds away from the poor, the category we have referred to as middle class will be larger and hence there will be more votes for the program, while if it transfers funds to the poor the category we call middle class will be smaller and the wealthy category will be larger and hence there will be fewer votes for the program. Of course, it is not only the middle class and wealthy who vote on the issue, the poor do also. If the poor favor universalization, then the loss of some of the voters from the middle class to the wealthy class by lowering the net payoff line would make little difference. The poor are about 10% of the population, they only need to have 41% of the remainder on their side to win.

The situation of the poor is ambiguous. First, we have pointed out that they gain considerably less from the universalization than the people in the lower end of the middle class. Second, it is quite possible they will lose, and third, it is extremely difficult to calculate exactly whether they will gain or lose.

The calculation problem is made even more difficult by the fact that almost all of the people who are experts in the field will be in favor of universalization because they will in one way or another gain if the service is universalized. The experts are apt to be either employees of the welfare service or potential employees or people who expect research grants from the welfare service, etc. There are occasional specialists in this field whose incomes do not either directly or indirectly originate in the welfare program itself, but their number is very small compared to the number of people who are specialists and whose incomes will actually increase whenever the welfare programs are expanded.

Thus, the possibility that the poor will lose out from the program is not likely to be emphasized very much, even if it is true. The poor are apt to be told they will gain whether they do or do not. They don't face an easy calculation problem like the lower-middle class and must depend on experts or learn to do rather complicated calculations themselves. Hence, they are liable to be deceived.

In this respect we have here only one example of a general problem of the poor in a democracy. People in general are poor because they are not too intelligent, lack motivation, etc. This not only makes them inept in a private marketplace, it also makes them inept in the political marketplace. Consequently, they tend to do poorly in the distribution of pork, which is such an important part of democratic politics. Perhaps as a result of their low general motivation or perhaps because they understand this situation, they tend to abstain from voting in any event. In general what they get out of democracy reflects not their real voting power, which tends to be wasted, but essentially charitable motives on the part of upper-income voters. These charitable motives, although real, do not seem to be very strong.

A Combined Package

But let me now complicate my model further. So far I have been assuming that the only points at issue are whether the health service shall be income tested or universal and the exact level at which the health service will be provided. Further, I have used a proportional tax system to finance the program. It is possible to combine either of these systems with different tax arrangements, with the result that the income shifts which I have been describing will not necessarily occur. For example, a switch from an income-tested to a universal program could be accompanied by an appropriate package of taxes so that even though it greatly increased the cost of the medical service, only the wealthy minority lost on the deal while everyone else gained.

It is fairly easy to demonstrate that such combined packages do not lead to any firm equilibrium. Suppose, for example, a bill were proposed that would provide the universal health care free and that a special tax to finance it was imposed, falling on only the top 49% of the population. We would have a 51% majority for the plan but the wealthy top 49%, being clever people, could offer to some particular group of 2% of the population twice what they are getting under the universal health program with the result that they would favor this new proposal and the wealthy, of course, would favor it also because their taxes would fall. Their taxes would fall particularly sharply if they arranged that this new, and in total rather small, payment be financed only by the people in the bottom 51% who are not also in the 2%. We can go on with various combinations—each of which will beat the previous one. Any distribution of tax and benefit that you care to name can be reached by a properly planned set of proposals. When it comes to income distribution, there is in fact no equilibrium solution if all proposals are available.

In the real world things are fortunately a good deal more stable. In part this is unexplained, but there are a number of partial explanations for the observed reasonable stability of income redistribution measures.

Redistribution Effects

The first of these partial explanations is the straightforward fact that income redistribution away from the wealthy pays more than income redistribution away from anyone else. There is simply more money there. The tax on the top 10% of the population has as its total possible yield more than a tax on any other 10% of the population. This being so, tax systems in a democracy have a strong tendency to fall particularly heavily on the wealthy. The proportional income tax which we have been using as our base and which except for the very top does not deviate too much from the reality in most democracies is, in fact, a tax which gets a good deal more money from the top 10% of the population than from any other bracket.

The transfer of funds from the wealthy, even though it is not a very large-scale phenomenon in absolute quantity, benefits mainly the middle class. When the poor are given special privileges, and they usually are in all societies, this reflects charity on the part of the middle class and wealthy rather than the political power of the poor. In any event, if we look at the actual history of the development of Social Security and other social welfare programs in the United States, it is fairly obvious that redistribution to the poor was not one of its major objectives (Weaver, 1977).

Medicare, a general program for all of the old, could be predicted to lead to a very sharp increase in the income of doctors and civil servants, not lower-income groups, and also a rearrangement of American medical resources in which the principal beneficiaries were older people who are not particularly poor. The older poor, were, of course, already receiving free medical attention. This increased demand for medical services combined with no increase in the number of doctors or hospitals in the short run surely meant that everyone else, including the poor, had a reduction in their medical care.

At the same time the Medicare was passed, Medicaid, an income-tested program which provided resources only for the poor, was also enacted. It seems likely for most of the poor that Medicaid counteracted the effect of Medicare. The net effect of the two programs was surely to benefit doctors and the older nonpoor. Whether the poor benefited or not is something which cannot be said for certain, but if they did benefit it was because of the existence of the income-tested program.

I would like to say that this phenomenon not only occurred in these two cases in the United States, and they are, of course, the two most significant examples of recent expansion in social welfare activity in the United States, but always and everywhere. Unfortunately I cannot, because I simply don't know enough. Here again empirical research is called for and unfortunately it is an extremely difficult type of empirical research. Substantially each social welfare program in each country must be looked at in great detail with great care and with a good deal of skepticism for statements made by its apologists to see whether this is a general phenomenon or not. Once above I suggested a good project for a doctoral dissertation. Here we have a set of good projects for maybe 200 doctoral dissertations.

As a start on empirical research on this phenomenon, I should like to discuss three studies which I have succeeded in turning up. The first of these concerns Germany in the period 1969 through 1975, which was the initial period of the Social Democrat–Liberal coalition government. This government passed a considerable number of redistributional laws and increased the size of the transfer sector quite considerably. Martin Pfaff's study (1978) of this period shows a net increase in inequality. The increased transfers, even though enacted by a basically left-wing government, benefited the middle and upper classes rather than the poor. This study is particularly notable because Pfaff's predilections are quite in the other direction.

That the same phenomenon has occurred in Britain under its current labor government is indicated by an article in the London *Economist* (1978). Between 1974 and 1976, a period in which once again a new left-wing (labor) government was enacting very large increases and rearrangements in the social welfare program in England, the number of poor in England almost doubled.

My third bit of evidence comes from Switzerland, where there are direct public votes on many issues. Werner Pommerehne (1978) has chosen a number of communes in Basel and examined the redistributional effect of direct popular voting on budgets. These votes were not all specifically on social welfare programs but they did have considerable distributional impact. Pommerehne's study raises a certain number of difficulties with respect to the definition of transfer or nontransfer patterns of taxation and expenditure. It is, however, clear from the results of his study that there is, at the very least, no strong tendency to transfer funds to the poor when the populace is permitted to vote directly on such issues.

As a last item, and here we go to the underdeveloped world, two Indian scholars (Jagannadahm and Palvia, 1978) calculated the Gini coef-

ficient for government employees and then for the pensioners (i.e., retired government employees). They found that the Gini coefficient for
the actual employees was much lower than for the pensioners. The apparent explanation is that inflation has tended to lower pensions and the
existing power holders in India, whether they are the civil servants, or
legislatures, have raised the wages and improved the pension prospects
of active civil servants while letting the pensions of the already retired
personnel deteriorate. This is not directly relevant to the income-testing
hypothesis, but it is in general accord with Pommerehne's results. The
legislature and civil service of India are much more concerned with their
own well-being and with middle-income groups than with the poor and
elderly pensioners.

Of course these are merely a set of samples. They are, however, the
only ones I could find in which the subject had been discussed at all. I
cannot say on the basis of this evidence that the phenomenon is general
but I suspect it is.

The Politics of Income Testing

In any event, if it is very general that universal programs benefit the
middle class and not the poor, it is not difficult to explain, and certainly
it is not difficult to explain in the case of the United States. People who
are interested in expanding social welfare systems from income-tested to
universal programs are characteristically interested in just that and not
particularly in helping the poor. Establishing the program requires political support which almost of necessity has to come from the group that
we have referred to as the middle class because that is the only group
which makes an unambiguous gain. This group will be smaller and less
enthusiastic about a program designed to increase the benefits of the
poor considerably, because there is simply that much less left for them.

Hence, people trying to introduce some kind of general health insurance are not likely to propose a program which will transfer funds from
the middle class to the poor. There is another alternative, however,
which is to finance it in such a way as to transfer funds from the wealthy,
preferably the truly wealthy not just the people whom I have nomi-
nated wealthy in my somewhat arbitrary category. The trouble with this
plan is that the richest group is probably the best informed, most politically influential group in the electorate. Further, it is a fairly small group
and hence able to organize much more efficiently than larger groups.

In general to try to get anything through Congress you should try to avoid antagonizing any sector of the population. Now, of course, there are things put through Congress despite disadvantaging specific groups; our whole energy program for example. But on the whole, this is something you would want to avoid. The national health program will be easier to put through Congress if the cost doesn't fall too conspicuously on the wealthy. On the other hand, if the cost doesn't fall too conspicuously on the wealthy, then it must fall on the middle class or on the poor. The proponents of the program then are likely to set up financing methods which lead to the whole program being mildly regressive.

It should be noted that insofar as the middle-class voters can succeed in getting funds from the wealthy, there is no obvious reason why they should pass them on to the poor. Thus, even if we do have a scheme which raises the cost to the upper-income groups, like the recent extension of the social security tax to all wages, there is no reason to believe that the poor rather than the middle class will benefit.

This last line of reasoning, while I find it persuasive, is clearly much less rigorous than the models I have used before. I have difficulty imagining how it could be tested. Detailed historical research of the sort that Carolyn Weaver (1977) did on the origins of the Social Security Act would be called for and unfortunately this type of historical investigation has the characteristic that it is always possible for different historians to disagree.

Conclusion

Any extension of social welfare activity provides a direct benefit to those who receive it and a direct cost on those who are paying for it. Those who are paying for it may well be the recipients, but in any event we have to net out the two sides of the budget. This is, of course, particularly important when we are contrasting an income-tested with a non-income-tested program, because the improvement in quality (if there is an improvement at all) for the people who have previously been receiving the income-tested service is apt to be much less than the gain obtained by people who were previously not receiving it because the income test barred them.

The third item that has to be netted out, of course, is the cost to the former recipients of the income-tested service, in that the additional budgetary cost of spreading the service over the population as a whole probably will mean that various other services which they would be entitled to either are contracted or at at least not expanded as rapidly as they otherwise would be. Only when we have completed this rather difficult computation can we tell whether the people who previously received the income-tested service benefit or are injured by the expansion to the society as a whole.

Fortunately, the calculations for the rest of the society are a good deal easier, although here again all three of these items are present. They will receive a benefit, they will pay taxes, and presumably the existence of this program will have effects elsewhere in the government budget that will benefit or injure them. In either case, however, it is usually fairly easy to at least work out the direction of the effects. With the poor the problem is much more difficult.

The calculation above, of course, involves simply the measurement of effects. When we consider the political forces which may lead to the expansion of a program it is, in general, clear that if people who are interested in expanding the program are trying merely to help the poor, they have chosen an inept way of doing it. Only if they feel that they can trick members of the middle and upper class into voting for a program to help the poor by that indirect method which is more generous than they are willing to give in a direct and open way, is it sensible. Politics, of course, involves a great deal of misinformation and a great deal of trickery and so the possibility that this is true cannot be totally ruled out, but it seems to me unlikely. It will not escape the reader that I personally think that in most of the cases in which income-tested programs have been converted into universal programs, the poor have been injured, and indeed that this is what was intended. I tend to think of them as programs which are aimed at benefiting the group which I have referred to as the middle class and in addition benefiting the factor suppliers— the doctors, welfare workers, professors of social work, etc. who will gain when such programs are extended.

I suspect that the other authors in this book feel quite differently on the subject. Indeed, I must complement Professor Garfinkel on his willingness to bring in what he must think of as a particularly perverse reactionary in order to present the other side. I trust, however, that the reader, having read my paper, will agree that even if my personal opinion on the matter is wrong, at any event the problem is in fact a difficult one and the matter would deserve a great deal of careful empirical study.

Discussion

ANTHONY DOWNS

Gordon Tullock's paper on the relative merits and drawbacks of income-tested versus universal programs exhibits his provocative and thought-stimulating style of writing, and thereby raises several key issues on this subject. As a long-time friend of Gordon's, I have always admired his vigorous use of what I call "proof by assertion," in contrast to the more mundane approach of proof through factual evidence, with all the limitations of the latter, narrower approach. In this paper, his proofs by assertion are cleverly wrapped in diagrams and model worlds containing small numbers of citizens, but they are nonetheless relatively unencumbered by facts. In part, this approach may be necessary because relevant empirical work is not available. And there is no doubt that this method does allow the author to focus on critical issues and express definite views concerning them.

However, I believe some of the conclusions he arrives at concerning those issues are either wrong or are the results of certain assumptions he makes at the outset that are not necessarily true in what he calls the real world. In these comments I will focus in particular upon his argument that shifting from an income-tested program to a universal program (1) always injures the relatively affluent; (2) always benefits those who are just above the poverty group; (3) is rarely espoused by persons whose real motive is to aid the poor; and (4) usually (though not always) re-

117

duces the net welfare of the poor. Like Gordon, I will use a model to illustrate my own approach to these conclusions. However, my model has been developed from actual data concerning the U.S. income distribution in 1976, and from data concerning spending on medical care in the United States at about the same period. Tables 4.1–4.6 lay out the initial income distribution and several alternative methods of providing a subsidized medical-care program similar to that discussed in Tullock's paper. The income distribution contains only 100 families, but they are distributed among income levels in a manner that roughly approximates the 1976 income distribution in two ways (see Table 4.1). The percentage of families in each part of the distribution is roughly the same as was true in the United States in 1976, and the total income received by each quintile of the distribution is about the same as that which prevailed among U.S. families in 1976. However, I have assigned specific incomes to each family, rather than ranges of incomes, to make subsequent calculations easier.

Other aspects of my model reflect some realities of health care in the United States in about the same period, but the model does leave out many other elements. It assumes the following:

1. The dollar cost of "adequate" health care in the United States at that time was about $900 per family, regardless of the actual health-care spending done by that family. This cost estimate was taken from the estimated urban budget for a four-person family for 1976 prepared by the Bureau of Labor Statistics; hence it somewhat understates actual per capita health-care costs, which are higher when all households—including the elderly—are taken into account. However, use of this figure does not influence the basic nature of the conclusions drawn.

2. In the absence of any health-care assistance programs, households with incomes $5000 and below would spend 10% of their incomes on health care; those with incomes from $5001 to $11,000 would spend 8%; and those with incomes above $11,000 would spend $900 plus 1% of their incomes. Such spending is shown in Table 4.2, labeled "No Health-Care Program." This assumes there is no charity providing health care for the very poor.

3. Society considers expenditure of 8.0% of a family's income on health care an "appropriate" amount and is willing under some circumstances to subsidize families for whom such expenditure would result in less than the amount needed to achieve "adequate" care—that is, less than $900.

4. Expansion of total spending on health care does not result in inflationary price adjustments that affect different income groups dif-

TABLE 4.1
Model Income Distribution

Family Income ($)	Number of Families	Sum	Total Income ($ thousands)	Cumulative Income ($ thousands)	% Families (By Census income groups)	% Income	Quintiles % Families	Quintiles % Income
0	1	1	0	.0	4 (below $3,000)	.00		
1,000	1	2	1	1		.06		
2,000	2	4	4	5		.24		
3,000	3	7	9	14	6 ($3000–4,999)	.54	20	5.1
4,000	3	10	12	26		.72		
5,000	4	14	20	46	8 ($5,000–6,999)	1.20		
6,000	4	18	24	70		1.44		
7,000	2	20	14	84	8 ($7,000–8,999)	.84		
8,000	6	26	48	132		2.89		
9,000	4	30	36	168	12 ($9,000–11,999)	2.17		
10,000	4	34	40	208		2.41	20	11.
11,000	4	38	44	252		2.65		
12,000	2	40	24	276	12 ($12,000–14,999)	1.44		
13,000	6	46	78	354		4.69		
14,000	4	50	56	410		3.37		
15,000	10	60	150	560	19 ($15,000–19,999)	9.03	20	17.
16,000	5	65	80	640		4.81		
18,000	4	69	72	712		4.33		
20,000	11	80	220	932	13 ($20,000–24,999)	13.25	20	22.
24,000	2	82	48	980		2.89		
28,000	4	86	112	1,092	18 ($25,000 and above)	6.74		
30,000	4	90	120	1,212		7.22	20	43
40,000	5	95	200	1,412		12.03		
50,000	5	100	250	1,662		15.04		
Total	100		1,662	1,662	100	100.0	100	100

TABLE 4.2
No Health-Care Program

Family Income ($ thousands)	Number of Families	Spending on Medical Care ($)		"Deficit" below $900 Minimum Care ($)	
		Each Family	Total	Each Family	Total
0	1	0	0	900	900
1	1	100	100	800	800
2	2	200	400	700	1,400
3	3	300	900	600	1,800
4	3	400	1,200	500	1,500
5	4	400	1,600	500	2,000
6	4	480	1,920	420	1,680
7	2	560	1,120	340	680
8	6	640	3,840	260	1,560
9	4	720	2,880	180	720
10	4	800	3,200	100	400
11	4	880	3,520	20	80
12	2	1,020	2,040	0	0
13	6	1,030	6,180	0	0
14	4	1,040	4,160	0	0
15	10	1,050	10,500	0	0
16	5	1,060	5,300	0	0
18	4	1,080	4,320	0	0
20	11	1,100	12,100	0	0
24	.2	1,140	2,280	0	0
28	4	1,180	4,720	0	0
30	4	1,200	4,800	0	0
40	5	1,300	6,500	0	0
50	5	1,400	7,000	0	0
Total			90,580 (5.45% of income)	0	13,520

ferently. This is probably an erroneous assumption, but I want to abstract from supply-shortage questions in this brief analysis. I will comment further on this subject below.

5. Households who would spend more than $900 for health care if there were no subsidies will continue to spend the same total amount when subsidies are provided, by adding private spending to whatever subsidies they receive to reach that amount.

6. In universal health-care subsidy programs, a subsidy of $900 is provided for every household, but neither more nor less than that amount on the average.

Given these assumptions, I have developed five different means of providing health care in this model world. They are

1. *No health-care program.* Every household pays for its own health care in accordance with the spending patterns mentioned above, and no transfer payments are made.

2. *A notched income-tested program.* This is the type of program Tullock refers to as "income tested." In it, the government subsidizes $900 worth of medical care for every household with an income below $5000 per year, but provides no subsidies for any other households. The subsidy is paid for by a tax proportional to income levied on all families.

3. *A gradual income-tested program.* In this program, the subsidy declines with income in accordance with the formula, $900 − .08 (income). For households with zero incomes, the subsidy equals $900; then it gradually declines, but all households with incomes below $11,250 receive at least some subsidy. Again, the subsidy is paid for through a tax proportional to income levied on all families.

4. *A universal program with proportional taxation.* In this program, every family receives a $900 subsidy, but must spend all $900 on health care. Families that would otherwise have spent more than $900 on health care continue to do so. The subsidy is financed through a proportional tax, as mentioned above.

5. *A universal program with progressive taxation.* This provides the same benefits as the preceding program but finances them through a tax with higher rates on high-income families than on low-income families.

Tables 4.2–4.6 present these five programs. A summary, Table 4.7, then compares the net benefits received by a family at each income level under all five arrangements. This table can be used to examine the conclusions Tullock arrives at in the context of a much more realistic simulation than he employed in his paper.

Careful examination of Table 4.7 leads to the following conclusions:

1. Tullock is correct in asserting that the most affluent families are the big losers from almost any form of health-care program that does not have regressive financing. In particular, his assertion that any shift from an income-tested program to a universal one is likely to adversely affect the affluent is borne out by the results of this simulation. A family with an income of $30,000 per year, for example, does best under no subsidy program, second best under a notched income-tested program (because the total subsidy to be financed is small), and worst under a universal program with progressive financing.

2. Tullock's belief that a shift from income-tested aid to universal aid probably harms the poor is strongly dependent upon his assumption of

TABLE 4.3
Notched Income-Tested Program (*tax rate* = .005415)

Family Income ($ thousands)	Number of Families	Medical Subsidy ($)		Medical Care Spending ($)		Taxes for Subsidy ($)		Subsidy Minus Taxes ($)
		Each Family	Total	Each Family	Total	Each Family	Total	Each Family
0	1	900	900	900	900	0	0	900.00
1	1	900	900	900	900	5.42	5.42	894.58
2	2	900	1,800	900	1,800	10.83	21.66	889.17
3	3	900	2,700	900	2,700	16.25	48.74	883.75
4	3	900	2,700	900	2,700	21.66	64.98	878.34
5	4	0	0	400	1,600	27.08	108.30	−27.08
6	4	0	0	480	1,920	32.49	129.96	−32.49
7	2	0	0	560	1,120	37.91	75.81	−37.91
8	6	0	0	640	3,840	43.32	259.93	−43.32
9	4	0	0	720	2,880	48.74	194.95	−48.74
10	4	0	0	800	3,200	54.15	216.61	−54.15
11	4	0	0	880	3,520	59.57	238.27	−59.57
12	2	0	0	1,020	2,040	64.98	129.96	−64.98
13	6	0	0	1,030	6,180	70.40	422.38	−70.40
14	4	0	0	1,040	4,160	75.81	303.25	−75.81
15	10	0	0	1,050	10,500	81.23	812.27	−81.23
16	5	0	0	1,060	5,300	86.64	433.21	−86.64
18	4	0	0	1,080	4,320	97.47	389.89	−97.47
20	11	0	0	1,100	12,100	108.30	1,191.34	−108.30
24	2	0	0	1,140	2,280	129.96	259.93	−129.96
28	4	0	0	1,180	4,720	151.62	606.50	−151.62
30	4	0	0	1,200	4,800	162.45	649.82	−162.45
40	5	0	0	1,300	6,500	216.61	1,083.03	−216.61
50	5	0	0	1,400	7,000	270.76	1,353.79	−270.76
Total	100		9,000		96,980 5.85% of income (up 7.1%)		9,000.00	

TABLE 4.4
Gradual Income-Tested Program (*tax rate = .00844765*)

Family Income ($ thousands)	Number of Families	Medical Subsidy ($)		Medical Care Spending ($)		Taxes for Subsidy ($)		Subsidy Minus Taxes ($)
		Each Family	Total	Each Family	Total	Each Family	Total	Each Family
0	1	900	900	900	900	0	0	900.00
1	1	820	820	900	900	8.45	8.45	811.55
2	2	740	1,480	900	1,800	16.90	33.79	723.10
3	3	660	1,980	900	2,700	25.34	75.03	634.66
4	3	580	1,740	900	2,700	33.79	101.37	546.21
5	4	500	2,000	900	3,600	42.24	168.95	457.76
6	4	420	1,680	900	3,600	50.69	202.74	369.31
7	2	340	680	900	1,800	59.13	118.27	280.87
8	6	260	1,560	900	5,400	67.58	405.49	192.42
9	4	180	720	900	3,600	76.03	304.12	103.97
10	4	100	400	900	3,600	84.48	337.91	15.52
11	4	20	80	900	3,600	92.92	371.70	−72.92
12	2	0	0	1,020	2,040	101.37	202.74	−101.37
13	6	0	0	1,030	6,180	109.82	658.92	−109.82
14	4	0	0	1,040	4,160	118.27	473.07	−118.27
15	10	0	0	1,050	10,500	126.71	1,267.15	−126.71
16	5	0	0	1,060	5,300	135.16	675.81	−135.16
18	4	0	0	1,080	4,320	152.06	608.23	−152.06
20	11	0	0	1,100	12,100	168.95	1,858.48	−168.95
24	2	0	0	1,140	2,280	202.74	405.49	−202.74
28	4	0	0	1,180	4,720	236.53	946.14	−236.53
30	4	0	0	1,200	4,800	753.43	1,013.72	−253.43
40	5	0	0	1,300	6,500	337.91	1,689.53	−337.91
50	5	0	0	1,400	7,000	422.38	2,111.91	−422.38
Total			14,040		104,100 6.0% of income (up 15%)		14,039.01	

TABLE 4.5
Universal Program, Proportional Tax (*tax rate = .0541516*)

Family Income ($ thousands)	Number of Families	Medical Subsidy ($) Each Family	Medical Subsidy ($) Total	Medical Care Spending ($) Each Family	Medical Care Spending ($) Total	Taxes for Subsidy ($) Each Family	Taxes for Subsidy ($) Total	Subsidy Minus Taxes ($) Each Family
0	1	900	900	900	900	0	0	900.00
1	1	900	900	900	900	54.15	54.15	845.85
2	2	900	1,800	900	1,800	108.30	216.61	791.70
3	3	900	2,700	900	2,700	162.45	487.36	737.55
4	3	900	2,700	900	2,700	216.61	649.82	683.39
5	4	900	3,600	900	3,600	270.76	1,083.03	629.24
6	4	900	3,600	900	3,600	324.91	1,299.64	575.09
7	2	900	1,800	900	1,800	379.06	758.12	520.94
8	6	900	5,400	900	5,400	433.21	2,599.28	466.79
9	4	900	3,600	900	3,600	487.36	1,949.46	412.64
10	4	900	3,600	900	3,600	541.52	2,166.06	358.48
11	4	900	3,600	900	3,600	595.67	2,382.67	304.33
12	2	900	1,800	1,020	2,040	649.82	1,299.64	250.18
13	6	900	5,400	1,030	6,180	703.97	4,223.83	196.03
14	4	900	3,600	1,040	4,160	758.12	3,032.49	141.88
15	10	900	9,000	1,050	10,500	812.27	8,122.74	87.73
16	5	900	4,500	1,060	5,300	866.43	4,332.13	33.57
18	4	900	3,600	1,080	4,320	974.73	3,898.92	−74.73
20	11	900	9,900	1,100	12,100	1,083.03	11,913.36	−183.03
24	2	900	1,800	1,140	2,280	1,299.64	2,599.28	−399.64
28	4	900	3,600	1,180	4,720	1,516.25	6,064.98	−616.25
30	4	900	3,600	1,200	4,800	1,624.55	6,498.19	−724.55
40	5	900	4,500	1,300	6,500	2,166.06	10,830.32	−1,266.05
50	5	900	4,500	1,400	7,000	2,707.58	13,557.92	−1,807.58
Total	100		90,000		104,100		90,000.00	

6.0% of income (up 15%)

TABLE 4.6
Universal Program, Progressive Tax

Family Income ($ thousands)	Number of Families	Medical Subsidy ($)		Medical Care Spending ($)		Taxes for Subsidy ($)		Subsidy Minus Taxes ($)
		Each Family	Total	Each Family	Total	Each Family	Total	Each Family
0	1	900	900	900	900	0	0	900
1	1	900	900	900	900	4.58	4.58	895.42
2	2	900	1,800	900	1,800	9.15	18.31	840.85
3	3	900	2,700	900	2,700	13.73	41.19	886.27
4	3	900	2,700	900	2,700	18.31	54.92	881.69
5	4	900	3,600	900	3,600	22.89	91.54	877.11
6	4	900	3,600	900	3,600	27.46	109.85	872.54
7	2	900	1,800	900	1,800	32.04	64.08	867.96
8	6	900	5,400	900	5,400	63.86	383.18	836.14
9	4	900	3,600	900	3,600	71.85	287.39	828.15
10	4	900	3,600	900	3,600	79.83	319.32	820.17
11	4	900	3,600	900	3,600	87.81	351.25	812.19
12	2	900	1,800	1,020	2,040	95.80	191.59	804.20
13	6	900	5,400	1,030	6,180	650.00	3,900.00	250.00
14	4	900	3,600	1,040	4,160	700.00	2,800.00	200.00
15	10	900	900	1,050	10,500	750.00	7,500.00	150.00
16	5	900	4,500	1,060	5,300	960.68	4,803.40	−60.68
18	4	900	3,600	1,080	4,320	1,080.77	4,323.06	−180.77
20	11	900	9,400	1,100	12,100	1,200.85	13,209.35	−300.85
24	2	900	1,880	1,140	2,280	1,695.02	3,390.05	−795.02
28	4	900	3,600	1,180	4,720	1,977.53	7,910.11	−1,077.53
30	4	900	3,600	1,200	4,800	2,118.78	8,475.12	−1,218.78
40	5	900	4,500	1,300	6,500	2,825.04	14,125.20	−1,925.04
50	5	900	4,500	1,400	7,000	3,531.30	17,656.51	−2,631.30
Total	100		90,000		104,100		90,000.00	

NOTE: The tax rate is as follows: $0–7,000, .004577; $8,000–12,000, .007983; $13,000–15,000, .05; $16,000–20,000, .06; $24,000–50,000, .07.

TABLE 4.7
Subsidy Minus Taxes: Net Position under Alternative Programs

Family Income ($ thousands)	Number of Families	No Health-Care Program ($)	Notched Income-Tested ($)	Gradual Income-Tested ($)	Universal, Proportional Tax ($)	Universal, Progressive Tax ($)
0	1	0	900.00	900.00	900.00	900.00
1	1	0	894.58	811.55	845.85	895.42
2	2	0	889.17	723.10	791.70	890.85
3	3	0	883.75	634.66	737.55	886.27
4	3	0	878.34	546.21	683.34	881.69
5	4	0	−27.08	457.76	629.24	877.11
6	4	0	−32.49	369.31	575.09	872.54
7	2	0	−37.91	280.87	520.94	867.96
8	6	0	−43.32	192.42	466.79	836.14
9	4	0	−48.74	103.97	412.64	828.15
10	4	0	−54.15	15.52	358.48	820.17
11	4	0	−54.57	−72.92	304.33	812.19
12	2	0	−64.98	−101.37	250.18	804.20
13	6	0	−70.40	−109.82	196.03	250.00
14	4	0	−75.81	−118.27	141.88	200.00
15	10	0	−81.23	−126.71	87.73	150.00
16	5	0	−86.64	−135.16	33.57	−60.68
18	4	0	−97.47	−152.06	−74.73	−180.77
20	11	0	−108.30	−168.95	−183.03	−300.85
24	2	0	−129.96	−202.74	−399.64	−795.02
28	4	0	−151.62	−236.53	−616.25	−1,077.53
30	4	0	−162.45	−253.43	−724.55	−1,218.78
40	5	0	−216.61	−337.91	−1,266.05	−1,925.04
50	5	0	−270.76	−422.38	−1,807.58	−2,631.30
Total subsidy		0	9,000.00	14,040	90,000	90,000
Total medical care spending		90,580.00	96,980.00	104,100.00	104,100.00	104,100.00
Tax rate		0	.005415	.00844765	.0541516	varies

a notched program rather than a gradual one. In a notched program, everyone with an income below a certain level receives full assistance; whereas everyone with an income above that level receives nothing. In contrast, in a gradual or graduated-aid program, the size of the subsidy gradually declines and eventually fades out as income rises. This means that many relatively low-income households do not receive a *complete* subsidy up to the full cost of "adequate" care, but must contribute something themselves. Hence they stand to gain a higher subsidy from a shift to a universal program that finances *everyone's* care up to that level of "adequacy." Also, the degree of progressiveness in the financing of the subsidy system influences how well they come out. For example, a family with an income of $3000 receives a net benefit of $883.75 under the notched income-tested program, but only $634.66 under a gradual income-tested program. It would receive $737.55 in net benefits from a universal program financed by proportional taxation. That means shifting from an income-tested program to a universal one would be desirable if the income-tested program was a gradual one, but undesirable if it was a notched one. But such a shift would be desirable in either case if the universal subsidy was financed with a progressive tax, since that provides a net benefit of $886.27 to this family. Although Tullock admits it is difficult to determine whether the lowest-income families would gain or lose from such a shift, he believes they would usually lose. This analysis tends to dispute that conclusion.

3. Tullock is correct in arguing that the biggest gainers from any shift to a universal program from an income-tested one are those families just above the level at which benefits ceased to be subsidized in the income-tested program. This is true whether the latter is notched or gradual. For example, a family with an annual income of $12,000 sustains net losses from both types of income-tested programs, since it is not eligible for benefits but must pay taxes. Hence moving to a universal program greatly assists such a family, because the health-care subsidy it receives is larger than the taxes it must pay.

4. The political support a universal program is likely to receive depends in part upon how progressively it is financed. The program that provides the highest net benefit for most families is the universal program with progressive tax financing. Those 60% of the families with incomes below $16,000 receive larger net gains from this program than from any other—but the 35% with incomes above $16,000 are more injured by this program than by any other. Hence they are likely to oppose it vehemently. Whether the intensity of their resistance can overcome the popularity of such a program with a majority of the families probably depends more upon particular circumstances when the issue comes up than upon the structure of the situation.

5. Shifting to a universal program tends to increase the total demand for whatever services are involved, such as health care in this example. This can result in a rather sudden imbalance in the market for those services, as Tullock points out. Although this model is not designed to analyze such an imbalance, it does illustrate that total health-care spending would be 15% higher under a universal program than under no program at all, and 7% higher than under a notched income-tested program. The imbalance is likely to be less under a shift from a gradual income-tested program, however—and most income-tested programs today are gradual rather than notched. Nevertheless, questions of inflation in prices caused by such imbalances are clearly important in considering the desirability of universal programs.

Another important aspect of shifting to a universal program is not discussed by Tullock at all because his approach abstracts from real-world arrangements, particularly those concerning health care, even though it is the sample service he discusses. Most households who are financing their own health care (under the "No Health-Care Program" alternative all would) will do so through some type of health insurance scheme to protect themselves from the heavy costs of catastrophic illness or injury. This is the best way for them to use at least some of their health-care expenditures in the most prudent manner. But once households use insurance schemes that involve third-party payments for services, their direct incentives to economize on the use of those services are reduced. Hence at the moment of choosing the amount of direct services to consume, they face a marginal cost that is below the full marginal cost of the resources concerned—so each such family tends to "over-consume" health care. This draws "excessive" resources into the health-care field from other economic sectors where no such distortion of economizing incentives exists. The distributional impacts of this distorted allocation of resources are hard to trace, especially since they are related to the contribution that rising health-care prices make to inflation generally. Dealing with this issue is beyond the scope of this discussion. However, it might have an important bearing upon the relative desirability of income-tested versus universal programs for assisting low-income households. (I am indebted to Louise Russell and Henry Aaron of the Brookings Institution for suggesting this aspect of the situation to me.)

Discussion

LARRY ORR

Gordon Tullock has written a paper that is stimulating and thought-provoking, often frustrating and occasionally downright outrageous, largely devoid of theoretical rigor and thoroughly lacking in empirical evidence. Like Tony Downs, in reading the paper I was struck by Tullock's liberal use of "proof by assertion" (to use Downs's apt phrase).

For all of that, the paper contains a number of observations which, while occasionally irrelevant to the theme of this conference and often overdrawn, are worth keeping in mind. These include his observations that

1. Income is not the only, or even the dominant, criterion on which transfers are made in this society; thus, many transfer programs benefit primarily the middle- and upper-income classes.
2. The expansion of one assistance program may well reduce the amount of resources devoted to another; my own research indicates, for example, that food stamp benefits to cash assistance recipients are offset dollar-for-dollar in lower cash benefit levels. Thus, the distinction between replacing current programs and adding a new program may not be as clear-cut as it might seem at first glance.

3. The net distributional outcomes of a shift from income-tested to universal transfers will depend heavily on the distribution of taxes levied to finance the (presumed) increase in the transfer budget.

At bottom, though, Tullock's paper is primarily devoted to a single, fairly straightforward, argument: The "poor" (defined as current transfer recipients) will very likely lose from a shift to universal transfers. He arrives at this conclusion by assuming that the transfer in question has a zero tax rate up to a notch, and that any expansion in transfers will be financed by a proportional tax on income. Given those assumptions, he is almost certainly right, at least for current recipients with nonzero incomes.

This, however, is not a very general case and, in the end, Tullock's tortuous argument yields results that are little more than illustrative of his main theme, that the more broadly you spread transfers, the less generous they are likely to be and/or the heavier the tax burden will be, for the poor as well as for everybody else.

Fortunately, for any specific set of program alternatives, it is not necessary to attempt to resolve the issue of winners and losers in this abstract, a priori fashion. Through the modern miracle of microsimulation modeling, the question of who gains and who loses under any particular tax–transfer scheme can be answered rather precisely—as witness the simulation modeling papers presented at this conference. Unfortunately, these efforts assume away an important—possibly the important—question. In comparing any two types of program via microsimulation, one must make some assumption about the relative size of the transfer budget available for each. If the amount of funds that the political system is willing to devote to a NIT is not the same as that which it will devote to, say, a CIT, then the distributional impacts simulated under the assumption that they are the same can be very misleading. Indeed, one of the central arguments of proponents of non-income-tested programs appears to be that much more generous transfer budgets are politically feasible for non-income-tested programs. While simulation studies can explore the distributional consequences of alternative budget constraints, it appears that we know very little about the actual budget constraint that would face a non-income-tested alternative to any given income-tested program. It seems important, then, to consider the motivations, and past and probable future behavior, of taxpayers and their elected representatives in legislating transfer programs.

The motivation of taxpayers with respect to transfers can, I would argue, be represented (at least heuristically) by a rather simple utility function:

$$U_i = W\,(Y_i,\ S_i) + V\,(Y_j,\ B_j,\ S_j),$$

where Y_i is the after-tax, after-transfer income of the ith taxpayer and S_i is its variability over time, Y_j is the pretax, pretransfer income of the jth other individual, B_j is the net transfer to the jth individual, and S_j is the variability of the jth individual's total income over time.

Viewed in these terms, it is apparent that there are two fundamentally different motivations for transfer programs. If the taxpayer's utility function is altruistic (i.e., if the first partials of Y_j and B_j are positive, at least for low values of these variables), the $V(\cdot)$ term provides the basis for redistributive transfer programs, such as AFDC.[1] But transfer programs of an essentially nonredistributive nature can also arise out of the $W(\cdot)$ term. That is, by accepting somewhat lower current income (Y_i), the taxpayer can establish transfer programs that reduce the variability of his own income over time (S_i).[2] These programs are of the type commonly known as "social insurance": Social Security, Unemployment Insurance, Workmen's Compensation, etc. We analyst-types have been far too successful in propagating (at least among ourselves) the perfectly plausible notion that social insurance programs aren't really insurance, but are simply transfers, thereby blurring the distinction between welfare and, say, Social Security. But although Social Security may not be insurance in any actuarial sense, it is not intended to be primarily an income redistribution program either—at least not in the sense of systematically transferring income from people with high (lifetime) income to those with low. In a very real sense, these programs *are* insurance: They insure against variability in lifetime income in much the same way that private health insurance does. The social insurance programs, then, can be viewed as collective consumption of "income variability insurance" by the (largely middle-class) taxpayers, for their own private benefit.

In his Introduction, Garfinkel identifies the social insurance programs as "non-income-tested," and displays, in Table 1.1, the huge disparity between outlays for these programs and those for the "income-tested" welfare programs. Looking at these budgetary figures, it is easy to leap

---

[1]See my article (Orr, 1976).

[2]If Y_i is defined as the taxpayer's lifetime normal income and if his or her benefits are offset against current taxes, the cost to the taxpayer of even major reductions in S_i may be very slight indeed; on average, for a self-financing program, the only costs to the taxpayer are administrative costs. It seems likely that in many cases these costs are much lower in a public program than for the alternative private market mechanisms available to the individual for reconfiguring his or her lifetime income stream in a similar fashion. This would explain a preference for collective, as opposed to private, action to achieve reductions in income variability.

to the conclusion that the taxpayer is somehow much more liberal with his/her money when it is spent on non-income-tested programs. Indeed, it seems to me that this simple comparison colors much of our thinking and discussion about income-tested versus non-income-tested programs. But if one bears in mind the fundamentally different motivations for the two sets of programs, the disparity is quite understandable, if not very encouraging to the redistributionist case. *Of course* the middle-class taxpayer is willing to spend more on programs for his/her own benefit than for those that give income to other people. But by the same token, he/she is not likely to be sympathetic to using those programs for redistributive purposes.

Moreover, if one considers carefully the form of the major social insurance programs, it becomes clear that the term "non-income-tested" is a gross misnomer, and even clearer why taxpayers prefer this form to the (income-tested) NIT form. The social insurance programs have been

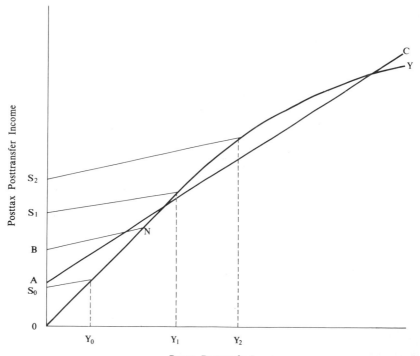

Figure 4.4. Diagrammatic comparison of NIT, CIT, and social insurance program. (Figure by University of Wisconsin Cartographic Laboratory.)

carefully tailored around those events—unemployment, disability, retirement, death—that account for the greatest variability in middle-class income over time, and they typically have high tax rates (usually referred to as "replacement rates" in this context). Thus, the amount of reduction in income variability "purchased" with each tax dollar is likely to be much higher, especially for a middle-income family, under these programs than under a negative income tax or credit income tax. More important, these programs are in fact income-tested, but in a rather unusual way: the guarantee (e.g., the "principal insurance amount" in Social Security) is based on past earnings, and therefore is *positively* related to income. Thus, the middle-income class enjoys much higher income floors under these programs than the lower-income classes.

A diagrammatic comparison of a NIT, a CIT, and a prototypical social insurance program is shown in Figure 4.4. Line $0Y$ denotes existing posttax posttransfer income; lines AC and BNY are the transfer schedules for a CIT and a NIT, respectively. The social insurance program, however, does not have a unique transfer schedule, since the guarantee is based on past earnings. Rather, an individual whose normal earnings are Y_1, will have a guarantee S_1, while an individual with earnings Y_2 will have a guarantee S_2. Clearly, the social insurance program does a much better job of offsetting major income losses for individuals who are very far above the NIT and CIT breakeven levels (i.e., for most of the middle- and upper-income classes).[3] Of course, a low-income individual at, say, Y_0 may well have a social insurance guarantee below that of either the NIT or CIT, but such individuals are apt to be a distinct minority of taxpayers.

The exact distribution of relative guarantees for equal-cost programs is, of course, an empirical matter; one cannot say a priori that a majority of taxpayer–voters will be better off under a social insurance program than under an equal-cost NIT or CIT. But given that social insurance programs almost certainly transfer only a small fraction of total benefits to those with low lifetime incomes, it seems highly likely that the vast majority of middle-income families would fare better under such a program in the long run than under an equal-cost NIT or CIT. It would be

---

[3]Small income losses may well not be offset at all by the social insurance programs because of the restrictive nature of their coverage; but most middle-income families would not fall below the NIT breakeven as a result of a small income loss, and the CIT only offsets a small fraction of any income loss because of its low tax rates. Moreover, the most serious risk of a small income loss (on an annual basis) for most middle-income families—short-term unemployment—is covered by social insurance.

extremely useful to resolve this question with microsimulation studies of the distribution of benefits by income over long periods of time.[4]

Of course, any attempt to "tilt" the benefit formulas of social insurance programs toward greater redistribution—by raising the replacement rates for low-income families and lowering those for the middle class—would erode the very features of these programs that middle-class voter–taxpayers find attractive, and could therefore be expected to meet stiff resistance.

If one defines a non-income-tested program as one in which gross benefits are invariant with income, then there are almost no examples of major non-income-tested programs in the United States today. Thus, it is difficult to know how generously the taxpayers would be willing to support, say, a CIT. But it does seem clear that the taxpayers would not willingly exchange any of the existing social insurance programs for a CIT; nor are they likely to allow those programs to be revamped to provide greater redistribution. It seems equally unlikely that they would opt for converting any of the existing income-tested programs into a CIT by substantially lowering the tax rates on these programs. All of the evidence from the past ten years of deliberations on welfare reform indicates that the taxpayers prefer high tax rates for welfare recipients. Congress appears quite comfortable with guarantees that range from 65% to 90% of the poverty line (depending on family type and place of residence). But one encounters stiff political resistance to providing benefits in these income-tested programs to families with incomes much above 150% of the poverty line. Indeed, the federal tax entry point is currently only slightly above the poverty line. Taken together, these preferences imply tax rates in the range of 45% to 60%, well above the level usually associated with a CIT.[5]

Any new non-income-tested program, then, would probably have to be adopted as an addition to the existing complex of programs. With no quid pro quo for the middle class, that seems highly unlikely: as Betson, Greenberg, and Kasten have shown, middle-class families are net losers under a CIT.[6] In any case, I have seen no persuasive evidence—at this

---

[4]The data limitations facing such studies are, of course, serious. However, longitudinal data such as the Panel Study of Income Dynamics at Michigan or the Parnes Survey allow studies of the distribution of Unemployment Insurance over periods up to twelve years, and the Office of Income Security Policy at HHS has created synthetic 40-year wage histories that might be used to study the lifetime distribution of Social Security benefits.

[5]Note that the credit income taxes simulated by Betson, Greenberg, and Kasten in their paper (Chapter 6 in this volume) have guarantees ranging from about 55% to 100% of the poverty line, tax rates between 28% and 41%, and breakeven levels (or tax entry points) of 200% to 245% of the poverty line.

[6]See Betson, Greenberg, and Kasten, Chapter 6 in this volume, Table 6.6.

conference or elsewhere—that the middle class wants to transfer a larger volume of resources to the poor than is transferred by the existing complex of programs. If anything, recent legislative history would seem to argue that the majority of taxpayers (or at least their elected representatives) are quite resistant to any major new expenditures for redistributive transfers. This should not be surprising, of course, since the taxpayers have had nearly thirty-five years to adjust these programs to match their preferences for redistribution and have, in fact, substantially increased the level of transfer income going to the poor within the last decade.

While I don't think that the middle-class majority is either being thwarted in its egalitarian urges by any inherent aspect of income-tested programs, or is passing up a Pareto optimal shift that would both be in its own (narrowly defined) self-interest and increase transfers to the poor, I don't want to end on a totally pessimistic note. There may well be (nonessential) features of the current set of income-tested programs that cause taxpayers to transfer less through that mechanism than they would in the absence of those features. I can think of two such features.

The first such feature is the widespread perception—and in many cases, fact—that the welfare system is very inefficient and poorly managed, that benefits are carelessly dispensed, and the system is highly susceptible to fraud and abuse. If taxpayers were convinced that need was being measured accurately and benefits paid accordingly, they might well be willing to devote more dollars to the system. This argues for management reforms of the system that make it more accurate and efficient and, as a result, improve its public image.

The second inhibiting feature of the current system also has to do in large measure with public perceptions. The multiplicity of current assistance programs, with frequently overlapping eligibility conditions, gives rise to multiple benefits to a minority of recipient families that can, in relatively infrequent cases, result in very high total benefits to an individual family. It may well be that these extreme cases are frequent enough and visible enough that taxpayers generalize from them and overestimate the generosity of the existing system. If this is the case, it argues for merging programs and simplifying the system—what has come to be known as "comprehensive welfare reform." A consolidated transfer program would even out the distribution of benefits, eliminate the "horror cases," and make the actual generosity of the system much more apparent.

Discussion

BENJAMIN I. PAGE

Any analysis of the politics of universal as opposed to income-tested programs to aid the poor must rest upon a coherent account of redistributive politics generally. In my view the politics of redistribution can be understood only by clearly distinguishing among three factors: who actually benefits; who is perceived (by whom) to benefit; and who has how much power over collective decisions.

A standard public-choice analysis resting upon assumptions of fixed (exogenous) preferences, perfect information, and a perfect political market runs into trouble by ignoring the latter two factors. Moreover, in its own terms it is inconclusive because there is ordinarily no majority-rule equilibrium among a full set of redistributive alternatives. With citizens voting out of simple self-interest, any proposal to take from some and give to others (say, to take $1000 each from the rich in group A and give $999 each to the poor in equal-sized group C, with $1 thrown in to win the votes of those in middle group B) will lose by majority vote against some other proposal (for example, $1002 from A, $1000 to C, and $2 to B), which in turn will lose to a third. In fact, any proposal can be defeated by *many* other proposals. The lack of equilibrium persists whether we treat the problem as one of a noncooperative majority-rule referendum, or a cooperative n-person game, or a matter of two-party electoral competition for votes.

When we add a bit of realism by considering Pareto optimal redistribution wih altruistic as well as narrowly self-interested motives, the configuration of preferences is no longer so patently incompatible with a determinative outcome, but neither is there any particular reason to expect that the problem of indeterminacy disappears. Why should altruistic preferences, any more than egoistic, be single-peaked? I see this as a difficulty with the theory, not as a troublesome feature of reality; in the real world, political decisions are made and remain stable over decades and even centuries. It is an important challenge for public-choice theory to come to terms with this reality.

In his present paper, as in much of his past work, Gordon Tullock evades the equilibrium problem by considering only choices over a very restricted set of alternatives, imposing an artificial single-peakedness upon preferences. This severely limits the utility of the analysis. If, in his examples, he treated tax schemes as endogenous—themselves subject to choice—and admitted more alternative distributions of benefits, it is not at all clear what social decisions would follow. We cannot tell whether universal or income-tested programs would be chosen; whether one of Tullock's particular outcomes, or some other.

At the same time, Tullock's presentation does illuminate an important aspect of redistributive politics: Some universal programs may have greater political appeal than some income-tested programs precisely because they give less to the poor and more to the middle class. Many of his apprehensions about national health service or health insurance proposals are well taken. The same is true of a credit income tax as opposed to a negative income tax, if there is a fixed budget constraint. (*Why* a budget constraint is another matter, touched upon below.) By giving more to the middle class the CIT may win political support at the cost of helping the poor less. Of course such political support may be necessary if any broad program is to be enacted.

Even here, however, the usefulness of Tullock's analysis is limited by its focus upon a very specific sort of income-tested program, with obvious flaws: one with a drastic notch at some poverty income threshold such that all below that threshold receive full benefits while all above it receive nothing. Since the debates over Nixon's Family Assistance Plan, if not before, most people have been aware of the evils of notches and their perverse effects upon work incentives. A catalogue of the welfare losses associated with such programs does not tell us much that is new. Nor does study of their politics generalize well to the politics of other programs. What we need is analysis of income-tested programs of a more realistic sort, with graduated benefits, to be contrasted with universal programs that are comparable in budgetary costs or benefit levels or in some other respect.

The difficulty for a simple analysis based on who benefits is that when income-tested and universal programs are made comparable, they quickly become identical and leave no differences to analyze. Any "universal" program of, say, a taxable $1000 demogrant, is exactly equivalent in economic effects to a tax-exempt "income-tested" grant, graduated by income level, of the $1000 minus that portion of it which would have been taxed away. While this is most obvious in the case of cash transfers, it can be made true of in-kind programs as well. "Universal" allotments of food stamps or medical-care stamps coupled with a progressive income tax system is much the same thing as an income-tested scheme of compulsorily providing such stamps in return for income-graduated payments. The difference is chiefly one of appearance and packaging— and, conceivably, of the political process involved in enacting one program or the other.

Even if we take marginal tax rates as the defining characteristic, with an "income test" signifying that the poor are subjected to higher implicit or explicit marginal rates than the nonpoor, the two types of program blend together as the kink (the difference between tax rates on rich and poor) becomes arbitrarily small. If there are any fundamental political differences between universal and income-tested programs, they are not likely to be found in the reactions of perfectly informed, equally influential citizens, because such citizens will perceive that the benefits of the two programs are identical (or nearly so) and act accordingly. Rather the differences must be found in how the packaging of the programs affects fiscal illusions and/or the power of various groups in the political marketplace. In order to get any leverage on the political question, we must enter the messy realm of information costs, transaction costs, market imperfections, and perhaps even endogenous preferences which can be manipulated through political action.

The first point to be made is that the poor are politically weak. Empirical studies show that the poor vote less and participate less in lobbying or contacting public officials. They are less well informed and less aware of whether or not their interests are being protected. They have fewer organized interest groups to represent them. Arguably they do not in this country even have a political party to represent their interests and mobilize them after the fashion of the social democratic parties of Europe.

The theoretical work of Anthony Downs and Mancur Olson—which in this respect has not been followed up nearly as much as one would wish—helps explain why this is so. Information costs and transaction costs in politics are less easily borne by the poor than the rich; to write a formal letter to a congressman, or to comprehend registration require- ments and get to the polls, or to read the *New York Times* and the *Wall Street Journal* is much easier for an attorney than a manual laborer. Moreover, the wealthy have the advantage of belonging to many producer-oriented organizations with selective benefits, which as a side effect can lobby government and (assuming an imperfect political mar- ket or one responsive to dollars as well as votes) can win favorable policies. The poor, on the other hand, are more inhibited from organiz- ing by the free rider problem (why should any individual pay to help a large group?) and the great transaction costs associated with their dis- persed population.

Thus the poor are always at a disadvantage and are unlikely to reap whatever benefits a one-man-one-vote social choice would seem to promise them. A major problem is how to increase their power. Certain differences among policy proposals—such as universality versus income testing—may, to some degree, affect political power. The disadvantage of the poor is greatest when information costs are highest and policymaking is most complex or invisible, as in tax policy, where ar- canely designed loopholes undermine progressivity. When policy alter- natives are made more clear and more visible, when information costs are reduced and the scope of the conflict is enlarged, the poor have more weight in the political process. Thus universal programs which promise $1000 demogrants or "free" medical care for everyone might help the poor to see where their interests lie and get mobilized. Similarly, the simplified administration inherent in some universal programs might ease access and encourage the poor to take advantage of available ser- vices. Few would fail to cash a check that came unbidden in the mail.

On the other hand, simple and visible proposals may be misleading. The poor may find themselves, as Murray Edelman argues, with sym- bols rather than reality. A national health insurance program devoted mostly to the middle class could deceive the poor in this way. Any plan to trick the rich into supporting income redistribution in the guise of universal programs seems rather unlikely to succeed—the rich are good at keeping track of where their money goes. Much better to tell the truth to the poor than try to lie to the rich. But this is not always simple. The wealthy and powerful may succeed at confusing the potential be- neficiaries of universal programs so that they oppose them; this could be read as one lesson of the 1972 McGovern difficulty with demogrants.

In this connection it must be acknowledged, as Tullock unkindly reminds us, that the political impetus for certain in-kind programs may come largely from service providers like doctors, social workers, and academics. In some cases the benefits to the poor may be small and political support may be gained only through misleading symbolic appeals.

Once we consider information costs and imperfect markets, the fixedness of policy preferences is called into question. The blunt fact is that most Americans don't want much income redistribution. It sometimes seems, in fact, that the only remaining warriors against poverty are to be found in certain recesses of HHS and in Madison, Wisconsin. So long as the public tolerates extreme inequality, the chances of combating it are slim. But there is reason to expect that such preferences could change in response to information: information, for example, about causes of poverty; about ways of avoiding work disincentives; about the illusory nature of budgetary "costs" of transfer programs (in a certain sense transfers cost nothing), and the general irrelevance of budget balancing; about the current extent of inequality and its devastating effects upon human beings. Dissemination of information by politicians and educators could have profound effects upon support for antipoverty programs. Of course power over the provision of information may be no more equally distributed than power over policymaking, to some degree perhaps thwarting an information-oriented strategy.

With regard to preference change, proposals for universal programs might play a part in building support for antipoverty policy by encouraging a rhetoric of "rights": universal rights to adequate food, health care, housing, jobs, and income. A substantial degree of equality might be achieved in this way without offending Lockean liberalism. Individualistic competition could proceed, seeking economic rewards beyond the minimum.

If I am correct that the political barriers to egalitarian policies involve powerlessness of the poor and recalcitrance among the general public, more will be needed in the way of remedies than simply coming up with efficient and attractive transfer proposals. The main work is to mobilize those of low income, and to educate the citizenry. At the same time it is possible that the rallying cry of universality, in support of a credit income tax proposal with a high guarantee level, might help on both fronts. If so, more power to the effort.

5

Social Policy Development in Europe and America: A Longer View on Selectivity and Income Testing

ARNOLD J. HEIDENHEIMER
with JOHN LAYSON

As Gordon Tullock has suggested in a preceding essay, the citizens of advanced Western systems have in common the fact that their citizenship is worth a very large amount in entitlements to public benefits. My aim in this paper is less to argue that the value of these entitlements is higher or lower in the United States or Western Europe, but rather that the entitlement "bundles" came to be quite differently constituted. My review of the development of social security and education policies is intended to illustrate how they came to be different and why the countries came to recognize claims to universal and selective programs in quite different ways.

The century since the 1880s can be subdivided into two periods. During the first half-century we can identify a pattern of increasing divergence, with West European citizenship generally accruing larger social security entitlements, while American citizenship came to be associated with claims to longer periods of postprimary education. The period since the 1930s has been one of greater convergence. More Americans have developed firmer claims to social security protection, while more Europeans have won effective opportunities to go on to secondary and university education (Heidenheimer, 1973). Income maintenance and social services have long been subsumed under welfare state development (Briggs, 1967, p. 29). The inclusion of education has been more contested, but the more direct contrast of education and social security entitlements offers broader opportunities for comparing American and European developments (see Flora and Heidenheimer, 1980).

We are concerned here with tracing how public programs came to become more universal, in the sense of unrestricted citizen entitlements, or remained more selective, in terms of a variety of selection criteria. Hence there is only a partial grid overlap with the categories of income-tested or non-income-tested. Generally the more universal the programs, the less income tested is access. But access to program benefits may be conditioned not only by income tests, but also by other criteria of status and labor force position. We are utilizing selective and selection usually in this broader sense of separating the sheep from the goats, but when appropriate in the sense of income-tested access.

If public services or facilities are scarce, income barriers can be one means of allocation. In the late nineteenth century eligibility for German social insurance was income tested. Participation was limited to industrial and comparably low-paid white-collar workers. Entrance to German public academic high schools was also conditional on an ability to pay moderate school fees. When these fees were dropped, attendance became non-income-conditional but still remained selective. Selectivity was class based and geared to cultural and linguistic tests given at an early age, which the lower-class students usually found a much tougher barrier than the fee levels had constituted.

A focus upon education and social security programs permits an examination of how long-term trends toward greater universality encompassed trade-off and substitution effects, as well as the limits set by clienteles and ideologies. Social security programs were generally introduced as categorical programs for the poor, and then extended up the social ladder to encompass the middle class. Post-primary education, by contrast, usually commenced as a selective benefit for the upper classes and then was universalized down the social ladder. During the period of divergence (1880–1930), the political culture of "young" America tended to offer greater opportunities to its youth, while "old" Europe tended to give priority to assuring the material support for its elderly.

In the era of convergence (since 1930), these political culture differences have diminished, but that does not mean that the utility of analyzing programs on the basis of income-test criteria has increased. As the citizenry have had increasing opportunities to select among benefits, they have apparently not developed general attitudes toward universal or income-tested programs. Rather, attitudes have varied widely in accord with different expectations of different clienteles (Coleman, Chapter 3 in this volume). Servicing the youth who go on to a differentiated occupational structure, the education system obviously must be selective, in a sense that the social security system does not have to be. The potential which the state possesses for reducing inequalities varies considerably, as between the life-cycle phases between the womb and the tomb, a factor which Wilensky's (1975) postulation does not explicitly consider.[1]

To render my tasks somewhat more manageable, the focus will be narrowed to four nations—the United States, Germany, Great Britain, and Sweden. These nations differ in their reliance upon universal programs. The United States has been the traditional leader in equalizing access to postprimary educational opportunities, and Germany has led in the introduction of social insurance. Great Britain and Sweden represent reasonably well-developed welfare states which combine many of the reforms initiated by the two leaders.

When and Why Social Insurance Benefits and Educational Opportunities Became More Widely Extended

A century ago, most income maintenance programs incorporated a means test. Administration by local governments, the Church, or private charities sought to separate the undeserving from the deserving poor. Relief was meant to be so stigmatizing that it would serve as a last resort only for the very poor, who would accept alternative private employment under any conditions at the earliest opportunity. Income maintenance programs without a means test were limited to a few subnational schemes or categorical national programs limited to a few select occupations. Nor had public mass education advanced much beyond the primary level.

The universalization of social insurance and educational opportunity has been closely associated with the urbanization and industrialization processes which have accompanied sustained economic growth. The capitalist development of agriculture overwhelmed the capability of local mechanisms to provide relief—forcing migration to urban areas and occupational shifts to industrial tasks. Urban and industrial de-

---

[1]As when he postulates that "a nation's health and welfare effort is clearly and directly a contribution to absolute equality," whereas a "nation's educational effort is only a peripheral contribution to equality [pp. 6–7]."

velopment created new insecurities associated with capitalist business cycles, technological change, and industrial accidents.

Governmental decision makers, however, have considerable discretion to recognize or ignore the "needs" of large sectors of the population. Economic development had created a "need" for economic security in earlier centuries, but the social insurance response was delayed until the late nineteenth century. Repression, cross-cutting nonclass cleavages, external scapegoating, could allow governments to ignore social problems. Then some "needs" could be met through public programs, others left to private efforts. Means-tested programs could meet the needs of the very poor, while the more privileged could resort to personal savings, private insurance, or employer-financed fringe benefits. Postprimary education could be limited to projected manpower needs, with selection processes heavily weighted toward the offspring of the upper classes. More specific and proximate reasons must be developed to explain the trends toward universalization in social welfare programs over the last hundred years.

The kinds of selection processes that operate to condition access to postprimary education opportunities and income maintenance programs have seldom been directly compared, perhaps because they seem to involve such very different sets of selection criteria. In the initial stages of welfare state development, universal education and social security appeared as alternative means of meeting some security and mobility needs of the population, but juxtapositions varied.

In the United States education was long viewed as a viable substitute for income maintenance and other social legislation (Welter, 1962, pp. 139, 241). The early growth of public education in the United States was intended to equalize economic opportunities. Persons who lacked the ability or character to avail themselves of these opportunities were relegated, with little sympathy and much stigma, to the mercy of private charity or the Poor Laws. Although Workmen's Compensation legislation expanded rapidly among the states in the early twentieth century, and pensions were endorsed in the Progressive party candidacy of Theodore Roosevelt in 1912, it took the Depression to render national universal old-age pensions and unemployment insurance and national categorical assistance a reality.

Just as the expansion of educational opportunity served as a substitute for social security in the United States, social security benefits were being offered to lower-class workers in Europe in lieu of broadened educational opportunities. At the start of the welfare state era in Europe in the late nineteenth century the clienteles for the two kinds of public programs were almost totally separated from each other by class-based formal and informal barriers. When Bismarck initiated social insurance on a categorical basis in the 1880s, only the lowest-paid workers were eligible for participation. At the same time the scarce postprimary educational opportunities were allocated through a rigid selection process based upon social class. Working-class children were vastly underrepresented in the academic secondary schools. Of those who graduated from such schools in Berlin in 1882–1886, only 1% were children of workers (Mueller, 1977).

By offering the workers old-age pensions similar to those which had previously been guaranteed mainly for educated public officials, Bismarck was in effect offering workers incentives *not* to utilize education and other mobility mechanisms for lifting their children out of the working class. Thus in Germany social insurance benefits were offered as a collective benefit to those groups whom social barriers had prevented from utilizing individual education opportunities which their taxes were helping to sustain.

The Coverage Extension of Four Major Social Insurance Programs

Countries varied considerably in the timing and sequence of their introduction of the various social insurance programs, and in the degree to which they subsequently expanded their coverage to larger population groups. Germany introduced health insurance in 1883, but delayed unemployment insurance until 1927. Britain introduced similar compulsory programs in these areas in 1911. The United States did not introduce unemployment insurance until 1935, and health insurance has so far been introduced only as a categorical program for the aged. Sequential patterns in which Western countries introduced these, as well as the other two basic social insurance programs, are given in Table 5.1.

TABLE 5.1
Sequence of Introduction of Social Insurance Programs

Program	12 West European Countries		Germany	United Kingdom	Sweden	United States
	First	Average				
Accident insurance	1884	1914	1884	1906	1901	1911
Sickness insurance	1883	1923	1883	1911	1891	—
Old-age insurance	1889	1922	1889	1908	1913	1938
Unemployment insurance	1911	1930	1927	1911	1934	1935

Usually accident insurance was introduced first, old-age pensions later, and national unemployment insurance last. In many cases, accident insurance was viewed by the owners of industrial enterprises as a preferable alternative to the rise in civil court litigation concerning industrial accidents. The elderly have long been viewed favorably by the makers of social policy, ever since Bismarck's original program guaranteed a pension to industrial workers at age 65. Unemployment insurance was usually last, because the availability of transfer payments to non-aged, able-bodied adults presented the most direct challenge to the ability of employers to secure a supply of cheap labor.

We can trace patterns of universalization in terms of dates at which countries had enrolled given proportions of the labor force (or the general population) under one or more of these four basic social insurance programs. Thus Germany, the leader, had enrolled 10% of the labor force in one program by 1885, 25% of the labor force in two programs by 1888, and 50% of the labor force in three programs by 1910. Similar thresholds were achieved in Britain in 1908, 1913, and 1926 respectively. In Sweden the relevant dates were 1899, 1914, and 1941. The United States was behind all these countries on all three thresholds, which it passed in 1913, 1937, and 1944, respectively.

Another comparative overview of the growth of coverage of these four programs for our four countries can be achieved through use of the weighted social insurance coverage index devised by Flora and Alber (1980). This index is constructed by adding the proportions of the labor force enrolled in the four basic programs, and weighting these figures in accordance to the relative importance of the programs; old-age insurance 1.5; unemployment and sickness medical insurance, each 1.0; accident insurance .5. As shown in Figure 5.1, the index displays graphically how the four countries compare with one another as well as with the 12-nation West European average, in coverage extension. If one uses the "European average" as a benchmark, it is evident that Germany maintained a clear lead in coverage from the 1880s until the 1930s, but then dropped somewhat behind in the 1950s. Britain and Sweden moved ahead around 1910, with Sweden maintaining that lead throughout the 1960s, and Britain falling behind.

Explanations of the growth of social insurance programs toward more universal levels of coverage build on theses which posit that

1. The more authoritarian central European systems were more likely to introduce social insurance at lower levels of economic development than their Liberal Democratic counterparts.

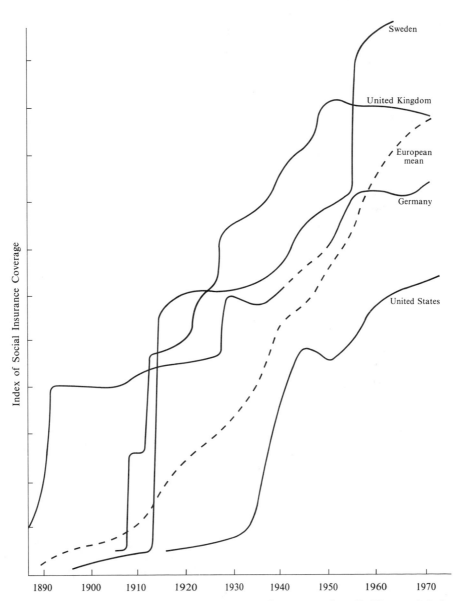

Figure 5.1. Index of social insurance extension. Taken in part from P. Flora and A. J. Heidenheimer (1981). (Figure by University of Wisconsin Cartographic Laboratory.)

2. The degree of trade union organization was initially, and to a degree remains, an important determinant of social insurance development.
3. Labor market changes have engendered a central concern for economic security, which did not diminish with growing societal prosperity.

INTRODUCTION OF SOCIAL INSURANCE

Social insurance was first introduced by Bismarck in Germany during the 1880s.

Other economically less developed, authoritarian regimes in central Europe were next to adopt social insurance. Their political leaders held traditional paternalistic attitudes toward the poor. Liberal Democratic institutions, in contrast, originally served as vehicles for increasing the political power of adherents of the anti-statist nineteenth century liberal philosophy until labor parties made effective bids for mass support, and then government office.

UNION DEVELOPMENT

The institutional variable which cross-national studies have found to be most strongly associated with social insurance adoption up to 1914 has been that of trade union development (Pryor, 1968, p. 475). The creation of union organizations, often closely aligned with political parties, proved conducive to the introduction and expansion of income maintenance programs. Early European social insurance was limited to manual and poorly paid nonmanual workers. In the absence of union development, politicians had less incentive to propose social insurance. Also, the categorical nature of European systems, which selectively limited social insurance to manual and poorly paid nonmanual workers, led Samuel Gompers to claim that "governmental regulation must tend to fix citizens into classes, and a long-established insurance system would tend to make these classes rigid" (see Rimlinger, 1971, p. 83).

"SECURITY" AS VALUE SYMBOL

The broadest "ideational" reason why more universal programs replaced selective ones seems to lie in the spread of the "security" concept as a societal value. During the twentieth century the concept of security has come to join terms like freedom, equality, and order in the repertory of Western "great words." The same economic changes which produced prosperity also induced frequent dislocations in the labor market with a consequent loss of agricultural and menial industrial jobs and frequent shifts in employment opportunities. As a consequence of these labor market changes, the population groups in situations of either "secure property" or "clear-cut poverty" have decreased, while those in situations of "insecure relative prosperity" have grown. These groups feel potentially threatened not so much by fear of falling below some "poverty line," as by the possibility of future relative need and deprivation. This interpretation helps to explain why, in the course of economic growth, social insurance expenditures have increased, and not decreased, as many people once expected (Kaufmann, 1970).

Patterns of Enrollment Growth in Postprimary Education

The United States, which "lagged" behind Europe in social security coverage, led in the expansion of secondary and university education capacity. Table 5.2 presents educational recruitment data for the United States and several European countries. It suggests that the expansion of education effectively reduced the severity of class-based selectivity in university enrollment. British secondary and university development utilized selection and recruitment criteria different from those in Sweden and West Germany, thus reducing class-based barriers to enrollment. In the postwar years, the expansion of West German secondary and higher education did lead to a reduction in the inequality of access. Similarly, in Sweden the expansion of secondary and higher education, coupled with explicit policies to heighten equality of access, reduced the ratio of selectivity between the offspring of the upper strata to their working-class contemporaries from 30:1 in 1950 to 9:1 in 1970 (Anderson, 1975; Heidenheimer, 1977).

TABLE 5.2
Relative Chances of Upper-Stratum and Lower-Stratum Youth Studying in a University

Country	Date	Ratio, Upper Stratum to Lower Stratum
Germany	1952–1953	82:1
	1958–1959	61:1
	1961–1962	58:1
	1964–1965	48:1
Sweden	1960–1961	26:1
United Kingdom	1961–1962	8:1
United States	1958	5:1

SOURCE: Organisation for Economic Co-operation and Development. 1970. *Group Disparities in Educational Participation*, Background Study No. 4. Paris: OECD, Committee for Scientific and Technical Personnel, p. 65.

Generally access to benefits has been broadened *up* the social pyramid for social security, but *down* the social hierarchy for postprimary education. I shall now discuss briefly the major social–economic influences upon the accessibility of higher education.

Selective tendencies in postprimary education were strengthened and perpetuated mainly by (*a*) strong social elite demand for higher education; and (*b*) sociocultural and economic barriers to lower-class enrollments. Universalistic tendencies, on the other hand, can be perceived as being strengthened by (*c*) increased permeability of educational institutions; and (*d*) increased labor market demands for "educated manpower."

ELITE DEMAND

Goals of status maintenance and career advancement seem to have strengthened upper-middle-class demands for university education in the nineteenth century, thus contributing to increased social selectivity compared to some preindustrial periods. This held most strongly for systems with highly developed bureaucratic career systems, like France and Germany; selectivity in England was maintained more by keeping the supply of university places limited and costly. In the United States, the value of college degrees was sometimes less evident. Though few lower-class students attended college during the transition period 1915–1925, according to Jencks and Riesman (1968), "it was college freshmen from poorly educated families who were actually more likely to earn degrees than were freshmen of well-educated families [p. 95]." Later, as the value of college degrees became more evident, American upper-middle-class parents also made "aggressive efforts to provide their offspring with a college education superior to that usually given to the middle-majority and poor [Wilensky, 1975, p. 5]."

SOCIOCULTURAL BARRIERS

Upper-class birth did not necessarily vouchsafe a command of classical languages, as Winston Churchill's school career illustrated, but high linguistic thresholds usually weeded out bright lower-class youth at an early stage. The expansion of the curricula of U.S. high schools in the early twentieth century caused the high school Latin teacher to become a largely extinct species one or two generations earlier than in Europe. Around 1900, while German medical faculties were still deeply split about admitting scientifically talented students who had not studied Latin, American college educators were encouraging substitution of prerequisities through adoption of the flexible "Carnegie unit" system. Tougher curricular requirements in secondary schools in Germany contributed to perpetuating the status quo in the distribution of educational opportunities between 1890 and 1960 (Kaelble, 1975).

EDUCATIONAL PERMEABILITY

The high permeability of the American system no doubt contributed to the larger proportion of youth of lower-class origins who were able to achieve more socially and economically rewarding degrees. Eclipsing the stratification built into European educational systems has necessitated reorganization attempts like the recent European policies to make the systems more comprehensive. Similarly, the "separate but equal" justification of black education was frontally attacked in the United States. But the subtler limits to permeability, as they were encompassed in highly diverse university admission procedures which before the *Bakke* case were seldom frontally challenged, remained much less visible in the American settings. The sharp, and in West European experience unparalleled, changes in recruitment to elite U.S. professional schools in the 1970s confirmed that they had previously, in effect, been practicing a categorical admission policy largely restricted to white males. In the European setting, legal challenges to the selectivity criteria used in allotting medical school places, as in recent German experience, have been both more frequent and more often successful.

DEMAND FOR EDUCATED MANPOWER

The large increases in the number of university students during the last part of the nineteenth century in Germany and the United States can be interpreted to support the thesis that more rapid economic development is translated into perceived increased opportunities for academic manpower. But a German–American contrast for the succeeding decades also suggests that the identification of manpower demands can be very different. American youth streaming into the new high schools evidently saw these degrees as providing leverage on the securing of white-collar positions, more than did the Gymnasium students with their "academic" goals.

In the Continental countries incentives for continuing education had long hinged on the fact that a very high percentage—often two-thirds or more—of the secondary and especially university graduates would find appropriate public sector positions for which their credentials qualified them. In the United States greater public spending also enhanced job opportunities. But the greatest expansive factor on the demand side was the tendency of various occupational groups to upgrade their "professional" status by increasing the kind of credentials they required for memberships. It is this kind of labor market pressure which helps explain Janowitz's (1976) statement that "massive support for the expansion of public education, including higher education, in the United States must be seen as a central component of the American notion of 'welfare' [p. 34]."

Trends toward Universality of Coverage in Social Insurance and Education

The available data can be presented to illustrate that the United States was "ahead" on education, and Europe on social insurance, while also demonstrating to what degree these benefits were accessible and utilized at various points in time.

Thresholds of Coverage

In the figures presented below I attempt to show graphically how the dynamics of welfare state development can be represented through national policy development profiles. Their construction was facilitated by my being able to draw on the refined measurements of historical participation in social security and educational programs which were developed by Jens Alber and Peter Flora, as well as by Arthur Banks (see Flora and Alber, 1971; Flora, 1974; Alber, 1976; and U.S. Department of Commerce, 1976). In order to impose simplicity on the massive data base, I decided to employ four threshold criteria which could be utilized to discriminate effectively as to the degree to which potential beneficiaries—the labor force in the case of social security, the primary school enrollees in the case of postprimary education—did, in fact, participate in these programs at various points in time.

For social security development, relevant thresholds (T/SS) were defined as follows:

T/SS_1 = Year when enrollment in *one* of the four major social security programs (accident, old age, sickness, and unemployment insurance) first encompassed 10% of the labor force;

T/SS_2 = Year when at least 25% of the labor force was first enrolled in two of the four major programs;

T/SS_3 = Year when at least 50% of the labor force was first enrolled in three of the four major programs;

T/SS_4 = Year when at least 60% of the labor force was first enrolled in *all four* major programs.

Relevant thresholds for education development were defined as follows:

T/E_1 = Year when, largely as result of growth and spread of primary education enrollment, adult illiteracy first declined below 20%;

T/E_2 = Year when secondary school enrollment first constituted at least 10% of primary school enrollment;

T/E_3 = Year when secondary school enrollment first constituted 25% of primary school enrollment;

T/E_4 = Year university enrollment first constituted 10% of primary school enrollment.

National Policy Development Profiles

A comparative look at the German and U.S. policy development profile shows that they do, indeed, reflect the policy choices and proclivities which we have been discussing from the perspective of entitlements. Whereas the American profile (Fig. 5.3) shows equivalent education thresholds being passed one or two generations before those on the social security scale, the reverse holds true for Germany (Fig. 5.2). The German profile is determined by the relatively long interval between the achievement of the equivalent thresholds. One of the German data point pairs, that comparing the third thresholds, embodies the longest interval—47 years—found in any of the pairs in all four profiles. In this case it illustrates that the data at which half the labor force was enrolled in three social security programs occurred almost two generations earlier than the time point at which secondary school enrollment was one-fourth as large as primary school enrollment. The average German T/SS–T/E lag is 33 years, and the second education threshold is achieved a full 15 years after the third social security threshold has already been passed.

The American profile is in spatial terms very much the converse of the German figure. Not only do the education thresholds lead the social security ones, but the large intervals are reciprocal. Where the German profile is broad in the middle, the American one is broadest at the ends. The interval between the first thresholds is the largest for any of the countries, 43 years. The same holds for the fourth threshold distance, which is somewhere between 32 years and infinity, depending on when the United States passes some kind of general health insurance law.

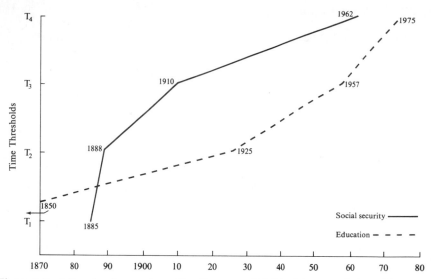

Figure 5.2. Policy development profile, Germany. Published by permission of Transaction, Inc. from *The Development of Welfare States in Europe and America,* edited by Peter Flora and Arnold J. Heidenheimer. Copyright © 1981 by Transaction, Inc. (Figure by University of Wisconsin Cartographic Laboratory.)

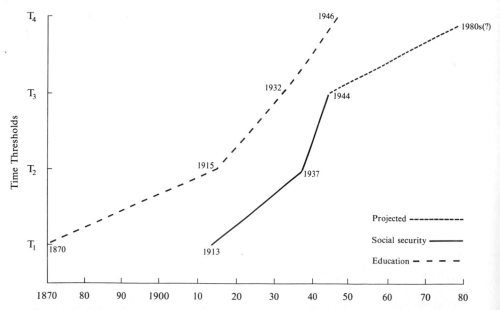

Figure 5.3. Policy development profile, United States. Published by permission of Transaction, Inc. from *The Development of Welfare States in Europe and America,* edited by Peter Flora and Arnold J. Heidenheimer. Copyright © 1981 by Transaction, Inc. (Figure by University of Wisconsin Cartographic Laboratory.)

154

Earlier the United States shows something of a tendency for social security thresholds to coincide roughly with the preceding education threshold points—i.e., T/SS_1 (1913) coincides roughly with T/E_2 (1915), T/SS_2 (1937) with T/E_3 (1932), and T/SS_3 (1944) with T/E_4 (1946).

In both Britain and Sweden, education thresholds lag behind social security ones, but much less sharply than in Germany. Both pursued a pattern of welfare state development in which education and social security entitlements were broadened on a more balanced basis. The relatively "steep" slope of the British policy lines (Fig. 5.4) reflects the relatively rapid transition to the welfare state there. The fact that the interval between the first and fourth social security thresholds encompasses the shortest time period, only 39 years, bears out that the Beveridge reforms in Britain culminated a process which may be seen to have taken almost twice as long in Sweden and Germany. The slim Swedish policy development profile (Fig. 5.5) may be interpreted as that of a policy follower which became an innovator. The uniqueness of the Swedish development is characterized by the profile tip, which is produced as the consequence of the convergence of the education and social security lines around 1970.

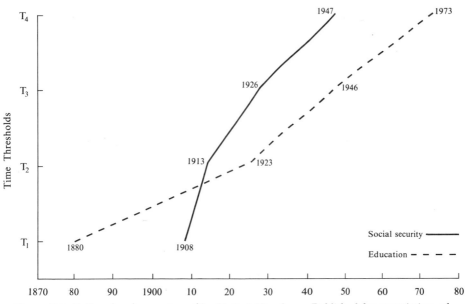

Figure 5.4. Policy development profile, United Kingdom. Published by permission of Transaction, Inc. from *The Development of Welfare States in Europe and America,* edited by Peter Flora and Arnold J. Heidenheimer. Copyright © 1981 by Transaction, Inc. (Figure by University of Wisconsin Cartographic Laboratory.)

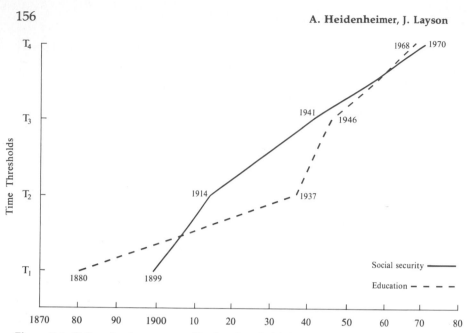

Figure 5.5. Policy development profile, Sweden. Published by permission from *The Development of Welfare States in Europe and America*, edited by Peter Flora and Arnold J. Heidenheimer. Copyright © 1981 by Transaction, Inc. (Figure by University of Wisconsin Cartographic Laboratory.)

Universality and Selectivity in Contemporary American Policies

In the previous analysis we have explored the utility of cross-national comparison to illustrate how the entitlements of Americans to various benefits varied by sector and over time.

In the contemporary setting, we find that the United States displays not only the expected greater internal diversity (which we cannot adequately explore here), but also a greater emphasis in selection in the kinds of programs utilized by different social and income groups. This is particularly true of income maintenance, where we find relatively greater reliance upon income testing, categorical assistance, and employer-provided and other private benefits, compared to Europe.

Categorical Emphasis in Income Maintenance

The previous sections documented the U.S. lag in the introduction and coverage of the four major social insurance programs. Other less systematic evidence reinforces the impression of the relative underdevelopment of universalization and consequent emphasis upon income testing in U.S. income maintenance programs. The United States, alone among the four nations under detailed consideration, lacks a universal family allowance. The income-tested Earned Income Tax Credit is instead targeted toward assisting the families of workers with incomes of less than $10,000 annually. The United States has also refused to embark upon an extensive public housing program. During the past several decades, the income limits upon U.S. public housing assistance have been lowered considerably in order to limit public housing to the poorest sectors of the population.

Comparing all benefits paid out in recent years under public "insurance type" and "assistance type" programs in the United States and West Germany, Stephan Leibfried (1978) has calculated that they constituted 8.7% and 2.8% of GNP in the United States, and 25.3% and 1% of GNP in the Federal Republic of Germany, respectively. In 1973, German social insurance outlays of DM 263 billion dwarfed social assistance outlays of DM 10.7 billion, while in the United States, assistance expenditures of $45 billion were a much larger proportion of insurance expenditures of $141 billion (Leibfried, 1978).

The development of social insurance and social service programs in the 1950s and 1960s caused the proportion of those drawing social assistance in countries like Sweden and France to drop to less than 4% of the population. In Germany in 1973, the figure was 3.3%. Where West Germany had 33 welfare recipients per 1000 population, the figure for the United States was 139 recipients per 1000.[2] Leibfried attributes the larger American figure in part to the greater success of recent American "outreach" programs to identify eligibles. Possibly the number of single-parent families, prime candidates for assistance, was larger and growing more rapidly in the United States. But by far the largest determinant of the different composition of the two national income maintenance programs is attributable to the greater development of the German social insurance programs, their coverages and their benefit levels.

In contrast to European countries like Sweden and Britain, which have in recent years adopted universal public supplementary pension (superannuation) programs, proposals for an integrated pension program have yet to reach the political agenda in the United States. Although the coverage of social security pensions is universal, minimum payout levels are quite low.

The Organisation for Economic Co-operation and Development (OECD) has compared the minimum old-age pension level in 1972–1973

[2]Most of the disparity can be traced to the U.S. reliance upon the income-tested Earned Income Tax Credit to aid lowly paid working families. Germany instead extends family allowances to all families. Still, single-parent family units receiving welfare constituted 0.5% of the German population in comparison with an AFDC caseload of 5.3%.

as a proportion of a standardized poverty line of two-thirds of the average disposable income for each nation. The U.S. minimum pension of 44.3% significantly trailed the levels of 70.9% in Germany, 77.0% in the United Kingdom, and 117.3% in Sweden (OECD, 1977b, p. 76). The elderly poor in the United States must rely on income-tested programs like Supplemental Security Income, Food Stamps, and, for a few, public housing.[3]

Unemployment insurance follows a similar pattern. Although U.S. payments vary widely from state to state, the average unemployed recipient received 51% of his previous gross earnings in 1974–1975 in comparison with 60% for his German counterpart. Between 1956 and 1974, on the average, only half of the total U.S. unemployed have been eligible for any UI payment (Mittelstädt, 1975, pp. 5–10). The U.S. economy, needless to say, also registered significantly higher rates of unemployment during these years.

How assistance is related to other income maintenance programs for one important target group, single-parent families, is spelled out comparatively in Table 5.3. Here we demonstrate how much more American one-parent families are reliant on social assistance, since they do not benefit from the predominantly universal programs such as family allowances, child maintenance, and housing awards of the kind drawn by their equivalents in three European countries. Relying exclusively on assistance and food stamps, the typical American one-parent family receives only two-fifths of the income of a two-parent family which is supported by the median adult male industrial-worker earnings of the father. The United States also has a larger proportion of all one-parent families drawing assistance—more than 50%, compared to about 40% for Britain and 20% for Sweden. Single-parent families in Europe also benefit from universal medical and housing programs. Their American equivalents are eligible for the income-tested Medicaid and the underfunded public housing assistance.

"Muffled" Selection within Higher Education

In education policy it seems as though some American programs are distinct in the degree to which they have been overtly selective in favor of certain target groups, in the name of universalizing access to all. In

---

[3]The more affluent in the United States are much more likely to be eligible for supplementary, usually private, pensions. The 45% of U.S. retirees receiving a second pension in 1974 had earned a median annual income (during the three highest earning years) of $11,315. This differed sharply from the other half, not enjoying such pensions, whose median preretirement income had been $7905 (Fox, 1979, p. 31).

TABLE 5.3

Estimated Monthly Income from National Income Maintenance Programs for Three "Model" Families (I, II, III)

Income Source	British Families			Swedish Families			German Families			U.S. Families		
	I	II	III	I	II	III	I	II	III	I	II	III
Assumed earnings		£82	£124		Kr. 1,667	Kr. 2,500		DM 1,000	DM 1,500		$482	$730
Family allowance	£4	4	4	Kr. 200	200	200	DM 25	25	44			
Child maintenance guarantee				460	460							
Housing allowance				148	140	75						
Maternity grant[a]	(2)	(11)	(2)	(90)	(465)	(90)	(50)	53	(50)			
Public assistance	52			575			626	(292)		$204[b]		
Other[c]		1								40		
Less national taxes		−9	−16		−290	−743		−200	−350		−66	−105
Net income per month	56	78	112	1,383	2,177	2,032	651	878	1,194	244	416	625
Net income as percentage of two-parent family income	50%	70%	100%	68%	107%	100%	55%	74%	100%	39%	67%	100%

SOURCE AND NOTES: A. J. Heidenheimer, H. Heclo, and C. T. Adams, *Comparative Public Policy* (New York: St. Martin's, 1975). Reprinted with permission from St. Martin's Press, Inc., Macmillan & Co., Ltd. This table includes only programs available nationally and, among these, excludes job-training grants, cash values of free school meals and milk, reduced day-care fees, and other rebates. Data are for 1971 in Europe and 1972 in the United States.

Family I is a lone, nonwidowed mother with two children, one just born and one of primary-school age. It is assumed that the mother lacks financial resources of her own, has no job, and receives no maintenance from the absent father. Family II is the same as I except that the mother is assumed to have wages equal to two-thirds of the median male industrial earnings. Family III is a two-parent family with children as in I and II. The wife is not working outside the home, and the husband is assumed to have median adult male industrial earnings in each respective country.

[a] Combines lump-sum grants available to all mothers and earnings-related benefits available to working mothers under national health insurance programs. The figures are in parentheses because they are prorated over 12 months, though benefits are normally payable only 14 to 26 weeks. Maternity grants are *not* added to the table's net income figures.

[b] Since public assistance payments vary by state, the figure here is for one state, Colorado, ranking midway between the highest and lowest states. At the two extremes of the range, the net income for Family I would be $130 in Mississippi and $330 in Michigan.

[c] Food Stamps in the United States; Family Income Supplements in Britain.

West European experience we do not seem to find any programs in which being a member of an educationally underrepresented group, such as working-class children, is weighed positively in selection processes as directly as it has been in the United States over the past decades. Since efforts to open up higher education to previously underrepresented groups have also engendered much conflict in Western Europe, it is useful to reflect on why none of the countries there have experienced a joining of the issues similar to the *Bakke* case in the United States.

Why is it that America has not only relied more on selective techniques in income maintenance, but has also been more overt and direct in the legal–administrative manner in which it has sought to use "affirmative action" and positive discrimination policies in education? Can this be attributed to the different legal systems and the manner in which constitutional issues have been raised, or more to the relatively unique character of American ethnic minorities, especially blacks?

These factors are undoubtedly important, but I do not believe that they can fully account for the much greater European reliance on seemingly universal techniques, such as the move toward comprehensive education and alternative educational routes—"Zweiter Bildungsweg"—which have there been relied on to reduce inequalities of opportunity. American "pluralism," in all its manifold ideological and institutional manifestations, undoubtedly permits the legislator greater flexibility in exploring many kinds of remedial approaches than is possible in the more legally and institutionally homogeneous European systems. But what *particular* aspects of pluralist practices most favored recourse to something approaching affirmative quotas?

Is it that the upper social strata themselves have enjoyed something much closer to affirmative quotas than has been the case in even the most selective European higher education institutions? Thus, at Harvard, alumni children have a five times higher admission chance than do other applicants. This has led a German observer, Ulrich Teichler, to contend that American higher education is differentiated in two ways from the general model of "meritocratic elitism prevalent in most Western systems [1978, p. 91]." On the one hand, the favoritism toward particularly wealthy applicants is frequent and unabashed; on the other hand, there is a great readiness to depart from set standards to allow the socially disadvantaged and lower achievers to enjoy a higher education. "This favoring of the privileged at prominent universities is amazing when one considers that continuing social inequality in the U.S. is, in comparison with most European countries, more characterized by meritocratical legitimization and is less affected by social legislation."

Teichler seeks to explore how the two kinds of discrimination might be interrelated, and asks: "Are efforts toward integration and positive discrimination for the disadvantaged more easily accepted when the privileged also receive positive discrimination in selection processes?"

This perspective suggests that, in analogy to Indian stratification, the advantaged access of the Brahmins to Harvard is compensated for by reserving a number of university places exclusively for members of the "scheduled castes." American social stratification is not castelike, and one reflection is that rules of classification are both flexible and opaque. The criteria affecting selection cannot be too explicitly related to ascriptive criteria, as the *Bakke* judgment once again affirmed. Sometimes, when selection takes place predominantly in a public higher education system, the selection criteria may be fairly explicit, but more typically they are applied in a muffled manner. It is this perpetuation of a series of distinct subsystems with muffled criteria of selection within a total system which offers more universal access than any other, that distinguishes the American higher education system.

The Arrested Development of Health Insurance

Are the consequences of this pattern of camouflaged or muffled selection within relatively universal programs related to any more general characteristics of the American policy development profile? If this is one of the unique characteristics of the American education system, is it just possibly related to any of the unique characteristics of the American social security system? The most obvious deviant case there, of course, is the American nonadoption of a noncategorical health insurance system. In Europe, the time lag between the first adoption of accident insurance and the adoption of a near-universal health insurance or service program was about 40 years. In the United States the lag is now about 70 years.

Brian Abel-Smith (1972) has sought to answer why "the patterns of financing and organizing medical care are so different in the United States from those in other countries [p. 219]." I agree with his deemphasis of the role of "political ideologies of relatively recent origins," and on the stronger shaping influence of nineteenth-century and earlier modes of health care delivery, the relative development of professional interests and labor-based consumer organizations, and the pattern of financial responsibility assumed by governmental authorities at various levels. Still, does his analysis, focused predominantly on health care systems themselves, adequately explain why, almost a half-century after adopting the other major social insurance programs, the United States has entered the 1980s without adopting a broad public health insurance program?

It seems to me, rather, that a more convincing explanation of why the United States has lagged particularly in the health sector emerges from the pattern of relative education and social security development as demonstrated in the U.S. policy profile. The unique strength of the provider-organized opposition to more universal public programs in the twentieth century seems to be *less* crucially linked to the lateness of social insurance programs, than to the *earliness* of *educational* expansion and the kind of stratification which subsequently developed.

The period around 1910 in Europe was one in which the rapid sprouting of social insurance structures made the time ripe for health insurance, which financed more employment of doctors. But in the United States this was a time when each day a new high school was founded, and the massive flow of students produced a flood which was checked, for the medical schools, by the imposition of admission quotas through the Flexner reform. A system of muffled selection was imposed so as to place recruitment under direct associational control, thus preparing the ground for the establishment of a professional monopoly which held sway for two generations. The American physicians became unique—in relation to both their European peers and other American professionals—in the degree to which they were able to develop professional control of their labor market, and in maintaining alliances that resist alternatives to the kind of selective health financing and delivery modes which they favored. It is significant that this provider elite has usually prevailed even when challenged by popular alliances led by presidents who were Harvard alumni. If at all, scoring for universal health insurance will require a dramatic performance which can carry the grudging support of the affluent medicos clustered around the fifty-yard lines of the continent's arenas of power.

Epilogue

In St. Louis, the *Post-Dispatch* carries on its masthead its founder's injunction to "never lack sympathy for the poor," but also to "never be afraid to attack wrong, whether by predatory plutocracy or predatory poverty." Under the fiscal pressures of the 1980s, public and private officials are curbing their sympathy for the poor in a very overt manner. They have closed public health centers which have catered to the blacks in the city and the working poor whites in the suburbs. The remaining capacity is reduced because the city's leading medical school withdrew most of its staff from the city hospital, which could not provide optimal working conditons or meet the payment levels that the physicians are used to receiving from middle-class clients and their insurers.

In Europe such cutbacks are also occurring, but they are much less based on playing the interests of the middle class against those of the "predatory" poor. There the conditions which have made the universal benefits useful to the poorer classes have been incorporated in legislation and more consistently maintained. There health insurance incorporates "first unit coverage," or very low copayment. Social security programs are supplemented for adequacy of benefits. Higher education benefits more frequently also cover the living costs of students. Providing benefits in this form, rather than through income-conditioned special programs, has special political advantages in a period of "low growth." If living standards have to be lowered, resultant burdens can be distributed through instruments more subtle than the meat-ax. If opportunities have to be constrained, the resultant hardships can be prevented from hitting specific age groups or the least affluent particularly hard.

Discussion

ROBERT J. LAMPMAN

Professor Heidenheimer's paper is an essay on the comparative historical development of social policies in four nations. The policies on which he concentrates are social insurance and postprimary education. His theme is that Germany led in social insurance from 1883 to 1930, and the United States has led in education since 1915. Sweden and the United Kingdom are now ahead of Germany in social insurance coverage and all three nations are following the American pattern of broader enrollment in secondary and higher education. Heidenheimer's paper is rich with hypotheses concerning the divergence and convergence of policy across countries over the past century.

I interpret his story as follows. The great breakthroughs in the development of modern welfare states were the opening of low-tuition secondary and higher education institutions and the beginning of governmental insurance against the costs of accident, illness, retirement, and unemployment. At the outset these education and insurance benefits were available to or were taken up by only a small fraction of the population, but the trend has been to make them more widely available. The extreme case of universal coverage is found in the British National Health Service, which is not really social insurance in the usual sense. Translated into the terms of this conference, two types of non-income-tested benefits came upon the scene; they were first received mainly by the nonpoor, but have gradually become more available to all, including the poor.

I think that is an important insight into the controversy under discussion here. Often the question has been, How can the non-income-tested programs be made to meet the needs of the poor? In many instances these programs were designed to exclude the poor by means of coverage, contribution, eligibility, and copayment provisions. Only after a right was firmly established for a minority of the middle class was it later extended to a majority of the population. But for these benefits to be meaningful to the poorest they often must be twisted around rather roughly. Old-age insurance must have a strong redistributional tilt; health insurance must have first-dollar coverage without copayment; higher education benefits must cover living costs of students. Security must be supplemented by adequacy of benefit. And opportunity must be followed by affirmative action.

Heidenheimer does not detail all the modifications of policy which have accompanied the extension of non-income-tested benefits. He does say that income-tested benefits still go to 3% or 4% of the population in European nations. I think his figure of 14% in the United States is too high, it should be stated as closer to 8% or 9%.

I suggest that we would have a better picture of the diversity of non-income-tested benefits if Heidenheimer had looked at such benefits as housing and child day care. Here quite often the benefits are distributed away from the poor by virtue of "creaming" policies for admission or by first-come, first-serve rules for claiming a tightly rationed set of places. The point is that in the real world non-income-tested programs are not generally pro-poor.

I applaud Professor Heidenheimer for highlighting education (both public and private) in his discussion of social welfare policy. I do wish that both he and Professor Garfinkel in his Introduction had seen fit to refer to the U.S. "social welfare expenditure" series published by the Social Security Administration (McMillan and Bixby, 1980). This series shows that public outlays for income support, education, and health care amount to 20% of GNP. It also shows that private expenditures for education, health insurance, and pensions are an additional 5% of GNP. This series plus the taxes and contributions to pay for the benefits gives us a better basis for comprehending the significance of income testing, and it also provides a better perspective on the cross-national position of the United States as a welfare state. For example, the low relative position indicated for the United States on the Index of Social Insurance Extension (Fig. 5.1) would be somewhat offset if there were a table showing that 40% of the health care bill is paid by government and another 30% is paid by private insurance.

Discussion: Ideology, Education, and Social Security

HAROLD L. WILENSKY

Professor Heidenheimer's paper is broad-ranging, stimulating, and diffuse. It contains many sensible observations about variations in educational development in the four countries as well as contrasts in British and American health care. Using data from the Historical Indicators of West European Democracies group, Heidenheimer constructs intriguing "policy development profiles" to picture thresholds of coverage for social security and education.

In explaining the general tendency toward universal coverage as well as divergences in program emphasis, Heidenheimer offers a long catalogue of causes. Beyond economic growth as it has affected the growth of public bureaucracies and the age composition of the population, he mentions the strength of labor movements and the working class; the role of landed elites; the role of the state in economic expansion; changes in labor markets, social stratification and mobility; elite demand for higher education and the need for educated manpower or high culture curricula; authoritarian or centralized versus liberal democratic states; relations among political parties, interest groups, and government bureaucracies; the sequence and timing of program adoption; and conservative, paternalistic, statist ideologies versus laissez faire ideologies.

For this discussion I shall concentrate on two topics prominent in the paper: (a) education versus social security and related programs; (b) the role of ideology and public opinion. Drawing on our continuing study of the politics of taxing and spending in nineteen rich democracies (Wilensky, 1975, 1976, 1978), I shall briefly summarize three arguments. First, education, especially at higher levels, is and is likely to remain essentially meritocratic while the rest of the welfare state remains mainly egalitarian. Second, we cannot explain national variations in contemporary social programs, including the mix of selectivity and universality, by differences in broad ideologies and mass preferences. Finally, if we want to simultaneously pursue three somewhat contradictory goals—decrease inequality, reduce stigma, and make the necessary social reforms politically feasible—we should strive for universality in basic pensions, health insurance and sickness benefits, and family allowances; and emphasize income testing in higher education, housing allowances or rent supplements, and the least popular program, public assistance. National differences in the mix of selectivity and universality suggest that the most-developed welfare states have done just that. My comments aim to supplement or modify the interpretation of public opinion by James Coleman (Chapter 3 in this volume) and the analysis of stigma by Lee Rainwater (Chapter 2), as well as Heidenheimer's essay.

The Big Trade-off: Social Security versus Higher Education

I have elsewhere shown that "welfare state laggards" like the United States tend to be education leaders and vice versa (1975, pp. 3–7). If we are to understand national differences in welfare state development we must be alert to this central trade-off—between investment in higher education and investment in the social security package. Heidenheimer confirms the point for his four countries, although it is clear that catch-up games are now producing some convergence (e.g., the recent expansion of education in Sweden, France, and Germany; the recent expansion of social security in the United States, Canada, and the Soviet Union).

The reason for this trade-off is that modern education is overwhelmingly meritocratic and vocational, a contribution to equality of opportunity, especially at the higher levels, while a nation's health and welfare effort is mainly egalitarian, a contribution to equality of results (Wilensky, 1975; Wilensky and Lawrence, 1979). A hundred years ago secondary schools were the main channel for upward mobility for minority groups and lower strata in the United States, and even now, with the falling rate of return to degrees, postsecondary education remains the main channel for social mobility. A careful study by Donovan (1977) demonstrates this function of secondary schools at the turn of the century. She specifies the populations and times for which education did or did not function as a means of mobility. She regressed the proportion of 14–17 year olds enrolled in all types of secondary education from 1870 to 1910 on the proportion of the economically active labor force in nonmanual jobs, taking account of variations by region, differential migration of educated labor, white and nonwhite. Her main conclusion: Established elites (native-born whites) could rely on ascription (family origin and related advantages) for access to white-collar jobs, but less-favored groups—the foreign born and blacks—got access to such positions only by achievement through secondary schools. A century later, as we know, the same educational road is traveled by blacks: Where it once took a high school diploma, it now takes a college degree for such minorities to secure entry to upper-level occupations.

To bring this trade-off argument up-to-date and make it cross-national, we must distinguish between primary, secondary, and post-secondary levels and, with the spread of mass higher education, pay attention to the riotous diversity of quality among colleges and universities.

At early levels of their development, the nations of Western Europe and North America did not have to trade education for welfare; universal primary education was widespread before national social security systems were invented. Universal primary school education for basic literacy and good citizenship was a demand of employers interested in a labor supply, Protestant sects and churches concerned that children be able to read the Bible, a labor movement interested in contradictory ideals of equality of opportunity and absolute equality, and the state interested in political integration and social control. Later the same interests would press for the spread of secondary education. But there would still be no direct trade-off between universal education at its lower levels and social security development. The relevant clue in my data is that for nineteen rich democracies, secondary school enrollment ratios in the period 1965–1972 were not significantly correlated with either social security spending as a percentage of GNP or per capita social security spending. Whatever effect the spread of universal secondary education had on social security development was indirect: The mobility functions of public secondary schools created political resistance to welfare state expansion.

For higher education, however, the trade-off is both direct and indirect. The postsecondary enrollment ratios for these nineteen countries *are* negatively correlated with welfare effort, especially in the mid-1960s.

Further, in the 15 rich countries for which we have data, the percentage of working-class sons and daughters in higher education is positively and strongly correlated with tax–welfare backlash; the more a country's working class can escape out and up through the colleges and universities, the greater chance for a successful antitax, antiwelfare, antibureaucratic movement. In other words, the more meritocratic the education system, the more resistance to the rest of the welfare state.

The question is whether the general push for equality and the specific demand for affirmative action will greatly weaken the meritocratic character of modern education. I would modify Heidenheimer's observations about "affirmative quotas" to suggest a pattern of favoritism for alumni children at selected wealthy private institutions such as Harvard combined with far more widespread affirmative action for minorities and women at every type of institution. But I doubt that this will swiftly transform higher education. The intense resistance by higher-quality institutions in the most egalitarian countries indicates that meritocracy marches on. Consider the boldest attempts at affirmative action, those of Eastern Europe, based not on race or sex but on social class—attempts which have foundered. For instance, for university entry in Poland in the late 1960s and early 1970s you could get points for being the son or daughter of a worker or peasant. At its peak, affirmative class action could account for between 10% and 20% of the score for tough entry exams, both written and oral. However, the system is now withering away. The reasons include (a) a backlash from Communist party officials and bureaucrats who are now old enough to have children entering college; (b) the trouble in securing sufficient resources for compensatory education for rural and lower-class students; and (c) the usual complexities of defining the categories. Resistance was greatest at elite institutions with highest academic standards (e.g., the University of Warsaw).

In short, higher education, even where egalitarian ideologies are much stronger than those of the United States, remains chiefly meritocratic—a contribution to equality of opportunity (enhanced mobility for those judged to be potentially able or skilled); it is only a peripheral contribution to absolute equality. In contrast, a nation's health and welfare effort is clearly and directly a contribution to absolute equality—the reduction of differences between rich and poor, young and old, minority groups and majorities (as indicated by the effect of OASDI in moving a large fraction of the aged out of poverty); it is only a secondary contribution to equality of opportunity.

It follows that if one's purpose is the reduction of occupational and income inequalities, the case for income testing is strongest for higher education, which disproportionately benefits the well placed and well off or those with good occupational prospects. Concretely, that means higher tuition charges in publicly financed universities coupled with enlarged subsidies for the less affluent, equally qualified students.

Does the Ideology of Economic Individualism Explain America's Reluctant Welfare State?

It is tempting to attribute our emphasis on income testing for income maintenance programs and our early development of mass higher education to our cultural values—our economic individualism, our unusual emphasis on private property, the free market, and minimum government—because they permeate so many areas of American life. Although they certainly shape our public debates, these values do not explain much of our resistance to adequacy and universality in social programs for the nonaged poor.

For the ideologies of all modern societies are a complex blend of contradictory themes, both meritocratic and egalitarian. Gallup polls typically tap economic individualism and collectivist sentiment in the same interview at the same moment. For instance in 1965 a national cross section of Americans clearly showed wide acceptance of proposals for national health insurance, federal responsibility to do away with poverty, and increased spending on urban renewal, along with majority sentiment that relief rolls are loaded with chiselers, that any able-bodied person who really wants to work can earn a living, and that we should rely more on individual initiative and less on welfare (Wilensky, 1975, pp. 28–49; cf. Coleman, Chapter 3 in this volume).

Such ambivalence is apparently built into the structure of modern society. As part of our cross-national study of the politics of taxing and spending, Richard Coughlin (1979) recently completed an analysis of all the more-or-less comparable sample surveys we could find in eight countries over the past 30 years and one we devised ourselves in 1975. The countries include a few welfare state leaders (West Germany, Sweden, Denmark, and the marginal case of France joining the big spenders), two middle-rank spenders (the United Kindgom and Canada), and two laggards (the United States and Australia). We found the same mass ambivalence, although there were modest differences in the ideological mix of economic individualism and collectivism. The surveys asked cross sections of these countries to choose between such alternatives as whether "government should see to it that everyone has a job and a good standard of living" or "government should let each person get ahead on his own." Or government should guarantee full employment, and so on.

The results: On these very broad ideological themes focused on government intervention and regulation of economic life, the mass of citizens express views that match their government's behavior. In countries that spend a lot and tax a lot to ensure a high minimum standard of living, people in larger majorities embrace the welfare state ideology. They also endorse the success ideology, although not as enthusiastically as Americans or Canadians do.

Moving to the middle-rank spenders—Canada and the United Kingdom (Britain)—the pro-welfare-state ideology scores medium in popularity and the success ideology is a little stronger than it is in Germany, France, and Sweden.

Moving down to the lean spenders, the pro-welfare-state majority is still there but the success ideology is a bit stronger.

In other words, in broad, abstract ideological themes, a country's mix of economic collectivism and economic individualism will match its social spending and taxing and the actual amount of government intervention.

But even here we must not exaggerate the national differences. In 1975, we asked cross sections of France, West Germany, Britain, and Denmark to choose between more spending on health and social security even if it meant more payroll deductions and other taxes versus cuts in taxes even if it meant reduced benefits and services. In every country, the supporters of increased social spending with more taxes outnumbered those who preferred cutbacks in both. The maximum spread was 13% between France, a medium-high spender, and Britain, a medium spender. Big spending was slightly more popular in France.

Although there is some congruence between broad ideology and levels of taxing and social spending, when we focus on specific issues—support for particular public policies—the structure of public opinion is strikingly similar across all these countries.

Briefly, in these eight countries, wherever we could find data, people love pensions and national health insurance; they are a little less enthusiastic about family allowances or children's allowances; and in Denmark, the United Kingdom, Canada, and the United States alike, they have serious reservations about unemployment compensation and are quite doubtful if not downright hostile to public assistance—which they think too often goes to the undeserving. Thus, comparing countries with different histories, cultural traditions, and political systems, we find only tiny differences in the answers to roughly comparable questions. In mass attitudes about specific social programs, capitalist America and social democratic Sweden are brothers (sisters?) under the ideological skin.

Similarly, issue-specific opinion surveys in the United States—both before and after Proposition 13—show rather stable, strong support for public spending wherever benefits are widely shared, but doubts about means-tested public assistance. Analysis by Jacob Citrin (1979) concludes, "There remain popular majorities for *more* spending on health, education, urban problems, environmental protection, and [solutions to] drug addiction... [p. 117]." Only public assistance payments (as well as space exploration and foreign aid) elicit a majority demand for cuts in current spending. Indeed, by 1978, already strong public support for national health insurance and a guaranteed job was growing and commitment to the existing social security program was unshaken.

The tension between meritocratic ("success") ideologies and welfare state ("collectivist") ideologies gives politicians an opportunity to play it either way.

If ideology and public opinion are not important sources of national variations in contemporary welfare states, we must look to variations in the structure of political economies, especially the degree of centralization of government and of the major economic blocs and the tax policies they pursue. For instance, Austria, Holland, Belgium, and Germany are characterized by more centralized and coordinated labor unions or labor federations, employer federations, and governments, with effective channels for national bargaining on broad social and economic policy. In financing the public sector they all avoid an overreliance on the most painfully visible and unpopular taxes (income taxes and property taxes on households). Contrast the United States, Britain, Switzerland, and Denmark: Not only are their political economies less "corporatist" but, at least up to 1971, they all relied heavily on income taxes and property taxes, thereby inviting intense tax–welfare backlash movements (see Wilensky, 1976).

Does a High Degree of Universality Reduce Stigma and Minimize Political Uproar?

It is my impression that the accent on universal versus income-tested transfers and services is closely linked to welfare effort (social security expenditures as a fraction of GNP) and welfare output (e.g., per capita social security expenditures, equal access to services, even measures of real welfare). In other words, what makes Sweden, the Netherlands, West Germany, Belgium, Austria, and Norway "welfare state leaders" (or, if you prefer, profligate spenders) is what also shapes their mix of selectivity and universality in social policy—a heavy weighting toward universality. None of these countries, of course, avoids income testing entirely. They merely fix the floor below which no one sinks at a reasonably high level. Further, they emphasize universality in the three most popular programs—pensions, health insurance, and family or child allowances.

Regarding the effects of universality on stigma, Lee Rainwater suggests an important hypothesis (see his paper, Chapter 2 in this volume). I would broaden and modify it as follows: What counts in reducing the political, social, and psychological costs of income testing and means testing is a high degree of universality in the three most important programs common to welfare state leaders. *Either*, as Rainwater suggests, broad coverage for family allowances, health insurance, and basic pensions creates a climate in which income-tested housing allowances, rent supplements, and other targeted benefits are not so stigmatized; *or*, if they are stigmatized, as the issue-specific attitudes I have reviewed suggest, the population falling through the net of universal programs is small, and the stigma cannot become a symbol for the mass mobilization of tax–welfare backlash movements and campaigns.

Since the United States cannot soon transform its labor, management, and government structures into more centralized, collaborative, consensus-making machines, what lessons can we draw from these cross-national comparisons? First, in financing, if you want to move quickly toward universality in income maintenance, move toward tax balance—rely more on social security payroll taxes and consumption taxes such as the European-style VAT (value-added tax). Second, in spending, continue the battle for national health insurance; adopt some form of taxable, universal child or family allowance as the centerpiece of income maintenance for the nonaged poor; and devise simpler forms of income testing for higher education, housing allowances or rent supplements, and public assistance. The up-front, straightforward, neat income-redistribution schemes that have dominated American discussion of both tax reform and social policy—prominent in the papers of this conference—are nowhere popular, not even in Sweden; in the United States, they are politically fatal.

6

A Simulation Analysis of the Economic Efficiency and Distributional Effects of Alternative Program Structures: The Negative Income Tax versus the Credit Income Tax

DAVID BETSON
DAVID GREENBERG
RICHARD KASTEN

Introduction and Major Findings

In this paper, we compare the distributional and efficiency implications of two frequently advanced schemes for redistributing income—the negative income tax (NIT) and the credit income tax (CIT)—by simulating their effects on a representative sample of the nation's households.[1] To facilitate this comparison, we simulate prototype NIT and CIT plans that are relatively simple, but quite comprehensive. They replace most existing welfare programs and substantially alter the existing federal income tax system. The essential difference between the NIT and CIT prototypes we examine is in the structure of their marginal tax rates. The simulated NIT imposes higher marginal tax rates on transfer recipients than on those who pay positive taxes, while the simulated CIT

---

[1]More abstract, theoretical approaches for making such comparisons may be found in the paper by Sadka, Garfinkel, and Moreland (Chapter 8 in this volume), and in Kesselman and Garfinkel (1978b).

ot distinguish between net taxpayers and transfer recipients in its tax rate structure.[2]

Our findings indicate that both the NIT and the CIT simulated plans would substantially redistribute income by increasing taxes paid by those with relatively high incomes and transfers received by those with relatively low incomes. Apparently, however, neither the simulated NITs nor the simulated CITs would affect economic efficiency, at least as measured by such indicators as aggregate hours of work, deadweight loss, and total earnings. The results for earnings, which are indicative of program effects on national economic output, are particularly striking. In contrast to most previous research suggesting that income redistribution would be associated with appreciable reductions in earnings and output, our findings imply that such adverse effects are likely to be negligible—and indeed, that small increases in earnings are quite possible.

The source of the contrast between our findings and those of others is that most studies of the effects of redistribution schemes on economic efficiency focus almost exclusively on transfer recipients. It is generally found that increased transfer benefits tend to cause such persons to reduce their work effort and earnings, and indeed, our simulation results are quite consistent with these findings. Unlike most other studies, however, ours has also examined the work responses of those who must support larger transfer benefits by paying higher taxes, and we have found that these persons partially compensate for the reductions to their incomes resulting from the taxes by increasing their hours and earnings. These increases, moreover, appear to be sufficiently large to offset most or all of the earnings reductions by transfer recipients.

These findings, if validated by further research, have at least two important policy implications. First, they imply that substantial reform of the existing tax–transfer system, involving considerable redistribution of income, can be made without causing substantial reductions in eco-

---

[2]A distinction between the NIT and the CIT that usually receives far more emphasis than differences in tax rate structures concerns various program administration features. For example, most NIT proposals would limit payments to net beneficiaries. In contrast, many CIT schemes involve demogrants that would be paid to everyone and then partially or wholly recaptured by the government through the positive income tax system. Although such differences may be of enormous political and psychological importance, they are not inherent to NIT and CIT programs and do not represent an essential economic difference. In principle, a NIT and a CIT could be administered similarly, even though they probably would not be in practice. In any event, simulations of the type that are reported here are unable to incorporate most administrative considerations, and we shall assume that the simulated CIT and NIT are administered identically.

nomic efficiency and in the output produced by the national economy. Second, they suggest that choices among alternative tax–transfer systems—between NITs and CITs, for example—probably must mainly depend on less objective factors than economic efficiency. For example, the simulations show that a NIT would benefit considerably fewer households than a comparable CIT, but that transfer payments under the NIT would be more focused on households with the greatest need, such as those households below the poverty line. Evaluation of such a trade-off must inevitably be quite subjective.

The following section of this paper describes the NIT and CIT plans we simulated for this paper and discusses some of the methodological issues confronting the simulation. The next section then presents the major results of the simulations. A final section contains our conclusions.

Methodology

The major methodological difficulty confronting this study is devising an appropriate basis for comparing two alternative types of redistribution schemes: the negative income tax and the credit income tax. Three basic steps are required. First, prototype NIT and CIT plans must be specified. Second, indices that can be used to rank the prototype plans must be developed. Third, it is necessary to obtain values for the indices. In this section, each of these steps will be discussed in turn.

Description of the NIT and CIT Prototypes

One problem in specifying NIT and CIT plans that are comparable is in deciding which program provisions should be held constant across alternative prototype plans and which should be allowed to vary. Our general approach is to allow as little to vary as possible, so that sources of different outcomes across alternative prototypes can be readily determined. For instance, comparisons between NITs and CITs are always made for prototypes with identical tax bases. Itemization is not permitted under any of the prototypes, for example, unlike the current tax system, both Unemployment Insurance payments and Social Security payments are treated as taxable income.

We have further constrained variation among the tax-transfer plans we compare by requiring them to be "self-financing." That is, the tax component of the plan must raise revenues that are sufficiently higher than those raised by the current system to allow any new obligations incurred under the transfer component of the plan to be fully met. Thus, budget deficits or surpluses will be unaffected by adoption of the plan.[3]

Given this self-financing principle, we make two different types of comparisons between NIT and CIT prototypes. The first of these holds the income guarantee—that is, the base level of support for those with no other source of income—constant between the CIT and NIT. The second comparison holds the aggregate net addition to government transfer expenditures constant. The two comparisons may be viewed as consistent with alternative, and extreme, assumptions about likely political outcomes. The equal guarantee comparison implies that no matter whether society ultimately decides on a NIT or CIT system, a similar level of support would be provided to those persons with no other source of income. The implication of the equal budget comparison, on the other hand, is that regardless of what income maintenance system is finally adopted, society will only be willing to spend a given amount of funds on transfer payments. Since the assumptions associated with the equal guarantee and the equal budget comparisons appear to be consistent with polar situations, the truth probably falls somewhere between them.

Since it is obviously not computationally possible to compare every feasible NIT and CIT and we must therefore restrict ourselves to a relatively small subset, findings that imply that either CITs or NITs are superior may merely reflect our choices of plans to compare, rather than differences that are truly inherent to the two alternatives. To minimize misleading conclusions that stem from this possibility, we attempted to select program characteristics for our prototype tax–transfer systems that fall within the politically feasible range. Our general strategy was as follows. We first designed a NIT prototype. The guarantee levels and the implicit tax rates that would be faced by transfer recipients under this prototype were selected so that they would be similar to those that have been considered during recent attempts to reform the welfare system. In order to facilitate comparisons among prototypes, however, our NIT plan is much simpler than the programs that would actually result from enactment of any recent welfare reform proposal. Unlike such proposals, for example, the NIT does not permit state supplementation of transfer benefits, even though many current recipients of welfare in

---

[3]Use of this self-financing principle is intended to reflect a long-run view of transfer policy. Although new transfers might initially be financed through deficit spending or by reducing government expenditures in some other area, over the long run positive taxes will be larger in the presence of these transfer payments than in their absence.

high-benefit states would be worse off. After developing the prototype NIT system, we then constructed two CIT prototypes, each of which could be compared to the NIT. As already indicated, guarantee levels in one of the CIT prototypes (CIT/G) and net transfer expenditures in the other (CIT/E) were set equal to those in the NIT.

In constructing the NIT prototype and the two CIT prototypes, it was assumed that each would replace the federal income tax system and most existing welfare programs, including Aid to Families with Dependent Children, Food Stamps, Supplemental Security Income, and General Assistance. Other federal tax programs, state and local taxes, and transfer programs that are not specifically directed toward the poor (such as Unemployment Insurance and Old Age and Survivors Insurance) are assumed to remain unchanged.

The prototype NIT plan guarantees a minimum income of $1374 per adult and $687 (half the adult amount) per child,[4] but faces all families receiving transfer payments with a benefit reduction rate of 50%. Families that receive transfer payments would not be required to pay any federal income taxes. Under this scheme, a two-parent family with two children and no other source of income would receive $4122, 75% of the poverty line for such families. These transfer benefits would be reduced by 50 cents for each dollar of income received from other sources. Since total transfer payments under the plan would be larger than under the existing welfare system, to maintain the self-financing principle mentioned earlier, it is necessary to raise additional tax revenues. This is accomplished in two ways. First, as indicated earlier, Unemployment Insurance and Social Security payments are included in the definition of taxable income, and itemized deductions are not permitted. Second, the marginal tax rate for all households not eligible for transfer payments is set at 23%, a rate just sufficient to raise tax revenues by the amount required to finance the new transfer obligations.

The major difference between the NIT prototype just described and CIT/G, the CIT prototype with a guarantee equal to the NITs, is that the tax structure of the CIT does not distinguish between those who do and those who do not receive transfer payments. All families, regardless of their income level, face a marginal tax rate of 34%, a rate that is again just sufficient to meet the new transfer payment obligations incurred under the plan. Not surprisingly, this 34% tax rate falls between the two rates associated with the NIT prototype.

The structure of CIT/E, the second of the CIT prototypes, is similar to

---

[4]Aged, blind, and disabled adults are assumed eligible for $1786, an amount 30% higher than the standard adult benefit. All dollar amounts are given in 1975 dollars.

that of CIT/G. However, unlike CIT/G, which provides for total transfer benefits that are much larger than those that would occur under the NIT prototype—$57.6 billion versus $38.5 billion—total transfer expenditures under CIT/E would be virtually identical to those under the NIT—$38.2 billion versus $38.5 billion.[5] As a consequence, the guarantee level associated with CIT/E is only three-fourths of that associated with CIT/G and the tax rate necessary to finance the transfer obligations that are incurred is only 28%, rather than 34%.

The three tax–transfer prototypes just described may be readily compared by examining their tax–transfer schedules, illustrative examples of which appear in Figure 6.1. The three schedules for the prototype systems that are represented in this figure are equally applicable to a two-parent family with two children and a single-parent family with four children. To allow comparison between the prototype systems and the existing tax–transfer system, Figure 6.1 also shows the 1975 Federal Income Tax schedule for the two-parent family[6] and the tax–transfer schedule that would have faced a single-parent family had they lived in Wisconsin in 1975 and been eligible for AFDC. Earnings are represented on the horizontal axis of the figure,[7] while transfer payments received, *less* federal income taxes paid at each earnings level, appear on the vertical axis.

It is apparent from Figure 6.1 that under any tax–transfer system, including the current one, there exists an earnings level—frequently referred to as the breakeven level—at which transfer payments and taxes are in exact balance and a family's income is unaffected by the system. At earnings levels below this breakeven point, a family receives positive *net* transfer payments (that is, transfers exceed taxes) and its income is augmented by the system; at earnings above the breakeven, the family owes net taxes and its income is reduced by the system. We shall refer to families with earnings below the breakeven level of a given transfer plan as transfer recipients and those with earnings above the breakeven as

[5]These estimates of net transfer expenditures allow for adjustments in hours of work and earnings that would result from implementation of the prototype plans.

[6]In diagramming this schedule it was assumed that two-parent families would not participate in any of the existing welfare programs even when they are eligible (actual participation in welfare among eligible two-parent families tends to be quite low), but that they would receive benefits from the Earned Income Tax Credit. It was further assumed that the family would begin to use itemized deductions once its taxable income reaches $30,000.

[7]For purposes of simplification, it is assumed that the families represented in Figure 6.1 have no sources of income other than earnings and transfer payments.

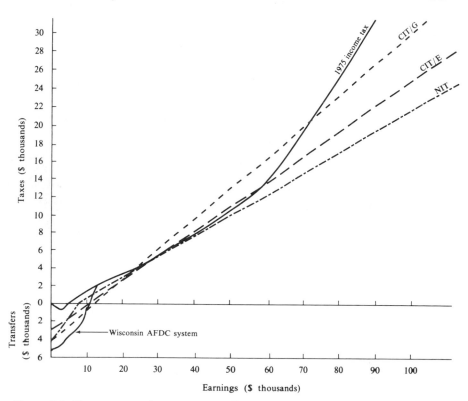

Figure 6.1. Three tax–transfer prototypes: NIT, CIT/G, and CIT/E. The 1975 income tax schedule and Wisconsin AFDC are provided for comparison. See text. (Figure by University of Wisconsin Cartographic Laboratory.)

taxpayers.[8] Since, as is obvious from Figure 6.1, breakeven levels vary between different tax–transfer systems, households may be classified as taxpayers under one system and as transfer recipients under another.

Perhaps the most interesting of the comparisons suggested by Figure 6.1 is that between the NIT and the existing tax and transfer systems. As

[8]Depending on how a tax–transfer system is actually administered, families below the breakeven point may only receive the *net* transfers they are due and those above the breakeven may only pay the *net* taxes they owe; or alternatively, families may *both* receive transfer payments *and* pay taxes. Since such administrative issues are beyond the scope of this study, however, we ignore gross flows and concern ourselves only with net flows. Thus, even though a household pays federal income taxes, it is nevertheless classified as a transfer recipient as long as the amount of transfers it receives exceeds the amount of taxes it pays.

may be seen, households with very high incomes would pay considerably less in taxes under the NIT than they do under the current system, while taxes for the very large number of tax units in the middle-income range (from around $10,000 to $50,000) would be quite similar under the two systems,[9] although taxes would generally be slightly higher under the NIT. The comparison becomes more complicated at the lower tail of the distribution, since welfare families who live in states with generous welfare programs, such as Wisconsin, would be considerably worse off under the NIT, but those who live in states with less generous benefits would be better off. Moreover, low-income households that do not participate in any current welfare programs, a characteristic of most low-income families headed by a male, would enjoy substantial increases in income under the NIT.

Although welfare recipients in high-benefit states would not be as well-off under the CIT/G prototype as they currently are, they and most other low-income households would be better-off under this tax–transfer system than under the NIT. Higher income households, on the other hand, would have to pay considerably higher taxes under the CIT/G system than under the NIT. Thus, one would expect the CIT/G prototype to produce a substantially more equitable income distribution than the NIT prototype.

The comparative distributional implications of the CIT/E and NIT prototypes are less obvious. As Figure 6.1 illustrates, families with no workers or very low earnings would tend to receive larger transfer payments from the NIT than from the CIT/E plan. Moreover, high-income households would also tend to be better-off under the NIT. Offsetting these differences, however, is the fact that the incomes of households with moderate earnings would be higher under the CIT/E prototype.

The comparisons in Figure 6.1 are limited to only a few illustrative households: two-parent families with two children and one-parent families with four children. Table 6.1 permits us to examine the effects of the three prototype programs on the disposable incomes and marginal tax rates of the entire population. In interpreting the predictions of changes in disposable income that appear in the table, it is important to recognize that they pertain to the initial impact of the prototypes before any adjustments in hours of work take place. Thus, a prototype's effect on disposable income is calculated by simply subtracting any change in federal tax obligations occurring under the prototype from any change in

[9]The reason for this is that the current tax system imposes progressive tax rates, while the prototype NIT represented in Figure 6.1 does not. We have, however, conducted simulations with prototype plans with progressive tax rates. (The results from these simulations are reported in Appendix C, which is available from the authors upon request.)

TABLE 6.1
Predicted Effects of the Alternative Prototypes on Tax Rates and Incomes in the Absence of Adjustments in Work Effort

Conditions under Current System

	Number of Households (millions)	Marginal Tax Rates	Transfers Less Taxes ($ billions)	Transfers Less Taxes ($ per person)	Level of Disposable Income ($ billions)	Level of Disposable Income ($ per person)	Change in Marginal Tax Rates NIT	CIT/G	CIT/E
Income class									
Under $2,000	17.1	.08	14.7	592	27.3	1,095	.42	.26	.21
$2,000–6,000	22.8	.12	3.4	101	89.2	2,647	.25	.22	.16
$6,000–14,000	30.1	.20	-19.8	-285	252.7	3,640	.06	.14	.09
$14,000–18,000	10.0	.23	-17.0	-589	130.8	4,529	.00	.11	.05
$18,000–40,000	15.7	.28	-55.0	-1,149	294.8	6,157	-.05	.06	.00
Over $40,000	1.6	.48	-26.7	-5,843	62.8	13,752	-.25	-.14	-.20
Transfer recipients	16.5	.20	21.5	547	92.8	1,677	.41	.23	.18
Taxpayers	80.7	.17	-121.8	-716	764.9	4,654	.01	.10	.05
All households	97.2	.18	-100.3	-479	857.6	4,096	.14	.16	.10

Change in Disposable Income Prior to Labor Supply Adjustments

	($ billions) NIT	CIT/G	CIT/E	($ per person) NIT	CIT/G	CIT/E	(percentages) NIT	CIT/G	CIT/E
Income class									
Under $2,000	10.33	12.39	5.29	415	498	212	38.0	45.6	19.5
$2,000–6,000	3.11	13.02	6.53	92	386	193	3.5	14.6	7.3
$6,000–14,000	-7.76	4.30	.48	-112	62	7	-3.1	1.7	0.2
$14,000–18,000	-4.61	-4.22	-3.12	-159	-145	-107	-3.5	-3.2	-2.4
$18,000–40,000	-7.36	-19.03	-10.56	-154	-398	-221	-2.5	-6.5	-3.6
Over $40,000	7.06	-.34	3.87	1,541	-75	845	11.3	0.6	6.2
Transfer recipients	16.98	37.88	18.37	285	405	219	18.3	20.6	11.8
Taxpayers	-16.22	-31.76	-15.88	-108	-274	-126	-2.1	-4.7	-2.3
All households	.76	6.12	2.49	4	29	12	0.1	0.7	0.3

183

transfer payments. If the prototype induces labor supply adjustments, however, the change in net transfer payments (that is, in transfers less taxes) that occurs under the program will ultimately diverge from the change in disposable income that takes place. If hours of work are reduced, for example, earnings would decline, reducing disposable incomes but increasing net transfers. The opposite would occur if hours of work increase.

There are at least two reasons for anticipating that adoption of any of the three prototypes would induce labor supply adjustments. First, as is evident from Table 6.1, each of the prototypes affects the marginal tax rates individuals face, thereby changing the return that they receive for an hour of work. This change in effective after-tax wage rates should induce workers to adjust their hours, increasing their work effort if their marginal tax rates decrease and consequently their effective wage rates increase, and decreasing their hours if the opposite occurs. Second, if net transfers decline (or net taxes increase), individuals would be expected to work more hours to offset, at least partially, this loss of income. Alternatively, if net transfers increase (or net taxes decline), they would be expected to work fewer hours. In the following section on results of our simulations, where we will examine the effects of the prototype tax–transfer systems on the income distribution in considerably more detail than we do here, we attempt to take full account of adjustments in work effort.

It is apparent from Table 6.1 that the initial impacts of three prototypes on tax rates and disposable incomes differ considerably, and that these differences vary by income class.[10] For example, the table indicates that negative income tax plans would result in substantially greater increases in the marginal tax rates that are faced by low-income persons and considerably greater decreases in the rates faced by high-income persons than either of the two credit income tax plans. However, marginal rates faced by families and individuals with incomes from around $6000 to $18,000 would be less affected by the NIT than by the CITs. The table also indicates that although all three plans redistribute income toward the two tails of the income distribution and away from the middle,[11] the NIT focuses much of the burden of this redistribution among

[10]The income categories that are used in Table 6.1 and in all later tables are based on prereform, pretransfer, pretax incomes.

[11]Disposable incomes at the lower tail of the income distribution tend to increase because the prototype plans all provide more generous transfer benefits than does the existing welfare system. Disposable incomes at the upper tail of the distribution increase because the prototypes examined in Table 6.1, unlike the existing federal income tax, are not progressive. There is, however, no inherent reason why NIT and CIT systems should not be progressive at higher income levels, and we have analyzed such systems (in Appendix C of this paper, available from the authors upon request).

households in the $6000 to $18,000 income range, while the two ~
concentrate the burden almost entirely among households in the $14,~00
to $40,000 range.

In Table 6.2, we indicate the percentage of households in various
categories whose incomes would increase under the three prototypes
and the percentage whose incomes would decline. Although it is apparent that the prototype plans would generally increase disposable incomes near the two tails of the income distribution, a sizable minority of
upper- and lower-income households would not enjoy these increases.
There are several reasons for this. For example, the disposable incomes
of some high-income households would fall because the prototypes,
unlike the existing tax system, include Social Security benefits in the tax
base and do not permit itemization. Another group with declining disposable incomes would be found among low-income, female-headed
families living in states with high welfare benefits. In general, the prototypes would provide these households with smaller transfer benefits
than the existing welfare system, even though most other low-income
households would be treated more generously.

The three prototype tax–transfer systems that have just been dis-

TABLE 6.2
Percentage of Households with Substantial Increases and Decreases in Disposable
Income in the Absence of Adjustments in Work Effort

	Number of Households	Percentage with Increases			Percentage with Decreases		
	(*millions*)	NIT	CIT/G	CIT/E	NIT	CIT/G	CIT/E
Income class							
Under $2,000	17.1	71.3	76.5	66.0	14.5	13.4	20.7
$2,000–6,000	22.8	28.8	57.2	42.2	14.7	4.6	8.1
$6,000–14,000	30.0	7.4	40.2	32.1	47.7	37.2	35.9
$14,000–18,000	10.0	0.5	20.2	15.4	67.8	60.0	52.4
$18,000–40,000	15.6	5.0	3.5	4.2	66.4	87.0	75.8
Over $40,000	1.6	78.8	23.8	45.4	15.1	69.8	33.2
Transfer recipients	—	65.2	79.6	67.1	12.1	6.8	12.1
Taxpayers	—	3.9	9.8	10.2	51.5	62.0	51.7
Family status							
Two-parent families	24.8	17.6	49.2	42.6	38.2	33.4	27.8
One-parent families	6.2	13.9	30.9	17.0	57.7	43.5	54.8
Childless couples	21.8	20.3	34.8	30.2	48.5	48.9	45.8
Single individuals	44.4	30.3	43.8	34.4	31.5	30.6	30.5
All households	97.2	23.8	42.3	34.4	38.7	31.7	34.8

NOTE: In making these calculations, only households with income changes of more than $300 are
counted as having a substantial increase or decrease.

cussed provide the source of most of the comparisons reported in this paper. However, to examine the sensitivity of our basic results, two additional sets of prototypes were also compared. The first of these are NIT and CIT prototypes that vary from the basic prototypes in terms of their guarantee levels or tax rates. This provides a test of whether the original NIT–CIT comparison is sensitive to changes in important programmatic parameters. The second set of results are for simulations of tax–transfer systems that represent intermediate points between the current system and the set of basic prototypes. These simulations suggest that several of the steps in the transition between the existing tax–transfer system and a comprehensive NIT or CIT are themselves major reforms having important distributional and efficiency implications.

Indices Used to Evaluate the NIT and CIT Prototypes

Any redistributive plans must attempt to satisfy a number of different and sometimes conflicting objectives. Consequently, one plan is likely to be superior to another in terms of some objectives and inferior in terms of others. Thus, an overall assessment of the relative merits of alternative plans is inherently difficult. In general, we measure the effects of the tax–transfer prototypes discussed above by simply providing indices of various program outcomes, leaving evaluation of the trade-offs to the reader.

The indices we use convey several types of information. [12] First, they indicate the effects of each tax–transfer prototype on the distribution of income, particularly on inequality in the size distribution of income and on poverty. A second set of measures is used to compare alternative tax–transfer systems in terms of the target efficiency of their transfer component (that is, the fraction of total net transfer benefits received by the poor). The final set of indicators measures changes in economic efficiency and in national output resulting from the adjustments in hours of work and earnings that are likely to follow adoption of a new tax–transfer system. These adjustments are indicative of a tax–transfer system's effects on the real resources used by the economy.

Simulation of the NIT and CIT Prototypes

Values for the various indices used in this study were obtained by simulating the effects of the NIT and CIT prototypes on a representative

---

[12]These indices are described in considerable detail in Appendix A, one of five appendices to this paper that are available from the authors upon request.

sample of the nation's households. These simulations were conducted by means of a computer model developed in the Office of Income Security Policy, within the Department of Health, Education, and Welfare (now Department of Health and Human Services). This microsimulation model allows for various interactions among income maintenance programs, positive taxes, jobs programs, and labor supply adjustments, and can use data on individual households to simulate the effects of substantial changes in existing tax and transfer programs.

Simulations of the prototype plans examined here proceed in three major steps.[13] First, a random 10% subsample from the Survey of Income and Education (SIE) is used to characterize preform status of a representative group of the nation's families.[14] In the second step, certain characteristics describing the sample families, such as their net wage rates (that is, their wage rates after taxes) and their disposable incomes, are adjusted to what they would be after the simulated reform plans were implemented, but prior to any adjustments in work effort. The third step consists of adjusting hours of work and earnings to account for labor supply responses to changes in effective after-tax wage rates and disposable incomes resulting from the simulated plans. The appropriate tax–transfer schedules are then used to recompute the postreform disposable income after all labor supply adjustments have taken place.

Since one of the major sets of indices that we use to compare the NIT and CIT prototypes depends on predicting their effects on hours of work and earnings, we shall discuss the third step at some length. The principal information that we use to predict adjustments in hours and earnings is based on statistical estimates of labor supply response parameters obtained from data collected in the Seattle–Denver Income Maintenance Experiment.[15] These Seattle–Denver estimates indicate how individuals

[13]Because of space limitations, the simulation model is only sketched here and certain features of the model that are not required for present purposes, such as its ability to simulate programs that guarantee jobs to various subsets of the population, are ignored. Greater detail, as well as an examination—and in some cases sensitivity tests—of major assumptions that underlie the simulation methodology are found in Betson, Greenberg, and Kasten (1980).

[14]The SIE, which has annual data for the calendar year 1975, consists of 160,000 families selected in such a way as to be representative of the national population. Many of the variables used to characterize the preform status of individual households, such as earnings, unearned income, and hours were obtained directly from the SIE. However, others, such as tax payments and tax rates, were derived by using schedules in conjunction with information from the SIE. Still others, including unemployment insurance amounts and benefit-reduction rates associated with existing transfer programs, were determined from statistically estimated prediction equations.

[15]These estimates are reported in Appendix B (available from the authors), where the statistical model used in computing them is also briefly described.

would adjust their work effort in response to given changes in their transfer benefits and their effective, after-tax wage rates. Although in principle the Seattle–Denver labor supply estimates can be applied to any tax or transfer reform measure, the data on which they are based suffer from certain limitations. The most important of these from the perspective of this study is that the experimental sample underrepresented high-income families. For example, only about 1% of the families in the Seattle–Denver sample had incomes above $15,000 when they enrolled in the experiment in 1970 and 1971, as compared to 22% of the nation's families, and there were less than half as many families in the $12,500 to $15,000 range as in the nation.[16] Thus, to simulate labor supply responses for higher-income households, it is necessary to extrapolate. Although in our judgment considerable confidence can be placed in using estimates from the Seattle–Denver experiment in simulating the labor supply effects of redistributive programs on lower- or middle-income families, less confidence can be placed on using these estimates to simulate effects on higher-income families.[17]

A second problem results from the fact that the Seattle–Denver sample included relatively few single persons, and those who were included are untypical of single individuals in general. To simulate the hours and earnings responses of single males and females, therefore, we use Seattle–Denver estimates based on male and female family heads, respectively. Thus, it is apparent that considerably greater confidence can be placed in simulation results for husbands, wives, and female heads—groups that are all well represented in the Seattle–Denver sample—than for single individuals.

We have used two different approaches to address the data limitations just discussed. First, we frequently report simulation results separately for husbands, wives, female family heads, and single individuals. This enables the reader to examine separately simulation findings in which he can place considerable confidence and those in which he cannot. Second, we have conducted a sensitivity test of our major findings

[16]In principle, the estimates based on the Seattle–Denver data are only directly applicable to families with incomes below the level at which the experimental payments ceased. However, these income levels were quite high, often exceeding $20,000.

[17]In our judgment, the Seattle–Denver sample is sufficiently representative of families with 1975 incomes of less that $18,000 that considerable confidence can be placed in labor supply estimates for this group (82% of the simulation sample from the SIE is included in this income range), but only moderate confidence can be placed in parameter estimates for families in the $18,000 to $25,000 range (11% of the simulation sample), and only very low confidence can be given estimates for families with incomes above $25,000 (7% of the simulation sample).

by recomputing some of the simulations on the basis of labor supply response parameters that were obtained from nonexperimental data sources.

Results from the Simulations

In this section, we present the results from the simulations of the NIT and CIT prototypes. The presentation is divided into three subsections. The first of these reports on the effects of the three basic prototypes on work effort. The next subsection examines the basic prototypes' effects on income, inequality, and poverty. The final subsection summarizes the results of various sensitivity tests of the major findings.

Effects on Work Effort

As noted earlier, the initial impact of a new tax–transfer system is to change the marginal tax rates and disposable incomes of individual families. As a consequence of these changes, which are reported by income class in Table 6.1, workers would be expected to adjust their hours. Predictions of the changes in person years[18] and earnings that would result from the effects of the three basic prototypes on work incentives appear in the first two panels of Table 6.3. Changes in earnings is a particularly useful index, since it indicates the potential effects of the prototypes on economic output. As may be seen, the predicted effects closely follow a pattern implied by Table 6.1. For example, since the marginal tax rates of those who shoulder the redistribution burden would only be moderately changed by any of the three tax–transfer systems, it would be anticipated that these persons would increase their work effort to replace part of the income lost through taxes. And indeed, Table 6.3 indicates that this would generally be the case. Low-income persons, on the other hand, are generally found to decrease their hours and earnings in response to rises in both their disposable incomes and marginal tax rates. Although tax rates under the NIT and CIT prototypes fall for tax units with incomes above $40,000, their disposable incomes are increased and, as a result, workers in these units would apparently reduce their hours and earnings. The CIT/G, on the other hand, is associated with reductions in both tax rates and disposable incomes for

---

[18]For purposes of these calculations, a person-year was assumed to equal 2080 hours.

TABLE 6.3
Predicted Effects of the Alternative Prototypes on Person Years, Earnings, and Deadweight Loss

	Level under Current System	Aggregate Change			Percentage Change		
		NIT	CIT/G	CIT/E	NIT	CIT/G	CIT/E
Person Years (millions)							
Income class							
Under $2,000	2.61	−.50	−.34	−.09	−19.2	−12.9	−3.4
$2,000–6,000	10.20	−.26	−.38	−.18	−2.5	−3.7	−1.8
$6,000–14,000	29.22	.19	−.53	−.23	0.7	−1.8	−0.8
$14,000–18,000	13.24	.32	.18	.16	2.4	1.4	1.2
$18,000–40,000	24.55	.71	1.57	.90	2.9	6.4	3.7
Over $40,000	2.26	−.16	.19	−.03	−7.1	8.4	−1.1
Transfer recipients	—	−.91	−1.31	−.56	−10.3	−6.6	−3.5
Taxpayers	—	1.22	2.00	1.10	1.7	3.2	1.7
All households	82.07	.31	.69	.53	0.4	0.8	0.6
Earnings ($ billions)							
Income class							
Under $2,000	7.08	−.78	−.36	.76	−11.1	−5.1	10.7
$2,000–6,000	45.48	−.50	−1.30	−.49	−1.1	−2.8	−1.1
$6,000–14,000	226.55	2.06	−2.04	−.52	0.9	−0.9	−0.2
$14,000–18,000	140.74	2.79	2.13	1.70	2.0	1.5	1.2
$18,000–40,000	337.10	6.55	16.49	9.08	1.9	4.9	2.7
Over $40,000	77.24	−6.69	−.14	−3.97	−8.7	−0.2	−5.1
Transfer recipients	—	−2.07	−4.88	−1.31	−5.7	−4.5	−1.6
Taxpayers	—	5.49	19.65	7.88	0.7	2.7	1.1
All households	834.18	3.42	14.78	6.57	0.4	1.8	0.8
Deadweight Loss ($ millions)							
Income class							
Under $2,000	122	484	144	67	397	118	55
$2,000–6,000	1,367	−900	−972	−1,090	−66	−71	−80
$6,000–14,000	1,612	−1,107	−845	−1,105	−69	−52	−69
$14,000–18,000	140	−2	151	56	−1	108	40
$18,000–40,000	271	−127	56	−58	−47	21	−21
Over $40,000	10	−7	−4	−6	−70	−40	−60
Transfer recipients	—	−716	−282	−871	−35	−14	−43
Taxpayers	—	−943	−1,188	−1,265	−64	−81	−86
All households	3,522	−1,659	−1,471	−2,136	−47	−42	−61

high-income families, and consequently, person years among families increase.

Table 6.3 indicates, as expected, that transfer recipients under the three prototypes would decrease their hours and earnings. Under all three plans, however, these decreases are apparently more than offset by increases by positive taxpayers. Hence, it appears that the net effect of the three plans is to increase work effort and economic output. This finding, however, as will soon be seen, should be treated with some caution.

If the three prototypes are ranked on the basis of their positive predicted effects on person years and earnings, the CIT/G plan would be first, the CIT/E second, and the NIT third. However, the differences between any two of the plans amount to less than one-half of 1% of initial person years and less than one-half of 1% of initial earnings.

The effects of the three plans on earnings can be further assessed by use of Table 6.4, which indicates how various subgroups contribute to the predicted effects. For example, it is evident from the table that the predicted positive effects of the prototypes on earnings and the relatively more favorable ranking of the CITs are both largely attributable to the estimated size of the increases in the earnings of wives who reside in

TABLE 6.4
Contribution of Different Family Status Groups to the Effects of the Alternative Prototypes on Earnings

Row		Change in Earnings ($ billions)		
		NIT	CIT/G	CIT/E
A	Husbands in families with incomes under $18,000	−.2	−2.2	−.9
B	Row A plus husbands in families with incomes over $18,000	−1.8	−.8	−1.4
C	Row B plus female family heads in families with incomes under $18,000	−.6	.1	.0
D	Row C plus female family heads in families with incomes over $18,000	−.6	.2	.1
E	Row D plus single individuals with incomes under $18,000	−.9	.1	.5
F	Row E plus single individuals with incomes over $18,000	−3.0	−.4	−.9
G	Row F plus wives in families with incomes under $18,000	.1	−.5	−.3
H	Row G plus wives in families with incomes over $18,000	3.4	14.8	6.6

tax units with incomes above $18,000. In fact, if these wives were excluded from the comparison, the positive earnings effects would be eliminated and the NIT would be ranked first.

Since tax units with incomes above $18,000 must pay higher taxes under the CIT prototypes than under the NIT, it would not be surprising if wives in such units would work more—and consequently have higher earnings—under the former plans than under the latter, even though they would also face somewhat higher tax rates under the CITs. Nevertheless, we are skeptical of the size of the CIT–NIT earnings differential that is predicted for these wives by the simulation model. As indicated earlier, this prediction is based on behavioral parameters from the Seattle–Denver experiment that were estimated from a sample of low- and middle-income wives. When these estimated parameters are extrapolated to higher-income wives, the predicted responses to income changes become very large, both in absolute terms and relative to compensated changes in wage or tax rates.[19] Given the major source of the total estimated CIT–NIT earnings differential and the fact that this estimated differential is a comparatively small fraction of total earnings, we tentatively conclude that there is little reason to choose either the credit income approach or the negative income approach on the basis of their predicted effects on work effort. The choice between these two approaches must be based on other factors.

The results reported in Tables 6.3 and 6.4 do have an important implication, however: They strongly suggest that substantial reform of the existing tax–transfer system, involving considerable redistribution of income, is possible without causing large reductions in the potential output produced by the economy.[20] In fact, if the results in Tables 6.3 and 6.4 are taken at face value, they imply that modest *increases* in earnings are possible. And, even a very conservative interpretation of the tables, in which the results for higher-income wives are strongly discounted, suggests that none of the three quite different simulated alternatives to the existing tax–transfer system is likely to have strong adverse effects on total earnings, and positive effects are quite possible.

So far we have focused on the changes in output that would be occasioned by changes in earnings resulting from adoption of a new tax–transfer system. Earnings changes, however, are not an appropriate

---

[19]For an illustration of this, see Appendix B, Table B–2, available from the authors upon request.

[20]In conducting the simulations, it was assumed that labor demand curves are perfectly elastic, and consequently, that employers would not respond to shifts in the supply curves they face. If employers' responses were allowed for in the simulations, the predicted changes in hours and earnings would probably be smaller than those reported here.

measure of whether society as a whole is better or worse off under a new system, since such changes must be accompanied by adjustments in the amount of time spent outside the labor market, and the value of this time serves as an important offset to gains or losses in output. However, the tax rates that are associated with any tax–transfer system create a gap between the amount consumers are willing to pay for the production that is achieved through an hour of work and the net return to a worker for giving up an hour of his time. This gap results in a socially nonoptimal division between work and nonwork time—usually referred to as "deadweight loss"—that will, of course, be affected by implementation of a tax–transfer system that changes the existing structure of tax rates.

Estimates of the potential effects of the three basic prototypes on deadweight loss in the economy are presented in the bottom panel of Table 6.3. These estimates suggest that deadweight loss under the existing tax–transfer system is relatively small, less than 3% of federal income tax revenues and less than one-half of 1% of total earnings. Apparently, all three prototypes would cause substantial percentage decreases in deadweight loss, implying that adoption of tax–transfer schemes of the type considered here would result in a modest improvement in economic efficiency. Differences among the three plans, however, are relatively small in absolute terms, not exceeding two-thirds of one billion dollars. Thus, it appears that there is little reason to choose either a NIT or a CIT on the basis of their relative effects on deadweight loss.

Effects on Income, Inequality, and Poverty

It was pointed out earlier that adjustments in work effort resulting from implementation of a new tax–transfer system would cause the effects of the new system on disposable income to diverge from those on net transfer payments. That this is indeed the case is evident from Table 6.5. On the one hand, reductions in work effort among most transfer recipients and low-income households cause their disposable incomes to be lower than would be the case in the absence of an adjustment in working hours—compare Tables 6.1 and 6.5—but their net transfer payments to be higher. On the other hand, most households that pay positive net taxes increase their hours of work, causing their disposable incomes to be higher than in the absence of an adjustment, but their net transfers to be lower. Consistent with the findings presented in Table 6.3, Table 6.5 indicates that the increases in disposable income among taxpayers exceeds the reduction among transfer recipients, resulting in a

TABLE 6.5

Predicted Effects of the Alternative Prototypes on Disposable Incomes and Net Transfer Receipts after Adjustments in Work Effort

	$ billions			$ per person		
	NIT	CIT/G	CIT/E	NIT	CIT/G	CIT/E
Change in Disposable Incomes						
Income class						
Under $2,000	9.89	12.01	5.73	397	483	229
$2,000–6,000	3.04	12.30	6.24	90	365	186
$6,000–14,000	−6.20	3.13	.18	−89	45	3
$14,000–18,000	−2.71	−3.02	−2.06	−94	−105	−71
$18,000–40,000	−2.78	−9.47	−4.68	−58	−198	−98
Over $40,000	2.26	−.72	1.08	495	−157	236
Transfer recipients	16.14	35.32	17.84	271	371	210
Taxpayers	−12.64	−21.08	−11.40	−84	−184	−92
All households	3.50	14.24	6.45	17	68	31
Change in Transfer Payments Less Federal Income Taxes						
Income class						
Under $2,000	10.65	12.37	4.99	428	497	200
$2,000–6,000	3.54	13.55	6.73	105	402	200
$6,000–14,000	−8.13	5.06	.68	−117	73	10
$14,000–18,000	5.30	5.00	3.64	184	174	126
$18,000–40,000	−8.79	−24.62	−13.02	−184	−514	−272
Over $40,000	8.54	−.56	4.80	1,871	−123	1,052
Transfer recipients	18.15	40.01	19.15	304	421	225
Taxpayers	−17.64	−39.22	−18.60	−118	−343	−150
All households	0.50	0.79	0.54	2	4	3

small positive effect on the overall income level. This positive effect occurs even though transfer payments and tax revenues under each of the prototypes were predicted to be nearly offsetting, so that for all practical purposes the programs are self-financing.

Table 6.6 compares the percentage of households under each of the three prototypes that would enjoy substantial income increases or suffer from substantial income decreases after adjustments in hours of work have taken place.[21] Possibly the most striking result in Table 6.6 is the

[21]It should be noted that not all households with increases in income would necessarily be better-off nor would all households with decreases necessarily be worse-off than in the prereform period, since in some cases these increases and decreases may be more than offset by losses and gains in time spent outside the labor market. However, unreported estimates, in which we tried to adjust for these gains and losses in nonmarket time,

TABLE 6.6
Percentage of Households with Substantial Increases or Decreases in Disposable Income after Adjustments in Work Effort

	Number of Households (*millions*)	Percentage with Increases			Percentage with Decreases		
		NIT	CIT/G	CIT/E	NIT	CIT/G	CIT/E
Income class							
Under $2,000	17.1	69.0	75.6	65.5	14.0	12.3	19.5
$2,000–6,000	22.8	27.4	54.2	39.8	13.5	4.1	7.1
$6,000–14,000	30.1	6.2	37.0	28.0	34.3	36.0	31.6
$14,000–18,000	10.0	0.9	17.3	12.5	34.1	49.6	35.6
$18,000–40,000	15.7	5.6	5.9	5.6	26.4	68.8	41.8
Over $40,000	1.6	60.0	27.7	39.9	20.0	53.2	28.8
Transfer recipients	—	62.2	77.1	64.8	11.4	6.1	10.9
Taxpayers	—	3.4	8.2	8.0	30.5	53.8	36.9
Family status							
Two-parent families	24.8	15.9	46.7	38.1	16.6	22.2	13.7
One-parent families	6.2	13.4	30.0	16.0	53.0	42.0	49.5
Childless couples	21.8	19.5	34.2	29.1	25.0	40.6	26.4
Single individuals	44.4	28.9	41.9	33.1	24.3	30.3	28.8
All households	97.2	28.9	40.7	32.4	24.3	31.3	25.7

NOTE: In making these calculations, only households with income changes of more than $300 are counted as having a substantial increase or decrease.

prediction that the earnings status of considerably more households would improve than deteriorate under the CITs, but that this would not occur under the NIT. The CITs appear clearly superior to the NIT at income levels between $2000 and $14,000, which contain a majority of households, while the NIT only clearly dominates the CITs at income levels above $18,000.

Table 6.6 also implies that single-parent families and childless couples would tend to be the major losers under all three plans, with two-parent families and single individuals comparatively better-off. Within each of

---

produced results similar to those appearing in Table 6.6 and are similar to those in Table 6.2, where no labor supply adjustments are allowed. A comparison of Tables 6.2 and 6.6 suggests, however, that once changes in work effort are taken into account, the fraction of households with either substantial increases or decreases in incomes declines. The reason for this is that hour and earnings adjustments generally tend to at least partially offset initial changes in income, since households enjoying increases in transfer payments or decreases in taxes usually decrease their work effort, and households whose taxes increase usually do the opposite. Thus, once hours adjustments are accounted for, the disposable incomes of many households are left substantially unchanged.

the demographic groups, fewer households would enjoy substantial increases in income under the NIT than under either CIT. However, except for one-parent households, fewer households would also suffer from income decreases. In other words, it appears that the NIT would leave more households with substantially unchanged incomes than would either CIT.

Table 6.7 presents several indicators of the effects of the current tax–transfer system and the three prototypes on income inequality and poverty.[22] All these measures indicate that although the current system already produces very large reductions in income inequality and poverty, adoption of any of the prototype plans would result in fairly substantial additional reductions.[23] Of the three prototype tax–transfer systems, the CIT/G plan appears to have the greatest effect on reducing income inequality and poverty, followed by the NIT plan, and then by the CIT/E plan. Although the CIT/G system is clearly far superior to its alternatives in terms of numbers of people removed from poverty, the CIT/G and NIT plans are fairly similar with respect to their effects on income inequality and on the poverty gap of those who remain below the poverty line.

Critics of credit income tax proposals often point to the fact that such plans are less target efficient than possible alternatives, such as negative income tax programs. These critics are supported by estimates of target efficiency that are reported in Table 6.7. As may be seen, a substantially larger percentage of total transfer would be received by the pretransfer poor under the NIT plan than under either of the CIT plans. However, all three prototypes are considerably less target efficient than the current system. The relatively high target efficiency of the existing tax–transfer

[22]Descriptions of these indicators may be found in Appendix A (available from the authors upon request). The comparisons between the prototypes and the current system implied by Table 6.7 are somewhat misleading, since participation of eligibles in existing transfer programs is well under 100%, but simulations of the prototype systems assume full participation. If actual participation in the prototypes were also under 100%, the simulation results would overstate their effectiveness in reducing income inequality and poverty.

[23]Although the income inequality measures reported in Table 6.7 allow for labor supply responses, comparable measures that do not allow for labor supply responses were also computed. A comparison of these two sets of estimates suggests that adjustments in work effort induced by the prototypes slightly lessen their effects on inequality. For example, in the absence of labor supply responses, the Gini coefficients predicted for the NIT, CIT/G, and CIT/E prototypes were .406, .394, and .418, respectively. A somewhat analogous result can be found in a study by Golladay and Haveman (1977) that allowed for adjustments in the level of demand for goods and services in response to exogenous changes in the size distribution of income. These demand adjustments were found to induce changes in earnings that tended to dissipate the initial redistribution of income.

TABLE 6.7
Predicted Effects of the Alternative Prototypes on Income Inequality and Poverty after Adjustments in Work Effort

	Pretransfer	Current System	NIT	CIT/G	CIT/E
Gini coefficient	—	.456	.409	.399	.419
Mean of log of welfare ratio	—	.651	.692	.732	.692
Variance of log of welfare ratio	—	.536	.393	.349	.427
Number of persons remaining in poverty (millions)	28.24	21.53	15.85	12.96	17.40
Poverty gap					
$ billions	23.38	9.86	5.42	4.41	7.61
Per poor person ($)	828	458	342	340	437
Percentage of total net transfer payments received by pre-transfer poor	—	73.8	57.2	44.2	47.7

system probably partially results from enforcement of various eligibility rules such as asset tests. In addition, most low-income persons would have higher guarantee and breakeven levels under the prototypes than under the existing system. Another partial explanation is that many persons who are eligible for transfer payments under existing programs do not choose to become recipients; such nonparticipants are more likely to be found among households above the poverty line than among those that are below. In the simulation of the prototype systems, it was assumed that all persons eligible for transfer payments would actually receive them. If some would not, the simulations probably understate the target efficiency of the prototypes.

Sensitivity Tests of the Major Findings

So far in this section, we have made a number of comparisons of a negative income tax prototype and two credit income tax prototypes. We now summarize the results of three different types of sensitivity tests of these basic findings. The first of these tests investigates the sensitivity of the findings to changes in two basic programmatic parameters: the guarantee level and the structure of the tax rates. The second examines tax–transfer plans that represent intermediate points between the existing system to the NIT and CIT/G systems. The third test indicates whether the results are sensitive to the use of other labor supply response parameters than those obtained from the Seattle–Denver Income

Maintenance Experiment data. Details on these three sets of sensitivity tests may be found in Appendices C, D, and E, respectively (available from the authors upon request). A summary of major findings from the sensitivity tests is presented in Table 6.8 and briefly discussed in the remainder of this section.

The first of the sensitivity tests is based on simulations of two pairs of additional tax–transfer prototypes. The first pair provides for higher guarantee levels than the NIT and CIT/G plans examined above, but are otherwise identical. The second additional pair is also identical to the NIT and CIT/G plans examined earlier, except for incorporating a progressive tax schedule. Thus, a total of three pairwise comparisons between equal guarantee negative income tax and credit income tax plans can be made.

Findings from these three pairwise comparisons are remarkably similar. For example, all three imply that the CIT is superior to its paired NIT in terms of numbers of households with substantially increased incomes, reductions in income inequality, and reductions in poverty. Each of the NITs, however, is more target efficient than its CIT counterpart. The major source of these differences is that negative income tax systems tax low-income households at higher rates and high-income households at lower rates than do credit income plans providing for equal guarantees (see Table 6.1 and Appendix C, which may be obtained from the authors). As a consequence, CIT/G plans redistribute much more income from high- to low-income families than do comparable NITs. As compared to CIT plans, however, in the NIT plans, the income that is redistributed is targeted on those who are below the poverty line.

The three simulated NIT prototypes and their CIT/G counterparts are all predicted to increase earnings and decrease deadweight loss. In fact, it appears that the high guarantee and progressive tax structure NITs and CIT/Gs would raise earnings by somewhat more than the NIT and CIT/G plans reported on earlier. The high-guarantee plans are somewhat less effective in reducing deadweight loss, however. In the three pairwise comparisons, the CIT/Gs are consistently predicted to produce greater earnings increases than comparable NITs, but the NITs consistently appear to cause greater reductions in deadweight loss.

Although all six prototypes are predicted to have favorable effects on earnings and deadweight loss, it is important to recognize that these improvements are generally modest. The earnings improvements never exceed 3% of prereform earnings levels and the reductions in deadweight loss are never more than one-quarter of 1% of prereform earnings. Differences between comparable NIT and CIT/G plans are, of course, even smaller. For example, the estimated differences in earnings

TABLE 6.8
Summary of Results from the Sensitivity Tests

Alternative Plans	Economic Efficiency			Target Efficiency	Income Inequality			
	Change in Earnings		Change in Deadweight Loss ($ billions)	% of Total Transfer Received by Pretransfer Poor	Percentage of Households with Substantial Income Changes		Gini Coefficient	Persons Remaining in Poverty (millions)
	Measure I ($ billions)	Measure II ($ billions)			Increases	Decreases		
Basic prototypes								
NIT	3.4	.1	−1.7	57.2	22.5	24.3	.409	15.9
CIT/G	14.8	−.5	−1.5	44.2	40.7	31.3	.399	13.0
CIT/E	6.6	−.3	−2.1	47.7	32.4	25.7	.419	17.4
High guarantee prototypes								
NIT	18.5	.4	−.5	47.5	38.5	36.2	.378	7.1
CIT/G	25.1	.8	−.2	41.3	48.2	33.8	.373	6.7
Progressive tax prototypes								
NIT	8.7	−.3	−1.7	57.2	23.6	16.4	.408	15.8
CIT/G	20.4	−1.1	−1.4	41.4	46.4	25.5	.395	12.5
Intermediate prototypes								
NIT	9.6	2.7	3.5	57.0	20.5	9.4	.409	15.7
CIT/G	27.5	−1.1	3.5	32.1	59.7	23.5	.392	10.7
Basic prototypes simulated with nonexperimental labor supply parameters								
NIT	19.1	14.6	−7.8	57.5	26.4	27.0	.413	15.9
CIT/G	−3.0	−4.2	2.9	44.0	39.0	39.8	.398	13.0
CIT/E	8.2	5.6	−3.7	47.8	32.8	34.7	.422	17.6

NOTES: Measure I uses the changes in earnings of the total population; Measure II uses the changes in earnings of the total population, but imputes a zero change to wives in units with incomes above $18,000. Only households with changes of over $300 are counted as having a substantial income increase or decrease. The Intermediate NIT and CIT/G prototypes are respectively similar to the basic NIT and CIT/G prototypes, except that they do not tax Unemployment Insurance and Social Security payments and they retain the existing progressive tax schedule. Results for additional intermediate prototypes are reported in Appendix D (available from the authors upon request).

are equal to only about 1% of total earnings. Moreover, virtually all the positive effects on earnings and the estimated differences in earnings are attributable to predicted increases in work effort by higher-income wives—predictions about which, as suggested earlier, there is reason for considerable skepticism. Even if the predictions for wives are discounted to a considerable degree, however, the simulations appear to imply that none of the six tax–transfer prototypes would have very detrimental effects on earnings or economic efficiency and, in fact, they could very well have modest positive effects.

Adoption of any one of the NIT or CIT tax–transfer plans examined so far would involve very extensive reforms of the nation's existing system. However, not all the components of the tax–transfer plans we have been examining are necessarily integral parts of a negative income tax or credit income tax system. For example, the simulation results presented so far are for tax–transfer systems that would expand the tax base by counting Unemployment Insurance and Social Security payments as taxable income. These plans would also eliminate the existing progressive schedule of tax rates associated with the federal income tax. It is quite feasible, however, to construct NIT or CIT systems that continue to leave Unemployment Insurance and Social Security payments untaxed and retain the present progressive tax schedule—and we have, in fact, simulated several such plans.

A primary reason for simulating these "intermediate" NIT and CIT plans is to see whether the findings reported above can be ascribed to our treatment of such issues as the taxation of Unemployment Insurance and Social Security payments or the retention of the progressivity found in the existing tax schedule, rather than to the more essential elements of credit and negative income tax systems. This does not appear to be the case. For example, the simulated intermediate NITs and CITs are predicted to cause earnings increases, as were the final versions of these plans. Indeed, the predicted increases are somewhat larger for the former plans than the latter. Again, however, the earnings increases are mostly attributable to predicted increases in the work effort of higher-income wives. Comparisons of intermediate NIT plans with their CIT/G counterparts are also quite consistent with our earlier findings. For example, the intermediate NITs appear to be considerably more target efficient than the intermediate CIT/Gs, but the latter are predicted to have a larger impact on income inequality and poverty and to engender larger increases in earnings.

So far, all our reported results have been based on simulations that utilized labor supply parameters estimated with data from the Seattle-

Denver experiment. In our judgment, the overall reliability of Seattle–Denver parameters is superior to any available alterna[tive]. Nevertheless, as indicated earlier, our confidence in extrapolating these parameters to households with incomes above $18,000 is relatively low. Hence, our final sensitivity test involves comparing findings based on the Seattle–Denver parameters with results computed with labor supply parameters that were selected from among those found in studies using nonexperimental data.

Simulations that were based on the nonexperimental parameters, like those utilizing the Seattle–Denver parameters, indicated that considerable redistribution of income is feasible under either NITs or CITs without large reductions in national output, and, in fact, that small increases are possible. However, the predicted effects of the prototypes on earnings and deadweight loss are quite sensitive to whether the Seattle–Denver or the nonexperimental parameters are used in the simulations. For example, while simulations using the Seattle–Denver parameters suggest that the CIT/G plan is superior to the NIT plan in terms of its effects on earnings, estimates based on the nonexperimental parameters indicate just the opposite. Since one of the criteria used in choosing the nonexperimental parameters was that they vary considerably from the Seattle–Denver parameters, these results are not particularly surprising. They do imply, however, that considerable uncertainty must exist about whether CITs or NITs would have superior effects on the national economy. When this uncertainty is coupled with the fact that estimates based on both sets of labor supply parameters indicate that differences in the earnings effects of the rival tax–transfer systems are unlikely to exceed 2% or 3% of total earnings in the economy and that differences in effects on deadweight loss are unlikely to be more than about 1%, there appears to be little justification to choosing between CITs and NITs on the basis of their implications for economic efficiency.

Conclusion

Table 6.8, which appeared in the last section, provides a useful summary of the major findings of this paper. One important set of findings, for example, is based on the alternative indices of economic efficiency reported in the first three columns of the table. First, the predicted effects that appear in these columns are relatively modest, never exceeding 3% of earnings under the current tax–transfer system and usually much smaller.[24] Second, most of the predictions suggest that adoption of the simulated plans would improve economic efficiency by causing earnings to increase and deadweight loss to decrease. In the relatively few cases where improvements are not predicted, the estimates imply that adverse effects would amount to no more than a minute fraction of total output in the economy. Third, differences between the predicted efficiency effects of comparable CITs and NITs are generally quite small. Moreover, the relative ranking of the CITs and NITs in terms of their effects on economic efficiency appear sensitive to the index used to measure economic efficiency and the set of labor supply parameters utilized to compute this index.

The implications of these findings for policy are significant. One such implication is that potential economic losses—measured in terms of earnings or deadweight loss—are not important obstacles to income redistribution, even if the redistribution is as comprehensive and sweeping as the tax–transfer prototypes we simulate. The findings also imply that the choice among alternative tax–transfer systems must be mainly based on other criteria than economic efficiency.

One potential criterion for this purpose is target efficiency; and as Table 6.8 suggests, the ranking of the alternative systems in terms of target efficiency is quite clear: NIT plans are ranked substantially ahead of comparable CIT plans. However, the CITs appear superior to comparable NITs when evaluated on the basis of the number of households that enjoy improvements in income. The reason for this is that CITs tend to redistribute income toward a larger number of households than do NITs, and although these households have relatively low incomes, many are nevertheless above the poverty line. The redistribution that takes place under a NIT is enjoyed by fewer households, but a larger proportion of those that do benefit have pretransfer incomes that are below the poverty line. This point is illustrated by a comparison of the basic NIT plan and CIT/E plan, two prototypes with comparable transfer expenditures. As Table 6.8 indicates, more households would have substantial income increases under the CIT/E plan than under the

---

[24]Even these relatively small economic efficiency effects could be attenuated by certain labor market adjustments not taken into account by the simulations reported in this paper. For example, we have not allowed for the possibility that employers will respond to changes in the supply conditions they face by adjusting the wages they pay, or that (in periods of high unemployment) workers who reduce their supply of hours to the market may be replaced by the unemployed, and those who increase their supply may join the ranks of the unemployed. For an example of a simulation study that did attempt to incorporate these possibilities, see Greenberg (forthcoming).

NIT plan, but the greater target efficiency of the latter results in persons remaining in poverty.

In the final analysis, the findings reported in this paper suggest that the choice between the CIT and NIT approaches to tax–transfer policy may largely depend on value judgments concerning the extent to which income should be redistributed and the manner in which any redistribution that takes place should be allocated among households. According to the simulation results, economic efficiency considerations need not be an impediment to redistribution under either approach. However, it does appear that allocation of a given amount of redistributed income would vary considerably between a NIT and a CIT, with poverty households receiving the greatest benefits under a NIT, but a larger number of households sharing the redistributed income under a CIT.

Discussion

EDWARD M. GRAMLICH

Two years ago, I attended an IRP-sponsored conference where David Greenberg presented an early version of some public employment simulations from the KGB model. One year ago I attended another IRP-sponsored conference where I was a discussant of a second version of the KGB model. This year here I am again at yet another IRP-sponsored conference discussing yet another version of the KGB model. I am beginning to think it's an annual rite of spring—every year I get crocuses on the lawn and a new KGB paper on my desk. And every year the marginal value of what new I have to say must go down, perhaps by a lot.

This year's KGB vintage, like the others, is a careful study of an interesting question with a rich and sophisticated model. As I said in one of those previous years, if the United States still had a CIA, it would be worried about falling behind in the simulation model race. As befits the theme of this year's conference, the model is put to work comparing different efficiency and equity aspects of an income-tested transfer plan, the NIT, with a universal plan, the CIT. As has been pointed out in Garfinkel's Introduction, the differences between the two in the realm of income maintenance involve both administration questions, which Betson, Greenberg, and Kasten ignore, and the internal structure of tax rates, which is what they focus on.

By this time model simulations of transfer plans are slightly old hat, particularly if you have been discussing them at annual IRP conferences, but the authors did add a lot to the paper, because they focused more on how to evaluate the simulation results from a policy perspective. In summarizing the paper, I will devote most of my attention to that aspect—how we use models to analyze transfer plans, and what we should think about NITs and CITs after reading this paper.

Figure 6.2 describes the three polar case plans analyzed by Betson, Greenberg, and Kasten. The present transfer–tax system (using the Wis-

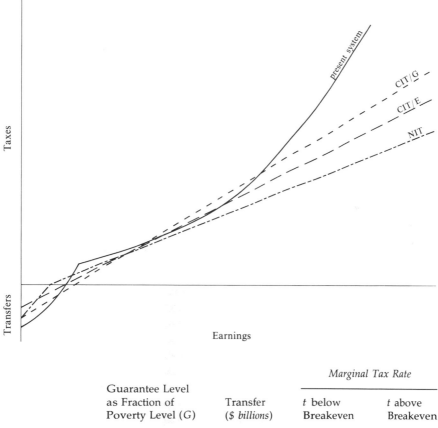

	Guarantee Level as Fraction of Poverty Level (G)	Transfer ($ billions)	Marginal Tax Rate	
			t below Breakeven	t above Breakeven
NIT	.75	38.5	.50	.23
CIT/G	.75	57.6	.34	.34
CIT/E	.55	38.2	.28	.28
Present system	?	22.4	?	?

Figure 6.2. Three tax–transfer plans analyzed by Betson, Kasten, and Greenberg: NIT, CIT/G, and CIT/E. (Figure by University of Wisconsin Cartographic Laboratory.)

consin AFDC program), features very high guarantee levels and rising marginal tax rates on high earnings (though we all know the tax does not look so progressive when we add capital income to earnings). The NIT to be analyzed has a guarantee of about three-fourths of the poverty line, marginal tax rates of 50% up to the breakeven level, and then a constant 23% marginal tax rate for positive taxpayers. This is contrasted with two different CIT plans—the generous one (CIT/G) keeps the same guarantee level as the NIT and simply taxes earnings at a 34% marginal rate, transferring $58 billion in the process—and the cheap one (CIT/E) lowers the guarantee level to about 55% of the poverty line, taxes all earnings at a 38% rate, and transfers $38 billion, by construction exactly the amount transferred by the NIT. Both totals are $16 billion more than was transferred in 1975, the comparison year, by the present undersubscribed mixture of AFDC, Food Stamps, and SSI. All plans are self-financing in the sense that total tax revenues are sufficient to cover all present-day expenditures plus any new transfer liabilities occasioned by the plan, leaving the size of the deficit constant. The authors also do a series of sensitivity tests to check for nonlinearities in the impact of their plans, but do not find much interesting there, so I will not bother with that part of the paper.

One problem that arises at this point is exactly what is meant by a transfer. Since each plan is self-financing, it redistributes spending power throughout the population. Some present-day transfer recipients get more, some less; and the same is true on the tax side. When the authors hold transfers constant at $16 billion, they are counting only the net gains in the transfer population, ignoring those of the taxpaying population (which are not transfers in the official accounts). The arbitrariness of this convention should be obvious.

The technical operations are easy to understand, if incredibly difficult to implement. The KGB model is a standard microsimulation model, with the labor supply responses from the Seattle–Denver Income Maintenance Experiment (SIME–DIME) built in. Incomes and tax rates are computed before and after the hypothetical program is put into effect, labor supply responses (both income and substitution effects) are calculated, hours and earnings are altered appropriately, and new information is generated. This posttransfer and postresponse information is used to evaluate the plans. The main problem at this stage is that since the SIME-DIME experiment did not include many high-income people, Betson, Greenberg, and Kasten had to extrapolate labor supply responses over this range and that is troublesome, yielding as it does very high income effects for high-income wives. The authors are sensitive to this difficulty, however, and tell us when to take their figures with a grain of salt.

They evaluate outcomes first with a series of efficiency measures. These are shown graphically in Figure 6.3 for a typical family whose wage rate is not altered by labor supply changes. One measure is the gross change in earnings at the initial level of hours (H_0), denoted by WZ for this family. Perhaps this number is interesting to some people, but it has no welfare significance at all because it ignores the value of any changes in leisure time, and hence does not even purport to measure economic efficiency in the conventional sense. For what it is worth, the authors do provide a surprise here. We may have all grown accustomed to thinking that transfer plans will lower earnings, but that is only when transfer plans are not self-financed. When they are, earnings rise and fall depending on the changes in marginal tax rates and disposable income in various families. In this case a transfer of spending power from

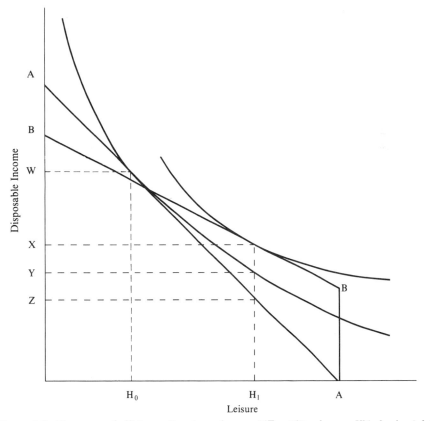

Figure 6.3. Measures of efficiency: Earnings change, WZ; utility change, XY; deadweight loss (change in disposable income less change in utility), YZ. (Figure by University of Wisconsin Cartographic Laboratory.)

high- to low-income families is in general accompanied by a transfer of hours worked the other way, with the change in overall earnings depending on the potential wage rate of those workers who change their hours. The authors find that because high-income wives have an apparently rather high income effect, not estimated but extrapolated, overall earnings changes are positive for all plans, for the CIT/G by as much as $15 billion. But all of these net positive changes are due to the unreliably estimated labor supply change of high-income wives, and none would have welfare significance even if they were reliably estimated, so it seems best simply to ignore this measure in comparing the plans.

Betson, Greenberg, and Kasten give two measures that try to value changes in leisure time. These are the change in the family's utility, XY (they call it compensating variation), and the deadweight loss, or change in disposable income less the change in utility, YZ. Both are evaluated at post-tax–transfer hours (H_1), and both can again be either positive or negative depending on whether the family is facing an increase or decrease in marginal tax rates and income under the plan. Without going into details, both add up to incredibly small amounts over the population as a whole, a fraction of 1%. Between the plans, there is essentially no difference on the deadweight loss measure—here all changes are a fraction of a fraction of 1%—and the generous credit plan has the largest positive effect on overall utility, a mere $4.2 billion out of disposable income of $850 billion. (If I have not perchance compared this number to the right base, it is still small relative to a properly constructed standard error.) The less generous credit plan has a slightly less positive effect, and it in turn has a very slightly more positive effect than the NIT of the same dollar transfer size. Hence for what it is worth, the CIT does seem to be "more efficient" than the NIT, though the margin of superiority is very small, and the meaning of transfers still very unclear. For practical purposes there is no efficiency difference between the plans, and no apparent reason for opposing any of them on grounds of efficiency.

Then Betson, Greenberg, and Kasten turn to some equity measures, illustrated approximately in Figure 6.4. The first is the decrease in the Gini coefficient, proportional to area $A + B$. The second, focusing just on the pretransfer poor, is simply their increase in transfer payments, proportional to area A. The third is the target efficiency of the plan, total transfers to the pretransfer poor divided by total transfers. If most of area C represents preplan transfers, this target efficiency measure would be slightly less than proportional to area $(A + C)$ divided by total transfers.

Of these measures, the most sensible seems to be the change in the Gini coefficient. What is desired here, under reasonable assumptions

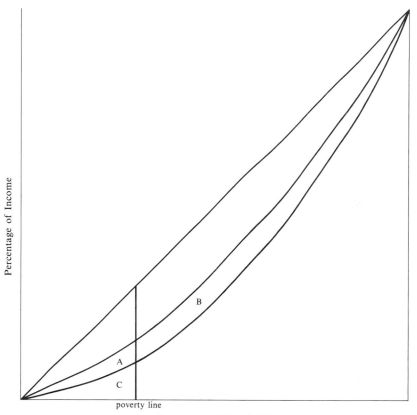

Figure 6.4. Measures of equity: Change in Gini coefficient, proportional to (A + B); change in poverty gap, proportional to (A); target efficiency, less than proportional to (A + C) ÷ transfers. (Figure by University of Wisconsin Cartographic Laboratory.)

about the taste for redistribution of those who favor more of it, is some measure of weighted redistribution—gross redistribution with heavier weights on those dollars that raise incomes of the lowest pretransfer-income families. Since the Gini coefficient is based on cumulative percentages, it does have this property: An equal size transfer to a very poor family will lower it more than will a transfer to a middle-income family; an equal size tax on a middle-income family will raise it more than a tax on a high-income family. Both poverty-based indices impute no value at all to any tax or transfer change for the nonpoor, even though those families may not be very well-off by any less official standard. The target efficiency measure has the additional flaw that it generally *declines* as the extent of redistribution *increases,* not a desirable property of an index of redistribution. One could correct for this problem by holding constant the scale of the transfer, but then the measure says exactly the same thing as the simple change in transfers to the pretransfer poor. So I will consider the target efficiency measure dominated by the change in transfers to the pretransfer poor and not worry about it further.

Betson, Greenberg, and Kasten then follow the standard procedure of just giving the information and letting policymakers make decisions. This information, purged of the irrelevant earnings change and target efficiency measures, is summarized for the three plans in Table 6.9. As was already mentioned, the relevant efficiency measures show such small overall effects as to remove themselves from consideration. The leading plan from an equity standpoint is clearly the CIT/G—the generous CIT plan. But it also entails the largest transfers, $19 billion more than the others. Holding constant their concept of transfers, $16 billion more than in the present system, we can see that both plans lead to a substantial amount of redistribution, but the NIT does win a slight overall victory.

At the technical level, I could devise an equity index better than either of theirs—simply a computation of how much utility changes at each pretax and transfer level. This is, in fact, close to some information the authors do present earlier in the paper for efficiency, but I didn't find a table that did it exactly right. Then the policymaker could insert his or her own weights, computing povertylike indices or Gini indices as the case merits, and there would be no need to choose between the different indicators.

But on a policy level, the conclusion does, I think, stand, that there is not much to choose between the two plans of constant approximate size.

TABLE 6.9
Comparison of Tax–Transfer Plans

Measures	NIT	CIT/G	CIT/E
Efficiency			
Change in overall utility ($ billions)	1.9	4.2	3.1
Change in overall deadweight loss ($ billions)	0.0	0.3	−0.1
Equity			
Change in Gini coefficient[a]	−0.050	−0.062	−0.038
Change in transfers to pretransfer poor ($ billions)	6.6	8.9	1.6

[a]Without labor supply response, to approximate utility changes more closely.

To the extent a choice can be made, the NIT gives slightly more weighted redistribution per dollar of transfer. But I think these differences are not major either, given the much bigger puzzles about how to define and hold constant transfers, whether income is a good measure of well-being, how to value leisure, measure family needs, etc. Ultimately the result of this analysis should, I think, be to leave policymakers free to make program choices based on factors that are not in the model—ease of administration, social stigma effects, and the like.

Discussion

HENRY AARON

This paper provides useful simulations of the differences among income maintenance proposals according to a number of well-established criteria. It grows out of highly professional work in developing a flexible model for analyzing labor supply response to various income maintenance proposals carried out by the authors at the Department of Health, Education, and Welfare. While I have a number of comments about this paper, none should be taken as criticism of the expert work performed by the authors on that model-work, which, in my opinion, would have earned them tenure at most departments of economics in the country.

The paper purports to compare the effects of income-tested and universal programs. In fact, however, it is a comparison of different guarantee-levels and rate schedules, any of which could have been generated by a program that was means tested or universal. The NIT plan is a "high guarantee–regressive rate schedule" plan; the CIT/G plan is a "high guarantee–moderate linear tax rate" plan. The CIT/E plan is a "low guarantee–low linear tax rate" plan. It is apparent that the guarantee could be provided as a matter of right or only upon a showing of need. The rate schedule could consist of two (or more) pieces, one attached to the means-tested program and one attached to the general tax system; or it could consist of one piece applicable to everyone. Moreover, the authors stress that the model they have developed and apply in this paper cannot take account of the administrative differences between a universal and a means-tested program. Because any given rate structure can be achieved within either a means-tested or a universal framework, the choice between these two approaches must hinge on administrative and political considerations, which the authors acknowledge are outside the scope of their paper. In short, the paper should be regarded as an exploration of the impact of different guarantees and different rate schedules, as measured by a variety of indices, and not as a comparison of universal and means-tested programs.

My second comment concerns the problems that the paper encounters because of the necessity of making a large number of simplifying assumptions. In order to simplify the modeling exercise (and in part because of the character of the data used in the exercise), it was necessary to ignore the fact that the existing welfare system, which is the "base case" for the paper, is highly varied across states. Instead, the authors "nationalized" the Wisconsin system and used that as a base of comparison with the various guarantees and tax rates of the NIT and CIT plans. Because they are largely administrative in character, work tests also could not be built into the analysis. To achieve a standard of comparison, the authors assumed the same income tax base in all cases and, in particular, that all transfer payments are taxable and itemized deductions are abolished. Each of those simplifications moves away from circumstances that are likely to obtain under any income maintenance reform and does so in ways that are likely to be significant for some of the measures the authors employ.

A bedeviling obstacle and the source of most complexity in recent efforts to reform the welfare system has been the inconvenient fact that benefits differ so widely from one state to another and the perception that it would be impossible and probably undesirable to erase such differences through a reform of the welfare or tax system. But these differences are correlated with wage rates, race, and other variables relevant to labor supply. The exclusion of such differences across states may have little effect on the differences among the plans under analysis, but it may have some bearing on the effects of all three plans.

The absence of work requirements is perhaps more troubling. It is hard to conceive of a credit income tax accompanied by a work requirement as a condition for receipt of the demogrant. Although such a linkage is logically possible, the essence of the credit income tax, and of the demogrant which it contains, is that the payment is made as a matter of right and without administrative complexities. In contrast, the linkage of work requirements with welfare or with a negative income tax is becoming increasingly common in public discussion and in practical application. But this important characteristic that distinguishes universal from means-tested programs cannot be incorporated into this analysis.

My third comment concerns the pendulum swing among analysts away from the concept of target efficiency as a measure of a program's effectiveness. We seem to have rejected altogether the naive evaluation of programs according to such crude measures as what fraction of additional public expenditures go to a particular target group in favor of recognition that we should be directly interested in how much a particular policy changes the distribution of income or economic efficiency, not in the fraction of an arbitrary set of dollars that accrues to a particular group.

I think that the pendulum has swung too far. Budgets for collective objectives have never been unlimited and they assuredly have limits today. Where budgetary resources are the binding constraint, rational maximization of our objectives will involve a calculation equivalent to an estimation of target efficiency whenever our objectives include income distribution.

My final comment is offered with considerable hesitation. I would urge those who advocate the credit income tax to recognize that they are promoting a Utopia, not presenting a practical program for action in the contemporary United States. The presentation of Utopias is a vital function of academic research. By presenting structures pure in form and logically conceived to promote clearly defined objectives, they clarify thinking and create models which practical reforms can be designed to promote. But because they ignore the numerous conflicting and complex values that actual institutions incorporate, they cannot be used as blueprints. The credit income tax ignores the countless complexities that inhere in the tax and welfare system that have proliferated in the face of efforts by reformers to remove them. The goal of simplicity has been singularly without appeal to the framers of our tax and welfare laws. And with the increase of our data-processing capability, it is not clear why its relative attractiveness should increase. One should not scorn the aesthetic attractions and economic savings of greater simplicity, but something else guides people's actions.

7

Taxpayer Behavior and the Design of a Credit Income Tax

JONATHAN R. KESSELMAN

Introduction

Imperfections in the income tax and transfer system have generated numerous reform proposals.* Yet even the proposed forms have serious deficiencies. An inflation-adjusted comprehensive income base, favored by many critics of the progressive income tax (PIT), would eliminate some distortions of taxpayer behavior and improve equity.[1] However, this reform leaves untouched the progressive tax rate schedule—a basic

*The author thanks Sheila Kesselman for helpful discussion of surtax, categorization, and other issues and for extraordinary editorial assistance; John Helliwell for penetrating comments on the taxation of corporate-source incomes; and Joseph Pechman for provoking thoughts about tax base erosion. All views and any errors are those of the author.

[1]Two recent major reappraisals of direct taxation (U.S. Department of the Treasury, 1977b; Meade, 1978) have tentatively favored an expenditure base over an income base. I thank Mervyn King for the observation that many of the practical advantages of the CIT arise independently of whether its base is income or expenditure. Still, the expenditure base is more likely to require departures from a uniform marginal tax rate for distributional purposes. A nonuniform rate schedule would confront the expenditure tax with incentive and administrative difficulties of its own. Moreover, the CIT facilitates inflation adjustments in the measurement of capital-source incomes and thereby diminishes one of the relative attractions of an expenditure tax.

source of incentive, administrative, and compliance difficulties of the PIT. There would remain incentives for the shifting of incomes between persons and across time. Progressive rate schedules also complicate the unified treatment of corporate-source incomes and the equitable treatment of fluctuating incomes. Critics of the existing cash welfare and in-kind transfer system have generally supported negative income tax (NIT) schemes. But the difficulties of implementing a NIT have become increasingly apparent. The concepts of tax unit, taxable income, and accounting and operational principles would have to be reformulated for consistency between the NIT and the PIT. Fundamental incentive and administrative problems result from the divergence between the NIT marginal tax rate and the PIT bottom bracket rates. Among other consequences, this poses incentives for families to split up. The NIT would require periodic income reports from all beneficiaries, more frequent than annual PIT returns, in order to avoid widespread overpayments.

A credit income tax (CIT) could rectify many defects of current tax and transfer programs while avoiding most drawbacks of a comprehensive-base NIT–PIT. Under a CIT uniform definitions and procedures would be applied to net beneficiaries and net taxpayers. All individuals regardless of their income would receive CIT credits. A uniform marginal tax rate would be applied to a comprehensive income base, with no personal exemptions, at all income levels. The CIT uniform tax rate could facilitate fundamental simplifications to the taxation of corporate-source, business, and investment incomes. It would also eliminate the need for PIT income-averaging provisions, NIT income-reporting forms, and anti-avoidance provisions for income or asset shifts required under the NIT and PIT. Compliance to the CIT would be considerably eased by the expansion of withholding of tax at source, the abolition of almost all nonbusiness deductions, and the automatic payment of credits. Most individuals would need no year-end reconciliation of their tax; the amounts withheld during the year would be their exact liabilities. These features would undermine most opportunities for individuals to avoid tax or to exploit transfers. Reduced avoidance and the simplified provisions of a CIT would ease the administrative and enforcement burdens. Hence, a relatively simple CIT could reduce the real resources used in operating the direct tax–transfer system.

Social equity of the tax–transfer system could also be enhanced by the CIT. First, eliminating many nonbusiness deductions would remove the inequities created by differential knowledge and utilization of the tax code. Second, providing subsidies to institutions based on their charitable receipts would eliminate the inequitable outcome of deductions under a PIT—the unequal subsidization of individuals' donations based on their marginal tax brackets. Third, a CIT should enjoy virtually complete participation of eligible persons. Through ignorance of their entitlements, fear of stigma, or distaste for bureaucratic procedure, some eligible persons are deprived of benefits under income-tested welfare; similar situations would arise under a NIT. Fourth, the CIT offers unprecedented responsiveness to changing individual needs. A net taxpayer automatically becomes a net beneficiary when his income falls to the level where his credit exceeds his taxes withheld. Fifth, the CIT uniform marginal tax rate provides equitable treatment of individuals with fluctuating incomes without the need for income-averaging provisions. Finally, the CIT could retain vertical equity despite its constant marginal tax rate. Substantial progressivity of *average* tax rates would remain, after netting out credits received from taxes paid by each unit. Moreover, part of the measured progressivity of the PIT is illusory, since progressive marginal rates tend in the long run to generate greater inequality of market-earned incomes. Like a proportionate income tax, a CIT will tend to preserve the lower dispersion of earned incomes that would be found in a no-tax economy.[2] In short, the CIT does not require the complex provisions of a NIT–PIT in order to achieve equity among individuals.

Goals of the Study

This study reviews the taxpayer distortions and administrative difficulties of the NIT and PIT. It investigates in detail the optimal programmatic and administrative design of a CIT. I also explore aspects of business, capital gain, and corporate taxation which expand the benefits of a CIT, as well as elaborations of the basic CIT to include a surtax at high incomes and categorical credit levels. My principal criterion in designing the CIT is to maintain simplicity without sacrificing social equity. Some advantages of simplicity are a reduction of taxpayer distortions, the associated economic inefficiencies, and administrative and compliance costs. I shall also identify situations where equity and simplicity may conflict under a CIT. Where it is instructive, I shall refer to tax–transfer provisions and problems in Britain and Canada as well as the United States. In examining compliance and avoidance responses, I focus on incentives such as the shifting of assets and income within the family; the choice of size and composition of the family unit in response

[2]A simple extension of the argument in Montmarquette (1974) confirms this result. Also see the treatment by Kanbur (1979).

to the tax unit definition; decisions to marry based on the treatment of married versus single status; and the timing and form of income receipts, deductible expenditures, sale of assets, and business organization. For the most part I shall sidestep the four economic incentives conventionally analyzed for tax–transfer schemes—work effort, human capital, savings, and investment behavior.[3] This study also does not examine the short-run political feasibility of adopting a CIT. A scheme as radical as the CIT is clearly not on next year's reform agenda. Yet if the potential social and economic benefits of a CIT are more widely understood, it may in time become a politically attractive course as well.

Antecedents of the CIT

Economists and tax practitioners have long recognized the advantages of a uniform marginal tax rate for ease of administration and minimal distortions of taxpayer behavior.[4] In their classic critique of progressive income taxation, Blum and Kalven (1953) attributed most complexities of tax legislation and many avoidance incentives to graduated marginal tax rates. The American Bar Association, in its 1960s project on substantive tax reform, recommended a comprehensive tax base coupled with constant or modestly graduated marginal rates (Willis, 1969). One form of this proposal, a "degressive" system, retained personal exemptions under a flat marginal rate schedule (Galvin and Bittker, 1969, p. 21). Uniform marginal tax rates, at least for a majority of the population, have been a central feature of "social dividend" and tax credit proposals in Britain and CIT plans in the United States. Previous studies have readily cited the simplifications that would stem from a proportionate tax on personal incomes. For example, the ABA report stated that "problems of shifting income forward or backward in time or outward to others, problems of bunched income, deferred compensa-

---

[3]See Betson, Greenberg, and Kasten (Chapter 6 in this volume) for a comparative evaluation of efficiency and distribution under NIT and CIT programs based on their labor supply incentives. Also refer to Masters and Garfinkel's view (1977), that "... the choice between a NIT and CIT should rest on noneconomic considerations rather than on differential labor supply effects between the two plans [p. 247, n.]."

[4]Adam Smith's (1976 [1950 ed., p. 310]) first maxim on taxation urged proportionate rates applied to all forms of income. While the CIT imposes a constant marginal tax rate on all income, it differs from a proportionate income tax on account of its credits. Kay and King (1978) highlight the difficulties caused by marginal-rate progressivity and high marginal tax rates in the current British tax system.

tion, and corporate distributions would diminish substantially in significance [American Bar Association, 1963, p. 10]." A committee of the London-based Institute for Fiscal Studies chaired by J. E. Meade (1978) observed:

> If all income... were subject to a single rate of tax, the administrative problems of the direct tax system could be simplified out of all recognition. Averaging would be unnecessary; a cumulative pay-as-you-earn (PAYE) scheme would have no point; the problem of the taxation of social benefits would disappear; the deduction of tax at source could remove most end-year adjustments of tax; close company problems would not arise; the treatment of trusts would be greatly eased; the treatment of married couples for tax purposes... would be greatly simplified... and much complicated anti-avoidance legislation would become unnecessary [p. 316].

Unfortunately, some of the earlier schemes have failed to allow tax relief for low-income units or have offered personal exemptions without fully examining the incentive and administrative implications. One variant proposed was to supplement a proportionate positive income tax with a NIT for the poor (Galvin and Bittker, 1969, p. 22). Since the marginal tax rate in the negative tax would have exceeded the constant positive tax rate, this plan recalled many of the problems of progressive taxation. A different method of providing tax relief and income support for lower-income units was contained in Lady Rhys-Williams's (1943) "social dividend" proposal. It proposed to pay out weekly allowances to all persons who were working, unable to work, or registered as available to work. To finance the scheme, Rhys-Williams advocated a flat marginal tax rate on all income supplemented by surtax rates on high incomes. Social dividend schemes were refined in Britain over the succeeding years, endorsed by the Liberal Party, and carefully considered by the Royal Commission on the Taxation of Profits and Income (Great Britain, Royal Commission, 1954). A similar proposal for a "tax credit system" later gained official support in a green paper by the Chancellor of the Exchequer (Great Britain, Chancellor of Exchequer, 1972), but this ultimately was not implemented.

Interest in social dividends and tax credits has led the British to investigate many administrative aspects. However, the development of a streamlined scheme has been hindered in Britain by three major concerns. First, the desire to exclude certain groups from receiving benefits implied nonuniversal coverage. Excluded groups were the employable who would not work and, in the green paper proposal, the self-employed and very low wage earners. Second, it was hoped to provide benefits high enough to supersede major elements of the existing transfer system. This goal in turn implied unacceptably high marginal tax rates to finance the scheme. Third, it was always intended to keep the surtax rates on relatively high incomes, so that many problems of progressive taxation would have remained. The Meade report rejected the plan for paying undifferentiated credits mainly for the second reason. It examined in detail an alternative two-tier scheme which would pay low-rate credits on an unconditional basis and higher credits conditioned on obstacles to full-time earnings, such as old age, involuntary unemployment, and sickness (1978, pp. 274–276, 279–294).[5]

In the United States Rolph (1967) proposed a constant marginal rate tax–transfer scheme called a credit income tax. He touted the scheme as an alternative to the negative income tax to redistribute income and "to minimize incentive problems associated with high marginal tax rates, and . . . to reduce radically the complexity of the present federal income tax law [p. 160]." In the 1972 presidential campaign, Democratic candidate George McGovern advocated a CIT plan. Although the redistributional effects of the policy have been studied by Okner (1975) and Watts and Peck (1975), there has been virtually no American analysis of the administrative and compliance aspects. This is in marked contrast to the extensive study given to the practical implementation of a negative income tax. The absence of serious study of the administrative and taxpayer incentive aspects of a CIT may reflect the superficial simplicity of the scheme. In contrast to British proposals, American CIT schemes have been advanced as universal demogrant programs. They would make payments to all residents irrespective of employment and would avoid the cumbersome delivery mechanism for credits suggested in Britain. Moreover, while British proposals retain surtax rates at higher income levels, most American plans contemplate a flat tax rate imposed at all levels on a comprehensively expanded tax base.

Definition of the Tax–Transfer Unit

There are two aspects to defining the family unit for the purposes of taxation or transfer programs. First, rules are required for aggregating individual incomes to determine the unit's tax liability or transfer claim.

---

[5]Another method of reducing the requisite basic tax rate is through the imposition of a surtax on high incomes. This approach is not mentioned in the Meade report, which examined a somewhat analogous expenditure tax. In this plan, a value-added tax is applied for the basic tax rate and is supplemented by filing for an expenditure tax surcharge on high-consumption family units.

Second, rules are needed for scaling the provisions of tax relief and transfer benefits to individual or family characteristics. In defining the tax–transfer unit, equity objectives must be considered along with administrative ease and minimal distortions of household behavior. The Meade report (1978) listed the most important criteria as follows:

> (1) The decision to marry or not to marry should not be affected by tax considerations. (2) Families with the same joint resources should be taxed equally. (3) The incentive for a member of the family to earn should not be blunted by tax considerations which depend upon the economic position of other members of the family. (4) Economic and financial arrangements within the family (e.g., as regards the ownership of property) should not be dominated by sophisticated tax considerations. (5) The tax system should be fair between families which rely upon earnings and families which enjoy investment income. (6) Two persons living together and sharing household expenditures can live more cheaply and therefore have a greater taxable capacity than two single persons living separately. (7) The choice of a tax unit should not be excessively costly in loss of tax revenue. (8) The arrangements involved should be reasonably simple for the taxpayer to understand and for the tax authorities to administer [pp. 377–378].

These criteria are equally relevant in assessing transfer programs. Under any particular tax or transfer structure, conflicts will inevitably arise in meeting these goals.

Aggregation of Incomes

A PIT permits no way of aggregating incomes which can satisfy criteria 1, 2, 3, and 6 simultaneously, or even fulfill conditions 1 and 2 together. The rules used to aggregate income in each country induce some avoidance responses (OECD, 1977a). The U.S. income tax permits limited aggregation in the form of splitting incomes between married persons. As the initial practice was excessively favorable to married partners with dissimilar incomes, different rate schedules are now provided for single and married people. These schedules penalize marriage when the partners have similar incomes. Exemptions may be claimed for the support of a child or other dependent. However, the inability to split incomes with immediate family members or relatives other than spouse has led to many avoidance devices. Some examples are anticipatory assignments of income, family partnerships, gift or sale of assets with leaseback, short-term trusts, and gifts of bond coupons or dividends on shares (Blum and Kalven, 1953; Gutkin and Beck, 1958). Shifting at-

tempts generally involve incomes from property, business, or investments rather than labor earnings. The Canadian income tax uses the
individual as the basis for the tax unit. Incomes are aggregated only
insofar as a claim for marital or dependent exemption is offset by the
relative's income.[6] Anti-avoidance measures are needed both to guard
against individuals' attempts to shift income and to preserve tax progressivity. For example, the income from assets transferred within the
family is attributed back to the donor for tax purposes. Payments to a
person for services rendered to the spouse's business are barred as deductible expenses. Still, several avoidance mechanisms have evolved,
such as interest-free loans between spouses (Aikman, 1978).

The income aggregation problem of the NIT is opposite to that of a
PIT. Progressive marginal rates create an incentive for individuals to
aggregate or average their total incomes. The NIT joins with a PIT at a
breakeven income level, below which the NIT marginal rate exceeds the
PIT first-bracket marginal rate. Thus, the NIT creates an incentive for
individuals to disaggregate their incomes, so long as some members of
the family can be pushed above the breakeven income level. In this
"nest egg" problem, a family would gain by dissociating itself from any
member whose own income bears NIT tax-offset greater than his
additional guarantee. If the NIT rules permitted persons freely to define
their own tax units, nonworking members even in high-income families
would draw NIT benefits. Every practical specification of a NIT has
required income aggregation among persons having specified relations.
These rules impose somewhat arbitrary expectations that individuals
will support other members of the family or household. In some cases,
such as a husband's failure to provide regular support to his family, this
may create undue hardship. Incentives for fictitious separations and
disincentives to marriage or to marital reconciliations may also arise. The
chief alternative, however, would be a return to bureaucratic snooping
into interpersonal relationships. Some such investigations would have
to be retained under any set of rules that does not permit free disaggre-
gation (Klein, 1971).

The CIT eliminates most of the income aggregation problems faced by
the PIT and the NIT. Because all individuals face the same marginal tax
rate under a CIT, they are not normally induced to shift incomes or
income-producing assets within or outside the family. The absence of
exemptions or standard deductions removes the inducement to shift

[6]Because the dependent's income can only reduce the net exemption he generates, this
is not income aggregation in the ordinary sense. Beyond a disregard level, the dependent's
earnings may face the marginal tax rate of the taxpayer claiming him. This violates criterion
3 on the Meade list.

modest amounts of income to dependents of the earner, as may arise under American and Canadian tax provisions. To minimize incentives to shift income toward persons having an overall loss from business or investment activities, the CIT would allow liberal loss carry-overs and loss offsets against earned incomes. Entities such as nontaxable trusts would not be permitted. Finally, intrafamily gifts would not be considered taxable income to the recipient. Under these CIT provisions, the tax–transfer authorities should be relatively indifferent to the methods that private individuals use to aggregate their incomes.

Scaling of Benefits

A PIT may contain personal exemptions or allowances, standard deductions, and nonrefundable credits. These features can be scaled according to the individual's age, family status, family size, or other characteristics. Personal exemptions in the United States follow a "per capita" structure, with special provision made only for old age and blindness. In Canada the size of exemptions hinges on family status, age, and income of the dependent. Scale economies may be implicitly recognized by offering a standard deduction or differentially large exemption for the filer. Transfer programs, such as categorical welfare, have typically scaled their benefits so as to ensure comparable living standards for families of different sizes and compositions. Most NIT proposals have scaled their guarantee levels in a similar fashion. The scaling of benefits for family size may encourage family fragmentation, discourage marriage, induce shifts of property, and raise program enforcement costs.

Under the CIT, credit levels would be determined by individuals' ages but not by their family size. Conditioning of benefits on age, an objective trait that is easy to verify, does not distort household behavior in any way. It might be argued that the savings from scale economies should accrue to persons choosing to live in larger units and should not be offset by the benefit structure. Nonrecognition of family size would augment economic efficiency and, to those who reject criterion 6, equity as well.[7] The CIT definition of the tax–transfer unit satisfies all of the Meade criteria except for item 6 and perhaps straining item 7. However, the choice not to scale for family size will work to the disadvantage of smaller family units, particularly unrelated individuals. If the CIT chose

---

[7]Refer to MacDonald and Sawhill (1978) for a discussion of neutrality and for a contrasting view of equity.

to scale its credits for family size, this would carry larger incremental costs than under a NIT. It would necessitate periodic communications between the CIT authorities and families, which would be a regular feature of the NIT in its income-testing function. The provision of special categorical credits conditioned on traits other than age is examined later in this paper.

Accounting Period and Procedures

A variety of goals related to accounting period and operating procedures have to be satisfied in structuring any tax or transfer program. Bawden and Kershaw (1971) summarized the major accounting design goals for a transfer program as follows:

> (1) Administrative costs are held to a reasonable level. (2) Most families will be able to report income and comply with regulations without assistance (i.e., the self-administrative features of the program are maximized). (3) Disincentive to work is minimized. (4) There is a reasonable responsiveness to the needs of recipients. (5) There is a close relationship between the operations of the national program and state or local public assistance programs. (6) Equity among all recipients is maintained [pp. 258–259].

Two other relevant goals are (7) The timing of income receipts and deductible expenses is minimally distorted; and (8) The arrangements are sufficiently simple for recipients to understand the consequences of anticipated actions. Most of these objectives are applicable to the PIT as well as to transfer programs. Item 6 relates to the fair treatment of units with fluctuating incomes relative to those with steady incomes having the same average level over a specified period. Closely related to this horizontal equity goal is a desire to minimize sporadic disbursements to units that would not be judged as needy over a longer span.

NIT Accounting Problems and Procedures

The NIT tax-offset rate exceeds the lower-bracket marginal tax rates of the PIT with which it would be joined. This divergence poses a serious conflict for the NIT in achieving horizontal equity and minimizing program outlays while also responding quickly to changes in families' needs. NIT payments would be most responsive if they were based on the family's recent, say monthly, income experience. However, this approach would result in monthly payments to many families with full-year incomes exceeding the NIT breakeven level. Annual reconciliations would have to be instituted. There would be difficulties in collecting overpayments from many lower-income units, and the unrecovered sums could substantially increase program costs. Moreover, the short accounting period required to maximize responsiveness would provide the greatest incentives for individuals to manipulate the timing of income receipts, deductible expenses, and working patterns. Alternatively, maximizing equity by basing NIT payments on the family's income for the preceding year or prospective year would be insufficiently responsive to changing family needs. The prospective-year income method would also require a year-end reconciliation (Bawden and Kershaw, 1971; Allen, 1973).

To attain a reasonable compromise between responsiveness and horizontal equity, a complex accounting system has been devised for the NIT. Families are required to file monthly income report forms (IRF) and to report annually some types of steady incomes. While IRFs could be filed less frequently, this would reduce the responsiveness of payments to changes in need. To achieve horizontal equity without annual reconciliations for overpayments, a carry-forward account is established for each family. This account registers the difference between the unit's income and its breakeven income for the preceding twelve months. NIT payments are based on the unit's average income for the preceding three months plus, if this average falls below breakeven, a fraction of any positive balance in the unit's account. Amounts remain in the unit's carry-forward account until they are used to raise average income for computing NIT benefits or for twelve months, after which they lapse (Asimow and Klein, 1970). A carry-forward procedure was satisfactorily implemented in all of the U.S. income maintenance experiments. Considerable experience was gained in the construction and administration of IRFs, and most families learned to complete them without continuing assistance (Kershaw, 1973, pp. 16–18). Thus, the scheme achieved a reasonable compromise of criteria 2, 4, and 6. Still, the need to process monthly IRFs for all beneficiaries raises administrative costs (criterion 1). And it is difficult to imagine that many recipients understand the carry-over procedure—which takes several pages to describe in a law journal and requires a computer to make the computations.

It has been asserted that the use of a three-month accounting period "dilutes" any work disincentives created by the relatively high NIT tax rate. As Bawden and Kershaw (1971, p. 262) and Allen (1973, pp. 53–54) argue, a beneficiary family will experience only one-third of the benefits impact from any short-term change in its work effort in the following month. However, the implications of this point for work incentives are ambiguous. Recipients who understand the system recognize that the benefit impact of a one-month change in earnings will be spread over three months. The total effect on benefits is identical to that of a one-month accounting period—the offsetting tax rate times the earnings change.[8] Recipients who do not comprehend the method of determining payments will be uncertain as to the benefit impact of contemplated changes in their work effort. Without a formal model of worker behavior, we cannot predict whether disincentives will be moderated or accentuated in the presence of this uncertainty. An accounting system could enhance work effort only by confusing recipients about the effective marginal tax rate.

PIT Accounting Problems and Procedures

Progressive marginal rate schedules pose problems for the PIT in withholding the proper amount of tax and in establishing horizontal equity. Fast responsiveness is deemed a lesser concern for tax liabilities than for transfer payments. Taxpayers are less likely than transfer recipients to be poor and in need of immediate relief following drops in income. The PIT can use either of two assessment methods, both of which have a one-year accounting period. Under the American and Canadian "current earnings" method, the worker's personal exemptions and standard deduction are divided into a number of equal amounts, one for each pay period. The employer withholds taxes from paychecks assuming that the worker's total annual earnings are at the current earnings rate on that job alone. Any part of exemptions or deductions not utilized by a worker in one pay period cannot be transferred to other pay periods. Hence, variations in income typically lead to over-withholding of taxes under a progressive rate schedule. This necessitates extensive year-end reconciliations of tax liabilities, which typically yield refunds of tax.[9] Despite the general tendency of the method to over-withhold tax, individuals can have tax due at year-end. This can result from their failure to pay sufficient estimated tax on income sources not subject to withholding or from their obtaining the

[8]This total does not discount the stream of benefits over the period. Also, we ignore the possibility that the household is liquidity constrained, which could introduce differential work responses contingent on the accounting system.

[9]Note that the use of current earnings assessment for a flat-rate income tax with exemptions would also necessitate annual reconciliations.

relief of personal exemptions and lower-bracket tax withholding rates in each of several jobs held concurrently. Of the 83.3 million U.S. returns filed for the 1974 tax year, 78.9% claimed refunds for overpayment of tax, 18.5% had tax due at the time of filing, and only 2.6% had neither a tax due nor an overpayment (U.S. Department of the Treasury, 1977a).

A "cumulative earnings" assessment method can improve the accuracy of tax withholding under a PIT and thus reduce the need for year-end reconciliations. One such system, called Pay As You Earn (PAYE), has been employed in Britain since 1944. The worker's exemptions and other allowances are split into 52 equal sums, one for each weekly pay period. The employer keeps a cumulative year-to-date record of each worker's earnings, tax allowances, and taxes withheld. Using this information, the employer can usually keep each worker's tax withholdings current with his cumulative earnings. For example, in the third week of the year, the employer compares the worker's cumulative earnings with 3/52 of his annual tax allowances and computes the tax due. If the worker's tax liability for the three weeks exceeds his taxes withheld over the first two weeks, the incremental tax is deducted from his paycheck. Conversely, a dip in the worker's earnings can lead the employer to supplement his gross pay on behalf of the tax authority; an unemployed worker can collect such refunds at an employment exchange. PAYE greatly reduces the need for year-end reconciliations, with typically only one-sixth of persons requiring a year-end assessment. However, this assessment method shifts most costs of compliance from taxpayers to employers. Over 400 code numbers are needed to designate workers' tax allowances. Individual workers' codes and changes in them have to be communicated to employers by the tax authorities. Whenever a worker changes jobs, his cumulative records must be transferred to the new employer (Great Britain, Royal Commission on the Taxation of Profits and Income, 1954, pp. 3–8, 26–31; Barr, James, and Prest, 1977, pp. 23–32). The administrative complexities and costs have spurred repeated reform efforts, including the 1972 proposal for a tax credit system.

To facilitate equity for persons with interyear income fluctuations, PIT systems commonly have devices to extend the accounting period beyond one year. These devices include net operating loss carry-back and carry-forward, spreading out of lump-sum compensation, installment sales method of reporting profit, last-in first-out inventory accounting, and carry-over of capital losses (Blum and Kalven, 1953, p. 17). The accounting period can be extended more explicitly through an income-averaging provision, which effectively averages the taxpayer's marginal rates for two or more years. The American system sets a threshold for income change before an individual is permitted to average, so that some distortive incentives remain (Goode, 1976, pp. 234–238). Several of the avoidance responses are discretionary family trusts, family corporations, and distorted billing practices (Blum and Kalven, 1953, p. 16). Canada allows the purchase of income-averaging annuities for certain forms of income as well as performing general averaging by computer. Other methods include block averaging as proposed by the Canadian Royal Commission on Taxation and a British plan for tax reserve certificates (Meade, 1978, pp. 137–139). Vickrey's (1947) proposed lifetime cumulative averaging scheme would extend the PAYE principle to a period longer than the year.

CIT Accounting Procedures

Because of its uniform marginal tax rate, the CIT automatically satisfies most of the eight accounting goals. Widespread source withholding of tax and universal payment of credits, as detailed in a later section, simplify families' compliance requirements. The absence of IRFs and other factors examined below should hold down CIT administrative costs. Horizontal equity for both intrayear and interyear income fluctuations is assured without numerous annual reconciliations or cumbersome income averaging. The payment of universal credits provides a floor for any family incomes that drop suddenly. As Meade (1972) has aptly observed:

> With the Social Dividend type of arrangement everyone is guaranteed the minimum-standard income every week... and the means-tested adjustment is then carried out solely by the taxation of their other income through the accepted machinery of the income tax authorities on a basis which does not require the same degree of precise, prompt response to meet a sudden or irregular change of income flow [p. 313].

The CIT states its marginal tax rate in a straightforward fashion, thus facilitating popular comprehension of the scheme. Relative to the three-month accounting period and carry-forward procedure of the NIT, it is not clear whether the CIT practice will diminish work incentives. Still, it is questionable whether accounting obfuscation should be used to stimulate work effort even if it is effective. The CIT can be readily integrated with other transfer programs by methods discussed in the next and a later section. Finally, a constant marginal tax rate poses minimal distortions to the timing of incomes, outlays, or work patterns.

Definition of Taxable Income

Any income tax or income-conditioned transfer program requires an operational definition of taxable income. The specification of taxable income can be judged against the following criteria for an ideal measure:

1. All net flows from labor, capital, property, or asset appreciation should be counted equally as income.
2. Discretion in the timing of income receipts (capital gain realizations and corporate payouts) and deductible expenses (depreciation accounting) should not materially influence discounted tax liabilities.
3. The form of business organization should not affect tax liabilities.
4. Inflation should not cause the tax system to introduce additional distortions to economic behavior.
5. Taxes should not distort the consumption and financial investment patterns of households.
6. Taxes should not distort the input and financing choices of businesses.
7. The income definition should be reasonably simple for taxpayers to comprehend and comply with; households with no business or self-employment income should not be expected to keep extensive records or to have tax expertise.
8. The taxable income measure should be relatively easy for the tax–transfer authorities to administer and enforce. Clearly, the administrative–enforcement task is eased by reducing taxpayers' opportunities to manipulate their taxable income.

Many NIT proposals have combined an expanded definition of taxable income with an unreformed PIT tax base. This combination can complicate the treatment of family units whose incomes move across the breakeven level or fluctuate around it. Further, it applies different standards of equity to beneficiaries and taxpayers. In contrast, a CIT sets the same definition of taxable income for net beneficiaries and net taxpayers. A uniform income standard avoids the cited administrative and equity problems. The CIT measure of taxable income would be a comprehensive one, modified only by the needs of simplicity in administration and compliance. My CIT provisions for taxable income are summarized in the rest of this section. Appendix 7.A provides a fuller discussion of each provision and justifies it in terms of the earlier criteria. Because an ideal NIT–PIT might also adopt a comprehensive tax base, not all of the potential advantages are unique to the CIT. Still, it will be shown that the CIT uniform marginal tax rate can facilitate broadening the tax base while simplifying the system—in several ways that the NIT–PIT cannot parallel.

Labor, Transfer, and Household Income

Households not running an organized business or making investments commonly receive several types of incomes. These forms include wages and salaries, employee benefits, public transfers and social insurance payments, and gifts and inheritances. Owner-occupied housing and home-production activities also generate implicit incomes which could be imputed for tax purposes. My CIT scheme would treat these income sources as follows:

1. Wages, salaries, vacation or holiday pay, and bonuses would be subject to source withholding at the CIT basic tax rate.
2. Employee noncash benefits that can be assigned to individual workers would be taxed by withholding from wages and salaries. Nonassignable benefits would not be taxed to employees but would also not yield deductions for their firms. These provisions would discourage the inefficient expansion of such benefits and the associated tax avoidance.
3. Benefits of any remaining public transfer programs would be nontaxable, as all recipients face the CIT uniform marginal tax rate.
4. The benefits of any remaining contributory social insurance schemes would be taxable. Contributions to these schemes would be nontaxable; reduced tax withholding would compensate for the employee's contribution without necessitating explicit deductions.
5. Net imputed incomes from owner-occupied housing would not be taxed. However, deductions for mortgage interest and property taxes would generally be disallowed.[10] Real capital gains on these properties would be taxed at the time of realization with a penalty for deferral of tax.
6. In defining taxable income, other imputed incomes from home-production and consumer durables would be ignored.
7. The receipt of gifts or inheritances would not constitute taxable

[10]Expanded revenue sharing to localities and school districts, which benefit from the deductibility of property taxes, might be desired. Also, as explained later, some mortgage interest would be deductible against property earnings under the "pooling" method.

income. This choice does not bar taxing such transactions through other policies such as an accessions tax.

Capital, Business, and Investment Income

Special problems arise in measuring capital-source incomes for tax purposes. Most attempts begin with the Haig–Simons definition of taxable income—the sum of current-period consumption plus accretions to real net worth. The operational problems include assessing annual changes in the nominal values of assets retained by the owners; isolating the changes in the real values of assets in times of inflation; apportioning shares of corporate retained earnings to shareholders; and offsetting the deferral value of postponing tax assessments until owners dispose of their assets. The measurement of capital-source incomes under the existing PIT, corporate tax, and capital gains tax has severely complicated tax administration and distorted taxpayer behavior. While some of the imperfections of the current system are the result of special-interest lobbies, others are inherent in the PIT form. The constant marginal tax rate of the CIT facilitates the integrated treatment of capital gains and corporate-source incomes.

The CIT offers the following provisions:

1. All preferences for capital-source incomes or savings would be abandoned, as the CIT takes a pure income base.
2. State and local bond interest, currently not subject to U.S. federal income tax, would be taxable.[11]
3. Tax would be withheld at the basic rate against interest paid or credited on savings accounts or term deposits minus the inflation rate. No inflation adjustment would be made for cash or checking balances not earning interest.
4. Business liabilities of fixed nominal value would give rise to an income imputation for their declining real value. Comparable adjustments for household debt would not be made.
5. Gains or losses on all assets would be taxed upon realization. Realization would be deemed to occur when the asset was transferred through sale, gift, bequest, or intercorporate distribution.

---

[11]Interestingly, most of the deficiencies from excluding such interest would disappear anyway with the introduction of a CIT. Its uniform marginal tax rate would eliminate the interpersonal inequities and the "inefficiency" of the exclusion in transferring revenues from the federal to lower jurisdictions (see Blum and Kalven, 1953, p. 18).

Computation of the taxable income would utilize Helliwell's (1969, 1973) suggested adjustments for price-level changes and tax deferral over the holding period.

6. Corporate income would be handled under the partnership method by withholding tax against earnings at the CIT basic rate. Dividends and retained earnings would then receive equal treatment, and capital gains on corporate shares would reflect only "goodwill gains."

7. In defining depreciation for tax accounting, capital assets would be allowed inflation adjustments. However, depreciation claims would be restricted to economic rates. These provisions of the CIT may complicate certain mechanical aspects of tax administration and compliance. Yet, they would bring fundamental simplifications to a vast range of individual, corporate, business, and investment taxation matters.

Deductions from Income

Comprehensive tax bases refer to the Haig–Simons definition in determining allowable deductions from gross incomes. Expenditures needed to earn incomes and personal outlays that do not yield consumption benefits are deductible. However, the treatment of expenditures which augment both earnings and consumer satisfactions is ambiguous (Vickrey, 1947, pp. 121–130). The deductions allowed by a CIT could depart substantially from those under a comprehensive base PIT. Deductions against business, self-employment, and rental incomes could be the same; persons with these income sources would still have to file detailed returns under a CIT. But the expenses of earning wages and salaries and costs of certain nonbusiness outlays could be handled differently. To avoid wide-scale filing for deduction claims, the CIT would eliminate some deduction types, make claims subject to high thresholds, or deliver the equivalent reliefs through subsidies. These procedures are patterned after the British tax credit proposal (Great Britain, Chancellor of the Exchequer, 1972, pp. 11–13). Implementing simplified deduction provisions could enhance horizontal equity; as Brown and Dawson (1969) have argued:

> The present tax system attempts to achieve equity essentially by allowing a wide variety of allowances and reliefs for different purposes. Allowances and reliefs cannot achieve equity unless people understand their entitlements. Thus rather than a conflict between equity and simplicity, it may well be necessary to have simplicity in order to achieve equity [p. 76].

The taxpaying public has been found to possess widely varying knowledge about and inclination to use particular deductions for which they qualify (Sandford, 1973, pp. 28–32). Restricting the deductions allowed under a CIT could thus reduce differential utilization by persons in similar circumstances. For each provision, the equity gains through simplification must be weighed against the loss of discriminatory power.

The principal provisions for deductions under a CIT are the following:

1. Interest paid on business-type or consumption-type debt would be deductible in amounts limited by the taxpayer's income from property sources.
2. Deductions for union and professional dues would be replaced by direct subsidies to the organizations. Deductions for special work clothing or tools would not be allowed to employees.
3. Commuting expenses would not be deductible, and a high threshold would be placed on deductions for job-related moves.
4. Child-care deductions would be replaced by direct subsidies to day-care centers, or alternatively they could be retained subject to a disregard level.
5. No deductions would be allowed for educational or training expenses.
6. No deductions would be permitted for households' medical, insurance, or personal casualty expenses. Insurance and casualty costs would remain deductible on properties yielding taxable incomes. An alternative specification would permit medical deductions subject to a high, income-related threshold.
7. Charitable contributions would not be deductible for the donor, but they would generate subsidies to qualifying organizations based on their charitable receipts.[12] Gifts of appreciated assets would be deemed realized for computation of capital gains tax.

Administrative Arrangements

Most proposals for general income transfers have involved cumbersome administrative methods. All NIT plans have required recipients to file frequent income report forms. This arrangement introduced a system of income testing distinct from that of the personal income tax.

---

[12]The subsidy rate on donations received would be $t/(1 - t)$, where t is the CIT basic rate.

Some individuals might fall under the provisions of the NIT and the PIT concurrently; any such overlap would increase compliance and administrative costs.[13] While the New Jersey experiment demonstrated the feasibility of these NIT features, they nevertheless complicated the program and obscured participants' understanding of it (see Kershaw and Fair, 1976). The social dividend schemes of Rhys-Williams and of the 1972 British green paper aimed to exclude employable persons who declined to work. Under the proposed tax credit system, workers were required to present credit entitlement papers to their employers or to social insurance agencies. Those institutions would have disbursed the credits in combination with pay or relief checks (Great Britain, Chancellor of the Exchequer, 1972, pp. 3–9). A CIT would eliminate many administrative complexities of the earlier schemes. Net beneficiaries and net taxpayers would be treated identically within the same administrative machinery. The principal administrative issues of a CIT concern the methods of tax withholding, the nature of taxpayer filing requirements, and the modes of credit payments.

Tax Withholding and Filing

Under the CIT, taxes on wages, salaries, taxable fringe benefits, dividends, interest, pensions, and annuities would be withheld at source wherever feasible. The uniform tax rate of the CIT means that the withheld amounts would fully satisfy the associated tax liabilities. Payers of interest incomes on nominally fixed financial assets would make the requisite adjustments for inflation in their tax withholding. To avoid delays in crediting interest and withholding tax caused by lags in reporting current price indices, the tax agency could extrapolate inflation rates for one month ahead. With these arrangements, tax filing requirements could be eliminated for the great majority of persons. Individuals receiving incomes from nonwithheld sources—self-employment, business, capital gains, rentals, foreign interest and dividends, and noninstitutional interest income—would still have to file returns. Persons receiving

---

[13]The problem of overlap arises whenever the NIT breakeven income exceeds the PIT tax threshold (personal exemptions plus allowable deductions, in the absence of credits). To avoid a "notch" or the interaction of the two marginal tax rates, a common solution has been to extend the NIT high tax rate for a range of lower-income net taxpayers (U.S. President's Commission on Income Maintenance Programs, 1969, p. 154; U.S. Congress, Joint Economic Committee, 1974, p. 213). The administratively simpler expedient of raising tax thresholds to the breakeven level can be very costly. Gottschalk (1978) examines these policy alternatives but does not deal with administrative issues.

substantial amounts from these sources would pay quarterly estimated tax. Deduction claims for moving expense and, under alternative provisions, child-care and medical expense, would necessitate some additional filing. If the thresholds for claiming deductions were conditioned on the individual's income, all payers would have to issue annual income statements. Otherwise these statements would not be needed.

An alternative to wide-scale abolition of filing would be mandatory filing of annual CIT returns by all adults. Universal filing, as originally suggested by Simons for the PIT (1950, pp. 118–120, 148), offers certain advantages. In the first part of the return, each filer would list amounts of income from which tax had not been withheld or sign a declaration that all income received was subject to withholding. Note that income from withheld sources would not have to be listed nor would income statements be needed. Parents would sign declarations for their dependent children. Although most filers would simply sign the declaration, this part of the return would serve as a reminder of the legal obligation to report all nonwithheld incomes. On the second part of the return, filers would list their capital asset holdings and any basis adjustments occurring within the year. For most filers this would entail little beyond occasional recording of home improvements. The annual inventories would ensure that adjustments to asset basis did not escape taxation in later years. They would also assist taxpayers or their estates in computing taxable gains at the time of realization. Incomplete asset records are reportedly a source of frequent problems for tax accountants (Sandford, 1973, pp. 94–95). Because of these advantages, the CIT should adopt universal filing.

Payment of Credits

Payment of periodic credits raises two major administrative questions—to whom and how frequently the payments would be made. Under the CIT each adult would receive his or her own credit payment directly. This approach sidesteps the issue of who controls family budgets and avoids the need to keep track of changing familial attachments. Payments on behalf of dependent children would be made to their mothers, except in cases where the mother was absent or irresponsible. This procedure was proposed by Rhys-Williams (1943, p. 165) and is followed in the Canadian Family Allowances program. The British green paper described the advantages of channeling child credits through the father's employer as lower administrative cost and speedier adjustment of credit levels (Great Britain, Chancellor of the Exchequer, 1972, pp. 19-20). Widespread public opposition to payment through fathers was conveyed to the select committee reviewing the tax credit scheme. Fortunately, under a CIT payment to mothers does not incur the administrative disadvantages present under the British scheme.

Setting the frequency of CIT payments raises considerations similar to those for a NIT. Two factors need to be balanced—making payments frequently enough to relieve families from excessive planning and budgeting, and minimizing the administrative costs of delivering payments (Bawden and Kershaw, 1971, pp. 260-261). The CIT and NIT present the same budgeting problems for units having no current income. Such units receive the maximum support levels which are not reduced by the taxes implicit in the CIT or NIT-PIT program. Families with incomes exceeding the breakeven level might face greater budgeting problems with a CIT than with a NIT-PIT. Tax withholding under a PIT would continuously provide the relief of exemptions, but under a CIT the comparable financial relief would arrive only periodically with credit checks. This situation suggests the desirability of more frequent payments under a CIT. However, the quantitative significance of this differential is questionable. If the frequency of payments were adequate for the budgeting of zero-income units, it should not pose undue strains for units having positive incomes.[14]

Control of Evasion and Fraud

Nonreporting and understatement of income receipts are common forms of evasion under the current PIT. In the United States in 1970, an estimated 6.5% of adjusted gross incomes—in addition to an indeterminate amount of capital gains—were illegally omitted from individual income tax returns (Goode, 1976, p. 33). Underreporting of incomes has been most widespread in situations where there is neither tax withholding nor information reporting (U.S. Department of the Treasury, 1979). A 1979 IRS study found almost 50% of workers treated as independent contractors not reporting any of their compensation for tax purposes; even interest and dividend incomes, subject to information reporting but not withholding, had as much as $14 billion not reported on tax

---

[14]Even with fortnightly payments, some individuals would occasionally need emergency assistance. Rather than establish a special relief program, it might be preferable to allow banks to make individual loans secured by prospective credit payments. Clearly, to avoid the possibility of destitution, the CIT legislation should set limits on the amounts and repayment rates for such borrowings.

returns each year (U.S. Congressional Budget Office, 1980, pp. 100–101). Obtaining full compliance in filing tax returns is a problem at all income levels in the United States. In 1972, 19% of families with incomes of $5000 and less who should have filed did not do so; for incomes over $20,000 the nonfiling rate was still 3% (U.S. Comptroller General, 1979, p. 10). There is also evidence of extensive underreporting of earnings to welfare authorities in the United States.[15] Because it would not withhold incomes at their source, a NIT would similarly be subject to widespread evasion through underreporting. Personal exemptions of the PIT would further minimize the amounts of tax withheld from low earners who were not fully reporting their earnings for the NIT.

A variety of factors in the CIT administrative design would lessen the incentives and opportunities for evasion. First, the broader application of source withholding would reduce the amounts of incomes escaping tax. Since taxes on financial accounts would be withheld at the standard rate, their owners would have no reason to falsify their identities or tax-identifying numbers. Second, the annual statements of assets held would ensure fuller reporting of capital gain incomes. Deductions for realized capital losses would be allowed only when the filer had properly reported the asset acquisition in his next annual return. It is unknown whether the CIT would fare better than the PIT in controlling evasion on other nonwithheld income sources. Its use of a lower marginal tax rate for high incomes might induce fuller reporting, although this advantage would be reversed at intermediate incomes, where the CIT rate exceeds that in the PIT. Third, by curtailing nonbusiness deductions, the CIT would undermine the current practice of evading tax through overstated claims. Fourth, the payment of universal credits would provide current registers of names and addresses to help enforce the filing requirement. Determined nonfilers would have to change their addresses and forgo credits as well as run the risk of being apprehended. Virtually all low-income units not currently filing would have a strong incentive to file, though the extent of their reporting of nonwithheld incomes is unknown. Finally, public confidence in the system's equity would be bolstered by its simplicity, uniform taxation of all incomes, and minimal avoidance opportunities. As Spicer and Lundstedt (1976) have shown, taxpayer feelings about the fairness of a tax program are important motivators of honest compliance.

Under traditional welfare programs individuals sometimes attempt to collect multiple benefits by filing with fictitious identities. The British

---

[15]Halsey et al. (1977) estimate that only 60% of beneficiary earnings in the range of $75 to $300 monthly per family was reported to welfare authorities in Colorado in 1970.

green paper scheme would have nearly eliminated this behavior by delivering credits through employers. With this arrangement a person would have to hold multiple jobs as well as multiple identities to secure additional credits. Conceivably, fraudulent multiple registrations might arise under a CIT, but its administrative procedure should keep them to a bare minimum. Individuals would register for credits only once in their lives. At the program's inception all registrations would be carefully verified through birth and death records. Perhaps the procedures used in establishing the initial Canadian Family Allowance registers could be followed (Schwartz, 1946, pp. 452–459). Thereafter, all native-born residents would be registered at birth, and immigrants could be registered upon receiving the appropriate residence visa. Registrations sought for persons not recently born or newly resident in the country would face special scrutiny. It is reassuring to learn that multiple claims are virtually unheard-of in the Canadian child and old-age demogrant programs.

Surtax Considerations

Applying a surtax on high incomes along with the basic flat-rate tax may be desirable for several reasons. First, public opinion, more concerned about the appearance than the reality of progressivity, might demand a surtax under a CIT. It is instructive that all British social dividend and tax credit proposals have retained a surtax. And following the first politically significant advocacy of a CIT in the United States, Watts (1972) suggested the addition of two surtax brackets. Second, the use of a surtax would permit a reduction in the CIT basic tax rate (see examples in Table 7.1).[16] Third, a surtax would afford the CIT greater flexibility in its incidence. This can be explained with the aid of Table 7.1, which presents estimates of alternative plans that reduce the number of tax brackets while raising the same revenues as the PIT. If the tax base were comprehensively expanded, low proportionate tax rates would suffice. However, even the proportional scheme with exemptions would shift substantial tax burdens from high-income to low- and middle-income units. The U.S. Department of the Treasury (1977b, pp. 160, 163) estimated that a three-bracket PIT scheme could mimic the distributional pattern of the current U.S. personal income tax. In the two tabulated

[16]Note that the tabulated surtax CIT schemes provide multiple brackets, unlike the type analyzed here. Also see the prototype labeled CIT/G in the Betson, Greenberg, and Kasten paper.

TABLE 7.1
Tax Rates in Plans Which Reduce the Number of Tax Brackets

Type of Plan	Tax Base	Tax Rate(s)	Exemptions or Credits/Year	Year of Data	Source
Proportional tax	All personal income	10.4%	None	1962	American Bar Association (1963, p. 10)
Proportional tax	Comprehensive income	13.9%	None	1965	Willis (1969, p. 33)
Proportional tax	Comprehensive income	14.35%	None	1976	U.S. Department of the Treasury (1977b, p. 159)
Proportional tax	Comprehensive income	19.35%	Exemptions $1,500 per capita	1976	U.S. Department of the Treasury (1977b, p. 159)
PIT	Comprehensive income	8% $0–4,600 25% $4,600–40,000 38% $40,000 plus[a]	Exemptions $1,000 per capita plus $1,600 per return	1976	U.S. Department of the Treasury (1977b, pp. 159, 162)
CIT	"Partial reform"	43.8%	Credits: $1,250/adult, $750/first or second child, $500/additional child	1970	Okner (1975, p. 89)
CIT	Comprehensive income	40.2%			
Surtax CIT	Comprehensive income	33.3% $0–50,000 40% $50,000–100,000 50% $100,000 plus	Credits $1,000 per capita	1972?	Watts (1972)
Surtax CIT	Comprehensive income	32.5% £0–4,000 35% £4,000–5,000 40% £5,000–6,000 42.5% £6,000 plus[b]	Credits: £76 age < 17; £188 age ≥ 17; £325 single and age > 65, disabled, widowed, sick, or unemployed	1966	Brown and Dawson (1969, pp. 80, 85)

NOTES: Definitions of comprehensive income vary among studies. For PIT and surtax CIT plans, tax rates refer to marginal rates on bracketed incomes.
[a] These apply to joint returns; for single returns the bottom two bracket rates become 8% for $0–2,800 and 22.5% for $2,800–40,000.
[b] This plan obtains partial financing through a wealth tax.

estimates for a CIT, the requisite tax rates are higher because they must finance the credits as well as generate the existing tax revenues. Okner's (1975, pp. 96–97) computations for several CIT schemes show a shift of tax burdens to middle- and upper-middle-income units; they also show an adverse impact on substantial numbers of units with incomes below $10,000.[17] Because a CIT provides net income transfers to the poor, it is unavoidable that some portions of the income scale will have increased tax burdens. A surtax could help to avoid increased tax burdens at moderate income levels.

Under the surtax CIT, incomes exceeding a specified threshold would face a marginal rate greater than the basic rate. Thus, the surtax logically recalls all of the potential complications of progressive income taxation. A surtax CIT can preserve most of the incentive and administrative advantages of the pure CIT by confining the surtax to a small part of the population and restricting it to a single rate. Assuming that the individual is the tax unit and that no more than 6% of the population fall within the surtax, we can get an idea of the requisite threshold levels. Canadian income taxes are levied on individuals and approximate the proposed CIT tax base more closely than the U.S. tax; thus, we shall illustrate the thresholds on the basis of Canadian data. In 1978, 5.5% of the total population had assessed incomes exceeding C $23,000, 4.2% exceeded C $25,000, and only 2.3% exceeded C $30,000 (Canada, Revenue Canada, Taxation, 1980, pp. 34–39). If we rescale for subsequent wage increases and the greater dispersion of U.S. incomes, it is apparent that high surtax thresholds are implied.

One might question whether high thresholds vitiate the arguments for a surtax. Applying a high threshold lessens the potential to reduce the CIT basic rate; the precise terms of this trade-off are derived in Appendix 7.B. Still, some reduction in the CIT basic rate would be feasible for any threshold level including quite high ones. Choice of the threshold level affects the CIT incidence pattern of net tax burdens. Although a surtax CIT can minimize the increased tax burdens at modest income levels implied by a pure CIT, the optimum threshold from this perspective may not be very high. Regardless, the desired incidence pattern may dictate a higher threshold. Finally, it is unlikely that thresholds of $20,000 or even $25,000 would undermine the appearance of progressivity. Incomes below these levels are not commonly regarded as lavish. In summary, it is uncertain whether thresholds high enough to minimize the administrative and incentive problems of a nonuniform

---

[17]See Table 6.2 in Chapter 6 of this volume for the impacts of CIT/G. More detailed breakdowns not in the chapter indicate that the decreases in disposable income of units of below $10,000 arise predominantly among childless couples and unattached individuals.

rate structure would dissipate the advantages of a surtax CIT. The conclusion will depend upon normative judgments as well as further empirical evidence.

The Tax–Transfer Unit

Imposing a surtax on the CIT raises a substantive issue of the appropriate tax unit for aggregating incomes. Conflicts among the criteria
described in the Meade report (listed earlier) reemerge. Use of the family
basis would avoid incentives for intrafamily shifts of assets (criterion 4),
but it would distort marital incentives (criterion 1) and allow a person's
earnings to affect the tax rate on other family members' work effort
(criterion 2). To avoid the latter disadvantages and to simplify tax administration and compliance (criterion 8), the surtax CIT would adopt the
individual as the tax unit. One problem of the individual as tax unit is
the incentive to shift income-generating properties within families
where at least one member falls in the surtax range. The difficulties of
tracing the original owner of each property and attributing to him the
derived income have been revealed by Canadian experience. Instead,
relatively rigid but simple attribution rules would be adopted (see
Meade, 1978, pp. 382, 392). Children's property income could be added
to the father's income, split equally between both parents, or attributed
to the higher-income parent. Property income of spouses could be taxed
as belonging to the higher-income partner or divided equally between
the two. Attributing half of total property income to each spouse would
tend to favor marriage in a greater range of circumstances.

Administrative and Accounting Procedures

All institutions paying incomes would issue annual statements to
help individuals determine whether they were above the surtax
threshold. Tax would be withheld from all feasible incomes at their
source. Employers could withhold tax at rates reflecting surtax for employees earning above the threshold. Because tax would be assessed by
the current earnings method, this would sometimes result in over-
withholding and require year-end refunds. While over-withholding
would be less frequent than for a PIT, it could be further reduced by
special rules to avoid applying surtax rates to workers whose earnings
only occasionally fluctuated above the threshold. The rules would be
proximate and much simpler than cumulative assessments (see Great
Britain, Chancellor of the Exchequer, 1972, p. 8). Incomes paid on finan-

cial accounts or securities would be withheld at the basic rate. This approach minimizes administrative costs and avoids the partitioning of individuals' portfolios into small holdings. Persons having incomes from nonwithheld sources or earning at rates above the threshold but not withheld at surtax rates would pay quarterly estimated tax.

A surtax CIT would adopt an annual accounting period. The accounting goals (listed earlier) are less easily satisfied by the surtax version than by the pure CIT. Yet, the use of a single surtax rate effective only at high incomes helps to minimize the drawbacks in three ways. First, horizontal inequities in tax burdens would be limited to persons whose yearly incomes fluctuated above and below the threshold over several years. For the bulk of the population, whose incomes vary but remain consistently above or below the threshold, no inequities would arise. Second, the single surtax rate restricts distortions in the timing of incomes and deductions to the relatively few persons who can cross the threshold through manipulation. Third, whereas under a NIT there are difficulties in responding quickly to individuals' changing incomes, the surtax CIT has no comparable problem. Because the surtax CIT kink in marginal rates arises at a high threshold, the affected persons are all net taxpayers with substantial incomes. This group has little need for fast responsiveness.

Use of a single surtax rate rather than a series of progressively graduated rates offers simplicity for taxpayers in planning their economic affairs and in their compliance with the system. A single surtax rate also implies a larger gap between the rates at the threshold. A larger gap aggravates the equity and incentive problems for the relatively few affected individuals. Hence, an income-averaging device would be desirable under a surtax CIT. Fortunately, the single surtax rate facilitates the structuring of a simple income-averaging system. We shall illustrate its principles for a five-year averaging period. An individual would be eligible to average if his income for the current year lay in the surtax range but was below the threshold in any of the four preceding years. He would gain by averaging if the four-year sum of the gaps between his taxable incomes and the thresholds for the respective years were negative. Once the taxpayer had determined his average taxable income for the base period, the averaging could be computed in three or four lines on the tax return.[18] A progressively graduated surtax scale with a high initial threshold would require a more complex averaging scheme.

---

[18]Tax forms could be printed from a central computer file with certain individualized information. One item would be the individual's cumulative averageable income. The other would be a listing of his previous year's asset inventory, so that the taxpayer could simply report changes in basis and acquisitions and dispositions of assets.

Income Definition

Several aspects of defining taxable income need to be reconsidered for the surtax CIT. Under the pure CIT, taxing the credit payments would merely reduce their net value equally for everyone—clearly, a pointless exercise. Under a surtax CIT child credits could be taxed to reduce tax differentiation by family size at higher income levels. The tax would be applied only to parents in the surtax range and at the difference between surtax and basic rates. To provide the same tax–transfer advantage for all children irrespective of parents' income, admittedly a normative choice, we opt against taxing any of the credits. Similarly, public transfer payments could be taxed under a surtax CIT. Because few of these payments go to high-income individuals, applying the surtax differential rate would yield small gains in revenue or equity. Hence, we again opt against their inclusion in taxable income. Both of these choices would obviate mailings of numerous income statements by the public transfer authorities. For reasons detailed in Appendix 7.A, the surtax CIT would tax dividends when paid but might tax corporate retained earnings only when share gains were realized. Subject to safeguards against dividend stripping, the corporate income tax would be abolished.

Allowable deductions and their partial replacement by subsidies raise some new issues for a surtax CIT. In computing the subsidies to charitable institutions based on their receipts, the program would apply only the CIT basic rate. Donors in the surtax range would not obtain any additional leverage for their contributions. Because donations do not affect ability to pay, this simple approach promotes equity. Union and professional dues and child-care expenses are legitimate costs of earning incomes. Under the surtax CIT the direct subsidies used to replace these deductions would be computed by the basic rate. Surtax filers could then itemize their expenses and obtain a credit based on the difference between the basic and surtax rates.

Categorization for Benefits

Basing credit levels solely on individuals' ages could create serious problems for the CIT. With credits high enough to meet the needs of persons having no private incomes, gross budgetary costs would be very large. The high tax rate needed to finance a noncategorical CIT might pose unacceptable work disincentives and barriers to compliance. The requisite basic rate equals the per capita credit plus the per capita general revenues to be raised through income tax, each expressed as a percentage of mean per capita taxable income (see Appendix 7.B). For example, setting the credits at 40% of average income and general revenue needs at 15% of average income imply a 55% basic rate. The tax rate can be reduced by providing high credits only for special categories and paying low credits to the general population. Continuing with our example, assume that the credits at 40% of mean income could be confined to 20% of the population, with the remainder receiving general credits at 15% of mean income. Then the average value of credits would be only 20% of mean income, and the basic rate could be reduced to 35%. The use of low, undifferentiated credits in a CIT would necessitate the continuation of categorical welfare programs.[19] Consequently, categorization is an unavoidable issue for reformed as well as traditional transfer programs.[20]

The trade-off between avoiding categorization and minimizing marginal tax rates is not unique to a CIT. It arises to the same degree for a NIT–PIT program. The trade-off is not a consequence of the CIT paying gross benefits in contrast to the NIT paying net benefits. An example will clarify this statement. Take a program administered along NIT–PIT lines but which applies a uniform marginal tax rate. Assume that the income guarantee of the NIT is set equal to the credit of the CIT and that both programs are noncategorical. While the CIT tests for income through the "tax" system, the NIT applies an income test in determining transfer payments. Still, the net budgetary costs and therefore the requisite marginal tax rates will be identical in the two programs. Providing special categorical benefits to a subset of the population and lower benefits for the rest would reduce marginal tax rates to the same extent in both programs. Appendix 7.B shows further that the NIT–PIT system cannot improve on this trade-off by imposing differential marginal tax rates on beneficiaries and taxpayers.[21]

[19]The Betson, Greenberg, and Kasten study projects major disposable income losses for the poorest single-parent families if categorical welfare were replaced by a NIT or CIT program even with relatively high undifferentiated support levels.

[20]For various reasons Masters and Garfinkel (1977, p. 243) favor the use of a work test under a CIT. They would exempt from the test only the aged, disabled, students, single parents, and one parent in two-parent families. Their approach carries the heavy administrative costs and compliance strains of applying a work test to most of the adult population, including nonaged wives who are childless or whose children are grown. Alternatively, a categorical CIT avoids the pressures for instituting a work test by offering lower credit levels for workers who might reduce their work effort contrary to the "work ethic."

[21]To argue that imposing very high marginal tax rates on low incomes in the NIT avoids the need for categorization despite high guarantee levels merely concedes our point. Namely, high marginal tax rates, for at least a part of the income scale, are required to avoid categorization. The efficiency issue of where in the income scale to impose the higher marginal tax rate is analyzed in Kesselman and Garfinkel (1978).

Role of Categorical Welfare

Could benefit categorization readily be accommodated within the CIT, or is a separate categorical program required? Let us begin by exploring the case where special beneficiaries are subjected to a higher marginal tax than the basic rate. This practice would reduce program net cost. It would also confine the higher marginal rates to individuals who are typically nonworking or less employable than the general population.[22] Applying differential marginal tax rates under a CIT would open the possibility for recipients to underreport their incomes. The resulting incentive, cost, and audit problems would be similar to those of a NIT but less severe; the gains from underreporting would be reduced to the gap between the basic rate and the higher rate. Differential tax rates for special beneficiaries carry no added administrative or compliance costs under a NIT. Income report forms are an integral feature of the NIT, even in the absence of differential marginal rates. Under a CIT differential marginal tax rates would necessitate some version of income report forms. This recalls part of the administrative–compliance costs inherent in the NIT. However, since categorical beneficiaries are typically nonworking and less likely to experience income fluctuations, these IRFs could be administered less frequently.[23] With differential tax rates, a separate categorical welfare program might help to preserve the popular image and comprehension of the CIT. It is debatable whether segregating special beneficiaries in this manner would be more stigmatizing than the NIT–PIT delineation between all beneficiaries and taxpayers. The total earnings of persons who would qualify for special benefits are small. Therefore, taxing them at a higher rate would yield only modest revenues and may not justify the associated administrative costs and taxpayer distortions under a CIT.

In the absence of differential tax rates for categorical beneficiaries, could the CIT accommodate these groups as easily as the NIT? We can evaluate this question by examining the two main operations in administering categorical benefits. First, an agency has to assess and periodically review the credentials of individuals claiming special needs. Since the

[22]The implications for work incentives are ambiguous. Many members of the categories are out of the labor force and are therefore not responsive to tax–transfer disincentives. Still, in terms of labor supply elasticities, female heads and the aged are more responsive than prime-age males. Yet, because these groups are less productive than prime-age males, concentrating higher marginal tax rates on them would reduce the economic losses (see Masters and Garfinkel, 1977).

[23]Note that the Canadian Guaranteed Income Supplement, an income-tested program for the elderly, has only annual IRFs.

NIT agency routinely maintains contact with all recipients, the certification function would fall naturally to it. However, there is no inherent administrative advantage to performing this function within the CIT agency. Certification would carry the same incremental costs if undertaken by the CIT agency or by a separate agency. It is unknown whether divorcing this function from the CIT would enhance the public acceptability of the program; of course, this might increase the stigma of receiving categorical benefits. Second, the transfer agency must disburse the higher benefits to certified persons. It would be administratively economical to combine the extra payment with either the basic NIT or CIT payment. If the categorical portion of each payment were denoted on the check stub, popular comprehension of the program's principles could be sustained. Canadian acceptance of Old Age Security as a demogrant program has not been undermined by the blending of payments from the income-conditioned Guaranteed Income Supplement program. In summary, there are no inherent administrative drawbacks to supplanting categorical welfare with a categorical CIT. But unless the CIT adopted simpler eligibility criteria for its categories, it would incur many of the same administrative costs as categorical welfare.

Categorization Criteria and Methods

I next offer some tentative thoughts on provisions for special benefit categories in a CIT. Among the most important groups requiring special credits are single-parent households. I shall deal with the typical case of female heads; single fathers would be treated identically. To qualify for this category a woman must have at least one preschool child or an older child unable to attend school owing to disability. Eligibility is restricted in this fashion because women are generally able to work once their children are all in school—as indicated by labor force participation statistics. The second criterion for female headship in a CIT would be nonsupport. Each woman would periodically report her major outlays including rent and declare that she had not received outside support. These statements would normally be accepted without investigation, but random audits would be conducted. We choose a criterion of support rather than marriage or cohabitation for several reasons. Outside support can be easily assessed except in cases where a woman had substantial previous assets. Tests of cohabitation are more difficult to implement and more intrusive than a support test. A marital test would be inappropriate in cases where the husband was absent or not providing support. And since cohabitation without marriage is an increasingly common and socially acceptable practice, a marital test would be inadequate. Of course, some incentives for family splitting and nonsupport are inherent in any of these criteria. Note that our suggested provisions would include a woman living with a man who contributes nothing toward household expenses. A cohabitation test would be needed to disqualify her. A single mother working full-time at a comfortable salary would also be entitled to special credits. If it were desired to exclude her, a differential high tax rate could be applied to special beneficiaries.

A special benefit category would be created for the disabled and chronically ill. As in categorical welfare and workers' compensation programs, eligibility would be based on medical evidence. A determination of partial disability would entitle the individual to a lower special credit. Disabled persons who are capable of earning low full-time wages in a sheltered work situation should obtain the full credit. This would encourage their working and possibly aid their rehabilitation. Some persons classified as disabled can still earn substantial incomes. The program could offset their special credits by a higher tax rate on their earnings or withdraw the credits if their earnings exceeded a threshold. Both courses would require income report forms and complicate program administration. In the case of the disabled, an annual retrospective test of earnings may be justified. It would attempt to make only a gross distinction of persons able to earn at normal rates. Disability credits would be paid irrespective of the presence of other working or employable family members. This procedure would avoid family-splitting incentives, minimize administrative costs, and help to defray families' costs of caring for disabled members.

The unemployed are the most difficult group to treat categorically. Freely granting special credits to all nonworking persons could cause serious disincentives, particularly for those with low wage opportunities, and give windfalls to those out of the labor force. To lessen the attractions of unemployment, the special credit would be set below full-time minimum wage earnings. Providing the basic adult credit in addition to special benefits ensures adequate support levels. A work test would be instituted to exclude persons voluntarily out of the labor force from receiving the categorical credits. This test would require each applicant to register for employment and to accept any suitable vacancy. Low-wage public employment projects to which registrants could be assigned would facilitate administration of the work test. Individuals would have to choose between receipt of the special credit and unemployment compensation. Because of the credit's relatively low level and the associated work test, the unemployed would typically prefer to draw the insurance benefits until they had exhausted their entitlements.[24] Voluntary idleness would not disqualify individuals from CIT basic credits. Since these credits replace personal tax exemptions, even idle wealthy bond-clippers should derive their benefits.[25] Family income or assets would not be considered in assessing an individual's eligibility for the special credit. These factors are contrary to the CIT philosophy and would complicate program administration.

A dual scale would be instituted for child credits to provide adequate support in families without an earning member. This provision would permit a relatively low general scale of child credits so as to minimize budgetary cost and the requisite basic tax rate. The general child credits would be set below the incremental costs of raising a child at the poverty threshold. The CIT would pay a higher scale of child credits for children in families where the head was a single parent or where both heads were disabled and/or unemployed. Single parents would receive the higher child credits even when all children had attained school age, although they would lose the special credit for themselves. This would help to compensate for the added burdens of home maintenance and child care of a single parent who is expected to work. A dual scale might provide an incentive for heads of larger families to remain unemployed, but this should be controllable through the relatively stringent work test. Any disincentives remaining for this group may be worth the budgetary savings. Administration of a dual scale for child credits requires no added information beyond the determination of parents' categorical status.

Costs of Administration and Compliance

The operation of any tax or transfer program imposes a variety of costs on society. Economists have traditionally investigated the efficiency costs associated with distortions of work effort, human capital, savings, and investment behavior. For example, Betson, Greenberg, and

[24]Alternatively, the CIT provisions could permit a reduction or abolition of unemployment insurance benefits. This choice depends upon one's philosophy about wage-related income replacement in social insurance programs.

[25]The British tax credit scheme would have disallowed credits to the voluntarily idle, the self-employed, and persons with meager earnings. For these groups it would have continued to provide personal allowances (exemptions).

Kasten (in Chapter 6) estimate the deadweight loss from labor supply distortions of the 1975 U.S. income tax–transfer system at $1.4 billion annually. These deadweight losses can also be evaluated for the CIT uniform marginal tax rate. A "high guarantee" CIT would pay credits equal to the poverty threshold—nearly $5500 in 1975 for a two-parent family with two children and no aged, blind, or disabled adults. Betson, Greenberg, and Kasten estimate that this scheme would raise the deadweight loss of the tax–transfer system by $1.1 billion to a total $2.5 billion, or less than 1% of program cost. The existing PIT–corporate tax system carries additional deadweight loss from distortions of savings, corporate finance, and interindustry resource allocations. Full integration of the corporate tax, as under the CIT, would reduce these components of efficiency costs, with annual gains as high as $5.6 billion (in 1973 dollars; see Fullerton et al., 1980). Moreover, it has been demonstrated that a PIT tends to increase the market premium on risky financial assets (Fellingham and Wolfson, 1978). Like a proportionate income tax, a CIT would decrease investors' risk aversion and facilitate efficient investment patterns. In the present study I shall focus on the administrative and compliance costs of tax and transfer programs, areas usually neglected by economists. The available evidence indicates these costs to be substantial and likely to exceed the more customary economic measures.

This treatment will distinguish administrative, compliance, and third-party costs (see Sandford, 1973, pp. 4–13). Administrative costs will refer to the resources expended by the public agency in collecting taxes and in distributing transfers. These costs include the wages, supplies, rents, maintenance, and depreciation spent in preparing and distributing forms and instructions, receiving and storing completed forms, assessing taxes or transfers, collecting taxes, issuing refunds or payments, auditing, and litigating. Compliance costs will refer to the resources expended by the parties liable to tax or eligible for transfers in satisfying the provisions of the program. These costs include cash outlays, time expended, and psychic discomfort for individuals and, additionally, diversion of regular staff and facilities for firms. A portion of compliance costs might be designated "avoidance" costs, although the distinction is often vague. These are costs incurred in attempts to minimize tax liabilities or maximize benefit entitlements which go beyond simple compliance. Avoidance behaviors include the shifting of assets within the family, the timing of income receipts including capital gain realizations, the formation of family corporations, and numerous other activities. For example, when parents shift assets to their children for tax reasons, they incur notary and registration costs as well as the psychic costs of lessened control. Third-party costs are expenses borne by parties other than those liable for the tax or eligible for the transfer. The most common forms are the expenses of employers and payer institutions in withholding tax and issuing income statements.

Costs of Existing Income Tax Programs

Administrative costs for income tax programs can be derived from agency operating statistics. Table 7.2 presents estimates of administrative costs for programs in the United States, Britain, and Canada. Because several tax programs are jointly administered in each country, there are difficulties in allocating total costs among the constituent programs. Goode (1976, p. 33) argues that, even with extreme assumptions about the allocation of administrative expenses, costs for the 1973–1974 U.S. individual tax were less than 1% of revenues. The 1943–1944 cost estimates for U.S. individual and corporate taxes were based on an "informal" breakdown by the IRS (Martin, 1944a). Applying the 1943–1944 ratios of administrative costs to 1976–1977 statistics, I estimate the recent cost of individual taxes at 0.96% of revenues. This figure supports Goode's estimate; still, it is probably inflated owing to the secular growth of average taxpayer liabilities and administrative improvements. The recent figures for "all federal" taxes in the United States (0.51%) and Canada (1.24%) reflect primarily the individual and corporate taxes. The figure given for the British tax (1.39%) is that for all taxes collected by the Inland Revenue; Sandford (1973, p. 45) argues that this approximates the individual tax alone. Higher administrative costs for individual taxes in Britain compared with the United States probably result from the use of cumulative assessment in the former. Surtax and capital gains tax, which are administered separately in Britain, are more costly.

Costs incurred by parties other than the tax-collecting agency are much more difficult to assess. Unfortunately, my search of the literature has not uncovered studies of the costs of avoidance behavior or the psychic component of compliance costs. The available estimates of compliance and third-party costs appear in Table 7.2. Martin's (1944b) figure for compliance costs for the 1941 U.S. individual income tax (1.2%) is admittedly a "guess." The 2.4% estimate for 1964 includes compilation and computational costs based on rates charged by a commercial tax assistance firm. A detailed study of British individual income taxes found compliance costs to be 3.9–7.3% of revenues. Because of self-assessment by American taxpayers, their compliance costs almost cer-

TABLE 7.2
Costs of Collecting Individual and Corporate Income Taxes in Three Countries

Type of Tax	Type of Cost	Estimated Cost	Country	Year of Data	Source
Individual	Administrative	1.68% of revenues	U.S.	1943–1944	Martin (1944a, p. 134)
Individual	Administrative	1.39% of revenues	Britain	1969–1970	Sandford (1973, p. 44)
All federal[a]	Administrative	0.51% of revenues	U.S.	1976–1977	U.S. Commissioner of Internal Revenue (1978, p. 134)
All federal[a]	Administrative	1.24% of revenues	Canada	1978–1979	Canada, Revenue Canada, Taxation (1980, p. 252)
Surtax	Administrative	1.89% of revenues	Britain	1970–1971	Sandford (1973, p. 8)
Capital gains	Administrative	2.58% of revenues	Britain	1970–1971	Sandford (1973, p. 8)
Individual	Compliance	1.2% of revenues	U.S.	1941	Martin (1944b, p. 203)
Individual	Compliance	2.38% of revenues	U.S.	1964	Willis (1969, p. 60)
Individual	Compliance	3.92% to 7.32% of revenues	Britain	1970	Sandford (1973, p. 44)
Individual	Third-party	0.68% of remittances	Canada	1960	Bryden (1961, p. 24)
Individual	Third-party	0.62% to 1.03% of revenues	Britain	1970	Sandford (1973, p. 44)
Corporate	Administrative	0.71% of revenues	U.S.	1943–1944	Martin (1944a, p. 134)
Corporate	Compliance	0.10% to 3.24% of taxable income[b]	U.S.	1960	Johnston (1963, p. 72)

NOTE: Meanings of terms and measurement methods differ by study; see the original sources.

[a] Primarily individual and corporate income taxes; in Canada the provincial income taxes (except for Quebec) are also collected by the federal government.

[b] Costs as a percentage of corporate tax revenues are approximately twice the tabulated values.

tainly exceed the British figures. Most third-party costs result from employers withholding income tax from paychecks. Cumulative assessment in Britain (0.6–1.0%) proved more costly than current-earnings
assessment in Canada (0.7%). Because of scale economies, the percentage costs for U.S. corporate compliance and Canadian third parties were
inversely related to firm size. Although the evidence is fragmentary, it
suggests that the total costs of collecting the U.S. individual income
tax—not counting psychic or avoidance costs—may exceed 6% of revenues.

Costs of Existing Income Transfer Programs

The administrative costs of income transfer programs can be computed from agency statistics. Table 7.3 summarizes the administrative
costs as a percentage of benefits paid under programs in the United
States, Britain, and Canada. No figures for the compliance or avoidance
costs of beneficiaries or third-party costs have been uncovered.[26] The
transfer programs are classified as "universal" or "tested." A universal
program does not apply extensive income tests or frequent reviews of
eligibility; its benefits may be restricted to a subset of the population
defined by age, disability, past contributions, or other easily verified
traits. A tested program has extensive income tests, frequent reviews of
eligibility, and/or conditioning traits that are relatively intrusive to verify. As seen in the table, universal programs have the lowest administrative costs in all countries. For example, the American universal program of veterans' pensions and compensation costs only 1.3% of benefits to administer. An individual's benefits from this program are highly
stable and, once approved, tend to continue for long periods. In contrast, the service-oriented tested program of U.S. veterans' welfare and
miscellaneous benefits has very high administrative costs (95.2%). The
lowest administrative cost tabulated pertains to a universal program,
Canadian demogrants (0.8%).[27]

[26]A good illustration of transfer-induced third-party costs arises in employers' added
costs of interviewing job applicants who are merely trying to fulfill interview quotas for a
work test.

[27]This estimate is biased upward because it includes costs attributable to other programs (see Table 7.3, note a) but is also biased downward because it appears to omit the
costs of issuing and mailing payment checks. An estimate for the total costs involved in
administering and disbursing Family Allowances in 1978-1979 is about 1.0% of gross
payments (see next footnote).

TABLE 7.3
Administrative Costs of Income Transfer Programs in Three Countries

Program Type	Country	Program	Total Benefits (millions)[a]	Administrative Cost as % of Benefits	Year of Data
Universal	U.S.	Old age, survivors, disability, and health insurance	$19,794	2.5%	1965-66
Tested	U.S.	Public assistance	$ 5,797	12.1%	1965-66
Tested	U.S.	Unemployment insurance	$ 2,132	11.8%	1965-66
Unclassified	U.S.	Workmen's compensation	$ 1,900	4.6%	1965-66
Unclassified	U.S.	State temporary disability insurance	$ 493	3.0%	1965-66
Tested	U.S.	Veterans' welfare and miscellaneous benefits	$ 62	95.2%	1965-66
Universal	U.S.	Veterans' pensions and compensation	$ 4,365	1.3%	1965-66
Universal	Britain	National insurance benefits	£ 3,775	3.8%	1973-74
Universal	Britain	Family allowances	£ 339	3.5%	1972-73
Tested	Britain	Supplementary benefits	£ 1,420	13.4%	1975
Tested	Britain	Family income supplement	£ 12	8.3%	1975
Tested	Britain	Local rent rebates	£ 134	5.2%	1975-76
Tested	Britain	Local rent allowances	£ 27	11.1%	1975-76
Tested	Britain	Local rate rebates	—	15.4%	1975-76
Universal	Canada	Family allowances and old age security	C$ 6,416	0.8%[a]	1978-79

SOURCES: U.S. data are from Merriam and Skolnik (1968, pp. 195–209, 231–234); British data are from Meade (1978, pp. 305–306); Canadian data are from Canadian Tax Foundation (1979, p. 118).

NOTES: Designations of program types are defined in the text. Total benefits are program expenditures excluding administrative expenditures, for the U.S. programs. Some programs, such as OASDHI, have secondary in-kind services along with cash transfers.

[a] The C$ 53.3 million reported for "administration—income security and social assistance" is attributed entirely to the two demogrant programs, although portions were spent in administering the Canada Assistance Plan and two income-tested programs for the aged. An earlier estimate—0.87% for 1956–1957—confirms the order of magnitude for the two demogrant programs combined (Vadakin, 1958, p. 71).

253

Projected NIT Costs

Previous studies have estimated the costs of administering a NIT program at less than 3% to greater than 10% of benefits. The lower estimate was based on an early NIT proposal to cover 10.5 million households. Annual administrative costs of $200 million were projected assuming quarterly income report forms but drawing little guidance from field operations (U.S. President's Commission on Income Maintenance Programs, 1969, pp. 61–62, 155). Higher estimates resulted from the income maintenance experiments and the use of monthly IRFs. The costs of administering more frequent IRFs were partially offset by reduced costs of auditing needed to ensure the accuracy of reported incomes. A detailed study of NIT organizational requirements placed "the total administrative costs well below $1 billion, probably in the neighborhood of $700 to $800 million, or about $150 per case per year [Kershaw, 1973, pp. 12, 21]." The NIT program proposed at that time would have paid *net* benefits averaging less than $1500 per case, so that administrative costs would be above 10%. Another study based on the New Jersey income maintenance experience projected the direct administrative costs for a similar national program at $90 per family per year in 1970 (Kershaw and Fair, 1976, pp. 17–18). Adding in the overhead costs of administration and allowing for subsequent inflation suggests total current annual costs over $200 per family or over $3 billion in aggregate. While the NIT restricts payments to a minority of the population, the operation of its breakeven income threshold extends coverage to large numbers of families above the poverty line. Still, these surprisingly high estimated costs must reflect primarily the requirements of income testing. Implementing benefit categories under a NIT would further increase its administrative costs. No estimates of NIT compliance or third-party costs are available.

Projected CIT Costs

The costs of operating a CIT can be appraised by examining its basic functions. These are the payment of credits, the optional application of categories, and the collection of revenues. The Canadian demogrant programs offer the best guide to the cost of paying CIT basic credits. The required administrative procedures are identical—initial registrations, printing and mailing monthly checks, recording address changes, and canceling registrations of emigrants and the deceased. I take the total administrative costs for the Family Allowance program of C$6.25 per family, which yields C$0.52 per monthly check issued.[28] This figure apportions a share of all ongoing administrative costs, including registrations, to each check. It is appropriate to use a cost estimate expressed in dollars per client rather than a percentage of benefits, as the latter clearly is sensitive to the benefit scales. Still, this figure may somewhat overstate the costs of administering credits under a CIT. Individuals are registered for Family Allowance at birth but their eligibility expires at age 18; under a CIT the registration is valid for a lifetime. I ignore this difference and apply the Canadian figure to estimate the cost of administering monthly basic credits for the U.S. population. Since all child credits would be paid to mothers, the total number of checks issued in each period equals the number of adults. The resulting estimate of the yearly cost of administering basic credits is about $800 million.[29]

Incorporating categorical credits in a CIT would increase administrative costs because of the need to assess individuals' eligibility. Although there is no firm basis for estimating these added expenditures, the administrative costs of categorical welfare programs offer an upper bound for the CIT. Categorical welfare has administrative complexities not present in implementing the CIT categories. For example, U.S. public assistance provisions have included frequent caseworker contact, tests of assets and cohabitation, and periodic income reporting. A categorical CIT would have none of these features—except income reporting if differential tax rates were imposed on special beneficiaries. Overall, the eligibility criteria for CIT categories suggested earlier are less demanding to administer than those characteristic of welfare. Hence, the administrative cost of CIT categorical credits should prove to be less than the 12% of benefits needed to administer U.S. public assistance. Similarly, the relative clarity and simplicity of the CIT categories should reduce compliance costs and psychic costs of beneficiaries.

The costs of tax collection under a CIT cannot be projected in any reliable way. Yet, we can establish that these costs would be far less than the total operating costs of the current PIT–corporate tax. Numerous features in the CIT design would minimize distortions of taxpayer be-

---

[28]This figure was cited by Monique Begin, Minister of National Health and Welfare, during questioning (Canada, *House of Commons Debates*, 1978, pp. 1629–1630). Comparisons with figures given by Mendelson (1979, pp. 73, 113) based on unpublished data support the presumption that Begin's figure includes the costs of issuing and mailing the monthly checks. Excluding these costs, Mendelson placed the 1976–1977 administrative costs of Family Allowances at C$3.06 per family.

[29]The estimate is based on just over 150 million civilian U.S. residents aged 19 or over in 1978 and has been converted at an exchange rate of US $0.85 per C$1.00. Note that comparisons with the projected NIT administrative costs for 1969 of about $750 million should consider the doubling of prices since that time.

havior; these have been cited throughout this study. Each of these features would reduce the costs expended by individuals in tax-avoidance maneuvers and the administrative costs of anti-avoidance measures needed under the current system. Eliminating exemptions and many nonbusiness deductions would lessen compliance costs. Relatively few people would ever have to hire tax advisers or tax-return preparers. A majority of returns would require little more than a signature under a CIT and additionally a listing of income receipts under a surtax CIT. The tax authority would have correspondingly reduced costs of reviewing, auditing, and storing tax-return information. The CIT would reduce employers' tasks of withholding tax against wage and salary payments. Employers would not have to obtain information from employees on the number of their dependents, as required under PIT withholding. Corporate-source incomes would be taxed directly by withholding at the CIT basic rate. As compared with the PIT–corporate system, the pure CIT would hence save individuals' compliance costs of reporting dividends and paying the associated taxes. The administrative costs of comparing company dividend statements with amounts reported on returns and auditing individuals for unreported dividend receipts would simultaneously be eliminated. These cost savings would also apply for individuals earning below the threshold of a surtax CIT.

Several features of the CIT would increase costs to particular groups but reduce the total costs borne by society. Requiring financial institutions to withhold tax and make inflation adjustments would increase third-party costs. However, the added costs would be modest for the majority of firms, which handle customer accounts by computer. Moreover, it is cheaper in the aggregate to have firms withhold tax than to have numerous individuals pay their own tax on financial incomes. The CIT would shift individual compliance costs onto third parties by converting some nonbusiness deductions into subsidies. Claims for subsidies would be made by institutions based on their charitable receipts, by various employee groups based on their dues, and by child-care centers based on their fees. The administrative, auditing, and aggregate compliance costs should be lower than where the tax agency has to deal with large numbers of claims by individual taxpayers. Using the Helliwell treatment of capital gains would increase taxpayers' computational tasks. Requiring taxpayers to report all asset acquisitions and changes in asset bases would also raise compliance costs. But these increases would be more than offset by reduced avoidance and administrative costs resulting from the neutral treatment of capital incomes. In summary, the CIT would reduce the overall costs of revenue collection below that of the existing PIT–corporate tax.

The Role of the CIT in Public Finance

Replacing the PIT–corporate tax with a CIT would have implications for many facets of public finance policy. I shall investigate the CIT in relation to stabilization policy, joint administration with other direct taxes, and tax reform without welfare reform. My evaluation will center on the ability of the CIT to perform these functions without sacrificing its essential neutrality and simplicity. I shall also consider which public transfer and social insurance programs could be replaced by a full-scale CIT.

Short-Term Stabilization

The stabilization properties of the CIT can be analyzed in terms of built-in features and suitability for discretionary changes (see Green, 1973). The CIT uniform marginal tax rate would relinquish the chief automatic stabilizer of progressive income taxation. Removing tax from the inflation component of capital incomes would further reduce the stabilizing properties of the CIT. The surtax CIT would reduce stabilization by deferring tax on corporate retained earnings until gains were realized. However, shareholders' realization of gains before cyclical peaks and the resulting tax payments might offset this effect. Despite the progressive rate schedule of the surtax CIT, a desirable adjustment procedure would eliminate its stabilizing properties. To prevent a secular increase in the fraction of population covered by surtax, the threshold would be raised routinely at the growth rate of nominal per capita income. With short lags in this adjustment, the surtax CIT would be no more stabilizing than a pure CIT. One element of the CIT might tend to promote stability, although its quantitative influence may not be large. The assured receipt of monthly credits by members of the working poor would help to cushion their consumption responses to income declines. In general, the automatic stabilizing properties of the current PIT–corporate tax would be greatly attenuated by a CIT. This is a direct consequence of the CIT design and hence cannot be rectified without loss of neutrality and simplicity.

The CIT basic rate or credit levels could be changed quickly to meet the needs of countercyclical policy. For minimal incentive effects, it would be preferable to adjust credit levels when revenue requirements changed.[30] Categorical benefits permit flexibility in varying the basic

---

[30]See Simons's (1950, p. 33) suggestion that rates be maintained for many years and exemption levels be varied for stabilization purposes.

credits while maintaining support levels for especially needy groups. Exactly offsetting changes would be made in the categorical credits. If the requisite variations in basic credits posed undue stress on the working poor, the CIT tax rate could be adjusted. Note that the comprehensive tax base of the CIT would allow small changes in the basic rate to produce large revenue changes. A surtax CIT could concentrate short-term tax changes on higher-income individuals. A rate-averaging provision for capital gains would minimize any incentive effects. However, as for a PIT, concentrating tax changes on the higher-income population may be relatively ineffective in altering aggregate consumption. To influence investment spending or other desired business behaviors, the CIT could implement subsidy policies. With full integration of the corporate tax and abolition of accelerated depreciation, the traditional tax incentives for business would no longer apply. In summary, the CIT can be used for discretionary stabilization without sacrificing its neutrality or simplicity.

Other Direct Taxes

The CIT could easily subsume other elements of the direct tax system. Most of the administrative and compliance costs of state income taxes could be reduced by joint operation under a federal CIT. Each state could choose its own tax rate but would have to accept the same tax base and tax unit as the national scheme. Taxes on wages and salaries would be collected on the basis of the individual's work location. Employers in each state would simply withhold tax at the basic rate plus the state rate. This would avoid the incentive effects and administrative complications of imposing a residential tax basis on states having substantial cross-border commuting. All other forms of income would be taxed on the basis of the individual's place of residence. Basing state taxes on financial incomes on the location of the assets—to facilitate withholding— would generate interstate competition for highly mobile assets. State tax on nonwithheld incomes would be paid at year-end filing and quarterly for larger receipts. States desiring to do so could supplement the national basic credits for their residents. Joint administration of state income taxes with a national CIT would not affect the neutrality of the latter. The distortions of taxpayers' choices of residential and work locations are already present in state income taxes.

The United States, Britain, and Canada levy payroll taxes to finance major pension and social insurance programs. Labor earnings are taxed at a proportionate rate up to a ceiling level of annual earnings. The CIT could easily absorb payroll taxes by adding percentage points to the basic rate. Several advantages would stem from this change. It would eliminate the ceiling on annual earnings subject to tax and bring non-labor incomes into the tax base. The broader tax base would neutralize current distortions of firms' input choices favoring nonlabor inputs and highly paid occupational groups. Because the existing payroll tax structure is regressive, this amalgamation might also overcome objections that the CIT is insufficiently progressive. The elimination of earnings ceilings on the consolidated payroll taxes would reduce administrative and compliance costs. Employers would no longer have to keep track of when each employee reached the ceiling or furnish breakdowns of payments under the ceiling. Taxpayers would no longer have to claim refunds of excess payroll taxes withheld from multiple jobs, as they now do in Canada and the United States. The amalgamation would not undermine any of the desirable properties of the CIT. However, it would likely necessitate new rules for benefit entitlements under the pension and social insurance plans.

CIT as Tax Reform

Up to this point I have described the CIT as a program to restructure the welfare and taxation systems together. Alternatively, the CIT could serve as a program of fundamental tax reform alone. In this role the CIT would set low basic credits, offer no categorical benefits, and leave the existing welfare system intact. If desired, the benefit scales of welfare could be reduced to neutralize the basic credits. Credits would be set at a level to create the desired tax thresholds, and the basic rate would be set to finance the credits plus the required net yields from income tax. For example, let us assume the chosen tax threshold for a single adult to be $4000 annually. Credits of $800 per adult would meet this threshold if the corresponding basic tax rate were 20%. Although the credits would serve mainly to replace exemptions and nonbusiness deductions, they would provide some net benefits to workers earning below their tax thresholds. Even with low credit levels, all the reduced administrative, compliance, and third-party costs of revenue collection would be realized under a CIT. In contrast, there would be little attraction to implementing a NIT at low support levels. The NIT is essentially an income transfer device with no tax simplification features.

Other Income Support Programs

Many existing income support programs could be phased out with the implementation of a full-scale CIT—one with high general credit levels or a categorical variant that could supplant traditional welfare. Dispensable programs in the United States include Aid to Families with Dependent Children, Supplemental Security Income, and General Assistance. Since Food Stamps are conditioned on family size and income, they could readily be absorbed in the general credit levels. In Canada the categorical provisions of Social Assistance, as well as the Guaranteed Income Supplement for the elderly, could be eliminated. Canadian demogrant programs of Family Allowances and Old Age Security could also be deleted. The basic CIT credits would be geared to age so as to provide higher levels for the elderly. This scaling would also allow the redistributional components of benefit scales for public old-age pension programs to be eliminated. Similarly, certain redistributional elements within the unemployment insurance system would have less justification under a full-scale CIT. Many people would still wish to retain the pure insurance aspects—that is, the *ex ante* nonredistributional provisions—of social insurance programs. Hence, it is unlikely that a CIT would completely dismantle contribution-linked old-age pensions, unemployment insurance, and workers' compensation. A CIT would probably retain health-care programs for the poor and the elderly, if not provide access on a universal basis.

Political Economy and CIT Implementation

A tax–transfer proposal as radical as the CIT is unlikely to be implemented in a single move.[31] Fortunately, the plan is amenable to gradual implementation. The main problems of transition are to avoid major shifts in groups' relative positions and to build support for successive changes. A first step would be conversion of personal exemptions into credits.[32] These could initially be nonrefundable so as to reduce the administrative requirements. Standard deductions could be increased to

[31]Nevertheless, Kurz (1977) presents the intriguing theoretical result that the problem of revelation of preferences will lead society to choose a CIT format. In his findings, the credit level is half the mean income, and the basic tax rate is 50%. His analysis does not consider any incentive problems other than the revelation of preferences.

[32]The shifting Canadian balance among credits, exemptions, and demogrants, particularly in the treatment of dependent children, and the associated administrative factors are critically reviewed in Kesselman (1979).

reduce itemized deduction claims. The tax base would be gradually expanded by including omitted income types and deleting unjustifiable deductions. Since these changes primarily affect higher income units, they would be compensated by reduced PIT higher-bracket rates. At a later stage standard deductions could be eliminated and lower-bracket tax rates raised. A simultaneous increase in the basic credit levels would help to compensate low- to middle-income units. Still, eliminating the standard deductions would favor larger families relative to smaller families—an intentional aspect of the CIT design. Interest and dividends could have tax withheld at source at the bottom-bracket rate after abolishing the "zero rate" bracket. Credits could be paid out on a refundable basis, with parallel decreases in categorical welfare support levels. The uniform rate and comprehensive base of the CIT would be achieved through further changes in tax rates and taxable income items. At this point the individual could easily replace the family as the tax unit. After attaining a uniform tax rate, the CIT would replace deductions for union and professional dues, child-care expenses, and charitable contributions with institutional subsidies. The substitution of categorical credits for categorical welfare would be the final step.

The CIT treatment of capital-type incomes involves major changes from current PIT–corporate provisions. Features of the CIT should ease some of the adjustment impacts. The market value of nontaxable bonds is determined by the marginal tax rate of persons at the margin of purchasing them (currently about 30%). If the CIT basic rate were close to this rate, the bonds could be phased out with minimal wealth impacts. Allowing inflation adjustments on capital gains would help to offset their full taxation. Indeed, these two changes together could reduce taxes on capital gains in inflationary periods.[33] Integrating the corporate tax in a CIT should be popular with shareholders. Dividends would no longer be doubly taxed, and the inflation adjustments in capital gains and depreciation accounting would help offset deferral charges on share gains.

Erosion of the Tax Base

Our analysis of the CIT has assumed a comprehensive tax base. However, influential groups with vested interests would oppose some of the

[33]U.S. corporate shares sold in 1973 yielded actual capital gains tax liabilities aggregating $1138 million. Against this, Feldstein and Slemrod (1978, p. 114) computed a yield of $1193 million from fully taxing the capital gains with inflation adjustments and no limitations on loss deductions. Deferral charges were not considered in this study.

moves toward a comprehensive base. This opposition might appear to threaten the financial viability of a CIT. A severely restricted tax base might raise the requisite basic tax rate to undesirable levels. Nevertheless, the marginal tax rates of a NIT–PIT could be equally sensitive to erosion of the tax base (see Appendix 7.B, "proportionate" erosion case). Therefore, a comprehensive tax base may be no more critical a financial prerequisite for a CIT than for a NIT–PIT.

Posing the erosion problem in an extreme form, would a CIT still be desirable if restricted to the current American tax base? Only personal exemptions would be eliminated, and standard deductions would be replaced by a disregard level for itemized nonbusiness deductions. Even with this "worst case" tax base, some net gains would stem from the CIT uniform marginal tax rate and individual tax unit. Source withholding on interest and dividend payments would fulfill the associated tax liabilities. Most persons would have their total tax liabilities satisfied without year-end adjustments. The individual tax basis would remove incentives to shift assets within families or to change family structures. The uniform tax rate would eliminate differential subsidies for charitable contributions, the inequities of failing to tax public transfers, the inefficient transfers of revenue to localities via tax-free bonds, and other distortions caused by progressivity. The major drawback to adopting a CIT with the restricted tax base might be an insufficiently progressive pattern of tax incidence.

Advantages of Simplicity

Around 40 years ago it was argued that extending the income tax to lower income units would promote "tax consciousness." It was felt that heightened awareness of taxation would elicit more responsible demands on public spending (Strayer, 1939, pp. 75–112). Families who had to save to meet income tax payments naturally knew their tax liabilities. The introduction of source withholding has not appreciably diminished the degree of tax consciousness (Strayer, 1939, pp. 139–146; Enrick, 1963, p. 170). However, the current tax–transfer system or a NIT–PIT relieves beneficiaries from tax, which encourages their feeling that budgetary growth is costless. In contrast, a CIT would augment tax consciousness by applying basic-rate variations for changed revenue needs to even the lowest income units. The simplicity of the CIT should further enhance voter responsibility. Rhys-Williams (1953) argued that "The only effective safeguard, both against abuse of the public services and evasion of taxation is a clear understanding, by everybody, of the principles under-lying the whole structure [p. 145]." The principles of a tax–transfer scheme could hardly be simpler or more comprehensible than those of a CIT. Current PIT–corporate provisions and NIT–PIT proposals fall be-yond most people's comprehension.

The simplicity of the CIT would provide some protection against pressures for special tax concessions. As noted by the Meade commis-sion (1978), "A tax system based on one or two simple clear-cut princi-ples will make unjustifiable concessions to special interests more obvi-ous and therefore easier to resist [p. 19]." Under a CIT lobby groups would be unable to obfuscate their arguments for tax relief by referring to progressivity, exemptions, or corporate tax complications. They would have to divert their efforts toward gaining direct subsidies. Many existing tax concessions would not likely have been approved in the form of outright subsidies (see Surrey, 1973). Consequently, concessions to special interests are less likely to arise under a CIT. The CIT uniform marginal tax rate might further moderate pressures for tax base erosion. It would eliminate the high nominal top-bracket rates of the PIT, which have generated many of the worst departures from a comprehensive tax base. Appending a NIT to the PIT–corporate tax would not mitigate incentives for base erosion. Indeed, a relatively high NIT offsetting tax rate might create new demands for concessions.

Potential and Limitations of CIT Form

Adoption of a CIT would yield large and diverse social and economic benefits. The CIT would provide income support for the working poor and replace categorical welfare with less intrusive means. Unlike the NIT, the CIT would respond immediately to dips in individuals' incomes and treat net beneficiaries and net taxpayers identically. The noncategor-ical portion of the CIT would enjoy the virtually complete participation rate of non-income-tested demogrant programs.[34] While its categorical aspect would face some of the same problems as a NIT or traditional welfare, the simpler qualifying characteristics and the absence of income testing in the CIT would offer decided advantages. Additionally, the CIT could supplant the PIT, the corporate income tax, and a portion of social

[34]A study of two Canadian income-security programs for the aged found 99–100% take-up of demogrants and only 83–89% take-up of income-tested transfers by eligible persons (Beavis and Kapur, 1977). Also see Meade (1978, p. 304).

insurance. A CIT could reduce private compliance and avoidance costs, socially unproductive tax consultancy, and tax–transfer administrative and enforcement costs. Rough figures suggest that administering credits to the entire population would be less costly than applying a NIT to a restricted group. The typical individual would register for credits once in his life, notify the agency of address changes for the mailing of monthly credit checks, and file a simple annual tax return. I think it would be very hard to imagine a less intrusive tax–transfer system. A CIT would further restore neutrality to a wide range of economic, financial, and social decisions confronting households and firms. The program would improve equity by eliminating opportunities for differential exploitation of current complex welfare and income tax provisions. The reduced incentives for evasion, fraud, avoidance activities, and tax base erosion under a CIT could go far toward restoring integrity to the tax–transfer system.

My evaluation has strongly favored credit income taxation over the current system, an improved PIT, and the NIT proposal. Therefore, in concluding, it is incumbent on me to review the limitations of the CIT form. The CIT credit scaling does not recognize scale economies of households and may unduly penalize smaller family units. It may provide excessive tax differentiation for larger families at higher incomes, although this could be remedied by taxing the credits under a surtax CIT. The single marginal tax rate of the CIT reduces the possibilities of graduating average tax rates net of credits. The surtax CIT can create greater rate differentiation, but it must maintain a high threshold to preserve gains in simplification. Under a CIT the use of direct taxation as an instrument of social policy would be limited primarily to income support. The comprehensive tax base eliminates a wide range of incentive features, from home ownership to corporate investment. Moreover, the replacement of certain deductions with subsidies reduces the control over amounts claimed. Subsidies to child-care centers would complicate linking payments to mothers' earnings, and subsidies to charitable institutions would bar ceilings tied to donors' incomes. Last, a CIT would attenuate the automatic stabilizing properties of the direct tax system. Some of these limitations could be reduced by introducing greater administrative and compliance complexities and greater distortions of taxpayer behavior. In designing the CIT, I have consistently opted for administrative simplicity and taxpayer neutrality. It remains for others to examine the administrative, taxpayer incentive, cost, and economic implications of CIT designs based on different views of equity or desirable program goals.

Appendix 7.A: Elements of Taxable Income for CIT

The considerations leading to the definition of taxable income for a CIT are detailed in this appendix. The eight general criteria for specifying taxable income have already been listed. I will draw heavily on previous analyses of a comprehensive income tax base. The cited literature provides additional background and, on some points, contrary views. My treatment is intended to be suggestive rather than exhaustive.

Labor, Transfer, and Household Income

EMPLOYEE BENEFITS

The CIT would differentiate between noncash benefits which are readily assignable to individual employees and those which ·cannot be assigned. Assignable benefits, such as employer payments of premia for life insurance[35] and pension plans[36] would be taxed by withholding from wages and salaries. The costs of nonassignable benefits, such as recreational facilities, would in effect be taxed by denying the employer deductibility for their costs. This approach would make employers neutral in the choice between compensating their workers via cash and noncash benefits; they would be willing to substitute fringe benefits dollar-for-dollar of *net* employee compensation. Hence, workers would be compelled to evaluate consumption via fringe benefits on the same terms as private purchases. A comprehensive base PIT could similarly tax assignable benefits. However, an ideal PIT has no fully satisfactory counterpart to the CIT device for taxing nonassignable benefits, because of workers' differing marginal tax rates and the divergent rate of tax on

[35]Life-insurance policies other than one-year term policies have a savings component. Current PIT provisions fail to tax most of the interest on policy reserves, which induces inefficient purchases of insurance as a savings vehicle. Proposals to tax the interest income might be facilitated by the uniform tax rate of the CIT (see Goode, 1976, pp. 125–133; U.S. Department of the Treasury, 1977b, p. 60; Meade, 1978, pp. 140–141).

[36]This method would apply to an employer's defined-contribution pension, which is assignable. Earnings of the fund could be taxed on the realization principle (see next subsection of this appendix) or on annual inflation-adjusted accruals. Employer contributions and fund earnings in defined-benefit pension plans would be treated with the CIT's method for nonassignable benefits. Other complications may bar such extensive changes (see Sunley, 1977, pp. 77–84; U.S. Department of the Treasury, 1977b, pp. 56–58; Meade, 1978, pp. 141–143).

business income. The failure to tax many employee benefits has encouraged their inefficient expansion under the PIT (see Goode, 1976, pp. 114–117; Sunley, 1977, pp. 76–92; Clotfelter, 1979).

PUBLIC TRANSFERS AND SOCIAL INSURANCE

Benefits of public transfer programs remaining under a CIT would not be taxed. Taxing these benefits at the uniform CIT rate would merely require them to be scaled up proportionately in order to maintain net levels of income support. This move would increase administrative costs but accomplish nothing on balance. The CIT would tax social insurance benefits upon receipt. Since employee premia produce no current consumption benefits and are not voluntary savings, they would be tax deductible. Employers could reduce tax withholding on wages and salaries to eliminate the need for explicit deduction claims. Because of the compulsory nature of social insurance, individuals cannot choose to divert savings into the plans to gain the benefits of tax deferral. If transfer components of social insurance programs were retained under a CIT, their levels would have to be raised to compensate for the tax. To maintain horizontal equity, the PIT would have to tax both transfer payments and social insurance benefits (see Goode, 1976, pp. 100–109; Sunley, 1977, pp. 92–105; U.S. Department of the Treasury, 1977b, pp. 58, 60–63).

IMPUTED RENTS AND INCOMES

The CIT would not tax imputed rents on owner-occupied housing. It would disallow all homeowner deductions and impose an inflation-adjusted capital gains tax on realizations. This approach would eliminate most of the current inequities against renters and inefficient incentives for use of housing services. For example, disallowing homeowner deductions in 1977 would have raised U.S. taxable incomes by 81% of the amount from imputing net rents (Hellmuth, 1977, p. 166). Additionally, the CIT approach avoids the administrative and compliance costs of imputing net rents. The difficulties of measuring imputed rents are so great as to make equity gains questionable (Goode, 1976, pp. 117–125; Kurtz, 1977; Merz, 1977; U.S. Department of the Treasury, 1977b, pp. 85–89; Meade, 1978, pp. 220–221). Because of still greater measurement problems, the CIT would not attempt to tax the imputed incomes from consumer durables, cash balances, food produced and consumed on farms, and household services for family use (see Goode, 1976, pp. 139–143). Clearly, a comprehensive base PIT could follow the same rules.

GIFTS AND INHERITANCES

Individuals' receipts of gifts and inheritances would not constitute taxable income under the CIT. This approach departs from the Haig-Simons treatment of gifts, one which has not commanded widespread acceptance. Applying the CIT uniform rate would levy taxes unrelated to the donee's economic circumstances and merely penalize giving. To assess accurately the donee's lifetime standing, a separate cumulative accessions tax would be appropriate. Of course, the PIT is not much better suited than the CIT for assessing the donee's true circumstances. The PIT tax rate varies but considers only the donee's income in the year of receiving the gift (see Goode, 1976, pp. 98–100; Meade, 1978, pp. 40–42, 137, 347, 392–395).

Capital, Business, and Investment Income

EXISTING DISTORTIONS

The current PIT treatment of capital, business, and investment incomes distorts taxpayer behavior. Taxing the inflation component of all capital-source incomes discourages savings and distorts the interindustrial allocation of investment. Preferential rates encourage the conversion of ordinary incomes to capital gains. Several devices are anticipatory redemptions of stock, sales of leases and service contracts, and low salaries for corporate owner–managers. Taxing capital gains at realization causes inefficient "lock-in" of funds. It inhibits firms from reallocating funds, households from shifting their portfolios toward desired risk-return holdings, and the transferring of homes and firms to owners who value them most highly. A required holding period, as in the United States, induces investors to realize losses quickly and to defer realization of gains. Differential treatment of capital gains has also necessitated complex anti-avoidance provisions. Certain gains are nonrecognized or rendered ordinary income, such as recapture of depreciation and intangible drilling costs. There are also provisions for collapsible corporations, corporate reorganizations, involuntary conversions, like-kind exchanges, and nontaxable dividend distributions (see Gutkin and Beck, 1958; Wetzler, 1977, pp. 127, 139–140).

Current capital gains provisions and nonassignment of retained earnings necessitate a corporate income tax. Since dividends are doubly taxed, corporations tend to lock-in their earnings. Reduction of double taxation through dividend exclusions (U.S.) and dividend tax credits (Canada) has been incomplete. Moreover, the nondeductibility of dividends for corporations distorts their choices between debt and equity financing. The extra burden of corporate tax discourages corporate business organization and reduces savings and capital accumulation. The differential impacts of corporate tax further distort interindustrial output and price patterns (see Fullerton et al., 1980).

REQUIRED ADJUSTMENTS

Neutral tax treatment of capital-source incomes requires fundamental changes from current provisions. The requisite adjustments depend on the nature of the asset. First are assets with fixed nominal values which pay or credit all current earnings to their owners. An adjustment is needed to remove the inflation component of earnings from the tax base. Second are assets with variable nominal values which pay out or credit all current earnings other than appreciation in value. Examples are works of art, undeveloped land, marketable bonds, and unincorporated businesses. These assets require a charge for deferral of tax until the gains are realized as well as an inflation adjustment. The full adjusted gain should be subject to tax. Third, corporate equities have variable nominal values but may retain a portion of current earnings. A method is needed to tax retained earnings or to safeguard against payout of dividends exceeding current earnings. The CIT provisions for these asset categories follow.

NOMINALLY FIXED ASSETS

The decline in the real value of savings accounts or term deposits would generate offsetting deductions. This inflation adjustment could be computed by the financial institution and incorporated into the CIT withholding. Negative real interest rates would yield net credits to the account. Inflation adjustments would not be allowed for cash or checking balances earning no interest, as their liquidity services are not taxable income. Fixed-nominal-value business liabilities would generate income imputations for their declining real values. Because interest on business debts is deductible, the imputed incomes merely reduce the net deductions to real interest paid. The CIT would not impute such incomes for household debt against owner-occupied housing and consumer durables. An imputation would be inappropriate, since interest on these debts would not usually be deductible under the CIT. This approach would also simplify CIT administration (see Helliwell, 1973, p. 169; Meade, 1978, pp. 114–115, 135–137).

An alternative treatment of nominally fixed assets could simplify compliance by exploiting the uniform marginal tax rate of the CIT. Nominal interest receipts would be fully taxable and nominal interest costs fully deductible. This treatment would rely on financial market adjustments to equalize the expected real net-of-tax yields on nominally fixed and variable assets. Lenders would be compensated for the tax paid on the inflation component of their fixed-asset incomes. Note that departures of actual inflation rates from expected rates would yield nondeductible real capital losses or nontaxable real capital gains under this procedure. While this may be a minor violation of equity, there are also inefficiencies for resource allocation. The market adjustment mechanism involves a shift of resources from nominally fixed to variable assets and corresponding intersectoral shifts of resources. It seems preferable to have financial institutions adjust for inflation than to invoke these distortions. Hence, the CIT would not exploit this aspect of its uniform rate—a potential not present in the PIT (see Feldstein, Green, and Sheshinski, 1978).

CAPITAL GAINS

The CIT would apply Helliwell's (1969, 1973) "realization" method for capital gains taxation. Changes in asset values would be fully taxed when realized, subject to certain adjustments. Transfer through gift, bequest, or intercorporate distribution, as well as through sale, would constitute realization. The cost basis of each asset would be written up for price-level changes over the holding period. The inflation-adjusted gain would then be multiplied by a penalty factor for the value of tax deferral.[37] Additionally, the CIT might tax the adjusted real gains at the five-year average basic rate. This feature would prevent discretionary realizations from exploiting rate variations. Since the basic rate is likely to be relatively stable from year to year, at least in peacetime, the importance of this feature is uncertain. And as noted by Vickrey (1947, pp. 146–147), investors may be unable to gain from predicting tax rate changes if tax policy is countercyclical.

The method of taxing capital gains under a CIT eliminates inefficiencies and inequities of existing treatment. Taxing at realization also avoids most of the problems of taxing at accrual—valuation difficulties, taxpayer illiquidity, and administrative complexity. The method removes the inequitable taxation of inflationary gains. Charging the taxpayer for deferral would drastically reduce lock-ins and conversions of ordinary incomes to capital gains. This method has been criticized for assuming a particular temporal pattern of asset appreciation (U.S. Department of

---

[37]The CIT uniform tax rate simplifies constructing tables of deferral factors. However, Helliwell (1973, p. 168) reports that these figures are not highly sensitive to the tax rate. Also see Wetzler (1977, pp. 152–153) and Meade (1978, pp. 132–135, 148–149).

the Treasury, 1977b, pp. 81–82).[38] Yet, any resultant timing distortions are of second-order compared with current deferral incentives. Short of implementing an accrual system, in which the actual appreciation pattern is assessed, no further improvement is possible.

CORPORATE SOURCE INCOME

Taxing dividends as paid and taxing share gains by the realization method does not resolve all distortions for corporate-source incomes. Corporations would have an incentive to retain earnings in early years and later pay out dividends exceeding their earnings. This maneuver would save shareholders the deferral charge on capital gains; yet, this might be more than offset by the loss of inflation adjustment. To avoid this incentive, the CIT would tax all corporate income at the basic rate. This method would fully integrate the corporate and individual income taxes. Because income would be taxed as it accrues, and dividends and retentions would be taxed equally, incentives to lock-in capital would disappear. Any tax-induced bias between debt and equity finance would also be eliminated. The CIT uniform tax rate avoids the conventional difficulties of the partnership integration method. No shareholder would have to pay additional taxes on retained earnings; there would be no need to apportion retained earnings across classes of securities; and it would not be necessary to keep track of share trades to assign earnings. In defining corporate income, inflation adjustments would be allowed on plant and equipment, but depreciation rates would be reduced to realistic levels. Small corporations would bear the same tax rate, since the CIT tax unit is the individual and not the corporation.

With the preceding arrangements for taxing corporate retained earnings, an adjustment is required to avoid taxing retentions again at the time shares are sold. Under the Helliwell method, the cost basis of shares is written up for inflation over the holding period. The cost basis must be further increased by the cumulative net retained earnings (or rise in book value) per share multiplied by approximately half the change in price level over the holding period.[39] Simple tables can provide the taxpayer with the figures needed for these calculations. This

[38]Brinner's (1973) proposal to base deferral factors on rates of appreciation of assets rather than a specified interest rate has been critiqued by Folsom (1978).

[39]A more refined method would rescale annual claims on retained earnings of shares to dollars of the cost-basis year and add them to the original cost basis. Then, at the time of realization, this cumulative adjusted cost basis would be scaled up to current-year dollars. However, if this level of complexity and paperwork were acceptable, it might be attractive to obtain annual share prices and to adopt full accrual accounting in the taxation of capital gains.

procedure ensures that mainly goodwill gains in corporate shares bear capital gains tax at the point of realization. Note that the procedure assumes relatively steady inflation rates and retained earnings rates. Shareholders who found these assumptions adverse might be given the option of deeming realizations on their shares at any time.[40]

Adoption of the partnership method poses similar problems for a surtax CIT as for the PIT. Under the CIT only high-income individuals would have to pay the incremental surtax on retained earnings. Still, the other administrative and compliance difficulties of the method would remain. To reduce these strains, an alternative approach may be better suited for the surtax CIT. Tax would be withheld at the CIT basic rate on dividends paid. Surtax payers could meet their incremental liabilities from net dividends received. Share gains, which now include cumulative retained earnings as well as goodwill gains, would bear capital gains tax when realized. Long-term and short-term shareholders in a firm would have divergent preferences as to reinvesting unusual transitory profits. Hence, it is not clear whether corporate funds will suffer from lock-in. Any firm distributing dividends greater than its current earnings would pay an additional tax reflecting the average deferral value on its cumulative retained earnings. Taxpayers in the surtax range would pay their extra liabilities. Aside from this safeguard against excess distributions, the surtax CIT could effectively abolish the corporate income tax.[41] Of course, some device would be required to capture tax on the retained earnings of foreign shareholders. For this reason, and to reduce the delays in tax collection, it may still be preferable to invoke a form of the partnership method under a surtax CIT.

Deductions from Income

INTEREST PAID

The CIT would allow taxpayers to deduct their interest payments in amounts not exceeding their net income from financial and business

---

[40]Even without this option, Meade (1978) has noted that ". . . if the taxpayer felt that this compulsory smoothing procedure was working against his interests, then, to the extent that he could control the timing of realisations, the remedy would lie in his own hands [p. 133]."

[41]This method follows the spirit of Simons's (1950) compelling argument for abolishing the corporate income tax if capital gains are fully taxed. Note that Simons (pp. 127–129, 134–136) carefully considered but rejected adjustments for deferral and price level in computing taxable capital gains.

assets. This "pooling" method offers the best compromise among tax-payer neutrality, administrative ease, and equity. No interest deductibility would cause assets to be sold, even when their yields exceeded borrowing costs. Allowing all interest to be deducted, as in the current American practice, encourages efficient holding of financial and business assets but confers benefits for consumer debt. It is unjustifiable to allow interest deductibility for owner-occupied housing and consumer durables, since their imputed incomes are not taxed. The Canadian tax attempts to disallow interest deductions for consumer debt by making deductibility contingent on "pairing" debt obligations with financial or business assets. Still, individuals with net business or financial assets manage to deduct interest on consumer debt by rearranging their loans. The CIT pooling procedure would eliminate the avoidance and enforcement costs by automatically allowing deductibility in this circumstance. Pooling provides incentives for efficient asset holdings and restricts the associated concessions for consumer debt (see Bale, 1973; Goode, 1976, pp. 148–152).[42]

WORK-RELATED EXPENSES

The CIT would restrict deductions for costs of earning wages and salaries. This would reduce administrative–compliance costs and the problems of distinguishing between necessary costs of earning and consumption outlays. Direct subsidies to worker organizations would replace deductibility of union and professional dues. This method would reduce the number of units for audit and obviate refunds to individuals. No deductions would be allowed for tools or special clothing supplied by the worker. This practice might impel firms to furnish essential items or raise compensation for the additional tax. No deductions would be allowed for commuting expenses, because residential choices have a large consumption component. Job-related moving expenses would be allowed, but the number of claims would be reduced by imposing high disregard levels (for example, $800 or 10% of first-year income in the new job). A disregard may not be inequitable, as workers often move for desired change of locality along with job changes (see Goode, 1976, pp. 77–96).

---

[42]For assets not producing substantial current income, such as undeveloped land, pooling might unduly constrain interest deductions. Either a carry-over provision for interest paid or optional use of the pairing method would be introduced. Certain business activities, such as self-employment, commingle incomes attributable to capital and labor. For these, the ceiling for deductions would be the depreciated value of tangible business assets times the loan interest rate rather than net business income.

CHILD-CARE EXPENSE

The CIT would replace child-care deductions with equivalent subsidies to child-care centers. This approach saves on filing, verification, and enforcement costs of the current system. It also prevents the deduction of "child-care" expenses incurred for routine housekeeping services. Because transfers would be paid directly to centers, it would be harder to restrict funding for children of working parents. To overcome this, parents would file with their center declarations that they are working. Directly subsidizing the centers distorts the parents' choice between in-home and out-of-home care. To provide relief for in-home care, the CIT might also provide deductions with disregards to eliminate small claims.

EDUCATIONAL AND TRAINING EXPENSE

The CIT would allow no deductions for educational and training expenses. Ideally, human capital investments would be treated like tangible capital investments; the initial costs should be depreciated over the useful life of the assets. Variants of this have actually been proposed (Vickrey, 1947, pp. 123–126; Goode, 1976, pp. 83–91), but they are inevitably complex. The major cost of most educational or training activities is the student's foregone earnings. The absence of tax on foregone earnings is like a fast write-off of an expense that should be capitalized. Students are typically in a low-income stage of their lives. Therefore, under a PIT they would fare better by imputing the foregone earnings and depreciating them over their principal earning years. The CIT uniform tax rate makes the current practice more favorable to students than the ideal method. The CIT disallowance of tuitions and training expenses would not necessarily damage equity or efficiency, as these costs usually have a large subsidy component.

MEDICAL EXPENSE AND CASUALTY LOSS

The CIT would not allow deductions for households' insurance or medical costs or their casualty losses. Properties yielding taxable incomes would continue to qualify for insurance and casualty deductions. These rules provide efficiency incentives and administrative–compliance savings without major loss of equity. Since most risks are insurable, they can be reduced to regular, predictable outlays. The enjoyment of nonbusiness properties has implicit insurance costs; hence they are a consumption expenditure. The CIT could alternatively allow medicalexpense deductions with income-related thresholds higher than the current American or Canadian disregards. The CIT uniform tax rate would yield a standard "coinsurance" rate for all persons in place of the PIT differential treatment. The CIT would eliminate current American tax incentives for making suboptimal outlays to reduce casualty loss risks and for underinsuring casualty or medical contingencies (see Goode, 1976, pp. 153–160; U.S. Department of the Treasury, 1977b, pp. 89–91, 97–98).

CHARITABLE CONTRIBUTIONS

The CIT would pay subsidies to qualifying organizations based on their charitable receipts. Gifts of appreciated tangible assets would be deemed realized for capital gains tax. These procedures would encourage private support for socially beneficial activities without the undesirable features of current American provisions. First, implicit differential subsidies from PIT deductions would be replaced by uniform subsidies on all receipts (see text footnote 12). Second, it would be easier to audit the organizations than the individual donors, who often inflate their claims for cash contributions. Third, the public benefits of the organizations might be scrutinized more closely with explicit public outlays in place of tax expenditures. Insofar as private donations affect the use of public funds, increased public review would appear justifiable. Fourth, the CIT would eliminate incentives to donate appreciated tangible assets without paying capital gains tax. Valuation problems would be greatly eased, as the deemed values would be inconsequential for the treasury. Understatements of value would reduce the subsidy of the donee institution as well as decrease the donor's capital gains tax (see Goode, 1976, pp. 160–168; U.S. Department of the Treasury, 1977b, pp. 95–97).[43]

Appendix 7.B: CIT Administrative Design and Marginal Tax Rates

Relations between three aspects of the CIT administrative design and marginal tax rates are explored in this appendix. The features include the level of surtax threshold, the presence of benefit categorization, and the degree of tax base erosion. It is shown that the last two factors face the same trade-offs in minimizing marginal tax rates in the CIT as in a NIT–PIT. Terms used repeatedly in our analyses are defined as follows:

[43]Alternatively, the CIT might not deem the realization of capital gains on appreciated gifts but provide subsidies based only on the donor's cost basis.

y = taxable income of a tax unit;

$f(y)$ = density function of the distribution of taxable incomes;

K = surtax threshold for surtax CIT; threshold of integration for NIT–PIT;

$F_2 = \int_K^\infty f(y)dy$ = proportion of population with taxable incomes of K or higher;

$\bar{y}_1 = \int_0^K yf(y)dy;$

$\bar{y}_2 = \int_K^\infty yf(y)dy;$

$\bar{y} = \bar{y}_1 + \bar{y}_2$ = population mean per capita taxable income;

t_1 = basic tax rate in surtax CIT; NIT offsetting tax rate in NIT–PIT;

t_2 = surtax rate in surtax CIT; positive marginal tax rate in NIT–PIT;

t_c = basic tax rate in pure CIT;

C = per capita credit (noncategorical);

R = per capita general revenue to be raised through income taxation.

Note that terms $\bar{y}_1$ and $\bar{y}_2$ are aggregate forms and not per capita mean values. Other notation will be introduced as needed. Except at one point, all the analyses ignore the work incentive and other behavioral impacts of variations in programs. Hence, the distribution of income, $f(y)$, will remain the same across program designs and program types. Throughout it is assumed that all programs have the same tax base and tax unit.

Surtax Thresholds

The pure CIT must satisfy the relation for budgetary balance:

$$t_c\bar{y} = C + R.$$

We now define a new term:

$$b = (C + R)/\bar{y},$$

and it is clear that t_c must equal b. The budgetary condition for a surtax CIT is

$$t_1\bar{y}_1 + t_2\bar{y}_2 + F_2(t_1 - t_2)K = C + R.$$

For a given threshold level K and ratio b, imposing a surtax at rate t_2 ($>b$) permits a relative reduction in the basic rate from t_c to t_1:

$$\frac{t_1}{t_c} = \frac{\bar{y}}{\bar{y}_1 + F_2 K} + \frac{t_2}{b} \left(1 - \frac{\bar{y}}{\bar{y}_1 + F_2 K} \right).$$

Necessarily, $F_2 K < \bar{y}_2$, so that $\bar{y}_1 + F_2 K < \bar{y}$, and the bracketed expression is negative. Higher surtax rates and lower values of b permit greater reduction in the basic rate (t_1). For a given threshold, the basic rate can be reduced by raising the surtax rate:[44]

$$\frac{dt_1}{dt_2} = \frac{F_2 K - \bar{y}_2}{F_2 + \bar{y}_1} < 0.$$

Keeping down the number of surtax filers minimizes administrative complexities and taxpayer distortions. However, fewer surtax filers lessens the potential for reducing the basic tax rate—one of the primary reasons for choosing a surtax format. The trade-off can be analyzed by taking a given, fixed surtax rate (t_2) and deriving

$$\frac{dt_1}{dK} = \frac{F_2 (t_2 - t_1)}{F_2 K + \bar{y}_1}.$$

This expression assumes a positive sign for the surtax CIT (with $t_2 > t_1$). Therefore, raising the threshold always requires a higher basic tax rate. Moreover, the rate at which the basic rate must be increased is proportional to the gap ($t_2 - t_1$). The basic tax rate (t_1) and the proportion subject to surtax (F_2) present an important policy trade-off. Using the inverse relation between the threshold and the proportion of population subject to surtax,

$$\frac{dF_2}{dK} = \frac{d}{dK} \int_K^\infty f(y)dy = -f(K) < 0,$$

we derive

$$\frac{dt_1}{dF_2} = \frac{F_2 (t_1 - t_2)}{f(K)(\bar{y}_1 + F_2 K)} < 0.$$

With an empirical distribution for $f(y)$, this expression can be evaluated to aid policy choice.

Benefit Categorization

We next take a categorical trait, such as disability, to show that the CIT and NIT–PIT face the same trade-off between benefit categorization

---

[44]Results such as this one are obtained by completely differentiating the budget equation, holding constant the pertinent variables (in this case $dK = 0$, hence F_2, $\bar{y}_1$, and $\bar{y}_2$ are unchanged), and rearranging terms.

and minimizing marginal tax rates. We assume that CIT credits and NIT guarantees are high enough to support zero-income disabled persons without a categorical transfer program. A noncategorical NIT or CIT would have to offer all individuals the common support level C. A categorical NIT or CIT could provide a lower support level, C', for able persons and reserve the level C for the disabled. Clearly, the noncategorical approach will require greater revenue and hence higher marginal tax rates.

The NIT–PIT system has a set of marginal tax rates. Incomes below level K face a relatively high NIT tax rate (t_1). Higher incomes face a progressive rate structure beginning at a rate below t_1. For simplicity of exposition, we shall assume a single marginal tax rate (t_2) in the PIT range of incomes above K. Keeping the two marginal tax rates in a fixed ratio allows us to identify a "higher" or "lower" marginal tax rate for the NIT–PIT ($t_2 = \theta t_1$ where θ is constant). The following proof can be extended to a schedule of progressive rates in the PIT; marginal rates in all brackets would maintain fixed proportions independent of benefit categories. The proof below shows that the sensitivity of "the" marginal tax rate to categorization is invariant between one and two rate brackets. It is intuitively clear that the argument remains valid with additional rate brackets. Similarly, the argument can be extended to a comparison of the surtax CIT and the NIT–PIT.

As in the earlier notation, $f(y)$ refers to the distribution of taxable incomes of the total population. The density functions for the income distributions of the able and disabled groups are $f^a(y)$ and $f^d(y)$, respectively. Some additional terms are defined:

$$F_2^a = \int_K^\infty f^a(y)\,dy;$$

$$F_2^d = \int_K^\infty f^d(y)\,dy;$$

F^a, F^d = proportions of the population who are able and disabled, respectively ($F^a + F^d = 1$).

Budgetary balance for a noncategorical CIT requires

$$t_c \bar{y} = C + R.$$

In the comparable categorical CIT, with marginal tax rate t_c', this becomes

$$t_c' \bar{y} = F^a C' + F^d C + R.$$

The two types of CIT have marginal tax rates in the ratio

$$\frac{t_c'}{t_c} = \frac{F^a C' + F^d C + R}{C + R} < 1.$$

If we depart from our original assumption of no labor supply responses, mean income will be $\bar{y}'$ under the categorical CIT. This yields

$$\frac{t'_c}{t_c} = \frac{F^a C' + F^d C + R}{C + R} \frac{\bar{y}}{\bar{y}'} .$$

Categorization tends to increase work effort because of its reduced income effect ($C' < C$) for the able population and its relative price effect ($t'_c < t_c$) for the entire population. The resulting $\bar{y}' > \bar{y}$ allows t'_c to be even smaller relative to t_c. Hence categorization permits a lower marginal tax rate because of the induced rise in the taxable income base as well as the lower budgetary requirement.

A noncategorical NIT–PIT satisfies budgetary balance with

$$t_1 \bar{y}_1 + t_2 \bar{y}_2 + (F^a F^a_2 + F^d F^d_2) (t_1 - t_2) K = C + R.$$

Using the proportionality assumption ($t_2 = \theta t_1$) yields[45]

$$t_1 [\bar{y}_1 + \theta \bar{y}_2 + (F^a F^a_2 + F^d F^d_2) (1 - \theta) K] = C + R.$$

The categorical NIT–PIT with marginal tax rates $t'_2 = \theta t'_1$ yields a similar budgetary condition:

$$t'_1 [\bar{y}_1 + \theta \bar{y}_2 + (F^a F^a_2 + F^d F^d_2) (1 - \theta) K] = F^a C' + F^d C + R.$$

Combining the marginal rates for the two types of NIT–PIT yields the ratio

$$\frac{t'_1}{t_1} = \frac{F^a C' + F^d C + R}{C + R} .$$

We therefore have the result originally sought:

$$\frac{t'_c}{t_c} = \frac{t'_1}{t_1} .$$

Ignoring differential incentive effects, the set of marginal tax rates in the NIT–PIT are as sensitive to categorization as the CIT marginal rate.

---

[45]The extension to N marginal rate brackets (1 in the NIT and $N - 1$ in the PIT) is straightforward. The terms are denoted $\bar{y}_i$, F_i^a, and F_i^d as defined above the ith bracket; K_i the lower income threshold for the ith bracket; and $t_i = \theta_i t_1$, where the θ_i are a set of constants ($\theta_1 = 1$). The left-hand side of the equation in the text becomes

$$t_1 \left[\sum_{i=1}^{N} \theta_i \bar{y}_i + \sum_{j=2}^{N} \sum_{i=2}^{j} (F^a F_j^a + F^d F_j^d) (\theta_{i-1} - \theta_i) K_i \right].$$

Tax Base Erosion

Erosion of the tax base may have different implications for the marginal tax rates required in CIT and NIT–PIT programs. We shall analyze a NIT–PIT having only two tax rates, a constant marginal rate in each subprogram. The analysis can be extended to a full schedule of progressive rates. It is assumed that a taxpayer's restricted taxable income (y_r) equals fraction $g(y)$ of his comprehensive taxable income (y):

$$g(y) = \frac{y_r(y)}{y} , 0 < g(y) \leqslant 1.$$

Function $g(y)$ is assumed to be continuous.[46] If the derivatives of $g(y)$ are single-signed, three cases can be distinguished:

$$g' \begin{cases} = 0 \text{ proportionate erosion} \\ > 0 \text{ progressive erosion} \\ < 0 \text{ regressive erosion} \end{cases}$$

Some additional terms are defined:

$$\bar{y}^r = \int_0^\infty g(y) \, yf(y)dy;$$
$$\bar{g} = \bar{y}^r/\bar{y};$$
$$\bar{y}_1^r = \int_0^K g(y)yf(y)dy;$$
$$\bar{g}_1 = \bar{y}_1^r/\bar{y}_1;$$
$$\bar{y}_2^r = \int_K^\infty g(y)yf(y)dy;$$
$$\bar{g}_2 = \bar{y}_2^r/\bar{y}_2.$$

In the absence of base erosion, the requisite CIT tax rate is t_c:

$$t_c\bar{y} = C + R.$$

With base erosion the required rate becomes t_c':

$$t_c' \, \bar{y}^r = C + R.$$

The ratio between the requisite CIT rates with and without erosion is

$$\frac{t_c}{t_c'} = \frac{\bar{y}}{\bar{y}^r} = \frac{1}{\bar{g}},$$

[46]The additional restriction $dy_r/dy > 0$ preserves the initial ranking of individuals in terms of their restricted incomes. This implies $g'(y) > -g(y)/y$ for all y.

which necessarily exceeds unity. For reasons noted in the categorization analysis, the two NIT–PIT rates bear the same ratio in the presence or absence of erosion:

$$t_2 = \theta t_1 \quad \text{and} \quad t_2' = \theta t_1'.$$

Budgetary balance in the absence of erosion requires

$$t_1 \bar{y}_1 + t_2 \bar{y}_2 + F_2 (t_1 - t_2)K = C + R.$$

Substitution for t_2 and rearrangement yield

$$t_1 [\bar{y}_1 + \theta \bar{y}_2 + F_2(1 - \theta)K] = C + R.$$

With an eroded tax base, we assume that the budget kink is reduced to maintain the same fraction of the population within the NIT:

$$K' = y_r(K) = g(K)K.$$

Budgetary balance now requires

$$t_1' \bar{y}_1^r + t_2' \bar{y}_2^r + F_2 (t_1' - t_2')g(K)K = C + R.$$

Substitution for $\bar{y}_1^r$, $\bar{y}_2^r$, and t_2' yields

$$t_1' [\bar{g}_1 \bar{y}_1 + \theta \bar{g}_2 \bar{y}_2 + F_2 (1 - \theta)g(K)K] = C + R.$$

We then derive the ratio

$$\frac{t_1'}{t_1} = \frac{\bar{y}_1 + \theta \bar{y}_2 + F_2(1 - \theta)K}{\bar{g}_1 \bar{y}_1 + \theta \bar{g}_2 \bar{y}_2 + F_2 (1 - \theta)g(K)K}.$$

We now compare the impacts of erosion under the two systems. If erosion is proportionate ($g' = 0$), then $\bar{g} = \bar{g}_1 = \bar{g}_2 = g(K)$, and

$$\frac{t_1'}{t_1} = \frac{1}{\bar{g}} = \frac{t_c'}{t_c}.$$

Proportionate erosion thus implies the same relative impacts on the marginal tax rates of the CIT and NIT–PIT. Further manipulation of terms yields the conditions with nonproportionate erosion:

$$\frac{t_1'}{t_1} \gtrless \frac{t_c'}{t_c} \quad \text{as} \quad (1 - \theta) \left(\left(\frac{\bar{g}_2 - \bar{g}_1}{\bar{y}_1 + \bar{y}_2} \right) \bar{y}_1 \bar{y}_2 + [\bar{g} - g(K)]F_2 K \right) \gtrless 0.$$

The typical assumption is that the NIT marginal tax rate exceeds the PIT marginal tax rate ($0 < \theta < 1$). Progressive erosion ($\bar{g}_2 > \bar{g}_1$) then tends to have more adverse effects on the NIT–PIT marginal rates than on the CIT basic rate. Conversely, regressive erosion ($\bar{g}_2 < \bar{g}_1$) will tend to be relatively more damaging to the CIT. These results can be stated only as tendencies on account of the ambiguous sign of $[\bar{g} - g(K)]$ under nonproportionate erosion. For definite results the income distribution and the function $g(y)$ must be known explicitly.

Discussion

JOSEPH A. PECHMAN

Kesselman has skillfully summarized the major advantages of a credit income tax with a comprehensive income tax base. He proposes that all incomes, including capital gains, should be taxable at full rates and that the personal deductions now allowed under the federal income tax (including the standard deductions) should be eliminated. He also recommends that the credit income tax (with a flat rate) should replace not only the present progressive income tax, but also the corporation income and payroll taxes. All this would greatly simplify tax administration and compliance and would eliminate many of the irritating practical problems of income taxation that plague the income tax in most countries.[1]

The flat rate credit income tax proposed by Kesselman would have many attractions. It would sweep away most of the present transfer payment system, integrate the individual and corporate income taxes, eliminate the need for tax returns from most individuals and simplify the returns for most of the remainder, and ease the problems of withholding for employers. Since the tax would be levied at a flat rate, there would be no averaging problems. The credits would be based on the

[1]All the advantages recited by Kesselman were discovered by Earl Rolph, when he first developed the credit income tax (see Rolph, 1967).

282

ages of individuals, thus eliminating the problems of how to treat the family equitably in different marital and dependency situations.

Unfortunately, the picture is not as bright as Kesselman paints it. He himself points out that the rate for the credit income tax would have to be set at a very high level in order to yield the requisite amount of revenue. For example, he points out that, if the credits were set at 40% of average income, and general revenue needs were 15% of average income, a 55% basic rate would be required. It is not clear how Kesselman arrived at these numbers, but they are somewhat higher than the rates needed for the United States. I have made similar calculations for 1977 and find that if a comprehensive income tax were used the flat rate needed for Kesselman's credit income tax would actually be 47%.[2] However, this 47% rate is a significant underestimate, because it assumes that all incomes would be taxed. If not, the required rate would be increased in proportion to the amount of income that would not be included in the tax base. Thus, if the present definition of adjusted gross income were used, the required rate would rise from 47% to 56%. I am not sure that Kesselman would agree that a 56% rate is out of the question, but I think that most people would find such a rate—or even a rate as low as 47%—out of the question.[3]

So the real question is whether the credit income tax idea can be used in some way with something like the present income tax base. It seems to me that the best that could be hoped for are relatively low credits, say, something like the tax value of the personal exemptions under the present income tax. In that case, the progressive rates would be needed simply to avoid a wholesale redistribution of the tax burden from the rich to the middle- or low-income classes. If Kesselman is counting on the eventual adoption of a full-scale credit income tax, which would fully replace the positive income tax, he is bound to be disappointed. There is a long distance between credits that are roughly equivalent to the tax value of the personal exemptions and the kind of tax originally envisaged by Rolph.

The question therefore remains: What advantage would there be to

[2]These calculations assume that the per capita credits would replace all social security benefits, unemployment insurance, food stamps, supplemental security income (SSI), and state welfare payments.

[3]These rates would be required to provide per capita credits of 40% of average income. If the per capita credits were reduced to 20% of income (or roughly the poverty line levels for 1971), the required rates would be reduced to 32% for the expanded tax base and 39% for the present tax base. These calculations assume that the per capita credits would replace food stamps, SSI, state welfare payments, and half the payments now made under the social security system.

beginning the long fight for Kesselman's ideal tax system by replacing the present exemptions with a tax credit? I see few advantages. Replacing the deduction by a credit would not solve the questions relating to the treatment of the family or averaging. Nor would pressures for retaining the eroding features of the tax law be less with a credit than they have been with the personal exemption.

In fact, I have grave doubts that the adoption of a credit in lieu of an exemption would improve the present income tax in any major respect. During the years 1975–1978, there was a small per capita credit in the federal income tax, but this was eliminated in the Revenue Act of 1978, effective January 1, 1979. The credit had been especially helpful to low-income people with large families and had narrowed the differences in tax liability between families of different sizes in the upper-middle and top brackets. The differences in tax for middle- and high-income families with the same income were already relatively narrow with the exemption, however, and the further narrowing of the differences by the adoption of the credit was resented. Even though the Carter administration recommended complete replacement of the exemption by a credit, the Congress disregarded that recommendation and restored the full exemption.

I agree with Kesselman that withholding should be expanded to include interest, dividends, and other incomes not subject to withholding under present law. But I see no evidence that Congress will be moved either by the substantive argument in favor of such a reform or by the possibility that a credit income tax would be more workable with a broadened withholding system.

In brief, I am sympathetic to Kesselman's proposal for trying to expand the tax base. I believe that this should remain on the tax agenda for the United States. It has unfortunately received a substantial setback in the last year, largely as a result of the unhappiness of the middle classes with inflation and its effect on tax liabilities and income distribution. It is to be hoped that the movement for tax reform will be revived at an early date. However, I very much doubt that a proposal for a modest credit income tax would have any influence on such developments. In fact, given the present mood in the country, I regret to say that the proposal for a credit income tax at a very high rate would probably further retard the movement toward income tax reform.

Discussion

EARL R. ROLPH

Some 27 years ago, a graduate student in economics at Berkeley by the name of Robert R. Schutz filed his Ph.D. dissertation, "Transfer Payments and Income Inequality" (Schutz, 1952), at the University of California–Berkeley library. Thus was born the idea of a credit income tax. His various proposed rate structures and credits (called "subsidies") were scarcely simple; he showed, however, that it was technically feasible to largely eliminate the social evil of poverty from American society if there was the will to do so.

During the intervening years, the idea of some type of credit income tax (CIT) has been floating about, as Professor Kesselman illustrates by his extensive bibliography. It is pleasant to know that even after candidate McGovern gave the idea a kiss of death, it continues to receive careful scholarly attention.

If we restrict our attention to the design of a CIT, as opposed, for example, to its long-run social and economic effects, there are a number of issues that require attention—such as the size of the credit or credits, the rate structure, including the case of one rate, the definition of the tax base, and the definition of the legal taxpayer. Of critical importance are the government transfer programs and other taxes that are to be eliminated if a CIT is to be installed. Kesselman addresses several of these topics.

Let me begin by considering a well-worn topic—the definition of the tax base. Kesselman tells us that his analysis is based on a comprehensive definition of income. But his idea of comprehensive and mine are far apart. For example, without giving any reason, he wishes to exclude gifts and bequests from income. Yet one can scarcely believe that a bequest is not gain to the recipient. Any claim that bequests are not practical to measure cannot be taken seriously. The annual amount of death-related transfers must be at least $100 billion per year; if so, we are not discussing peanuts. If the argument is that such transfers are already taxed, as some have suggested (Goode, 1976, pp. 99–100), the argument, besides being irrelevant, is not correct for most of such transfers. At the federal level, the exemptions in the estate tax law exclude all but a small portion of estates, and the estate tax law itself has become a shambles, as experts well know.

Kesselman also tells us that a CIT would not include the net imputed income from owner-occupied houses. Again no reason is given. Such income has been included in the income tax base in Sweden and in other countries. The experience of these countries could be studied with the idea of seeing whether it is practical and desirable to do likewise in the United States or Canada. Either Kesselman or I must have misapprehensions about the proper definition of income for tax purposes, whether the tax scheme in question is a NIT, PIT, or CIT. Yet income must be defined. In all cases, failure to include some gains in income leads to inequities and distortions. The reasons for including imputed income in the tax base are essentially the same for any income tax design that attempts to be equitable. Any supposed special simplicity of a CIT does not apply to hard-to-define types of income such as implicit income from consumer durables in general.

Let me throw out a few suggestions in the hope that scholarly attention be paid to including some types of nonmarket personal activities in the definition of income. Even that dedicated believer in comprehensive income taxation, Henry Simons, threw in the sponge when it came to including the value of leisure activities in income (Simons, 1938, pp. 52–53). It is true that a precise calculation of the value of one's time spent in nonmarket activities requires information that may be impossible to obtain. Yet it does not follow that nothing can or should be done. Consider, for example, the fact that in the United States, many occupations now have an average workweek of 35 hours and sometimes, even for supposedly full-time work, 32 hours. Except in rare instances are average workweeks less than the 40 hours optimal from the point of view of productivity.[1] Standard workweeks might be officially defined for various occupations. Workers, then, would be asked to report as presumed wages on their tax returns, the amount they would have earned if they had worked the standard workweek. Such a provision, besides reducing the discrimination against workers who work, say, a 40-hour week or more, would serve as a deterrent to those labor union officials who wish to reduce the workweek as a device to enforce the union wage scale. The same tax treatment would be appropriate for time taken off for strikes; such a provision would be especially pertinent for England, Scotland, and Wales, as well as for Canada and the United States.

Premature retirement might also be handled by less gentle tax treatment of pensions and annuities received by persons retiring at early ages. Attention might be given to unusually long vacations taken by professional and self-employed business people. I appreciate that the research into such topics is highly risky; there may be no payoff. But if such attention results only in fewer papers on trivial topics in public finance, there may be a Pareto improvement.

Kesselman does not explicitly discuss the issue of the definition of the legal taxpayer under a CIT except to suggest that it be the individual person. In the United States, at least, this problem must be addressed. What would we do about foreigners who legally work in the United States, such as the "green card holders" who live along the Mexican border and work in the fields in California? Presumably under a CIT they (or their employers) would be liable for tax on the wages earned within this country. But what about the credit? Should it be denied or should it be apportioned to the number of days each person works in the United States? My inclination is to disallow the credit. A much larger problem is posed by illegal aliens. By definition, these people are not supposed to be in the country at all. Depending on whose figures one believes, their numbers run into the millions. Clearly if such people obtain income in the United States, they should be liable for tax. But again, what about the credit or credits? If a main goal of a CIT is to reduce the inequality of the after-tax, after-credit income distribution among citizens of this country, as opposed to the goal of reducing the income inequality of all people living in the North American continent, illegals should probably not be entitled to the credit.

---

[1]Edward Denison holds, "The curves for males imply that output per hours is a maximum at 38.4 hours a week and output per worker is a maximum at 52.7 hours. The corresponding points for females are 34.7 and 49.0, respectively [Denison, 1974, p. 39]." These numbers are for full-time nonfarm wage and salary workers. If leisure is defined as subtracting hours from work that has a nonnegative productivity, a workweek of 40 hours would seem to be a reasonable minimum for both men and women.

Yet another fundamental issue concerns what other taxes are to be modified if a CIT is installed. Obviously one does not want to have both a PIT and a CIT. But do we want, for example, a corporation income tax? Kesselman takes for granted that the answer is no. But this position is not obvious. Let me outline my preferred combination of a CIT and a corporation income tax. Define corporate net earnings before distributions as the tax base for any domestic corporation. Subject each corporation to a tax formula at the single CIT rate, say, for example, 30%. Treat all distributions made by the corporation, such as interest and dividends paid to "native persons," on a collection-at-the-source basis. Individual taxpayers are to be instructed to "gross-up" such payments and treat the difference between that total and the interest and dividends received as prepaid taxes. Owners of shares of stock report pretax retained earnings per share as income and treat the tax per dollar of such retained earnings as prepaid taxes. This integration of the corporate tax and CIT extends only to native persons; they are defined as people who are fully liable for tax under the CIT. Others, such as nonprofit organizations and foreigners, are allowed no offset against the corporate tax. For example, an American corporation whose stock is owned entirely by nonprofit organizations would be required to settle a tax liability equal to 30%, if that is the tax rate, of its net earnings before distribution. This plan is consistent with a CIT, but because it generates positive tax revenuc it may not be strictly accurate to say that the corporate tax is abolished under a CIT. The corporate tax is abolished only for those domestic corporations whose shares are held only by U.S. citizens.

In principle, a CIT could live happily alongside of other large-scale revenue producers, such as some variety of a value-added tax (VAT). An origin-principle VAT, for example, can be shown to reduce wages, salaries, rents, and corporate earnings relative to GNP and NNP when the economy has fully adjusted to the tax. This means that what workers see as their wages are reduced in unseen ways by the VAT. As long as a nontrivial set of per capita credits is installed, the desired degree of income inequality can be achieved. In fact in societies in which personal income taxation is not feasible, a combination of a general VAT and a system of credits can accomplish much the same results as can a CIT alone.

A central question in the design of a CIT concerns the credit structure and the tax rate or rates. Many of the administrative and economic advantages of a CIT are lost even if there are only two rates, such as the standard rate and surtax rate examined by Kesselman. For example, even with uniform per capita credits, a two-rate pattern immediately raises the knotty problem of the definition of the unit for taxation. If the unit is to be each person, incentives for income splitting within the family are created. If the family is to be the unit, it must be defined, and however this is done, a member with a large income may have incentives to break away from the unit. Problems of income averaging are again introduced. With a one-rate system, withholding can be pushed as far as social costs of doing so dictate, with the consequences of greater compliance and equity.

The size of the credit or credits depends critically on which other government transfer programs are to survive. If I understand Kesselman's position, he seems to be suggesting that a CIT is to be pasted on top of existing public transfer programs. Schutz, by contrast, was prepared to eliminate social security programs; and for all practical purposes he proposed putting the Department of Agriculture out of business. His was a formula for "small government" and of large reductions in the inequality of the personal income distribution. I see little point of retaining the present highly expensive and inefficient income redistribution devices if a CIT comes into being. If the size of the credit or credits is to be nontrivial, the retention of present transfer programs and the imposition of a CIT would require a high tax rate. Those people who are in the upper portions of the income distribution are scarcely likely to support a CIT if it means that they are to be made much worse off. Just how far students of public finance might wish to go in suggesting the elimination of other transfer programs is not an easy question to answer; but an answer is essential if a CIT is ever to have any chance of being enacted. Obviously in the United States large parts of the present social security programs would have to go or be drastically modified.

Kesselman, in assessing the limitations of a CIT, mentions that it may burden small families unduly. As compared to the present U.S. federal individual income tax, a CIT would almost certainly increase the tax liability of high-income two-person American families. But to reduce the burden on families with children, a CIT could be designed to provide credits for children that are a function of age of the child, subject to the condition that upon reaching a certain age, the person obtains the same credit as other adults. In addition, if we take the "slow-growth" goal seriously, the credit per natural child could be made to depend upon the number of children. Much of the sting of a CIT on small families could be alleviated by such measures. If older people—I avoid that horrid Washington word "aged"—are to be treated as gently under a CIT as they are under current income tax laws, the adult credit can be increased when the recipient reaches some defined age.

I do not believe that economies of scale in consumption should be a basis for different tax treatment as Kesselman suggests. It would not be surprising to find that consumption economies of scale may hold for groups up to 100 in number. Boardinghouse living arrangements may be much cheaper than single-family living arrangements. There are, however, diseconomies of scale in group living for the commodity "privacy"—a rather important commodity to most people. These may or may not be offsetting. In any event, they are matters of taste that the government has no good reason to try to influence.

Although it may be true that a CIT has a smaller built-in flexibility than a PIT, consider how potentially powerful it is as one feature of an arsenal for demand management. Quick stimulation can be achieved by slightly increasing the per capita credits. Everyone's buying power is increased. If the economy needs to be dampened, the tax rate may be temporarily increased. It is hard to imagine a fiscal device that is more powerful than a CIT.

Just in case one is inclined to view a CIT as a social panacea, consider some implications arising from possible alienation of the credit. There are always some people in this world who, if they were presented with any sum of money, would within a short time end up broke. Presumably the credit would be an entailed asset to the person in the sense that he/she could not make an enforceable contract to sell the right to the credit to another for some sum of money. But suppose there are loan sharks around who enforce their own agreements. Portions, possibly all, of the credit could be alienated by the recipient at, perhaps, 10% weekly interest rates. The same problem arises with other devices that transfer income to low-income people. How serious this problem might become I do not know; but almost certainly, some people will end up with a disposable income that is less than the credit.

Kesselman seems to believe that a CIT calls for subsidies of certain activities, such as child-care centers and labor unions. His remarks on these subsidies leave me utterly in the dark. If parents wish to send their children to child-care centers, let them pay for the service. The child's credit helps the parents support the child. About the last subsidy arrangement I could possibly bring myself to support would be government payment of union dues. Let union members pay their own dues.

Professor Kesselman is to be congratulated on a first-rate research job. My comments merely imply that if I had been given his assignment, I would have written a paper with a somewhat different emphasis.

8

Income Testing and Social Welfare: An Optimal Tax–Transfer Model

EFRAIM SADKA
IRWIN GARFINKEL
KEMPER MORELAND

In the United States at the present time, most Americans would agree with the view that it is the responsibility of government to ensure a certain minimum level of living below which no one should be allowed to fall.* (This is not, of course, to say that there is agreement concerning what that level should be.) Government can meet this responsibility in two ways: (1) by providing minimum standards of income, goods, and/or services for only the poor—an income-tested approach, or (2) by providing them for everyone regardless of income—a non-income-tested approach.

The income support system in the United States currently follows both strategies. AFDC, Supplemental Security Income (SSI), Food Stamps, and Medicaid are restricted to those with low incomes. Public education, Social Security, and Unemployment Insurance are open to people regardless of income.

Until recently the consensus of economic experts was that income-tested programs are more efficient than non-income-tested programs. This consensus apparently stemmed from the widespread use of the

*The authors wish to thank Kenneth Arrow and Peter Diamond, discussants at the conference, for many stimulating comments and suggestions. Thanks are also due to John Bishop and Paul Menchik for suggestions which led to a better use of the data.

target efficiency measure—a conceptually flawed measure of technical rather than economic efficiency.[1]

Kesselman and Garfinkel (1978) have established the possibility that non-income-tested tax–transfer regimes are more efficient than income-tested ones. By an income-tested transfer–tax regime, Kesselman and Garfinkel mean one in which marginal tax rates on the poor exceed those on the nonpoor. Higher tax rates on the poor are a consequence of limiting transfer payments to poor people, that is, of income-testing benefit payments. In a continuous world where there are finer divisions than the poor and nonpoor, income testing occurs when marginal tax rates—both implicit and explicit—decrease as income increases. A transfer–tax system is non-income-tested if marginal tax rates are either constant or increase as income increases. Put in these more general terms the issue of income testing becomes simply, What is the pattern of optimal income tax rates by income class?

Kesselman and Garfinkel found that the efficiency of income testing depends upon how the compensated wage derivative of labor supply (the change in labor supply per unit change in the wage rate) varies by income class. If this derivative either increases or remains constant as income increases, then income testing is economically efficient. If it decreases as income increases, depending upon the rate of decrease, income testing may be inefficient. They also found that for reasonable values of the differences across income classes of the compensated wage derivative of the labor supply, the economic efficiency gains or losses from income testing are likely to be so small as to be inconsequential for policy purposes.

The purpose of this paper, therefore, is to reexamine the welfare aspect of income testing within the framework of the general equilib-

---

[1]Target efficiency has been used by some of the most prominent economists in the field of income maintenance to evaluate alternative transfer programs (see Barth, 1972; Haveman, 1973; Musgrave, Heller, and Peterson, 1970; and Rea, 1974). Only Rea presents measures of both target efficiency and economic efficiency.

Target efficiency is defined as the proportion of total transfer benefits which accrue to some target group—usually the pretransfer poor. Target efficiency thus refers not to economic efficiency but to some notion of technical efficiency.

Even as a measure of technical efficiency, though, the target-efficiency ratio is flawed. Its denominator, total transfer benefits, is not necessarily a useful measure of inputs or costs. In an income-tested program, total transfer benefits paid are a measure of the cost to government and might approach the net cost of the program to nonbeneficiaries. In a non-income-tested program, while total transfer benefits are a measure of the cost of the program to government, they do not gauge the net cost of the program to the net losers. Thus, as long as ultimate interest lies in the well-being of people rather than the accounts of government, target-efficiency ratios will not be a good measure of technical efficiency.

rium optimal income tax literature. The Kesselman–Garfinkel analysis relies upon a model with only two skill classes and makes pure efficiency comparisons without recourse to a social welfare function. But this advantage is achieved at a cost. Specifically, Kesselman and Garfinkel fix the utility level of the poor and examine the effect of income testing on the utility level of the rich. Their results are *not* invariant to the level at which the poor man's utility is fixed. In contrast, in this paper we ask the question whether income testing improves or reduces total social welfare. We also examine the robustness of our results to alternative specifications of the social welfare function. In those cases in which income testing is an optimal policy, we offer a measure of the welfare loss incurred in the absence of income testing. Similarly when non-income-tested regimes are optimal, we calculate the welfare loss incurred by adopting a particular income-tested regime.

In the following section we discuss the optimal income-tax–transfer model. The third section explains how the calculations are made and the fourth presents our results. The paper concludes with a brief summary and section on policy implications.

The Model

The Individuals

We consider an aggregate model of our economy in which there are only two commodities, consumption (x) and labor services (y). There are I individuals in this economy, all having the same preference over bundles of x and y. These preferences are represented by a twice continuously differentiable utility function $u(x, y)$, where $\partial u/\partial x > 0$ and $\partial u/\partial y < 0$. Consumption is assumed to be a normal good. Individuals differ in their wage rates. We denote w_i the wage rate of person i. The individuals were arranged in the following order: $w_1 < w_2 < \ldots < w_I$.

Our model differs from others in that it allows households to have some unearned incomes (such as rent, interest, etc.), in addition to earned income. The unearned income of person i is denoted by A_i. It should be noted here that since individuals were ranked according to their wage rates, it is not necessarily true that $A_1 < A_2 < \ldots < A_I$. Indeed, we do not assume the latter. As we shall see in the next section, the presence of unearned incomes invalidates the standard result from the optimal tax literature that gross income is an increasing function of the wage rate.[2] This could potentially complicate the calculations of optimal tax rates.

The Tax–Transfer System

The gross income of individual i is denoted by z_i. This includes both earned and unearned income so that $z_i = w_i y_i + A_i$, where y_i is the amount of labor services supplied by household i. The income tax in this model is piecewise linear and it does not distinguish between earned and unearned income. Because there are only two linear pieces (income brackets) to this income tax, it can be described by four parameters, two parameters for each of the two linear pieces. These are denoted by G_P, τ_P, G_R, and τ_R as follows: $(1 - \tau_P)$ and $(1 - \tau_R)$ are the marginal tax rates at the low and at the high income brackets, respectively, and $-G_P$ and $-G_R$ are the (usually negative) lump-sum taxes at the low and at the high income brackets, respectively. (G_P is a guaranteed income for the poor; G_R may be thought of as a "shadow" guarantee in the sense that if the rich man's income ever fell to zero he would collect not G_R but G_P. Geometrically G_R is simply the intercept obtained by projecting the linear tax at the high income bracket back to the vertical axis.) The gross income level at which the two linear parts of the income tax intersect is denoted by $\bar{z}$. Thus, $\bar{z}$ is defined implicitly by

$$-G_P + (1 - \tau_P)\bar{z} = -G_R + (1 - \tau_R)\bar{z},$$

which can be solved explicitly to obtain

$$\bar{z} = \frac{G_R - G_P}{\tau_P - \tau_R}. \tag{1}$$

Employing (1), we can formally write the income tax as

$$T(\bar{z}) = \begin{cases} -G_P + (1 - \tau_P)\,z \text{ if } z \leqq \dfrac{G_R - G_P}{\tau_P - \tau_R} \\[2ex] -G_R + (1 - \tau_R)\,z \text{ if } z \geqq \dfrac{G_R - G_P}{\tau_P - \tau_R}. \end{cases} \tag{2}$$

After-tax income, $z - T(z)$, is therefore

$$z - T(z) = \begin{cases} G_P + \tau_P\,z \text{ if } z \leqq \dfrac{G_R - G_P}{\tau_P - \tau_R} \\[2ex] G_R + \tau_R\,z \text{ if } z \geqq \dfrac{G_R - G_P}{\tau_P - \tau_R}. \end{cases} \tag{3}$$

[2]See Mirrlees (1971) or Sadka (1976a).

When the kink in the income tax occurs exactly at the breakeven income (i.e., $T(\bar{z}) = 0$), we say that the tax system is fully integrated. Otherwise, it is not fully integrated. For the four tax parameters, the restriction for a fully integrated income tax is

$$-G_P + (1 - \tau_P)\,\frac{G_R - G_P}{\tau_P - \tau_R} = -G_R + (1 - \tau_R)\,\frac{G_R - G_P}{\tau_P - \tau_R} = 0. \quad (4)$$

Since (4) can be solved for, say, G_R in terms of the other three parameters, we can thus define a fully integrated tax as a tax satisfying the constraint

$$G_R = \frac{1 - \tau_R}{1 - \tau_P}\, G_P. \quad (5)$$

If the income tax imposes a higher marginal tax rate on the poor than on the rich (i.e., $\tau_P < \tau_R$), we call it a negative income tax (NIT). A fully integrated NIT is a NIT which satisfies (5). Fully integrated and nonfully integrated NITs are illustrated in Figure 8.1. By an income-tested tax–transfer program we mean a NIT program (a fully or nonfully integrated one). Finally, we call an income tax with a constant or increasing marginal tax rate and a (usually) negative lump-sum tax (namely, $\tau_P \geqq \tau_R$ and $G_P \leqq G_R$) a credit income tax (CIT). In the text we analyze only the fully integrated case. In our Appendix, we explain that in our model the nonfully integrated case does not shed much light on the income-testing issue.

The Household Income–Leisure Choice

Each individual i is assumed to choose his (x_i, y_i) bundle by maximizing his utility $u(x_i, y_i)$, subject to his budget constraint. Without any taxes the budget constraint is

$$x_i = w_i y_i + A_i. \quad (6)$$

His choice of x_i and y_i are then functions, $X(w_i, A_i)$ and $Y(w_i, A_i)$, respectively, of his wage rate, w_i, and lump-sum income, A_i. These functions are the same for all individuals. With a piecewise linear income tax, his budget constraint is either

$$x_i = \tau_P w_i y_i + \tau_P A_i + G_P \quad (7)$$

if individual i is "poor" (i.e., at the low-income bracket), or

$$x_i = \tau_R w_i y_i + \tau_R A_i + G_R, \quad (8)$$

if individual i is "rich" (i.e., at the high-income bracket). Thus, if we can be sure that individual i is poor, then his x_i and y_i are $X(\tau_P w_i, \tau_P A_i$

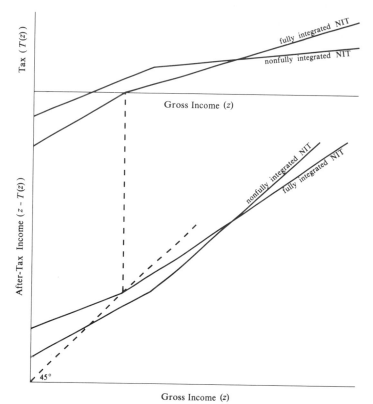

Figure 8.1. Fully and nonfully integrated negative income tax (NIT) regimes. (Figure by University of Wisconsin Cartographic Laboratory.)

$+ \ G_P$) and $Y(\tau_P w_i, \tau_P A_i + G_P)$, respectively, where $\tau_P w_i$ is his net wage rate and $\tau_P A_i + G_P$ is his net lump-sum income. Similarly, if we are sure that individual i is rich, then his x_i and y_i are $X(\tau_R w_i, \tau_R A_i + G_R)$ and $Y(\tau_R w_i, \tau_R A_i + G_R)$, respectively. However, whether an individual will be poor or rich depends not only on his wage and unearned income, but also on all four tax parameters (τ_P, G_P, τ_R, and G_R).

Therefore, in our calculations, the demand x_i and supply y_i are determined in two steps. First, for any combination of τ_P, G_P, τ_R, and G_R we determine the sets $P(\tau_P, G_P, \tau_R, G_R)$ and $R(\tau_P, G_P, \tau_R, G_R)$ of poor and rich individuals, respectively. An individual i belongs to $P(\tau_P, G_P, \tau_R, G_R)$ if his gross income $z_i = w_i y_i + A_i$ is strictly less than $\bar{z}$. He belongs to $R(\tau_P, G_P, \tau_R, G_R)$ if $z_i > \bar{z}$. When $\tau_P < \tau_R$, it is possible for an individual to be indifferent between being poor and being rich. In this case we arbitrarily pick $z_i < \bar{z}$ and classify this individual as poor. When

$\tau_P > \tau_R$, an individual may choose to be exactly at the kink in the income tax schedule (i.e., $z_i = \bar{z}$). The set of such individuals is denoted by $K(\tau_P, G_P, \tau_R, G_R)$. (In an appendix available upon request, we describe how to find the sets $P(\cdot)$, $R(\cdot)$ and $K(\cdot)$ and show that it is possible to do so before first finding x_i and y_i.) Once these sets are determined, the choice of individual i of x_i and y_i is then given by

$$x_i = X(\tau_P w_i, \tau_P A_i + G_P) \text{ and } y_i = Y(\tau_P w_i, \tau_P A_i + G_P)$$
$$\text{if } i \in P(\tau_P, G_P, \tau_R, G_R);$$
$$x_i = X(\tau_R w_i, \tau_R A_i + G_R) \text{ and } y_i = Y(\tau_R w_i, \tau_R A_i + G_R)$$
$$\text{if } i \in R(\tau_P, G_P, \tau_R, G_R); \qquad (9)$$
$$x_i = \bar{z} \text{ and } y_i = \frac{\bar{z} - A_i}{w_i}$$
$$\text{if } i \in K(\tau_P, G_P, \tau_R, G_R).$$

Optimality

The social welfare function is assumed to be

$$W = \sum_{i=1}^{I} \frac{u(x_i, y_i)^{(1-\epsilon)}}{1 - \epsilon}. \qquad (10)$$

Roughly speaking, ϵ on the right-hand side is an index of inequality aversion. The higher the ϵ, the higher is the aversion to inequality. The Arrow–Pratt measure of absolute risk aversion for $u^{1-\epsilon}/(1 - \epsilon)$ is increasing in ϵ and one may expect higher marginal tax rates $(1 - \tau)$ and lower negative lump-sum taxes $(-G)$ as ϵ increases (see Helpman and Sadka, 1978). As ϵ goes to infinity, the criterion (10) approaches the Rawlsian max-min criterion. In our calculations we consider several alternative values for ϵ and the max-min criterion.

The government is assumed to have fixed revenue needs, so that its budget constraint is

$$\frac{1}{I} \sum_{i \in P(\tau_P, G_P, \tau_R, G_R)} [-G_P + (1 - \tau_P)(w_i y_i + A_i)] + \frac{1}{I} \sum_{i \in K(\tau_P, G_P, \tau_R, G_R)} [-G_P + (1 - \tau_P)\bar{z}]$$

$$+ \frac{1}{I} \sum_{i \in R(\tau_P, G_P, \tau_R, G_R)} [-G_R + (1 - \tau_R)(w_i y_i + A_i)] \geq B \qquad (11)$$

where B is the government's revenue requirement per individual.[3]

To find the optimal piecewise linear tax, one has to find τ_P, G_P, τ_R,

[3]Notice that in the fully integrated case the second summation in the left-hand side of (11), of course, vanishes.

and G_R which maximizes (10) subject to constraint (11), taking into account that x_i and y_i are as defined in (9). The optimal fully integrated tax is found by further adding the constraint (5).

Finally, we estimate the welfare loss incurred by using a CIT when a NIT is optimal and vice versa. To do this we first find the optimal fully integrated piecewise linear tax. Denote by $\hat{W}$ the level of W obtained with this optimal tax. Suppose that this optimal tax is a NIT (i.e., $\tau_P >$ τ_R). Next we must compare this NIT to some CIT. The choice is arbitrary. But one CIT that has great appeal for comparison purposes is where τ_P $= \tau_R$. This is the case of maximum tax simplification and also represents a tipping point. While we focus on other cases below, we shall explain our technique here by continuing with this example.

If we try to design a CIT in which $\tau_P = \tau_R$ and which sustains a level $\hat{W}$ for our social welfare function, we shall not be able to generate the required revenue B. Thus, if we want to achieve $\hat{W}$ via this CIT, we shall have to surrender some amount of revenue. This loss in revenue can serve as a reasonable measure of the welfare cost of replacing the NIT with a CIT in which $\tau_P = \tau_R$. Formally, after finding $\hat{X}$, we solve

$$\max_{\tau, G} \frac{1}{I} \sum_{i \in I} \ [-G + (1 \ - \tau) \ Y(\tau w_i, \tau A_i \ + \ G)] \tag{12}$$

subject to

$$\sum_{i=1}^{I} \frac{1}{1-\epsilon} \ u \ [X(\tau w_i, \tau A_i + G), \ Y(\tau w_i, \tau A_i \ + \ G)]^{1-\epsilon} \geqq \hat{W}. \tag{13}$$

Denote the maximum level of (12) by $\bar{B}$. Then $B \ - \bar{B}$ is the welfare cost per individual of adopting the CIT rather than the NIT.[4]

Calculations

Data

The wage and unearned-income distribution were taken from the 1976 Current Population Survey (CPS) for heads of households (male or female) who are not retired, or full-time students, or handicapped. These individuals were arranged first in an increasing order according to their wage rates and then grouped into five quintiles. For each quintile

[4]This measure of the welfare loss is inspired by the works of Diamond and McFadden (1974) and, especially, Pazner and Sadka (1978).

the average wage rate and average unearned income were calculated. Our economy was then composed of five individuals who were given the average wage rate and the average unearned income of each of the five quintiles. It should be noted that the quintiles were constructed according to the wage-rate distribution and not the unearned-income distribution, so that while we have $w_1 < w_2 < \ldots < w_5$, we do not necessarily obtain $A_1 < A_2 < \ldots < A_5$. Unearned income included interest, dividends, rent, veterans payments, unemployment insurance payments, pensions, alimony, and child support. The average wage rates and unearned incomes are presented in Table 8.1.

We also present in Table 8.1 the average annual labor supplies of each of the quintiles. The average labor supply increases with the wage rate up to the fourth quintile and then drops for the highest quintile. This pattern is very similar to our calculations of the labor supplies under the optimal tax coefficients for the constant elasticity of substitution (CES) utility function (see Table 8.3 below). A comparison between Tables 8.1 and 8.3 also indicates that the magnitude of the labor supplies that we have calculated are very similar to the average labor supplies in the 1976 CPS.

To choose an appropriate value for B (the government's revenue need per each head of household who is not retired or a full-time student or handicapped), it was assumed to be the average actual tax collected in calendar year 1975 from each such head of household. To calculate this figure we had to decide how to treat the social security tax (employee's share). We followed two approaches. One approach was to assume that individuals treat their payments to social security as an income tax. In this case the *effective* income tax which determines their labor supply is the sum of the personal income and the social security taxes. In calendar year 1975, the personal income tax (less the earned income tax credit) was $121.34 billion and the social security tax added $41.40 billion for a

TABLE 8.1
The Wage and Unearned-Income Distribution

	Hourly Wage Range ($)	Average Hourly Wage Rate ($)	Average Annual Unearned Income ($)	Average Annual Labor Supply (*hours*)
Bottom quintile	0– 2.86	1.52	782	1,782
Second lowest quintile	2.87– 4.27	3.56	681	1,958
Third lowest quintile	4.28– 5.77	4.98	693	2,044
Fourth lowest quintile	5.78– 7.69	6.63	733	2,065
Top quintile	7.70–333.33	11.74	1,348	1,978

total of $162.74 billion. In order to obtain B, we first divided the latter figure by 56.963 million, which is the number of heads of households who are not retired or full-time students or handicapped. The result was then multiplied by the ratio of total taxes paid in 1975 by these heads of households to total taxes paid by all individuals. Our estimate for this ratio was 0.726, which was the ratio of the total income of these house-holds to the national personal income. In this way we obtained a value of $2074 for B. It should be understood that the optimal tax coefficients which we calculated for this B are the effective coefficients. For instance, the optimal marginal tax rate which we found should be regarded as the sum of the personal income and the social security marginal tax rates.

An alternative approach is to assume that individuals believe that their payment to social security is essentially an old-age insurance and hence that they do not view these payments as a tax at all. Therefore, the $41.40 billion social security tax should not be added to the personal income tax in calculating B. If this is done, we find a value of $1546 for B. Optimal tax coefficients were also calculated for this value of B.

Finally, we have calculated our optimal tax coefficients for five alter-native values of ϵ: 0.2, 0.4, 0.6, 0.8, and 1.4. Often, we also carry out the calculations for the max-min criterion ($\epsilon = \infty$). Occasionally, we also consider the other extreme case, where $\epsilon = 0$. In the latter case the social marginal utility of full income (inclusive of the value of leisure) is con-stant, and the society becomes indifferent to full-income inequality.[5] However, the social marginal utility of actual income (exclusive of the value of leisure) is usually diminishing and the society aspires for a more equal distribution of actual income.[6] Thus, the case when $\epsilon = 0$ does not usually imply that no minimum income should be guaranteed to the poor, as we shall see in the next section (see Table 8.4).

Specification of the Utility Function and Its Parameters

In calculating the optimal tax coefficients, we employ a CES utility function

$$u(x,y) = [\beta x^\rho + (1 - \beta)(\bar{y} - y)^\rho]^{1/\rho} , \tag{14}$$

where the elasticity of substitution is $\sigma = 1/(1 - \rho)$. $\bar{y}$ is the individual's endowment of leisure, or the maximum amount of hours that he can work; it is the same for all individuals—60 hours per week, 52 weeks per

---

[5]The constancy of the social marginal utility of full income follows from the linear homogeneity of the utility functions (14) and (17) in ($x, \bar{y} - y$).
[6]See Sadka (1976b).

year, for a total of 3120 hours per year. Our CES utility function yields the following consumption demand and labor supply function:

$$X(\tau w, \tau A + G) = \frac{\tau w \bar{y} + \tau A + G}{1 + \tau w \left[(1 - \beta)/\beta \tau w\right]^{1/(1-\rho)}} \quad (15)$$

and

$$Y(\tau w, \tau A + G) = \bar{y} - \frac{\tau w \bar{y} + \tau A + G}{\tau w + [(\beta \tau w)/(1 - \beta)]^{1/(1-\rho)}} . \quad (16)$$

With the CES utility function the values of two parameters, β and σ, have to be determined. Here we considered two cases: when β and σ vary across income classes; and when β and σ are the same for all individuals.

In the first situation, we employed the findings of Masters and Garfinkel (1978). They studied, among other things, the dependency of the compensated wage elasticity of the labor supply on various demographic variables. In our terminology this elasticity can be written as

$$\theta = \frac{W}{Y} \left(\frac{\partial Y}{\partial W} - Y \frac{\partial Y}{\partial I} \right), \quad (17)$$

where $W = \tau w$ is the net wage rate and $I = \tau w \bar{y} + \tau A + G$ is full income. Given the demographic composition of each of our quintiles, we employed Masters and Garfinkel's findings in order to estimate the θ of each quintile. These estimates are presented in Table 8.2. We then calculated β and σ for each quintile by requiring them to yield our estimates of θ and the labor supplies in the last column of Table 8.1.

Specifically, to find the pair (β, σ) for a certain quintile, we solved these two simultaneous equations:

$$\theta(\tau w, \tau A + G; \beta, \sigma) = \text{Estimated } \theta \text{ (from Table 8.2);} \quad (18)$$

TABLE 8.2
The Compensated Wage Elasticity (θ) and the Elasticity of Substitution (σ)

	θ	Case I ($B = \$2,074$)				Case II ($B = \$1,546$)			
		τ	G ($)	β	σ	τ	G ($)	β	σ
Bottom quintile	0.26	0.79	1,916	0.9245	0.4653	0.85	1,916	0.9245	0.4689
Second lowest quintile	0.21	0.67	1,697	0.9363	0.4976	0.73	1,656	0.9367	0.5014
Third lowest quintile	0.15	0.75	1,060	0.9807	0.4092	0.81	1,019	0.9818	0.4108
Fourth lowest quintile	0.11	0.755	1,012	0.9979	0.3108	0.815	967	0.9982	0.3118
Top quintile	0.10	0.72	1,822	0.9999	0.2589	0.72	2,668	0.9999	0.2553

NOTE: In Case I FICA is viewed as a tax; in Case II FICA is not viewed as a tax.

$$Y(\tau w, \tau A + G; \beta, \sigma) = \text{Average Labor Supply (from Table 8.1).} \tag{19}$$

In order to solve (18)–(19) for (β, σ), we first had to determine the actual τ and G faced by each quintile in 1975. For all but the bottom quintile, τ and G were calculated exclusively from the federal income tax tables (for married filing jointly, claiming a total number of three exemptions and taking the standard deduction). Since the federal income tax schedule is not linear, $1 - \tau$ and $-G$ were taken as, respectively, the slope and the intercept of the line which is tangent to the tax schedule at the point where the quintile in question actually was in 1975. This procedure is justified in view of the quasi-concavity of the individual's utility function, which gives rise to well-behaved indifference curves. In determining the actual τ and G for the bottom quintile, we also took into account various income-tested cash and in-kind transfer programs (such as food stamps, AFDC, and the earned income credit).

Table 8.2 presents the actual values of τ and G and our estimates of β and σ. In fact, we calculated two alternative values of (τ, G) and hence of (β, σ), depending upon whether the employee contribution for social security (FICA) is viewed as a tax or not. Recall that a similar distinction was made with respect to B, the government's revenue requirement. In Case I, FICA was considered as a tax and we found B to be $2074. Correspondingly, when we calculate optimal tax rates for this value of B we employed our estimates of β and σ under the assumption that FICA is indeed viewed as a tax. Similarly, in Case II we had $B = \$1546$ and we used our estimates of β and σ under the assumption that FICA is not regarded as a tax.

When β and σ are the same for all individuals, we followed the suggestions of Stern (1976) that β is between 0.95 and 0.995 and σ between 0.35 and 0.50 (see also his references). In the text, we present results for $\beta = 0.98$ and $\sigma = 0.50$.[7]

Results

In Table 8.3 we present the optimal tax rates (τ), guarantees (G), breakeven levels of income $(\bar{z})$, labor supplies (y), and before- and after-tax income (x and z, respectively) for the variable β and σ case. The

[7]We also calculated results for all possible combinations of $\beta = 0.95, 0.98, 0.99, 0.995$ and $\sigma = 0.35, 0.40, 0.45, 0.50$, but found that the pattern of the results was more or less invariant with respect to this range of values of β and σ. We also computed optimal tax rates for a Cobb–Douglas utility function (i.e., $\sigma = 1$).

TABLE 8.3
Optimal Tax–Transfer Programs for a CES Utility Function with Variable β and σ

	$\epsilon = 0$		$\epsilon = 0.2$		$\epsilon = 0.4$		$\epsilon = 0.6$		$\epsilon = 0.8$		$\epsilon = 1.4$		Max-Min $(\epsilon = \infty)$	
	$B =$ $2,074	$B =$ $1,546	$B =$ $2,074	$B =$ $1,546	$B =$ $2,074	$B =$ $1,546	$B =$ $2,074	$B =$ $1,546	$B =$ $2,074	$B =$ $1,546	$B =$ $2,074	$B =$ $1,546	$B =$ $2,074	$B =$ $1,546
τ_P	.92	.95	.51	.50	.41	.65	.48	.55	.43	.49	.42	.40	.14	.14
τ_R	.92	.95	.62	.66	.57	.39	.43	.35	.38	.33	.22	.26	.10	.11
G_P ($)	−1,070	−919	3,142	3,566	4,012	3,554	4,241	4,455	4,727	4,951	5,226	5,732	6,673	7,100
G_R ($)	−1,070	−919	2,437	2,425	2,924	6,195	4,649	6,435	5,142	6,504	7,028	7,069	6,983	7,348
z ($)	−13,380	−18,380	6,413	7,131	6,799	10,155	8,156	9,900	8,293	9,707	9,011	9,552	7,759	8,256
y_1 ($)	2,341	2,302	1,476	1,365	1,157	1,422	1,151	1,154	958	972	792	616	0	0
y_2 ($)	2,157	2,141	1,879	1,887	1,825	1,751	1,639	1,635	1,550	1,554	1,465	1,389	513	404
y_3 ($)	2,122	2,118	1,984	1,995	1,959	1,900	1,822	1,848	1,769	1,810	1,670	1,734	1,332	1,295
y_4 ($)	2,086	2,099	2,047	2,068	2,043	1,930	1,989	1,923	1,972	1,923	1,829	1,884	1,746	1,777
y_5 ($)	1,948	1,953	2,020	2,022	2,037	2,053	2,066	2,071	2,082	2,083	2,100	2,104	2,171	2,178
z_1 ($)	4,340	4,280	3,025	2,857	2,541	2,942	2,531	2,536	2,238	2,258	1,986	1,718	782	782
z_2 ($)	8,359	8,301	7,371	7,398	7,178	6,915	6,514	6,501	6,198	6,212	5,895	5,624	2,505	2,119
z_3 ($)	11,259	11,242	10,573	10,628	10,449	10,155	9,765	9,898	9,502	9,707	9,011	9,331	7,326	7,141
z_4 ($)	14,560	14,648	14,305	14,441	14,275	13,531	13,921	13,485	13,808	13,484	12,860	13,221	12,307	12,517
z_5 ($)	24,216	24,273	25,060	25,084	25,256	25,452	25,606	25,663	25,789	25,801	25,997	26,050	26,836	26,913
Mean Income ($)	12,547	12,549	12,067	12,082	11,940	11,799	11,667	11,617	11,507	11,492	11,150	11,189	9,951	9,894
x_1 ($)	2,922	3,147	4,685	4,994	5,053	5,467	5,456	5,850	5,690	6,057	6,060	6,419	6,782	7,210
x_2 ($)	6,620	6,967	7,007	7,307	7,015	8,049	7,368	8,031	7,392	7,994	7,702	7,981	7,024	7,397
x_3 ($)	9,288	9,761	8,992	9,439	8,879	10,155	8,848	9,899	8,753	9,707	9,011	9,464	7,698	8,100
x_4 ($)	12,324	12,997	11,306	11,956	11,061	11,472	10,635	11,155	10,389	10,953	9,858	10,506	8,214	8,725
x_5 ($)	21,209	22,140	17,794	18,980	17,320	16,121	15,659	15,417	14,941	15,018	12,748	13,842	9,667	10,308
Percentage of Net Beneficiaries	20%	20%	20%	20%	20%	40%	40%	60%	40%	40%	40%	60%	60%	60%

results are presented for seven values of ϵ, the inequality aversion parameters, and two values of B, the government's revenue need.

In all but three cases, the tax rate on the nonpoor exceeds or is equal to that on the poor. The CIT is optimal. The difference in tax rates ranges from zero to a high of 26 percentage points. Except in the $\epsilon = 0$ case, both tax rates are quite high. In the max-min case the tax rates are virtually confiscatory. Even in the other cases, the tax rates range from a minimum of 34% to a maximum of 78%. As expected, the tax rates more or less increase as aversion to inequality (ϵ) increases.

The guarantee to the poor is relatively high. Except for the case where $\epsilon = 0$, the guarantee varies from a low of about $3000 a year to a high of about $7000 a year. (When $\epsilon = 0$, the tax rates on the poor and on the rich are equal to each other and are very small. The guarantees to the poor and to the rich are, of course, equal to each other and negative. Essentially, we have a head tax in this case.) As expected, the guarantees to the poor and to the rich both increase with ϵ.[8] Similarly, the lower the value of taxation required to finance other government-provided goods and services (namely B), the higher are usually the guarantees.

The optimal income tax, or more approximately, the optimal tax-transfer system has a breakeven level of income below the mean income. The difference between the breakeven and the mean income shrinks as ϵ increases to a low level of less than $2000. Consequently, the number of the net beneficiaries in the optimal tax–transfer system (those whose tax–transfer incomes after taxes exceed their tax–transfer incomes before taxes) increases with ϵ. Most commonly, 20% to 40% of the population are net beneficiaries.

With one exception (namely, when $\epsilon = 0$), the optimal labor supplies increase as the wage rate increases. (In three other cases, the fifth quintile's optimal labor supply is slightly lower than the fourth.) The poorest wage class works substantially less than the rest of the population. (Again, the case of $\epsilon = 0$ is an exception.) Furthermore, the greater the aversion to inequality as measured by ϵ, the less the poor work, and hence the greater the divergence between their life-styles and that of the rest of the population. Indeed, in the max-min case the poor do not work at all; and the near-poor work very little. The explanation for this result is simple. As the guarantee and tax rate increase, the ability of the poor to afford to forego work increases while the rewards they derive from work decrease. Whether such a large divergence in life-styles is consistent with a broader notion of equality is an important question which unfortunately cannot be addressed within the confines of our formal model.

[8]For a general result of this sort, see Helpman and Sadka (1978).

As mentioned earlier, we also simulated optimal income taxes for the constant β and σ case. Alternative values of β between 0.95 and 0.995 were combined with various values of σ between 0.35 and 0.50. Table 8.4 presents the optimal tax rules and guarantees for $\beta = 0.98$ and $\sigma = 0.50$. In all cases, the optimal tax rate on the poor exceeds that on the nonpoor. This result holds for all our simulations with constant β and σ, including the case of a Cobb–Douglas utility function, which is a special case of the CES function (i.e., $\sigma = 1$). Thus, the NIT is optimal when both β and σ are constant. Another interesting feature of the results in Table 8.4 is that the guarantee to the poor and to the rich are no longer negative in the case where $\epsilon = 0$. In fact, G_P can reach as high as $5000 a year. This is not surprising in view of our earlier discussion of this situation.

A comparison between the tax rates and the guarantees in Tables 8.3 and 8.4 shows that the poor face a significantly higher tax rate in the constant (σ, β) case than in the variable (σ, β) case. The difference is around 15% to 20%, except in the $\epsilon = 0$ case, where it jumps to 50% to 56%. The guarantee to the poor is significantly lower in the variable (σ, β) case. Except in the case $\epsilon = 0$, where it reaches $6000 a year, the difference between the guarantees to the poor in the two cases is between $1000 and $3000 a year. The fact that both the marginal tax rate on the poor and the guarantee received are higher in the constant (σ, β) case than in the variable (σ, β) case explains why the NIT is optimal in the former case, while the CIT is optimal in the latter case. Comparing τ_R and G_R in the two cases does not suggest any clear-cut pattern.

Next, we consider the magnitude of the welfare losses incurred by adopting an income-tested tax–transfer schedule when a non-income-tested system is optimal and vice versa. The choice of the nonoptimal income-tested (non-income-tested) system to simulate is, of course, arbitrary. Recall that we generally found non-income-tested systems to be optimal when the substitution elasticities more or less declined with the wage rate and income-tested systems to be optimal when the elasticity was constant. A natural comparison then, which highlights the importance of whether the substitution elasticity declines with the wage rate, is to use the difference in the optimal tax rate parameters derived from the constant elasticity case as constraints in the maximization problem in the declining elasticity case and vice versa. We also compare the optimal tax in each case with the linear tax (i.e., $\tau_P = \tau_R$). The welfare losses are then calculated as explained earlier. In Tables 8.5 and 8.6 we present welfare losses in absolute terms and as percentages of government's revenue and national gross earnings.

When β and σ are variable (where the optimal tax is usually a CIT), the welfare losses of adopting a linear tax (Table 8.5A) are generally low

TABLE 8.4
Optimal Tax Coefficients for $\beta = 0.98$ and $\sigma = 0.5$

	$\epsilon = 0$		$\epsilon = .2$		$\epsilon = .4$		$\epsilon = .6$		$\epsilon = .8$		$\epsilon = 1.4$		Max-Min ($\epsilon = \infty$)	
	$B = \$2,074$	$B = \$1,546$	$B = \$2,074$	$B = \$1,546$	$B = \$2,074$	$B = \$1,546$	$B = \$2,074$	$B = \$1,546$	$B = \$2,074$	$B = \$1,546$	$B = \$2,074$	$B = \$1,546$	$B = \$2,074$	$B = \$1,546$
τ_P	0.44	0.42	.36	.32	.30	.32	.30	.42	.29	.39	.35	.34	0.12	0.12
τ_R	0.61	0.63	.55	.61	.52	.61	.52	.49	.52	.46	.39	.41	0.22	0.23
G_P (\$)	4,287	4,916	5,211	5,714	5,781	5,714	5,781	5,535	5,845	5,858	5,913	6,366	7,404	7,776
G_R (\$)	2,989	3,136	3,664	3,277	3,964	3,277	3,964	4,867	3,951	5,186	5,549	5,691	6,562	6,804

TABLE 8.5
Welfare Losses Caused by Nonoptimal Tax–Transfer Programs when β and σ Are Variable

	$\epsilon = 0$		$\epsilon = 0.2$		$\epsilon = 0.4$		$\epsilon = 0.6$		$\epsilon = 0.8$		$\epsilon = 1.4$		Max-Min ($\epsilon = \infty$)	
	$B =$ $2,074	$B =$ $1,546	$B =$ $2,074	$B =$ $1,546	$B =$ $2,074	$B =$ $1,546	$B =$ $2,074	$B =$ $1,546	$B =$ $2,074	$B =$ $1,546	$B =$ $2,074	$B =$ $1,546	$B =$ $2,074	$B =$ $1,546
A. Welfare Losses of a Linear Tax ($\tau_P = \tau_R$ and $G_P = G_R$)														
Total ($ billions)	0	0	0.48	1.04	0.55	0.10	0.32	2.47	0.41	3.94	3.32	6.44	3.55	2.91
As percentage of government's revenue	0	0	0.3	0.9	0.3	0.1	0.2	2.0	0.2	3.2	2.0	5.3	2.2	2.4
As percentage of gross national earnings	0	0	0.05	0.12	0.06	0.01	0.04	0.29	0.05	0.47	0.41	0.79	0.50	0.41
B. Welfare Losses of a Tax with a Value of $\tau_P - \tau_R$ as in the Optimal Tax for the Case of Constant β and σ														
Total ($ billions)	0	0	0.25	0.99	0.21	1.53	3.22	3.62	9.93	5.48	4.96	9.16	8.46	34.97
As percentage of government's revenue	0	0	0.2	0.8	0.1	1.3	2.0	3.0	6.1	4.5	3.0	7.6	5.2	28.8
As percentage of gross national earnings	0	0	0.03	0.1	0.02	0.2	0.4	0.4	1.1	0.7	0.6	1.1	1.1	4.9

TABLE 8.6
Welfare Losses Caused by Nonoptimal Tax–Transfer Programs When β and σ are Constant

	$\epsilon = 0$		$\epsilon = 0.2$		$\epsilon = 0.4$		$\epsilon = 0.6$		$\epsilon = 0.8$		$\epsilon = 1.4$		Max-Min ($\epsilon = \infty$)	
	$B =$ $\$2,074$	$B =$ $\$1,546$	$B =$ $\$2,074$	$B =$ $\$1,546$	$B =$ $\$2,074$	$B =$ $\$1,546$	$B =$ $\$2,074$	$B =$ $\$1,546$	$B =$ $\$2,074$	$B =$ $\$1,546$	$B =$ $\$2,074$	$B =$ $\$1,546$	$B =$ $\$2,074$	$B =$ $\$1,546$
	A. Welfare Losses of a Linear Tax ($\tau_P = \tau_R$ and G_R)													
Total ($ billions)	1.01	1.85	2.07	2.34	2.78	1.64	2.93	0.62	2.26	0.77	0.44	1.14	16.31	21.05
As percentage of government's revenue	.6	1.5	1.3	1.9	1.7	1.4	1.8	0.5	1.4	0.6	0.3	0.9	10.0	17.3
As percentage of gross national earnings	.1	.2	.2	.2	.3	.2	.3	.07	.2	.08	.05	.1	2.0	2.6
	B. Welfare Losses of a Tax with a Value of $\tau_P - \tau_R$ as in the Optimal Tax for the Case of Variable β and σ													
Total ($ billions)	1.01	1.85	0.40	1.49	0.20	11.62	3.73	9.56	3.26	8.26	12.52	9.91	31.36	27.08
As percentage of government's revenue	0.6	1.5	0.2	1.2	0.1	9.6	2.3	7.9	2.0	6.8	7.7	8.2	19.3	22.3
As percentage of gross national earnings	0.1	0.2	0.04	0.2	0.02	1.3	0.4	1.0	0.3	0.9	1.4	1.1	3.9	3.4

($0.3 to $1 billion); in three cases they reach about $3.5 billion and in one case they even exceed $6 billion. The welfare losses of adopting a nonoptimal CIT (Table 8.5B) are substantially higher. They are especially high for high levels of ϵ and in one of the two maxi-min cases they even reach $35 billion!

When β and σ are constant (where the optimal tax is a NIT), the welfare losses of adopting a linear tax are usually between $1 and $3 billion and most often they are less than $2 billion. The max-min case is an exception ($16 to $21 billion). Adopting a CIT with the value of $\tau_P - \tau_R$ as in the variable (β, σ) case results in quite high welfare losses.

Finally, a brief comparison of our results with those of Garfinkel and Kesselman (1978) is in order. They argue that the compensated wage derivative of the labor supply function[9] is lower for the rich than for the poor. They also found that if this derivative falls sufficiently fast with the wage rate, then a fully integrated NIT is inefficient. Recall that our findings show that the variable (β, σ) is more favorable to the CIT while the constant (β, σ) is more favorable to the NIT. Thus, for our results to be consistent with those of Garfinkel–Kesselman, it must be the case that the compensated wage derivative of the labor supply falls, roughly speaking, more rapidly with the wage rate when β and σ are variable than when they are constant. Strictly speaking, whether the compensated wage derivative falls more rapidly in the variable (β, σ) case than in the constant (β, σ) case is an ambiguous question because the compensated wage derivative depends on τ and G. It is not obvious what τ and G should be employed in investigating this question. We calculated the compensated wage derivatives for our various wage classes both at the actual τ and G in 1975 (see Table 8.2) and at the various optimal τ and G. Although a clear-cut pattern did not exist, our calculations certainly suggest that this derivative is falling more rapidly in the variable β and σ case. For instance, at the actual τ and G in 1975, the compensated wage derivative is about 20 times as high for the poorest individual as it is for the richest one in the variable (β, σ) case, while the same ratio is only about 5 in the constant (β, σ) case.

Summary, Qualifications, and Policy Implications

Our results are broadly consistent with the Garfinkel–Kesselman findings in favor of the CIT. For most values of our inequality-aversion

[9]In our terminology, this derivative is

$$\frac{\partial y}{\partial(\tau w)}\bigg|u$$

and it can be calculated from (16) by applying the Hicks–Slutsky equation.

parameter (ϵ), the CIT is optimal, when the elasticity of substitution between leisure and consumption (σ) falls across wage classes (and β rises). Making use of the best available labor supply estimates for a variety of demographic groups, we found that σ indeed falls and β indeed rises across wage classes, starting from the lowest wage class and moving upward.

Higher elasticities than those found by Masters–Garfinkel are some-what less favorable to the CIT although even here the non-income-tested tax–transfer schedules were optimal far more often than income-tested ones. (Owing to space limitations, these results are not presented in this paper.) Only when the elasticity was constrained to be the same for all wage classes were income-tested tax–transfer schedules consis-tently optimal.

In general, the welfare losses of adopting a non-income-tested regime (such as a linear tax) when the income-tested regime is optimal are not very large. If this result continues to hold up in future research, the choice between income-tested and non-income-tested tax–transfer schedules will depend much more heavily on other criteria. Nearly all of these other noneconomic considerations favor non-income-tested pro-grams.[10] Here we discuss only two: equality of opportunity and the dignity and self-respect of beneficiaries.

Taxation reduces the opportunity of individuals to improve their own lot through hard work and sacrifice. The higher the tax rate, the greater the reduction in opportunity. Placing the highest tax rates on the poor via income-testing transfers, therefore, exacerbates already existing in-equalities of opportunity.

A cost of participating in welfare programs is loss of pride. So much stress in this country is placed on economic success, that to declare oneself poor is proclaiming oneself a failure. As a consequence, many who are eligible for welfare benefits do not claim them and among many who do, a negative self-image is fostered.

Because the noneconomic considerations favor non-income-tested programs, the results presented in this paper which also favor non-income-tested programs should be subjected to careful scrutiny.

For example, the model in this paper is unrealistic in several respects which could affect the results. Perhaps the two most important are that the model consists of individuals rather than families and no account is taken of the effect of taxation on savings. The labor supply literature indicates that wives of all income groups have higher substitution elas-ticities than husbands. The substitution elasticity of all family members,

---

[10]See the other papers and discussions in this volume.

therefore, might decrease less rapidly with family income than the substitution elasticity of family heads decreases as wage rates increase. Similarly, if saving is more responsive to taxation than labor supply, this would tend to make the optimal tax rates on the well-to-do lower. We intend to incorporate these and other similar considerations in future work.

Still, the results presented in this paper are sufficient to call into question the consensus among economic experts that transfer programs which provide benefits only to those with low incomes are more efficient than those which provide benefits to all regardless of income. At the very least, this paper serves the function of shifting the grounds of debate away from preoccupation with the concept and measure of target efficiency to a concern with "real" economic efficiency.

Appendix: Nonfully Integrated Tax–Transfer Systems

Our calculations for nonfully integrated tax–transfer systems are presented in Table 8.7 for a CES utility function with $\beta = 0.98$ and $\sigma = 0.5$.

In this case, the marginal tax rate faced by the richest individual is zero ($\tau_R = 1$). In essence, the income tax on the richest quintile becomes a head tax (equals $-G_R$), which ranges in value from about \$8000 to about \$17,000. As might be expected, the head tax increases with ϵ and it is usually higher for the higher value of β. All the other quintiles are "poor" in the sense that their gross income is below the kink in the tax schedule. (This, however, does not mean that all of them are net transfer recipients because the kink in the tax schedule occurs above the break-even point in the nonfully integrated case.) They have a guaranteed income (G_P), which ranges in value from about \$5000 to about \$8000, and they face a marginal tax rate ($1 - \tau_P$), which lies between 50% to about 85%. As expected, the income guarantee and marginal tax rate are increasing with the inequality-aversion parameter ϵ.

Strictly speaking, the results presented in Table 8.7 indicate the superiority of the NIT over the CIT. We further present in the bottom panel of Table 8.7 the welfare losses incurred when a linear CIT (namely, a CIT with $\tau_P = \tau_R$) replaces the NIT, as the percentages of government's revenue losses from total revenues and from GNP. These losses are quite significant: 7.3% to 16.7% of total government's revenue or 1.2% to 2.2% of gross earned income (except in the max-min case, where they are even higher). These losses are much higher than those incurred when the optimal fully integrated NIT in the constant (β, σ) case was replaced by a linear CIT (see Table 8.6).

TABLE 8.7
Tax Parameters for Optimal Nonfully Integrated Systems and CIT Welfare Costs (A CES Utility Function with $\beta = 0.98$ and $\sigma = 0.50$)

	$\epsilon = 0.2$		$\epsilon = 0.4$		$\epsilon = 0.6$		$\epsilon = 0.8$		$\epsilon = 1.4$		Max-Min ($\epsilon = \infty$)	
	B = $2,074	B = $1,546	B = $2,074	B = $1,546	B = $2,074	B = $1,546	B = $2,074	B = $1,546	B = $2,074	B = $1,546	B = $2,074	B = $1,546
τ_P	0.42	0.50	0.42	0.50	0.42	0.44	0.40	0.40	0.31	0.32	0.14	0.15
τ_R	1.00	1.00	1.00	1.00	1.00	1.00	1.00	1.00	1.00	1.00	1.00	1.00
G_P ($)	5,500	5,000	5,500	5,000	5,500	5,700	5,700	6,100	6,600	6,900	7,760	8,080
G_R ($)	−10,512	−8,511	−10,512	−8,511	−10,512	−9,566	−10,767	−10,089	−12,390	−11,587	−17,244	−16,362
Percentage of loss from government's revenue	7.3	9.0	9.2	9.7	10.3	12.9	10.9	13.6	13.1	16.7	39.6	52.9
Percentage of loss from gross earning	1.21	1.11	1.53	1.20	1.71	1.61	1.82	1.72	2.24	2.16	7.46	7.50

However, we feel that a nonfully integrated system is not an appropriate framework for evaluating the relative merit of a linear CIT compared to a NIT. Therefore, we also believe that the figures in Table 8.7 are not good indicators of the welfare costs of the linear CIT. Our calculations of nonfully integrated systems rather emphasize the importance of the result about the optimality of a zero marginal tax rate at the top end of the income ladder. Sadka (1976a) has shown that any tax system which taxes the richest individual with a positive rate at the margin will be improved (according to any individualistic social welfare function) by reducing this rate to zero. Thus, any linear CIT can be improved by adjusting the marginal tax rate at the top end of the income range to zero. Performing such an adjustment results in a rather strange NIT system where the four lowest quintiles face the same (positive) marginal tax rate and the highest quintile faces a zero marginal tax rate. Such a strange NIT system is not exactly a "conventional" one; it is not what people usually have in mind when they talk about a NIT system. A "conventional" NIT looks more like our fully integrated NIT, where the first or perhaps also the second lowest quintiles faced one marginal tax rate and the rest faced another (lower) marginal tax rate. Limiting (as we did) the number of brackets in the tax–transfer system to only two, one can choose between either a conventional NIT or a nonfully integrated NIT, which places the same marginal tax rate on all, except on the richest person. Thus, it seems to us more accurate to interpret the costs presented in Table 8.7 as indicating that adjusting a linear CIT in order to comply with the principle of zero marginal tax rate at the top end of the income ladder is far more important than changing a linear CIT to a conventional (fully integrated) NIT: Given the choice between a zero marginal tax rate on the richest individual and a conventional NIT, the former alternative is an overwhelming winner.[11]

[11]This result is in sharp contrast to Mirrlees (1976), who understates the importance of having a zero marginal tax rate at the top end of the income distribution.

Discussion

PETER DIAMOND

The authors take a model of the economy and calculate the optimal two-piece linear income tax.[1] For some parameters of both utility functions and the social welfare function they find that the optimal tax has a lower marginal rate on low-income people than on high. This tends to support CIT relative to NIT. For others, they find the reverse. The former predominate when the utility function varies with skill in a way to mimic labor supplies by income bracket. The latter predominate when the utility function is the same for all. This difference is an important finding of this paper. Then they calculate the optimal linear tax and conclude that the welfare loss from a single slope rather than two is generally small, permitting one to favor CIT over NIT if there are other reasons for such a preference.

I will divide my summary and discussion into three sections. First I will discuss the assumptions of the model relative to other assumptions that might have been made with this sort of model. Second I will ask the question, What size welfare loss is small when comparing the two different optimal taxes? Third I will again discuss the assumptions, concentrating on those commonly made in this class of models.

---

[1]They concentrate on a fully integrated tax. Full integration means zero tax at the breakpoint between the two marginal tax rates.

314

Assumptions of the Model

The model has five workers. (I will return to this number below.) Each worker has an exogenous marginal product of labor per hour. While this is commonly assumed in many optimal tax models, there are exceptions. If wages depend on the capital stock, if higher-income workers have higher marginal propensities to save, and if the government is not using other fiscal tools to optimize the capital stock, then concern for the capital stock is likely to result in a less progressive tax (i.e., strengthen the case for NIT).

Properly evaluating the effects on the capital stock involves consideration of other tax and debt tools that affect capital accumulation. Thus, it is slightly easier to discuss the second source of wage endogeneity on my list. Workers of different skills are unlikely to be perfect substitutes for each other (adjusted for relative skills). That is, having more labor supplied by skilled workers may raise or lower the marginal product of unskilled workers. When there do not exist exogenously defined weights for labor aggregation, then labor supplies of different skills need to be considered as different commodities. Optimal taxation will generally involve different ad valorem tax rates on different labor skills. The use of an income tax involves a constraint on the relative taxation of different labor skills. When optimal taxes are calculated subject to such constraints, the effect of labor supplies on relative wage rates becomes an integral part of optimal tax considerations. Before we can evaluate this effect we would need more information on whether an increase in the supply of higher-skilled workers raises the marginal products of lower-skilled workers, presumably by making better use of them, or lowers their marginal products by shifting them to other jobs where they are less valuable. Limitations on labor allocations (e.g., unions) may make the substitution effect larger by moving lower-skilled workers out of the unionized sector to lower-paid jobs.

The wage rate is assumed to be the same for any level of labor supply. This ignores the fact that wages for full-time work will generally be higher than those for part-time work, with overtime, when available, generally paying even more. For higher-income workers where the wage differences may not be so large, this may not be important as long as labor supplies are measured appropriately. For low-income workers (or elderly workers), this may be an important distinction, especially if learning on the job differs greatly between full-time and part-time jobs. This is a relatively unexplored dimension of optimal tax considerations. I suspect the issue is more the appropriate measure of labor elasticities than their use in optimal tax considerations. Let me reiterate. If full-time work is to be encouraged much more than part-time work and if full-time wages are much higher than part-time wages, then one may use the bottom end of the tax structure very differently from the current disregard system followed by the highest tax rates.

In addition to a wage, each of the five has an exogenous level of lump-sum income. This income is fully included in taxable income and is markedly higher for the top worker than for the other four. Since this is treated as lump-sum income, there is a large payoff to taxing it heavily. Presumably this fact adds considerably to the attraction of a higher marginal rate on high-income workers. Since this income is not really exogenous, once the intertemporal setting is recognized, the model presumably overstates the case for CIT.

The tax structure, wage rate, and unearned income give each individual his budget constraint (and are chosen subject to the government budget constraint).[2] The next step is to give each worker a utility function. As in previous studies, the Cobb–Douglas case is easy to calculate, but unsatisfactory in its workings. Thus they also consider the CES case, which is the basis of my remaining discussion. Following part of the optimal tax literature, they give each of the workers the same CES parameters. The elasticity of substitution is taken to lie between .35 and .5. While it greatly simplifies the formulation of the welfare function to assume the same parameter for each worker, one can question its appropriateness. Then the authors allow the elasticity of substitution to vary with the wage rate in a way that mimics labor supply by income class. It is an important finding of this paper that the desirable structure of progressivity is changed by the introduction of varying elasticities in this way. Of course, this introduction also involves a particular cardinalization of the different utility functions in forming the social welfare function.

Given the numbers of families in the other simulations reported at this conference, it is natural to wonder about the importance of having only five workers. (Of course, one wouldn't attempt optimization with the large models used in the other simulations.) There are several ways in which one could ask the question. Given the wage, the choice of a single worker with the average level of unearned income is a proxy for a distribution of lump-sum income levels. By going to ten workers rather than five one could test the importance of this assumption. I suspect that this aggregation is not important, although this is an unexplored area.[3]

---

[2]It is curious that the employee and employer values of the social security tax are treated differently by the authors in their discussion of the government budget.

[3]On the other hand there has been examination of the biases from aggregation of production sectors.

The second question is the use of a single worker with average wage as a proxy for a distribution of wages. My guess is that in the interior of the wage distribution, use of a one-worker approximation may be important for the location of the breakpoint (and thus for the size of zero-income transfer, given full integration), but it is probably not important for the optimal tax rates themselves.

However the story may be different at the lower extreme of the wage distribution, since income distribution is so important for the level of social welfare. The use of a single worker with $1.52 hourly wage and $782 in unearned income for a wage distribution from 0 to $2.86 and some (unstated) spread in unearned incomes may be very important for the results. This concern is heightened by the fact that the bottom worker has gross income of $2000 to $3000 in the central cases ($\sigma \neq 0, \infty$), along with a guaranteed transfer of about $3000 to $6000. To test this concern, one could add a sixth worker with zero wage and zero unearned income. This would focus on a key issue, the distribution of income among the poor.

The results on the nonfully integrated NIT also suggest that the use of a single person to represent the top 20% of the income distribution has a major effect on the results—permitting a lump-sum tax and zero marginal tax rate for so much of the population.

The Size of the Welfare Loss

Optimal tax simulations generally try to quantify the value of having the optimal tax. Before turning to Sadka, Garfinkel, and Moreland's method and results, let me cite two general findings in these simulations. First, the social welfare function is generally pretty flat in a sizable band around the optimal tax rate. Missing by 5 points on the optimal tax doesn't generally matter very much. (The CIT–NIT tax differences are larger than this.) Second, there is generally a large welfare penalty for the tax rates that are much too high, but that doesn't concern us here.

To quantify the loss from a shift to a nonoptimal tax, the authors calculate the additional resources needed by the government to allow the same level of social welfare with CIT as with the optimum. Going from varying CIT tax rates to a single tax rate for everyone has a welfare loss of $.1 to $6.4 billion, with a median between $1 and $2.5 billion. This is not a trivial sum in absolute terms. We can express it as a percentage of various larger things and it will look smaller. If one wants to compare this with administration costs, it is best done in absolute—not percentage—terms, since the savings from a uniform rate will only come from some of taxable income because we will not have a uniform rate everywhere. Of course, to make the sum big we can take the present discounted value over the expected life of the system.

Since it seems to me improbable that we will move to a proportional income tax, one would really want to focus on the bottom half of the income distribution in terms of both gains and losses from nonconstant marginal tax rates.

Limitations of the Optimal–Tax Approach

In the first section of my discussion, I considered several changes in the assumptions which might affect the conclusions. They involve minor modifications of the model, both in conceptual framework and computational difficulty. In this section, I want to discuss two possible limitations of the optimal-tax approach to this question. The conference already has papers on political decision making, stigma, and social cohesion; three elements that are omitted in the literature on optimal taxation. I want to single out two other elements that seem to me worth serious consideration.

It is easy and common to model an equilibrium at a fixed point in time. Once one starts to think about intertemporal behavior of economies (with uncertainty), however, the analysis becomes complicated at a rapid rate. Capital accumulation is the most obvious consideration. But life-cycle considerations for labor supply may also be important; particularly where the learning of habits and skills is important for both productivity and labor disutility and the return to current work lies partially in the future in both higher future pay and pensions.

The second omitted element I want to mention is labor demand. The speed of response of employers to changes in the character of labor supply must be an important part of the design of redistribution policies. This refers to both the skill mix of the labor supply and the supply of part-time rather than full-time labor, particularly by women and teenagers. If, as one suspects, labor productivity is significantly affected by the design of jobs (capital equipment, location, and organization) for the skill and hours mix available, then the model needs significant modification of both the definition of labor market equilibrium and the concentration on labor supply.

Discussion

KENNETH J. ARROW

The paper by Efraim Sadka, Irwin Garfinkel, and Kemper Moreland is an excellent application of economic theory to a problem of fundamental economic importance. The notion that redistribution by income taxation is limited by the inefficiency it creates is, of course, an old one, but the operational problem of seeking an optimal tax was only tackled in the immediately classic paper of Mirrlees (1971).

The analysis turns basically on two elements, a specification of the utility function for consumption and leisure, which determines the inefficiency in responding to income tax rates, and a criterion function for the choice of income tax rates. Individualistic ethics requires that the criterion be a function of the utilities of the individuals, the same utilities which the individuals maximize by their consumption-leisure choices. Once the problems are stated in this broad form, all relevant criteria are included, and there is no room for partial criteria such as "target efficiency." Indeed, virtually any reasonable economic analysis distinguishes sharply between exhaustive expenditures and transfers; to treat them on a par, as budget totals do, is a clear confusion. The only vague justification is the correct view that any budget item must be financed by taxation (apart from the relatively small budget deficit) and hence induces inefficiency. But if the inefficiency is specifically allowed for, "target efficiency" becomes an otiose concept.

The following sections deal with comments on specific aspects of the paper.

What Is Income Testing?

The paper claims to be a measure of the efficiency loss, if any, in abandoning income testing. But the definition of income testing used is surely very strange; it is a higher marginal tax rate on the poor than on the rich. While there is an explanation for this definition, it arises out of a particular history and has no fundamental basis.

Indeed, any program of taxes and transfers which aims to redistribute income, if only to alleviate poverty, is by definition income tested. This is true whether the marginal tax rate is increasing, decreasing, or constant. It is semantically or administratively possible to separate a fixed demogrant from the tax system which finances it and say that the demogrants constitute a non-income-tested system; but from the economic point of view of this paper, this is an evasion (though the distinction may be important for sociological or psychological reasons). And if one were to make the separation, then the progressivity of the tax system would be irrelevant.

It is clear that the identification of "universality" with decreasing marginal tax rates is the outgrowth of the many income-tested welfare programs. These indeed do have high implicit marginal income taxes on the poor, and these taxes fall to zero for those rich enough not to be eligible. But if one started with the income tax system rather than the welfare system, one would be tempted to give just the opposite definition; the lower marginal rates at the lower end of the scale are an income-tested program for redistributing from the rich to the poor (or at least to the middle class).

On a related point, I wonder at the emphasis on fully integrated tax–transfer systems. Once the elementary point that taxes can be negative as well as positive is grasped, there seems no especial reason for a change in rates to take place just at the point where taxes are zero. The restriction to fully integrated systems seems to be very strong.

The Important Lesson of the Analysis

The emphasis on the choice between "negative" and "credit" income taxes (in the authors' terminology) obscures what I consider to be much the biggest lesson. It is nothing less than a major rethinking of the meaning of progressivity in taxation. As I have mentioned above, redistributionist aims have been associated with *increasing* marginal tax rates. Now we learn that optimal redistribution requires *decreasing* marginal tax rates. One cannot complain that the aim of redistribution has been overlooked; it is there in the measure of inequality-aversion, though of course the factor of incentives has also been given explicit representation.

Though the analytic details are necessarily involved, one can step back and see the reasons for the new doctrine. Essentially, incentives are affected by marginal tax rates,[1] but redistribution is measured by average tax rates. If taxes are assumed to be positive numbers, then average and marginal tax rates move together so that the traditional view is right. But as soon as Milton Friedman or Lady Rhys-Williams or whoever is to be given credit made the simple observation that taxes could be and indeed effectively were negative, a new mathematical possibility arose. A constant marginal rate with a guarantee meant an increasing average tax. Even decreasing marginal rates are compatible with progression in the average tax sense. (I would recommend to the authors that, in their tables, they show the average as well as the marginal tax for each income class; it would avoid misunderstanding.)

The extreme implication of this new viewpoint is found in Sadka's (1976a) theorem that the marginal tax rate on the highest wage category should be *zero,* all taxation there being lump-sum. This is illustrated in the present paper in the Appendix. While the logic is unexceptionable, there is an implication which will be difficult to justify politically; the average tax rate will be decreasing for sufficiently large incomes. Hence, there will not be progression uniformly throughout the income structure even in the sense of average tax rates. The magnitude of this effect will depend on assumptions about labor supply in the high brackets, as discussed in the next section.

The Labor Supply Assumptions

It has been a common view that the elasticity of supply of labor in the higher-wage groups is very low. There have been interview studies in the past by Saunders (1951) and Break (1957) which concluded that taxes

---

[1]This statement might be misunderstood. Of course, a lump-sum transfer will usually also have an effect on the incentive to work; leisure is a normal good. But there is no efficiency loss in this reduction of work offered. The point made is that marginal tax rates create inefficient incentives.

had relatively little effect on the willingness of corporation executives and professionals to work. This effect derives in part from the indivisibility of many jobs, so that working less is not really an option, and from the motives for labor. There is nothing paradoxical or contrary to neoclassical economics in assuming that the marginal disutility of labor, especially of an interesting kind, may be zero or even negative. The idea that productive activity is an essential part of individual self-definition and satisfaction is common to many otherwise divergent viewers of human nature, from Aristotle to Marx.

The utility functions used in the study are certainly somewhat special in nature. There are all homothetic in consumption (equals posttax income) and leisure (defined rather arbitrarily as 60 hours per week less hours worked per week). (The functions would have a different shape if the point from which leisure was measured were altered.) For example, these utility functions imply that an increase in unearned income will increase consumption and leisure in the same proportion. If labor supply elasticity is very low in the high-income groups, then this result would fail; an increase in unearned income might be mostly taken out in consumption (or in savings in a dynamic model).

Clearly, if supply elasticities were low or even zero, marginal tax rates need not fall so sharply.

A Remark on Unearned Incomes

There is much to be said on the role of unearned incomes. To the extent that they arise from past savings, a fully dynamic model is needed to get at savings motives.

I will not enter into these questions here. I am surprised at the unearned income figures in Table 8.1. The level in the lowest quintile is determined by transfer payments, no doubt, but the relative constancy over the next three quintiles is surprising. Most surprising of all is the relatively low figure for the highest quintile. The average annual wage income there is about $25,000; if their unearned income arises from savings earning only 5%, the representative individual's assets would be $26,000, which seems very low.

To test the model more fully, I would have thought that a joint distribution of wages and unearned income could have been used. A wide dispersion of unearned incomes for each wage level could have been tried, to see if the results are sensitive to averaging over unearned income levels for given wages.

The Measurement of Welfare Losses

In the paper, welfare losses are measured in terms of compensating variations in the government budget available for exhaustive expenditures. For small variations, of course, all the measures one can think of are equivalent. For larger variations, however, this particular measure seems to introduce alien considerations. What about measuring losses in terms of the lump-sum transfers necessary to restore the original level of welfare?

Let T and T' be two tax schedules. For a given individual, let $V_i(A_i)$ and $V_i'(A_i)$ be the utilities attained, considered as functions of unearned income. (We hold the wage rates, w_i, constant in what follows; they represent an unalterable characteristic of the individual.) Suppose T is preferred on welfare grounds, so that

$$\sum_i [V_i(A_i)]^{1-\epsilon} > \sum_i [V_i'(A_i)]^{1-\epsilon}.$$

The less efficient tax schedule could yield the same utilities as the more efficient if the unearned income of individual i were increased by h_i, where

$$\sum_i [V_i(A_i)]^{1-\epsilon} = \sum_i [V_i'(A_i + h_i)]^{1-\epsilon}.$$

Among the many unearned income increments which satisfy this condition, choose that which minimizes the amount of lump-sum transfer, $\sum_i h_i$. The measure would be close to those of Hicks and others in the traditional literature.

9

Income Testing of In-Kind Transfers

BRIAN ABEL-SMITH

Introduction

There is no internationally agreed upon definition of what constitutes a social service, and even within countries there is debate about the appropriateness of definitions used in official statistics. Inevitably there is room for argument about, for example, the distinction between a social service and a public amenity and on how correction services should be classified. This paper is confined to the main services which would be widely accepted as social: (*a*) personal health care; (*b*) personal social services (including counseling services, day nurseries, services for children not cared for by their own parents or parent, and residential, domiciliary, and community services for the aged, disabled, and mentally ill or retarded); (*c*) education (including preschool and post-compulsory education); and (*d*) housing.

A Definition of Income Testing for Services

The concept of income testing when applied to services is harder to define than it may initially appear. The term income testing is presumably deliberately selected to distinguish it from means testing, where capital assets are also taken into account. Paying for services which are free at time of use by income-related taxes is not the subject under discussion. Compulsory insurance contributions are a form of income tax with special features. The contribution can be flat-rate or earnings-related (with or without a threshold of income from which payment has to be made). Investment income will normally be excluded and the right to use a particular service may depend upon the payment of the contribution. Alternatively, insurance coverage in the sense of right to use the service may be universal, but the poor could be exempt from actually paying any contributions and the near-poor may only have to pay reduced contributions.

A further complication arises when there is a ceiling beyond which contributions are not required. For example, 30% of the population of the Netherlands are not covered by national health insurance because their incomes are above the ceiling. In the case of Ireland there are three groups of coverage: The lowest income group receives free health care; an intermediate group is entitled to free in-patient and out-patient hospital care and to subsidized out-of-hospital medicine but has to purchase other health care in the private market; and the highest income group has no compulsory insurance. I assume that a service which is free at time of use should be regarded as universal even where this is not strictly true because use is restricted to the payers of the contribution (and their dependents).

All these different forms of income testing involved in the process of collecting compulsory levies, some of which may be service-specific, are assumed to be outside the scope of this conference, which is confined to the issue of whether services at time of use should be available free on a universal basis or on an income-tested basis. The income testing may be done by the provider (the school, the hospital, or the counseling agency) or by a separate agency to whom application is made either before or after receiving the service.

Income testing can be applied to particular parts of services (e.g., dentistry, spectacles, preschool education). It can also be applied to only part of the cost (e.g., when charges are made for pharmaceuticals, the poor can be exempt). A service can be universal for some categories of users (the aged, children, etc.) and income tested for others.

Income testing can be tapered or untapered. For example, a service can be free up to a defined low level of income and fully charged for above it. Alternatively there can be a sliding scale so that the poor obtain free services, the near-poor subsidized services, and those above these levels of income pay the whole cost or the whole of a nominal charge. Or the taper can be more gentle so that the cost is reduced or the charge lowered up to or beyond average income.

The Policy Objective

It is assumed that whatever arrangement is chosen for paying for services (income tested or universal) the policy objective is to enable both the poor and the near-poor to receive the service and that they should not be deterred from using it by the financing mechanism. Second, it is assumed that the service available to them should be of good standard—in no respect worse than the majority of average citizens would want to receive in the case of health, education, and personal social services, and little worse in the case of housing. These assumptions are made on the premise that the objective is to help the poor and that it is inequitable for the near-poor to fare worse than the poor in the services available to them.

It is particularly important that the poor should not be deterred from using services which are made available because their professionally determined need for most of these services is on average greater than that of the average citizen. For example, on average, their health status is lower, their children start school with educational disadvantages, and among the poor are disproportionately to be found elderly, disabled, and mentally handicapped persons.

The Case for Income Testing

The Target-Efficiency Argument

If the better-off paid for their own services rather than receiving them free, it is argued, more tax money would be available to help the poor and the near-poor if the same taxes were levied. The money might be used to raise levels of income support for those not at work and for those with one earner, low earnings, and/or large families. Alternatively, it might be used to extend the range of services available to the poor, to raise their quality, or to seek out underusers.

To this argument there are two objections. First, the capacity of the better-off to pay taxes would be reduced because they had to buy their own services instead of receiving them free as a universal service. But if taxes were not lowered to the full extent of the saving on services for the better-off, there would still be a surplus *theoretically* available to provide better services for the poor. The second objection is that the better-off may be willing to pay more taxes when a good standard of services is available to them as well as the poor than if the use of the tax-financed services were restricted to the poor and near-poor. Probably the force of these objections varies in different societies, and the question cannot be resolved by quoting the experience of one country as if it were a guide to another.

The Argument Based on Who Uses the Service

The case for income testing is strongest in those services where the cost of service use is skewed toward the better-off and weakest where the cost of service use is skewed toward the poor. For this purpose it is not relevant to examine the question of how far the "value" to users is below the cost of providing the service. How does the cost per head of different social services vary by income group? The following analysis is based on British experience and may not be applicable elsewhere.

The need for the services for the long-term sick, the disabled, and the mentally handicapped arises out of a condition which has caused inability to earn. The need for services is continuous and adds to ordinary living expenses. There is therefore only a weak case for income testing such services.

In Britain under the National Health Service, wholly reliable data based on income groups are not available for the study of short-term health care. This is partly because there is no administrative need to calculate the cost of health care used by different individuals in a national service. Moreover, there are major conceptual problems in deciding how income level should be defined for this purpose: Income during the week or month of sickness? During the year when the sickness occurred? Past normal income? Or prospective income? There is evidence that perceived illness is considerably greater in the lower-income group. On the other hand, there is evidence which suggests that particular health services and especially more costly services are used by the higher social classes more than by the lower social classes (Le Grand, 1978). Probably there is little variation by income group.

It may seem at first sight that in compulsory education the cost of service use is roughly equal in different income groups subject to differences in family size. But the attendance record of children from poorer families is lower than that of children from better-off families. And teacher time may be disproportionately devoted to the more "gifted" child and to children who have acquired wider vocabularies from their home background. For these and other reasons universal compulsory education may favor the children in better-off families. In addition, the use of preschool education tends to be higher in the higher income groups than in the lower.

Post-compulsory education is used disproportionately more by children of parents in higher income groups than by those whose parents are in lower income groups. Similarly, those who continue in education achieve, on average, higher incomes than those who do not. The most costly university courses, such as medical education, are used disproportionately by the children of high-income parents, and they in turn achieve high incomes themselves with the qualifications obtained with the education.

Thus, if the argument is accepted, the case for income testing is greatest for post-compulsory education (particularly for the later years), next for preschool education, next for short-term health care, leaving a much weaker case for personal social services and perhaps the weakest case of all for services provided to those who are chronically or permanently unable to work.

The Argument for Equity in Services Received

If the better-off have to buy their own services, according to this argument, they will choose the level of service they are prepared to pay for. It is clear that the better-off and more articulate tend to receive more costly services for a given type of need (as professionally defined) than the poorer and less articulate. As mentioned above, this is the case with the British National Health Service. This may be because they live in areas where professional staff also want to live, so that high-quality staff is more easily recruited or contracted than in poorer areas. It may be because they are better informed on the quality of different services which are available. Or it may be because they articulate their demand more insistently, are more skilled in complaining, are favored by those who authorize resources, or there may be other reasons. Income testing can prevent this type of inequity. The better-off may still decide to *purchase* something better than is provided for the poor, but if they are spending their own money this cannot be said to be an abuse.

What the *average* citizen is prepared to pay for could provide a market criterion to indicate the level of service to aim at for the poor. To this argument there are three objections. First there may be benefits to society as a whole from higher standards of service than the average citizen is prepared to pay for (e.g., external benefits in health and education). Second, the assumption that the average citizen's capacity to pay for services is not affected by the need for them may be erroneous. This is clearly not the case when there is major medical or social need. Third, the assumption that there is effective choice and that the average citizen is knowledgeable enough to exercise it is also questionable. In the case of health care there may not be effective choice when the choosing is done by the doctor rather than the patient. Moreover, patients are also in a poor position to know whether doctors choose appropriate services or what criteria are used by different doctors in choosing.

The main cash benefits are intended to provide maintenance or to maintain the living standards of families or individuals when absence from work is socially sanctioned. This is the function of old age and survivors' pensions, unemployment benefits, and sickness and disability benefits. Cash benefit is intended to pay in whole or part for ordinary living expenses. When, however, such an individual is admitted to an institution such as an old-age home, home for the disabled, nursing home, or hospital, it would involve duplicated provision to provide free care, thus the resident of the institution should be charged on an income-tested basis for the ordinary living costs covered by the institution provided there is a genuine saving[1] and the resident is left with money for personal spending. Similarly, when a child is admitted to a children's home, an income-tested charge may be levied on the parents to recoup the costs which would have been incurred on the child if he had remained at home.

The Case for Universal Services

Stigma

Stigma is important for two reasons. First it can lead to deep resentment against the whole social system. Second, the prospect of the stigma of being income tested can be a barrier to use—for example, the risk is taken that an illness will go away without paid professional help. The strength of the barrier depends upon a number of different factors.

---

[1]An alternative is for the cash benefit to be reduced because institutional care is provided. This is the practice adopted in Britain for hospital care. Weekly cash benefit is reduced after a period of eight weeks' residence in hospital. It has often been suggested in Britain that patients should (as in Belgium) make a daily payment to hospital even for short stays (under 8 weeks) in view of the home savings in daily living expenses which occur when the patient is in hospital. This has been resisted in Britain on the grounds that home savings are not as large as is often assumed, vary considerably between individuals, and can be negative. For example, if the mother is admitted to hospital, extra payments may be made to a homemaker, or a relative may be invited to live free, which absorbs the home savings. Second, the actual cost of catering by the father for the family (excluding the mother) may be higher than when the mother is present and does the catering, because he

First, it depends upon the perceived merit of using a particular service. The student who has won admission to a university may have no hesitation in applying for financial support because to want to take further education is socially approved behavior. To be unable to find the money for other expenses such as medical care, school clothing, or meals at school is a confession of failure in a society which expects people to pay their way. The man who cannot pay for his wife and children has failed as a provider.

Second, the stigma of using income-tested services depends on who becomes aware of the perceived failure. If separate services such as hospitals, schools, or counseling agencies are provided for the poor, not only the staff of the income-testing office but the staff of the service (doctors, nurses, teachers, counselors, etc.) and the local community are aware of who has had to resort to them. For these and other reasons segregated services for the poor should be avoided. But they are arguments against a particular form of providing income-tested services, not all forms. In one service however, community stigmatization is hard to avoid. This is the provision of public housing when eligibility and rent depend on income tests. It is for this reason that in Britain housing need rather than income is used to allocate public housing (though inevitably they are related). It is also for this reason that the more progressive public authorities have attempted to build for all social classes and charge full-cost rents to high-income tenants. But the extent of higher-income housing has not been sufficient to prevent particular estates attracting a certain amount of stigma. The extent of stigma is probably much lower in Britain now that a third of families live in public housing than in the United States, where public housing plays a very small role.

Stigma can also arise in a service used by the whole community. For example school meals are provided in nearly all British schools. Such meals are charged for but poor children can obtain them free. Where schools have separate queues for children who pay and children who do not, or the dinner money is collected in class, poor children become known to their classmates. For these and other reasons, some parents pay for meals which their children would be eligible to receive free.

---

is an inexperienced caterer and has restricted cooking skills. Third, extra costs may be caused by the admission of a member of the family to hospital. There are the transport costs of visiting the hospital. There are also the conventionally required gifts of flowers, fruit, etc. to the patient. Finally there is what has been called the "trousseau effect." Admission to hospital is for most people the only time when their most private possessions are on public view. As a result new nightgowns, dressing gowns, bed jackets, and toilet requisites are purchased of a quality considerably above what would normally be used at home, and these new items are worn out or used at a faster rate.

The degree of stigma also depends on the form of income test. If the test is simply to separate two categories—those entitled to a free service and those not so entitled (in other words there is no income taper) the attitudes of the staff administering it are likely to be more stigmatizing. Their role is one of gatekeeper—to keep out those not eligible. Inevitably they tend to view claimants more suspiciously then if their task were simply to assess how much should be paid, and this suspicion adds to stigma. An income test for services of this type is undesirable for this reason. Moreover, it does not meet the policy criterion stated above of providing some service to the near-poor.

Stigma can therefore be reduced by separating the process of income testing from the actual provision of the service. For example all tenants in Britain, public or private, can apply for income-tested rent subsidies. In France patients have to make a copayment of 20% or 25% of cost for certain health services. The provider submits the bill and the patient claims 75% or 80% from the national health insurance system. The poor can, however, claim the remaining 20 to 25% from the local public assistance agency. The provider does not therefore know who is obtaining free services. It so happens however that public assistance in France involves considerable stigma—probably because it is very much a residual service and has no income taper. An agency operating a tapered income test for copayments could be established.

The Horizontal Distribution of Income

Our societies have developed many different devices to help relieve parents of part of the costs of supporting their dependent children. Generally the earliest have been free education and allowances for children in the income tax. Many countries provide family allowances. Since World War II several European countries have been assimilating child tax allowances into one tax-free benefit payable for each child. From April 1979 Britain has fully adopted this system of cash aid to children. One of the main arguments for assimilation was that child allowances in the income tax disproportionately helped the better-off, since this form of indirect cash aid is not available to those below the tax threshold. Thus if it is desired to reduce the cost of child support going to better-off families, the simplest step—though not necessarily the easiest politically—is to abolish child allowances in the income tax. The arguments that the responsibility for maintaining dependent children reduces the capacity to pay income tax and that financial help for children from public authorities should be concentrated on the poorer families are not compatible. If education were made into an income-tested rather than universal service, this would be equivalent to a negative child tax allowance or negative family allowance. It would turn upside down the argument that those with family responsibilities have less taxable capacity, an argument which should logically be applied to indirect as well as to direct taxes.

Two major changes have occurred, however, in both our societies since World War II. First, there has been a trend toward higher relative earnings of women, partly as a consequence of legislation for equal pay for men and women and partly as a consequence of improved job opportunities for women. For this and other reasons the proportion of married women at work has been increasing. While previously marriage led to the withdrawal of women from the labor force, now this does not typically occur until the birth of the first child. Increasingly the period in which an earner (normally the mother) withdraws from the labor force to care for dependent children is seen as a temporary rather than a permanent break in employment.

The question increasingly raised by women's organizations as an issue of women's rights is whether society has an obligation to secure that all mothers have a genuine option to resume paid work without loss of seniority after a period of a year or more of maternity leave. In other words the question posed is whether child-minder costs should be paid either in part by the employer as a fringe benefit or wholly by government. A low earner may receive no financial advantage from working because the full cost of day care at a professionally acceptable standard may amount to more than net earnings (after tax and the costs of going to work have been deducted). Thus typically a woman without special skills finds that she contributes more to family income by caring for her own children than by earning and paying for their care.

If the aim were simply to secure that every parent should have some cash incentive to take paid work, then day care and/or education services for young children could be income tested on the earned income of the lower earner (in the case of a couple) or the sole earner in the case of one-parent families. The woman who could command high earnings would, of course, be able to pay the full costs of day care out of her earnings. But the more children she had who needed the service, the higher her earnings would need to be. If, on the other hand, the aim is to secure that women with children should have the right to the same spending power as low-earning women who do not have children, this points to a universal service. If it is right for maternity leave or benefit to be universally available, it can be argued that either this should continue until the child starts compulsory education or, as an option, day care should be provided as a universal service.

Why has society made provisions for education on a universal basis but not for preschool care, which is crucially important for progress later at school? The arguments for preschool care shade into those for investment in the right to educational opportunities, discussed below. How far should the costs of child rearing be borne by society as a whole in an age when women can so readily control their fertility and so many do so?

Income Maintenance in the Face of Unpredictable Risk

Many cash benefits provide for contingencies which cannot be predicted by the individual—maintenance when sick or unemployed or the risks of being a survivor. What cannot be predicted is if and when it will occur and even more important when it will end. The same is true of the "need" for health and social care. But there are further additional features: (a) Serious illness[2] destroys earning capacity so that major needs for health and social care come on top of and at the same time as the need for income support. (b) The cost of meeting these needs cannot be predicted. No one knows in advance how much health and social care (as professionally assessed) he will need, and at what time. It may not even be possible to predict this at the time of the onset of illness. Will the illness respond to treatment or will heavy costs for health and social care continue throughout life? These costs can, even with the existing level of professional knowledge, be very high in relation to average earnings. A week of health care can consume a year's earnings and a year of care the earnings of a lifetime. And there is every reason to expect that future costs will be substantially higher than present costs.

Because of the special characteristics of supply and demand, the *total* costs of health and social care cannot be privately insured. Any private

[2]Some needs for health care (dentistry and spectacles) do not normally cause incapacity for work and others (contacts with physicians leading to diagnostic tests and/or pharmaceuticals) may not do so. Moreover, many such needs (dentures, crowns, fillings, and spectacles) are nonurgent, postponable and not costly in relation to annual income. There may also be an element of moral hazard—e.g., dental neglect or broken spectacles. Charging for such services (with the charge waived for the poor) is less likely to cause hardship. It is presumably for this reason that such services tend to be selected for charges or copayments under compulsory health insurance with a provision that the public assistance agency will pay the cost for the poor. When the charges for health care are low, the administrative costs of charging can absorb a disproportionate part of the revenue.

policy has to be limited in one or more respects—for example, days of hospital care, duration of policy, excluded risks. Inability to "afford" most goods can be remedied by saving up to buy them later on. In the case of health services there may be no chance of earning or saving unless treatment is purchased now.

Thus the social aims of social security and fringe benefits are frustrated if health care costs are not underwritten. What such measures are intended to provide is a guarantee of living standards not of income status. It is the latter which the serious illness of an uninsured or underinsured family member undermines. The white-collar worker or the executive does not want to find his living standards reduced to below those of a blue-collar worker by having to pay for the costs of his kidney dialysis or his wife's multiple sclerosis.

Similar arguments apply in education and personal social services. Should parents find their living standard radically lowered because they have a mentally handicapped or severely disabled child needing specialized social care and special education? It is for this reason that the costs of unpredictable and not wholly insurable services should be met on a universal basis.

Universal Health Care and Society

Society has a duty to prevent ill-health whenever possible and particularly to prevent and treat communicable disease to prevent the spread to other people. People cannot know in advance of obtaining medical advice whether their ill health is due to communicable disease or not and prevention is more likely to be carried to the desirable limit if everyone is in regular contact with the health care services. The absence of money barriers encourages the seeking of advice and thus helps to protect others from communicable diseases.

The causes of much of the need for health care lie deep in the fabric of society. Many of the cause agents are unknown. It is, however, clear that advanced industrialized societies have developed many diseases which were virtually unknown a century or more ago and are only found on a very small scale or not at all in rural developing countries. This suggests that a wide variety of diseases have been created by society—by our environment, by the food we eat, and by the life we lead. Only in a few cases, where the necessary evidence exists, is it possible to transfer the costs of damaged health to those who can be held responsible for it—such as motorists, suppliers of faulty goods, employers who cause identifiable industrial disease, and manufacturers of damaging foods and pharmaceuticals. Thus society has a duty to pay for ill-health because much of it is caused by persons acting in good faith and not knowing that their actions are causing ill-health in others. Universal health care contributes to social cohesion.

Money barriers lead some people to delay in seeking health care. Conditions which could be treated if presented early become untreatable when presented late. If society makes provision for the poor to be protected from this risk, it is inequitable not to extend this protection to all.

An income-tested service is inequitable. It helps those who are not insured while denying or restricting help to those who have taken out good insurance cover at substantial financial sacrifice.

The need for health care is a bad and not a good. It is in a different category from everything else in the individual preference schedule and thus should be provided for separately outside it, according to a collective preference schedule.

Educational Opportunities

Historically, education in Britain became compulsory before it became free, but it was made free because it was compulsory. It was the answer found to the problem of enforcement on poor families who argued that they could not afford school fees or they could not manage without the benefits of child labor or both. The underlying premise was that *society* had an interest in securing that all children were educated.[3]

In our more affluent and credential-conscious society, it can be argued that if compulsory education were income tested the problem of enforcement would not pose insoluble problems or at least more insoluble problems than it does at present: It is now perhaps more common

---

[3]The classic case for free or nearly free education was made by John Stuart Mill in 1848, though he modified his views eleven years later in his essay "On Liberty" (1859):

There are certain primary elements and means of knowledge, which it is in the highest degree desirable that all human beings born into the community should acquire during childhood. If their parents, or those on whom they depend, have the power of obtaining for them this instruction, and fail to do it, they commit a double breach of duty, towards the children themselves, and towards the community generally, who are all liable to suffer seriously from the consequences of ignorance and want of education in their fellow-citizens. It is therefore an allowable exercise of the powers of government to impose on parents the legal obligation of giving elementary instruction to children. This, however, cannot be fairly done, without taking measures to insure that such instruction shall always be accessible to them, either gratuitously or at a trifling expense [p. 954].

for the intentions of the legislature to be flouted by willful children than by willful parents. Thus the considerations which originally led to free universal education in the compulsory ages may no longer be compelling.

A stronger argument may be found by examining the likely consequences of income testing. If education were income tested (whether voucher financed or not), governments would be in a much weaker position to prevent the extensive development of schools which were segregated by race, by religion, and by parental income. In neither of our countries is government prepared to forbid parents from sending their children to schools where they pay the cost, provided that educational standards are met. But the requirement that parents must pay taxes for schools they do not use as well as fees to schools they do use makes the scale of fee-paying schooling not too obstructive. If schools were income tested this would no longer be the case as it would no longer be acceptable to secure a near monopoly of local schools. The quality of schooling would vary sharply by parental income and the children of near-poor families would start adult life with relative educational handicaps. It would also be extremely difficult to secure that the children of the poor fared any better. Thus the case today for *free* compulsory education rests heavily on the case for equalizing educational opportunities to promote social integration. And they apply to care and education before the age of compulsory education as well as after it.

A universal service enables the bulk of educational resources to be distributed according to the professionally assessed educational needs of children rather than the income-backed aspirations of their parents. Of course not everyone would agree that all these aims are desirable.

The arguments for free health services for children are similar to the arguments for free educational services. Health defects can limit the ability of a child to benefit from education. The earlier defects are found and treated (where this is possible), the greater the benefit the nation will obtain from its investment in education. In so far as free education is intended to provide equal opportunities, this objective can be frustrated if the child is absent from school because of illness which is treated too late or inadequately because of the cost. Moreover opportunities in life can be restricted because of poor health just as they can be by limited education, and poor health can be a reason for lack of educational attainment. Parents cannot know in advance that their child will be born with spinal bifida, a faulty heart valve, or will be brain-damaged by a disease or even by immunization. Very substantial costs may need to be incurred to give a child with severe heart defects the opportunity to develop as normally as possible and compensate for disabilities to the fullest extent possible.[4]

Universal services can select for above-average provision of service on the basis of professionally determined need without worrying about whether the user or the user's family is willing to pay all or part of the extra cost. In the education services, for example, extra teaching resources can be allotted to children resident in disadvantaged areas, to children who are deaf, blind, partially sighted, dyslectic, aphasic or who suffer from some other handicap, to slow learners, to children whose parents speak a different language from the language of instruction, or to children of very high intelligence. In the health service, discrimination may also be geographical: for example, it is the aim of policy in England, among other considerations, to allot higher resources for the National Health Service to regions and areas with above average age-standardized mortality (Great Britain, Her Majesty's Stationery Office, 1978a) and to concentrate preventive services for children on neighborhoods where infant mortality is high and attendance at child clinics low. Any treatment, however expensive, can be given to any patient without worrying about the ability of any patient or family to pay the cost. In addition, hospital stays can be extended for reasons of medical education or research without worrying about charges falling on the user.

As pointed out earlier, on the grounds of the vertical distribution of income, there is the strongest case for income testing post-compulsory education on two grounds. First, use increases substantially with parental income. Second, on average, the lifetime earnings of the average student are considerably higher though earnings are foregone during the period of extended education.

The snag with parental income testing is that parents are under no legal obligation to pay the share of the costs which they are assessed as being in a position to pay. Moreover, better-off parents are in a position to dictate whether their child, without resources of his own or ability to raise a loan, should have further education, and if so, the form that education will take. They may be willing to support a course in law or medicine but not in sociology or fine arts. Thus if the service is income tested, the child of poor parents will be able to apply for any type of course, knowing that financial support will be available, and continue in education as long as educational institutions are prepared to provide the

---

[4]The fact that everything possible is not done for the health of children in the United States is well documented in a recent book by Silver (1978). Even the provision of free health care for children does not mean that all is done to safeguard their health, as shown in a recent British report, *Fit for the Future: The Report of the Committee on Child Health Services* (Great Britain, Her Majesty's Stationery Office, 1976).

service, while the child of well-off parents is subject to any restrictions his parents choose to impose (assuming that no loan is available). The child from the more affluent family remains dependent on his or her parents while the child of poor parents is dependent on the paying agency. It is for these reasons that the income testing of parents can obstruct the opportunities of the young. And in the case of older students it becomes absurd.

The alternative is income testing on the current income of full-time students. This would only lead to small savings in the public cost of the system from those students who have inherited assets or enter higher education after they have acquired substantial savings from previous work on which they receive an income. For these reasons the benefit is unlikely to justify the administrative cost and aggravation.

The third alternative is financing by loans, to be repaid out of later work income on an income-tested basis. This falls within our definition of a universal service if the loans are universally available. The repayment becomes a service-specific tax. It should be noted in passing that this is not an attractive option for any government to *introduce* because of the long gap in time before any substantial repayments take place. The government has to incur the odium of introducing the system and face the opposition of student organizations in the knowledge that the fiscal gain from repayments will accrue to later administrations— assuming that they have not responded to the political pressure to repeal the scheme.

We are not, however, concerned here with the likelihood of such a scheme commending itself to politicians, but with its merits. The main arguments used against the loan system of financing are

1. It could lead to a fall in the output of certain categories of highly qualified manpower which could not be quickly remedied. Selected courses could, however, be subsidized once an undesirable trend was identified.
2. It would encourage the emigration of highly qualified personnel to escape the obligation to repay. The force of this argument, however, is not strong in the case of the wealthier industrialized nations.
3. It would lead students to seek too much paid work to reduce the extent of borrowing, with the result that they do not derive the fullest possible benefit from the education provided. Colleges could, however, attempt to restrict time devoted to earning.
4. It might discourage students from poorer families from applying for loans through lack of confidence that they will achieve suffi-

ciently high earnings to repay them with comfort. This assumes that such students are more risk-averse.

5. There would be considerable problems in tracing those liable to pay. High levels of default would discredit such a scheme.

6. A special problem is how to assess repayments from those who marry. If the assessment for repayment is on the joint income of the married couple, the scheme ends up as a negative dowry. For this reason the assessment to repay might be only on the earnings of the person who originally received the education.

One can conclude that the arguments against loans repaid out of later income are largely but not entirely administrative.

Conclusion: Income Testing as a Scarce Resource

How can these opposing arguments be reconciled? The main argument in favor of income-tested services was that more tax money could, in theory, be made available to help the poor. Whether the better-off would approve this use of their money rather than have it back in their own pockets to help pay for the services which had now become income-tested is much more questionable. A second argument was that if the better-off had to pay for their services they would choose the level of service they were prepared to pay for. The third argument, which only applied to residential services, was to prevent duplication provided by cash benefits and enforce the obligation on parents to maintain their children.

The case for universal services was based on a variety of considerations which applied to different sections of the population. One argument was in terms of the benefits to the poor and near-poor: Income testing tends to involve stigma unless what is sought is particularly meritorious, though tests can be devised which limit the extent. Stigma is important not just in terms of subjective feelings but in terms of the objective fact of creating a barrier to use. A second series of arguments involved benefits to those who are neither poor nor near-poor—protecting the living standards of parents during periods of child rearing (particularly women's earnings) and ensuring that living standards are guaranteed against unpredictable risks. A third series of arguments was in terms of gains to society as a whole (not just service users) from investment in the right to educational opportunities and all the social gains from universal health care. These last two series of arguments are a major challenge to the second argument in favor of income-tested services. In effect, they posit that what the better-off are prepared to pay for is not an appropriate criterion for establishing the level of service to be provided to the better-off or to the poor or near-poor. Even more important, they pose fundamental questions about values—about the sort of societies we want to have. How far should society share in the costs of child rearing—a particularly important question in view of the current low birth rates in most highly industrialized societies? What importance do we attach to the maintenance of living standards in all sections of society? How much do we believe in the right of the next generation to be given the maximum opportunity to make the best they can of their lives?

The question which must be faced is that income testing is a scarce resource. An income test without any taper would provide free services only for the poor and require the near-poor to pay the whole cost of the services they use. This would not meet the policy objective of equity for the near-poor. It would also, for reasons stated earlier, be more stigmatizing. But while a universal service adds to the marginal rate of taxation throughout the whole range or at the higher end of the income distribution, any income taper adds to the marginal tax rate at the lower end. If the taper is gentle, the administrative cost becomes large because of the number brought into the system. If the taper is tough the cumulative tax rate can become intolerable. This can also happen if a family is claiming several income-tested services, each with a moderate taper. Thus if it were decided that the case had been made for income testing every social service, the cumulative effect of all the different income tests could be socially, if not also economically, intolerable. Even if it were proved that a high cumulative tax rate did not discourage effort, it seems nevertheless socially undesirable, if not inequitable, for poorer people to be put in a position such that extra hours of work, less pleasant work at higher rates of pay, more difficult work, or more work done on piece rates leads to negligible extra reward.

Therefore if the cumulative tax rate is regarded as a scarce resource, it should not be "wasted." There is no objection on these grounds to income testing ad hoc claims for unanticipated social service needs such as help with a dental bill or a wheelchair. But it is wasteful to use the cumulative tax rate on continuing needs for services which do not help all the poor. Not every family has children currently being educated. Not every family has a member with a *regular* need for some type of health or personal social service. On the other hand, every poor family needs cash and virtually every family has housing. Hence income testing should be reserved for uses which help virtually all the poor all the time, such as help with housing costs (including property taxes) and fuel bills and for lightening the load of service-specific contributions—particularly social security contributions whether for cash benefits or health insurance.

Housing cost is a particularly strong candidate for an income-tested subsidy because the original distribution of income results in large numbers of families being unable to afford housing that is regarded as socially adequate by the standards of the time. The problem may be made worse by government action, in the form of taxes falling on house property which raise still further the cost of housing. Government action to drive really bad housing off the market (in Britain under Public Health Act powers, or in the United States by code enforcement) may only replace one set of evils by another if adequate housing is beyond the reach of those displaced.

The case is reinforced by the argument that young children should be protected from bad housing caused by the low income of their parents (generous allowances for children can be built in when making the income assessment). An additional consideration is that pay levels and job prospects do not rapidly adjust to changes in rent levels. Subsidies to rents may enable people to stay in high-rent areas where jobs are available rather than move to low-rent areas where they are not. Thus such subsidies *may* be cost effective in terms of saving cash support for the unemployed. But actions which help to reduce unemployment may be considered socially desirable even when they are not cost-effective in this sense.

A special feature of housing, not shared by most other services, is the great variations in the amount that people pay to use very similar kinds of housing. Inflation coupled with fixed-interest mortgages makes the disparities even more extreme. Subsidies based only on income and family circumstances could be ineffective or wasteful: If set on the basis of average rents and average expenditure on mortgages, the subsidy would be too low to achieve its purposes for large numbers of households; if set high enough to be adequate for everyone, a single scale would be grossly extravagant by giving those with very low annual costs—such as homeowners who have paid off their mortgages—far more than they need. An income-tested subsidy needs therefore to be related to annual housing expenditure as well as income and family circumstances. Fuel costs become closely related to housing costs when the system of heating is part of the property. Thus fuel costs could be built into the same system of income-tested subsidy.

If, therefore, income testing is more target-effective when it helps virtually all the poor all the time, it follows that it should not be applied to recurring social service needs which not all the poor need to use, such as education, the bulk of health care, day nurseries, and other personal social services (except when it is applied to prevent duplicated provision for ordinary living expenses by cash benefits or to enforce the obligation to maintain children—the third point made in favor of income testing services).

This would seem to be the best means of directing maximum help to the poor. How far our societies are actually prepared to go along this road is another question. What it implies is that a universal structure of social services in-kind is needed for a whole variety of reasons including not only the advantage to users who are poor, near-poor, and above these levels of income but to society as a whole. Income testing should be used to redistribute resources through the way services are financed and through special benefits which reach all the poor.

Perhaps the most profound summary is that made by Richard Titmuss in 1968:

> The challenge that faces us is not the choice between universal and selective social services. The real challenge resides in the question: what particular structure of universalist service is needed in order to provide a framework of values and opportunity bases within and around which can be developed socially acceptable selective services aiming to discriminate positively, with the minimum risk of stigma, in favour of those whose needs are greatest [p. 135].

Discussion

EVELINE M. BURNS

I confess to having had considerable difficulty in preparing appropriate comments on Abel-Smith's paper. This was due partly to the range and variety of the ideas and issues covered so that it was not easy to select among them or indeed to determine what was his main thrust. I also have to admit that I was unable to fathom his organizational system. But it was also due to my own intellectual problem in accepting the universal-selective dichotomy which is today the conceptual "in-thing," especially among the social work intellectuals. To me, "universal" means exactly that, namely, that a service is available to everyone. A selective service is one available only to limited groups, who may be selected on the basis of age, or sex, or physical condition, or intellectual competence, or residence, or citizenship, or family size, or income status, etc. The current meaning of "selective" is however to define a service that is available or charged for only on the basis of income status. This is the concept that Abel-Smith has adopted, quite understandably in view of the subject of the conference, and in what follows, if I use the term at all, it will be in that sense. But I do wish we could develop some other terminology that more precisely describes the distinction we wish to make. Perhaps "free versus income-conditioned" services would be better.

It should be noted that income testing is a device that can take two forms and serve two ends. First, it can be used to restrict access to the service or program to persons with incomes below a specified level. Limiting the scope of a compulsory health insurance system to persons with incomes below a certain level is one example, restricting the benefits of Medicaid to persons with some specified level of income is another. Second, income testing can also be used to permit access to the service but to reduce the benefit secured by the richer by levying a variable charge for its use. It is this second form of income testing which appears to be the main concern of Abel-Smith's paper, and here I ran up against a third problem in commenting on it, for it seems to me that in some parts of his paper he is talking about whether there should be *any* charge for a service and sometimes about whether that charge should be income-conditioned and thus income tested. Both issues are important but they are not identical.

Should There Be Any Charge for a Service?

The first issue to be decided is surely whether there should be any charge at all for a service. In favor of doing so, a number of considerations can be adduced.

First, there is the purely financial advantage. It is a way of raising money to support the service that may meet with less resistance than collecting the funds from the general tax system, because people may pay more gladly if they see that they are getting a direct benefit in return for what they pay. Even here, however, Abel-Smith points out what concerns people is the cumulative tax rate, and among the richer there may still be resistance if the combined charges due to the general tax system and the payment of the service charge come to be felt oppressive.

Whether or not it would pay to make a charge for purely financial reasons depends among other things on the costliness of the service. If the cost is relatively low (e.g., free or subsidized travel on buses or subways), it could be held that the costs of either limiting access to the service by income status or collecting a charge would outweigh the financial gains. On the other hand, a service such as health care, or basic education, or some of the components of such services, could be very costly and justify a charge on the grounds of making a needed contribution to the financing of the service.

Second, making a charge for a service could be defended, and often is, on the grounds that it fosters economy in the use of the otherwise free service. As Abel-Smith reminds us, this argument is valid only if the service falls into one of the following three categories:

1. Its nature and quality are known to the potential users (and this is clearly not the case in regard to some social services, e.g., health or legal services).

2. The potential consumers are the people who in fact decide the extent of the demand for the service. The most obvious departure from this requirement is of course in the health services, where it is typically the providers, not the users, who determine the extent of demand for the service. About the only exception to this situation occurs when medical prosthetics or equipment, and perhaps drugs, are lost or damaged because of the carelessness of the user (e.g., lost or broken eyeglasses or dentures).

3. A final requirement which will determine whether or not there is any significant problem of overuse is that the service must be pleasant or desirable. To many people immunizations and inoculations, for example, are unpleasant and to be avoided and so overuse of the service is scarcely a problem.

Third, making a charge can also be used as a way of excluding some people from any access to the program. Those affected however will be mainly the poor of course. And it is doubtful if this purpose would make sense in the social services, the vast majority, if not all of which, have presumably been developed because the society believed that they met minimal needs of the population, for health, education, shelter, etc., not currently being met because of limited income.

A fourth argument in favor of making a charge for a service is that it lends itself to variation by income status and the possibility of securing other desired objectives such as equity or income redistribution. These I shall discuss when I deal with income testing per se.

Should a Charge Be Income Conditioned (and Tested)?

Having made the decision to impose a service charge, the next question is whether it should be income adjusted (and tested) or uniform for all users. Here a number of considerations must be taken into account.

How important is it that the service be used by all who are eligible (which may include the entire population or some category defined other than by income)? If there is a danger that the uniform fee may create a financial barrier to the use of the service to the extent that is believed to be in the public interest, varying the charge by reference to income status, and making it zero in the case of the poorest, may achieve the desired objective.

Thus it is often held that charges made for visits to the doctor will discourage use of preventive services or lead to the postponement of consultations and treatment that might avoid more costly medical services later.

Importance is often attached to conserving resources, either real or financial, by limiting the benefits of a service to those who are deemed most "needy." This is the so-called economic "efficiency" consideration, that in an effort to help the admittedly needy, one should not at the same time give benefits to those who are not needy.

Abel-Smith's treatment of the cumulative tax rate as a scarce resource, the use of which must be limited to priority needs, is intriguing in this connection. This would seem to be an argument in support of using income testing to determine eligibility (i.e., to exclude persons with income above some specified level) rather than in support of making an income-adjusted charge.

It may be believed important to retain the middle classes as users of the service, thereby having among the users a group who are accustomed to good-quality service and who can exert some pressure in favor of high standards, thus avoiding the danger that "a service only for the poor is apt to be a poor service." If so, income-tested charges are a way of keeping the middle classes in the program yet limiting the net benefit they derive.

Income-conditioning may be a necessary way of achieving some of the objectives sought in making a charge for a service. Thus a uniform deductible or copayment, imposed in the interest of controlling usage of a health service, may, if it is to be within the means of the poor, be no deterrent at all to the richer. If it is meaningful to higher-income receivers, it may be an unbearable burden to the low-income receivers. Varying the charge by income helps to avoid this dilemma.

Similarly, making a charge variable by income with zero rates at some levels avoids the "all or nothing" cutoff and the accompanying "notch" problems created by an income-limited "access" policy. This may be especially appealing in the case of the social services. For unlike the cash transfer programs, it is not easy to avoid or modify the "notch" problem by tapering off the benefit as income increases. Abel-Smith suggests that some parts of a service might be free and others income tested, but services do not readily lend themselves to such divisions. One can hardly envisage for example a gradual reduction of the basic education service benefit as income increases. The benefit has to be "all-or-nothing." So you offer the entire service but make an income-tested charge.

There may be other social objectives that can be attained by income testing for the social services. As Abel-Smith suggests, there may be a concern about income redistribution. It appears to be generally accepted that the rich should pay proportionately more than the poor in the way of taxes to support the general services of government. And in fact the income tax *is* income tested. Thus it can be argued that for consistency the same policy should be applied to charges for the use of the social services. The counter-argument is that it is highly uneconomic and administratively cumbersome to make such income-tested charges—social service by social service—and if income redistribution is indeed the goal, it can be attained more effectively by making the service free and adjusting the income tax rates and brackets to attain the desired degree of income redistribution.

There may be a concern about equity. It may be held that the charges should reflect the use made of the service. As Abel-Smith points out, there is some evidence that at least in the case of two of the social services in Britain, namely the health service and post-elementary education, and perhaps even elementary education, the rich use these services more extensively than the poor. If this is so, equity considerations would suggest that any charge made should vary by income.

At the same time, there are some negative considerations to be taken into account in deciding whether or not a service should be income-conditioned and tested. One is the psychological effect of the requirement to undergo a test of income. It has often been argued that although income testing, which may include a zero charge for the poorest, may remove the financial barrier to use of the service, the test is regarded as so demeaning that it deters many people from use of the service. Thus in the United States food stamps, and to a lesser extent SSI, are substantially underused by those financially eligible, and this is generally attributed to reluctance to submit to the income test.

But one may ask why the test is held to be demeaning—why the means test should be so mean. There appears to be no feeling that the test in the income tax is demeaning, nor do people appear to feel this way about an income test for an award (e.g., a university scholarship). The income tax involves a self-declaration, and detailed evidence of the accuracy of the declaration, other than production of the W-2s, is required only on a sample basis. Not every income tax payer has to produce documents, supporting evidence from other people—landlords, neighbors, etc.—and the many other kinds of proof that can be required of applications for public assistance.

Furthermore, the definition and scope of income, and often resources, utilized in the most common form of the test, namely, in public assistance or SSI, is much more inclusive and rigorous (including the cash value of help from relatives and friends) than is the case in the income tax. Is it conceivable that if the social services were to use the same definition as the income tax, the test would not be regarded as so demeaning?

Dislike of the income test, so often identified with the public assistance procedures, is also due to the manner in which it is administered. In public assistance the object of the test is to restrict eligibility: to keep people out of the system. In many, if not most jurisdictions, this objective is reflected in the treatment of the applicant, who is, so to say, regarded with suspicion, as a possible cheat or abuser, and treated by the administrator with scant courtesy at best. But the object or policy in the case of the social services is to ensure use of a service that has been deemed to be needed by those covered. Is it conceivable that a test could be devised and administered in a way that is not felt to be demeaning?

The identification of an income test with public assistance leads to another question: Why is it that a test is regarded as demeaning when applied to public assistance but not, apparently, when applied to scholarships? The answer seems to lie in the nature of the service. There is something good about obtaining education. Receipt of the service casts no slur on the recipient; on the contrary, it suggests something commendable about the recipient. But receipt of income-tested cash payments seems to many people to be proof of personal inadequacy, namely an inability or unwillingness to earn enough income for self-support.

A second consideration that may argue against the use of income testing in the social services concerns the policy and administrative problems of operating an income test. Decisions have to be made determining the income levels at which the marginal rates should apply and what the specific rate differential should be. There is the technical problem of avoiding notches and selecting the period of accounting to use in determining income status—whether to be prospective or retrospective, and over what unit of time. All these are common to the test as applied to the income security programs and have been thoroughly discussed at earlier sessions of the conference and will not be elaborated here. But there is an additional problem in the social services: Should the test, the brackets, and the marginal rates be the same for all social services? There are also technical problems in the way of collecting income-tested charges in the case of services where the benefits accrue after a period of time. Abel-Smith has illustrated this in his discussion of collecting charges for higher education either in cash or more particularly in the form of loans.

Some Unanswered Questions

Finally, there are several questions that I hope Abel-Smith will elucidate or elaborate on in the course of the discussion.

What is the relevance of the public–private discussion to decisions as to whether or not to income-test? It is not clear to me that the issues raised by income testing are different according to whether a service is publicly or privately provided. The only significant difference I can see is that a publicly provided service is more accountable. The public service must make publicly available the standards and definitions of the test and must account for the sums raised. The private physician who income-tests does not publish or make otherwise generally available a schedule of his income-related charges, nor does he report on the extent to which his charges are income tested and the numbers of his patients who pay less than full charges.

Last, I hope that Abel-Smith will clarify for us where he stands on income testing as applied to the various social services. At one point he indicates his belief that the "case for income testing is greatest for post-compulsory education... next for preschool education, next for short-term health care, leaving a much weaker case for personal social services and perhaps the weakest case of all for services provided to those who are chronically or permanently unable to work." Are we to assume that he would not income-test compulsory education or the remaining health services? Even after most diligent reading of the paper I was unclear as to the criteria that led him to this list of priorities. And where does he stand on housing subsidies or day care or foster care for children or legal services or counseling, and similar supportive services?

Discussion

MARTIN REIN

At an abstract level, policy analysts have identified two critical issues in the design of income support programs: unrestricted cash grants versus in-kind benefits; and income testing versus universal entitlement. Superficially, these issues seem intuitively clear and self-evident. But consider each in turn. Either we make available services such as education, medical care, or public housing or we provide cash to purchase these and other goods and services.[1] These cash or in-kind benefits can be distributed to all citizens or residents of the society (i.e., on the basis of universal entitlement), or selectively to those in economic need by the concept of need. The concept of need restricts entitlement benefits to low-income families by establishing several levels of family income which serve as a standard of eligibility for families of different sizes and composition. There are clearly many other rules for selecting, but when the dichotomy between universal and selective is employed the term "selective" is intended to mean that economic resources (income and/or assets) serve as a test of eligibility.

Policy analysts assume these twin dichotomies are conceptually interesting and administratively useful in designing programs. They then

[1]One economist equates in-kind transfers with price subsidies and cash transfers with income subsidies (Wiseman, n.d., p. 456).

351

set out to provide intellectual arguments for and against each choice. Theory and practice diverge. In practice all kinds of ambiguities emerge at the boundary separating each programmatic form. It is not simply a matter of choosing between cash or in-kind benefits; rather there is a "continuum of transfers ranging from cash, cash with advice, vouchers, in-kind provision, and, finally, compulsion [Thurow, 1977, p. 98]." When we turn to selectivity by income testing we find that it could be achieved either at the point of consumption, in the allocation of expenditures, or at the point of financing, where the role of taxation becomes critical. Thus virtually all programs are income tested at either the taxation or the expenditure level. But an important point is that what looks like selectivity on the consumption side can be undone by the system of taxes (see footnote 4). Even when we agree to restrict our discussion to the expenditure side rather than a simple dichotomy of universal or income testing, there are at least three different principles of distribution. Benefits can be distributed neutrally regardless of income (children's allowances are an example); they can be distributed positively, so that the more you earn the more you get (this is the principle on which wage-related insurance benefits rest); or negatively, so that the less you have the more you get (this is the principle on which welfare-type programs are premised).

These boundary complications are of course recognized by all people who have seriously thought about the problem of the design of income support programs. It is therefore not the purpose of this paper to further refine the policy dichotomies. Rather, I want to argue that the policy dichotomies of cash versus in-kind and universal versus selectivity by income testing become most meaningful in the following three circumstances: First, when the choices are embedded in the economic and political context in which decisions are taken. That is to say, when choices are examined within the context of institutional events from which they arise. It is an illusion to search for general, lawlike rules which are stripped from their context. Second, when it is recognized that there are many different ways of providing benefits, and thus the specific form of the program needs to be detailed. I will try to elaborate this point by focusing on the many different ways that income-tested programs can be distributed. It will not be at all obvious that it is income testing that unifies the variations in programmatic form. Third, when there is a sharp disparity between theory and practice. This discrepancy is particularly striking, and I might add disturbing, when we contrast intellectual arguments for in-kind benefits which are based on theories of pure public goods, merit goods, external benefits to donors, and the practice of cashing out in-kind benefits in order to determine their contribution to the distribution of money income and real welfare levels. In practice the procedures for cashing-out disregard altogether the benefits to donors on which the theory of in-kind benefits so critically depends.

By focusing on *context*, *form*, and *practice* I want to distinguish between analysis, which tends to be abstract, and real-life circumstances, which tend to be bound by situations. The argument has implications for the practice of analysis, which should pay serious attention to the institutional setting in which programmatic design is invented.

The Case for Income Testing

Before examining the context in which income testing takes place I want to review the general case for income testing of in-kind benefits. I have already suggested that there is a continuum of in-kind benefits, and by implication that the different types of in-kind benefits require different intellectual justification. I cannot hope in this brief paper to focus on all programs along the continuum. I therefore limit this discussion to earmarked or restricted transfers. Between unrestricted cash grants and public provision of compulsory in-kind benefits (as in the case of presecondary education), we find cash grants which are earmarked for specific consumption in such varied fields as housing allowances, university grants, reimbursement and exemptions for drugs, eyeglasses, dental care, and food. What, then, is the intellectual rationale for restricted cash transfers? There are two general arguments for earmarked income-tested benefits.

The strongest general case in favor of income testing is to be found in those situations where the per capita value of benefits is greater for higher-income than low-income groups (i.e., when there are vertical inequalities in the per capita distribution of services).

The second general argument for income-tested benefits is that they prevent or compensate for externalities. In his thoughtful paper in this volume, Abel-Smith offers some examples in the field of housing. Housing allowances can protect children from the bad housing caused by the inadequate income of their families. They protect workers in tight markets from exorbitant rent which might force them to relocate to low-rent, job-scarce areas where they are likely to become unemployed. So important are these and other externalities to society that Abel-Smith believes that it is legitimate to disregard the use value of the benefits to the consumer. We will return to this important observation later in the paper in the discussion of the relationship between theory and practice.

Income testing also has disadvantages. It adds to both the marginal and the cumulative tax rates, thus creating problems of work incentives (the severity of which is difficult to demonstrate) and a sense of unfairness (it is wrong to subject the poor to very high marginal tax rates, even if it does not affect their willingness to work). We therefore need to be extremely cautious in using this potentially egalitarian tool, since redistributive aims can conflict with efficiency and fairness. Abel-Smith has suggested one criterion for deciding which program should be income tested, namely, that the service must be one that everyone uses. In other words, the case for income testing is strongest when the goods and services to be distributed selectively are those which are universally used by all individuals. Education at the postsecondary level provides a good example of a situation where vertical inequalities can exist. Because not everyone makes use of advanced education, the program meets only one standard of income testing, not both. In the case of housing, two principles of widespread use and unequal distribution reinforce each other. Thus it is housing subsidies that provide the prototypical example for income testing.

Before examining the context in which income-tested housing allowances take place I want to offer some critical comments on each of these rationales.

It is useful to provide some comparative factual information on the central justification for means testing (i.e., it should redress vertical inequalities as measured by per capita subsidies). A review of data on the per capita distribution of educational expenditures in Britain and the United States suggests some interesting contrasts. Grants to students in Britain at the postsecondary level are distributed to all students who qualify for advanced education. The size of the grant, however, depends upon parental income. It is income tested. Before 1977 all students received a minimum award of £50 per year regardless of parental income.[2] This system produced subsidies four times as large for low-income students compared to higher-income students.[3]

In the United States, Hansen and Weisbrod (1969b) cashed out the cost of education to the state of California and then related these costs to the parental income of university students. They found that the children

[2]Since 1977 three important policies have been introduced: (a) the minimum award has been raised from £50 to £200; (b) university fees are automatically paid for all home students, while overseas students must pay tuition fees which have been substantially raised; (c) the marginal tax rate on the parental means test at the higher-income levels have been reduced to offset the loss of tax exemptions for students, which came about as a result of the elimination of tax exemption and the creation of the new Child Benefit scheme.

[3]Students whose parental income represents 75% of the average earnings of male manual workers receive on average a maintenance grant, after the parental contribution was taken into account, of £1100. By contrast, students with parental incomes of 300% of the average earnings of male manual workers receive an average maintenance of £233 (Great Britain, Her Majesty's Stationery Office, 1978b, p. 50).

of better-off families get a larger per capita subsidy than those of lower-income families. The main reason for this outcome was that parental income was positively correlated with participation rates (the children of well-off parents were more likely to go to college), staying power (they were more likely to complete their education), and selection (they were more likely to be enrolled in the high-cost sector of both public and private education).[4]

It is not clear that these data suggest that Britain has a more egalitarian educational subsidy system than does the United States. They do seem to call attention to two different institutional arrangements for distributing in-kind subsidies. Student grants subsidize the individual student, permitting him to go to any institution he can get in to, without concern for fee and maintenance expenditures. Subsidies to institutions look universalistic and egalitarian, but in fact they are not. One might speculate that the number of students in the high-benefit group is likely to be quite small. To understand the egalitarian impact of such a system we want to know how the total amount of money is spent by government for student aid that is distributed to students coming from different income groupings. It is the share of total expenditure by income class that might be more revealing about vertical inequalities than is the measure of the per capita benefit.

The choice of a measure of inequality is particularly important because it implies a model of equality. At least three models of equality are relevant. First is the concept of equality as a means of improving the real welfare level of a whole income class. From this perspective we want to know what percentage of the total class makes use of the benefit and what proportion of the total money they receive. Equality of opportunity is a second conception of equality. Here the per capita measure seems important. The underlying rationale for this model of equality is to increase the individuals' chances of moving out of their income class rather than improving the position of the class as a whole. The concept of equality that underlies this conception is that of reaching those who are "best off" within a class in order to equalize their opportunity to leave the class. The third conception of equality seeks to distribute resources to those who are "worst off" within a given income class. The

---

[4]Hansen and Weisbrod's findings were criticized by Pechman (1970) for their failure to take into account the system of financing the educational subsidies. When taxes are taken into account, Pechman finds that the subsidies that well-off families receive are offset by the taxes they pay. The striking pattern of vertical inequality and the value of subsidies to the well-off families gets washed out when both taxes and benefits are taken into account. Of course, the Pechman findings depend on the critical assumption that all income classes pay an equal proportional tax for education. Since the tax is not earmarked, there is no way of testing this assumption.

model is that of compensation for misery and misfortune rather than equalization of opportunity or the reduction of class inequalities. In this conception of equality it is the sous-proletariat that is the target of reform. This is essentially an anti-"creaming" conception of equality.

The discussion of models of equality raises questions about whom income-test programs should seek to reach and what is the intellectual reason for wanting to reach any particular group. In brief, then, I have suggested that there are at least three different types of groups that could be reached: the class as a whole; the best-off within a class; or the worst-off within a class. Simply focusing on vertical inequalities obscures the target of means-tested programs.

We also need to pay attention to the reason for wanting to reach any particular group. The primary rationale for equalizing subsidies in education and housing is that of investment.[5] We hope that the subsidies will help each person contribute to society his maximum potential human capital. Educational subsidies can also contribute to a stable society by encouraging upward mobility across income classes and creating thereby the sense that society is not divided along rigid class lines. If the investment objective is central, then the argument about vertical inequalities becomes subordinate to it, and examples of where income-testing programs should be developed multiply. For example, children in low-income households suffer from poor nutrition more than do children in other households and this handicaps their capacity to study. If, then, we are worried about the relationship between nutrition and learning, this suggests that we should have means-tested school meals. Indeed, the case for income testing based on an investment argument can lead us to search out all of the negative consequences of low income and to justify this action as an attempt to redress the negative consequences of inequalities. Meritocratic considerations are more likely to enter when the aim is individual mobility.

The argument that income testing is justified whenever vertical inequalities exist, even when the cost of the service is much higher than the actual user is prepared to pay for it, is derived from the theory of externalities and the investment rationale. I want to call this phenomenon "discounting," which in its general usage means a deduction in the value of a service.[6] The basic argument about externalities appears to be that when investment and subjective use value conflict as goals, it is the

[5]There are other rationales based on the principles of consumption, compensation, and fairness. The individual rather than society is seen as the primary beneficiary of public intervention.

[6]Most economists use the concept of discounting to refer to time delays. I do not intend that the concept refer to time, but rather to subjective use value.

principle of investment which should override the users' preference. This answer seems to be unsatisfactory. There is a considerable amount of cynicism with respect to the distribution of public services and a deep feeling that services are not provided with uniform equality across income classes; that they are not effective in meeting investment aims (however these might be defined); and that individuals in all income classes may not be getting their money's worth from the in-kind benefits provided by government.

The traditional argument in support of in-kind benefits does not seem to help very much here, either. The case for the public provision of pure public goods exists when "exclusion is impossible... consumption is nontrivial. My neighbor's enjoyment . . . does not subtract from my enjoyment... [and when] identical amounts must be consumed [Thurow, 1977, p. 86]." As we have seen, this argument is convincing in the case of social welfare. The model applies most clearly to national defense and not to social welfare expenditures where goods are sold in the market and also in both the private and the not-for-profit voluntary sector. Indeed, the history of social welfare is a history of the efforts by voluntary agencies to prevent a takeover by government. Advocates of private social work believed that it could provide a substitute for government authority and thereby promote individual responsibility for protection against economic adversity. The Community Chest movement flourished in the United States during the 1920s and was inspired by the idea that voluntarism could substitute for government programs. In practice the idea proved faulty because the Chests were never able to provide adequate services even in good times, and of course they collapsed altogether during periods of economic recession, when they were needed most.[7] The introduction of public social welfare programs had essentially nothing to do with the theory of pure public good.

But what of the argument that public programs produce externalities and that they are best understood as benefits for the donors rather than the users? If this rationale for program intervention is accepted, then the case for in-kind benefits rests on some theory of donor satisfaction. It is to this issue I want to return in the concluding section of the paper.

The Context of Income-Tested Programs

I want briefly to compare the development of income-tested programs in Sweden and Denmark in order to argue that the institutional context in which programs develop must be taken into account if we are

---

[7]For a discussion of these issues, see Lubove (1968).

to appreciate why income-tested programs were introduced and to understand what consequences follow after their introduction.

Swedish social policy during the 1960s has been heavily biased in favor of rental units.[8] The key tool of equalization is an income-tested housing allowance, which reduces the rent burden and protects families from rent increases.[9] Eighty percent of a marginal rent increase is covered by the allowances. Half of all families with children receive allowances and virtually all families with only one earner receive these benefits. The value of the benefit varies with the size of the family, the level of rent, and family income. This type of comprehensive and extensive income testing seems to be designed to exclude the top of the income distribution rather than including the bottom.

In 1973 the level of means-tested programs offset the level of tax exemptions to homeowners, creating a situation where public subsidies between rental and owning units were broadly similar.[10] On a per capita basis owners received an average in Swedish kroner of SKr 250 and renters SKr 220.

Why then did Swedish policy turn to income testing? The income-tested housing allowance was largely developed to correct inequities within the rental sector and was inspired by the belief that everyone should have access to good-quality housing. Later this aim was further redefined, when the quality of the unit was dropped as a condition of entitlement and the allowance became a general cash subsidy. The active manpower policy, which encouraged geographic mobility to get jobs, also created housing bottlenecks in areas of high employment. The housing allowance facilitated the implementation of labor market policy; this, in turn, contributed to the prevention of unemployment. Finally, in the late 1960s, concern about poverty and low income among families with children led to an interest in making child allowances more selective. But there was strong resistance to modifying these universal benefits, and the cost of sharply increasing the benefits seemed prohibitive. Income-tested housing allowance was an alternative to universal children's allowances as a way of reaching low-income families with chil-

---

[8]The example is drawn from a report by Esping-Andersen (1978). I have also enormously profited from several extended discussions with the author.

[9]The Swedish Housing Allowance program does have an asset test based on the value of the home, thus the program is, in fact, a means-tested, rather than income-tested, program. Wealth in excess of SKr 75,00 is added to income. Since the asset test is set relatively high, this justifies referring to the program as income tested.

[10]Even if there was no bias on the expenditure or output side, there may be bias on the input or financing side. To the extent that the financing is progressive, the net bias favors renters.

dren. Concern about inequities in the per capita distribution of public subsidies in housing played only a minor role.

Dissatisfaction and restlessness with the housing policy and the sense that policy should not be biased in favor of homeownership has been growing since 1975. The housing market seems saturated, and people are dissatisfied with the large suburban rental units. "Specific criticisms were that increasingly the buildings were too high, too close together and too stereotyped in appearance.... What was being produced ... was a hard, anonymous and anti-life environment [Dairn, 1979, p. 8]." Since there is virtually no population growth, any shift in policy might lead to the abandonment of the existing rental units; this would be an enormous waste of resources. It would appear that extensive means testing and bias toward rental units led to a policy stalemate and to a shift in practice. By 1978 single-family homes almost totally dominated new construction.[11] A surplus of flats in high-rise buildings now exists. In this context a possible remedy might be to increase further the bias to renters through an even more generous means-tested housing allowance that would decrease the cost of rental units and compensate renters for the externalities of suburban block living.

Danish housing policy, by contrast, provides a clear example of a policy biased in favor of homeownership. Owners receive a per capita subsidy in Danish kroner of Dkr 500. Renters receive per capita subsidies of only DKr 60. At the same time, rent controls were abolished in the 1970s, thus further reinforcing the bias in favor of owners. The bias in favor of homeownership reinforces the traditional values of the ownership of small property.

In the United States, homeownership represents a kind of modern Jeffersonian argument. Owners, like farmers, have a stake in the community and thus serve as a ballast for political stability, and ownership contributes to the more effective rearing of children by giving children a sense of stability as well as the additional space in the child's own home. In Danish housing policy, it was the concern for privacy rather than the American celebration of ownership that seemed to play a critical role.

The review of housing policy in Denmark by Esping-Andersen suggests that the ownership bias had the effect of undermining the welfare state and producing considerable economic and political disruption. Economically it led to land speculation and the fueling of inflation by the use of productive capital in this nonproductive sector. Politically,

---

[11]It is interesting to note that no society seems to means-test exemptions for housing allowances. This would, in effect, be a policy of giving more tax exemption to lower earners than higher earners.

it divided owners and renters and created a strong movement of discontent in the left wing of the Social Democratic group, who are largely renters. To redress the imbalance created by liberal tax incentives to private homeowners and the elimination of rent controls, a set of compensatory programs was designed in the form mainly of means-tested rent subsidies to lower-income and large families. These subsidies provide a clear example of the intellectual arguments for means testing advanced by Abel-Smith, but intellectual arguments and political realities conflict. Esping-Andersen reports that rising incomes eroded rent subsidies for many families. Rent subsidy policies thus bred frustration more often than satisfaction. During the early 1970s, the pressure on the Social Democrats to alter their housing policy became so intense that they were forced to introduce a bill which would reduce the favorable tax advantage accruing to homeowners. The policy backfired because many Social Democrats had acquired their own homes by the earlier tax-exemption policies, and they were reluctant to relinquish the gains they had achieved. The efforts to introduce more egalitarian policy exacerbated equity politics when groups vied to maintain their relative advantage. In brief, the introduction of income-testing programs for renters to redress the vertical inequalities created by tax-exempted homeownership programs created political polarization, backlash politics, and a movement to the political right.

In Sweden, by contrast, concern about quality of housing, about bottlenecks in manpower policies, and about child poverty seemed to inspire the development of an extensive means-tested housing allowance. Policy did not try to equalize per capita inequities in housing subsidies. In this context, income testing and a renters' bias were politically acceptable. But the policies contributed to a new problem—the erosion of the quality of the physical environment of suburban high-rise rented apartments.

A review of the context in which income-tested housing allowances developed in Sweden and Denmark suggests the following three general conclusions: (a) Countries turn to income testing for reasons other than the reduction of vertical inequalities and the avoidance of externalities.[12] (b) The introduction of income testing produced negative side effects. In Sweden it contributed to an erosion in the quality of living; in

---

[12]In Britain, the case of housing allowances (rent and rate rebates) was largely justified on the grounds that the universal subsidies for public housing, which produced low rents, were too costly. When government reduced housing subsidies and rents increased, low-income groups experienced hardships. It was not politically acceptable to let the poor suffer the consequences from raising rents without some program to protect

Denmark to political polarization. (*c*) These negative reactions only partly depended on the income-tested programs per se. The more critical factor was the nature of unanticipated events.

The Forms of Income-Testing and Universal Programs

It is of course a mistake to assume that the income-tested housing allowance programs in Denmark and Sweden were identical. They differ in important ways in terms of the value of benefits, the proportion of the population receiving the benefits, and the aggressiveness with which eligible clients were contacted. In the discussion which follows I want briefly to identify seven different dimensions on which income-tested programs differ from one another. Then I want briefly to show that there are also important variations in the form of the universal programs as well.

1. We need to distinguish between income-tested and means-tested programs. An income-tested program uses only income as a criterion for determining eligibility. By contrast, a means-tested program depends upon an extensive asset test. Swedish policy analysts are eager to point out that the housing allowance is an income- and not a means-tested program, suggesting that this type of program is more politically acceptable to both taxpayers and recipients than the means-tested welfare program (Social Help). One of the ways that means-tested programs are liberalized is to reduce the asset test by a series of disregards (i.e., assets, earnings, and income that are not taken into account in determining eligibility). When the disregards are very high, the practical distinctions between an income test and a means test dissolve.

2. The size of the population covered is a critical aspect of an income-tested program. Swedish housing allowances reach half of all families with children. This contrasts very sharply with welfare-type housing programs in the United States, which reach less than 10% of the population. The extent of coverage is important because it defines what the program is as a social phenomenon.

3. The value of the benefits in an income-tested program is obviously important. This value cannot be measured only in absolute terms, but also in relation to its contribution to the family income. Housing

---

them. The rationale for income testing was based on the political necessity of protecting the consumption of the poor when general subsidies were removed and was much less concerned with the broader arguments about per capita inequalities in the distribution of housing benefits.

allowances only contribute a small portion of total family income. By contrast, many means-tested programs like welfare account for large portions of the total family income.

The combination of coverage and generosity gives the program its distinctive character. For example, a program may give "much" to few people (the American welfare system) or "little" to many people (Swedish Housing Allowance).

4. Most income-tested programs use categories of inclusion other than simply income. Perhaps the most important distinctions concern attachment to the labor market. In Britain, the Supplementary Benefits program is only available to those individuals who are primarily out of work. By contrast, the Family Income Supplement is available only to those individuals who *are* at work. Similar distinctions exist in Sweden between mandatory and voluntary social help programs. In brief, then, social categories as well as income categories define the universe of eligibles.

5. The extent of discretion is perhaps the most controversial of all features in income-tested programs. Discretion enters income-tested programs in order to achieve the ideal of individualization. At the same time, income-tested programs strive for a degree of uniformity. There is thus a conflict between the goals of individualized need and providing uniformity of benefits. However, the exercise of discretion is costly because it takes up a great deal of staff time, is a source of grievance among recipients, and produces glaring inequities in the distribution of benefits. Moreover, it has been the critical focus toward which welfare rights organizations have mobilized their efforts. Thus the discretionary grants have contributed to the politicization of income-testing benefits. Income-tested programs differ quite sharply in the extent to which they rely upon discretionary grants.

6. Income-tested programs can serve as a general "safety net," to meet all of the economic necessities which other programs fail to do. Alternatively, they could be restricted and specifically directed towards a single item of consumption, such as education, housing, medical care, etc. Much of the general criticism about income testing is directed at general rather than specific income programs. However, general programs also have earmarked features. For example, housing is paid as incurred in many welfare programs, and this is in effect a restricted program nested in a general program.

7. Sometimes, general income-tested programs serve as an automatic "passport" to entitlement for specific income-tested programs. In Britain, specific income-tested programs which are secured through the "passport" route have participation rates of 70–80%. By contrast, spe-

cific or earmarked income-tested programs which require separate eligibility review often have disturbingly low take-up rates.

What is more, we cannot assume that all universal programs are similar. In fact, most universal programs are not universal at all, but depend upon broad social categories of eligibility other than income. In most universal programs citizenship or residence serves as a category of restriction. For example, in order to be eligible to receive a serious and expensive surgical operation in Britain some form of residence must be established. However, because emergency medical care can be received free on demand for both nonresidents and noncitizens, the British Health Service comes closest to the ideal of a universal program. But it is only practitioner services that are free on demand in the British system. Access to specialist services is available only by referral from the practitioner.

Consider another case—namely that of universal Child Benefits, which are available to all children under 16. However, they are also selectively available to children 16 to 19 years of age who are in full-time study. These selective Child Benefits are designed primarily to relieve the economic burden of parents who keep these young persons at school. Child Benefits in these age groups are strikingly selective when compared to the universe of all children. Consider the following figures: only 58% of 16-year-olds receive Child Benefits; 28% of 17-year-olds and only 10% of 18-year-olds. Presumably, these "universal" educational benefits are more likely to go to children who live in higher-income families than to those in low-income families. In this sense universalism reinforces income inequalities.

In brief, then, it is a mistake to rely upon a simple dichotomy of income-tested versus universal programs. Much depends upon the form in which each of these types of program is devised. These issues of design are critical in determining political acceptability, the economic costs, and the social consequences of the development of each of these types of programs.

The Analysis of In-Kind Benefits in Practice

When we leave the field of earmarked cash benefits and the various forms of income testing and universal benefits, we enter into what is perhaps the most controversial of all the issues in the design of income support programs, namely, the subject of in-kind benefits. In the United States, whatever intellectual arguments have been developed in support of unrestricted cash grants, in fact expenditures for in-kind benefits have grown at a more rapid rate and account for a larger proportion of total social welfare expenditures. I have tried to argue that the critical question in income testing is the problem of discounting: how to take into account the fact that people value services less than their actual cost to the public.

Admittedly, the problem of measuring discounting is extremely complicated, partly because of the fact that those who pay taxes and those who receive benefits are different individuals. We therefore cannot simply equate the burden of paying taxes and the pleasure of receiving benefits when different individuals are involved in each activity.

Consider two major efforts to cash out the value of in-kind benefits. In Britain, the Central Statistical Office has devised a procedure for allocating in-kind benefits to different income classes as part of their effort to examine trends in the redistribution of household income. Essentially they allocate current cost to average use of individuals based on age and sex. Over the years they have improved these estimates by securing better information on the use made of particular health and education facilities. The Commission on Income Distribution and Wealth observed critically that "benefits that households obtain from these services may only approximate broadly the cost of their provision." This analysis led the commission to reach the following gloomy conclusion: "Where the value of the service lies partly in its ready availability and partly in the actual use made of it, there is no agreed method of valuing the benefits [Great Britain, Royal Commission on the Distribution of Income and Wealth, 1976, p. 26]."

In the United States the question of cashing out in-kind benefits has arisen largely in relation to an effort to measure the extent of poverty. Edgar Browning cashed out the value of education, medical care, and other in-kind benefits. He concluded that poverty has been eliminated in the United States. Martin Anderson, at the Hoover Institution, reached much the same conclusion. Still the issue remains of whether attributing cash values to in-kind benefits is appropriate and, if so, how it is to be calculated. (See Smeeding, 1982, for a critique and review of alternate methods for valuing in-kind benefits.) A study contracted by HEW concludes that "no value on principle can provide measures of nontransferable in-kind income which are based, as money income is, on exchange values. Unless it is absolutely required in a particular income distribution application, therefore, it seems best not to add together the measures of money income and in-kind income, no matter what valuation principle is used [Cooper and Katz, 1978]."

These methodological problems have not discouraged work in the area. Economists at the Institute for Research on Poverty have tried to take account of two problems—the failure to take into account discounting and the arbitrary inclusion of education as an in-kind benefit, because it cannot be translated into current consumption value. Sheldon Danziger and Robert Plotnick have excluded educational benefits and tried to cash out the value of in-kind benefits by taking into account the actual market value of these benefits to users. For example, if a program costs a thousand dollars and the consumer only values it at $500, then $500 is added to the income of the user of the program and the remaining $500 is treated as a "dead loss." By this procedure they conclude that only 6% of American families are poor (Danziger and Plotnick, forthcoming).

Both the British procedure for cashing out in-kind benefits and allocating current costs to individuals based on age, sex, and use of programs, and the American attempt to cash out in-kind programs as a way of measuring their effectiveness in reducing poverty fail to take into account the value of the benefits to donors. In this respect, the theory of public goods and the theory of externalities are unrelated to the actual empirical studies carried out by economists, and the analytic work and the theoretical work are divorced from each other. Admittedly there are practical reasons for the problem, namely the difficulty of translating theory into practice. However, the value of in-kind benefits to donors and the contribution of these values to the distribution of real well-being is an important, if unresolved, problem in our understanding of the distribution of in-kind benefits. If the donors were rewarded, then we would have the reverse of a backlash, namely, an expansionist welfare state, a cycle of benign reinforcement. Of course, the problem is more complicated. Some give freely and others feel that they are being "done in" by being forced to give. It is this conflict among donors that shapes our social program and gives it its special character of complexity.

Politically, the problem centers on the question of overload and backlash. Where the discount rate is high, is there a risk that a vicious circle will (has) set in whereby (a) the taxpayers feel overwhelmed by their burden; (b) service recipients feel aggrieved because they place little value on the services received; and (c) analysts inform the society that it is corrupt because, despite high public expenditures, benefits accruing to those at the bottom are deemed slight?

In conclusion, then, the analysis of policy tends to be on an abstract level dichotomizing between universal and income-tested; between cash and in-kind benefits. I have argued that the analysis of program design requires that it be embedded in a context, that attention be given to the complexities of form, and that practice be related to the theory. An analysis stripped of context and situation cannot provide answers to the design problems faced in real life. The high level of these dichotomies of generalization does not account for real-life complexities. On the other hand, the efforts to inform the programmatic design by grounding it in the details of experience inhibit the capacity to develop general rules. However, experience provides taut guidelines for understanding when general rules should be violated and when they make sense. Much more attention needs to be given to the relationship between abstract analysis and programmatic design.

10

Financing Health Care

STEPHEN H. LONG
JOHN L. PALMER

National health insurance (NHI) has been a subject of American political debate for the past five decades without legislative resolution.* Proposals for NHI date from the Great Depression, when the public became keenly aware of the financial risks of ill health as well as unemployment, retirement, and other problems of its increasingly industrialized way of life (Hirshfield, 1970). During the New Deal, when only 6% of the population was covered by private health insurance, other social insurance programs were passed instead of NHI, which was deemed too costly for federal taxes to support. Since the 1930s, each decade brought with it new pressure for NHI, but no legislation. The reluctance of the United States to develop an NHI program is not for lack of models, since all major Western nations have adopted national health insurance or national health service programs since 1940. Likewise, our lack of an NHI program is not for want of proposals; an HEW publication listed 18 bills pending before the 94th Congress (Waldman, 1976). Separate NHI legislation was introduced by President Jimmy Carter, Senator Edward Kennedy, and Senator Russell Long in 1979. Yet political commentators see

*The authors acknowledge helpful comments on earlier versions of this paper by Karen Davis, David Emery, Irwin Garfinkel, Theodore Marmor, Maurice MacDonald, Timothy Smeeding, Burton Weisbrod, and Barbara Wolfe.

little chance of passage for any of the proposals. This lengthy and intensive history of deliberations suggests that NHI is an important but extremely complex and difficult issue.

This paper develops the main themes of the universal versus income-tested debate in the context of national health insurance, and discusses their relevance to the choice among alternative approaches to NHI in the 1980s. The first section presents some background on American health care financing in general and government health programs in particular.[1] In response to the problems in the current system, a set of social goals has emerged against which any NHI approach may, in principle, be evaluated. A description of these goals appears in the second section. The third section discusses the meanings of universal and income-tested national health insurance and the fourth briefly characterizes the generic types of NHI that have been proposed in the United States. The alternative approaches are assessed in the fifth section, in which we pay particular attention to the insights provided by the universal versus income-tested perspective. The paper closes with a summary and conclusions. Our analysis is largely qualitative, and even speculative at times, because of the current lack of hard evidence on many of the related issues. We hope, however, to have organized and sharpened the universal versus income-tested debate in the context of NHI.

Current Arrangements for Financing American Health Care and Their Problems

During the postwar period in the United States an elaborate patchwork system of health care financing has evolved. Gross enrollments in private hospitalization insurance plans (i.e., double counting persons with multiple policies) grew from 82 million in 1950 to 209 million in 1976, while premiums grew from $1 billion to $39 billion over the same period (Carroll, 1978). Government responsibility for health care shifted from a role of providing public health, research, and care for a few categorical groups (particularly veterans and the active military) to that of the primary insurer of the aged and the poor. National health expenditures have grown from $12 billion or 4.5% of GNP in 1950 to $163 billion or 8.8% of GNP in 1977 and continue to rise rapidly.[2] The average

---

[1]Readers familiar with the health care sector will find little new here. The section is intended for the benefit of readers more familiar with various cash transfer programs than with health care.

[2]The source of all health expenditure data in this section is Gibson and Fisher (1978).

annual rate of increase for the period was 9.9%, half of which was due to price increases.

This $163 billion of national health expenditures can be viewed in terms of the uses of the funds or the sources of the funds. Among the uses are hospital care (40% of total expenditures), physicians' services (20%), dental services (6%), drugs (8%), nursing homes (8%), and a residual of administrative costs, public health, research, construction, and miscellaneous personal health expenditures. The sources of funds include government at all levels (28% of total spending was federal and 12% state and local), private insurance (nearly 30%), and direct patient payments (30%). The relative importance of the sources in financing particular types of health care varies considerably, with government and private insurance payments combined financing 92% of hospital services, 61% of physicians' services, but less than 20% of dental services and drugs.

The tremendous growth in private health insurance, strongly encouraged by the tax-exempt status of employer-paid premiums, has gone a long way toward covering the employed population and their families against the basic costs of hospitalization and surgery (roughly three-quarters of all policies are acquired through employment groups).[3] Yet even with this coverage and government provision for the aged and poor, between 18 million and 26 million Americans remain uncovered against the basic costs of hospitalization. Furthermore, coverage against catastrophic costs has lagged substantially behind the growth of basic coverage. In 1976 there were only 70% as many major medical policies as basic hospitalization policies. Additionally, insurance policies have a strong bias toward first dollar coverage and toward higher-cost institutional care (as opposed to lower-cost ambulatory and preventive care). Thus, there are many gaps remaining in private insurance coverage of the population.

Public Programs

Current government health programs are of three sorts: (1) insurance programs, including Medicaid, Medicare, and Workers' Compensation; (2) direct service delivery programs, including Neighborhood Health Centers, Maternal and Child Health, Veterans Administration and Defense Department programs; and (3) tax expenditures which encourage

[3]In addition to its nearly $40 billion in premium revenues in 1976, the private insurance industry served as a financial intermediary for a significant proportion of the claims under government health insurance programs. The substantial size of this industry makes it a force to be reckoned with in the design of NHI.

purchase of private insurance and insure against certain medical expenditures.

The insurance programs are methods of augmenting the private resources of eligibles in order to give them improved financial access to medical care; that is, they employ a demand-augmenting strategy. Medicaid is a federal–state matching-grant program with state administration subject to federal guidelines. Eligibility is closely linked with the cash transfer programs in the states, principally giving benefits to low-income mothers and dependent children, and low-income aged, blind, and disabled. Therefore, Medicaid is targeted toward a subset of the low-income population. There is generally no patient cost-sharing in Medicaid; that is, the program reimbursement for treatment by a provider is considered full payment for the service. One of the major problems in Medicaid is the low participation rates among providers due to reimbursement restrictions—in many cases physicians' reimbursements are less than 50% of their customary charge (Burney et al., 1978; Sloan, Mitchell, and Cromwell, 1978). Since only a fraction of physicians treat Medicaid patients, it can be argued that we currently have a two-class system of U.S. medical care (Medicaid patients represent over 10% of all visits for only one-third of general practice physicians, and Medicaid visits exceed 30% of all visits for only 10% of U.S. physicians).

Medicare combines two programs, one of hospital insurance financed by payroll taxes and a second of medical insurance financed by general revenues and premiums paid by participants. These programs—enrolling 26 million persons—involve nearly universal eligibility among the aged (over 22 million enrollees), and also include nonaged participants eligible through disability and chronic renal disease. Medicare benefits are subject to partial patient payment through its deductibles, coinsurance, and premiums, though these are usually paid by Medicaid for the low-income eligibles. Seventy-three percent of the nonpoor purchase supplementary insurance which fills in the program's substantial cost-sharing (and thereby removes its function of rationing utilization). This leaves the low-income, non-Medicaid eligible aged and disabled with less complete coverage, especially against large medical bills.[4]

In contrast to the insurance programs are a number of government programs that deliver services directly to population groups; programs that are supply-augmenting. Most of these programs involve provision of medical care from government-owned facilities and by salaried employees. The largest of these programs are the Veterans Administration health care for veterans and the Department of Defense care for military

[4]Link, Long, and Settle (1979) examine patterns of Medicare supplementation by income and a number of other characteristics.

personnel and their dependents, which together represented over 13% of government expenditures on health. Eligibility for these programs is based upon past or current military service and is without regard to income level. There is also significant state and local spending on various types of hospital care and public health activities, including school health programs. Other programs such as the Indian Health Service, Neighborhood Health Centers, and the Maternal and Child Health Program are targeted to particular populations or areas and frequently are designed to serve lower-income or other special-need groups.

While not included in official government accounts of health expenditures, a third class of programs having major impacts on the present health care financing system are the "tax expenditures" for private insurance and medical expenditures.[5] Employer-paid premiums to private health insurance plans are excluded from the personal income tax base along with other paid fringe benefits. The foregone federal revenue in the case of health insurance amounts to about $6 billion (U.S., Executive Office of the President, 1979). Over the post–World War II period this tax expenditure has been a major cause of the growth of employment-related private health insurance. The other tax expenditure for health that is of quantitative importance is the personal income tax deduction for medical expenses in excess of 3% of income. This program was intended to provide a form of insurance for very high medical expenditures by reducing the income tax liabilities of taxpayers hit by large medical bills. With the rise of health expenditures relative to personal income, however, an increasing proportion of itemizers claiming the deduction do not have unusually high medical expenses (Mitchell and Vogel, 1975).

If we include tax expenditures in our total, government expenditures for the three classes of programs in 1977 were roughly $40 billion for the insurance programs (62%), $17 billion for the direct service programs (26%), and $8 billion for the tax expenditures (12%).

Major Goals and Other Considerations of NHI

There seems to be considerable agreement among students of NHI on its three major goals:[6] (a) access for all persons to acceptable-quality medical care; (b) control of rapidly rising medical costs; and (c) coverage

---

[5]See Steurle and Hoffman (1979) for an excellent discussion of the background, costs, and effects of tax expenditures in health.

[6]However, as recently as the 1960s cost control would not have been considered a primary goal.

of all families for catastrophic loss. In addition, we note the following considerations which, if they are given sufficient weight, can constrain achievement of the major goals: (*a*) minimizing increases in the federal health budget, while (at worst) holding constant state and local contributions; (*b*) minimizing disruption of the present private market system of financing and delivering health care—notably the role of private health insurance and the independence of providers; and (*c*) achieving a "fair" distribution of program costs.

The Goals

Access to acceptable-quality medical care has been justified for both equity arguments—for example, "health care is a right"—and efficiency arguments regarding investments in the productive capacity of the nation's labor force.[7] The efficiency argument is particularly strong with respect to perinatal care and the health of the young. In the school age population, good health is considered an input to the educational process. During the late teens to middle age, it is less clear that national financing of medical care will be as cost-effective, at least for the general population, as changes in life style achieved through health education (Fuchs, 1974). However, among disadvantaged groups there may remain significant benefits to be gained from additional medical treatment (Davis and Schoen, 1978). We described above a number of gaps in private insurance coverage and in the workings of present public programs, particularly Medicaid, that imply either limited financial access to care, or access limited to a second-class form of care. Achieving financial access, however, is merely necessary, but not sufficient, to assure receipt of care. There remain supply-side barriers to care—including unavailability of personnel or facilities or transportation to them, and discrimination—that must be overcome to assure genuine access. This suggests that an effective NHI program will include special incentives for supply-side changes or support direct government provision in a manner that assures a single class of acceptable-quality care.

Control of rapidly rising medical costs has apparently risen above the goal of access as the number-one health issue of this day. The lines are beginning to be drawn between those who see cost control as a prerequisite to NHI and those who see NHI as a prerequisite to effective cost control. In the eyes of the public the biggest health problem is the steady and rapid rise of health *expenditures*, though surely some of the in-

---

[7]While some would state this goal as strongly as "equal access to equal-quality care," many others would be satisfied with the weaker statement we have chosen.

creased expenditures are a measure of increased services providing satisfaction to consumers. Hence, the problem of cost control is to find effective mechanisms first to control the rise in medical care prices, and second to control the rise of "undesirable" or "needlessly costly" procedures or treatments while somehow allowing the continued expansion of "desirable" and "cost-effective" services. The orders of magnitude here are striking. We noted above that rising prices accounted for half the growth in health expenditures since 1950. Since the end of the Economic Stabilization Program in 1974, the medical care component has exceeded the all-items CPI by roughly 3% per year, with hospital charges and physician fees rising at an even higher rate than other medical care services.

The need for coverage against catastrophic loss has increased.[8] As prices for medical care rise and with rapid technological change in methods of treatment, the costs of care for major illnesses have become very large in both absolute terms and as a percentage of family income. Yet the gaps in insurance coverage, as noted above, are even greater for catastrophic than for basic health care expenditures. These gaps in coverage are due to a failure of the private market to provide adequate catastrophic insurance to some individuals (notably those without access to employer or union groups), since the threat of adverse selection drives premiums too high for individuals to purchase the insurance. Public sector action to assemble the group through compulsion creates a market that the private sector does not provide.

Other Considerations

National health insurance has the potential to increase the federal budget substantially, since only 28% of current national health expenditures are federal (three-quarters of these expenditures are for Medicaid and Medicare). Aside from any impact of NHI on total national health expenditures, it is clear that NHI is likely to involve substantial increases in federal budget costs, as many existing health expenditures of population groups other than the aged, disabled, and Medicaid-eligible poor are transferred through the federal budget. In addition, NHI is likely to induce new expenditures through improved access to services for certain population groups, increases in demand resulting from lower effective prices for care, and rising market prices and quantities of care pro-

---

[8]Unanticipated expenditures on medical care can often consume a very large amount of family assets and current income, as well as interrupt earnings if primary workers become ill. Numerous definitions of catastrophic loss are used, some referring to some absolute level of expenditure and others to a percentage of family income (say 10%).

vided as a result of provider responses. Unless these induced costs are offset by cost controls and/or redistributions of previous quantities among population groups, there will be further increases in budget costs. Since so much of the potential change in the federal budget from NHI would be due to transfers of costs, it is important to clearly understand the particular financing mechanisms of any NHI plan.

The impact of NHI alternatives on state and local health expenditures is also an important consideration, since 12% of national health expenditures are financed by state and local governments. In particular, the states pay about 45% of Medicaid costs. This is significant because many of the NHI schemes concentrate on improving coverage for the Medicaid-ineligible poor and near-poor, hence having important potential to either add to or substitute for current and future state expenditures (and, perhaps, the current state role in administering the program).

Another consideration is the extent of disruption of current market arrangements. At the very least this seems important to political acceptability. The magnitude of the present private insurance industry argues for, at least, an undiminished role in claims administration. Whether a substantial underwriting role must also be maintained is less clear. Provider groups—particularly the short-term general hospitals and the physicians—have an obvious interest in the amount of potential NHI-induced disruption of their location, operation, and practice; their control over education, licensing, and peer review; and especially their reimbursement systems. While many other goals may seriously conflict, minimal disruption from the current system for providers may be a constraint on political acceptability.

Finally, a fair distribution of program costs must be achieved through the mix of NHI financing sources. The notion of "fair" remains vague here, but depends heavily upon the distribution of current health care expenditures. The potentially large budget costs involved and the wide array of potential financing instruments available suggest that it should be simultaneously feasible and important to design NHI financing to achieve a fair distribution of burdens.

The Universal and Income-Tested Concepts as Applied to NHI

Among the complex and difficult issues that must be addressed in designing any NHI proposal are eligibility, financing, benefits covered, reimbursement of providers, the roles of federal and state governments and private health insurance companies, and cost-control mechanisms. The distinction between universal and income-tested forms of a program manifests itself primarily in eligibility decisions and secondarily in financing decisions. Should only lower-income persons be eligible for the program, or all Americans? Even if eligibility is extended to all citizens, it is important to determine the extent of participation by various income groups. For example, suppose the government created a public health insurance plan open to the voluntary participation of all citizens at a tax-subsidized "fair" premium, but the resulting enrollment largely consisted of the unemployed and the poor. Is a program that is ex ante universal but voluntary, and ex post limited to the participation of certain groups a universal program? For our purposes, no. We define a universal national health insurance program as one involving the participation of most, if not all, citizens in the same plan or in minimally equivalent plans. In contrast, income-tested plans limit eligibility to persons falling below a given income level in a means test.

Premiums and cost-sharing provisions, when they are used, may treat all participants equally or their level may rise with family income.[9] In the latter case an element of income testing is introduced into the program. Premiums are solely a financing mechanism and hence income testing of premiums is not conceptually different from raising funds through a progressive income tax, a payroll tax, or by some other means.[10] However, cost-sharing may have important implications for patient utilization and, if it is collected by the provider, has impacts on access to care and stigma. Advocates of cost-sharing point to two advantages: (a) Patient sharing in costs may lead to economizing behavior in

[9]A premium is a prepayment for services that may or may not be used; but if services are used they will be reimbursed by the third party (insurance company, government) in accord with certain rules. Cost-sharing refers to a class of arrangements by which insured patients share some of the risk of payment for services with the insurer. Common forms of cost-sharing include deductibles, which must be paid by the patient before insurance reimbursement begins; coinsurance, which specifies a constant percentage of each bill to be paid by the patient; and copayment, which specifies a constant absolute amount to be paid by the patient each time a certain service is consumed.

[10]But, a premium is a head tax on labor and hence is one of the most regressive means of financing. Because the impact of employer–employee premiums is so severe for low-wage workers—and especially for minimum-wage workers to whom the premium "tax" cannot be shifted backwards in the form of lower wages—the adverse employment effects of premiums are expected to be large (see Mitchell and Phelps, 1976; Emery, Long, and Mutti, 1979). Thus, when premiums are a part of the financing package they are generally income tested in some manner to reduce these adverse effects on low-wage workers (and/or the firms employing them).

utilization decisions, thereby holding total expenditures down; and (*b*) placing a share of costs directly on patients instead of financing them through taxes reduces the on-budget cost of the program (as does the device of mandating private health insurance coverage through employers). Opponents of cost-sharing argue that it discourages utilization of necessary services (particularly preventive care) and/or the savings in utilization are not sufficient to justify the higher administrative costs of collecting the cost-sharing. Most plans compromise by exploiting the on-budget cost reductions of cost-sharing for the nonpoor and by reducing or eliminating cost-sharing for the poor.

We have distinguished between universal and income-tested approaches to NHI on the dimensions of eligibility-participation and cost-sharing on the financing side. This yields four general cases:

Eligibility/Participation	*Cost-Sharing*
1. Income-Tested	Yes
2. Income-Tested	None
3. Universal	Yes, Income-tested
4. Universal	None

Medicaid is an example of an income-tested program in which cost-sharing is prohibited for most eligibles and for most services. However, since 1972, states with eligibles who qualified by their income rather than through categorical eligibility under a federally assisted cash program were allowed to impose modest copayments for all services (including hospital and physician services) to the former class of eligibles, and for special optional services (including prescription drugs and eyeglasses) to all eligibles. While several states (including California and New York) experimented with cost-sharing, no state has permanently adopted the copayments for basic services.

There are numerous examples of universal programs with income-tested cost-sharing. We explained above that the overlap between Medicaid and Medicare eligibility effectively relieves Medicaid-eligible Medicare enrollees from payment of premiums and cost-sharing; thus Medicare is, for the aged, a universal program with income-tested cost-sharing. Most NHI plans, as we shall see below, also fall into this category. Finally, a few NHI alternatives—perhaps best known is the Kennedy plan (formerly called Health Security)—propose universal eligibility and no cost-sharing. As we hope to demonstrate below, however, there are many other dimensions of NHI plans that do not relate to whether or not they are means tested but still have important implications for various population groups.

In the Introduction to this volume, Irwin Garfinkel discusses a number of issues suggested by the examination of the universal versus income-tested distinction at a conceptual level. The major hypotheses are

1. Greater income redistribution is possible under universal programs, particularly to the lower-middle-income groups who in income-tested programs fall just above income levels for benefits but still pay taxes.
2. However, if there are serious budget constraints that limit the total expenditures under the program, income-tested eligibility allows greater income to be transferred to the poor.
3. Income-tested programs may promote stratification of society along class lines.
4. Income-tested programs often result in stigma, that is, psychological harm to their recipients.
5. Income-tested programs involve rapid phase-outs of benefits above some income level, leading to high marginal tax rates and, therefore, substantial disincentives to work.

Anticipating some of our conclusions, we find only partial support for these hypotheses in the NHI case. For example, the insights on income redistribution and budget constraints seem to hold under NHI. But, while issues of class stratification and stigma are very important in health care delivery, they are not determined by the universal or income-tested nature of a plan. Moreover, the distinction between universality and income testing appears irrelevant to one of the most important goals of NHI, cost control.

Alternative Approaches to NHI

The range of national health insurance proposals spreads from narrow proposals that would marginally extend Medicaid to reduce the number of uninsured persons and prevent financial catastrophe for families to very broad proposals that would achieve these objectives and attempt to implement or encourage changes in the organization and delivery of health care services (especially including changes in reimbursement methods). The details of various plans have been given elsewhere (Davis, 1975; Waldman, 1976). In this section we shall describe the salient features of four generic forms of NHI that are broadly characteristic of the relevant NHI alternatives: expanded Medicaid plus catastrophic coverage, tax credit for premiums or expenses, mixed public–private, and complete public sector. The discussion is framed to highlight the universal versus income-tested distinction.

Expanded Medicaid Plus Catastrophic Coverage

Plans offering the most marginal changes from the current health care financing system would federalize Medicaid to achieve uniform income-tested eligibility, thereby filling some of the worst gaps in health insurance coverage for the poor, and would institute a universal program of catastrophic insurance through employer group plans and a residual federal plan. The plan introduced by Senators Russell Long and Abraham Ribicoff is the major example of this form of NHI.

The medical assistance (low-income) component of the plan is an ideal example of our category 2 plans, that is, with income-tested eligibility under a single national standard and, aside from some minimal copayments on ambulatory services, imposing no cost-sharing. This would represent a substantial improvement over Medicaid by moving away from (a) the categorical and highly differing income standards for eligibility; (b) variability in even the level of basic hospital and physician benefits; and (c) differing but often inadequate reimbursement levels. For the nonpoor, nonaged population the plan depends upon the voluntary continuation of the present system of employer–employee private insurance (it does not mandate minimum employment-based insurance). Thus, as in nearly all NHI plans, the combination of the coverage under the plan and private market purchases of health insurance are seen by supporters to provide "universal" coverage.

The catastrophic component would provide universal coverage for the entire population. Under the Long–Ribicoff plan the definition of catastrophic costs is specified in days of hospital care and dollars of physician and other medical services. After these deductibles are met, cost-sharing would be paid up to an annual dollar limit. Cost-sharing under the catastrophic plan for the medically assisted would be paid by the government, providing an element of income testing to the definition of catastrophic expenses.

Tax Credit Plan

Tax credit plans would provide federal personal income tax credits for either (a) premiums paid to qualified private insurance plans; or (b) high medical expenses (which effectively turns the IRS into an insurance company). Several recent plans based upon tax credits have been proposed by Robert Dole, John Danforth, and Alain Enthoven, though several earlier plans, including one sponsored by the American Medical Association, used this device.[11]

Plans offering tax credits for the purchase of private insurance depend critically upon government regulation of the characteristics of plans qualifying the taxpayer for the credit. At a minimum the regulation would assure adequate catastrophic coverage. Medicare would be retained for the elderly. Medicaid would either be altered to subsidize premiums paid by the poor, or replaced by a system of income-tested vouchers for the purchase of insurance, similar, in principle, to vouchers for education or housing. Such plans include income-tested cost-sharing for poor and nonpoor by varying in accord with income the percentage of the actual premium allowed as a credit. For example, if the tax credit were worth only 80% of the premium for a plan meeting minimum benefit standards, the plan would clearly include significant cost-sharing. This is expected to bring about consumer cost-consciousness. Alternatively, there is an incentive for HMOs or other prospectively paid institutions to enter and compete for consumers by offering better benefits or lower premiums than traditional insurance reimbursement under fee-for-service practice.

Premium tax credit plans allow voluntary participation, though the financial incentives to purchase a qualified plan are likely to bring about universal coverage. Differences in the ability of premium tax credit plans—all of which incorporate universal eligibility and income-tested cost-sharing—to achieve the goals of NHI will depend critically upon the kinds of insurance plans chosen by consumers and the resulting responses of medical care providers.

In contrast to tax credits for insurance premiums are plans providing refundable tax credits for medical expenses. Legislation of this sort was previously introduced by Senator William Brock and has been discussed by academics under the label "major risk NHI" (see Feldstein, 1971; 1977b). The goal of such plans is to provide insurance for high health care expenses through the personal income tax (where high expenses are defined on an income-related basis) and to remove the current tax subsidies for employer-paid basic coverage. Benefits would be available to persons who would otherwise not have filed a tax return, since the tax credits are refundable. Hence the tax credits for expenditures promise to be universal NHI programs and are generally designed to include

---

[11]For a carefully argued explanation of this approach, see Enthoven (1978).

income-related deductibles and maximums on family out-of-pocket expenses per year. Supporters of the plans argue that they will lead to a sharp decline in current insurance coverage of basic benefits through repeal of the subsidy for employers and an obvious improvement in coverage of catastrophic expenditures.[12] This shift in the kind of insurance coverage is argued to result in a new cost-consciousness among consumers and providers of medical care. Over time, then, hospitals and physicians would be expected to alter the costs and intensity of services in response to the greater market discipline.

Mixed Public–Private Plans

As under the expanded Medicaid and catastrophic plans, the mixed public–private plans depend upon private coverage of the employed population and dependents. However, in order to bring such coverage up to minimum standards (i.e., in benefits, cost-sharing, and reimbursement provisions), these plans mandate employer coverage for full-time workers and their families. Examples of plans in the mixed public–private category include the Nixon administration plan of 1974, plans sponsored by the American Hospital Association (AHA) and the Health Insurance Association of America, and the approach proposed by the Carter administration.[13]

Coverage of the aged under these plans is achieved either by continuation of Medicare (or a program very similar to it) or by combining the aged and the poor in a single federal insurance program. Most plans provide for federal insurance of the poor replacing Medicaid and thereby making improvements much like those of the expanded Medicaid–catastrophic form of NHI (though in the AHA plan the poor are covered under contract with private insurance companies instead of by a government-administered plan). Persons neither covered by employer plans nor by virtue of their age or poverty status are generally offered

[12]The critical assumption here is that relatively few consumers will purchase supplementary insurance to fill in the cost-sharing once they face the full market cost of providing it. Evidence to the contrary includes (a) the extensive supplementation of Medicare in the United States, and (b) that substantial supplementation occurred in Canada after employer insurance payments became taxable in that country (we owe this second point to Ted Marmor).

[13]See Davis (1975) and Waldman (1976) for descriptions of the earlier plans. The Carter proposal would occur in phases, with the first phase, S.1812 (U.S. Senate, 1979b), being of the expanded Medicaid plus catastrophic type. Subsequent phases would add additional population groups and improve the mandated private coverage by expanding it from only catastrophic to a full range of benefits.

the option of voluntary enrollment in the plan for the poor upon payment of a premium. All of the plans provide for income-related cost-sharing, though the magnitude and form of the cost-sharing varies widely, and this feature leads to quite different implications for cost control and income distributive effects of the plans. Therefore, the plans involve universal eligibility and income-related cost-sharing, placing them in our group-3 category in the classification above.

Although the mixed public–private form of NHI appears to be considerably more expansive than the more marginal expanded Medicaid–catastrophic form, the federal budget costs of the two forms are quite similar. This result occurs because the coverage added to the federal budget by each form involves the same population group, the Medicaid-ineligible poor. The other gains in coverage for the nonpoor under the mixed public–private approach are largely kept off the federal budget through the device of mandated employer coverage. Thus, while this form is more clearly universal in participation (by virtue of employment-based coverage being mandated by the program), its federal budget costs need not be significantly higher. This is contrary to the usual presumption that universal transfer programs imply significant increases in the federal budget relative to income-tested programs. The mechanism created by the mixed public–private plan is, of course, that the new taxes (called "premiums") imposed on employers and employees are not a part of the budget. The exact federal budget increments will depend upon the definition of the poor used, the degree of income-related cost-sharing, whether or not the catastrophic portion of a plan is financed in a manner that puts it on or off the federal budget, and the extent of various subsidies designed to minimize adverse employment effects of the mandated premium.

Complete Public-Sector Plans

In contrast to the above approaches to NHI, all of which depend to some extent on the existing system of private-employment-based financing and eligibility for health insurance, the complete public-sector form provides for a single plan under which the entire population is eligible. The public-sector plans sever the link between financing and eligibility, and in so doing resolve a number of the difficult administrative issues generic to most of the approaches described above. However, complete public-sector plans also involve substantial institutional changes which carry with them considerable political opposition from entrenched provider and insurance groups, and correspondingly greater uncertainty about their implications for the quantity, quality, cost, and distribution of health care services in the United States. Examples of such plans include the Kennedy–Mills compromise bill of 1974, the Health Security Plan, and Senator Kennedy's 1979 Health Care for All Americans Act.[14]

The most important feature of those complete public-sector insurance plans that have been proposed is universal eligibility for a single, uniform plan (or set of equivalent alternative plans) covering a comprehensive range of health services. Medicaid and Medicare would be eliminated. While financing of care for various population groups may come from employer–employee payroll taxes (or "earnings-related premiums" in the language of the new Kennedy proposal), federal general revenues, or state and local taxes, eligibility for the plan is not tied to the source of financing, nor is the source of financing known to the provider when care is given. This is accomplished, for example, by issuing each participant a health insurance "credit card." Some plans provide for income-related cost-sharing (Kennedy–Mills), while most others impose no cost-sharing. Hence the plans fall into groups 3 and 4 of our universal versus income-tested taxonomy. The private insurance industry is, at most, relegated to a financial intermediary role under these plans.[15]

Compared to the mixed public–private plans, the incremental federal budget costs of the complete public plans will be much greater by transferring to the federal budget most costs currently financed through private employer–employee premiums.[16] This will be true both of plans with and without cost-sharing, though the incremental budget costs of

[14]Davis (1975) discusses Kennedy–Mills and Health Security. The latter is also described by Waldman (1976). The current Kennedy proposal, S.1720 (U.S. Senate, 1979a), modifies the Health Security model to provide a nominal role for the private health insurance industry and is, in part, financed by employer–employee "earnings-related" premiums. We have excluded from the domain of this paper any consideration of proposals for some form of a national health service, similar to that of Great Britain. While such a strategy has been proposed by Representative Ronald Dellums and has the support of a committee of the American Public Health Association, it seems to have no political viability for at least the next decade in the United States.

[15]This appears to be true as well under the insurance consortia created by the new Kennedy plan, given the extensive government regulation of the participating companies in these consortia. However, it would seem that private insurance could be given an underwriting role under area budgets if this were desired. The government could simply open coverage of an area to competitive bids by single insurers or consortia of insurers, who would then bear the risk of covering the population on an open-enrollment basis.

[16]The Health Care for All Americans Act would, in form, avoid having its employer–employee taxes counted as revenues to the U.S. government, since they are to be paid directly to consortia of private insurers. However, in substance, the earnings-related premiums are taxes, particularly since eligibility for NHI is separate from payment of an employer–employee premium.

the latter type will be especially high (unless the costs of additional utilization are offset by administrative cost savings). Reimbursement under completely public NHI plans would either (*a*) be similar to that of Medicare, though the increased government leverage provided by having most provider payments go through the plan may improve control over fees and budgets; or (*b*) involve some type of prospective area-wide budgets, allocated by quasi-governmental boards or agencies which would determine institutional budgets and provider fee schedules for the fee-for-service sector.

Assessment of NHI Alternatives

Given the four generic approaches to NHI—Expanded Medicaid and Catastrophic (EMC), Tax Credit (TC), Mixed Public–Private (MPP), and Complete Public Sector (CPS)—what can be said about their contribution to achieving the above described goals of NHI? This section assesses the four approaches in general terms, largely avoiding reference to the details of any particular plan.[17]

Access to Acceptable-Quality Care and Reduction of Stigma

It has frequently been argued that the United States has a two-class system of medical care. The poor are relegated to hospital emergency rooms, crowded outpatient clinics, and "Medicaid mills" with long waits, no continuity of records or staff, and inadequate preventive care. In spite of this characterization, the Medicaid and Medicare programs have been credited with significant improvements in utilization of services among their respective beneficiary groups (Davis and Schoen, 1978). What contribution can NHI make to further improvements in access to care, and do the approaches to NHI have different implications for a continued dual-quality system?

The critical element in uniform access is that providers of care, particularly physicians, view patients as being equal in the reimbursement offered and resource cost involved in receiving reimbursement. Rela-

[17]For example, we ignore details of benefit packages, definitions of poverty, schedules for phasing in premiums and cost-sharing, if any, specific financing mechanisms, and issues of administrative feasibility. While such details are extremely important to an assessment of any particular plan, discussion of them would have involved limiting this paper to consideration of only two or three plans.

tively low Medicaid physician fee schedules have been blamed for many physicians dropping out of the Medicaid program, forcing patients to travel farther or turn to institutional sources for ambulatory care. To give another example, various states experimented with cost-sharing in their Medicaid programs but dropped the procedure when physicians refused to participate because of the difficulty of collecting copayments from the patients.[18] Had the state Medicaid programs been able to reimburse the physicians in full and subsequently collect the cost-sharing from enrollees, there would not have been the same effect on access.[19]

Achievement of the equal access goal is not necessarily tied to the universal or income-tested nature of NHI. Nearly all forms of NHI would at a minimum federalize Medicaid and upgrade reimbursement to Medicare standards. While this is an improvement, Medicare reimbursement of physicians presently allows participating providers to bill the patient directly for the amount of fees in excess of the Medicare reasonable charge. To continue this procedure creates a potential financial access problem for the poor and a cost control problem for the system. However, to alter the procedure by forcing physicians to accept fees below their customary charges runs the risk of causing them to drop out of the program unless a significant share of their market offers the same level of reimbursement. Thus, while it may well be in conflict with the cost-control goal, achievement of access to comparable-quality care argues for fully comparable reimbursement policies for most or all patients. This condition, while it could conceivably be met by any NHI approach, is generally not adequately met by EMC proposals and it is unclear whether or not it would be met by regulation of private insurance under the TC-for-premium approach. Even in the universal MPP approach this condition may not be met by plans that use a separate insurance program for low-income eligibles unless their reimbursement methods are carefully coordinated with those in the mandated private plans. The larger the population covered by the low-income public-sector plan, the less of a problem access will be, since the enrollees would represent a significant proportion of most providers' markets and thus nonparticipation is not a viable option. Only in the CPS approach—the extreme case of a universal plan—where there is a single

[18]It is interesting to note that in a universal plan with income-related cost-sharing, if providers were required to collect the cost-sharing (say, a modest copayment) they would actually favor low-income patients, since they have lower billing costs. However, copayments have not been proposed for universal plans, only income-tested plans.

[19]A similar problem exists currently in several states which ask participating pharmacists to collect a fifty cent copayment on each prescription. The number of participating pharmacists has fallen, thereby reducing access.

public insurance agency or strictly uniform reimbursement guidelines is the financial access goal almost surely achieved.[20]

Even if identical financial access were provided, however, implementation begins with the prior market distribution of providers across the social landscape, more concentrated in the higher-income areas of cities and in the suburbs. It is not clear that improved ability to pay on the part of previously uncovered or inadequately insured groups will be sufficient to bring about the geographic redistribution of providers in the long run. We know that unequal, albeit improved, ability to pay under Medicaid has not been sufficient. Most plans will probably have to be supplemented by differential reimbursement rates among regions or direct supply intervention to even approach accomplishment of the access goal. The latter class of approaches may either be organized separately from the NHI program or as a part of plans like the Kennedy CPS plans that call for special authorities to administer area-wide budgets and perform planning functions. However, at least according to some observers (Cooper, 1975) similar planning authorities in the British National Health Service have been unable to fully eliminate geographic disparities in access.

Closely related to the goal of equal access is the reduction of stigma—a familiar issue in the literature on transfer programs but one that is somewhat less familiar in the health care area. Income-tested forms of NHI are likely to continue some of the stigma felt by current Medicaid recipients. However, even the EMC approach would serve the present Medicaid and Medicare populations under a single plan, probably reducing recipients' perceptions of being lumped solely with other "welfare" cases, unable to provide for themselves.[21] Some MPP plans, though universal in approach, would create a public plan similar to that of the EMC approach and thus fare no better in reducing stigma.

The approaches that go the farthest toward reducing stigma are those that separate eligibility for a particular kind of insurance from its financing. These include (a) the TC; (b) MPP where the public plan's enroll-

---

[20]Our discussion has abstracted from the issue of outright discrimination against the poor or "welfare" population by providers, even when reimbursement policies are equal. If there were widespread discrimination of this sort, then it would not be sufficient to have equivalent reimbursement policies across plans, but there would actually have to be a single plan or, at least, no way for providers to determine the basis of a patient's eligibility for coverage.

[21]As an aside, however, it is interesting to ask how the aged—many of whom "contributed" through Medicare H.I. payroll tax during their working years—would feel about being lumped together with low-income eligibles. Would they suffer a reduction in self-esteem?

ment includes the self-employed, the unemployed, and some private employees along with the poor and the aged; and (c) the CPS approaches. Under these plans the identification of an enrollee as poor or eligible for a subsidy is limited to instances of enrollment with the insurance carrier or, in the TC for expenses, to contact with the Internal Revenue Service.[22] The closer an approach comes to identifying access to health care as a socially established right and the farther NHI financing can get from its ties to employment (either an earned fringe benefit in current employment or an earned right of past employment in the case of Medicare), the less stigmatizing an NHI plan will be. Here we have seen that universal plans are probably necessary to reducing stigma, but universal eligibility is probably not sufficient for this task.

Control of Rapidly Rising Medical Costs

Clearly the most difficult to achieve of the three major NHI goals is sensible cost control. As argued above, sensible cost control allows desirable increases in utilization and technological change to occur, while screening out undesirable increases in price and quantity or intensity of service. Effective and efficient cost control in an NHI plan presumably will require the use of several or all of the following instruments: patient cost-sharing, departure from cost reimbursement of institutions and usual and customary fee-for-service reimbursement of physicians, encouragement of innovative methods of delivery including HMOs, equipment and facility review, benefit packages offering substitutes to costly institutional care, and national or area-wide health budget ceilings.

Cost-sharing—through deductibles, coinsurance, or copayments—is viewed as an important part of the cost-control strategy of most NHI plans. To impose patient sharing in the costs of care brings about more cost-conscious behavior on the part of patients and their providers, who are at least aware of average levels of cost-sharing, if not that of every patient. The economic literature has established the effectiveness of cost-sharing in reducing utilization in the short run, and probably in the long run as well.[23] While the direction of change is known, estimates of

[22]Or to contact with a special fund to handle cash flow problems of the ill between tax returns (see Seidman, 1977).

[23]See, for example, the studies by Scitovsky and Snyder (1972), Beck (1974), and Newhouse and Phelps (1976). The first two use the relatively rare natural experiments for data. The last uses microdata and statistical controls and compares its results to those of earlier studies using survey data.

the price elasticity of demand vary widely, and the subject is plagued with data problems (particularly on the marginal price). For example, the estimates apply to different income groups, different types of cost-sharing or even general price variables, and different medical services or providers. Furthermore, it has been argued (but not adequately demonstrated) that the imposition of cost-sharing on ambulatory care leads to postponed preventive care, but that ultimately costs rise when the illnesses not seen earlier become more serious (and expensive) acute-care cases.

If one accepts the long-run effectiveness of cost-sharing—especially the use of coinsurance—as a cost-control device (the weight of the evidence favors this view), then one will oppose on these grounds the CPS plans with no cost-sharing and the EMC approach, which leaves current employer–employee first dollar coverage untouched. Yet many other plans are subject to similar criticism. To design an NHI plan that imposes cost-sharing in the first instance is not to guarantee it in the last; this requires prevention of consumers and their employers from purchasing insurance to supplement the NHI plan by filling in the cost-sharing, much as middle- and upper-income Medicare eligibles do now. The primary approach to reducing supplementation is to repeal both the exclusion of employer insurance from taxable personal income and the deductibility of individually paid premiums. The success of this last approach is especially crucial to the cost-control mechanism in the TC-for-expenses plans, which offer no public coverage until reasonably large income-related deductibles have been exceeded. However, repeal of the tax expenditures for insurance should be an element in any of the universal plans (though it has clear equity implications for newly covered workers who find themselves paying premiums and higher taxes for their new coverage). We conclude that cost-sharing will probably be an effective cost-control mechanism if purchase of supplementary insurance can be prevented. The EMC and CPS, the income-tested and the most universal plan respectively, do not utilize this approach. The other universal approaches depend on cost-sharing as a key cost-control measure.

The second major instrument of cost control is reimbursement policy. Here, it is argued, reimbursement of institutional providers should be changed to a prospectively set rate for either patient days or per patient based upon industry averages, the characteristics of the particular institution, and tied to temporal changes in the general price level (Lave, Lave, and Silverman, 1973; Fuchs, 1974; U.S. Congressional Budget Office, 1979). It must be recognized that all specific formulas, even if generally effective in slowing the rise in institutional costs, run the risk of encouraging unexpected behavioral responses of institutions (Berry, 1976). A number of experiments in prospective reimbursement of institutions are currently under way in individual states; they should greatly improve our knowledge of this issue.

Turning to reimbursement of professional providers, many argue that strict fee schedules should be established for providers billing under fee-for-service, and that initially fees should be based on average, not usual or customary fees.[24] Furthermore, participating providers must be required to accept the scheduled fee as full payment for their services; that is, no additional billing of patients can be allowed. We mentioned above that some observers argue for cost control as a prerequisite to NHI, while others argue that NHI is a prerequisite to cost control. The force of the latter argument derives from the observation that centralized control over a substantial proportion of the payments to any provider group is necessary, otherwise strict reimbursement controls will only harm the beneficiaries, as we discussed above, in regard to physician reimbursement under Medicaid. This is one of the most forceful arguments favoring universal over income-tested approaches to NHI. To accomplish uniform fee schedules the approach must either be to establish a single public plan, CPS, or to utilize under the MPP and TC approaches the regulatory powers of the government to make adoption of the uniform fee schedule a prerequisite to status as a plan qualifying under mandated employer coverage in the former case or for tax credits in the latter case.[25]

Prepaid health plans and other innovative delivery modes should be encouraged as a substitute for the conventional postpaid and fee-for-service system. There is ample evidence to suggest that such arrangements have created the economic incentives or, at any rate, the environment in which costly hospitalization has been reduced; and there is some evidence to suggest that ambulatory utilization has not increased at all in such settings, and certainly not so much as to offset the savings on institutional care (Gaus, Cooper, and Hirschman, 1976). Encouragement can take several forms. First, it can be established that such set-

---

[24]See Dyckman (1978) for a description of the inflationary bias created by current insurance reimbursement schemes for physicians' fees and an argument for reimbursement at the average fee.

[25]We are simply unable at this point to predict the effectiveness of such regulation over the many possible plans that might present themselves for certification. Our intuition suggests that it may indeed by more difficult to achieve a single uniformly administered fee schedule for a few hundred employer–employee plans than for one national NHI plan. Certainly the inability of HEW in recent years to even *certify* HMO applicants at nearly its desired rate suggests that our caution is not unwarranted.

tings can be reimbursed by government NHI plans and are among the qualified providers under NHI forms that subsidize or mandate private coverage. Encouragement of this sort will obviously be stronger under the several universal than under income-tested programs, especially if employers are mandated to offer a qualified HMO or other prepaid plan as an available alternative to each employee. Second, it is critically important that prepaid plans be allowed to compete for enrollees on an equal footing with conventional insurance plans. That is, if prepaid plans must offer open enrollment or community rating, then conventional insurance must not be allowed to base rates upon the illness experience of each particular employment group. Finally, NHI plans may offer special government subsidies or loans for the creation or early operating costs of HMOs and other prepaid plans. Cost control by means of innovation in prepayment and delivery is available to all NHI plans, but appears to be depended upon most heavily under the Enthoven plan and certain MPP alternatives.

It is interesting to note in our discussion the contrast in cost-control mechanisms between two tax-credit-for-premiums plans, both of which strive for universal coverage. The AMA plan would rely heavily on the present private insurance system and its reimbursement policies, including reimbursement at physicians' usual and customary fees. This plan would expressly forbid any federal supervision of medical fees. In contrast is the Enthoven plan which, by setting the tax credit level well below the actuarial value for the nonpoor population, would encourage in an open enrollment period competition among a variety of area health insurers, HMOs, and any other new delivery forms that chose to compete for enrollees. The success of the latter plan is, of course, highly dependent upon the ability of the private market to respond to this challenge. What is interesting is that the major difference between these two plans comes not in their form or eligibility, but in the cost-control devices (if any) they rely upon. This example suggests that the universal versus income-tested framework is an irrelevant distinction to an important issue in the NHI debate.

One of the goals of NHI is the coverage of catastrophic medical costs. Yet success in achieving this goal may imply conflict with cost control. How can a plan simultaneously encourage coverage of very large medical bills and discourage excessive medical costs due to an increasing supply of hospital beds or the duplication of underutilized high-technology facilities? The instrument currently used to cope with the problem is Certificate of Need (CON) review of applications for new equipment or facilities. One study found CON to be ineffective in reducing the total volume of investment; instead, it reduced the expansion in bed supplies but increased investment in new services and equipment (Salkever and Bice, 1976). This is probably due to the greater emphasis of current CON laws on controlling bed supplies. Most NHI plans could continue devices like CON, but the CPS plans that establish regional authorities for administering budgets would appear to have more potential for effective comprehensive planning, since they would possess substantially more information on patients, providers, costs, and coverage.

The regional authorities established under the Kennedy CPS plans would be charged with administering area-wide budgets derived from a national budget constrained to grow only at the rate of general price increase. In plans with no cost-sharing, this is clearly the designers' hope for cost control. While we have no experience in America with such cost caps, the British National Health Service has used a top-down system of budgeting with some success. In contrast is the universal plan of Enthoven, which subsidizes only a portion of the health care costs of each individual, forcing consumers to face the full costs of additional insurance at the margin. This approach depends upon consumer cost-consciousness, competition among insurers for enrollees, and insurers' pressure on the behavior and reimbursement rates of providers; that is, it represents a "bottom up" approach. The CPS and MPP approaches rely primarily on faith in the ability of government regulation, while the TC approach relies primarily on faith in market forces through the creation of proper incentives.[26] Unfortunately there is very little direct evidence to indicate the optimal mix of market incentives and government controls. In its absence we are left with a difficult choice that depends more on our values and educated guesswork than on our positive economics.

Coverage for Catastrophic Loss

No one form of NHI appears to offer an advantage in the coverage of unusually high medical expenses as long as universal eligibility is achieved. Above, we noted that achievement of adequate catastrophic protection may conflict with the cost-control goal. The only exception is the particular approach of a catastrophic plan favored by Long and Ribicoff which, for the nonpoor, defines catastrophe without respect to

[26]Neither position is an absolutely extreme one. The MPP approaches use cost-sharing at least in part because of its effect on consumer cost-consciousness, and both MPP and CPS plans would encourage prepaid plans in competition with retrospective payment. The Enthoven TC plan relies on regulation of insurance and prepaid groups to achieve several minimum standards for the qualified plans.

income. This formulation of the cost-sharing imposes unreasonably severe burdens on families just above the low-income level who have very high medical expenses. All other plans handle this problem by employing an income-related ceiling on family out-of-pocket expenses for cost-sharing both in public plans and in regulated private insurance plans; and in the case of CPS plans without cost-sharing there is obviously full coverage.

Increases in the Federal Budget

The prevailing view in the debate over universal versus income-tested programs is that the latter involve substantially smaller increases in the federal budget than the former. If there are political limits on the tolerable federal budget increase for any one program, then more aid could be given to the poor under the income-tested alternative. As we have argued above, however, since there already exists a substantial private health insurance market, the incremental budget costs of NHI depend not so much upon whether the program employs universal or income-tested eligibility, but instead upon other factors: (a) whether coverage for the employed and their dependents is mandated for the private sector or brought through the federal fisc in the form of premiums, payroll taxes, or tax credits; (b) the degree of patient cost-sharing and how rapidly it is phased in as beneficiary income rises; (c) the effectiveness of cost-control mechanisms in the plan (we have argued above that universal plans may offer more leverage for controlling costs); (d) whether current state contributions to health care financing, particularly those for Medicaid, are captured as a financing source for the NHI plan; and (e) the definition of low income for eligibility, subsidized premiums, and reduced cost-sharing where these are applicable.

To illustrate this point with a specific example we cite HEW cost estimates of prototypical NHI plans (U.S. Department of Health, Education, and Welfare, 1978a). The "Target Plan" prototype described in the document is of the EMC form, establishing a federal health insurance plan for the aged and poor, a universal catastrophic program, and a limited children's health program. The "Publicly Guaranteed" prototype is of the MPP form, mandating employer–employee private-sector coverage for basic benefits, creating a residual public plan that would cover the poor, the aged, and small employment groups, and establishing a government "reinsurance" plan to cover catastrophic expenses of participants in both the private and public basic care plans. The HEW cost estimates indicate that the income-tested Target Plan would, if fully implemented, add $32.5 billion to the 1980 federal budget, whereas the universal Publicly Guaranteed Plan would add $34.0 billion. Both plans provide the same coverage for the poor and the aged. However, if the universal plan had brought the mandated private payments through the federal budget, the incremental federal cost of the plan would have been increased to roughly $100 billion.[27] Elimination of cost-sharing would add roughly another $15–20 billion, bringing the *incremental* federal budget costs of a CPS plan, without cost-sharing, to about $115–120 billion in 1980.

Moreover, all of the above estimates assumed that present contributions of state and local governments to covered services—about $7 billion, mostly in Medicaid funds—could be "captured" to finance the plans by substituting for current federal expenditures in other health areas. If fiscal relief to the states is required in the transition, the federal budget costs of each plan would be higher by this amount.[28]

To clarify our earlier distinction between transferred and induced costs, all of the above plans covered health services estimated to cost about $156 billion prior to NHI. Most of the incremental federal costs described above are indeed transfers, since estimated induced costs under the plans range from $16 billion under the income-tested plan to under $30 billion for the CPS plan with no cost-sharing.

Therefore, it is incorrect to assume that all universal NHI plans will necessarily involve substantially higher on-budget costs than will income-tested NHI plans. By mandating private expenditures outside the federal budget universal eligibility may be attainable without significantly different federal budget expenditures. Although this conclusion holds for the MPP form of NHI, the TC and CPS approaches are indeed more likely to add substantial amounts to the federal budget. With total expenditures on services usually covered by NHI falling in the $150–170 billion range (in 1980 dollars), transfer of a substantial share of these costs to the budget is indeed a major increase and a political liability of

[27]The HEW estimates assume that mandated premiums can be paid to a public corporation and hence be kept "off budget." We have simply assumed that these payments in fact must flow through the budget.

[28]It is also worthy of mention to a conference on transfer programs that the cost estimates described here assume that the Carter administration's Program for Better Jobs and Income had been passed, substantially raising the incomes of families below and around the poverty line. Without welfare reform and without changing the assumed levels of eligibility for income-tested plans and schedules for subsidized premiums and cost-sharing, the additional federal costs of the above plans might have been $5–10 billion higher in the EMC and MPP forms, but not substantially increased in the CPS forms, because the whole population is already covered on the federal budget (one author's estimate—not an HEW number).

very considerable magnitude in view of the prevailing attitude toward expansion of federal spending.[29]

Equity and Efficiency in Financing

Two hypotheses resulting from the universal versus income-tested perspective can be examined in the context of financing.[30] The first, bearing upon equity in financing, is that universal programs are more income-redistributive, especially to lower-middle-income groups. A second hypothesis is that income-tested programs are characterized by relatively large work disincentives when compared to universal programs, a problem of efficiency in NHI financing.

Mitchell and Schwartz (1976) have examined the redistributive impacts of the major NHI alternatives under consideration in the mid-1970s. Their estimates, presented in Table 10.1, have been titled to match three of our generic types and will be used to illustrate some essential redistributive effects of NHI.[31] Variation in the net benefits accruing to any income class is a result of two factors: cost-sharing and the progressivity of the premiums, payroll taxes, and income taxes used to finance NHI.

Cost-sharing is obviously a regressive form of financing, since the incidence of illness does not rise proportionately with income; in fact lower-income persons are more likely to be in poor health. Therefore, plans that remove cost-sharing by replacing it with more progressive means of financing will result in greater redistribution of income (such as the CPS plan in Table 10.1). However, cost-sharing also affects the level of consumption benefits through its effect on utilization of services. Plans that impose cost-sharing, but excuse low-income enrollees from it, will result in a redistribution toward lower incomes on the benefit side when compared to plans without cost-sharing. This point is illustrated by the benefits column of Table 10.1, where benefits fall with income in

[29]In fact, the latest Kennedy plan relies on mandated employer premiums in the hopes, claims one staff member, that they may be kept off budget. While not a substantive change in the Kennedy approach to financing, this change in presentation may indicate that the fully federal plans involve on-budget costs that are politically unacceptable.

[30]We are especially grateful to Barbara Wolfe for suggestions leading to improvement of this section of the paper. It is at her suggestion that we include Table 10.1, which she also refers to in her discussion.

[31]The Mitchell–Schwartz estimates are limited to a hypothetical family of four composed of a nonaged head who is the only worker. Therefore, the aged and most Medicaid recipients are excluded from the calculations. We report the authors' estimates of the total incidence of NHI plans.

TABLE 10.1

Estimates of Income Redistribution under Three Forms of National Health Insurance for a Family of Four (*1975 dollars*)

		Payments		
Family Income	Taxes[a]	Out-of-Pocket and Other Costs[b]	Consumption Benefits[c]	Income Redistribution[d]
Expanded Medicaid and Catastrophic[e]				
3,000	25	15	960	920
6,000	65	525	860	270
9,000	120	750	860	−10
12,000	170	820	860	−130
20,000	310	840	860	−290
50,000	1,070	1,000	860	−1,210
Mixed Public-Private[f]				
3,000	460	180	1,040	400
6,000	640	350	950	−40
9,000	690	350	950	−90
12,000	730	360	950	−140
20,000	880	360	950	−290
50,000	1,780	440	950	−1,270
Complete Public Sector[g]				
3,000	190	0	1,160	970
6,000	410	0	1,160	750
9,000	660	10	1,160	490
12,000	880	20	1,160	260
20,000	1,570	40	1,160	−450
50,000	3,880	200	1,160	−2,920

SOURCE: Estimates of Mitchell and Schwartz (1976) are reprinted with the permission of the Rand Corporation, Santa Monica, Calif.

[a] All figures from their Table 2, p. 7.

[b] Figures derived from their Tables 2 and 3, pp. 7, 10.

[c] Estimates from their Table D.1, p. 38, rounded to the nearest $10.

[d] Our calculations, based on previous columns. These figures vary by small amounts from Mitchell–Schwartz's Table 4, p. 12, for the second and third plans due to rounding.

[e] Based upon their estimates for Long–Ribicoff plan.

[f] Based upon Nixon administration CHIP plan.

[g] Based upon Kennedy–Corman Health Security Plan.

the EMC and MPP plans, but are constant over income classes in the CPS plan. Unless price elasticities of demand are very large and the groups excused from cost-sharing extend well beyond the lowest income group, however, the progressivity of other financing mechanisms is likely to outweigh the mild progressivity of imposing cost-sharing on the nonpoor.

Progressivity of the remaining financing methods is usefully divided into two components: that attributable to the expenditures for the working population and their dependents, and that covering costs of the rest of the population (i.e., the aged, poor, and nonpoor families without workers). Under the present system, health expenditures of families with workers are largely financed through employer–employee health insurance premiums; a regressive mechanism since premiums are a fixed dollar obligation regardless of income. NHI plans financed by employer–employee payroll taxes in lieu of premiums will redistribute income from higher- to lower-income families. This effect is illustrated by comparing the taxes column by income in Table 10.1 (which includes both premiums and payroll taxes) for the MPP and CPS plans, where the former relies on premiums and the latter uses payroll taxes. Finally, the magnitude and progressivity of taxes to cover health care costs of families without workers will affect net benefits by income class. Relatively greater dependence on income taxation and the larger amounts to be financed explain the very large net costs for the higher-income classes in the CPS plan when compared to the other plans in Table 10.1.

To summarize our findings on income redistribution under income-tested and universal plans, the income-tested (EMC) plan was indeed redistributive from high- to low-income families as hypothesized from the experience with cash programs.[32] Yet the two universal plans (MPP and CPS) have quite different redistributive outcomes depending upon their design; particularly the use of premiums versus payroll taxes and the presence or absence of cost-sharing. The CPS plan is consistent with the hypothesis that universal programs will result in net benefits for lower-middle-income groups (e.g., $6000 to $12,000 in the table). But the MPP plan, also based upon universal eligibility, yields net losses in those income groups. Therefore, the income redistributive effects of NHI are less a result of the universal or income-tested nature of a particular plan than they are a result of the particular cost-sharing and financing mechanisms used.

A second premise in the universal versus income-tested debate that relates to financing is that income-tested programs involve relatively higher implicit marginal tax rates and consequent work disincentives for the poor, but that universal programs by virtue of their substantially larger budgets result in relatively larger increases in the tax rates over middle- and upper-income groups. Does this reasoning apply in the case of national health insurance?

Work disincentives for the poor may arise in NHI from (*a*) income-

---

[32]The illustrative plan in Table 10.1 blunts this point slightly, since it represents a combination of an income-tested plan for the poor and a universal catastrophic plan. Estimates for the former taken alone would be even more redistributive.

tested premiums; (b) income-tested eligibility for benefits; and (c) from income-related cost-sharing. The gradual phasing in of premium payments by income will have analogous effects to an additional tax on income over the given income range between forgiveness of premiums and full payment. We would, thus, expect there to be concomitant reductions in labor supply. However, on questions of eligibility and cost-sharing, there may be an important difference between transfers of health insurance and transfers of other goods or services, or cash. While the consumption benefits of other transfer programs are known with relative certainty, the benefits of health insurance are relatively uncertain and depend upon the health status of the recipient and other members of the immediate family. To take the extreme example, suppose a recipient expected to remain perfectly healthy throughout an accounting period and that he were risk neutral. Then the prospect of reduced health care benefits for each extra dollar of earnings is unlikely to affect labor supply behavior. However, if the recipient expected to be in worse health than the average beneficiary, or if he were sufficiently risk-averse, then the value of health benefits to him will exceed the actuarially fair premium and a program offering reductions in benefits with increased wage income will have substantial labor supply effects. We need to amass more evidence on labor supply under income-tested health programs before a conclusion can be reached. Research on this subject is made particularly difficult because of the interaction between eligibility for our principal income-tested health program, Medicaid, and the various cash transfer programs which also employ income testing of benefits.

Work disincentives under NHI may not be limited to the poor. The nearly complete acceptance of income-related cost-sharing by the universal NHI programs may lead to similar qualitative effects on labor supply. In this case, the range of incomes over which cost-sharing is phased in may span to over twice the poverty level. Again, little is known about these responses, nor about how they vary by exact form of cost-sharing.

In all three areas of income-tested premiums, eligibility, and cost-sharing, the trade-offs are analogous to those in cash transfer programs. If the range of incomes over which the phasing out of eligibility or in of full payments is relatively narrow, then the plan will usually fare better on cost for the poor, but worse on grounds of work disincentives.

The sheer magnitude of NHI suggests that plans involving transfer of substantial sums from the private sector to the government through tax financing will indeed involve significant effects on personal tax rates and hence on decisions to work and to invest. For example, if one-half of the incremental budget cost of a complete public-sector plan with no cost-sharing were to be financed from federal general revenues (as proposed in the Health Security Plan), it would imply an increase in general revenue requirements of between 20 and 25%! We leave the efficiency effects of such an increase in taxes to the imagination of the reader.

Summary and Conclusions

Our commission to write this paper involved applying the universal versus income-tested distinction to national health insurance, "testing" the hypotheses arising in the cash transfer case to the NHI context and assessing the relevance of the distinction to the NHI debate. We began with a description of the current health care financing system—an elaborate patchwork of public and private financing mechanisms—in order to clarify that much in any NHI programs would not be new, in the sense of doing something that has not been done before, but that they largely would change and add to a complex set of existing institutional arrangements. The goals of NHI—increased access, cost control, and coverage of catastrophic costs—were discussed along with some other considerations likely to arise in the political arena. Universal and income-tested approaches to NHI are primarily distinguished by eligibility determination methods, but secondarily through whether or not use is made of income-tested cost-sharing. Four prototypical approaches to NHI programs were discussed: expanded Medicaid plus catastrophic, tax credit, mixed public–private, and complete public sector. The first represents an income-tested program, while the last three are different forms of universal programs.

While some of the hypotheses arising from the universal versus income-tested distinction found support in our examination of NHI, others did not. The hypothesis that universal programs will be more redistributive than income-tested programs, particularly to lower-middle-income groups, was not wholly supported by the estimates found in Mitchell–Schwartz (1976). Whereas one universal plan was far more redistributive than the income-tested plan, the other was less redistributive and actually left lower-middle-income working families worse off than under the income-tested plan. We conclude that the income redistributive effects of NHI depend more upon the particular design of cost-sharing and financing than upon the universal versus income-tested nature of any plan.

A similar conclusion emerges from consideration of the hypothesis that income-tested programs will transfer greater resources to the poor than universal programs when budget constraints are severe. We show that the move from an income-tested to a universal program need not involve the substantial political liability of increased federal budget costs, provided that the NHI program is of the mixed public–private variety. While to academics the distinction between on-budget payroll taxes and mandated (but off-budget) premiums may seem more one of form than substance, recent experience in NHI politics suggests that form is of importance in this instance.

Three sources of potential work disincentives under NHI have been identified: income testing of premiums in universal plans, income testing of eligibility for benefits, and income-related cost-sharing. While the first is expected to operate like any tax, the second and third may have different behavioral implications than the sources of implicit marginal tax rates in other cash and in-kind transfer programs. This is because most benefits under NHI programs will only be used should illness strike. This probabilistic nature of health care consumption complicates analysis of the efficiency of income-tested approaches and has not been the subject of previous research. Thus while the work-disincentive hypothesis has merit in the NHI context, as it does in cash transfers, we have no quantitative evidence on its importance.

The argument that universal programs correct the tendency toward two-class systems fostered by income-tested transfers is not particularly relevant to NHI. Two-class care remains an important issue, but its solution does not depend upon adoption of a universal program. Rather, the achievement of a single-class system lies in the assurance that services from all providers are eligible for coverage and that all providers receive the same reimbursement across all covered patients, at least in any given market area.

Current income testing of Medicaid surely involves some stigma for recipients. The ability of income-tested NHI to reduce stigma seems limited, though pooling the aged and poor in a single federal plan—as suggested in some plans to increase the income-tested enrollment—would surely reduce stigma by making the poor less distinct from those who had earned eligibility through prior payments. Universal plans offer greater hope for reducing stigma, particularly if they separate eligibility from financing. Thus universality is not sufficient; the degree to which stigma is removed depends upon design features within the class of universal plans.

We find that the universal versus income-tested perspective arising from the cash transfer case is not wholly applicable to NHI. Several of its hypotheses were found to have little or no support in the context of NHI.

To close, we ask a slightly different question: Is the universal versus income-tested perspective valuable in clarifying the debate over what kind of NHI we want in the United States in the 1980s? Again, the evidence is mixed. The perspective on the disadvantages of income testing leads us to conclude that universal plans go much further than income-tested plans toward satisfying the goals of NHI, if one leaves aside the other considerations of political realities we identified above. This is not altogether surprising, however, since the goals of NHI were developed with reference to the existing income-tested government plan for the poor and the patchwork of financing for other groups. Yet when we begin to concentrate on which universal form of NHI is best, the answers depend less upon issues raised by the universal versus income-tested debate than upon questions of the efficacy of market competition versus government regulation, for example. And it is, perhaps most of all, on the mechanisms to attain cost control that the current NHI debate hinges an issue upon which the universal versus income-tested perspective is relatively silent.

Discussion

BARBARA L. WOLFE

I would like to commend the authors for increasing our understanding of income testing versus universal programs as applied to national health insurance (NHI). They have clarified a number of issues, including differences between programs where the payment mechanism is universal and those where benefits are universal.

Turning now to points that might be modified, I will start with the goals cited for NHI.

The first goal, "access for all persons to acceptable-quality medical care," leaves unanswered a number of fundamental definitional questions. What do we mean by acceptable quality? Equal quality or a threshold level? How do we define quality? In terms of inputs (i.e., number of doctors or number of hospital beds) or by outcome (i.e., the effect on health)? The last is obviously harder to measure but presumably is what we should be interested in. Does access refer only to financial access along with some minimum supply guarantee, or is it more inclusive and aimed at equalizing utilization? If it is aimed at equalizing utilization, does this refer to the number of annual visits, or equal utilization for any given health problem? As the authors mention, quality control is an important factor when comparing universal versus income-tested health insurance programs. In both types of program, if the choice of provider is left to the individual (in various tax credit plans for example) or groups, the less well-informed (often the poorest) may receive a poorer quality of service either because "quality" is difficult to judge, or because providers are in short supply in their vicinity, or the most conveniently located services are of generally lower quality (possibly due to turnover).

A further set of questions relates to whether this goal includes all types of medical care—including outpatient mental health care, organ transplants, and all future technological changes—or a more limited set. These are questions that plague policymakers today.

The second goal, control of rapidly rising medical costs, is probably more appropriately termed control of rising medical expenditures. "Costs" refer to the way a good is produced. (Is it the least costly combination of inputs for example?) "Expenditures" refer to price times quantity. Most policies discussed generally influence expenditures. Copayments, for example, may reduce quantity demanded.

The third goal, coverage for all families for catastrophic loss, may be a too readily accepted goal. As Zook, Moore, and Zeckhauser (1980) have pointed out, "high-cost illnesses differ widely in terms of clinical options, controllability of resource utilization and predictability (the repeaters). Insurance schemes should reflect those differences [p. 72]." The population with catastrophic expenditures accounts for 40–50% of all hospital charges in a given year, and many of the persons in this category show harmful habits (such as alcoholism). Thus a catastrophic plan may subsidize such habits. The prevalence of harmful habits in medical records in the Zook, Moore, and Zeckhauser study suggests that a need to change incentives to encourage preventive measures may be an important aspect of insurance design. For certain problems, lower-cost settings may be as effective as hospitalization; for others, special facilities may provide economies of scale.

Care should be taken that the secondary goal of "minimizing disruption of the present private market system of financing and delivering health care—notably the role of private health insurance and the independence of providers" does not prevent any change whatsoever. This is particularly so for expenditure control. Perhaps this goal could be modified to "gain cooperation of providers." Realistically, we do need to be aware of this constraint, but not so much that our hands are tied.

Next, there is a good deal more conflict between goals than the authors recognize (unfortunately). The authors for example note what is probably the best-known conflict—between equal access and controlling expenditures of medical care. In order to control expenditures, many suggest using some form of coinsurance to reduce demand somewhat. However, coinsurance among those with low incomes would mean less care for low-income individuals. Another area of conflict between goals is between expenditure control and coverage for catastrophic loss. If all catastrophic medical expenditures are covered, this may lead to larger expenditures.

On a larger point, the authors do not discuss the justification for government intervention in medical care delivery to the poverty population or population in general. One argument stems from the asymmetry or lack of information on appropriate medical care. The fact that information is available only at very high cost leads to certain forms of government involvement, such as quality regulation (licensing for example) and subsidization of certain types of care. Another set of arguments have to do with externalities. Perhaps the most commonly recognized of these are externalities in consumption from immunizations—and the government's response of providing public health services (direct provision) plus certain requirements of school districts (laws regarding compliance). Another externality has to do with the idea that citizens do not wish the less fortunate to be without adequate care so are willing to subsidize care for the disadvantaged.

This last point may be important in weighing universal versus income-tested programs. It suggests that policies which are targeted at particular low-income groups—income-tested programs—would be most acceptable to the public, that is, the contributors to the programs.

Moving on, the authors promise but have not yet provided us with estimates of the distributional impacts of the various types of bills. A 1976 Rand paper by Bridges Mitchell and William Schwartz does provide some estimates.[1] We find the following picture using Mitchell and Schwartz's consumption estimates which are based on (a) coinsurance and deductibles; (b) coverage of service; and (c) financing of each of a variety of plans.

The important points one can get from these figures are as follows: (a) The coinsurance rate is the important factor in redistributing care. A universal program—such as a complete public-sector program—redistributes care less than those that impose a coinsurance plan on the nonpoor. (Compare the benefits in the first row to the rows for higher-income groups under the three plans.) Thus, both the expanded Medicaid plus catastrophic and mixed public–private result in more redistribution of care than the complete public sector. (b) Methods of financing are very important in determining the distributional impact. Three methods of financing are generally cited: premium, payroll tax,

---

[1]In response to my criticism, the authors have amended their paper by adding Mitchell and Schwartz's table (Table 10.1).

and income tax. Premiums are the least progressive (are regressive), payroll taxes are less so, and are proportional in part, while income taxes are most progressive. (It should be remembered that when we discuss universal versus income-tested, we are referring *only* to the benefit side.) (c) The figures also highlight a point frequently forgotten: the importance of out-of-pocket costs. An example of this is transportation. If transportation costs are substantial, those with lower incomes may still be unable to have equal access to medical care. (And, if provider location preferences remain, these costs [direct transportation] are likely to be greater for rural and low-income individuals who have further to travel.) Thus for service programs, what does universal really mean? Perhaps not just a plan for *all*, but requiring supplementary funds or services for truly equal access.

Finally, little is really said in the paper on two other health-related issues—public education and preventive medicine. On preventive medicine, any deductible or coinsurance is thought to decrease preventive care, which may lead to greater costs later on. This would be true both for universal and income-tested programs that included various forms of copayment. A way around this might be to have certain services provided without these costs—for example, immunizations, well-baby care, obstetric care. Alternatively, each individual might be permitted limited free care over a several-year period—the inverse of a deductible—and then face copayment. Certain types of health education may also reduce costs by increasing compliance, earlier recognition of diseases, need for preventive care, and so forth. Many forms of insurance do not cover consumer education—a policy which may ultimately increase costs.

In closing, may I suggest that the authors have improved our understanding of the issues involved in health insurance. They have shown that the budget implications are not clearly in favor of universal or income-tested programs. Decisions on which plans best accomplish objectives depend on a weighting of the objectives.

11

Single-Parent Households under Alternative Transfer and Tax Systems

HAROLD W. WATTS
GEORGE JAKUBSON
FELICITY SKIDMORE

A major reason given by proponents of universal as opposed to income-tested benefit programs (such as a credit income tax) is that they erase invidious distinctions among citizens. Instead of dividing society into various categories—by reserving different programs for different kinds of people as defined by different demographic characteristics, different social ills, different levels of income—the universal programs provide all people access to the same alternatives. Of course, any credit income tax that does succeed in changing the distribution of income by definition has to treat the rich differently from the poor. The point is that under such a program everyone faces the same credit and tax features of the system. It is the combination of the two that yields a different net benefit (or net tax) depending upon one's position in the income distribution.

But categorical distinctions, invidious though they may be, are an important feature of the current system. One group that has been traditionally recognized as requiring special attention is single-parent households, headed predominantly by women. To go from the categorical status quo to a universal income support system would render single-parent households substantially worse off in terms of posttax and posttransfer income relative to other groups in the population than they currently are.

It is the concern of this paper to examine the distributional consequences for children in one- and two-parent households of the proposed
radical reforms of the tax and transfer system introduced by Betson,
Greenberg, and Kasten in this volume (Chapter 6) and possible methods
of changing those consequences.

We begin with a discussion of why single-parent households need
special policy attention and the problems that must be resolved in the
design of policies for them. The next section discusses how the resolution of these problems over the last 30 years of social welfare policy has
led to the current configuration of income support policies. We then
discuss the basic distributional consequences of the status quo as of
1975, placing particular emphasis on the differential treatment of households with children depending on whether one or two parents are present. This contrast is shown in two ways. One uses net redistribution
functions that show how the net impact of current tax and transfer
policies alters the adult equivalent income levels in the one- and two-
parent tax units. The second simply shows the distribution of children
by adult equivalent income level between children in one- and two-
parent units.

The next sections use the same tools to show how a credit income tax
(CIT) and a negative income tax (NIT) would modify these net redistributions and distributions. As will be seen, the status quo tends to
favor one-parent units at any given level of predistribution resources
and CIT and NIT reform proposals tend to overcompensate for this
unequal treatment and, on balance, favor the two-parent unit. Indeed,
at maximum benefit levels comparable to those proposed in recent legislation, a large number of one-parent units would end up much worse off
than at present. We then develop two alternative benefit programs for
single-parent households to be added onto the original CIT or NIT to
redress the balance. The following section shows how each alternative
alters the distributional picture when combined with a CIT and a NIT,
and then explores the distributional consequences of adding, instead, a
universal children's allowance scheme (both with and without a tax
"clawback" feature) to a CIT or a NIT.

All these simulations take as given the current situation (at least as
reported) with respect to alimony and child support payments made and
received. The limitations of the data base give us no alternative. The tax
rates for the basic CIT and NIT used in the simulations are set so that the
programs have a zero net cost (in terms of taxes paid) compared with the
status quo. The various policy add-ons in our simulations, however, do
require additional funds. We, therefore, also calculate the net cost of
each alternative and the amount the tax rate would have to be increased

under the various schemes for them to "pay for" themselves. Such an exercise highlights how remedies based on general revenue for the income deficiencies of single-parent households require the taxpaying public to pay for absent parents' lack of responsibility—and produce, as a consequence, perverse incentives with respect to marriage, divorce, and remarriage.

This dilemma leads to our final section, which is a more speculative discussion of (a) policies that might achieve the enforcement and reinforcement of the financial responsibilities of both parents to their children, and (b) the problems that would remain, even then, for the income support system.

Why Single-Parent Households Present a Special Problem for Society

Households with children are different from other households in that they are responsible for building the human capital of the next generation. Because children become the citizens, parents, workers, taxpayers, and public dependents of the future, it is in society's self-interest that children be raised so as to ensure their productivity and viability as future adults and parents. Research is demonstrating increasingly clearly that a substantial part of human development, for better or for worse, is related to the household environment and the material and human inputs that make up that environment. Further, policy initiatives over the last 15 years have made it clear that effective extrafamilial compensation for the consequences of childhood deprivation is expensive at best and may be impossible (Advisory Committee on Child Development of the National Research Council, 1976; Keniston et al., 1977).

So far the argument applies to two-parent as well as one-parent households. And, as we know, many children are being brought up in two-parent households that are poor. Why, then, should one-parent households as a group be treated differently from two-parent households of the same income status?

First, single-parent households by definition have only one parent and often only one adult to shoulder all the financial and nonfinancial burdens of the household. Thus, the total productive time potentially available for earning and/or for housekeeping and child nurturing is less for one parent than for two. Most of the children in one-parent households these days have, of course, two parents. But, as a consequence of family breakup, their parents are parts of two separate households. Any sharing of parental responsibility, thus, becomes a matter of *in-*

*ter*household rather than intrahousehold concern. Even when both partners enter into this sharing in good faith, the interhousehold nature of it creates obvious inefficiencies and frictions. Such a situation also facilitates the abandoning of responsibility by the parent who does not have the day-to-day care of the children.

Added to these factors is the reality that most single-parent households are headed by women. As such, these family heads on average command lower wages in the labor market, first to the extent that they have developed their market skills and qualifications less, and second, to the extent that they suffer sex discrimination.[1] And the inequity may be aggravated by incremental discrimination on account of their single parenthood (employer expectations of higher absenteeism, lower reliability on the job, and so forth).

But once it is granted that society should ensure some kind of parity between one-parent and two-parent households, a host of difficult problems arise with respect to what kind of parity and how it should be achieved.

First, although the single-parent household is becoming a much more common occurrence—it has been estimated that nearly one-half of the children born in the early 1970s will live in a one-parent household at some time before they are 18—there is still general agreement in our society that a two-adult household is, other things equal, the preferable environment for the raising of children. Stepparents do, after all, provide important substitutes for absent biological parents in terms other than any contribution they may make to direct economic support (role models, time inputs to nurturing, etc.). Acceptance of this principle implies that any specific benefit system at least should not provide positive incentives for family breakup and that, equally, social policy should avoid erecting unnecessary barriers to remarriage and perhaps should go so far as to provide incentives for minimizing the duration of single-parent status.

Second, children are products of a union between two parents. With current life expectancies, most children will continue to have two biological parents throughout their childhood. It seems reasonable, therefore, that public policy should be designed to promote the responsibility of both parents for their children, whether or not they both remain in the same household.

---

[1]Labor market discrimination by sex is not, in our view, directly relevant to the subject of this paper. Such discrimination should, therefore, be dealt with by affirmative action and other remedies in the labor market, not by transfer systems designed to increase equity among families.

Third, whether mothers (particularly single parents) should work is inextricably entwined with the issue of single-parent support, although there seems no clear societal consensus on how the work issue should be dealt with. Traditionalists and many child development experts feel that children (particularly when young) are better off if their mothers take care of them rather than work for pay and that, if the mothers are single parents, society should provide the financial support to enable them to do that (Fraiberg, 1977). Many people, in contrast, feel uncomfortable as taxpayers about paying for a benefit program that enables single parents to stay at home rather than being out "earning their living." And women's rights advocates take the view that women (including mothers) have as much right to undertake paid work as any other adult in society and that a benefit system should not be structured so that it distorts their work choice.

Fourth, many single-parent households are poor, but many are not. Does society have a responsibility only to ensure an income *floor*, or does society have a further responsibility to achieve parity between one-parent and two-parent households throughout the income distribution?

Finally, at the same time that the increasing incidence of divorce is making the experience of living in a single-parent household much more common and therefore "normal," the prevalence of remarriage is making it a transitory state for most. Thus, although single-parent households as a group are conspicuously less well off than two-parent households, they are a shifting population. Clearly, the shorter the duration of single-parent status, the less important are the disadvantages of that status, the more widely spread and "normal" these disadvantages will be and, thus, the less will be the need for policy intervention.

The manner in which all these problems are resolved determines the shape of public policy toward the single-parent household and, in turn, the distribution of income between children being raised by two parents and children being raised by only one.

The History of Public Policy toward Support of Children in One-Parent Households

Concern at the national policymaking level with the plight of children in single-parent households dates back to 1935, when the President's Committee on Economic Security designed the social security system which, by and large, remains in place today. It was the time of the Great

Depression, jobs were hard to come by, and it was so generally agreed as to need no discussion that what jobs there were or could be created should go to able-bodied men, with first priority given to those with dependents.

The committee was concerned to provide income support to those population groups that were not expected to work—one might go so far as to say expected not to work. The committee saw the "core" of their program as their planning for children (Schorr, 1966, p. 4). Not surprisingly, therefore, one of the groups they chose to assist (in a program then called Aid to Dependent Children) was young, fatherless households below a certain income level. Eligibility depended on household income being below a certain level and upon the establishment of long-term single parenthood.[2] Many such households in 1935 were the result of the death of the father rather than merely his absence; this was, in any case, considered the typical single-parent household. In assisting these families, the committee was simply institutionalizing the traditional consensus that widows with children were worthy of help.

As can be readily seen, the assumptions behind this first policy initiative were that mothers should not work in the labor market but rather take care of their children; that if they were too poor to do this on their own, the government should step in and assist them. Since the women were widows, there was no need to worry about absent fathers shirking support payments. The problem of possibly perverse incentives with respect to marriage and remarriage went unnoticed.

The form of the assistance program was federal grants-in-aid to the states rather than a uniform federal system. This was because, in addition to the cash transfer components, the committee created social insurance programs (to be financed out of contributions from earnings) that were expected, when fully functioning, to take care of the bulk of economic hardship—insurance against old age and disability, survivors' benefits for widows and other dependents, and unemployment insurance. The assistance segment for single-parent households was thus expected to shrink back into a small residual to become once again the responsibility of the individual states. This was, however, not to be. The 1940s saw shortened waiting periods for establishing single-parent status, and the liberalizing of the program to include illegitimate children. They also saw rising birth rates and increasing incidence of illegitimacy and family breakup.

The AFDC caseload and budget grew as the program became by

---

[2]The other two groups were the aged and the blind—also traditional objects for public and private compassion.

default the only major benefit program available for helping poor children. But since it was designed for fatherless households, it was only helping children in single-parent households. Thus it came in for increasing criticism, and the incentive structure embedded in it came in for increasing scrutiny.

The first major focus for the dissatisfaction was that AFDC (then still ADC) was increasingly going to single-parent households that were not the result of death but of divorce or desertion. This seemed to carry the implication that somewhere out there were fathers who had run out on their parental responsibilities, leaving the bill to be paid by the taxpayer. The discontent resulted, in 1950, in the Notice to Law Enforcement Officials (NOLEO) Amendment to Title IV D of the Social Security Act. This amendment required the states, as a condition for continuing to receive federal funds for state-administered welfare, to notify the law of all cases of women applying for ADC, and it required a woman to take legal action against the father of her child in order to be eligible for aid. To make enforcement easier, all the states subsequently made formal agreements or enacted legislation to make it possible for absent parents to be sued for support wherever they lived, without extradition and without the suing parent having to go to the absent parent's current state of residence (Cassetty, 1978, pp. 7–8).

The next focus of discontent was on the exclusionary nature of the program—restricting aid to those needy families with only one resident parent—in the face of the evident fact that many households with children and two parents were also poor. In 1961, in consequence, further social security amendments established the unemployed-parent segment of what was now called AFDC, permitting, at state option, households with a present able-bodied father to be eligible for aid if that father were unemployed. The possible work disincentives and subsidization of laziness in such a program were much in the mind of public policy makers at this stage of the game. The eligibility for AFDC–UP was thus extremely restricted, requiring among other things a substantial history of prior employment in a job covered by the Unemployment Insurance program. It was also left up to the individual states whether to institute such a program, with the result that some states have never had AFDC–UP and some others have instituted such a program and then abandoned it.

This development also had the effect of focusing public attention on the possible work disincentives for mothers embedded in the AFDC program. "What every family needs most is a wage earner, so the argument goes, and, implicitly, this role takes precedence over others like mothering or homemaking [Bell, 1977, p. 226]." In 1967, therefore, came further amendments to the Social Security Act establishing the Work Incentive (WIN) program, to provide work or training for AFDC mothers, and cutting the effective tax rate on any money earned. To facilitate their working, deductions for day care were also allowed and, to a limited extent, subsidized day-care slots were provided. The year 1967 also saw further stiffening of the provisions with respect to absent-parent support by means of amendments requiring state welfare agencies to set up a unit to establish paternity of each illegitimate child receiving AFDC and to secure support from the father once identified.

With minor modifications this situation with respect to support for single-parent households remains in effect today. The Food Stamp program and the Earned Income Tax Credit have lessened but certainly not removed the single-parent two-parent distinction in our public assistance system. Combining AFDC with the other parts of the transfer system (categorical and noncategorical), then, we have the following situation. Households headed by single persons, if their income is below a certain income level, are eligible for a categorical transfer program (AFDC) because of their single-parent status. In return for this, the caretaking parent must sue the absent parent for child support and cooperate with authorities in those efforts (which seem from the evidence available to barely cover the costs of their collection). The parent with the children is also subject to a work test depending on the ages of the children.

Above the income cutoff level for AFDC eligibility, there is no special public provision for the single-parent household—either with respect to enforcement of child-support obligations by the absent parent or with respect to financial assistance. The single exception seems to be the HHS parent locator service, which came into effect as a result of the 1974 social security amendments and is available to nonbeneficiaries of AFDC at cost.

For a subset of two-parent households that are poor, AFDC–UP is available in some states—although the take-up rate is low, compared to an AFDC take-up rate by eligibles of practically 100%. Otherwise, the major assistance program is the Food Stamp program which, along with the earned income credit, is available to anyone on the basis of income and family size.

The poor single parent, therefore, belongs to a favored category in the current system, but the incentive structure is in the direction of keeping her (or his) income below a certain level to retain eligibility and keeping her (or his) single-parent status for the same reason. The caretaking parent is also subjected to invasions of privacy with respect to the identity and whereabouts of the absent parent that are not suffered by her or his better-off counterparts but, by the same token, she does have public help in efforts to enforce child-support obligations.

The Distributional Consequences of the Status Quo

The data base for the empirical work in this section and the next is a 10% sample of the 1976 Survey of Income and Education (SIE). The data and the microsimulation methodology used are described in more detail by Betson, Greenberg, and Kasten in Chapter 6 in this volume. The survey data have been modified and augmented to make the total benefits of major public programs match independently estimated aggregates. The microsimulation methodology involves a case-by-case approach to the approximately 20,000 nuclear families[3] in the sample, including a labor supply response to the guarantee and tax rate estimated with data from the Seattle–Denver Income Maintenance Experiment.

The focus, as we have said, is on the differential treatment accorded children in one-parent households vis-à-vis children in two-parent households.

In order to make comparisons across households, we needed a way to normalize income to account for differences in household size. One alternative was to look at per capita income. The disadvantage of this measure is that it treats all individuals in the household alike and makes no allowances for the economies of scale commonly assumed to exist in household consumption and welfare. The alternative we have chosen is to normalize income by the poverty line. Although this measure has obvious limitations, it has the advantages of not only adjusting for economies of scale, but also of fairly widespread, if sometimes grudging, acceptance and use.

The poverty lines we used are those that appear in the Current Population Survey (CPS) of 1975, supplemented from the "poverty standard" used in the Food Stamp program to allow differentiation by household size for sizes larger than six.[4] We used the resulting set of "poverty

---

[3]A nuclear family is defined to be head, spouse (if any), and own children (if any). Note that this is a more restrictive definition than the standard Census Bureau definition of the family, but one which more closely approximates the filing units for current cash assistance programs and the tax system. We prefer to refer to such units as households, since families in fact clearly extend across household boundaries. Children are defined as persons under 18 years of age.

[4]Let X = four-person poverty line; Y = four-person poverty standard from the Food Stamp program; Z = increment in the Food Stamp program; I = our increment. Then $I = (Z)(X)/Y$.

lines" to normalize income and defined a welfare ratio for each household as measured income divided by our constructed poverty measure.[5] For most purposes we group the welfare ratios into 18 intervals (upper endpoints are closed):

(1) 0.0–.25	(7) 1.50–1.75	(13) 4.0–4.5
(2) .25–.50	(8) 1.75–2.00	(14) 4.5–5.0
(3) .50–.75	(9) 2.0–2.5	(15) 5.0–6.0
(4) .75–1.0	(10) 2.5–3.0	(16) 6.0–7.0
(5) 1.00–1.25	(11) 3.0–3.5	(17) 7.0–8.0
(6) 1.25–1.50	(12) 3.5–4.0	(18) over 8.0

Several weaknesses in the data and methodology should be mentioned. First, as with all large-scale national surveys, the income data are collected for the previous year, usually some time in the spring, and may reflect the experience of a family composed somewhat differently from the family that is observed in residence at the time of the survey. This mismatch may be of more consequence in case-by-case simulations than for single descriptive aggregates. Second, we are using only a 10% sample of the SIE, which appears to afford enough precision for our rough comparisons. The full SIE, however, could provide substantially greater precision, which would be worthwhile for a full simulation of the policy alternatives we consider.

Third, while there is at present no equally well-accepted alternative to the use of the poverty thresholds for normalizing income, at least two qualifications should be noted. Whereas the poverty thresholds are patently concerned with defining equivalence at the low end of the income scale, there is much less justification for our applying the same proportionate normalization throughout the income distribution. We would contend, however, that because our interest focuses on children in one- and two-parent low-income households, it is better, if some error is inevitable, that we aim for an appropriate adjustment for the low-income groups. In any case, our strategy—even at the high-income end—is probably better than a simple per capita adjustment.

---

[5]For a nuclear family living alone and consisting of under seven persons, our measure is very close to the official poverty line for 1975.

It has been suggested that using 1975 data is distorting because of the bad recession. Although the high unemployment rate in that year might have affected the *level* of redistribution called for by these plans, the fundamental nature of the universal plans (i.e., redistribution from one- to two-parent households) would have remained unchanged, and our comparisons, similarly, would be little affected.

Additionally, because our analysis focuses on comparing one- and two-parent households, it is clear that the relative values of the poverty thresholds for these two household types has a direct effect on our statements about which group is or might be treated "more favorably." If, for instance, the poverty line for a one-parent household is judged to be too high relative to a two-parent household with the same number of children, then an adjustment that reduced the former would result in generally higher welfare ratios for the one-parent household. Poverty-line approximations that depend on the numbers (not the ages) of the household members might be subject to a similar bias and could be similarly adjusted. An income concept that attempted to reflect the additional adult human resources available in a two-parent family (e.g., looking at "full income"), in contrast, would tend to bias upward the numerator of the two-parent welfare ratio and hence make them look better-off than they do under the normalization we use.

There is, finally, no end to the questions one might raise about any attempt to define equivalence between these two types of households. We would emphasize that the main focus of our concern here is on *comparing* alternative policy approaches among themselves and with the status quo. These comparisons are not affected in important ways by our choice of normalization because they do not depend on characterization of absolute levels of welfare for either group. So long as the same normalization is used in all cases it is possible to say whether one policy or another does more for one- or two-parent households. The normalization *can* affect the relative location of whole distributions, and so the notion of distributional parity we introduce later in the paper should be modified if one believes the poverty thresholds are substantially biased in reflecting equivalent material living environments for one- and two-parent households with children. But even if the scales were adjusted to produce parity in the existing distributions, the same adjustment for the alternative policies would produce a wider disparity, and the policy contrasts would remain.

The income transformation function for the status quo is shown in Figure 11.1. In figures of this type the horizontal axis shows the welfare ratios before the effects of the tax–transfer system, and the vertical axis shows post-fisc welfare ratios. The diagonal represents a neutral transformation (that is, no change). The vertical distance between the transformation curve and the diagonal represents the effects of the tax–transfer system (in percentage terms, since the scales are logarithmic). The mean welfare ratio for the sample population falling into each interval is plotted against the midpoint of that interval.

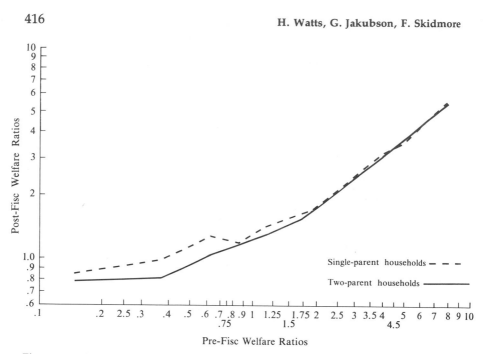

Figure 11.1. Income transformation function for the status quo. (Figure by University of Wisconsin Cartographic Laboratory.)

Logarithmic, or "ratio," scales were chosen for displaying the trans-formation functions.[6] This choice highlights the effects at the low-income end of the scale, and that is where our policy concern is greatest. We also plotted cumulative distributions of children by welfare ratio on logarithmic probability graphs and have found that the conformity to log-normality is quite good at least for the central part of the distribution.

We see from Figure 11.1 that for a substantial portion of the income distribution, above welfare ratio (WR) = 2, the transformation functions for single-parent households and for two-parent households are virtually identical. Below that level, however, there is a systematic bias in favor of single-parent households relative to two-parent households.[7]

---

[6]Some basic properties of logarithmic graphic representation should be mentioned here: (a) Distances on a ratio scale can be interpreted as percentage differences; (b) slopes on a double-log diagram represent elasticities; (c) on the assumption that the utility of an extra adult-equivalent dollar is inversely proportional to the welfare ratio, equal differences imply equal increments of well-being.

[7]To the extent that the data base omits lesser and in-kind benefit programs, for which the take-up rate is known to be higher for one-parent than two-parent households, our estimates will understate the bias.

In addition to the basic differences in level of support, there appears also to be a different incentive structure facing the two groups. Two-parent households appear to face a transformation function with an essentially increasing slope. For them, the elasticity of post-fisc income with respect to pre-fisc income is increasing as income increases, meaning that earnings gains add more, proportionately, to well-being the higher the welfare level. Single-parent households, in contrast, face a transformation function with a kink in the neighborhood of $WR = .6$ and then again near $WR = .8$. Very poor households, thus, can make themselves better-off by earning more, but at some point they hit a downward-sloping range. Possibly this reflects the fact that the income cutoff for AFDC eligibility is lower than the income level at which benefits cease, and also that some units are not covered.[8] For households above that range, the curve turns back up again, and the elasticity of post-fisc income with respect to pre-fisc income is again positive.

Perhaps we can get a better feel for the magnitude and shape of the differential treatment accorded to one- and two-parent households if we examine the differences between the group means over the first eight intervals of the welfare ratios (WR under 2). Figure 11.2 plots that relationship. With the exception noted above, the difference is very large for the poorest (for a household of four, $.2 \times \$5496 \doteq \$1100$) and declines as income rises to twice the poverty line.

Figure 11.3 shows the status quo frequency distributions of children in one- and two-parent households. Again, figures of this type are plotted with a logarithmic scale on the abscissa for welfare ratios and probabilities on the ordinate. Quantiles of the distributions can be found by finding the appropriate probability on the ordinate, reading across to the curve, and then reading down to the welfare ratio. For example, the median of the distribution of children in single-parent households is approximately $WR = 1.2$ and for two-parent households approximately $WR = 2.1$. The flatter the curve, the more unequal the distribution; and the further the curve is to the right, the wealthier the group. Figure 11.3 shows the familiar result that children in single-parent households are in general poorer than children in two-parent households.

As summary measures we can examine the log-mean and log-variance of the distributions. Table 11.1 shows these for the total population as well as for children in both types of household. Table 11.1 clearly shows the differences between the welfare ratio distributions of children by household type. The similar variances are reflected by the fact that the

---

[8]It is also possible that the negatively sloped segment is only apparently negative, given the sampling error.

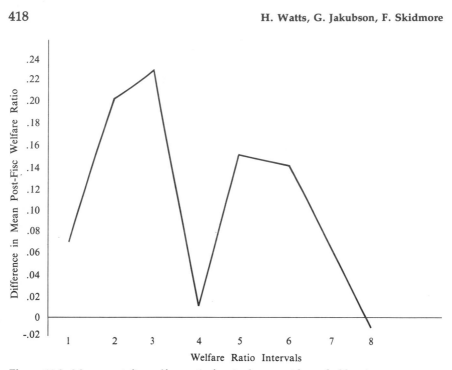

Figure 11.2. Mean post-fisc welfare ratio for single-parent households minus mean post-fisc welfare ratio for two-parent households, over the first eight intervals. (Figure by University of Wisconsin Cartographic Laboratory.)

two distributions have a similar shape, and the difference in means by the positioning of the curves.

For illustrative purposes we calculate for various ranges the mean plus or minus one standard deviation and the mean plus or minus two standard deviations for each distribution expressed as welfare ratios. These are shown in Figure 11.4.

The Consequences of Credit and Negative Income Tax Schemes, with Categorical Modifications for One-Parent Households

This section summarizes the findings from a variety of simulation experiments which are essentially variants of the simulation carried out by Betson, Greenberg, and Kasten.[9] The basic problem is posed by the

[9]Sections 4–6 of our longer paper (Watts, Jakubson, and Skidmore, 1979) present our simulations in detail. The tables and diagrams used to describe the status quo in this chapter are paralleled in our other paper for each of the variations.

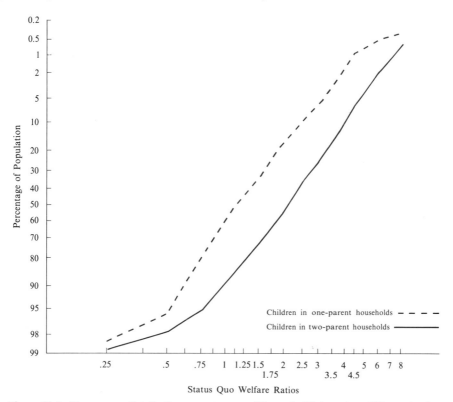

Figure 11.3. Frequency distributions—status quo. (Figure by University of Wisconsin Cartographic Laboratory.)

fact that both the CIT and the NIT are noncategorical programs and, as scaled in these simulations, redistribute a substantial amount of transfer funds to two-parent households at the low end of the scale. They thus provide little improvement and in some cases even reductions in benefits for one-parent households compared with the status quo. For the transformation functions described above, the CIT shifts the curve up-

TABLE 11.1
Log-Mean and Log-Variance of the Status Quo Welfare Ratio Distribution

	Log-Mean	Log-Variance
Total population	.65	.54
Children in one-parent households	.18	.35
Children in two-parent households	.76	.32

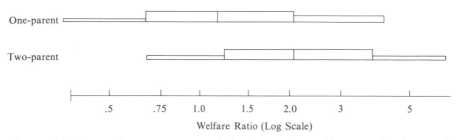

Figure 11.4. One- and two-sigma intervals for the post-fisc welfare ratio distribution of two kinds of households. (Figure by University of Wisconsin Cartographic Laboratory.)

ward substantially for the two-parent households, giving them more at every (low) level of income. For one-parent families the effect is mainly to smooth out the transformation without any substantial increase in its level at the low end. The NIT variant has much the same effects in both cases, except that the shift from high to low tax rates at the tax breakeven point produces a more pronounced convexity in the transformation function for the NIT.

Whether one regards the normalization that we have used as approximately correct (but recognizes that there may be continuing political reasons for the apparent favoring of one-parent families), or one challenges the normalization in such a way that the status quo is itself taken as the best approximation to equitable treatment, it is clear that the CIT or NIT reforms would mark a sharp change in policy—one indeed that improves the relative status of two-parent households with children.

We have explored alternative ways of reducing or even offsetting that sharp change. Two of these (Plans I and II) are essentially categorical augmentations of the benefit schedule that apply only to single-parent households. The other two (Plans III and IV) are of the children's-allowance variety and provide increases in basic credits for all children regardless of their family or income status. Both types of augmentation

TABLE 11.2
Dollar Add-On to the Credit for a Single-Parent Household with a Nonworking Parent under Plan II

Number of Children under 6	Number of Children 6 to 13			
	0	1	2	3+
0	—	$ 600	$ 800	$1,000
1	$1,000	1,300	1,500	1,800
2+	1,500	1,800	1,900	200

offer some possibility of offsetting the favoritism of two-parent families—the first quite obviously, and the second depending on the proposition that the ratio of children to adults is higher in single-parent households.

Plan I is an age-graded guarantee (credit) which treats a child more like an adult the closer he or she is to adulthood. Instead of 50% of the adult guarantee, a child under six receives 60%, a child between six and thirteen receives 70%, and a child over thirteen receives 80% of the adult guarantee:

$$\text{Credit} = (NUMA + .6NKLT6 + .7NK613 + .8NK14)(1374)$$
$$NUMA = \text{number of adults}$$
$$NKLT6 = \text{number of children under 6}$$
$$NK613 = \text{number of children between 6 and 13}$$
$$NK14 = \text{number of children 14 or over}$$

Plan II has a two-schedule add-on for single parents with children, which also varies by age of child, but in the opposite direction. The dollar value of the add-on for a household with a nonworking parent[10] is shown in Table 11.2. For a household with a working parent, the add-on is equal to $1000 per child under six and $500 per child between six and thirteen, not to exceed 50% of earnings.

The rationale behind this program alternative is to give the single parent a more effective choice between allocating productive time to market versus nonmarket activities by giving him/her a larger guarantee when the children are young—the time when it is most difficult for a single parent to join the labor force—and reducing the guarantee as the children grow older. If the parent chooses to work, the increased guarantee could be used to offset expenses for child-care and homemaker services; if the parent chooses not to work, the increased guarantee would (partially) offset the loss of market income.

The basic children's allowance simulated (Plan III) is an age-graded credit similar to Plan I, but paid to all households with children. Children under six receive the basic 50% of the adult guarantee; children between six and thirteen receive 65%, and children over thirteen receive 85% of the adult guarantee. We also attempt to achieve the same end at lower cost by imposing a "clawback" onto the basic children's allowance (Plan IV)—for each dollar of earnings, a 10% surtax is imposed on families with children until the original allowance is recouped. The extent to which the clawback mechanism enables us to achieve the same

---

[10]Working was defined as having earnings equivalent to at least one quarter of full-time work at the minimum wage ($1040 in 1975).

goal at lower cost depends upon the extent to which single-parent households have lower earnings than two-parent households.

All of these plans are financed by an increase in the positive tax rate sufficient to pay for the increased transfers.

The categorical augmentations (Plans I and II) are relatively effective in reducing the shift in relative treatment of one- and two-parent households. Plan II, which turns out to be much more costly than Plan I, even restores a substantial part of the existing apparent favoritism toward the one-parent households, as measured by the transformation functions. Plan I requires a 0.3 percentage point addition to the flat rate of the CIT (and Plan II adds 0.5), and only slightly more to the positive tax segment of the NIT.

The basic costs to be financed in the case of Plans I and II are essentially the same for both the CIT and NIT simulations. This is because most of the beneficiaries of the supplementation are below the NIT breakeven point, and the augmentation takes the form of increasing the initial guarantee or credit level. (This result should hold for any augmentation which affects primarily those whose income falls below the breakeven point for the NIT, e.g., the aged and disabled.)

The children's allowance alternatives prove to have a relatively weak effect in reversing the policy shift induced by the noncategorical CIT or NIT. The variant without the clawback (Plan III) is somewhat more effective in this respect than Plan IV, but the costs, as measured by required tax rate adjustments, are then substantially greater. Plan III calls for more than one additional percentage point on the tax rate when added to the CIT and nearly two for the positive segment of the NIT. Even at this rate of cost, the children's allowance does much less to redress the existing imbalance in the apparent treatment of one- and two-parent households.

It should be recognized that all of these variants, as well as the unaugmented CIT, provide a distributional improvement for children, whatever their type of household, in the sense that the mean of an estimated log–normal distribution is raised and the variance reduced. For the unaugmented NIT, the variance is still reduced, but so is the log-mean. The augmentations serve to raise the log-mean of the one-parent households an additional amount and reduce the variance somewhat as well.

The Remaining Dilemma and a Possible Solution

As the previous section has shown, for a given level of pretransfer income normalized for family size, a noncategorical CIT or NIT would reverse the current policy of favoring one-parent households relative to two-parent households. While the universal nature of such reforms would place a more reliable floor under the resources available to households in general, at any politically feasible maximum benefit (guarantee) level, they would at the same time make one-parent households worse off absolutely than they are under the current income support system. Our simulations have also shown how specific categorical add-ons could approach horizontal equity between one- and two-parent units and even restore the existing bias.

Such categorical solutions, however, severely compromise the very features that make a noncategorical approach attractive. These are (a) that the size of the credits depend only on age; and (b) that the tax rate is constant over a wide enough range so that the tax does not depend on either the unit to which the income is attached or the time period during which it is received. This means that there are no incentives to misrepresent or alter one's living arrangements or the timing of one's income receipts. In consequence, it removes a major reason for public authorities to invade individual privacy in search of fraud. An additional advantage of the CIT, though not the NIT, is that the somewhat lower marginal tax rates over the low and moderate income range reduce the work disincentives of the current system for that population.

The reintroduction of a categorical add-on brings back the very "separation bonus" the NIT and CIT were designed to remove. There are many questions about the meaning of the "independence effect" of NIT benefits on divorce and separation that apparently shows up in the Seattle–Denver Income Maintenance Experiment data. But they do, at a minimum, highlight the apparent sensitivity of family stability to the terms on which transfer payments are made and suggest a cautious attitude toward automatic benefits for one-parent households.

The dilemma is sharpened when one notes that the credit tax does little toward narrowing the differential between the distributions of children in one- and two-parent units. While it tends to reduce the dispersion in each group, the overlap of the distributions is actually reduced. The categorical augmentation reduces the disparities at the low end, but leaves the distributions quite distinct.

The root of the difficulty may be that we are trying to design a public policy to offset the consequences of a failure of our various institutions to define and enforce parental support responsibilities. We are trying to treat the symptom, not the cause. It can be, and has been, argued that the present welfare system reinforces abandonment of responsibilities of the absent parent. But this is certainly not the only culprit of the current system. There is evidence of very haphazard and ineffective administration of child-support arrangements in our courts as well. And this phenomenon is by no means limited to low-income parents. Whether because of the apparent willingness of the public to assume minimal support for children when it is not forthcoming from an absent parent or because of the lack of effective sanctions against such abandonment, the consequences are evident in the disparity of the economic well-being distributions of children in one- versus two-parent households. Further and more direct evidence of this is provided in the extensive work of Sawhill (1977) and Cassetty (1978).

We regard it as extremely questionable whether any equitable and politically acceptable solution to the problem of assuming adequate resources for children in one-parent households can be found unless more effective attention is given to the issue of private responsibilities. Sentiment for better enforcement of child-support agreements is testified to by the recent laws providing federal resources and mechanisms for locating parents who are delinquent. But the problem goes deeper than the enforcement of court orders. The issue of adequate support, given the economic status of the two parents, is unresolved. The judgments being enforced may themselves be inadequate in view of the relative economic status of the parties involved. There also remains the issue of whether the children of a subsequent union should have first or second priority relative to those who claim support from an absent parent. Finally, should the custodial parent be required to take such an aggressive role, often at considerable cost in time or money, in order to secure what should be automatically due a child from a parent?

We are led toward a search for policies that can more effectively define and enforce the primary responsibilities of parents for the support of their children, recognizing that there will remain a role for a public transfer system, but that the goal of such a system should be to pursue the advantages of universality as much as possible. If the flow of support payments from absent parents at all income levels can be increased substantially, the disparity in the economic status of children could be substantially reduced and a part of the need for public support would be eliminated. But the goal should not be limited to the reduction of net public transfers to one-parent households. The appropriate objective is an approach to full sharing of the responsibility for support of children by both living parents, within the limits of their respective abilities to provide that support. If this goal can be achieved, then universal and noncategorical redistribution policies can be applied without prejudice to children living with one parent, with both parents, or even with neither parent.

Empirical analysis of these issues is hampered by the shortage of data that permit linking one-parent households with their appropriate absent-parent units. The Michigan Panel Study of Income Dynamics (PSID) has been exploited and has yielded some very important insights, even though the sample is small and may be biased toward those with the stability and predictability that permit continued participation in a longitudinal panel. Even these data, however, suggest that if one adopts the approach of equalizing the economic status of both households, absent parents are currently paying substantially less than they should. Fully 40% of absent parents, for instance, report no contributions to their children's support (Sawhill, 1977, p. 2). Further evidence should be forthcoming in the future. The Census Bureau has expanded its coverage of support and alimony receipts in the SIE conducted in 1976 (their analysis of which is expected sometime this year) and has more ambitious plans for future waves of the CPS, Decennial Census and SIPP.

Although remedying the lack of data is extremely important in developing the specific details of policy proposals, it may be questioned whether more or better data are really necessary in order to consider whether the basic idea of joint parental responsibility should be more vigorously enforced. The facts we have quoted are enough to establish that the most mimimal principles of joint responsibility are widely and flagrantly violated. Do we need more evidence in the hope of finding some merit in a right of unilateral abandonment? Such a right has never been declared, of course, but it is being widely exercised, and it is in direct conflict with the right of each child to support and maintenance from two parents. It seems to us that it is impossible to achieve reasonable goals of adequacy and equity for children living with only one parent without a much more effective system for enforcing parental responsibilities. So long as it is relatively easy for parents to abandon those responsibilities and thereby shift the burden to the public, that same public is unlikely to endorse programs that can give children in one-parent families adequate economic support without at least some of the restrictive, degrading features of the current system.

If, in contrast, there could be general confidence that parental responsibility was *not* being evaded, and that public programs were not being abused, there would be some likelihood that those children who are most in need (in all types of family) would receive more generous public support. The only other alternative consistent with equal treatment would be for the public sector to assume full responsibility for the economic support of all children, and that does not seem a solution that accords with widely held values in this society or that has any precedents.

Consequently, we suggest that first priority should be placed on development of policies that can effectively assure that each child has access to the resources of both parents provided they are living and not totally disabled. The following combination of proposals is put forward as a way of accomplishing this objective in the context of a fully integrated credit tax system, but one that preserves the basic structure of benefits for children with deceased or disabled parents that are provided under social security and veterans' programs. Some of our proposals could even be introduced within the current income support system.

The basis for any such policy formulation in our view must be explicit recognition and systematic application of the principle that every child has an inalienable right to support from two parents. Stated so simply, the principle seems to us completely consistent with basic values shared by virtually everyone in our society. That this "right" is violated in the case of death or permanent and total disability of one or both parents is recognized by the current transfer system, which regards such deprivation as the basis for a claim on public resources. Indeed, the law even allows claims for such support to be assessed on third parties if the death or disability resulted from willful or negligent behavior. Where this right is violated by willful or negligent behavior of parents in the form of nonacknowledgment of parenthood or abandonment, however, the current system takes a different attitude. The only recognized claim to public resources is means-tested—i.e., paid only if the custodial parent has a sufficiently low income—and any support obligation by the absent parent is frequently defaulted on totally or in part. There is also no remedy for the child when an act of commission or omission by the custodial parent, such as failure to identify the other parent or seek support, violates this right.

Our policy proposal has three parts.

First, publicly agreed upon normative standards of child support should be developed to guide both public policy formulation and family court proceedings. A possible method would be for a blue-ribbon commission, perhaps presidentially appointed, to examine the issues and develop such standards. One issue that must be tackled is how to define equitable sharing of the total resources available to custodial and noncustodial parents in providing material support for children. Sawhill (1977) has considered this issue and recommended that per-adult-equivalent disposable income be equalized across split households. This seems to be one defensible principle; there may be others. Additional issues relate to how support over time should reflect subsequent changes in, for instance, realized earnings of each parent and their separate current family responsibilities. A second kind of standard is needed that sets a minimum of support that would enable a one-parent household to reach as high a level of living as our policies effectively set as a social minimum for a two-parent family. The latter might be interpreted, for instance, as the per-adult-equivalent net income from employment and transfers for a two-parent family with one earner employed at the minimum wage. Although this minimum might well lie below the base amount of support provided for children of deceased parents, the payments to survivors should, in any case, be considered as a closely related issue.

Second, some form of child support insurance (CSI) should be added to our social insurance portfolio. This program would assure that any child not living with both parents would receive at least the minimum support defined above (paid to the custodial parent or other guardian). The benefits of this program could be defined on a simple per-child basis or they could be defined in a schedule that reflected ages and/or numbers of children. In any case, the CSI would reduce these benefits at the rate of, say, 70% of any child support payments actually made by the absent parent(s) up to the "breakeven" level, at which the benefit became zero. The benefit-reduction rate of less than 100% is intended to leave a monetary incentive for the custodial parent to seek and the absent parent to pay child support. Otherwise, the child support payments would be nontaxable to the recipient (i.e., not included as income); they would not, in any case, be deductible by the paying parent. Income should be taxed once in any case, and with a flat-rate tax it does not matter where. But taxing at the earning source would eliminate in the normal case the need for a reporting requirement for support payments received. For beneficiaries of the child support insurance, however, separate (and perhaps quarterly) reports of support received could be required.

Third, and finally, the obligation to support one's children could be enforced universally and impartially by an entirely separate mechanism. We recommend that the annual income tax return (which would in any case be universally required of adults in a credit income tax system) include an affidavit of compliance with support standards for *each* child registered as the responsibility (via biological or adoptive parenthood) of that adult. The support standard could be met in the following ways: (*a*) by living with and sharing a household with the child; (*b*) by complying with a court-approved support agreement; (*c*) by making payments at least equal to the minimum support standard defined above; (*d*) by an appropriate combination of the above, each covering distinct periods of time and together covering the entire year.

For each child *not* supported in one of these ways, a surtax would be assessed on all taxable income. This "penalty" tax would be strictly additive to the regular flat tax rate for the credit tax scheme, but would be limited so that the combined rates would never exceed, say, 70%. The assessment of this tax would not be connected with either the fact or amount of any child-support insurance benefits being paid for such children, nor would the amount of surtax affect the benefits paid for such children. Clearly it would be in the interest of the noncustodial parent to pay the surtax only if that amount were smaller than the cost of complying with the support standards. This argues for the penalty rate being set high enough to make regular compliance optimal for all but the lowest-wage absent parents. But, even for them, the surtax would at least assure that there is a nonzero cost of procreation even if the resulting children cannot be or are not supported directly.

Effective administration of these provisions might well require a registry of parenthood which would associate the social security number (SSN) of each adult with the SSN of each child the adult is responsible for either on natural or adoptive grounds. Such a registry could be maintained (or built up) by assigning an SSN to each newborn child (or immigrating child) and linking that number and name to the SSN of both parents. With such a registry the annual tax forms could include an affidavit for each child by name and/or it would be possible to carry out audits of completeness in reporting on parental responsibility.

Designation of the father of a newborn would normally be made by the mother, subject to appeal by the named father.[11] There may be cases where the mother refuses for some reason to designate the father, preferring to retain full responsibility. It is not clear whether this will be a large enough problem to warrant special provisions to discourage such refusals. It is clear, however, that it constitutes straightforward violation of the child's right to support from *two* parents. How that right should be balanced against rights to privacy of the mother or anonymity of the father is a complex problem, but our strong inclination is to give priority to the child's rights if there is a major conflict. The system itself could provide effective confidentiality and protection of privacy for the noncustodial parent in cases where the support standards are met.

With a system of this kind in place it seems possible that a universal credit tax could carry the main burden of vertical redistribution without recourse to categorical treatment of one-parent households. Children deprived of support of the second parent, whether because of death, disability, insufficient income or just plain cussedness, would be assured at least a minimum of support in lieu of (or to supplement) the parental contributions. The official standards for "normal" support, together

[11]Modern methods of cell biology promise almost foolproof determination of paternity in contested (or uncertain) cases.

with a universal system for penalizing evaders, should reduce the disparities at the moderate and higher levels of living, and also reduce the claims made for public support. Sawhill (1977, p. 41) has estimated, for instance, on the basis of a series of "equitable" formulae for the sharing of child support between formerly married parents, that fulfillment of child-support responsibility as defined by reasonable formulae could amount to an average increase in current income of the household that includes the child(ren) of over 25%. Finally, there would be a firm basis for confidence that parents, including absent ones, cannot evade or abandon support responsibilities, and that the residual burden of the child support insurance is resulting in benefits to those whose needs are real and not the result of willful or fraudulent behavior.

Some advocate a program that would place the Internal Revenue Code in the position of defining equity between the separate households of formerly married parents. The tax system, under such a regime, would assess and collect the formula-determined liability of the absent parent and disburse that amount, supplemented as necessary to meet a minimum standard, to the custodial parent. We feel that this rather radical usurpation of the traditional functions of the courts cannot be justified even by the unsatisfactory current performance of that system with respect to the setting and enforcement of child-support obligations.

While we favor the development and promulgation of normative standards for assessing child support, we recognize that such proceedings properly involve many individual and idiosyncratic considerations and that these are the province of the judicial system. We are, moreover, convinced that embedded in the statistics showing the current shortcomings of child-support practice there are many absent parents who are meeting their obligations more generously than any uniform system would be likely to require, and are being otherwise responsible in sharing the child-rearing burdens. We feel optimistic that the development of normative standards and their recognition by the courts and the litigants can do much more to promote responsible and generous behavior than would the option of melding it all into one impersonal (and, we would venture, universally begrudged) tax bill.

It is unfortunate that we do not have data that permit simulation of the consequences of a system like the one we have outlined. Comparisons of cost and impact would be very useful, but even with appropriately linked household data, estimated effects would have to rely on conjectures about changes in private child-support transfers. There is no obvious reason why the support insurance scheme would cost any more than the age-modal benefits (Plan I) that were simulated. While the minimum support levels might produce larger benefits for those without *any* support from the absent parent, the amounts would be smaller for those who receive some support under our Plan I because of the present low effectiveness of child-support enforcement. The added revenues from the penalty surtax might well be very small, but they would provide enough potential revenue to make the pursuit of evaders worth the time of IRS auditors. On balance, the support-enforcement system should not require major new expenditure on staff beyond what would be required for a credit tax. The initiative of a child–parent registry might require substantial start-up expenditures, but it could yield immediate economies in establishing a credible and fair support-enforcement process. And long-run benefits would accrue in the form of more equitable sharing of resources and responsibilities among parents, which in turn would reduce the distributional disparities that exist and reduce the number of cases that require supplementation from public funds.

The expectation that appropriate support levels will be defined and effectively enforced may also have an effect on the rates of formation and dissolution of families, although we have no good basis for saying how much (or even in what direction). The independence of the prospective single parent with custody might be enhanced somewhat, but the limits of independence for the noncustodial parent would be sharply reduced. Remarriage rates for custodial parents might well be increased by more adequate and universal child support, but the absent parent might be less inclined to remarry if new family obligations did not diminish responsibilities for support of the original family. But again, the criterion should not be whether more or fewer marriages are made and/or dissolved. The basic trends in family formation are affected by many other influences, and we do not recommend trying to manipulate all of them. But it is important that public transfers not be used to implicitly subsidize family dissolution and the abandonment of responsibility that has frequently accompanied it.

Conclusion

The burden of our argument in this paper has been that, in the absence of public policy intervention, single-parent households have lower incomes than two-parent households, although there are strong arguments that their financial needs, for a given household size, are greater. Current public policy, in the form of AFDC, does recognize the validity of these arguments—not only by redressing the balance at the low end of the single-parent household income distribution but, in fact, by giving these single-parent households preferential treatment.

Universal reforms like the CIT, and noncategorical but income-tested reforms like the NIT, preserve and in some income ranges exacerbate the income inequality of the current pretransfer situation. So do universal child-support programs like the children's allowance.

We have developed two program designs that, if added onto non-categorical programs like the CIT and NIT, would restore the preferential status of the single-parent household within the framework of a universal transfer system. Such alternatives, however, bring back the dilemma that any preferential treatment for single-parent households creates incentives for family dissolution and the abandonment of financial responsibility for one's children. This consideration led us also to design a possible set of policies that could remove the incentive to desert one's children financially when a marriage breaks up and equalize more effectively the post-split economic well-being of each parent's current household.

Such a system would not, however, completely take care of the argument that single-parent households need additional money income to compensate for the lack of a second parent. Within the context of non-categorical income support and effective fulfillment of the absent parent's financial responsibility, thought must still be given to the question: Does society have a remaining obligation to the parents and children who must live for any extended period of time in a one-parent household? If divorce and remarriage are widespread and follow hard upon the heels of one another, this problem loses at least some of its urgency. But for one-parent households of lengthy duration, society may well want to answer, Yes. If so, we have identified two alternative routes that might be followed. The first (Plan I) focuses on the needs of the children and increases the size of the transfer as the child and his or her needs grow to increasingly adult proportions. The second (Plan II) focuses on the consequences, not of the presence of the child, but of the absence of the second parent. This plan, thus, scales support inversely to the age of the child—recognizing that older children are at home less and when at home require less parental time input. Its major advantage is, in line with emerging social preferences, that it does provide the nurturing parent with a less distorted choice between work in the market and work at home.

Both, of course, will cost the taxpayer something. But in the context of effective fulfillment of private obligations, the cost will be less than our simulations imply. In the interests of equity among children, whatever the shape of the household to which they belong, it may be well worth paying.

Discussion

JUDITH H. CASSETTY

Summary of Alternative Systems

The Watts, Jakubson, and Skidmore paper represents an attempt to resolve one general dilemma created by replacing the present categorical system of transfers with one which is universal: that low-income one-parent families, which are favored under the present systems, would, under a CIT or NIT such as that developed and explored by Betson, Greenberg, and Kasten, be made worse off relative to two-parent households.

The authors justify their position that one-parent families should not be economically disadvantaged with respect to two-parent families on the following grounds:

1. The total productive time potentially available for earning, house-keeping, and child nurturing is less for one parent than for two.
2. Most single-parent households are headed by women who, most likely, have developed their market human capital less and suffer sex discrimination and incremental discrimination due to employer expectations of higher absenteeism and unreliability. The end result, of course, is that they command lower wages in the labor market.

432

Once it is granted, however, that society should promote parity between one- and two-parent households, other questions arise as to what kind of parity and how it should be achieved. These questions include the following: How can parity be achieved while providing no incentives for families to break up and avoiding barriers to remarriage? How can parity be achieved in such a way as to promote the responsibility of *both* parents, though they live in separate households? How can parity be achieved without distorting the market work choices of women? And finally, should parity be promoted only to ensure an *income floor* for single-parent families, or between one- and two-parent households *throughout* the income distribution.

With these issues in mind the authors proceeded to estimate the distributional consequences of several modifications of the basic CIT and NIT—modifications designed to preserve as much family stability as possible, reduce market choice distortion for women, and restore economic balance between one- and two-parent families.

As a basis of comparison, Watts, Jakubson, and Skidmore took a look at the distributional consequences of the present system, using SIE data and the microsimulation methodology employed by Betson. The authors began by developing welfare ratios for one- and two-parent households with children, based upon income and poverty levels and family size. The welfare ratios of both types of families were compared before the effects of the tax–transfer system (pre-fisc) and after the effects of the tax–transfer system (post-fisc). It was found that for a substantial portion of the income distribution (above welfare ratio 2), the transformation functions for one-parent households and two-parent households were virtually identical. Below that level, however, there was a systematic bias in favor of one-parent households relative to two-parent households. In addition to the basic differences in level of support, there were kinks in the transformation function for one-parent households which were attributed to different incentive structures facing this type of household.

Further analysis focusing on the children in these two types of households established that, overall, children in one-parent households are substantially worse off under the present system than those in two-parent households—the welfare ratio median being 1.2 for the former, 2.1 for the latter.

The authors then turned to a comparison of the distributional consequences of the status quo and that of the CIT as proposed by Betson, Greenberg, and Kasten. Their analysis revealed that the CIT as proposed by Betson and his colleagues would reverse the status quo which favors the one-parent household at the lower end of the income distribution and would, instead, favor the two-parent household at every welfare ratio interval. In addition, the kinks in the curve for one-parent households would be removed owing, possibly, to the removal of the work disincentives inherent in the present system, but the level of support accorded one-parent households would be drastically lower than that under the present system. Additional analysis, not reported here, which focused upon the frequency distribution of children in one- and two-parent households, showed that while no unit was below welfare ratio .75 under the CIT, children in one-parent households would be treated unfavorably relative to children in two-parent households under the CIT and, furthermore, children in one-parent households would be worse off under the CIT than they are under the current system!

Next, the authors developed four income support alternatives for one-parent households to be grafted onto the basic CIT as proposed by Betson, Greenberg, and Kasten. Plan I is an age-graded guarantee (or credit). That is, a child under 6 would receive 60% of the adult guarantee, a child 6–13, 70%, and over 13, 80% of the adult guarantee.

Plan II has a two-schedule add-on for children which is also age-graded but in the opposite direction. That is, in order to provide the single parent with a more effective choice between allocating productive time to market versus nonmarket activities, a larger guarantee would be provided when the children were young—the time when it is most difficult for a single parent to join the labor force. If the parent chooses to work, the increased guarantee could be used to offset expenses for child-care and homemaker services. For the single parent who chooses not to work, the larger guarantee would partially offset the loss of market income. The per-child guarantee would be reduced as the child aged, the reverse of Plan I, in order to foster reattachment to the labor force.

When Watts, Jakubson, and Skidmore augmented the CIT with Plan I for one-parent families—that which increased the per-child guarantee as the child aged—they found that for all but the lowest welfare ratios (below .75), one-parent households are treated very much like two-parent households at equivalent pre-fisc money incomes and household sizes. Plan II turns out to be much more generous, favoring, in most instances, one-parent households above two-parent households under the CIT. When Plan II is compared with the current tax–transfer system, the one-parent/two-parent differential is not as great as under the current system at the lowest range of welfare ratios, reflecting a real lessening of inequality among the poorest families. Unfortunately, both Plan I and Plan II augmentation of the CIT would be considerably more costly, necessitating an increase in the tax rate from 34% for Plan I to 34.51% for

Plan II in order to recapture the zero net cost feature of the CIT proposed by Betson, Greenberg, and Kasten.

Turning to the distributional effects of a negative income tax, Watts, Jakubson, and Skidmore found that for two-parent poor households, the level of support was higher than under the current system but below that under a CIT, owing to the higher tax rate under the NIT (50% versus 34% for the CIT). The authors found the situation to be markedly different for one-parent households, however. While facing a concave upward transformation function without the kinks of the current system, their absolute level of support was lower under the NIT than under the CIT and much lower than under the current system. The disadvantage faced by one-parent households relative to two-parent households was found to be less under the NIT than the CIT. Compared with the status quo, however, one-parent households were substantially worse off than two-parent households at the lowest welfare ratios, though the differential declined as the welfare ratio increased. The frequency distributions for children in one- and two-parent households showed greater within-group inequality for children in one-parent households and also showed that these children were generally poorer than children in two-parent households under the NIT. Furthermore, children in one-parent households were poorer under the NIT than under either the CIT or the current system.

When Plan I was superimposed on the NIT, much of the disparity between one- and two-parent households was alleviated in the lower welfare ratios, and their income transformation functions almost coincided between $WR = .4$ and $WR = 1.2$. Below that range, two-parent households were favored and above that range one-parent households were favored.

Compared to Plan I with the CIT, Plan I with the NIT better reduced the disparity between one- and two-parent households among the poorest of them, owing to the difference in the tax rate. In addition, Plan I under the NIT reduced income inequality among children in poor one-parent households and raised their incomes as well.

When the NIT was augmented by Plan II, it raised the level of support for one-parent households above that under the current system and favored one-parent households over two-parent households over most of the range of welfare ratios. Furthermore, Plan II under the NIT reduced income inequality among children in poor one-parent households the most and raised their incomes the most as well.

The additional costs ($3.7 billion) of Plan I would necessitate an increase in the positive tax rate of from 23.19% to 23.7% in order to retain the zero net cost feature, and for Plan II, from 23.19% to 24.08%.

Two additional plans—variations of a children's allowance—were also developed by the authors for the purpose of examining their impact upon one- and two-parent households under either the CIT or NIT. The basic components of the children's allowance include an age-graded credit paid to all households with children, those under 6 years of age receiving 50% of the adult guarantee, 6–13 receiving 65%, and those over 13, 85%. This plan will heretofore be referred to as Plan III. Plan IV would be similar but would have a "clawback" feature under which each family with children would be subject to a 10% tax on earnings up to the point where the children's allowance was recouped.

The income transformation functions under these two allowance plans, added to the CIT, produced no severe disincentive effects under Plan III, but Plan IV slightly lowered the support level for the lower welfare ratios. Relative to the current system, one-parent households under the CIT plus Plan III were slightly favored, and under Plan IV were about the same as they are under the status quo.

When Plans III and IV were superimposed on the basic NIT, the level of support was higher for two-parent households over most of the welfare ratio distribution than under the NIT alone. Compared to the status quo, Plan III favored two-parent households over the lower range of welfare ratios (less than 3) and Plan IV favored these two-parent families until about $WR = 1.8$. In other words, single-parent households, under both children's allowance plans combined with the NIT, were worse off than under the current system. A comparison of one- and two-parent households revealed that for both the CIT and NIT, Plan IV (with clawback) creates less disparity between these two types of families than the children's allowance without the clawback feature (Plan III).

Examination of the frequency distributions of children in the two types of families indicated that children in one-parent households did better under the CIT without the clawback but better under the NIT with the clawback feature of the children's allowance.

The additional cost of Plan III would necessitate an increase in the positive tax rate from 34% to 35.15% but under Plan IV (with clawback) from only 34% to 34.15% under the CIT. Under the NIT, comparable increases would be from 23.19% to 25.14% (Plan III) and to only 23.44% under Plan IV.

The Remaining Dilemma and a Possible Solution

As the Watts, Jakubson, and Skidmore paper has demonstrated, for a given level of pretransfer income normalized for family size, a noncategorical CIT or NIT would reverse the current policy of favoring one-parent households relative to two-parent households. While the universal nature of such reforms would place a more reliable floor under the resources available to households in general, at any politically feasible maximum benefit (guarantee) level, they would at the same time make one-parent households worse off absolutely than they are under the current income support system. The authors' simulations also demonstrated how specific categorical add-ons could approach horizontal equity between one- and two-parent units and even restore the existing bias.

The authors readily pointed out, however, that such categorical add-ons toward the end of promoting parity between one- and two-parent households, would likely contribute substantially to family instability to the extent that women with children are responsive to these incentives, as the Seattle–Denver experiment seems to suggest they may be.

Thus, the basic dilemma is highlighted: Reducing inequities between one- and two-parent families will likely contribute substantially to family splitting. Such a consequence, the authors note, would be less apt to result if we were not attempting to treat the symptom instead of the cause. That is, we are trying to design public policy to offset the consequences of a failure of our various institutions to define and enforce parental support obligations. The authors go on to note the growing body of evidence indicting the legal/judicial system and its haphazard and ineffective enforcement of the parental support obligation across income classes. It is larely due to the wholesale unwillingness of absent parents to provide any, let alone adequate, support and society's unwillingness to enforce support laws that we find the very large income differentials between one- and two-parent households throughout the distribution and not just at its lower end. Thus, the authors conclude it is unlikely that any equitable and politically acceptable solution to the problem of assuring adequate resources for children in one-parent families can be found unless more effective attention is given to the issue of private responsibilities. Given a full sharing of these responsibilities by both living parents, the authors argue, universal and noncategorical redistribution policies could be applied without prejudice to children living with one parent, both parents, or neither parent, for that matter.

Toward the end of fostering child-support responsibilities among parents, Watts, Jakubson, and Skidmore propose a three-part program. The first part would necessitate the development of normative standards for child support toward the end of equitable parental sharing of economic responsibility for children. These standards might be based upon a formula for equalizing per-adult equivalent disposable income across split households with a minimum set at that level which would enable a one-parent household to reach the same level of living as that minimum which our society sets through minimum wage and public transfer policies for a two-parent family.

The second part of the authors' proposal would establish a form of child support insurance (CSI) to be added to the social insurance portfolio, which would provide payments which would be reduced by say, 70% of any child-support payments actually made by the absent parent.

Third, enforcement of the support obligation would be universal and impartial, through a mechanism separate from the Social Security Administration or Internal Revenue Service. Affidavits of compliance would be required on an annual basis, as would registration of paternity by the mother at a child's birth, subject to appeal by the designated father. The support obligation would be met (a) by living with and sharing a household with the child; (b) by complying with a court-approved support agreement; (c) by making payments at least equal to the minimum support standard defined above; or (d) by an appropriate combination of the above, each covering distinct periods of time and together covering the entire year.

For each child *not* supported in one of these ways, a surtax would be assessed on all taxable income of the noncustodial parent. Clearly it would be in the interest of this parent to pay the surtax only if that amount were smaller than the cost of complying with the support standards. The surtax would at least assure that there is a nonzero cost of procreation even if the resulting children cannot be or are not supported directly.

The incentives for unmarried mothers to cooperate in the designation of the fathers of their children is another issue. It is not clear to what extent refusal, or, most probably, a claim of ignorance as to identity of the father, would be a serious enough problem to warrant special provisions. The authors are clear, however, that the child's right to be supported by both parents should be given priority over the right to privacy of mothers and the right to anonymity of fathers.

One major advantage of this proposed program, in addition to the fact that it would better promote equal sharing of economic responsibility for children between both parents than that promoted by the present enforcement system, is that with a system of this kind in place it seems possible that a universal credit tax could carry the main burden of vertical redistribution without recourse to categorical treatment of one-parent households. In other words, the authors suggest that parity between one- and two-parent families might be realized in a more straightforward, direct fashion, by adopting a system which would promote parity between each pair of parents who no longer live together or may never have lived together. Other advantages of the proposal include probable reduced long-term public costs of support for one-parent families and an increase in the level of public confidence in the appropriateness of transfers to such families.

Though the authors anticipate large start-up costs for a program of this kind, they perceive no obvious reason why this program would cost any more than the age-graded supplement to the CIT that they simulated. Clearly, however, one should anticipate an increase in the "independence effect" for prospective single parents and a sharp reduction in options for noncustodial parents. This, in turn, would be likely to increase remarriage rates for custodial parents and decrease them for absent parents, if new family obligations do not reduce the support obligation for the former family.

A Critique of the Child-Support Insurance Plan

Though it is probably true that the advantages of the child-support insurance plan proposed by the authors will outweigh the disadvantages, it is imperative that future research be directed at estimating the redistributional consequences of such a program and variations thereof, a necessity recognized by the authors.

What has not been suggested, and was clearly outside the scope of the paper, is that with and without the child-support insurance proposal, future research must also be directed at estimating one- and two-parent household welfare ratio differentials *after* adjustments have been made for the effects of wage discrimination due to sex and single-parent status. For, while the authors admitted early in their introduction that such discrimination accounts for much of the difference in the relative economic well-being between one- and two-parent families, the child-support insurance plan, like other attempts to restore parity between these two types of families by superimposing a categorical program on a universal one, fails to address one of the more basic problems—that women are generally ill-equipped to compete with men in the labor market and receive lower pay when they do. To the extent that the economic disparity between one- and two-parent households is attributable to labor force and wage discrimination against women—especially those who are heads of households—child-support transfers may be both an inappropriate and inadequate solution to the problem. At the very least, we need to know how much of the variance in the economic disparity between these two types of families is attributable to each of these factors.

Furthermore, though we may certainly wish for equal sharing of the economic responsibility for children between parents who don't live together, the extent of the responsibility on the part of the noncustodial parent—usually the father—is implicitly a function, at least partially, of the willingness and ability of the custodial parent—usually the mother—to engage in market work. In other words, the size of the "bite" on Dad in the form of child support would largely be contingent upon Mom's earnings. This is not to say that attempts to restore parity between one- and two-parent households via the mechanism of insuring parity between the two sides of a former household are not presently worthy pursuits; rather, that we might achieve parity between these two types of families more quickly and with less direct cost if we simultaneously pursued equal opportunity and wage policies in the labor market *and* policies which seek the adoption of equitable normative standards for child support.

Though a federalized universal child-support insurance program of the sort proposed by the authors may indeed be an idea worth pursuing because of its value in fostering parental responsibility, it need not be pursued mainly on the grounds that it promotes parity between one- and two-parent households. Though this may be *one* effect, strictly speaking, child support alone cannot insure this kind of parity. It is doubtful that policies which pursue parity between the two households of a split family would eliminate altogether the income disparity between one- and two-parent families in the aggregate, as the authors seem to suggest. The economic needs of some families will always outstrip the ability of absent parents to support them. This is true for several reasons which include both the number of children in the family and limitations on the earnings of the female head. To the extent that women's earnings are artificially restricted by discrimination in the labor market, greater child-support transfers are necessary in order to reduce the gap in economic well-being between one- and two-parent families. If policies seeking parity between such families were adopted, they would be tantamount to forcing many absent parents to compensate, via the child-support transfer, for the consequences of discrimination in the labor market.

Similarly, to the extent that disaprity in economic well-being between one- and two-parent families is attributable to the latter having two wage earners rather than one, policies which promote parity between these two types of families would be inequitable. Thus, future research should also be directed at determining the extent to which categorical add-ons for one-parent families reduce the disparity between the two types of families when two-parent families contain only one wage earner and one-parent families are headed by women *and* by men with no wives present.

Furthermore, whereas there is little political constituency for a universal NIT or CIT outside the halls of academia and government, there is even less for a universal child-support system. The belief that intrafamily transfers are a strictly private matter, except in the case of welfare recipients, is deeply entrenched in both the mind of the public and within our legal institutions. This is best exemplified by the successful defeat of the Social Security Administration's attempt to force the states to adopt uniform standards for child-support payments in each state. The tradition of judicial discretion in the matter of setting child-support payments on a case-by-case basis is virtually inviolable. Though community property and no-fault divorce laws may represent the beginning of the end to this highly discretionary, subjective, and adversarial process, resistance to the federalization and universalization of child support is likely to be pronounced, no matter how rational the notion. The fact that the private system of enforcement of the child-support obligation has been such a total failure, however, can be an effective tool for countering the arguments against its continuance.

Granted that a child-support transfer system such as that proposed by Watts, Jakubson, and Skidmore is an idea whose time has come, the suggestion that child-support insurance become a part of the social security system, while perfectly logical, may not be appropriate during a time when the system has come under increasing criticism for waste and target inefficiency. There is no obvious reason why both payment dispersals and enforcement of the support obligation could not be handled by the IRS, especially if this agency is deemed the likely choice for administering a CIT or NIT at some time in the future. Similarly, there appears to be no good reason why, under a universal child-support system such as the one proposed, the adjudication process should not be circumvented altogether except in cases such as paternity appeal by alleged fathers. In fact, the authors themselves acknowledge that there is overwhelming evidence to the effect that the legal/judicial system has failed miserably in the setting of equitable amounts of child support. Why then, should they have suggested that the courts retain control over the adjudication of support? Given the tendencies of the courts to set minimal amounts of support, what reason is there to believe that they would not continue to do so? What means are available for ensuring that universal child-support standards, developed by the proposed "blue-ribbon commission," would be adopted and uniformly enforced by these same courts?

Likewise, given that the IRS will assess the child-support surtax on noncompliant obligors, they will, in effect, be involved in the enforcement process—oftentimes placing themselves in a position of internal conflict and conflict with the courts. If variance in court-ordered support as a proportion of the obligor's income is as great as research seems to suggest, then acknowledging the preeminence of a court order for support will result in the IRS treating persons differently, for tax purposes, who would otherwise be treated the same. Again, I do not believe the authors have built a convincing case for allowing the courts to retain control over the adjudication and enforcement of child support. A far more parsimonious, equitable, and efficient solution to the problem suggests that the IRS handle this function.

Another, perhaps more serious, problem exists with the child-support insurance plan as proposed. Registration of paternity of a child at birth and an automatic child-support collection and transfer system implies a nontransferable, centralized identification and income accounting system for which there is both growing support and growing opposition from many sources. Though an identification system is of key importance to a universal child-support program toward the end of promoting full sharing of parental economic responsibility, the implications of such a system are broad and, to many, alarming. The right to privacy in matters such as where one lives, how much one earns, who fathers a child, and who knows these things, is deeply entrenched. A system which violates this right may, understandably, create political and ethical dilemmas. Great care should be exercised by those who seek to reform the child-support transfer system to see to it that the basic right to privacy in these matters is protected to the maximum extent possible.

Finally, a word is necessary in regard to the authors' suggestion that a child-support insurance plan would likely offset some of the marital-dissolution consequences inherent in a transfer system which reduces the costs of marital breakups for women—the so-called independence effect. A public guarantee that payments for child support would be made by the absent parent to the custodial parent would reduce marital dissolution only to the extent that *men* are the initiators of splitting and women have custody of the children. A guarantee of child support, especially in amounts that would approximate parity, would more likely increase dissolution rates to the extent that women are the initiators of such. If large numbers of women who are presently trapped in unhappy marriages can be "liberated" by a public guarantee of reliable and equitable child support, the benefit to society can be viewed as far greater than that under the present system, in which women bear a disproportionate share of the economic burden of family dissolution. The net effect on marital dissolution rates and its magnitude, of course, is presently unknown.

Furthermore, to suggest that normative standards be adopted which would establish economic parity between the parents of a child is to suggest that, in most cases, amounts in excess of 40% of the absent parent's income would be transferred to the custodial parent and children, if one defines parity in terms of the equalization of welfare ratios as the authors implied. On the other hand, if we were to adopt normative standards which split equally the real costs of raising a child with no adjustments for either income differentials between men and women or for compensation for the personal cost of child care on a day-to-day basis for the custodial parent, we would reduce the "bite" on Dad, but such a notion of parity would not begin to approximate horizontal equity.

In summary, the value of one-parent household add-ons to a basic CIT appears, on balance, positive. Furthermore, programs such as child-support insurance are not only worthy for normative reasons but may serve to reduce incentives for family dissolution to the extent that men are the initiators of such dissolution.

It is not necessary, however, to reform the present transfer system in order to promote economic parity between two parts of a family that has split. A universal, federalized child-support program need not be tied to "welfare reform." It is important to remember, though, that pursuing such child-support policies may reduce *some* of the aggregate economic disparity between one- and two-parent families but cannot be expected to eliminate it altogether. It may be more fruitful to pursue multiple strategies for addressing the problem of income inequality between one- and two-parent families. It is imperative, however, that those concerned with reforming the child-support transfer portion of the system take special care to protect the right to privacy of all parties involved—a right which we have heretofore violated, with relative impunity, in the case of large classes of persons in our society.

Discussion

ROBERT I. LERMAN

Over the last decade, poverty in the United States has declined among two-parent families and the elderly. Unfortunately, among mother-headed families, poverty has jumped substantially, from 1.5 million families in 1969 to nearly 2.5 million families in 1978. The majority of poor children now live in families with at least one parent (almost always the father) missing. Moreover, the poverty is generally more severe and more chronic in one-parent than in two-parent families.

On the policy side, one-parent families have commanded the vast bulk of government transfers going to the able, nonelderly poor. Yet such outlays have failed to prevent a rise in the number of poor, one-parent families. One reason is that welfare programs for mother-headed families, especially AFDC, have an awful name with the public. The current AFDC approach does not attract either the support of recipients or of professionals and analysts dealing with the program. So the issue the authors address is ripe for new policy options, not only because existing programs do poorly but also because this group's poverty is so intractable.

The authors analyze two policies (an old and a new) that would move from current income-tested solutions to universal solutions. The first is the credit income tax (CIT). The authors directly compare the CIT with the negative income tax (NIT) using alternative benefit formulas which scale guarantees differently by family size and composition. The key issue is how well the universal CIT does relative to the NIT and the current system in helping the poor, reducing overall inequality, and achieving equity between one- and two-parent families.

Unfortunately, these simulations say more about the authors' assumptions than about how adequate or equitable are alternative benefit formulas. To see this, we must begin by examining carefully the welfare ratios (WR) which the authors use as their index of family welfare. The definition of WR is family income divided by the poverty line relevant to the specific family. Poverty lines rise with family size at a rate that declines with each additional member. More important for the simulations, poverty lines do not distinguish between adults and children. Thus, a one-parent family of four is said to require the same income to escape poverty as a two-parent family of four. Having made poverty lines the mechanism for scaling income into welfare, the authors seem to forget this decision when setting initial guarantee levels for the NIT and CIT alternatives. Here, they begin with adult benefit levels that are twice the level of child benefit levels. These imply that CIT and NIT guarantees are higher for two-parent than for one-parent families of equal size.

When one performs a microsimulation with these formulas and calculates distributional effects by WR, it is not surprising that the one-parent families come out behind. After all, their CIT or NIT payment is lower *at any WR* than is the CIT or NIT payment to two-parent families. To avoid sizable differentials in distributional implications, the authors devise age-graded benefit levels that raise the children's benefit relative to the adult benefit. Again, not surprisingly, the adjusted formulas improve the outcomes for one-parent relative to two-parent families, but not enough to make up the full difference.

The distributional comparisons also suffer from an inconsistency between what the authors say in the text and what they do in the simulations. According to the text, there is a need to supplement the basic benefits of one-parent families to take account of their higher child-care costs and other work expenses. (A broader way of expressing this idea is to notice that counting an adult's leisure would tend to imply that the full income of a two-parent family exceeds that of a one-parent family with the same money income.) The authors must mean that the simple WRs do not accurately represent the welfare of one-parent families relative to the welfare to two-parent families. This would seem to call for adjusting incomes of one-parent families downward to take account of special work expenses or adjusting their needs upward. This the authors fail to do. So, on the basis of their own comments, the comparisons are unfair to one-parent families.

One further problem is relevant not only to this paper but also to the conference paper by Betson, Greenberg, and Kasten (Chapter 6). That is the reliance on data based on incomes and work experience in 1975, by far the worst year for the economy since World War II. Although the authors of both papers claim to perform simulations which take account of labor supply effects, it is very difficult to judge whether the results reflect what could be expected in a normal year. The choice of the Survey of Income and Education (SIE) data base, which is available only for one year, would be understandable if the authors needed the SIE's unusually large sample size. But, in fact, neither paper used the full SIE sample size; each used a sample smaller than the Current Population Survey, which is available for normal years.

Let us now turn to the second, more innovative universal policy for helping poor one-parent families. It is one which emphasizes the cause of poverty among one-parent families, namely the absence of income from the second parent. By viewing their problem as primarily one which faces mother-headed families at *all* income levels, the authors point out that improved child-support collection would be a sensible universal program with important side benefits for the poor. With effective collection procedures in place, absent fathers would have to provide payments to fill much of the income gap now filled by AFDC. The authors' child support insurance (CSI) program would then provide supplementary support for those one-parent families whose child-support receipts are below some minimum level.

The authors generally do a good job of explaining and defending their proposal. But they should have emphasized two key advantages of the proposal. First, the program could reduce the stigma now faced by many AFDC recipients. Instead of falling into the class of poor, dependent mothers relying on taxpayer generosity, many current AFDC recipients would become part of the general class of mother-headed families. They would even receive much of their income in the same way that middle-income mothers heading families do. Second, the program could result in much better work incentives for low-income mothers heading families. The authors do not say whether earned income would reduce CSI payments. But, even if the CSI program were to count earnings, the earnings of low-income mothers would be worth much more under the new proposal than they are now under the AFDC program. The improvement in work incentives would certainly stimulate many mothers to earn more and to raise the living standards of their children.

These two omissions are less crucial than the authors' failure to make the child-support idea the key universal option for dealing with income deficiencies of one-parent families. There have been many simulations of CITs and NITs; as noted earlier, those in this paper add only a moderate amount of insight to the issues. On the other hand, little quantitative analysis has appeared on the child-support collection ideas. While the authors are right to point to data limitations, they could have exploited data from the Michigan PSID, from the Seattle–Denver Income Maintenance Experiments, and from the Department of Health and Human Services existing projects. The authors could have tried to estimate the quantitative dimensions of the problem facing mother-headed families not on welfare.

I agree with the authors that shifting toward a universal child-support-enforcement and insurance scheme has excellent potential for helping low-income families in a more effective and humane way than current welfare programs. However, showing the potential benefits of this approach requires going beyond their research.

12

Income Testing in Income Support Programs for the Aged

DAVID BERRY
IRWIN GARFINKEL
RAYMOND MUNTS

The federal system of old-age income support in the United States has two principal components: Old Age and Survivors Insurance (OASI) and Supplemental Security Income (SSI).* In OASI, widely known as social security, eligibility and benefits depend primarily on past earnings in occupations covered by the program. These occupations now represent about 90% of the labor force (*Social Security Bulletin, Annual Statistical Supplement, 1975,* 1977, p. 44). The SSI program took effect in 1974 with the purpose of putting a floor under the incomes of the aged, blind, and disabled poor. Benefits in the program are limited to those with low incomes and assets through an income test and an asset test, which together are referred to as a means test. In OASI, both rich and poor are eligible because benefits are not means tested, although there is a retirement test that reduces benefits for people whose current earnings exceed a given amount.

OASI now dwarfs SSI. In 1977, OAI benefits (which did not include survivors' benefits) for the aged totaled $52 billion, over 20 times as large

*The computer programming for this project was done by John Flesher and Mike Watts. Joseph Quinn provided helpful comments on an earlier draft. Jennifer Warlick provided estimates of her SSI participation model based on the variables available in our data. We extend special thanks to Richard Burkhauser for valuable help in understanding the data set that we used and for comments on several earlier drafts.

as the $2.5 billion in SSI benefits for the aged (*Statistical Abstract of the United States: 1978*, 1978).[1] However, the future roles of the two programs are much debated.

At the core of the debate are questions about the most desirable way of achieving two goals in social policy toward the aged. The first of these—the earnings-replacement or insurance goal—is that retired workers' incomes should not fall too far below preretirement levels. The second—the social adequacy or welfare goal—is to prevent people's incomes from falling below a minimum standard, that is, to eliminate poverty. There is a conflict between the two goals, however: If all retired workers had the same earnings-replacement rate (ratio of benefit to preretirement earnings), some of their incomes would fall below the minimum standard, and their benefits could be raised only by lowering benefits for high-income workers or by increasing the total outlay of the system.

Since the 1935 Social Security Act, the provisions of OASI have reflected a concern with social adequacy as well as earnings replacement. Currently, benefits rise with preretirement earnings, but the benefit structure is progressive in that earnings-replacement rates are higher for low-income workers than for high-income workers. There are other provisions as well that are intended to promote social adequacy: the minimum benefit, the special minimum benefit, and dependents' benefits.

Some analysts of our old-age income support system maintain that with the enactment of SSI, social security no longer needs to be concerned with social adequacy. Accordingly, they propose a two-tier system which would consist of an expanded SSI program and a revised OASI program in which benefits would become strictly proportional to past earnings. They argue that relying solely on income-tested benefits for redistributing income to the aged poor would be more target efficient than the present system—that is, a greater proportion of those benefits intended to aid the poor would actually go to the poor.

Other analysts, however, are concerned about the stigma felt by participants in welfare programs such as SSI and the high tax rates implicit in the provisions of these programs. Some propose a double-decker system which would pay a flat-rate pension to all citizens reaching retirement age plus a benefit strictly proportional to past earnings. The flat-rate pension would be large enough to eliminate or greatly reduce the need for an income-tested program such as SSI. Many advocates of such a system believe that it would redistribute more income to the poor and near-poor than either the present system or a two-tier system.

[1] The figure for OAI is from Table 533, p. 340; the figure for SSI is from Table 563, p. 356.

Should social adequacy continue to be a concern of OASI? If so, to what extent? If not, should we move toward a two-tier or a double-decker system? These are critical questions in the debate over how best to achieve the goals of earnings replacement and social adequacy for the aged.

This paper is concerned with the relative impacts of the present system and the two-tier and double-decker alternatives on income distribution both within the aged population and between the aged and non-aged. Its principal focus is on the distributional effects of income testing. We find that the relative distributional effects of the three systems are quite sensitive to the choice of parameters we hold constant in comparing them. In particular, we find that whether or not income testing brings about higher incomes for the poor depends upon the parameters which are held constant.

These and other results derive from a set of microsimulations of models of our present system and the two-tier and double-decker alternatives. The simulations use U.S data for 1972 which have been linked to social security annual earnings data beginning with 1951. They take account of two behavioral effects of the system: (a) the decision of an individual or couple eligible for SSI whether or not to participate in the program; and (b) intrafamily transfers. They do not take account of changes in time spent working that would occur in response to changes in the systems.

Before we present the results of our simulations, we shall review in more detail the current debate in the United States over alternative income support programs for the aged. We then describe the three system models that we simulate, deal with the critical problem of what to hold constant when making comparisons among them, and describe our data and simulation methodology. Finally, we present our results.

Should Social Adequacy be a Concern of OASI?

Three social adequacy or welfare features of OASI have been strongly criticized: the progressiveness of the benefit structure, the minimum benefit, and dependents' benefits.

The Progressive Benefit Structure and Minimum Benefit

Under OASI, an insured person's benefit is computed from an earnings index which is contructed so as to reflect both the number of years he or she has been employed in occupations covered by the program and the level of earnings during those years. The benefit rises with the earnings index, but earnings-replacement rates are higher for people with low earnings indices than for those with high earnings indices. Specifically, the annual benefit for a person reaching age 62 in 1979 was 90% of the first $2160 of indexed earnings, 32% of the next $10,860, and 15% of the remainder.[2] It is argued that this progressive benefit structure and the minimum benefit ($1460 in 1978) are inefficient devices for aiding the poor; they work to the advantage of many middle- and upper-income retirees who have low earnings indices because they have spent most of their careers in occupations which are not covered by OASI, particularly the federal and some state civil services (Pechman et al., 1968; Munnell, 1977). An obvious answer to this problem—bringing such occupations under social security—would be politically difficult to achieve.

Another criticism of the progressive benefit structure and the minimum benefit stems from the fact that they reduce rates of return on contributions for high- and upper-middle income workers relative to the average rate of return for all workers. As the system matures and the rate of population growth declines, the average rate of return on contributions will fall.[3] It is argued that this will cause rates of return for high- and upper-middle income workers to be so low that the system will lose much of its public support. Furthermore, the low rates of return for these workers will increase their tendency to view contributions as taxes rather than forced savings, and will therefore act as an incentive against working (Feldstein, 1977a).

In the 1977 social security amendments, Congress froze the minimum benefit at its December 1978 level for future beneficiaries. It also increased the special minimum benefit and mandated automatic cost-of-living adjustments in the benefit in the future. The special minimum benefit, which became effective in 1973, is for long-term workers only.

---

[2]The bracket widths are adjusted annually according to the growth of average wages (Snee and Ross, 1978, p. 13).

[3]Since payroll taxes are used concurrently to pay benefits to retired workers, average benefit levels depend, among other things, upon the number of people in covered employment relative to the number collecting benefits. With an expanding population and a broadening of OASI coverage throughout the economy, the *relative* number of people in covered employment has been large enough that benefit levels have represented fairly high rates of return on past contributions. However, the rate of population growth is declining and OASI coverage is nearly complete, so that the number of people making contributions relative to the number collecting benefits will fall in the future, thus reducing rates of return.

In 1979, its annual amount was $138 times the number of years of covered employment above ten and up to thirty (Snee and Ross, 1978, p. 14).

Dependents' Benefits

The spouse or dependent child of an insured worker may collect a benefit equal to 50% of that worker's benefit, if the benefit based on his or her own earnings record is lower. Benefits of this type have received one of the same criticisms directed toward the progressive benefit structure and the minimum benefit: They are not target efficient in aiding the poor, since they are payable to rich as well as poor families.

Perhaps a more serious criticism of benefits to spouses, however, is that they are inequitable. Working wives often find that their benefits are no greater than those of their nonworking counterparts, and that their social security contributions therefore have been wasted. Even if a married woman's past earnings are sufficient to entitle her to a benefit greater than 50% of her husband's, the difference between her benefit and that of a nonworking wife does not fully reflect the value of her contributions. With increasing numbers of women in the labor force, these inequities are being more widely felt. Moreover, it is argued that the fact that many working wives receive little or nothing in return for their contributions reduces their incentive to work and undermines public support for OASI (Feldstein, 1977a).

A TWO-TIER SYSTEM

These criticisms have led some experts to propose changing the OASI benefit structure so that benefits would become strictly proportional to past earnings. The underlying principle of such a change is that OASI should be concerned only with earnings replacement; the minimum benefit, dependents' benefits, and, presumably, the special minimum benefit would be eliminated. With this change in OASI, an expanded SSI program would bear the responsibility for achieving social adequacy (Pechman et al., 1968; Feldstein, 1977a; and Munnell, 1977). Such an arrangement has been referred to as a two-tier system.

SSI benefits are currently reduced by one dollar for each dollar of income other than current earnings, including social security benefits, above $240 per year. Because of this, workers who receive both OASI and SSI benefits can receive only $240 per year in return for the payroll taxes they paid while working. This problem would affect more workers in a two-tier system than in the present system; a change to a proportional OASI benefit structure would reduce OASI benefits for low-wage workers, so that more workers would collect SSI benefits. Munnell's (1977) proposal for a two-tier system deals with this problem by reducing the SSI benefit-reduction rate on income other than current earnings to 50% from its current 100% (the $240 annual disregard is eliminated). (Readers who are unfamiliar with the SSI program should refer to our Appendix).

Several advantages are claimed for the two-tier approach. First, it would be more target efficient in aiding the aged poor than the current system; a larger proportion of those benefits intended to aid the poor would actually go to the poor, because all such benefits would be income tested. Second, the burden of income support for the aged poor would be shifted toward higher-income groups, since payroll tax revenues would no longer be used for redistributional purposes and the use of general revenues would increase because of the expansion of the SSI program. Finally, because there would be a proportional relationship between OASI contributions and benefits, public support and work incentives would increase.

Critics of the two-tier approach argue that SSI participants are stigmatized because applying for benefits is associated with personal failure. They point out that a large proportion of the people eligible for SSI choose not to participate in the program, and they attribute much of this to a desire to avoid stigma and the inconvenience of applying for benefits. Welfare programs such as SSI, it is contended, accentuate class distinctions by singling out the poor for treatment under a set of rules that do not apply to the rest of society. Moreover, beneficiaries of welfare programs in the United States, because of their low economic status, have little political power and therefore have great difficulty in bringing about improvements in the programs, including more adequate benefit levels (Schorr, 1977). The two-tier approach also has the disadvantage that in SSI, the benefit-reduction rates applied to current earnings and other income are equivalent to tax rates; they therefore discourage work and saving.

A FLAT-RATE PENSION PROGRAM

An alternative to SSI for achieving social adequacy is a flat-rate pension program; such a program would pay an equal benefit to all old people. The proponents of a flat-rate pension program see several advantages in such a program over SSI. One is that it would not have the stigmatizing means test. In addition, the level of benefits would be of interest to all, which would be advantageous to the poor (Burns, 1965a; Schorr, 1977). Moreover, the discouragement of work and saving caused by the implicit tax rates in SSI would be absent.

Finally, some people advocate a flat-rate pension program because they believe it would reduce overall income inequality. One reason given is that the burden of income redistribution would be shifted toward higher-income groups because the pension would be financed with general revenues. This advantage is shared with the two-tier system; however, the shift toward general revenue financing would be much greater with a flat-rate pension. In addition, a flat-rate pension would raise the incomes of the poor more than a welfare program such as SSI with a guarantee of the same amount. First, all of the poor would receive a pension, while under a welfare program, some would choose not to collect benefits because of stigma or inconvenience. Second, benefits for the poor would be higher because they would not be reduced on account of outside income. Indeed, a shift to a flat-rate pension program from a welfare program with an equal guarantee would bring net benefits to all of the aged except the very wealthy, after subtracting the tax increase necessary to finance the program.

A DOUBLE-DECKER SYSTEM

Alvin Schorr (1977) has proposed a system that would combine a flat-rate pension with an earnings-related benefit computed by compounding payroll taxes at some rate of interest. A similar approach would be to compute the earnings-related benefit directly from an earnings index, with a strictly proportional relationship between them. A system combining a flat-rate pension program and an earnings-related benefit program is sometimes referred to as a double-decker system.

In both the two-tier and double-decker systems, the earnings-related benefit program is not concerned with social adequacy. The distinction between the two is that the former uses income-tested benefits to promote social adequacy while the latter uses the flat-rate pension. This gives rise to two further distinctions: First, in the double-decker system, earnings-related benefits do not bear the sole responsibility for earnings replacement for high-income earners, as they do in the two-tier system, but are supplemented by the pension. Second, the combined earnings-replacement rate in the double-decker system (based on both the earnings-related and non-earnings-related benefits) falls as the earnings index rises for all beneficiaries; in the two-tier system, this is only true for those receiving bottom-tier benefits.

It should be noted that both the two-tier and double-decker alternatives have precedents among foreign social security programs. Indeed, the range of alternatives embodied in foreign programs is very wide (see Callund, 1975, or U.S. Department of Health, Education, and Welfare, 1978d).

Should social adequacy continue to be a concern of OASI? If not, should we move toward the two-tier or the double-decker alternative? The answers to these questions depend on a host of factors, including the relative amounts of public support that the alternatives can command; this, in turn, depends on people's values. To some, including ourselves, the answers depend partly on the relative impacts of the systems upon the distribution of income among the aged.

Models of the Three Systems

The debate over alternatives is the basis for our choice of three system models as the focus of our simulation study: (*a*) a status quo model; (*b*) a two-tier model consisting of a proportional earnings-related benefit program (top tier) and an income-tested benefit program such as SSI (bottom tier); and (*c*) a double-decker model consisting of a proportional earnings-related benefit program and a flat-rate pension program. We

TABLE 12.1
Characteristics of Simulated System Models to Provide Benefits for the Aged

| | | Earnings-Related Benefits | | | |
| | | | Additional Benefits | | |
Model	Basic Structure	Spouse	Surviving Spouse	Divorced Spouse	Retirement Test[a]
Status quo	OASI as under 1977 amendments	50%	100%	50%	$3,100 disregard, 50% tax rate
Two-tier	Proportional to indexed earnings	none	100%	none	$3,100 disregard, 50% tax rate
Double-decker	Proportional to indexed earnings	none	100%	none	$3,100 disregard, 50% tax rate

| | Non-Earnings-Related Benefits | | | |
| | Guarantee ($) | | Income Test | |
Model	Individual	Couple	Current Earnings	Other Income
Status quo	1,800	2,700	$780 disregard, 50% tax rate	No disregard, 100% tax rate
Two-tier	1,800	2,700	$780 disregard, 50% tax rate	No disregard, 50% tax rate
Double-decker	1,800	2,700	none	none

[a] Applies only to people under age 70.

will simulate these models with data for 1972, because of the availability of a unique data set for that year (see below). The models are summarized in Table 12.1.

The Status Quo Model

In the status quo model, the OASI benefit structure incorporates the basic provisions of the 1977 social security amendments.[4] (The progressive benefit structure has been described above.) The minimum benefit ($950 in 1972 dollars) is included, despite the fact that it will be frozen in 1979, because it is a feature of OASI which has come under attack by proponents of the two-tier system. (We do not include the special minimum benefit because our annual earnings data begin with 1951; nobody who was 65 or older in 1972 could have had enough years of covered employment after 1950 to qualify for a special minimum benefit any greater than the regular minimum.) The spouse's and divorced person's benefits are 50% of the insured person's benefit and the surviving spouse's benefit is 100%. The retirement test reduces benefits for those under age 70 by 50% of current earnings above the disregarded amount of $3100.[5]

In SSI we set the guarantee levels for individuals and couples at $1800 and $2700. These are larger than the actual amounts, and near the U.S. government official poverty lines for 1972,[6] because of our interest in comparing programs that would largely eliminate poverty among the aged. We follow actual practice, however, in setting the guarantee for a couple 50% greater than for an individual. The benefit-reduction rates ("tax rates") are 50% for current earnings above $780 per year and 100% for other income.[7] We do not include the provision that reduces SSI

---

[4]For details, see Snee and Ross (1978).

[5]The actual disregarded amount was $2100 in 1972. Under the 1977 amendments, the disregard is raised in yearly increments to $6000 in 1982. Thereafter, it will be adjusted automatically in the same proportion as the growth of average wages. The $3100 amount for 1972 is obtained by applying such an adjustment to the 1982 amount, using actual covered wage growth from 1972 to 1977 and the wage growth projected for 1977 to 1982 by the Social Security Administration at the time of the amendments (see Snee and Ross, 1978, pp. 13–14).

[6]The poverty lines for aged individuals and couples in 1972 were $2005 and $2530 (U.S. Department of Commerce, 1973, p. 143).

[7]Recall that the $240 disregard for "other income" is eliminated under Munnell's (1977) proposed two-tier system. We eliminate it in the status quo model as well as in the two-tier so that our simulation results will not reflect a difference between the models which we do not consider to be inherent. The $780 disregard for current earnings is the actual amount. We do not convert it to 1972 dollars because it is not adjusted for inflation in actual practice.

benefits by one-third for people living in the homes of others; nor do we include the asset test or state supplements to SSI, because our data do not include asset or state variables.

The Two-Tier Model

In the two-tier model, the earnings-related benefit is strictly proportional to the earnings index. Benefits for widows and widowers are available under the same provisions as in the status quo model, but there are no benefits for spouses or divorced persons.[8] The retirement test provisions are also the same. The bottom-tier program is the same as the SSI program in the status quo model, except that the implicit tax rate on income other than current earnings (including top-tier benefits) is reduced to 50%, in keeping with the Munnell (1977) proposal noted earlier. (Hereafter, for convenience, we refer to "income other than current earnings" as "unearned income.")

The Double-Decker Model

In the double-decker model, the flat-rate pension amounts for individuals and couples—the guarantee levels—are the same as the guarantees in the status quo and two-tier models. As in the two-tier model, the earnings-related benefit is proportional to the earnings index. Earnings-related benefits are lower than in the other models, because with everyone receiving a flat-rate pension, earnings-replacement rates (based on combined benefits) comparable to those in the other models can be achieved with lower earnings-related benefits. As in the status quo and two-tier models, a surviving spouse is entitled to an earnings-related benefit equal to 100% of that of the deceased spouse.[9] Spouses and divorced persons are entitled only to flat-rate pensions and to earnings-related benefits based on their own earnings records. The retirement test applies only to earnings-related benefits, under the same provisions as in the status quo and two-tier models.

---

[8]We do not know what provisions proponents of a two-tier system would make for benefits for surviving spouses. For this reason, we use the same provisions in the two-tier model as in the status quo in order to focus on differences in other aspects of the model.

[9]In countries with double-decker systems, surviving spouses' benefits are considerably less than 100% of the deceased spouse's benefit. Our rationale for departing from this practice is given in footnote 8. The question remains, however, as to whether a lower surviving spouse's benefit is not a desirable feature of a double-decker system, given the availability of the flat-rate pension.

In all three system models, annual earnings indices are computed according to the provisions of the 1977 amendments. Under this method of computation, a person's earnings index depends on the number of years spent in covered employment as well as the level of earnings during those years.[10]

People are assumed to begin collecting both earnings-related and non-earnings-related benefits at age 65. Where earnings-related benefits are concerned, there are no delayed retirement credits or actuarial reductions for early retirement.[11] In all three models, earnings-related benefits are financed with payroll taxes and non-earnings-related benefits with income taxes.

The Problem of What to Hold Constant

The choice of what to hold constant in comparing the models corresponds to a political choice. Should we guarantee that the incomes of the aged poor will not fall below a certain level? Should we see to it that the middle- and upper-income aged have incomes that are not below some given proportion of their preretirement incomes? Should the size of the transfer from the nonaged to the aged be held below some limit? These critical questions guide our choice of parameters to be held constant.

The first of these parameters is the *guarantee*, or the income floor provided by the non-earnings-related benefit program. We will use the term to refer to the standard for an individual, the amount for a couple being 50% greater. We choose the guarantee because of its large impact on the incomes of the aged poor.

The second parameter that we hold constant is what we call the *high-income replacement rate*—the earnings-replacement rate for a representative high-income earner. It is computed from the average earnings

[10]Our earnings history data include annual covered earnings beginning with 1951 and total covered earnings for 1937 to 1950. A description of how we take into account the data from both periods in computing earnings indices is available from us upon request.

[11]The failure to take account of the effect of benefit provisions on people's decisions on when to retire may have had a significant effect on our results, since the incentives affecting the retirement decision vary among the models. Aside from incentive effects, it should be noted that a given overall percentage reduction in earnings-related benefits due to early retirement has different effects on costs in different models, since the total amount of earnings-related benefits varies. This is not trivial, since the overall reduction of OASI benefits for early retirement was 5% in 1972 (*Social Security Bulletin, Annual Statistical Supplement, 1972,* 1974, p. 104), and, as shown by our results, the total amount of earnings-related benefits in the double-decker model is less than in the other models by $20 million or more.

index of insured primary earners in the top fifth of the income distribution of the aged, and the corresponding benefit. It is based on only earnings-related benefits in the status quo and two-tier models; in the double-decker, it is based on the combined benefit. We choose the high-income replacement rate because of its influence on the economic positions of the upper-income aged.

The final parameter to be held constant is the *cost to the nonaged*—the transfer from the nonaged to the aged. The magnitude of this transfer depends on the budget cost of benefits, the relative amounts of income and payroll taxes used to finance benefits, and tax provisions affecting the aged.

In any of the system models, the values of any two of the parameters determine what the third must be. Because of this, we can hold only two parameters constant in comparing the models. We therefore make comparisons in three ways. In the first, cost to the nonaged and the high-income replacement rate are constant, and the guarantee is allowed to vary. In the second, the guarantee and cost to the nonaged are constant, and in the third, the high-income replacement rate and the guarantee are constant.

The parameters are held constant by setting them at *benchmark values*. The benchmark guarantee level was chosen in the specification of the models to be $1800. For the other two parameters, benchmark values are determined in the first simulation of the status quo model (see the next section).

As indicated in the preceding section, retirement-test provisions are the same in all of the models. Income tax provisions are also held constant: In all of the models, benefits are taxed and the special aged exemption is eliminated. These changes from actual provisions are made in the double-decker model because of the payment of a flat-rate pension to all of the aged, and in the other models to make them comparable to the double-decker.

Data and Methodology

The Data

The data used are from the 1973 CPS/IRS/SSA Exact Match Data Set, which links data from the Internal Revenue Service and the Social Security Administration to the March 1973 Current Population Survey data.

The social security data include annual covered earnings from 1951 to 1972 and total covered earnings for the period 1937–1950.

Our sample consists of family units with at least one person 65 or older in 1972 and unrelated individuals meeting the same age criterion. Younger people, in families where they are present, are of interest to us because their incomes affect the well-being of the old people living with them. There are 9890 aged persons (65 or older) and 7666 family units (including unrelated individuals) in our sample.

Methodology

Basically, our simulations consist of computing benefits and federal income and payroll tax payments under the system models we have described. The outputs of the simulation program include income distribution among the aged, budget costs, and changes in federal income and payroll tax rates. Additional results are cost to the nonaged, the guarantee level, and the high-income replacement rate. As noted earlier, only two of these are held constant in a comparison among the models; the third, therefore, constitutes a basis for comparison.

The simulation routine begins with the computation of benefits under the provisions of the system model at hand. Where non-earnings-related benefits in the status quo and two-tier models are concerned, a problem arises from the fact that there is less than full participation in the current SSI program. We use Warlick's model, which predicts the probability that a person or couple eligible for SSI will decide to participate in the program, to establish the proportion of eligible couples and individuals that will collect non-earnings-related benefits in the status quo and two-tier models.[12]

The next stage in the simulation routine is to compute, in three steps, federal income and payroll *tax payments*. This is done for all family members, since the incomes of those under 65 affect the well-being of the aged members. First, we compute both types of tax payments under actual 1972 rules, the income tax rules being modified by the inclusion of benefits in taxable income and the elimination of the special aged exemption. Second, we compute the changes in income and payroll tax rates relative to 1972 levels that are necessary to finance the difference

[12]See Warlick (1979). We extend special thanks to Jennifer Warlick for estimating for us a variant of her model based on the data available for our study. We use the predicted probability of participation for each eligible individual or couple to split the sample weight into amounts representing participants and nonparticipants.

between simulated and actual benefit levels. For this purpose, it is assumed that the actual level of non-earnings-related benefits in 1972 was zero.[13] Third, we adjust the tax payments according to the changes in rates.

Cost to the nonaged is computed from the tax rate changes. It is equal to the change in 1972 tax payments by the nonaged that would arise from the rate changes, with one modification: Since the payroll tax rate change is based on the difference between total simulated earnings-related benefits and the total of actual social security benefits for the aged (estimated from the data), cost to the nonaged also includes the portion of actual payroll tax payments by the nonaged which went toward actual social security benefits for the aged.

Tax payments and cost to the nonaged are computed in such a way as to satisfy a balanced-budget condition: Any change in the budget cost of benefits, from one simulation to another, is equal to the change in cost to the nonaged plus the change in tax payments by the aged. Thus, any change in cost to the nonaged implies an equal change in net benefits— benefits minus taxes—for the aged.[14]

A *measure of economic well-being* is computed from total family income, including simulated benefits, net of federal income and payroll taxes. Total family income is adjusted for family size by a formula which lowers the incomes of large families relative to those of small families, so that the adjusted incomes represent levels of economic welfare controlled for family size.[15] A family's adjusted income is attributed to each of its aged members for the purpose of computing income distribution.

This procedure implicitly assumes that family income is shared evenly among all members, a reasonable assumption for families with aged heads, including aged individuals and couples. Where elderly people live in the homes of younger relatives, we think it is more reasonable to assume that there is only partial sharing of income between the two groups. We determine the magnitudes of these intrafamily transfers by applying the procedure set forth by Moon (1977a, pp. 57–59).

---

[13]This is a trivial assumption. The SSI program did not exist in 1972, and Old Age Assistance payments (both federal and state shares) totaled $1.9 billion (*Social Security Bulletin, Annual Statistical Supplement, 1972,* 1974, p. 146), which amounts to 2% of federal income taxes for that year (U.S. Department of the Treasury, 1974, p. 22). More important, the small error that results is of the same magnitude in all simulations and therefore does not affect our comparisons.

[14]A description of the computation of tax rate changes, tax payments, and cost to the nonaged is available from us upon request.

[15]In the family-size adjustment, family income is multiplied by the ratio of the poverty line for a two-person family to the poverty line for the family's own size.

The high-income replacement rate is based on the average earnings index of those primary earners in the top fifth of the income distribution of the aged who have attained insured status under OASI. For this purpose, we assume that primary earners are men. We further limit the group to 66-year-olds, for three reasons: (a) in the status quo model, people of different ages who have the same real (inflation-adjusted) earnings indices have different real benefits; (b) among the aged, the relatively young have had more years of coverage under OASI; and (c) the proportion of people working drops rapidly after age 65; the 66-year-olds, therefore, are more representative of all of the aged in the top fifth of the income distribution than are the 65-year-olds (many of those who are still working will no longer be in the top fifth when they retire).

From the average earnings index of this group, we compute the corresponding benefit; the ratio of this benefit to the earnings index is the high-income replacement rate. In the status quo and two-tier models, only earnings-related benefits are used for this purpose; in the double-decker, the combined benefit is used. In all cases, the primary insurance amount (PIA) is used—the earnings-related benefit based on a person's *own* past earnings that would be payable if he or she retired and began collecting benefits at age 65. In all simulations, the high-income replacement rate is based on the same average earnings index—the one computed in the initial simulation of the status quo model. This is important, because in the status quo and double-decker models, earnings-replacement rates decline as the earnings index increases.

The benchmark values of the high-income replacement rate and cost to the nonaged are the values arising from the initial simulation of the status quo model—the "benchmark simulation." (Recall that we have already chosen the benchmark guarantee level to be $1800.) The specifications of the status quo model in this simulation are modified: Benefits are not taxed and the special aged exemption is present so that the benchmark value of cost to the nonaged is based on a model closely resembling what currently exists in the United States.

Setting cost to the nonaged at its benchmark level (within .2%) is accomplished by adjustment of either the guarantee or the high-income replacement rate, whichever is being allowed to vary. In the two-tier and double-decker models, adjustments in the high-income replacement rate occur through changes in the proportionality factor relating PIAs to earnings indices. Similarly, in the status quo model, such adjustments involve equiproportional changes in all PIAs (except those based on the minimum, which stay constant). In the double-decker model, changes in the guarantee are accompanied by adjustments in earnings-related benefits (specifically, in the proportionality factor that determines PIAs), so that the high-income replacement rate stays at the benchmark level.

Major Results

Values of Variable Parameters

Table 12.2 presents the values of the guarantee, the high-income replacement rate, and cost to the nonaged that arise from three sets of simulations of the three system models. We will refer to these simulation sets as the variable guarantee case, the variable replacement rate case, and the variable cost case. ("Variable replacement rate" is shorthand for "variable high-income replacement rate" and "variable cost" is shorthand for "variable cost to the nonaged.") Remember that whichever parameter is allowed to vary, the other two are held at their benchmark levels. The benchmark value of the guarantee is $1800; of the high-income replacement rate, .43; and of cost to the nonaged, $36.0 billion. Recall that the latter two values have arisen from the "benchmark simulation" of the status quo model, in which benefits are not taxed and the special aged exemption is present (and the guarantee is set at $1800). Because the income tax base is expanded in the present simulations, the

TABLE 12.2
Guarantee, Cost to the Nonaged, and High-Income Replacement Rate

Model	Guarantee ($)	High-Income Replacement Rate	Cost to the Nonaged ($ billions)
	Variable Guarantee Case		
Status quo	3,250	.43	36.0
Two-tier	2,700	.43	36.0
Double-decker	2,170	(.12)[a] .43	36.0
	Variable Replacement Rate Case		
Status quo	1,800	.51	36.0
Two-tier	1,800	.54	36.0
Double-decker	1,800	(.21)[a] .47	36.0
	Variable Cost Case		
Status quo	1,800	.43	30.9
Two-tier	1,800	.43	30.0
Double-decker	1,800	(.17)[a] .43	34.3

[a] Number in parentheses indicates the portion of the high-income replacement rate accounted for by earnings-related benefits.

parameter values in the status quo model diverge from their benchmark levels when they are allowed to vary.

In the variable guarantee case, the status quo and two-tier models have much larger guarantees than the double-decker; the income tests in the former models reduce costs, and the savings are used to raise the guarantees. Since the non-earnings-related benefit program in the status quo model has a 100% tax rate on unearned income as compared with only a 50% tax rate in the two-tier model, the cost savings resulting from the income test are larger in the status quo, and so, therefore, is the guarantee.

The advantage to the poor of income testing in this case appears to be quite large, judging from the differences in guarantees. However, the tax rates as well as the guarantees affect the economic well-being of the poor. As shown below, the differences in average incomes of the poor are much smaller than the differences in guarantees.

In the variable replacement rate case, income testing leads to larger values of the high-income replacement rate, since the cost savings are used to raise earnings-related benefits. One might expect the high-income replacement rate to be largest in the status quo model, which has the highest tax rates in the non-earnings-related benefit program and therefore the lowest outlay for this program. Because of the welfare features of OASI, however, earnings-related benefits for primary earners in the upper-income groups must be lower than in the two-tier model. In the double-decker model, the payment of the pension to all of the aged leaves a low budget for earnings-related benefits, so that the high-income replacement rate is smaller than in either of the other models. The portion of the high-income replacement rate accounted for by earnings-related benefits in the double-decker model is .21 in this case.

In the variable cost case, income testing leads to lower costs to the nonaged. The two-tier model at $30 billion is $4.3 billion cheaper than the double-decker. The status quo model is somewhat more expensive than the two-tier, despite the higher tax rate on unearned income in its non-earnings-related benefit program, because of the welfare features of OASI.

Budget Costs and Tax Rate Changes

Table 12.3 shows budget costs separately for earnings-related and non-earnings-related benefits along with percentage changes in income and payroll tax rates. Note that the relative budget costs of earnings-

TABLE 12.3
Budget Costs and Percentage Changes in Tax Rates

Model	Budget Costs ($ billions)		Percentage Changes in Tax Rates	
	Earnings-Related Benefits	Non-earnings-Related Benefits	Payroll Tax Rates	Income Tax Rates
Variable Guarantee Case				
Status quo	34.8	9.7	0	0
Two-tier	30.1	15.6	−8	5
Double-decker	8.2	41.2	−47	30
Variable Replacement Rate Case				
Status quo	41.2	2.0	11	−7
Two-tier	38.2	5.7	6	−4
Double-decker	14.1	34.2	−37	23
Variable Cost Case				
Status quo	34.8	2.2	0	−6
Two-tier	30.1	6.7	−8	−2
Double-decker	11.8	34.2	−41	24

NOTE: Tax rate changes are expressed relative to the rates in the benchmark simulation of the status quo model rather than actual 1972 rates.

related and non-earnings-related benefits vary substantially from one model to another. Vis-à-vis the status quo model, the share of total budget cost accounted for by earnings-related benefits declines in the two-tier model; consequently, the two-tier model depends less heavily on payroll taxes. This is one of the advantages of the two-tier model cited by its proponents. The double-decker model shifts the balance even more; non-earnings-related benefits in that model are 2.5 to 5 times as large as earnings-related benefits, which implies substantial decreases in payroll tax rates and comparable increases in income tax rates. Note that in the variable guarantee and variable replacement rate cases, in which cost to the nonaged is constant, the double-decker model has larger total budget costs than the other models; this is because the non-aged bear a smaller proportion of total income taxes than of total payroll taxes.[16] As a result, the guarantee and high-income replacement rate in

[16]The proportions in 1972 were .91 for income taxes and .97 for payroll taxes. With the expansion of the income tax base for the aged in the simulations, the proportion of income taxes paid by the nonaged falls to about .85. The figure for actual income taxes in 1972 is based on data in U.S. Department of the Treasury (1974, pp. 22, 205). The figure for payroll taxes is based on data obtained from the Office of Research and Statistics of the Social Security Administration and data in U.S. Department of Health, Education, and Welfare (1974, pp. 54–56).

the double-decker are larger than if this model had a total budget cost close to those of the others.

Income Distribution

Table 12.4 shows mean adjusted income[17] of aged individuals by quintile, with the top and bottom quintiles split into deciles.[18]

VARIABLE GUARANTEE CASE

In the variable guarantee case, consider first the different distributional effects of the status quo and two-tier models. In the top three income groups, average incomes are higher in the status quo model, even though the high-income replacement rate is constant. This reflects the welfare features of OASI, which work to the advantage of people other than the group for whom the high-income replacement rate is computed—primary earners (men) in the top quintile.

In the two-tier model, the absence of any welfare features in the top-tier program allows a higher budget for non-earnings-related benefits than in the status quo model (See Table 12.3). The groups that benefit from this, however, are the second and third quintiles rather than those at the bottom of the income distribution; the relatively low tax rate on unearned income in the two-tier model brings about higher benefits in the second and third quintiles but requires a lower guarantee than in the status quo. Though the guarantee is $550 lower in the two-tier model (see Table 12.2), the first decile has an average income in that model only $180 less than in the status quo, and the second decile has the same amount in both models; this is because the effect of the lower guarantee is mitigated by the lower tax rate on unearned income.

Now compare the status quo and two-tier models with the double-decker in the variable guarantee case. Because of the higher guarantees in the models with income tests, the lowest two deciles have higher average incomes in these models than in the double-decker. However, as in the comparison between the status quo and two-tier models, the differences in incomes are less than the differences in guarantees. This is

[17]The computation of adjusted income is described in the section on data and methodology.

[18]The first quintile is the lowest fifth of the aged when they are ranked by income, the second quintile is the next lowest, and so on. Likewise, the first decile is the lowest tenth, etc.

People are assigned to the same quintile or decile in all simulations. This is done for computational convenience, despite the fact that the ranking by income actually changes somewhat from one simulation to another.

TABLE 12.4
Mean Adjusted Income of Aged Individuals by Quintile ($)

	Status Quo Model	Two-Tier Model	Double-Decker Model
Variable Guarantee Case			
First decile	3,140	2,960	2,770
Second decile	3,680	3,680	3,290
Second quintile	4,090	4,440	4,160
Third quintile	5,350	5,560	5,550
Fourth quintile	7,550	7,400	7,650
Ninth decile	10,720	10,450	10,710
Tenth decile	20,680	20,280	19,550
Variable Replacement Rate Case			
First decile	1,900	2,090	2,530
Second decile	2,650	2,920	3,090
Second quintile	3,930	3,990	4,120
Third quintile	5,670	5,500	5,580
Fourth quintile	7,980	7,810	7,720
Ninth decile	11,200	11,030	10,810
Tenth decile	21,410	21,210	19,920
Variable Cost Case			
First decile	1,820	2,020	2,490
Second decile	2,500	2,780	3,020
Second quintile	3,580	3,680	4,000
Third quintile	5,260	5,070	5,440
Fourth quintile	7,550	7,280	7,580
Ninth decile	10,790	10,510	10,680
Tenth decile	20,990	20,640	19,780

NOTE: The top and bottom quintiles are split into deciles.

partly because the flat-rate pension in the double-decker model is not reduced by tax rates on other income, and partly because all of the aged poor receive a pension. In the status quo and two-tier models, in contrast, the participation rates in the non-earnings-related benefit programs arising from the Warlick model are 60–75%.

The relatively low average incomes of the poor in the double-decker model have counterparts in generally higher incomes in the middle and upper-middle classes, reflecting the fact that the flat-rate pension is received by all of the aged. The tenth decile, however, has a markedly lower average income in the double-decker model than in the others, because of the large income tax increase.

Our general conclusion from these comparisons: In the variable guarantee case, the models which use income testing—the status quo and the two-tier—transfer more income to the poorest groups than the model without an income test—the double-decker; income testing in this case makes possible a higher guarantee.

VARIABLE REPLACEMENT RATE CASE

Now consider the status quo and two-tier models in the variable replacement rate case. With the guarantee constant, the low-income groups have higher average incomes in the two-tier model because of the lower tax rate on unearned income in the bottom-tier program. The higher budget for non-earnings-related benefits in the two-tier model requires a lower outlay for earnings-related benefits, which is reflected in lower incomes for the upper-income groups.

When the status quo and two-tier models are compared with the double-decker in the variable replacement rate case, the effects of income testing are apparent. The absence of an income test in the double-decker model leads to higher incomes for the poor, especially in the lowest decile, where the average income level is $440 greater than in the two-tier model and $630 greater than in the status quo. The reason for the differences is the double effect of the income test: the reduction of benefits for those with outside income and the discouragement of many people from participating in the bottom-tier program. (It should be noted, however, that in the comparison between the two-tier and double-decker models, a poor person or couple that participates in the income-tested benefit program under the two-tier model and has no outside income receives a larger total benefit in that model than in the double-decker; although there is a 50% tax rate on earnings-related benefits in the two-tier model, these benefits are more than twice as large in that model as in the double-decker—as shown in Table 12.2, the replacement rate attributable to earnings-related benefits is .54 in the two-tier model and .21 in the double-decker.) In the upper end of the income distribution, incomes are correspondingly lower in the double-decker model than in the other two.

VARIABLE COST CASE

In the variable cost case, the two-tier model transfers more to the poor than does the status quo, and the double-decker transfers more than either of the other two; the reasons for this are the same as in the variable replacement rate case, in which the guarantee is also constant. For the wealthier groups, average incomes are higher in the status quo model than in the two-tier, because of the welfare features of OASI and the constant high-income replacement rate. Between the two-tier and double-decker models, incomes are larger in the double-decker up through the ninth decile, reflecting the difference in cost to the nonaged between the two models of $4.3 billion (see Table 12.2). As in the other two cases, the top decile in the double-decker model shows the effect of a large income tax increase.

Our conclusion from the variable replacement rate and variable cost cases: When the guarantee is held constant, the model which does not have an income test—the double-decker—transfers more income to the poorest groups than the status quo and two-tier models. The income tests in the non-earnings-related benefit programs in the latter models discourage some people from participating and reduce benefits for those that do.

Distributional Results by Marital Status

Behind the changes in aggregate income distribution among the three models, the changes for different demographic groups vary. An important demographic characteristic in this regard is marital status, since provisions that differentiate between married and single people are different in different models. Table 12.5 presents the mean adjusted incomes of married individuals, widows, and widowers in the same income classes as in Table 12.4, for the variable cost case. We examine the breakdown for this case because the task is simpler with the guarantee and high-income replacement rate constant.[19]

Between the status quo and two-tier models, the income changes in the lowest three income classes do not differ substantially by marital status. From the third quintile up through the tenth decile, however, there are large differences. Vis-à-vis the status quo model, average incomes of married persons in these groups fall by $340 to $460 in the two-tier model because of the absence of spouse benefits. The changes for widows are negligible; both models have survivors' benefits. For widowers, however, there are noticeable increases in the fourth quintile and ninth decile. We cannot give more than a speculative explanation for this without more detailed examination, which we have not done.

Between the two-tier and double-decker models, the differences in income changes for married persons and surviving spouses in the upper-income groups arise because the flat-rate pension in the double-

[19]In the other two cases, the explanation of differences in income changes by marital status is more involved; there are differences in either the guarantee or the high-income replacement rate as well as in provisions that differentiate between married and single people. In the variable replacement rate case, the differences in income changes by marital status are present from the lower-middle-income classes up through the highest; in the variable guarantee case, they are present throughout the income distribution.

TABLE 12.5
Mean Adjusted Incomes of Married Persons, Widows, and Widowers by Quintile—
Variable Cost Case ($)

	Status Quo Model		Two-Tier Model		Double-Decker Model
	Married Persons				
First decile	1,770	(160)	1,930	(470)	2,400
Second decile	2,680	(280)	2,960	(190)	3,150
Second quintile	3,680	(70)	3,750	(310)	4,060
Third quintile	5,310	(−340)	4,970	(430)	5,400
Fourth quintile	7,530	(−430)	7,100	(370)	7,470
Ninth decile	10,770	(−420)	10,350	(240)	10,590
Tenth decile	21,410	(−460)	20,950	(−840)	20,110
	Widows				
First decile	1,830	(220)	2,050	(470)	2,520
Second decile	2,430	(290)	2,720	(270)	2,990
Second quintile	3,480	(130)	3,610	(310)	3,920
Third quintile	5,220	(10)	5,230	(250)	5,480
Fourth quintile	7,620	(−20)	7,600	(140)	7,740
Ninth decile	10,900	(20)	10,920	(−20)	10,900
Tenth decile	19,270	(−30)	19,240	(−910)	18,330
	Widowers				
First decile	1,730	(170)	1,900	(470)	2,370
Second decile	2,420	(280)	2,700	(180)	2,880
Second quintile	3,550	(140)	3,690	(290)	3,980
Third quintile	5,190	(30)	5,220	(240)	5,460
Fourth quintile	7,530	(150)	7,680	(80)	7,760
Ninth decile	10,820	(170)	10,990	(−100)	10,890
Tenth decile	21,600	(0)	21,600	(−1,290)	20,310

NOTES: People are assigned to the same income classes as in Table 12.4. Figures in parentheses are differences between figures in adjacent columns.

decker model is increased by 50% for couples. This increase affects married couples in the lower-income groups as well, but so does the 50% increase in the guarantee in the two-tier model; hence the insignificant differences in income changes between married persons and survivors in these income classes.

Some Qualifications

In this section we discuss some qualifications to our simulation results.

The Problem of Participation in SSI

Some analysts of the social security system have stated that the expansion of the SSI program that would occur with a switch to a two-tier system might bring about an increase in the participation rate. The reason, it is argued, is that since many middle-income aged would become eligible for benefits (because of the reduction of the tax rate on unearned income), SSI would no longer be viewed as only a poor people's program, and the stigma from participating would therefore decline or disappear. This calls into question our use of the Warlick model to predict participation rates, because the model applies to the current system, in which the SSI program is fairly small.

We have therefore carried out additional simulations of the two-tier model under the assumption of full participation in the bottom-tier program (SSI). The income distribution results from these simulations are presented in Table 12.6; the results for the two-tier model with partial participation and for the double-decker model are reproduced from Table 12.4, in parentheses for comparison. We first discuss the changes within the two-tier model brought about by full participation, and then point out how these changes affect the comparisons between that model and the double-decker.

In the variable guarantee case, the transition to full participation requires a reduction in the guarantee to hold cost to the nonaged constant. The overall effect is that average incomes decline throughout the distribution, which is surprising given that cost to the nonaged is constant. The reason for this is that while the effect of the guarantee reduction ($470) is offset by the increase in participation, total intrafamily transfers to those eligible for SSI benefits decrease.[20] The slight declines in the upper-income groups are possible because some SSI beneficiaries live with wealthier relatives or friends.

In the variable replacement rate and variable cost cases, incomes in the lower groups rise with the transition to full participation, because the guarantee is constant. In the poorest decile, the increase exceeds $400 in both cases. In the upper-income groups, the higher income taxes required by the larger outlay for bottom-tier benefits cause slight de-

[20]The latter occurs because of the interaction of the participation rate model and the intrafamily transfer formula. Under this formula, the intrafamily transfer to an aged person is inversely related to his or her pretransfer income. In the present case, the decline in transfers to those who just begin to participate in SSI outweighs the increase in transfers to those already participating, whose pretransfer incomes fall because of the reduction in the guarantee. Total intrafamily transfers under full participation are about the same as in the double-decker model, in which all of the aged collect non-earnings-related benefits.

TABLE 12.6
Mean Adjusted Income of Aged Individuals by Quintile—The Two-Tier Model with
Full Participation in the Bottom-Tier Program ($)

	Two-Tier Model with Partial Participation	Two-Tier Model with Full Participation	Double-Decker Model
	Variable Guarantee Case		
First decile	(2,960)	2,870	(2,770)
Second decile	(3,680)	3,420	(3,290)
Second quintile	(4,440)	4,290	(4,160)
Third quintile	(5,560)	5,410	(5,550)
Fourth quintile	(7,400)	7,310	(7,650)
Ninth decile	(10,450)	10,430	(10,710)
Tenth decile	(20,280)	20,270	(19,550)
	Variable Replacement Rate Case		
First decile	(2,090)	2,500	(2,530)
Second decile	(2,920)	3,050	(3,090)
Second quintile	(3,990)	4,020	(4,120)
Third quintile	(5,500)	5,370	(5,580)
Fourth quintile	(7,810)	7,600	(7,720)
Ninth decile	(11,030)	10,800	(10,810)
Tenth decile	(21,210)	20,850	(19,920)
	Variable Cost Case		
First decile	(2,020)	2,460	(2,490)
Second decile	(2,780)	2,970	(3,020)
Second quintile	(3,680)	3,870	(4,000)
Third quintile	(5,070)	5,130	(5,440)
Fourth quintile	(7,280)	7,260	(7,580)
Ninth decile	(10,510)	10,470	(10,680)
Tenth decile	(20,640)	20,480	(19,780)

NOTE: Figures in parentheses are reproduced from Table 12.4.

clines in incomes. In the variable replacement rate case, this effect is strengthened by a fall in the high-income replacement rate from .54 to .50.

These changes substantially alter the comparisons between the two-tier and double-decker models. In the variable guarantee case, the average incomes of the lowest three groups are still greater in the two-tier model, but the differences are, at most, half as large as before (the guarantee in the two-tier model is now only $70 larger than in the double-decker). In the variable replacement rate and variable cost cases, the income differences in the lowest two deciles are now trivially small, and in the second quintile they are only slightly larger.

Retirement Test and Income Tax Provisions

In this section we present our conclusions from an examination of the sensitivity of the original simulation results to the choice of retirement test and income tax provisions. The sensitivity analysis is based on two sets of simulations. In each of these, the models have the same provisions as in the original simulations, except in one, the retirement test is eliminated; in the other, there is no expansion of the income tax base (benefits are not taxed and the special aged exemption is present).

In both of these sets of simulations, it is only in the variable guarantee case that the comparisons among the models differ significantly from those arising from the original simulations. In that case, as shown in Table 12.7, the guarantees are reduced, relative to their levels in the original simulations, in order to bring cost to the nonaged back down to the benchmark level after its initial increase.

Table 12.8 shows the income distribution results from the simulations without the retirement test and from those without the expanded income tax base. In both sets of modified simulations the lower income groups show declines in incomes relative to the original simulations that vary widely among the models, reflecting the differences in guarantee reductions. This changes our initial comparisons between the models that have income tests—the status quo and the two-tier—and the one that does not—the double-decker.

In the simulations without the retirement test, the income differences between the two types of models decline substantially in the lowest two income classes; in the first decile, no significant difference remains. There are two reasons for this: (*a*) The guarantees in the status quo and two-tier models exceed that in the double decker *by smaller amounts* than before; and (*b*) earnings-related benefits in the double-decker model

TABLE 12.7
Guarantees—Simulations Without the Retirement Test and Without the Expansion of the Income Tax Base, Variable Guarantee Case ($)

Model	Original Simulations	No Retirement Test	No Expansion of the Income Tax Base
Status quo	(3,250)	2,790	1,800[a]
Two-tier	(2,700)	2,440	1,880
Double-decker	(2,170)	1,990	920

NOTE: Figures in parentheses are reproduced from Table 12.2.
[a] This amount is from the benchmark simulation.

TABLE 12.8

Mean Adjusted Income of Aged Individuals by Quintile—Simulations Without the Retirement Test and Without the Expansion of the Income Tax Base, Variable Guarantee Case ($)

	Status Quo Model		Two-Tier Model		Double-Decker Model	
			No Retirement Test			
First decile	(3,140)	2,690	(2,960)	2,690	(2,770)	2,640
Second decile	(3,680)	3,250	(3,680)	3,420	(3,290)	3,160
Second quintile	(4,090)	3,840	(4,440)	4,200	(4,160)	4,090
Third quintile	(5,350)	5,330	(5,560)	5,420	(5,550)	5,520
Fourth quintile	(7,550)	7,700	(7,400)	7,490	(7,650)	7,680
Ninth decile	(10,720)	11,070	(10,450)	10,780	(10,710)	10,820
Tenth decile	(20,680)	21,250	(20,280)	20,830	(19,550)	19,810
			No Expansion of the Income Tax Base			
First decile	(3,140)	1,870	(2,960)	2,210	(2,770)	1,790
Second decile	(3,680)	2,560	(3,680)	3,000	(3,290)	2,410
Second quintile	(4,090)	3,740	(4,440)	3,960	(4,160)	3,790
Third quintile	(5,350)	5,590	(5,560)	5,430	(5,550)	5,560
Fourth quintile	(7,550)	8,070	(7,400)	7,780	(7,650)	8,030
Ninth decile	(10,720)	11,410	(10,450)	11,100	(10,710)	11,360
Tenth decile	(20,680)	21,820	(20,280)	21,400	(19,550)	21,290

NOTE: To facilitate comparison, figures from Table 12.4, which reflect inclusion of the retirement tests and expansion of the income tax base, are reproduced in parentheses. Figures for the status quo model without the expansion of the income tax base are from the benchmark simulation.

have been raised to hold the high-income replacement rate constant with a lower guarantee, although such benefits are still lower in the double-decker than the other models. This result seems to severely weaken our original conclusion that income testing leads to greater incomes for the poor in the variable guarantee case by making possible a higher guarantee. Specifically, the influences of the countervailing factors mentioned above—the failure of many of the aged poor to collect income-tested benefits for which they are eligible and the reduction of such benefits for those who claim them—are relatively stronger than in the original simulations, for the two reasons above. As explained below, however, the original conclusion still stands.

In the simulations without the expansion of the income tax base, the income differences between the status quo and double-decker models for the lowest two deciles are greatly reduced, the reasons being the same as for the simulations without the retirement test. Between the double-decker and two-tier models, however, the lowest two income classes have relatively larger incomes in the two-tier than before, since the guarantee in that model declines by a smaller amount than in the double-decker. These results further demonstrate that the benefit to the poor of income testing depends on other provisions in the models being compared, even though these provisions are the same in all of the models.

The changes in the retirement test and income tax provisions also affect the comparisons between the status quo and two-tier models. While the lowest decile had a higher average income in the status quo in the original simulations, the difference between the two models for this group is eliminated or reversed in the modified simulations. In the second decile, the original equality between the two models gives way to relatively high incomes under the two-tier model. These changes in the comparisons arise because of the greater declines in the guarantees in the status quo model.

The Effect of Income Tax versus Payroll Tax Financing of Benefits

In interpreting the simulation results presented in this section (as well as other sections), it is important to remember that in the cases where cost to the nonaged is held constant, the total budget cost of the double-decker model is substantially larger than those of the other models because, as explained above, a relatively large proportion of total benefits in the double-decker is financed with income tax revenues. The impact of this on our comparisons of the average incomes of the poor between the double-decker and the other two models is felt primarily in the variable guarantee case. In that case, the guarantee in the double-decker is substantially larger than it would be if the total budget cost of that model were close to the costs of the others.

The effect of this is that our simulation results understate the benefit to the poor of income testing by itself in the variable guarantee case. Therefore, our original conclusion that income testing raises the average incomes of the poor in the variable guarantee case still stands, despite the simulation results presented in this section.

Isolating the Effects of the Welfare Features of OASI

The criticism of the current OASI benefit structure by proponents of the two-tier system raises the question, What differences between the distributional impacts of the status quo and two-tier models are attributable to the welfare features of OASI alone? In order to provide an answer, this section examines the results of simulations of the status quo model with the tax rate on unearned income in the non-earnings-related benefit program reduced to 50%. With this change, the non-earnings-related benefit programs in the two models are the same.

Table 12.9 presents the distributional results of the simulations of the modified status quo model, along with the original results for both the status quo and two-tier models. In the variable guarantee case, the reduction of the tax rate on unearned income in the status quo model brings about higher incomes in the second and third quintiles, but requires a reduction in the guarantee from $3250 to $2330, so that incomes

TABLE 12.9
Mean Adjusted Income of Aged Individuals by Quintile—The Status Quo Model with a 50% Tax Rate on Unearned Income in the Bottom-Tier Program ($)

	Original Status Quo Model (100% Tax Rate on Unearned Income)	Modified Status Quo Model (50% Tax Rate on Unearned Income)	Two-Tier Model
Variable Guarantee Case			
First decile	(3,140)	2,710	(2,960)
Second decile	(3,680)	3,510	(3,680)
Second quintile	(4,090)	4,280	(4,440)
Third quintile	(5,350)	5,520	(5,560)
Fourth quintile	(7,550)	7,560	(7,400)
Ninth decile	(10,720)	10,730	(10,450)
Tenth decile	(20,680)	20,680	(20,280)
Variable Replacement Rate Case			
First decile	(1,900)	2,220	(2,090)
Second decile	(2,650)	3,070	(2,920)
Second quintile	(3,930)	4,030	(3,990)
Third quintile	(5,670)	5,550	(5,500)
Fourth quintile	(7,980)	7,830	(7,810)
Ninth decile	(11,200)	11,030	(11,030)
Tenth decile	(21,410)	21,150	(21,210)
Variable Cost Case			
First decile	(1,820)	2,180	(2,020)
Second decile	(2,500)	3,000	(2,780)
Second quintile	(3,580)	3,870	(3,680)
Third quintile	(5,260)	5,310	(5,070)
Fourth quintile	(7,550)	7,550	(7,280)
Ninth decile	(10,790)	10,760	(10,510)
Tenth decile	(20,990)	20,860	(20,640)

NOTE: Figures in parentheses are reproduced from Table 12.4.

decline in the lowest two deciles. Between the modified status quo and the two-tier models, the lowest three groups have higher incomes in the two-tier, since that model has a higher guarantee ($2700) than the modified status quo and the same tax rates. Note how this differs from the comparison between the original status quo model and the two-tier.

The two-tier model transfers more income to the poor in the variable guarantee case than does the modified status quo; the absence of welfare features in its earnings-related benefit program reduces cost and therefore allows a larger outlay for non-earnings-related benefits, which in turn leads to a higher guarantee than in the modified status quo, since the tax rates in the two models are the same.

In the variable replacement rate and variable cost cases, the reduction of the tax rate on unearned income in the status quo model raises the incomes of the lower groups because the guarantee is constant. A slight income tax increase affects the upper-income groups in both cases, and this is reinforced in the variable replacement rate case by a reduction in earnings-related benefits. Vis-à-vis the two-tier model, the lowest three groups in both cases had lower average incomes in the original status quo model, but their incomes are higher in the modified status quo.[21]

The modified status quo model transfers more income to the poor in the variable replacement rate and variable cost cases than does the two-tier; as in the variable guarantee case, the lower-income groups have higher earnings-related benefits in the modified status quo model because of the welfare features of OASI, but in the variable replacement rate and variable cost cases, the guarantees as well as the tax rates in the two models are the same.

Conclusion

In this paper we have estimated through microsimulation the relative costs and distributional impacts of models of our current old-age income support system and two alternatives. Our principal focus has been on the question of who benefits from income testing. Our main findings are these:

---

[21]It is readily noticed in the variable replacement rate case that the total of the income figures in the modified status quo model is somewhat greater than in the two-tier model; married couples have a larger share of total benefits in the status quo model, and couples' incomes are attributed to both spouses. Because of economies of scale, the family-size adjustment only partially offsets the effects of this on the total of the income figures.

1. One cannot predict which groups in the aged population will benefit from income testing without specifying which parameters are to be held constant in comparing alternative old-age income support programs. Although income testing leads to greater target efficiency, it does not necessarily work to the advantage of the poor.

2. In the variable guarantee case, income testing leads to higher incomes for the poor; when the guarantee is held constant, however, the models with income tests provide less income for the poor than the one without, and bring about higher incomes for either the upper-middle income groups or the nonaged. (One must be cautious in attributing the differences in distributional impacts to differences in benefit levels; it must be taken into account that overall tax payments for the aged are much larger in the double-decker model than in the others. This is especially true in the top decile, where differences in income tax payments between the double-decker and the other two models dominate differences in benefit levels in all three cases.)

3. The comparisons between the two-tier and double-decker models depend crucially upon the participation rate in the bottom-tier program in the two-tier model—the expanded SSI program. In the original simulations, in which there was only partial participation in SSI, the lowest income groups experienced substantial differences in income between the two models in all three cases. In the simulations with full participation in SSI, however, the differences between the models in average income for these groups are trivially small in the cases where the guarantee is constant, and only slightly larger in the variable guarantee case.

4. The relative incomes of the poor under the models with income tests and the one without depend on the retirement test and income tax provisions in the variable guarantee case. The conclusion still stands, however, that income testing raises the average incomes of the poor in the variable guarantee case.

5. One cannot make a general statement about the relative incomes of the poor under the unmodified status quo and two-tier models in the variable guarantee case. In the cases where the guarantee is constant, though, it is generally true that the two-tier model provides more income for the poor than does the unmodified status quo, because the non-earnings-related benefit program in the two-tier model has a lower tax rate on unearned income.

6. In the comparison between the two-tier model and the status quo variant with an identical non-earnings-related benefit program, the welfare features of OASI in the status quo model lead to lower average incomes for the poor in the variable guarantee case, but higher incomes for the poor in the cases where the guarantee is constant.

The common thread in these findings is that it is difficult to make assertions about the relative distributional impacts of alternative income support programs for the aged—and, in particular, about the distributional effects of income testing—that are *generally* valid. The relative distributional impacts of alternative programs depend on what is held constant in comparing them; one's answer to the question of what *should* be held constant depends on a political or value judgment.

Appendix: Basic Provisions of the Supplemental Security Income Program

Under the federal SSI program, benefits are available to the aged (65 or over), blind, disabled, and poor. Eligibility is restricted to those whose "countable" assets are less than $1500 (individuals) or $2500 (couples). Excluded from countable assets are a home; personal effects and household goods of $1500 or less; an automobile of $1200 or less; and life insurance with face value of $1500 or less. This is the "asset test." An eligible person or couple with no income from other sources receives a benefit equal to the "guarantee," which is adjusted annually for inflation. In 1978, the guarantees for individuals and couples were $2270 and $3410; these amounts are approximately 75% and 90% of the poverty lines for individuals and couples, respectively. The guarantees are reduced by one-third for those living in other people's households. Benefit payments are reduced by 50% of wage, salary, and self-employment income—"earned income"—above $780 per year. For other income—"unearned income"—the benefit reduction rate is 100% and the disregarded amount, or "disregard," is $240 annually. This is the "income test." The benefit reduction rates are sometimes referred to as "tax rates," because in reducing the net gain from an increase in income from other sources, they have the same effect. Most states supplement the federal payments, in widely varying amounts. (For more details on the federal provisions, see *Social Security Bulletin, Annual Statistical Supplement, 1975,* 1977, pp. 35–40.)

Discussion

ALICIA H. MUNNELL

The Berry, Garfinkel, and Munts paper explores the relative impact of alternative income support systems on the income distribution of the aged population and between the aged and nonaged. Specifically, the authors are concerned about the distributional effects of income testing. Their overall conclusion is that income testing does not necessarily lead to higher incomes for the low-income aged.

While I found their paper extremely interesting and feel that simulations of this type are an essential step in evaluating alternative proposals, I do not think that their work supports their conclusions. The authors emphasize the fact that the relative distributional effects are very sensitive to the choice of parameters held constant in the comparison. However, choosing which parameter to hold constant is equivalent to making an assumption of how to redistribute the monies saved by income testing. When these funds are used to raise the basic guarantee in the non-earnings-related portion of the scheme, the low-income aged gain from income testing. Not surprisingly, when these funds are used to raise the earnings-related benefits or to reduce the overall level of taxation for both the aged and nonaged population, the position of the low-income poor is not improved by income testing. Thus the paper presents evidence on how the low-income elderly would fare under three alternative assumptions of how the funds saved by income testing

481

welfare benefits are distributed. The paper should not be interpreted as an evaluation of the distributional effects of income testing per se. Let me try to clarify this point by briefly summarizing the paper.

The authors examine several alternative income support programs for the aged, some of which have been put forth by those critical of the welfare features of social security. Critics have argued that the minimum benefit and progressive structure of OASI are inefficient devices for aiding the poor. Furthermore, as the system matures, its progressive features will reduce the rate of return on contributions for middle- and high-income workers, which might substantially undermine support for the program. Dependents' benefits, like the progressive features, suffer from lack of target-efficiency as well as create serious inequities.

These alleged deficiencies in the current program have led some critics to advocate a two-tier system with a proportional wage-related OASI benefit structure augmented by an expanded SSI program. This two-tier approach has several advantages. First, it would ensure that a greater proportion of benefits intended for the poor would actually go to the poor. Second, a larger portion of income support for the aged poor would be financed through the progressive income tax. Third, a direct relationship between contributions and benefits would increase support for the program. Finally, a proportional earnings-related system would permit people to opt out of the program.

Some of those concerned with the stigmatizing effects of means-tested programs have suggested a universal pension for all aged as an alternative to SSI. Since everyone would be interested in the basic guarantee under such a scheme, proponents argue that benefits would be more generous than under a program targeted at the poor. Moreover, a universal pension would avoid the adverse incentive effects caused by the high implicit tax rates in SSI. Finally, the problem of low participation in SSI because of the stigma or general inconvenience of applying for benefits would be eliminated, since the universal pension would automatically be paid to all aged.

In an attempt to evaluate the merits of alternative approaches, the authors have simulated the distributional effects of three prototype plans (see Table 12.10). These include (a) a modified version of the current system where earnings-related benefits are taxable and the retirement test is somewhat less stringent (SQ); (b) a two-tier system consisting of a proportional earnings-related benefit program and a welfare program smaller than SSI (TT); and (c) a double-decker system consisting of a proportional earnings-related benefit program as in TT but with a universal flat-rate pension program instead of the means-tested SSI program (DD).

TABLE 12.10

Characteristics of Simulated Income Support Systems for the Aged

	Status Quo (SQ)	Two-Tier (TT)	Double-Decker (DD)
Non-earnings-related benefits			
Guarantee			
Individual	$1,800	$1,800	$1,800
Couple	$2,700	$2,700	$2,700
Income test			
Earned	$780 disregard 50% tax	$780 disregard 50% tax	None
Unearned	No disregard 100% tax	No disregard 50% tax	None
Reductions	None	None	None
Tax treatment	Not taxable	Not taxable	Taxable
Earnings-related benefits			
Basic Structure	OASI as of 1977	Proportional to indexed earnings	Proportional to indexed earnings
Additional benefits			
Spouse	50%	None	None
Surviving spouse	100%	100%	100%
Divorced spouse	50%	None	None
Retirement test	$2,930 disregard 50% tax	$2,930 disregard 50% tax	$2,930 disregard 50% tax
Tax treatment	Taxable and no special aged exemption	Taxable and no special aged exemption	Taxable and no special aged exemption

On the basis of 1972 data from the CPS/IRA/SSA exact match data file, the authors simulate the impact of implementing each of these schemes. In order to make the comparisons meaningful, certain parameters must be held constant across programs. The authors elected three alternatives: (a) the guarantee for an individual in the bottom-tier benefit program; (b) the high-income replacement rate (HIRR), which is the replacement rate for the representative high earner; and (c) the cost to the nonaged, which is the amount of the transfer from the nonaged to the aged.

Since establishing the value for any two of these three parameters predetermines a value for the third, only two parameters can be held constant at one time. Thus, the authors present three sets of comparisons: with cost and HIRR constant, with cost and guarantee constant, and with guarantee and HIRR constant.

Table 12.4 in the Berry, Garfinkel, and Munts paper summarizes the major results. Where cost and HIRR are constant, the revenues gained from taxing benefits and eliminating the additional deduction are used to raise the guarantee, and income is redistributed to the aged poor. In this set of simulations, the two-tier system yields the highest mean adjusted income for the low-income groups because means testing permits a considerably higher guarantee than all the other systems except SQ; also, the TT system has only a 50% tax rate on social security benefits whereas SQ has a 100% rate. Moreover, the TT system results in a 8% reduction in payroll tax rates and a 5% increase in income tax rates, which benefits the poor. The DD system involves a dramatic reapportioning of the two taxes—a 47% reduction in payroll taxes offset by a 30% increase in income tax rates.

In the second set of simulations, the authors conclude that income-testing the bottom-tier benefits actually reduces the incomes of the aged poor. This conclusion is based on the fact that the DD system yields higher mean adjusted income for the low-income aged. Since the guarantee is held constant for all programs, the ultimate income distribution hinges on the income testing. The double effect of the reduction of benefits for those with outside income and the low participation rate for potential beneficiaries in the bottom tier is the reason for the poor performance of the two-tier system.

The authors cite the results of the third set of simulations as corroborative evidence that income testing does not necessarily help the poor, since once again the mean adjusted income for the aged poor is higher under DD than under TT. This set of results must be interpreted with care, however, since the costs of the three programs differ substantially. DD costs 16% more than TT.

The remainder of the paper includes simulations with alternative assumptions such as elimination of the retirement test; no taxation of benefits; and lower guarantee. All these simulations reveal the same pattern as the original results—namely that income testing aids the poor when the cost and the HIRR are constant, but reduces the income of the low-income groups when the alternative sets of parameters are held constant.

In their overall conclusions, the authors put equal weights on the results of each of their three sets of simulations. Since low-income groups gain only when the funds released from income-testing welfare benefits are used to raise the guarantee and lose whenever these funds are used to raise wage-related benefits or to reduce overall taxes, the score is consistently 2 to 1 against income testing. On this basis, the authors conclude that income testing would not help the low-income aged.

My concern with this conclusion is that no one has proposed a two-tier system without a simultaneous expansion of SSI. Therefore, in my opinion the first set of simulations, where money saved from income testing is used to raise the bottom-tier benefits, is the only relevant basis for evaluating the alternative proposals—at least on academic grounds. In the real world, the other two sets of simulations may represent politically realistic outcomes and it may be useful to have documented that income testing per se will not help the poor unless the funds saved are used to raise bottom-tier benefits.

The two-tier approach may have substantial drawbacks, but it should not be rejected because it leads to lower incomes for the poor in two out of three sets of simulations. One of the main disadvantages seems to be the low participation of potential beneficiaries; perhaps alternative administrative procedures could be devised to ensure that benefits reach a greater proportion of eligible recipients. Moreover, SSI is a relatively new program and part of the low participation might be the result of potential beneficiaries' lack of familiarity with the various provisions of the program.

A second disadvantage of the two-tier approach, but one not mentioned in the paper, is the danger associated with a program dependent on annual congressional appropriations. Redistributon through social security financed by the earmarked payroll tax has traditionally been safeguarded from budgetary cutbacks, whereas a redistributive program financed by general revenues would be exposed annually to potential reductions. This significant risk is a compelling reason to consider the offsetting advantages of a two-tier approach very carefully.

On the other hand, arguments about the stigma associated with means-tested programs for the aged seem less persuasive. In the case of AFDC, it seems quite plausible that critics might view recipients as young able-bodied persons capable of working and therefore be critical of those on welfare. For the aged, blind, and disabled, however, society's attitude seems quite different. These groups are not expected to work, and it would be surprising if the public placed much emphasis on distinguishing between those who received a government check from the earnings-related social security program and those who received a government check from the means-tested SSI program. Since the recipient's view of his benefits in large measure mirrors that of society, it seems unlikely that means-tested programs for those not expected to provide for themselves by working would be as socially divisive as often suggested.

One last factor, not addressed in the paper, is how to deal with the fact that a proportional benefit formula will not yield equivalent rates of return once characteristics such as the lower life expectancy, etc., of low-income groups are taken into account. While it would be interesting to calculate precisely how much progressivity would be required to yield equal rates of return, I am not sure whether it would be socially desirable to maintain progressivity for this reason.

In short, I am not totally convinced that the two-tier approach is the way to go. However, my reluctance stems from these last considerations and not from the results of the simulations in the Berry, Garfinkel, and Munts paper.

Discussion

LAWRENCE H. THOMPSON*

This conference is focusing on differences between means-tested transfer programs and universal transfer programs. Transfer programs for the aged population represent a particularly appropriate focus for such a discussion. They deserve to receive more attention than they have so far either in the professional literature or at this conference. In these comments, I will first discuss my reasons for holding this view. I will then discuss briefly the paper by Berry, Garfinkel, and Munts, and close by posing some additional issues which I believe deserve further attention.

I believe there are at least five reasons for focusing a discussion of means-testing and universal programs on programs for the aged. First, there is—or at least there should be—far broader interest if the debate is about programs for the aged. Almost all of the aged in our society receive benefits from at least one government transfer program, and most nonaged people in our society expect one day to be the recipients of these transfers. In contrast, many do not expect to be recipients of the means-tested transfer programs currently available for the nonaged. A debate over whether the transfer programs for the aged should be

*The views expressed herein do not necessarily reflect the view of the U.S. Department of Health and Human Services or the Social Security Administration.

means-tested or universal is not an academic exercise; rather it is a debate over the form in which the vast majority of the population will receive transfer income.

Second, focusing on transfer programs for the aged population allows one to move more easily beyond the question of the initial distributional impact of each alternative to questions of the effect on program and labor force participation rates, social cohesiveness, and so forth. As a group, the aged are net recipients under our present income transfer system, and adjustments in the relative role of means-tested and universal programs for the aged will not alter that situation. Among the nonaged, however, the present transfer system creates both winners and losers, and adjustments in the mix of income transfer programs will alter the composition of the net winners and net losers.

While it is obviously important to discuss the effect of our transfer policy on the distribution of income, distributional questions are not the only important element of transfer policy. Yet a debate over broad alternative approaches to income transfer programs for the nonaged frequently involves greater attention to understanding the distributional effects than to understanding the other effects of the alternatives suggested.

It may be that concern over the distributional effects of an alternative income transfer strategy will invariably dominate any discussion in which people believe (whether correctly or not) that there is a significant change in the composition of winners and losers. If that is so, it may be easier to debate issues of basic program structure if the debate is focused on programs for the aged, the segment of the population where distributional changes will be the least significant.

Third, a movement either to greater reliance on means-tested programs or to greater reliance on universal programs represents a far more limited change for the aged than is generally realized, and a far more limited change for the aged than for the nonaged. While we may debate the merits of instituting a universal means-tested program for the nonaged, we already have one in place for the aged—the Supplemental Security Income program (SSI), which is essentially a negative income tax. In comparison to the kinds of changes being discussed at this conference, modifying SSI to assure all aged individuals a poverty-level income is a relatively modest change. It would cost an estimated $6 billion (in 1979 dollars) and involve essentially no change in the basic program structure.

Many proponents of universal income transfer programs favor a double-decker system for social security, under which there is a universal benefit paid to everyone and a supplementary benefit paid in proportion to earnings in employment covered by social security. It is possible to design such a system for this country which, if introduced, would involve surprisingly little modification in the structure of social security benefits.

At present, social security benefits are computed by applying a three-step formula: For workers turning 62, becoming disabled, or dying in 1979, the formula was 90% of the first $180 of average indexed earnings, plus 32% of average indexed earnings between $180 per month and $1085 a month, plus 15% of the remainder. That formula could be rewritten so that it provided a $162 flat grant to everyone eligible for social security plus 32% of average earnings in excess of $180. For all people insured for social security, except those very intermittent workers whose average indexed monthly earnings are less than $180, the rewriting of the formula in this way produces virtually the same monthly social security benefits as the present formula does.

Although it can have some very major implications for the way in which social security is financed, converting from our present social security system to a double-decker system like that outlined above represents a fairly modest change in the structure of social security benefits. Some 95% of the men now turning 65 are insured for social security benefits and a similar fraction of the women now turning 65 are insured either for worker benefits or for spouse benefits. Thus, under a double-decker, a small fraction of the population now turning 65 would get first-deck benefits, though now they are not eligible for social security, and another small fraction who are now eligible for social security but who because of very intermittent attachment to employment covered by social security have average monthly earnings of less than $180 would get more. However, for the great bulk of social security recipients, benefits under the new double-decker system would be very similar to those received under the present system.

It is possible to design a double-decker system which will shift a significant portion of the current responsibilities of the means-tested SSI program to the non-means-tested social security program with only a modest increase in total transfer costs. For example, a recent HEW report, *Social Security and the Changing Roles of Men and Women* (1979), examined a double-decker which incorporated a $122 universal flat grant and a second-deck benefit equal to 30% of average indexed earnings. The long-range cost of the double-decker alternative was estimated to exceed the total cost of the present system by roughly one-half of 1% of taxable payroll, an increase of only 4% over the projected cost of the present system. It was estimated further that the double-decker would reduce 1984 SSI expenditures from $6.7 billion to $3.9 billion. In effect, about 40% of the increase in social security cost was offset by reductions in expenditures in the SSI program. Another double-decker model was prepared for the Advisory Council on Social Security (U.S. Department of Health, Education, and Welfare, 1978c). It featured a first-deck benefit of $200 for an individual and $300 for a couple, and a second-deck benefit equal to 24% of average earnings. It was estimated that this would increase total costs by only one-tenth of 1% of payroll, and replace almost 90% of the total SSI benefits otherwise payable in 1984.

The fourth reason for focusing on the aged is that certain concerns involving the treatment of women under social security, the lack of universal coverage, and the financing of the program can be addressed more easily in the context of either a double-decker system or a two-tier system than they can in the context of the present income transfer system for the aged. Both the issues of concern to women's groups and some of the problems which arise as a result of the lack of universal coverage can be addressed fairly adequately by making the portion of the social security benefit which is financed by the payroll tax proportional to earnings, as is done with the second deck in a double-decker or as is done with the social security portion of the two-tier approach.

There is also a great deal of concern about the social security payroll tax increases scheduled for 1981 and the additional increases scheduled to occur in 1985 and 1990. If these increases are to be avoided, and if the present scheduled benefit payments are to be met without significant reductions, then there will have to be an introduction of general revenue financing of some portion of present social security benefit payments. Either the double-decker or the two-tier model can be a way to increase the use of general revenues for supporting the incomes of the aged. Either alternative involves greater reliance on the general revenues for financing the adequacy elements of our income transfer system, either through general revenue financing of the universal first deck of the double-decker or through general revenue financing of the enlarged means-tested program implicit in the two-tier model.

Moreover, we see increasing concern among high earners about the return that they receive under social security on their payroll tax payments. Either the two-tier or the double-decker models will produce a higher return on payroll tax payments for high earners, and either may therefore address their concern. As discussed above, either change also involves greater use of general revenues, however. Thus, high earners who are from high-income households may actually end up paying a greater fraction of the total transfer cost than they now do.

It is interesting that for a variety of reasons, including those I have just mentioned, one of the two large groups which represent the elderly, the American Association of Retired Persons, has recently endorsed a gradual movement toward the two-tier model.

A fifth reason for focusing on the aged is that it allows us to discuss the advantages and disadvantages of a means test as it is applied in the SSI program rather than as it is currently applied in the AFDC or Food Stamp program. This may reveal to us that some of the objections to means testing are to means testing as currently performed in specific programs rather than to means testing per se.

There has been great concern at this conference about the stigmatizing aspects of the current welfare system for the nonaged. But SSI was created, in part, to reduce the stigma on the aged. For instance, there are no lien laws under SSI; recipients of SSI are not, in effect, mortgaging their property in order to pay back any assistance they receive. There are liberal asset exclusions. People are no longer asked about the value of their houses and, at least compared to the AFDC program, most other assets are treated more liberally. Administrative responsibility for the program was lodged with the Social Security Administration, in part, to allow those aged in need of assistance to deal with the same agency that administered the social insurance program.

Earlier in this conference one participant observed that we rarely advertised the availability of our welfare program and that this policy was a sign of society's intention to stigmatize recipients. Yet, with SSI, we do advertise its availability. We advertise it in a way designed to reduce stigma and to encourage people to participate in the program.

I believe that SSI is less stigmatizing than the programs it replaced and that it could be made even less stigmatizing through elimination of the one-third reduction for living in another's household and through further liberalizations in the liquid asset test and the treatment of household goods. The real question which we should face at this conference is, If SSI is less stigmatizing than other welfare programs are, and if minor changes could make it even less stigmatizing than it now is, is it still objectionable? And if it is not objectionable, is our objection to the AFDC program inherent in the structure of AFDC or is it a function of the way it is currently administered?

Berry, Garfinkel, and Munts present an interesting analysis of some of the cost and distributional effects of making major changes in income support programs for the elderly. They examine the effect of a two-tier model, a double-decker model, and modest modifications in our present structure on three variables—the total cost to the nonaged of income transfers to the aged, the incomes of the lower-income aged, and the earnings replacement offered higher-wage earners.

Given the variety of the indicators they were looking at, it is not surprising that their results show no one structural approach to be unambiguously superior to the others. It is interesting to note, however, that when the two structural approaches were constrained to perform equally well on two of the three indicators, the double-decker approach and the two-tier approach tended to perform better on the third indicator than did the present system. This result, as well as the entire Berry, Garfinkel, and Munts analysis, suggested several questions, which I would hope could be addressed more fully in the future. I shall close by noting one particular issue involving the double-decker which allows me to sketch briefly some of these questions.

Most proponents of a double-decker model assume that the first deck will be financed from the general revenues and the second deck will be financed from payroll taxes, and that assumption underlies my earlier discussion of this approach. For instance, many of my statements about the double-decker, such as its ability to address the concerns involving the treatment of women, are true only if the double-decker is so financed.

Many of the opponents of the double-decker oppose it precisely because the first deck is to be financed entirely from the general fund. They believe that payroll tax financing of all or a substantial fraction of social security benefits is necessary to guarantee that social security benefits are not subjected to a means test by a future Congress. Essentially, their argument is that workers can see regular deductions being made from their paychecks over their working lifetimes in order to finance the social security program, that the workers expect that by making these payments they are earning a right to receive their own social security benefits when they reach retirement age, and that, as a result, imposition of a means test at some future date would be politically impossible.

Many proponents of the double-decker reject this scenario. They argue that social security is now nearly universal and that its very universality provides adequate protection against means testing. Thus, they view the structure of the program and its method of finance as independent issues, not interdependent issues.

It would be useful for us to delve more deeply into issues involving the relationship between program structure, program size, and the method of program finance, of which this issue is but one example. What can we say about the dynamics of the political process and the odds that it would eventually produce means testing of a double-decker benefit? What does this imply about a credit income tax? Is there any relevant foreign experience? Do the results of the Berry, Garfinkel, and Munts paper suggest that, even if what started out as a double-decker did eventually or for a time become converted into a two-tier model, the resulting structure might be preferable to the present structure? If not, why not? Is there a relationship between the structure of the transfer programs available to the aged and the cost that the nonaged (all of whom expect—or at least hope—to be aged one day) are willing to bear? Would they be willing to bear a greater cost if they were sure that they themselves would eventually qualify for benefits, as is the case under the present system and as would be the case under the double-decker? Would they be willing to bear a greater cost if they were sure that the increment was going to the truly needy among the aged population? Or would they demand a contraction in income support for the aged if they viewed today's tax as being independent from tomorrow's benefit? Does the structure of financing affect the cost that the nonaged are willing to bear? Are they willing to put more or less into a transfer system that is dominated by a payroll-tax-financed social security program than they would be willing to put into either of the alternative structures, which rely less extensively on the payroll tax and more extensively on general revenues?

13

Conclusion

IRWIN GARFINKEL

In this chapter, I attempt to pull together what the conference papers, formal comments, and informal discussion at the conference has taught us about the income-testing issue. The first two sections are organized around the conference papers. In the first section, the effects of income testing on stigma, social cohesion, the well-being of the poor, and economic and administrative efficiency are discussed. The papers and discussions relating to these major issues are briefly and critically summarized. My own views on what we now know are then presented. In the second section criteria for judging which particular programs should and should not be income tested are developed and then applied to four areas covered by conference papers. Again each paper and the discussions are briefly summarized and followed by my own comments. Finally, in the last section I argue that we have too much income testing in our overall income maintenance system and present a reform agenda designed to reduce the role of income testing.

The Major Issues Reviewed

Stigma

Do income-tested government transfer programs carry with them serious, negative, psychological consequences for the recipients? Lee

Rainwater argues (in Chapter 2) that though the actual evidence for and against is weak, it appears that many, but not all, income-tested programs generate unfavorable attitudes toward—and hence differential treatment of—participants, and that participants themselves come to share society's negative attitudes toward them. Allen in his discussion questions whether the evidence supports even this modest conclusion. My own summary judgment is as follows.

Some income-tested programs stigmatize some beneficiaries. Anecdotes, news accounts, case studies, and survey data on program participants and potential participants all confirm the existence of stigma. Social psychological theory and research suggest that stigmatization can result in severe psychological costs. But there is little direct evidence on the stigma effects of welfare.

Perhaps the most interesting policy question is, What accounts for the apparent difference in stigma across programs? Based on Rainwater's paper, the formal discussants' comments, and discussion at the conference, I would stress the following: (a) the degree to which the program's beneficiaries violate society's norms and values; (b) the proportion of the population covered by the program; and (c) the nature of program administration.

A program that aids individuals who violate society's norms is likely to be stigmatizing. To the extent that merely being poor is a violation of society's norms, income-tested programs by their nature tend to be stigmatizing. Yet the same logic implies that categorical income-tested programs such as veterans' pensions and Basic Educational Opportunity Grants that aid individuals who are or have been engaged in behavior valued by society should be less stigmatizing than noncategorical income-tested programs. Whether the behavior is valued sufficiently to completely eliminate stigma is not clear. Nor is it clear how much, if at all, income testing will increase stigma in cases where the category itself (like disability) is stigmatizing. [1]

How does the proportion of the population covered by a program affect stigma? If a program covers most of the population it cannot and hence will not be stigmatizing. It is virtually impossible to conceive of a

---

[1] For example, how much more stigmatizing is disability assistance than disability insurance? Was the temporary unemployment assistance program much more stigmatizing than unemployment insurance? Would a program that provided aid to all single parents be much less stigmatizing than AFDC? Finally, if stigma is a function of aiding individuals who violate society's norms, the degree of stigma should vary with the degree to which social norms are violated. One norm that most AFDC mothers violate is that family heads should work. Rainwater, therefore, speculates that if AFDC mothers worked more (which they would do in a non-income-tested program in which implicit tax rates would be greatly reduced), AFDC would be less stigmatizing.

situation in which a large majority of the population violate society's norms. Even if such a situation were to arise, it would not be stable. Either behavior or the norm would change. Furthermore, it seems reasonable to assume that the larger the proportion of the population covered by an income-tested program, the less stigma will be connected to it.[2]

There are numerous aspects of program administration that will affect stigma, including the intrusiveness of application forms and ongoing relationships, the behavior of functionaries, the relative emphasis placed upon detecting fraud versus ensuring that beneficiaries get what they are entitled to, and the extent to which the status of beneficiaries is known to the public. Food stamps, for example, have high potential for stigmatizing because spending them is a public act. Advertising the availability of benefits, as was done in the case of SSI, conveys the message that claiming benefits is a socially valued behavior. (Whether this message is strong enough to overcome previous attitudes is another matter.) Conversely, constant publicity about the prevalence of cheating and fraud in welfare conveys the message that to claim benefits makes one suspect.

How these administrative factors interact with one another and with the other factors which determine the extent of stigma is not well understood. The only generalization I would venture is that income-tested programs that either aid groups who are or have been engaged in socially valued behavior or aid large percentages of the population have less stigmatizing administrative regimes.

Social Cohesion

Coleman (in Chapter 3) presents the argument that income-tested programs create a sharp distinction between beneficiaries and non-beneficiaries as well as an alternative argument that non-income-tested programs run a greater danger than income-tested programs of splitting society into the governing and governed class. He finds, however, that the empirical evidence neither supports nor refutes either proposition. Jencks in his discussion goes even further. He not only questions the relevance of Coleman's data, especially with respect to the second ar-

[2]For example, if SSI were liberalized to the point of aiding half or more of the aged population, would it be less stigmatizing? I would guess so. Moreover, I suspect that AFDC became less stigmatizing in the mid-1960s and 1970s because of the increased proportion of single mothers who became eligible owing to increases in benefit levels and decreases in effective tax rates.

gument, but questions the very usefulness of the concept of social cohesion.

While I agree with most of what Jencks says, it is worth addressing the a priori aspect of Coleman's argument that non-income-tested programs lead to a split between the governors and governed. Coleman's argument is based on two propositions: (a) Non-income-tested programs increase the proportion of GNP funneled through the government and thereby increase the size and/or power of the bureaucracy; and (b) non-income-tested programs increase central control (federal as against state or local) and thereby further separate the governing from the governed class. Both propositions are in my judgment questionable.

Consider the latter first. While centralization, *ceteris paribus*, increases the distance between the governors and the governed, centralization does not necessarily result from either income testing or non-income-testing. Public elementary and secondary education is non-income-tested and decentralized. Food stamps are income-tested and centralized. I must add, however, that the reforms I propose in the last section would increase centralization in most respects. (This is in my judgment a regrettable, but acceptable, cost of achieving other worthwhile ends.)

It is true that non-income-tested programs have bigger budgets than income-tested programs, and therefore increase the proportion of GNP which is funneled through government. It does not follow, however, that either the size or the power of the bureaucracy is enhanced thereby.[3] For example, if we were to eliminate itemized tax deductions in the federal income tax, we could reduce both the size and power of the IRS bureaucracy while increasing tax revenues. Further, although a credit income tax would substantially increase the budget and the proportion of GNP funneled through government, Kesselman (in Chapter 7) convincingly argues it would result in substantial administrative savings. Both the size and the power of the bureaucracy would be reduced.

Income-tested programs create large bureaucracies that exercise great power over their beneficiaries. By their nature, income-tested programs must check into more detail to determine both eligibility and benefits than comparable non-income-tested programs. For in income-tested programs, eligibility and benefits depend upon at least income and frequently assets as well. The more information an agency collects on indi-

[3]Coleman, in his comments on this chapter, strongly disagrees. He says: "... the logical flaw in your argument is the failure to recognize that an increase in tax revenues ipso facto gives more power to the federal government, for it means that a larger fraction of the country's income is in government hands. This creates the potential (which is what I argued) for mistreatment of citizens, whose power is thereby decreased. (An economist should recognize that money = power)." Letter dated October 6, 1980.

viduals, the more labor-intensive and larger it must be. The more information the agency requires to make a decision affecting the well-being of that individual, the more power the bureaucrats in that agency have over the lives of beneficiaries. For information must be elicited, processed, and interpreted by the bureaucrat. The more information he needs, the more decisions the bureaucrat must make. And the more decisions he makes, the more powerful is the bureaucrat. No program that served Americans of all income classes would conduct unannounced midnight bed checks to determine if someone was eligible for benefits or defrauding the government. We can be grateful that the Supreme Court outlawed this barbaric practice in the AFDC program, but we should not forget that it used to happen.

In general, the trade-off in shifting from income-tested to non-income-tested programs would seem to entail a shift from a situation where the bureaucracy has enormous power over the lives of poor people to a situation where the bureaucracy has a little power over the lives of people from all income classes.

Therein, of course, lies the danger to which Coleman calls our attention. Exactly how "little" is that power? And will it grow worse as the welfare state matures? The power that the Social Security bureaucrat wields in administering OAI benefits or that bureaucrats in every other industrialized country in the world wield in administering children's allowances seems small enough. On the other hand, the power of public school teachers and administrators in the lives of pupils and parents is much larger. So each case must be judged on its individual merits. On balance, shifting to a largely non-income-tested transfer system like that described at the end of this chapter would in my judgment reduce the power and size of the bureaucracy.

The Well-Being of the Poor and Political Reality

As noted in my Introduction, target efficiency was designed to measure not efficiency but how pro-poor programs were.[4] Pro-poor was used synonymously with the proportion of benefits going to the poor. The total amount transferred to the poor—surely a more relevant mea-

---

[4]See Weisbrod (1969). The economists who developed the concept and measure of "target efficiency" were located at the University of Wisconsin, Madison—an economics department long noted for its concern about and research on income-distribution issues. Because of that concern and resulting research expertise, when the federal government declared a "war on poverty" and sought to develop a research organization to help give the country guidance on how to wage that war, the Office of Economic Opportunity chose to locate that facility at the University of Wisconsin.

sure of the effect on the economic well-being of the poor—was ignored. Underlying the argument that income testing is more pro-poor is the implicit assumption that budgets for income-tested and non-income-tested programs are identical. If the same amount of total budget expenditure is available for income-tested and non-income-tested programs, income-tested programs will naturally provide more aid to the poor.

If the total budget available for a non-income-tested program is much larger than that available for an income-tested program, however, the former might transfer more to the poor even though the poor received a smaller proportion of total benefits. Both the Berry, Garfinkel, and Munts paper (Chapter 12) and the Betson, Greenberg, and Kasten paper (Chapter 6) illustrate this point with examples of target-efficient income-tested programs being less pro-poor than non-income-tested programs. Although this should discourage utilization of target efficiency as an equity as well as an efficiency criterion for evaluating income testing, criteria which are easy to measure, even if they are poor measures of anything we care about, die hard.

Larger budgets for non-income-tested programs are a necessary but not a sufficient condition for non-income-tested programs to be more pro-poor than income-tested ones. Tullock (in Chapter 4) argues quite convincingly that conversion of an income-tested to a non-income-tested program may either help or hurt the poor depending upon (a) how the new benefits are financed; (b) the relationship between the new and old benefit structures; and (c) the effect of the shift on the scope of other programs which aid the poor. He also argues that in general, the poor and upper class will lose while the lower middle class will be the biggest gainer. His conclusion with respect to the poor is questionable.

Because Tullock's model gets complex at times, I will review it here. The following two examples show how the choice of the tax to be used to finance the programs alters how income testing affects the poor. Suppose that the guarantees (benefits to persons with no other income) in the income-tested and non-income-tested programs are identical and the extra budget cost of the non-income-tested program is financed by a consumption tax. The poor with no other income will be worse off, since they will have the same income, but prices, inclusive of taxes, will have risen. On the other hand, if an income tax is used and the benefit is not taxable, the poor with no other income will be equally well off under income-tested and non-income-tested programs with identical guarantees.

The effect on the poor of converting from an income-tested to a non-income-tested program will also depend on the kind of income-tested program being replaced. Most income-tested programs, such as Food

Stamps, SSI, and AFDC, reduce benefits gradually as earnings increase. But some, like Medicaid, provide full benefits to eligibles and zero benefits to ineligibles. The latter type of benefit structure has been referred to as notched; while, following Abel-Smith (see Chapter 9), the former may be called tapered. The effect on prior beneficiaries who work on converting these two types of programs to a non-income-tested program will differ. Again, suppose that the guarantees in the income-tested and non-income-tested programs are identical. The extra budget cost of the non-income-tested program is financed by an income tax, and the guarantee is not taxable. Prior beneficiaries who work and were receiving benefits from the notched income-tested program will be worse off under the non-income-tested program, since they will get the same basic benefit, but pay extra taxes to help finance it. This is the case to which Tullock devotes most of his attention.

But note that prior beneficiaries who work may be either better or worse off from converting a tapered income-tested program to a non-income-tested program. If, for example, the benefit-reduction (or tax) rate in the tapered program is 50% and the total tax rate in the income tax including the additional rate required to finance the extra benefits of the non-income-tested program is less than 50%, prior beneficiaries will be better off under the non-income-tested program. Indeed, unless the non-income-tested program is financed by a regressive tax, conversion from a tapered income-tested to a non-income-tested program will generally improve the status of working poor beneficiaries. For, as noted above, income-tested programs by their nature—in order to confine benefits to the poor—impose higher benefit-reduction rates on beneficiaries than the tax rates imposed on nonbeneficiaries to finance the program.

Downs estimates that the poor will gain rather than lose from converting from Medicaid to a non-income-tested national health insurance program.[5] His results may be reconciled with Tullock's model by noting that Downs takes account of the fact that in practice many of the poor are not eligible for and therefore receive no benefits from Medicaid, whereas Tullock's model assumes all of the poor participate in income-tested programs.

The Berry, Garfinkel, and Munts paper (Chapter 12), a simulation analysis of the income-distributional effects of income-testing old-age benefits, further demonstrates that it is impossible to say in general

---

[5]In further contradiction to Tullock's assertions, empirical evidence indicates that Medicare and Medicaid increased the share of medical services going to the aged and poor, respectively (see Davis and Schoen, 1978).

whether income testing helps or hurts the poor. The key problem in comparing income-tested to non-income-tested programs concerns what to hold constant. If the programs are not similar in some respects it makes no sense to compare them. But deciding what to hold constant is equivalent to making a political choice about who is to gain and who is to lose from income testing.

If costs to the nonaged are held constant, then the cost and benefits of shifting from income-tested to non-income-tested programs must be borne either by the poor aged or non-poor aged. If guarantees are also held constant, the poor aged get greater benefits from the non-income-tested program, because it has a lower benefit-reduction rate. If the earnings-replacement rate to upper-income aged is held constant, the poor get smaller benefits from the non-income-tested programs because the guarantee must be lower.

Which of these political outcomes is most likely? Equally persuasive cases could be made for assuming that if we switched to a non-income-tested income support system for the old, (a) we would not increase the costs to the nonaged; (b) we would not reduce the earnings-replacement rate to the upper-income aged; and (c) we would not reduce the guarantee to the poor. But it is impossible to make the switch and not do either a, b, or c, or some combination thereof.

This discussion suggests that the political arguments both for and against income testing are weak; it further casts doubt on the generality of Tullock's prediction that in general switching from income-tested to non-income-tested programs will hurt the poor.

On the other hand, Heidenheimer's historical examination of the development of income maintenance and education policy in Germany, Great Britain, the United States, and Sweden during the last 100 years (Chapter 5) appears to provide some support for two other Tullock contentions.

The major theme of Heidenheimer's paper is that there is a trade-off between education, especially higher education, and social security. The United States led in the former area and lagged in the latter. Germany led in the latter and lagged in the former. Although there has been a fair amount of convergence between the two countries, notable differences remain. These differences provide evidence for Tullock's contention that increases in public expenditures in one area may lead to decreases in expenditures in another area. Consequently it is possible that even if the shift from an income-tested to a non-income-tested program were of direct benefit to the poor, they might indirectly be hurt owing to cutbacks in funding for other programs of benefit to them. Heidenheimer's observation that the development of comprehensive social security coverage in Europe is most closely related to the strength of the labor movement is also consistent with Tullock's argument that those with incomes just above the eligibility line for income-tested programs, the lower middle class, stand to gain the most from converting to a non-income-tested program.

One final point. There are obviously times when a fiscal budget constraint will be binding. During such times, the poor are better served by expanding income-tested benefits. It appears that we have now entered such a period. But it is instructive to recall that target efficiency was invented and came into vogue during the latter part of the Johnson presidency, when "tax" increases were ruled out by the president. Then and now, the assumption of a fixed budget for welfare reform appeared to be an accurate reflection of reality. Yet payroll taxes were raised again and again to finance the six huge increases in Old Age Insurance benefits between 1965 and 1973. Reality may have been defined too narrowly. If welfare reformers had sought to reform welfare by expanding existing or creating new nonwelfare programs, the story might have been different.

Labor Supply Aspects of Economic Efficiency

Whereas non-income-tested programs raise tax rates on upper-income families, compared to income-tested programs, they lower taxes on lower-income families. The economic efficiency of income-testing, therefore, depends upon an analysis of whether it is more efficient to have higher tax rates on low- or high-income families.

Both the Betson, Greenberg, and Kasten paper and the Sadka, Garfinkel, and Moreland paper compare credit income tax to negative income tax programs. The negative income tax (NIT) is income tested; it has a higher tax rate on low-income than on high-income citizens. The credit income tax (CIT) is non-income-tested; it has either a constant tax rate or a higher tax rate on upper-income citizens.

Both papers also focus their analyses of the efficiency of income testing on the effects of tax rates on work effort or labor supply. For the effects on labor supply hold the key to the puzzle of who should pay the highest tax rates.

To see this, consider what would be efficient in the following opposite extreme cases: Either the most productive members of the economy will work hard no matter how much you tax them, or they will quit work entirely if you tax them in the slightest. Obviously, high tax rates on the most productive will be more efficient in the former case.

From the point of view of total productivity, a loss of one hour of labor of the most productive worker is more costly than the loss of one hour of labor of the least productive worker. If they responded equally, therefore, it would be efficient to place the highest tax rates on the least productive members. Only if the poor cut back on work more than the rich in response to the same tax rate will it make sense from an efficiency point of view to place higher tax rates on the rich than on the poor. Moreover, even if the poor are more responsive to taxes than the non-poor, whether income testing is efficient or not depends upon how more responsive the poor are, as compared to how less productive they are. Because both papers are rather technical, they are summarized here.

Betson, Greenberg, and Kasten use the microsimulation model developed at the Department of Health and Human Services for the purpose of calculating the costs of alternative welfare reform proposals. The model takes a random sample of the U.S. population and calculates the change in each person's income and labor supply that would result from either NIT or CIT. The predicted labor supply changes are based on evidence from the Seattle–Denver Income Maintenance Experiment.[6] Unlike previous simulations, which examined only the labor supply changes of beneficiaries, the Betson, Greenberg, and Kasten simulation also examines the labor supply changes of taxpayers who must finance the program.

The results are rather startling. First, considerable redistribution via either a NIT or a CIT is possible without a substantial loss—and indeed maybe even with an increase—in GNP as measured by total earnings. Increases in labor supply and earnings on the part of middle- and upper-income families—especially wives—in response to the increased taxes required to finance the programs are large enough in some cases to more than offset the decreased earnings of transfer beneficiaries. (This suggests that studies which ignore the labor supply response of taxpayers are seriously flawed.) As the authors and their discussants note, the GNP increases are based upon a very large increase in upper-income wives' labor supply in response to a decline in family income. The labor supply behavior of these wives is based upon an extrapolation of the labor supply schedule derived from mostly lower- and lower-middle-income wives in the Seattle–Denver experiment. However, such a large increase in labor supply is inconsistent with other empirical re-

[6]The Seattle-Denver Income Maintenance Experiment was the largest of four income maintenance experiments conducted by the U.S. government to measure the effects of income maintenance programs on the work effort of low-income people (see Keeley et al., 1978).

search.[7] Even when they assume no change in labor supply of the upper-income wives, however, Betson, Greenberg, and Kasten find only small decreases in GNP.

Second, the differences in economic efficiency between the CIT and NIT are very small. The CIT generally leads to somewhat higher GNP than comparable NIT programs. Since total earnings do not reflect the value of leisure, the authors develop two other more comprehensive measures of efficiency. According to both of these measures, the NIT is superior. But in all cases, the differences are very small, leading to the conclusion that the choice between income-tested and non-income-tested tax–transfer regimes should be made on other criteria. Gramlich in his discussion argues this case succinctly and persuasively.

Whereas Betson, Greenberg, and Kasten compare a few specific NIT and CIT plans, all of which may be inefficient, Sadka, Garfinkel, and Moreland find the most socially desirable (given values about inequality—see below) and efficient tax–transfer regime, determine whether it is income tested or not, and then calculate the efficiency loss which results from departing from the optimal regime.

In order to answer the question of what is the optimal pattern of tax rates by income, Sadka, Garfinkel, and Moreland construct a very simple model of the economy, consisting of five persons. Nonaged, able-bodied family heads in the 1976 CPS were arrayed by wage rates and divided into quintiles. Then the average wage rate, labor supply, and unearned income for each quintile was calculated and assigned to each of the five persons representing each quintile. These family heads are then taxed enough to provide their share of federal taxes which finance programs other than the transfer programs examined. The problem then consists of finding what combination of taxes and transfers maximizes the well-being of the five people in this economy.

But, of course, the question arises, how do you compare the well-being of the five different people? Economists handle the issue by resorting to what they call a social-welfare function. The social-welfare function tells the economist—or more precisely the computer—how to weight the well-being of each person. An egalitarian social-welfare function, for example, would, at the least, give more importance to an improvement in, say, the well-being of the poorest, than the richest person. How does the economist know how egalitarian we should be? Economists don't, of course. So Sadka, Garfinkel, and Moreland let the values reflected mathematically in the social-welfare function range

[7]No other cross-sectional study shows a backward-bending labor supply curve for married women (see Cain and Watts, 1973).

from not caring a whit about inequality to willingness to sacrifice improvement of everyone else in society if it benefits (no matter how little) the poorest. One interesting finding was that their results hold no matter what one believes about inequality.

The well-being of the five people in this economy depends only on their income and leisure. Like Betson, Greenberg, and Kasten, Sadka, Garfinkel, and Moreland simulate changes in labor supply in response to changes in tax–transfer regimes. They use two different sets of labor supply estimates: one taken from a study by Masters and Garfinkel (1977) in which the poor respond more than the nonpoor to tax rate changes, and the other in which the responses of the poor and nonpoor are identical. In the latter case, not surprisingly, they find the NIT is optimal. In the former—and, they believe, more realistic—case, they find the CIT is optimal. Like Betson, Kasten, and Greenberg, they conclude that in most cases the efficiency loss of being wrong—that is, of having a regressive marginal tax rate structure if a proportional or progressive structure is optimal, or vice versa—is small, usually well under 1% of GNP. While Diamond in his discussion notes that in absolute magnitude 1% of GNP is hardly trivial, I am inclined to agree with Gramlich, that it is small compared to the likely margin of error, given the crudeness of our measurement ability at this stage of economic science.

How do we reconcile Sadka, Garfinkel, and Moreland's best estimates, which suggest the CIT is optimal, with Betson, Greenberg, and Kasten's estimates, which suggest the NIT is optimal? The difference could be due to different estimates of labor supply or to the fact that the Sadka, Garfinkel, and Moreland paper is more general, or to the fact that their analysis is limited to the nonaged able-bodied population whereas the Betson, Greenberg, and Kasten analysis covers everyone. At this point we don't know which explanation is the most appropriate.

Further, as Sadka, Garfinkel, and Moreland and their discussants note, there are weaknesses in their paper. For example, in their economy only family heads work. But in the real world there are two-worker families. Similarly, labor supply is not the only variable that changes in response to tax rates. So might savings. This is also a problem in the Betson, Greenberg, and Kasten paper. For the time being we conclude that the best economic research on the issue indicates that income-tested programs, which impose the highest tax rates on the poorest people, are, at the very least, not clearly superior to non-income-tested programs on economic efficiency grounds, and indeed that non-income-tested programs may be more efficient.

Administrative and Behavioral Aspects of Economic Efficiency

The Kesselman paper (Chapter 7) compares economic efficiency under two tax–transfer regimes. The first system pays out gross transfer benefits to everyone and finances both transfers and other government goods and services through a proportional income tax with a comprehensive tax base. The second system pays out net benefits only to low-income persons and finances both these transfers and other public expenditures through progressive personal and corporate income taxes with highly eroded tax bases. The former regime he calls a credit income tax, the latter a negative income tax. The latter is also a pretty good description of our current system.

Kesselman argues that the CIT is superior because of the administrative savings of adopting a CIT in lieu of a NIT on the order of $2 billion annually. He also shows the CIT to be superior to the NIT in creating fewer incentives for distorting behavior. Because the income-tested NIT regime has two or more different marginal tax rates, it induces some people to (*a*) change their marital status or living arrangements; and (*b*) alter the timing of income receipts to maximize their benefits and/or minimize their taxes. For example, consider a husband, wife, two-child family where the husband earns $8000 per year while the wife earns nothing. Under the NIT with an eligibility level of $8000 or less, such a family would gain financially by splitting. Under the CIT, the family receives benefits and faces the same tax rate regardless of whether it splits. Under the NIT with an eligibility level of $8000 or less and with benefits based on monthly income, a family head would prefer a half-year job which pays $5000 to a year-round job which pays $8000, in order to qualify for benefits. Under a CIT, the family would be better off taking the $8000 job. Indeed, the head would be financially indifferent between year-round and half-year jobs that paid $5000. Benefits received, taxes paid, and total income would be the same. All of this is a consequence of the constant marginal tax rate in the CIT.[8]

One problem with a credit income tax (even one with a fairly high guarantee) as compared to a NIT combined with a progressive income tax is that upper-income people might be substantially better off under the former. For this reason—and political acceptability—Kesselman considers the costs of adding a surtax on high incomes. The surtax elimi-

[8]The advantages of a constant marginal rate have been used in the past by conservatives to argue for a proportional rather than a progressive income tax (see Blum and Kalven, 1953).

nates the constant marginal tax rate and thereby recreates incentives to alter marital status, living arrangements, and the timing of income receipts. In Appendix 7.B Kesselman mathematically examines how the surtax affects the basic requisite CIT tax rate. In the text he argues that one surtax imposed on relatively high incomes would not severely compromise the advantages of a constant marginal tax rate, because few people would be affected at the income threshold for the surtax rate. But it is not clear to me that one surtax will be sufficient to solve the distributional problem.

We might also ask, if a surtax at the top is not very costly, why should one at the bottom be so costly? The answer would seem to be that—with one exception—it wouldn't, so long as the surtax wasn't too steep. For, the higher the surtax rate, the greater would be the costs of administration, compliance, and avoidance. Kesselman apparently has in mind rather low surtax rates of 10–20%. A surtax rate of 30–40%, which is the magnitude of the difference in tax rates in welfare and the lowest rates in the current income tax, will have much greater adverse effects. Moreover, a surtax at high incomes does not involve the same administrative complications that arise out of a higher tax rate on the lowest incomes. For in the latter cases in order to make regular payments during the course of the year and avoid overpayments, special income-reporting provisions are needed.

Kesselman also argues that there are gains in both equity and efficiency in making distinctions among groups of people even though such treatment may create incentives for changing behavior. If society believes that some groups "need" more than others, the cost of failing to provide higher guarantees to the more needy group is either lower support for them or higher tax rates on everybody to finance the higher guarantees for everyone. The same trade-off between categorical treatment of individuals for benefits and higher marginal tax rates is shown to arise under the NIT regime in Appendix 7.B. Note in this connection that a categorical non-income-tested approach can avoid the high tax rates of a noncategorical, non-income-tested approach to which Pechman refers in his discussion.

It is obvious that the aged have on average greater need for income support than the nonaged, based on their reduced ability to work and their lower earnings capacity. Fortunately, benefit differentials based on age do not have adverse behavioral effects (with the possible exception of incentives for fraud), because people cannot change their age. Single-parent families are also more needy than two-parent families of equal size. Because they have only one adult, their capacity to earn in the market and work in the home is more limited (Garfinkel and Haveman, 1977). Yet, making special provisions for single parents creates incentives for the formation of single-parent households. Both the Kesselman paper and the Watts, Jakubson, and Skidmore paper (Chapter 11) discuss how this potential adverse incentive effect might be minimized. In any case categorization introduces adverse incentives equally to both the NIT and CIT.

Income-Testing Particular Programs

What if we wish to provide minimum guarantees for several goods and services—like health, education, housing, and food—as well as cash guarantees in general and for several contingencies—such as old age, disability unemployment, and sickness? If we provide all of these guarantees in income-tested programs, the cumulative tax rates on the poor would be quite high. As Abel-Smith says, income testing is a scarce resource. But so is non-income-testing. If we provide minimum guarantees in a large number of different non-income-tested programs, everyone will face quite high tax rates. Even if it is optimal for the overall system to have proportional or progressive tax rates, it may be that some combination of income-tested and non-income-tested programs is optimal and therefore that income testing is optimal in some particular cases. Moreover, it is worth exploring in which particular cases the arguments for non-income-tested programs are strongest and vice versa. In this section I shall first discuss some general considerations in ranking programs as to the desirability of income testing, and then review the case for and against income testing in four areas covered by papers presented at the conference: (a) national health insurance; (b) a noncategorical minimum income guarantee; (c) categorical supplements for the aged; and (d) categorical supplements for single-parent families.

General Considerations

Abel-Smith (in Chapter 9) argues that programs (a) which are likely to stigmatize the poor if provided on an income-tested basis and/or (b) which insure against unpredictable risks; and/or (c) which subsidize goods which provide external benefits should be provided on a non-income-tested basis. Programs which would redistribute from poor to rich if provided on a non-income-tested basis should be income tested. Finally Abel-Smith concludes that income testing should be reserved for those services which benefit all or most of the poor regularly.

Not surprisingly, all these criteria—except one—boil down to the program's effect on stigma, the distribution of income, and efficiency.[9]

Stigma and income distribution can be dealt with briefly. Abel-Smith argues, as above, that stigma is most severe if it is public. Further, publicness is inherent when the good or service is provided in a segregated fashion. Consequently, Abel-Smith argues for making eligibility for the good or service non-income-tested and then income-testing either subsidies or charges. For example, public housing should be provided to citizens of all income levels, but rents should be subsidized on an income-tested basis. Long and Palmer in their paper (Chapter 10) make a similar argument in the national health insurance area for making eligibility universal but possibly income-testing cost-sharing provisions.

The income distribution criterion has most application to higher education, for it is the most clear-cut example of a government-subsidized good which the well-to-do get much more of than the poor. Whether non-income-tested subsidies to higher education actually redistribute from poor to rich when the distribution of taxes required to finance the benefits is also considered is not clear.[10] Nevertheless, the case for income-testing higher-education benefits remains stronger than the case for income-testing other goods and services for two reasons. First, even if non-income-tested higher-education benefits don't redistribute from poor to rich, it is likely that they redistribute less from rich to poor than would equal-sized subsidies for goods that are consumed at the same rate by different income classes. Second, as noted above in the discussion of stigma, income-tested benefits for higher education are less stigmatizing than most other income-tested benefits. If this conclusion holds, it has profound implications for many states which continue to provide large institutional and therefore non-income-tested subsidies to

---

[9]Only Abel-Smith's argument that income testing should be reserved for those services which all or most of the poor consume regularly, appears unrelated to stigma, the distribution of income, and efficiency. Despite correspondence with him on this point, I fail to understand the relevance of this criterion. Indeed, one could argue that income-testing goods which are used infrequently by the poor is preferable. The high marginal tax rates which accompany income testing would only infrequently have effect. Furthermore, in general, in-kind subsidies are better candidates for income testing.

[10]Although a study of higher education in California by Hansen and Weisbrod (1969a) seemed to suggest this, a reanalysis of their data by Pechman (1971) suggests that even in this case, non-income-tested subsidies redistribute from rich to poor. The analysis is complicated further by considering the long-run impacts of additional higher education on income distribution. For, even if non-income-tested subsidies redistributed from poor to rich in this generation, by increasing the number of people who get higher education, the subsidies should reduce the relative wage of those with higher education and thereby reduce inequality in the next generation (see Conlisk, 1977).

higher-education institutions. Such subsidies must be justified on the basis of efficiency gains alone, not from the desirability of avoiding income testing.

Economic-efficiency considerations will be discussed at greater length. Three issues will be addressed: (*a*) the labor supply of the group being aided; (*b*) special considerations with respect to in-kind transfers; and (*c*) the relationship of efficiency to insurance.

LABOR SUPPLY

To examine the economic efficiency of an income-tested program, one must measure its labor supply effects on the group being aided. Marginal tax rates should be higher on groups not expected to work than on groups that are expected to work. This follows from the discussion of the relationship of labor supply and productivity to income class, discussed earlier. Recall that whether marginal tax rates should be higher for groups with low productivity depends upon how much less productive and more responsive to tax rates they are compared to more productive groups. In the extreme case, if the value of a person's labor is zero, it doesn't matter how elastic the supply. Placing a 100% marginal tax rate on such a person is sensible from an economic efficiency point of view.

If we don't expect a group to work, that is close to saying that we think their net market productivity is low. The disabled are the most clear-cut case. But for different reasons, during the Great Depression people also felt that the aged and single mothers were unproductive in market work. Every old man who worked, it was felt, was doing nothing more than taking a job from a younger, more needy man with a family to support. In other words, given unemployment rates and the equity judgment that scarce jobs should go to those with a family to support, the net output of the aged was zero. Quite consistently, the Old Age Insurance and Old Age Assistance programs and later the Disability Assistance and Insurance programs all taxed earnings at 100%. Similarly, people felt that single mothers should stay home and raise their children. In economic terms, women were judged to be more productive in the home than in the market. The tax rate in ADC was also set at 100%.

In subsequent years, though the market productivity of aged men increased, the proportion of them who worked steadily decreased while the proportion of married women who worked in the market steadily increased. The consensus that the aged should not work was reinforced and solidified. The consensus that single mothers should stay home and raise their children eroded. Indeed, it is possible that a new consensus is emerging: Single mothers with no children under age 3 (or perhaps 6) should work. The decrease in tax rates in AFDC during the last twenty years is consistent with the decline in the belief that single mothers should stay home. The decrease in tax rates in the Old Age Insurance and Old Age and Disability Assistance programs is incongruous. To summarize, work-related efficiency considerations suggest that higher tax rates should be placed on those not expected to work than on those expected to work. Among those expected to work, higher tax rates should be placed on high earners only if low earners are so much more responsive than high earners that the difference more than makes up for their lower productivity. Finally, note that the same consideration would apply to tax rates among those expected not to work. For even though we may not expect the aged, disabled, and, in the past, female heads of households to work, some do.

IN-KIND TRANSFERS

One big difference between cash and in-kind subsidies with regard to the efficiency of income testing is that subsidizing everyone's consumption of a particular good or service will lead to increases in everyone's consumption of that good or service. As noted above, the question of whether it is more efficient to give cash to all or only to the poor hinges on whether it is more efficient to place higher tax rates on the poor or rich. With respect to in-kind transfers the efficiency question also depends upon whether the nonpoor will underconsume the good in the absence of a subsidy. In cases where the consumption of a good by a particular individual benefits others in society (what economists refer to as an externality), underconsumption will occur in the absence of subsidization. The classic example of such a good is inoculations against infectious disease. Abel-Smith proceeds as if externalities and underconsumption are the norm and therefore rejects the argument that failure to income-test will lead to overconsumption.

Although there are goods where externalities exist, many goods, such as consumption of fuel for heating, lighting, and private transportation, do not ordinarily confer external benefits. In such cases, general subsidization through a non-income-tested program would create inefficiencies. In view of the current concern about energy conservation on the one hand and increasing pressures for providing fuel and utility subsidies to the poor on the other hand, the general principle that Abel-Smith appears to reject takes on an added importance.[11]

[11]Non-income-tested energy subsidies would create severe inefficiencies and should be rejected on that ground alone. Yet lifeline rates (in which public utilities charge less per unit for small amounts of energy consumption than for large amounts) may both promote efficiency by increasing incentives for conservation and reduce costs to the poor. And, lifeline rates are not income tested.

Cash and in-kind subsidies differ in another important respect which affects the efficiency of income testing. In-kind subsidies are more costly to administer than cash subsidies. At the very least, evidence of consumption of a particular good must be presented or the particular good must be purchased and supplied. As a consequence, it seems unlikely that the administrative savings from avoiding an income test will outweigh the extra costs of administering an in-kind program for everyone. In general, therefore, unless the good would be underconsumed in the absence of a subsidy, in-kind subsidies are more likely to be efficient if income tested.

INSURANCE

The reason programs which insure against unpredictable risks should be provided on a non-income-tested basis is also closely related to economic-efficiency concerns. The classic argument for non-income-tested social insurance programs is that the private market will not provide such insurance coverage because of self-selection (on average those who are most in danger of needing the insurance will purchase it more often than those least in need) and because at the price required to cover the administrative costs of providing such insurance there would be an insufficient number of buyers. If the differential participation rates between those who expect and those who don't expect to need the insurance is great enough, the insurance costs may be so high as to virtually preclude the formation of a market. This seems to be the explanation for the absence of widespread availability and utilization of catastrophic health insurance, despite the fact that most Americans seem willing to pay additional taxes to secure this kind of health insurance protection. Twenty years ago in his classic article, "Uncertainty and the Welfare Economics of Medical Care," Kenneth Arrow (1963) used the same line of reasoning to argue that private markets cannot efficiently provide health insurance in general, not just catastrophic insurance. (The health insurance issue will be pursued below.) In short, the government-run programs which insure against unpredictable risk—compared to leaving such concerns to the market—are simply better, more efficient ways of doing business.

Specific Programs

HEALTH CARE

Prior to 1965, whether the federal government should provide medical care to the poor was a hotly debated political topic. Today no major political figure suggests that we should not assure minimum levels of health care to the poor. The overwhelming majority of American people favor doing so. Currently we have an income-tested health care program for all the poor: Medicaid; and a categorical non-income-tested program for the aged: Medicare. When the conference was convened, the issue in the United States was which, if either, of the models to pursue. Although the election of President Reagan has removed the national health insurance issue from center stage at least temporarily, the principles discussed here remain valid.

A major theme of the Long and Palmer paper (Chapter 10) is that the issue of what kind of national health insurance (NHI) program to have in the United States turns on other questions in addition to—and probably more important than—that of income testing. Not that the income-testing issue is irrelevant. Income-tested programs can, they note, frustrate achievement of a consensus objective for our health care system: equal access to health care for all Americans. Income-tested reform programs are more likely to stigmatize beneficiaries. Medicaid, they assert, already does stigmatize the poor. Furthermore, as Wolfe notes in her discussion, in practice this and perhaps all income-tested personal health care programs also result in inferior quality of care for the poor—a violation itself of her notion (as well as that of others) of equal access.

Rather, Long and Palmer argue that "it is, perhaps most of all, on the mechanisms to attain cost control that the current NHI debate hinges; an issue upon which the universal versus income-tested perspective is silent." Though I agree with the first part of the statement, the second overstates the case.

The logic of Long and Palmer's argument and the discussion at the conference suggest that it is possible that only certain kinds of non-income-tested national health insurance programs, or a non-income-tested universal national health service, stand a good chance of bringing an end to the phenomenal explosion in medical-care costs we are experiencing. In their paper and at the conference two general alternative approaches to controlling costs were identified: (a) create incentives for consumers to conserve through the use of coinsurance, deductibles, and charges; or (b) create incentives for providers to conserve by limiting the total resources available to them.

Both income-tested and non-income-tested approaches to national health insurance can create incentives for consumers to conserve through the use of coinsurance, deductibles, and charges. (As Long and Palmer—and Burns in her discussion in Chapter 9—note, it is possible to income-test cost-sharing in a program in which eligibility is not income tested.) But the desire of consumers to pay most personal health-care costs in advance and the desire of consumers–citizens–taxpayers for catastrophic health insurance coverage, combined with the failure of the market to provide such coverage, suggest the possibility that such market-oriented incentives may not suffice. If the market-oriented incentives don't work, that leaves the approach of limiting total resources available to providers. Income-tested approaches cannot achieve this because they deal with only part of the health care market. Non-income-tested approaches (such as the AMA and Enthoven tax-credit proposals) that simply involve the government in financing care, but do nothing on the supply side, also cannot limit total resources. Non-income-tested approaches (including the Kennedy complete public-sector approach and a national health service) in which the government uses its financing of all personal health care to either exert large control over or actually provide the care itself can clearly stop the escalation in costs. Indeed, Long and Palmer note that to limit costs, the British National Health Service has used a top-down system of budgeting with some success.

Of course, it is possible that independent measures aimed at restructuring the supply side, such as encouraging the development of HMOs, will be just as effective in limiting costs. But it is also possible that such measures will not be as effective.

In short, we probably are now consuming too much personal health-care service and the best way to cure that may be for the government to assume responsibility for financing personal health care for all in order to limit the supply available to all.[12]

A GUARANTEED MINIMUM INCOME: AID TO THE WORKING POOR

The Food Stamps program is a noncategorical income-tested federally guaranteed minimum income—in food purchasing power. Even before the purchase requirement had been eliminated, the benefits were almost equivalent to cash in terms of their effect on food consumption. The purchase requirement had a much bigger effect on keeping people out of the program than on changing people's consumption habits (Mac-Donald, 1977). For all practical purposes, therefore, the Food Stamps program can be considered a negative income tax, except that it is more costly to administer and far more stigmatizing.

Presidents Nixon and Carter proposed that food stamps be replaced by a cash negative income tax, which in practice amounted to proposing to extend cash welfare eligibility to intact families with children and to provide a federal floor under such welfare payments. President Reagan proposes to cut back food stamps for the working poor by allowing

[12]See Garfinkel (1972). For an alternative perspective see Feldstein (1973) and Wildavsky (1977).

fewer work-related deductions and placing a ceiling on total income for the purpose of determining eligibility. Indeed, his administration appears to be challenging the consensus of the 1960s among income maintenance experts that some kind of income maintenance benefits should be extended to the working poor.

Why provide income maintenance benefits—though not necessarily income-tested benefits—to the working poor? Quite simply, in the absence of such benefits, these families will be unable to achieve what our society judges to be a minimally decent standard of living. Furthermore, providing benefits to the working poor enables us to minimize the adverse incentives which arise out of providing benefits to those not expected to work, which are high enough to assure them a decent standard of living. One problem with categorization is that it creates incentives to change behavior to qualify for the favored category. The larger the difference in benefits between the disabled and able-bodied, the unemployed and employed, and single and two-parent families, the greater the incentive to become or remain disabled, unemployed, and a single parent.

The case for providing benefits to the working poor remains as strong today as it was in the 1960s. Yet the case for providing these benefits on an income-tested basis is weak. Indeed the analysis in this and preceding chapters points exactly in the opposite direction. In particular, both the Sadka, Garfinkel, and Moreland paper and the Kesselman paper suggest that a non-income-tested credit income tax might be superior to an income-tested negative income tax on efficiency grounds. In addition, the CIT is likely to be less stigmatizing. Finally, it is worth noting that President Reagan's budget director, David Stockman, as of 1978 at least, accepted the case for aiding the working poor and argued eloquently for doing so through a non-income-tested approach (Stockman, 1978). In this light, the question suggested by Pechman's discussion takes on added significance. Is it possible to design a credit income tax with a guarantee equal approximately to the Food Stamps guarantee (about $700 per person per year in 1981) which has no more than one or two surtax rates and which does not redistribute from the middle- to upper-income groups? And, if not, would a credit income tax with a more progressive rate structure still dominate a negative income tax on administrative and other efficiency grounds?

SUPPLEMENTS TO THE AGED

The case for categorical supplements to the aged is worth restating: If one group is more "needy" than another, the cost of failure to treat categorical groups differently must be either that benefits are too low for the needy group, or that taxes on everyone are too high. Starting at about age 55 or so, earnings capacity, on average, decreases with age, which is to say the need for income support or supplementation increases with age. (The decrease, however, unlike the abrupt change in benefit entitlement in our current system, is a gradual one.) The case for paying higher benefits as age increases (after 55 or so) is, therefore, a strong one. But should the supplements be income tested or not? Note that it is possible that the supplements should be income tested even if the noncategorical basic cash guarantee is not income tested and vice versa.

Administrative and stigma considerations suggest that the supplements for the aged should not be income tested. The aged appear to be more sensitive to and deterred by the stigma associated with income-tested programs. Administrative simplicity in cash programs always favors non-income-tested programs. This argument is further strengthened if the underlying cash program is non-income-tested.

Work-related efficiency considerations, however, suggest that the aged, who are not expected to work, should probably face higher marginal tax rates than the nonaged. This would certainly apply to the very old or frail elderly. For the overwhelming majority of the very old, market productivity is close to or equal to zero. But note that even though they are not expected to work, many 65-year-olds are quite productive. Further, as the ratio of those over age 65 to those 25–65 increases during the next 30–40 years, and as the health of those over age 65 improves, our attitudes about whether the aged should work are likely to undergo change. Already many are proposing that the retirement age be 68 rather than 65.

The foregoing discussion suggests that tax rates as well as guarantees should increase with age. From the point of view of economic efficiency, therefore, the current retirement-test provisions in OAI appear to be upside down. The tax rate is now 50% for earnings in excess of $5000 per year for those less than age 72 and zero for those over age 72. Similarly, extra exemptions for the aged in the personal income tax also appear to be an inefficient way to aid the aged. Higher benefits are more appropriate. Note that higher tax rates on the aged as a group need not imply that aid to the aged be income tested in either the administrative or economic sense. It is possible that tax rates on all the aged, not just those with low incomes, should be higher than tax rates on the nonaged. This depends upon how supply elasticities and productivity vary by income class within the aged population. Even if, as I suspect,[13] it is more

[13]I am assuming that individuals who do brain work are more likely to be employable than those who do physical work. They are certainly better rewarded.

efficient to place higher tax rates on low-income aged, it may be that this can be achieved satisfactorily through a retirement-test mechanism.

SUPPLEMENTS FOR SINGLE-PARENT FAMILIES

Both the Watts, Skidmore, and Jakubson paper and the Kesselman paper confront the dilemma that, on the one hand, the lower earnings capacity of single-parent families increases their need vis-à-vis equal-sized two-parent families and thereby creates a case for paying them higher benefits, while, on the other hand, paying higher benefits to one-parent families creates an unfortunate economic incentive for two-parent families to become single-parent families.

Watts, Skidmore, and Jakubson show that current policy favors low-income single-parent families, and that either a noncategorical negative income tax or credit income tax would eliminate the current favorable treatment. They then examine the budget costs and distributional effects of a variety of income-tested and non-income-tested supplements to single-parent families. Perhaps their most important empirical finding is how small are the marginal budget costs of not income-testing supplementary benefits to single-parent families, given that the basic benefit is not income tested.

In the concluding section of their paper, Watts, Skidmore, and Jakubson argue that the only way to simultaneously provide higher benefits to single-parent families and minimize the financial incentives to split is to have the absent spouse pay for the supplement to the single parent. That's what child support is supposed to accomplish. But as they and others have documented, most absent fathers pay no child support, and among those who do, most pay less than the courts have ordered. After noting the abysmal failure of our current judicial system and AFDC to enforce parental responsibility for child support, they suggest a three-part non-income-tested approach which could be incorporated into the existing system or as a supplement to either the NIT or the CIT. In the following section, I present an alternative proposal designed to achieve the same objective. Here I focus on the issue of whether or not income support to single-parent families should be income tested or not.

The key question is, Do we expect single mothers to work? If so, income testing is probably inappropriate. If not, a high guarantee, high tax rate, public child support program would be efficient insofar as work is concerned. Even in this case, however, a non-income-tested approach might be superior because of efficiency gains in other areas. In particular, most experts agree that the most efficient child support enforement tool is wage garnishment (Chambers, 1979). By extension, therefore, the most efficient way to collect child support payments would appear to be to collect is as a tax through the wage withholding system, like the social security payroll tax. If a government agency collects child support taxes from nearly all absent parents, it will pay benefits out to nearly all custodial parents. In this case it may be administratively inefficient to have an additional and separate income-tested program.

Implications for Policy

In both the academic and policy worlds a consensus emerged in the late 1960s that income-tested programs were somehow "superior" to non-income-tested programs. Yet the conference papers and discussions suggest that, at the very least, serious consideration should be given to reforms which reduce the role of income testing in our tax–transfer system. Indeed, all three panelists of the last, summing-up session at the conference went much further.[14] One went so far as to say that he was convinced that the burden of proof ought now to lie with those who advocate income testing! . . . Perhaps.

What has the conference taught us about the effects of income testing on stigma, social cohesion, the economic well-being of the poor, and efficiency? The following is a brief summary.

- Income-tested programs are more likely than non-income-tested programs to stigmatize the poor. There is ample evidence of stigma in some income-tested programs. A priori reasoning and casual observation suggest that the degree of stigma varies by program, depending upon (*a*) the extent to which the program's beneficiaries violate society's norms; (*b*) the proportion of the population covered by the program; and (*c*) the administrative nature of the program. Unfortunately, we have virtually no evidence on the prevalence or severity of stigma in various programs.

- Social cohesion may be either weakened or strengthened by income testing. A priori reasoning suggests that income testing increases the division between beneficiaries and taxpayers. There is some disagreement about whether a priori reasoning suggests income testing decreases the division between bureaucrats and the rest of the population. Empirical evidence sufficient to support or refute either a priori contention does not exist.

[14]I must confess that two out of the three panelists were and remain good friends, while the third was before and remains now a staunch advocate of the non-income-tested approach. Yet I did not stack the deck. For both of my friends had been part of the consensus that income-tested programs were better. At the very least, they had been skeptical of my arguments in favor of non-income-tested programs.

- Income testing may be either harmful or helpful to the economic well-being of the poor. Particular political circumstances, not general laws, will determine whether the poor will fare better or worse from a particular income-tested or non-income-tested program.

- Income testing may be either efficient or inefficient in terms of work and output depending upon how much more the poor respond to tax rates compared to how much less productive they are—both in relation to the nonpoor. Empirical evidence does not support the intuitive view that income testing is likely to be more efficient.

- A noncategorical cash program is likely to be cheaper to administer if it is not income tested. In particular, a credit income tax would be cheaper to administer than a combination negative income tax and personal income tax.

- Except where a non-income-tested program is needed to prevent a good or service from being underconsumed or overconsumed (e.g., health care), it is more reasonable to income-test in-kind than cash programs, since in-kind programs require a somewhat complex administration in any case.

- Administrative and stigma considerations suggest that categorical supplements to the aged should not be income tested. Yet efficiency considerations related to labor supply suggest income testing may be appropriate, especially for the very old.

- Categorical supplements for single-parent families are not a good candidate for income testing if the parent is expected to work. Even if the parent is not expected to work, a non-income-tested approach may be more efficient in terms of enforcing the responsibility of absent parents to pay child support.

- Higher education is a good candidate for income testing because (a) stigma is likely to be low, and (b) non-income-tested subsidies are likely to be less pro-poor than income-tested subsidies.

- Whether programs which subsidize personal health care should be income tested or not depends in part on whether it is preferable to control costs through incentives to consumers or to providers. The former may be achieved by either approach. Non-income-tested approaches may have an advantage in achieving the latter.

Does this put the burden of proof on the advocates of income testing? Again, perhaps. Cash non-income-tested programs designed to aid those expected to work appear to have the edge in terms of efficiency and stigma. But the advantage is not clear-cut. Even more important, the edge in stigma is not "value free." Stigma may serve a "useful" social function. As Rainwater notes, stigma does serve to discourage behaviors which violate social norms. For example, stigma reinforces the values of self-support and independence. Yet, how effective a deterrent is stigma? How does its effectiveness compare to positive incentives? And finally who gains and loses from utilizing negative sanctions like stigma versus positive incentives like low tax rates? We have practically no direct knowledge on the first two questions. Yet, we know that the poor would benefit from positive incentives and bear the costs of negative sanctions while the reverse is true for the well-to-do. Advocates of the poor, therefore, will seek to achieve desired social ends through positive incentives rather than through stigma. Therein enters a value judgment.

Economic and administrative efficiency considerations, however, are by themselves, value free. Therefore, since non-income-tested cash programs appear to be more efficient, the assertion that the burden of proof now lies with the advocates of income testing is probably justified.

But note two further roles of values. First, the credence given to these findings on efficiency is as likely to depend upon values as on scientific judgment. This will always be the case where the scientific evidence is not clear-cut. Second, even if it is granted that cash non-income-tested programs have the edge in efficiency, it does not follow that they are preferable to income-tested programs. For non-income-tested and income-tested tax–transfer regimes have different distributional effects. If the guarantees in the systems are the same, the poor, near-poor, and lower-middle-income groups will have more income under a non-income-tested regime with a proportional or progressive tax rate structure. Upper-middle- and upper-income groups will have less income under the non-income-tested regime. Consequently, the choice between income-tested and non-income-tested regimes inevitably depends upon value judgments concerning the distribution of income as well as upon scientific knowledge.

Indeed my values, and I believe those of the majority of Americans, are such that non-income-tested tax–transfer regimes would be preferable even if they were slightly less efficient than income-tested tax–transfer regimes. The two critical values are equality of opportunity and integration.

The poor can earn less in the market than the nonpoor. Regressive marginal tax rate structures exacerbate this inequality. They take away a bigger share of whatever additional money the poor make (even if this is done in the process of aiding them) than is taken away from the nonpoor. Regressive tax rates therefore stack the deck against the poor making it the way Americans are supposed to, through work. This constitutes a violation of my notion of equality of opportunity.

Regressive is almost a dirty word. Regressivity is more excusable if it is imposed in the process of aiding the poor, but it is still not very attractive. It is especially ugly when imposed on those whom we expect to work. For in this case what we give with one hand we take away with the other.

Non-income-tested programs integrate beneficiaries into the social mainstream; income-tested programs segregate them. Income-tested programs place beneficiaries in separate programs. They create special bureaucracies to deal with the poor alone. Owing to the higher tax rates, they create incentives which in proportional terms are greater for the poor than for the nonpoor to work less at legitimate steady jobs where their incomes must be reported and to work more at intermittent, informal, and even illegal, jobs where earnings need not be reported.

The foregoing leads me to conclude that the following four-part non-income-tested reform agenda should be given serious consideration.

First, in order to achieve a non-income-tested, noncategorical minimum income guarantee, the current personal income tax and Food Stamp programs would be replaced by a credit income tax (CIT) with an income guarantee equal to Food Stamps—about $700 per person. The per capita tax credits—essentially income grants to all families—would replace both the personal exemptions in the current income tax and the Food Stamp program and would be paid in monthly installments to all persons in the manner that children's allowances are paid in other countries. The tax base would be made comprehensive by eliminating itemized deductions as well as the personal exemption and by making income from all sources (except the credits themselves) taxable. The tax rate would be identical on all except the very highest incomes. This is similar to the CIT discussed in Chapters 6 and 7, except the basic benefit is much lower.

This is a major change, and would accomplish several objectives by itself. Making payments to everyone would solve the nonparticipation and application problems in the current system, simplify benefit administration, and eliminate stigma. The comprehensive tax base and constant marginal tax rate (for most of the population) would simplify tax administration, result in a slight increase in tax payments for upper-income families while allowing for a decrease in marginal tax rates on the earnings of upper-income families, and an increase in labor supply in the aggregate.

Second, the credits would be increased with age beginning at age 55 so that by age 65 they would be equal to the present level of SSI plus food stamps. This would replace the SSI program for the aged. These credits can be thought of as a replacement for the current minimum benefit in the Old Age and Survivors Insurance (OASI) program. This change would permit the rest of the OASI program to focus on the earnings-replacement objective rather than the current mix of objectives: earnings replacement and minimum income. Furthermore, it would entail a substantial cutback in payroll taxes.

Third, a social child support program would be adopted in lieu of the current AFDC program. Under it, all absent parents would be required to pay a child support tax. The tax would be administered by the Internal Revenue Service and its employer withholding system. All children with a living absent parent who was legally liable for paying the child support tax would be entitled to receive a benefit equal to either the absent-parent tax or a minimum, whichever was larger. In cases where the absent parent paid less than the minimum benefit, the difference would be financed from general revenues.

This child support system would more effectively accomplish what AFDC intends: adequate income guarantees for children in one-parent families. Responsibility for these children would tend to be shifted from taxpayers in general to absent spouses, single parents would not face the high AFDC tax rate, stigma would be reduced, welfare administration would be simplified, and the burden on the court system would be reduced.

Fourth, adoption of a non-income-tested national health insurance system or a national health service would complete the changeover to a largely non-income-tested tax–transfer system.

This reform package provides a very low income guarantee to two-parent families without a disabled head. Clearly the guarantee is inadequate if the head becomes unemployed or ill. For two reasons, my own preference is to provide a low-wage guaranteed job in combination with a low-income guarantee for those expected to work rather than a high-income guarantee. First, doing so will keep overall tax rates lower. Second, reinforcement of the work ethic will require that a high-income guarantee be accompanied by a work test, which is undesirable on administrative grounds. The combination of a guaranteed-jobs program that offers a minimum wage and the low-guarantee CIT would enable those expected to work, but unsuccessful in finding a regular job, to achieve an income level somewhat above the poverty line.

As a package, these proposals reduce marginal tax rates on low-income workers, consolidate and simplify both tax and transfer programs, and transfer some of the burden of child support now borne by taxpayers to absent parents. Most important, they further the antipoverty effort in a way that reduces reliance on income-tested transfers and for those expected to work emphasizes the importance of earned income.

References

Abel-Smith, B. 1972. The history of medical care. In E. W. Martin (ed.), *Comparative development in social welfare*. London: Allen and Unwin.

Adams, J. S. 1965. In L. Berkowitz (ed.), *Advances in experimental social psychology*, Vol. 2. New York: Academic Press.

Advisory Committee on Child Development of the National Research Council. 1976. *Toward a national policy for children and families*. Washington, D.C.: National Academy of Sciences.

Aikman, M. G. 1978. Income splitting among family members. *Report of proceedings of the twenty-ninth tax conference, 1977*. Toronto: Canadian Tax Foundation.

Alber, J. 1976. The development of social security in Western Europe, HIWED Report No. 4, Cologne, mimeo.

Allen, J. T. 1973. Designing income maintenance systems: The income accounting problem. In U.S. Congress, Joint Economic Committee, *Studies in public welfare*, Paper No. 5 (part 3). Washington, D.C.: U.S. Government Printing Office.

Alston, J. P., and Dean, K. E. 1972. Socioeconomic factors associated with attitudes toward welfare recipients and the causes of poverty. *Social Service Review, 46*, 1–11.

Alves, W. M., and Rossi, P. H. 1978. Who should get what? Fairness judgments of the distribution of earnings. *American Journal of Sociology, 84*, 541–564.

American Bar Association (Section of Taxation). 1963. Resolutions on substantive tax reform approved by council of the section of taxation and board of governors of the American Bar Association. *Bulletin of the Section of Taxation, Annual Report, American Bar Association, 16*, 4–20.

Anderson, A. C. 1975. Sweden examines higher education: A critique of the U-68 report. *Higher Education, 4*, 393–408.

Anderson-Khleif, S. 1978. Income packaging and lifestyle in welfare families. *Family Policy Note No. 7*, Joint Center for Urban Studies of MIT and Harvard. Cambridge, Mass.: Joint Center.

Arrow, K. 1963. Uncertainty and the welfare economics of medical care. *American Economic Review, 53*, 941–973.

Asimow, M. R., and Klein, W. R. 1970. The negative income tax: Accounting problems and a proposed solution. *Harvard Journal on Legislation, 8*, 1–31.

Bakke, W. E. 1940. *Citizens without work*. New Haven, Conn.: Yale University Press.

Bale, G. 1973. The interest deduction dilemma. *Canadian Tax Journal, 21*, 317–336.

Ball, R. 1968. Some reflections on selected issues in social security. In *Old age income insurance*, U.S. Congress, Joint Economic Committee, Subcommittee on Fiscal Policy. Washington, D.C.: U.S. Government Printing Office.

Barr, N. A., James, S. R., and Prest, A. R. 1977. *Self-assessment for income tax*. London: Heinemann Educational Books.

Barr, S. 1968. Budgeting and the poor: A view from the bottom. In R. Perrucci and M. Pilisuk (eds.), *The triple revolution*. Boston: Little, Brown.

Barth, M. C. 1972. Universal wage-rate subsidy: Benefits and effects. In *The economics of federal subsidy programs* (Part 4). Joint Economic Committee, 92nd Congress, 2nd Session. Washington, D.C.: U.S. Government Printing Office.

Barth, M. C., Carcagno, G. J., and Palmer, J. L. 1974. *Toward an effective income support system: Problems, prospects, and choices*. Madison, Wis.: Institute for Research on Poverty.

Bawden, D. L., and Kershaw, D. 1971. Problems in income reporting and accounting. In L. L. Orr, R. G. Hollister, and M. J. Lefcowitz (eds.), *Income maintenance: Interdisciplinary approaches to research*. Chicago: Markham.

Beavis, D., and Kapur, V. 1977. An analysis of the take-up rates of the Old Age Security (OAS) and Guaranteed Income Supplement (GIS) programs. Canada, Health and Welfare, Staff Working Paper 7706, Ottawa, Canada.

Beck, B. 1966. Welfare as a moral category. *Social Problems, 14*, 258–277.

Beck, R. G. 1974. The effects of copayment on the poor. *Journal of Human Resources, 9*, 129–141.

Bell, W. 1977. AFDC: Symptom and potential. In A. L. Schorr (ed.), *Jubilee for our times*. New York: Columbia University Press.

Berglind, H., et al. 1975. *Socialvarden I Tre Kammuner*. Stockholm: Sociological Institute of Stockholm University.

Berry, R. E. 1976. Prospective rate reimbursement and cost containment: Formula reimbursement in New York. *Inquiry, 13*, 288–301.

Betson, D., Greenberg, D., and Kasten, R. 1980. A microsimulation model for analyzing alternative welfare reform proposals: An application to the Program for Better Jobs and Income. In R. Haveman and K. Hollenbeck (eds.), *Microeconomic simulation models for public policy analysis: Vol. 1, Distributional impacts*. New York: Academic Press.

Blum, W. J., and Kalven, H., Jr. 1953. *The uneasy case for progressive taxation*. Chicago: University of Chicago Press.

Boland, B. 1973. Participation in the Aid to Families with Dependent Children Program, Paper No. 12. U.S. Congress, Joint Economic Committee, Subcommittee on Fiscal Policy. Washington, D.C.: U.S. Government Printing Office.

Brazer, H. 1969. The federal individual income tax and the poor. *California Law Review, 57*, 422–449.

Break, G. F. 1957. Income taxes and incentives to work: An empirical study. *American Economic Review, 47*, 529–549.

Brehm, J. A. 1966. *A theory of psychological reactance*. New York: Academic Press.

Briggs, A. 1967. The welfare state in historical perspective. In C. I. Schottland (ed.), *The welfare state*. New York: Harper and Row.

Brinner, R. 1973. Inflation, deferral and the neutral taxation of capital gains. *National Tax Journal, 26*, 565–573.

Brown, C. V., and Dawson, D. A. 1969. *Personal taxation, incentives, and tax reform*. London: Political and Economic Planning.

Bryden, M. H. 1961. *The costs of tax compliance*. Canadian Tax Papers No. 25. Toronto: Canadian Tax Foundation.

Buchanan, J. M. 1972. The inconsistencies of the National Health Service. Reprinted in J. M. Buchanan and R. D. Tollison (eds.), *Theory of public choice: Political applications of economics*. Ann Arbor: University of Michigan Press.

Buchanan, J. M., and Tullock, G. 1977. The expanding public sector: Wagner squared. *Public Choice, 31* (Fall), 147–150.

Burlage, D. 1978. Reduction of income following marital separation: The financial alternatives. Ph.D. dissertation, Harvard University, Cambridge, Mass.

Burney, I., et al. 1978. Geographic variation in physicians' fees; payment to physicians under Medicaid and Medicare. *Journal of the American Medical Association, 240*, 1368–1371.

Burns, E. 1965a. Needed changes in welfare programs. Institute of Government and Public Affairs, paper MR-44, University of California–Los Angeles.

Burns, E. 1965b. Social security in evolution: Towards what? *Proceedings of the Industrial Relations Research Association*. Madison, Wis.: IRRA.

Cain, G., and Watts, H., eds. 1973. *Income maintenance and labor supply*. New York: Academic Press.

Callund, D. 1975. *Employee benefits in Europe*. Essex, U.K.: Gower Press.

Canada, *House of Commons Debates*. 1978. 4th Session, 30th Parliament, November 29, Vol. 122. Ottawa: Supply and Services Canada.

Canada, Revenue Canada, Taxation. 1979. *Taxation statistics, 1979 edition*. Ottawa: Supply and Services Canada.

Canadian Tax Foundation. 1979. *The national finances, 1978–79*. Toronto: Canadian Tax Foundation.

Carroll, M. S. 1978. Private health insurance plans in 1976: An evaluation. *Social Security Bulletin, 41* (Sept.), 3–16.

Cassetty, J. 1978. *Child support and public policy*. Lexington, Mass.: Lexington Books.

Chambers, D. 1979. *Making fathers pay*. Chicago: University of Chicago Press.

Citrin, J. 1979. Do people want something for nothing: Public opinion on taxes and government spending. *National Tax Journal, 32*, Supplement, 113–129.

Clotfelter, C. T. 1979. Equity, efficiency, and tax treatment of in-kind compensation. *National Tax Journal, 32*, 51–60.

Coe, R. D. 1977. Participation in the Food Stamp program among the poverty population. In G. Duncan and J. Morgan (eds.), *Five thousand American families—Patterns of economic progress*. Vol. 5. Ann Arbor: Institute for Social Research, University of Michigan.

Coleman, R., Rainwater, L., and McClelland, K. 1978. *Social standing in America*. New York: Basic Books.

Coles, A. S. 1978. The inner relationships among work, welfare, and higher education: An exploratory case study. Unpublished paper, Harvard University, Cambridge, Mass., June.

Commission of the European Communities. 1977. The perception of poverty in Europe. Brussels, March.

Conlisk, J. 1977. A further look at the Hansen–Weisbrod–Pechman debate. *Journal of Human Resources, 12*, 147–163.

Coons, J., Clune, W., and Sugarman, S. 1970. *Private wealth and public education.* Cambridge, Mass.: Harvard University Press.

Cooper, C., and Katz, A. J. 1977. The cash equivalent of in-kind income. Cooper and Company, Stanford, Conn.

Cooper, M. H. 1975. *Rationing health care.* New York: John Wiley and Sons.

Coughlin, R. M. 1979. Social policy and ideology: Public opinion in eight rich nations. In R. F. Tomasson (ed.), *Comparative studies in sociology,* Vol. 2. Greenwich, Conn.: JAI Press.

Dahrendorf, R. 1968. On the origin of inequality among men. *Essays in the theory of society.* Stanford, Calif.: Stanford University Press.

Dairn, A. 1979. Why do Swedish suburbs look the way they do? *Human Environment in Sweden,* No. 9. Feb.

Danziger, S., and Plotnick, R. Forthcoming. *Has the war on income poverty been won?*

Davies, B. 1976. *Universality, selectivity, and effectiveness in social policy.* London: Heinemann and Company.

Davis, K. 1975. *National health insurance; benefits, costs, and consequences.* Washington, D.C.: The Brookings Institution.

Davis, K., and Schoen, C. 1978. *Health and the war on poverty; ten-year appraisal.* Washington, D.C.: The Brookings Institution.

Denison, E. 1974. *Accounting for United States economic growth.* Washington, D.C.: The Brookings Institution.

Diamond, P. A., and McFadden, D. L. 1974. Some uses of the expenditure function in public finance. *Journal of Public Economics, 3,* 3–21.

Donovan, M. 1977. And let who must achieve: High school education and white collar work in nineteenth century America. Ph.D. dissertation, University of California–Davis.

Doob, A. N., and Ecker, E. P. 1970. Stigma and compliance. *Journal of Personality and Social Psychology, 14,* 302–305.

Douglas, P. 1927. *Wages and the family.* Chicago: University of Chicago Press.

Dyckman, Z. Y. 1978. A study of physicians' fees. Washington, D.C.: Council on Wage and Price Stability.

Economist (London). 1978. Sept. 8, p. 108.

Emery, E. D., Long, S. H., and Mutti, J. H. 1979. Payroll taxes, the minimum wage, and National Health Insurance premiums: Short-run employment impacts by industry. Health Studies Program Working Paper W-79-7, Syracuse University, May.

Enrick, N. L. 1963. A pilot study of income tax consciousness. *National Tax Journal, 16,* 169–173.

Enthoven, A. 1978. Consumer-choice health plan. *New England Journal of Medicine, 298,* 650–658, 709–720.

Erickson, K. 1966. *Wayward Puritans.* New York: John Wiley and Sons.

Esping-Andersen, G. 1978. Social class, social democracy, and the states. *Comparative Policies,* Oct., pp. 42–58.

Farina, A., Holland, C. H., and Ring, K. 1966. The role of stigma and set in interpersonal interaction. *Journal of Abnormal Psychology, 71,* 421–428.

Farina, A., and Ring, K. 1965. The influence of perceived mental illness on interpersonal relations. *Journal of Abnormal Psychology, 70,* 47–51.

Farina, A., Sherman, M., and Allen, J. G. 1968. Role of physical abnormalities in interpersonal perception and behavior. *Journal of Abnormal Psychology, 73,* 590–599.

Feagin, J. R. 1972a. God helps those who help themselves. *Psychology Today, 6* (November), 101–111.

———. 1972b. America's welfare stereotypes. *Social Science Quarterly, 52,* 921–933.

Federal Council on the Aging. 1975. *The interrelationships of benefit programs for the elderly.* Washington, D.C.: U.S. Government Printing Office.

Feldstein, M. S. 1971. A new approach to national health insurance. *Public Interest,* No. 23 (Spring), pp. 93–105.

———. 1973. The welfare loss of excess health insurance. *Journal of Political Economy, 81,* 251–280.

———. 1977a. Facing the social security visits. *Public Interest,* No. 47 (Spring), pp. 88–100.

———. 1977b. The high cost of hospitals—and what to do about it. *Public Interest,* No. 48 (Summer), pp. 40–54.

Feldstein, M. S., Green, J., and Sheshinski, E. 1978. Inflation and taxes in a growing economy with debt and equity finance. *Journal of Political Economy, 86,* S53–S70.

Feldstein, M. S., and Slemrod, J. 1978. Inflation and the excess taxation of capital gains on corporate stock. *National Tax Journal, 31,* 107–118.

Fellingham, J. C., and Wolfson, M. A. 1978. The effects of alternative tax structures on risk taking in capital markets. *National Tax Journal, 31,* 339–347.

Flora, P. 1974. *Indikatoren der Modernisierung.* Opladen, Federal Republic of Germany: Westdeutscher Verlag.

Flora, P., and Alber, J. 1970. Modernization, democratization and the development of welfare states in Western Europe. In P. Flora and A. Heidenheimer (eds.), *The development of welfare states in Europe and America.* New Brunswick, N.J.: Transaction Press.

———. 1971. Modernization, democratization and the development of welfare states in Western Europe. In A. S. Banks (ed.), *Cross polity time series data.* Cambridge, Mass.: MIT Press.

Flora, P., and Heidenheimer, A. J., eds. 1970. *The development of welfare states in Europe and America.* New Brunswick, N.J.: Transaction Press.

Folsom, R. N. 1978. Neutral capital gains taxation under inflation and tax deferral. *National Tax Journal, 31,* 401–405.

Fox, A. 1979. Earnings replacement rates of retired couples: Findings from the Retirement History Study. *Social Security Bulletin, 42* (Jan.), 17–39.

Fraiberg, S. 1977. *Every child's birthright: In defense of mothering.* New York: Basic Books.

Friedman, M. 1962. *Capitalism and freedom.* Chicago: University of Chicago Press.

Fuchs, V. R. 1974. *Who shall live? Health, economics, and social choice.* New York: Basic Books.

Fullerton, D., King, A. T., Shoven, J. B., and Whalley, J. 1980. Corporate and personal tax integration in the United States. In R. Haveman and K. Hollenbeck (eds.), *Microeconomic simulation models for public policy analysis: Vol. 2, Sectoral, regional, and general equilibrium models.* New York: Academic Press.

Gallup, G., ed. 1972. *The Gallup poll: Public opinion 1935–1971.* 3 vols. New York: Random House.

———. 1976a. *The Gallup international polls: France, 1939, 1944–1975.* New York: Random House.

———. 1976b. *The Gallup international polls: Great Britain, 1937–1975.* 2 vols. New York: Random House.

———. 1978. *The Gallup poll: Public opinion, 1972–1977.* 2 vols. New York: Random House.

Galvin, C. O., and Bittker, B. I. 1969. *The income tax: How progressive should it be?* Washington, D.C.: American Enterprise Institute for Public Policy Research.

Garfinkel, I. 1972. Equal access, minimum provision and efficiency in financing medical care. *Journal of Human Resources, 7,* 242–249.

Garfinkel, I., and Haveman, R. H. 1977. *Earnings capacity, poverty, and inequality.* New York: Academic Press.

Gaus, C. R., Cooper, B. S., and Hirshman, C. G. 1976. Contrasts in HMO and fee-for-service performance. *Social Security Bulletin, 39* (May), 3–14.

Gergen, K. J., and Jones, E. E. 1963. Mental illness, predictability and affective consequences as stimulus factors in person perception. *Journal of Abnormal Psychology, 67,* 95–104.

Gibson, R. M., and Fisher, C. R. 1978. National health expenditures, fiscal year 1977. *Social Security Bulletin, 41* (July), 3–20.

Goffman, E. 1963. *Stigma.* Englewood Cliffs, N.J.: Prentice-Hall.

Golladay, F., and Haveman, R. 1977. *The economic impacts of tax-transfer policy: Regional and distributional effects.* New York: Academic Press.

Goodban, N. 1977. Social psychological effects of welfare. Unpublished paper, Department of Psychology and Social Relations, Harvard University.

Goode, R. 1976. *The individual income tax.* Washington, D.C.: The Brookings Institution.

Gottschalk, P. T. 1978. Principles of tax transfer integration and Carter's welfare-reform proposal. *Journal of Human Resources, 13,* 332–348.

Gouldner, A. W. 1960. The norm of reciprocity: A preliminary statement. *American Sociological Review, 25,* 161–178.

Great Britain, Chancellor of the Exchequer. 1972. *Proposals for a tax credit system.* Cmnd. 5116. London: Her Majesty's Stationery Office.

Great Britain, Her Majesty's Stationery Office (Abel-Smith). 1976. *Fit for the future: The report of the Committee on Child Health Services.* Cmnd. 6684. London: HMSO.

Great Britain, Her Majesty's Stationery Office. 1978a. *Sharing resources for health in England.* London: HMSO.

Great Britain, Her Majesty's Stationery Office. 1978b. *Hansard* (parliamentary debates), Dec. 14.

Great Britain, Royal Commission on the Distribution of Income and Wealth. 1976. Report No. 4, Second Report on the Standing Reference. Oct., Cmnd. 6626.

Great Britain, Royal Commission on the Poor Laws. 1909. *Report.* London: His Majesty's Stationery Office.

Great Britain, Royal Commission on the Taxation of Profits and Income. 1954. *Second report.* Cmnd. 9105. London: Her Majesty's Stationery Office.

Great Britain, Supplementary Benefits Commission. 1977. *Low incomes: Evidence to the royal commission on the distribution of income and wealth.* London: Her Majesty's Stationery Office.

Green, C. 1967. *Negative taxes and the poverty problem.* Washington, D.C.: The Brookings Institution.

Green, C., and Lampman, R. 1967. Schemes for transferring income to the poor. *Industrial Relations, 6,* 121–137.

Green, M. C. 1973. Implementing income supplements: The case for a tax credit approach. *Canadian Tax Journal, 21,* 426–440.

Greenberg, D. Forthcoming. Employers, the unemployed, and the effects of transfer programs on hours of work. Technical Analysis Paper, Office of Income Security Policy, Department of Health and Human Services, Washington, D.C.

Greenleigh Associates. 1960. *Facts, fallacies, and future: A study of the Aid to Dependent Children program of Cook County, Illinois, and addenda.* New York: Greenleigh Associates.

Gurin, P., Gurin, G., Lao, R. C., and Beattie, M. 1969. Internal-external control in the motivational dynamics of Negro Youth. *Journal of Social Issues, 25,* 29–53.

Gutkin, S. A., and Beck, D. 1958. *Tax avoidance vs. tax evasion.* New York: Ronald Press.

Hall, A. 1976. *The determinants of participation of single-headed families in the AFDC program.*

SRI memorandum 32, Center for the Study of Welfare Policy Research. Menlo Park, Calif.: SRI.

Halsey, H., Kurtz, M., Spiegelman, R., and Waksberg, A. 1977. *The reporting of income to welfare: A study in the accuracy of income reporting.* Research memorandum 42. Menlo Park, Calif.: SRI.

Handler, J. F., and Hollingsworth, E. J. 1968. How obnoxious is the "obnoxious means test"? The views of AFDC recipients. Institute for Research on Poverty Discussion Paper No. 31, Madison, Wis.

Hannan, M., Tuma, N., and Groenveld, L. 1977. Income and marital events: Evidence from an income-maintenance experiment. *American Journal of Sociology, 82,* 1186–1211.

————. 1978. Income and independence effects on marital dissolution: Results from the Seattle and Denver Income-Maintenance Experiment. *American Journal of Sociology, 84,* 611–633.

Hansen, W. L., and Weisbrod, B. A. 1969a. The distribution of costs and direct benefits of public higher education. The case of California. *Journal of Human Resources, 4,* 176–191.

————. 1969b. *Benefits, costs, and finance of public higher education.* Chicago: Markham.

Haveman, R. H. 1973. Work-conditional subsidies as an income-maintenance strategy: Issues of program structure and integration. In U.S. Congress, Joint Economic Committee, *Studies in public welfare,* Paper No. 9 (part 1). Washington, D.C.: U.S. Government Printing Office.

Hausman, L. J. 1977. Rules and practices for the taxation of income and assets in income-like subsidies for housing, medical care, and higher education. In Federal Council on the Aging, *The treatment of assets and income from assets in income-conditioned government benefit programs.* Washington, D.C.: U.S. Government Printing Office.

Heidenheimer, A. J. 1973. The politics of public education, health and welfare in the U.S.A. and Western Europe: How growth and reform potentials have differed. *British Journal of Political Science, 3,* 315–340.

————. 1977. Achieving equality through educational expansion. *Comparative Political Studies, 10,* 413–432.

Heidenheimer, A., Heclo, H., and Adams, C. 1975. *Comparative public policy.* New York: St. Martin's.

Helliwell, J. F. 1969. The taxation of capital gains. *Canadian Journal of Economics, 2,* 314–318.

————. 1973. Towards an inflation-proof income tax. *Report of proceedings of the Twenty-Fourth Tax Conference, 1972.* Toronto: Canadian Tax Foundation.

Hellmuth, W. F. 1977. Homeowner preferences. In J. A. Pechman (ed.), *Comprehensive income taxation.* Washington, D.C.: The Brookings Institution.

Helpman, E., and Sadka, E. 1978. The optimal income tax: Some comparative statics results. *Journal of Public Economics, 9,* 383–393.

Hirshfield, D. S. 1970. *The lost reform; the campaign for compulsory health insurance in the United States from 1932 to 1943.* Cambridge, Mass.: Harvard University Press.

Hoagland, G. W. 1980. The effectiveness of current transfer programs in reducing poverty. Paper presented at conference, Welfare Reform, Goals and Realities, Middlebury, Vermont, April 19.

Hollenbeck, K. M. 1975. *An analysis of the impact of unemployment and inflation on AFDC costs and caseloads.* Washington, D.C.: Mathematica Policy Research.

Homans, G. C. 1958. Social behavior as exchange. *American Journal of Sociology, 63,* 597–606.

Jagannadahm, L., and Palvia, C. M. 1978. *Problems of pensioners.* New Dehli: Bhanurha.

Janowitz, M. 1976. *Social control of the welfare state.* New York: Elsevier.

Jasso, G. 1978. On the justice of earnings. *American Journal of Sociology, 83,* 1398–1419.

Jencks, C., and Riesman, D. 1968. *The academic revolution*. New York: Doubleday.

Johnston, K. J. 1963. *Corporations' federal income tax compliance costs*. Bureau of Business Research Monograph No. 110. Columbus: Ohio State University.

Kaelble, H. 1975. Chancenungleichkeit und akademische Ausbildung in Deutschland. *Geschichte und Gesellschaft, 1,* 121–149.

Kanbur, S. M. 1979. Of risk taking and the personal distribution of income. *Journal of Political Economy, 87,* 769–797.

Kaufmann, F. 1970. *Sicherheit als soziologisches und sozialpolitisches System*. Stuttgart: Enke.

Kay, J. A., and King, M. A. 1978. *The British tax system*. Oxford: Oxford University Press.

Keeley, M., Robins, P., Spiegelman, R. G., and West, R. W. 1978. The labor supply effects and negative income tax programs. *Journal of Human Resources, 13,* 3–36.

Kelley, H. 1967. Attribution theory in social psychology. In D. Levine (ed.), *Nebraska symposium on motivation, 15,* 192–238.

Keniston, K. 1977. *All our children*. New York: Harcourt Brace Jovanovich.

Kershaw, D. N. 1973. Administrative issues in establishing and operating a national cash assistance program. In U.S. Congress, Joint Economic Committee, *Studies in public welfare,* Paper No. 5 (part 3). Washington, D.C.: U.S. Government Printing Office.

Kershaw, D. N., and Fair, J. 1976. *The New Jersey income-maintenance experiment: Vol. 1, Operations, surveys, and administration*. New York: Academic Press.

Kesselman, J. R. 1979. Credits, exemptions, and demogrants in Canadian tax–transfer policy. *Canadian Tax Journal, 27,* 653–688.

Kesselman, J. R., and Garfinkel, I. 1978. Professor Friedman, meet Lady Rhys-Williams: NIT vs. CIT. *Journal of Public Economy, 10,* 179–216.

Kleck, R. 1966. Emotional arousal in interactions with stigmatized persons, *Psychological Reports, 19,* 1226.

———. 1969. Physical stigma and task-oriented interactions. *Human Relations, 22,* 53–60.

Kleck, R., Ono, H., and Hastorf, A. 1966. The effects of physical deviance upon face-to-face interaction. *Human Relations, 19,* 425–436.

Klein, W. 1966. Some basic problems of negative income taxation. *Wisconsin Law Review,* Summer, pp. 776–800.

———. 1971. Familial relationships and economic well-being: Family unit rules for a negative income tax. *Harvard Journal on Legislation, 8,* 361–405.

Korpi, W. 1978. Poverty research in the United States: Critical notes from European perspective. Committee on Evaluation of Poverty Research, National Research Council, National Academy of Sciences, Washington, D.C.

Kurtz, J. 1977. Comments on William F. Hellmuth. In J. A. Pechman (ed.), *Comprehensive income taxation*. Washington, D.C.: The Brookings Institution.

Kurz, M. 1977. Distortion of preferences, income distribution, and the case for a linear income tax. *Journal of Economic Theory, 14,* 291–298.

Lave, J. R., Lave, L. B., and Silverman, L. P. 1973. A proposal for incentive reimbursement for hospitals. *Medical Care, 11,* 79–90.

Le Grand, J. 1978. The distribution of public expenditure: The case of health care. *Economica, 45,* 125–142.

Leibfried, S. 1978. Public assistance in the United States and the Federal Republic of Germany: Does social democracy make a difference? *Comparative Politics, 11,* 59–76.

Levitan, S. A. 1977. The unemployment business is the message. Address at Washington Journalism Center, Washington, D.C., Dec. 14. Processed.

Lidman, R. 1975. Why is the rate of participation in the Unemployed Fathers segment of Aid to Families with Dependent Children (AFDC-UF) so low? Institute for Research on Poverty Discussion Paper No. 288-75, Madison, Wis.

Lindsay, C. M., and Zycher, B. 1978. More evidence on Director's Law. Unpublished paper, University of California–Los Angeles.

Link, C. R., Long, S. H., and Settle, R. F. 1979. Health insurance among the aged and disabled. Health Studies Program Working Paper #W-79-8, Syracuse University.

Long, S. H., and Cooke, M. 1978. Financing national health insurance. U.S. Department of Health, Education, and Welfare, paper prepared for the Secretary's National Advisory Committee on National Health Insurance. Mimeo.

Lubove, R. 1968. *The struggle for social security 1900–1935*. Cambridge, Mass.: Harvard University Press.

MacDonald, M. 1977. *Food, stamps, and income maintenance*. New York: Academic Press.

MacDonald, M., and Sawhill, I. V. 1978. Welfare policy and the family. *Public Policy, 26*, 89–119.

McMillan, A. W., and Bixby, A. K. 1980. Social welfare expenditures, fiscal year 1978. *Social Security Bulletin, 43* (May), 3–17.

McPherson, C. B. 1962. *The political philosophy of possessive individualism*. London: Oxford University Press.

Martin, J. W. 1944a. Costs of tax administration: Statistics of public expenses. *Bulletin of the National Tax Association, 29*, 132–147.

————. 1944b. Costs of tax administration: Examples of compliance expenses. *Bulletin of the National Tax Association, 29*, 194–205.

Masters, S., and Garfinkel, I. 1977. *Estimating the labor supply effects of income-maintenance alternatives*. New York: Academic Press.

Meade, J. E. 1972. Poverty in the welfare state. *Oxford Economic Papers, 24*, 289–326.

Meade, J. E., chairman. 1978. *The structure and reform of direct taxation*. Report of a committee of the Institute for Fiscal Studies. London: George Allen and Unwin.

Mendelson, M. 1979. *The administrative cost of income security programs: Ontario and Canada*. Toronto: Ontario Economic Council.

Merriam, I. C., and Skolnik, A. M. 1968. *Social welfare expenditures under public programs in the United States, 1929-66*. Research Report No. 25, U.S. Department of Health, Education and Welfare, Social Security Administration. Washington, D.C.: U.S. Government Printing Office.

Merz, P. E. 1977. Foreign income tax treatment of the imputed rental value of owner-occupied housing: Synopsis and commentary. *National Tax Journal, 30*, 435–439.

Michel, R. C. 1980. The participation rates in the Aid to Families with Dependent Children program. Urban Institute Working Paper 1387-02, Washington, D.C., Aug.

Middleton, R., and Allen, V. L. 1977. Social psychological effects. In H. W. Watts and A. Rees (eds.), *The New Jersey income maintenance experiment: Vol. 3, Expenditures, health, and social behavior; and the quality of the evidence*. New York: Academic Press.

Mill, J. S. 1848. *Principles of political economy*, 1909 edition. London: Longmans Green.

Mirrlees, J. A. 1971. An exploration in the theory of optimum income taxation. *Review of Economic Studies, 38*, 175–208.

————. 1976. Optimal tax theory: A synthesis. *Journal of Public Economics, 6*, 327–358.

Mitchell, B. M., and Phelps, C. E. 1976. National health insurance: Some costs and effects of mandated employee coverage. *Journal of Political Economy, 84*, 553–571.

Mitchell, B. M., and Schwartz, W. B. 1976. The financing of national health insurance. Rand Corporation Report #R-1711-HEW, Santa Monica, Calif.

Mitchell, B. M., and Vogel, R. J. 1975. Health and taxes. An assessment of the medical deduction. *Southern Economic Journal, 91*, 660–672.

Mittelstädt, A. 1975. *Unemployment benefits and related payments in seven major countries*. OECD economic outlook, occasional studies. Paris: Organisation for Economic Co-operation and Development.

Montmarquette, C. 1974. A note on income (labor) inequality: Income tax systems and human capital theory. *Journal of Political Economy, 82,* 620–625.

Moon, M. 1977a. *The measurement of economic welfare: Its application to the aged poor.* New York: Academic Press.

———. 1977b. The treatment of assets in cash benefit programs for the aged and disabled. In Federal Council on the Aging, *The treatment of assets and income from assets in income-conditioned government benefit programs.* Washington, D.C.: U.S. Government Printing Office.

Mueller, D. K. 1977. *Sozialstruktur und Schulsystem.* Göttingen: Vandenhoeck & Ruprecht.

Munnell, A. 1977. *The future of social security.* Washington, D.C.: The Brookings Institution.

Musgrave, R. A., Heller, P., and Peterson, G. E. 1970. Cost effectiveness of alternative income maintenance schemes. *National Tax Journal, 23,* 140–156.

Newhouse, J. P., and Phelps, C. E. 1976. New estimates of price and income elasticities of medical care services. In R. N. Rosett (ed.), *The role of health insurance in the health services sector.* New York: National Bureau of Economic Research.

New York Times. 1978. Census doubts middle incomes are squeezed by costs of college. Mar. 13, p. A14.

OECD. *See* Organisation for Economic Co-operation and Development.

Okner, B. 1975. The role of demogrants as an income maintenance alternative. In I. Lurie (ed.), *Integrating income maintenance programs.* New York: Academic Press.

Open University. 1971. *Money, wealth, and class.* Stockholm: Open University Press.

Organisation for Economic Co-operation and Development. 1970. *Group disparities in educational participation.* Background Study No. 4. Paris: OECD Committee for Scientific and Technical Personnel.

———. 1977a. *The treatment of family units in OECD members countries under tax and transfer systems.* Paris: OECD Committee on Fiscal Affairs.

———. 1977b. *Public expenditures on income maintenance programmes.* Studies in Resource Allocation, No. 3. Paris: OECD.

Orr, L. 1976. Income transfers as a public good. *American Economic Review, 66,* 359–371.

Ozawa, M. 1977. Social insurance and redistribution. In A. Schorr (ed.), *Jubilee for our times.* New York: Columbia University Press.

Pazner, E. A., and Sadka, E. 1978. Excess burden and economic surplus as consistent welfare indicators. Foerder Institute for Economic Research, working paper No. 8-78, Tel Aviv University.

Pechman, J. A. 1970. The distributional effects of public higher education in California. *Journal of Human Resources, 5,* 361–370.

———. 1971. The distributional effects of public higher education in California. *Journal of Human Resources, 5,* 361–370.

Pechman, J. A., Aaron, H., and Taussig, M. 1968. *Social security: Perspectives for reform.* Washington, D.C.: The Brookings Institution.

Pettigrew, T. F. 1980. Social psychology's potential contributions to an understanding of poverty. In V. T. Covello (ed.), *Poverty and public policy.* Cambridge, Mass.: Schenkman Publishing Co.

Pfaff, M. 1978. Patterns of inequality in income: Selected determinance, countries, and policy issues for the 1980s. Paper prepared for ASSA (Association of Social Science Associations) meeting.

Pommerehne, W. 1978. Public choice approaches to explaining fiscal redistribution. Paper presented at 34th Conference of the International Institute of Public Finance, Hamburg, Germany, Sept.

Potter, H. R., Coudy, W. J., and Larson, C. J. 1968. The study of subsistence living in

Montgomery County, Indiana: Final report, Institute for the Study of Social Change, working paper No. 18, Purdue University, Lafayette, Ind.

Pryor, F. L. 1968. *Public expenditure on communist and capitalist nations.* Homewood, Ill.: Irwin.

Public Opinion. 1978a. *6*, May–June.

———. 1978b. *6*, July–Aug.

———. 1978c. *6*, Sept.–Oct.

Puide, A. 1977. Attityder till socialhjalp: En Matodstudie. Sociological Institute, Stockholm University.

Rainwater, L. 1970. *Behind ghetto walls.* Chicago: Aldine.

———. 1974. *What money buys.* New York: Basic Books.

Rainwater, L., Rein, M., and Schwartz, J. Forthcoming. *Economic well-being in the welfare state: A study of family income packaging in Sweden, Great Britain, and the United States.*

Rea, S. A., Jr. 1974. Trade-offs between alternative income maintenance programs. In U.S. Congress, Joint Economic Committee, *Studies in public welfare,* Paper No. 13. Washington, D.C.: U.S. Government Printing Office.

Reddin, M. 1978. *Universality and selectivity: Strategies in social policy.* National Economic and Social Council. Dublin: The Stationer's Office.

Reich, C. 1966. The new property. *Public Interest,* No. 3 (Spring), pp. 57–89.

Reich, D. 1977a. *Applying for public assistance in New York City.* New York: Community Service Society.

———. 1977b. The needy get iciness. *New York Times,* Sept. 19, OpEd page.

Rein, M. 1972. *Conflicting aims of AFDC-UF.* Publication No. 11. Chestnut Hill, Mass.: Social Welfare Regional Research Institute, Boston College.

Rhys-Williams, J. 1943. *Something to look forward to.* London: MacDonald and Co.

———. 1953. *Taxation and incentive.* London: William Hodge and Co.

Rimlinger, G. V. 1971. *Welfare policy and industrialization in Europe, America and Russia.* New York: John Wiley and Sons.

Rolph, E. 1967. The case for a negative income tax device. *Industrial Relations, 6,* 155–165.

Sadka, E. 1976a. On income distribution, incentive effects and optimal income taxation. *Review of Economic Studies, 43,* 261–267.

———. 1976b. Social welfare and income distribution. *Econometrica, 44,* 1239–1251.

Salkever, D. S., and Bice, T. W. 1976. The impact of certificate-of-need controls on hospital investment. *Health and Society, 54,* 185–214.

Sandford, C. T. 1973. *Hidden costs of taxation.* Publication No. 6. London: Institute for Fiscal Studies.

Saunders, T. H. 1951. *Effects of taxation on executives.* Boston, Mass.: Division of Research, Harvard Business School.

Sawhill, I. V. 1977. Developing normative standards for child support and alimony payments. Urban Institute Working Paper No. 992-04. Washington, D.C.

Schorr, A. L. 1960. *Filial responsibility in the modern American family.* Washington, D.C.: U.S. Government Printing Office.

———. 1966. *Poor kids.* New York: Basic Books.

———. 1977. The strategy and hope. In A. Schorr (ed.), *Jubilee for our times.* New York: Columbia University Press.

Schultze, C. L., Fried, E. R., Rivlin, A. M., and Teeters, N. H. 1972. *Setting national priorities: The 1973 budget.* Washington, D.C.: The Brookings Institution.

Schutz, R. R. 1952. Transfer payments and income inequality. Ph.D. dissertation, University of California–Berkeley.

Schwartz, E. E. 1946. Some observations on the Canadian Family Allowances Program. *Social Service Review, 20,* 451–473.

Scitovsky, A., and Snyder, N. M. 1972. Effects of coinsurance on physicians' services. *Social Security Bulletin, 34* (June), 3–19.

Segalman, R. 1968. The Protestant ethic and social welfare. *Journal of Social Issues, 24,* 125–141.

Seidman, L. S. 1977. Medical loans and major-risk national health insurance. *Health Services Research, 12,* 123–128.

Sheehan, S. 1977. *Welfare mother.* New York: New American Library.

Silver, G. A. 1978. *Child health: America's future.* Germantown, Md.: Aspen Systems Corp.

Simons, H. C. 1938. *Personal income taxation.* Chicago: University of Chicago Press.

———. 1950. *Federal tax reform.* Chicago: University of Chicago Press.

Sloan, F., Mitchell, J., and Cromwell, J. 1978. Physician participation in state Medicaid programs. *Journal of Human Resources, 13* (Supplement), 211–245.

Smeeding, T. 1982. *Alternative methods for valuing in-kind transfer benefits and measuring their effect on poverty.* Bureau of the Census Technical Paper No. 50. Washington, D.C.: U.S. Government Printing Office.

Smith, A. 1776. *The wealth of nations,* 1950 edition. Vol. 2. London: Methuen.

Snee, J., and Ross, M. 1978. Social security amendments of 1977: Legislative history and summary of provisions. *Social Security Bulletin, 41* (March), 3–20.

Social Security Bulletin, Annual Statistical Supplement, 1972. 1974.

Social Security Bulletin Annual Statistical Supplement, 1975. 1977.

Spicer, M. W., and Lundstedt, S. B. 1976. Understanding tax evasion. *Public Finance, 31,* 295–304.

Spivak, J. 1979. Farmer force. *Wall Street Journal,* Jan. 2, p. 1.

Statistical abstract of the United States: 1978. 1978. Washington, D.C.: U.S. Government Printing Office.

Statistical abstract of the United States: 1979. 1979. Washington, D.C.: U.S. Government Printing Office.

Stern, N. H. 1976. On the specification of models of optimum income taxation. *Journal of Public Economics, 6,* 123–162.

Steurle, E., and Hoffman, R. 1979. Tax expenditures for health care. *National Tax Journal, 32,* 101–115.

Stockman, D. 1978. Welfare is the problem. *Journal of the Institute for Socioeconomic Studies, 3* (Autumn), 39–50.

Strayer, P. J. 1939. *The taxation of small incomes: Social, revenue and administrative aspects.* New York: Ronald Press.

Sunley, E. M., Jr. 1977. Employee benefits and transfer payments. In J. A. Pechman (ed.), *Comprehensive income taxation.* Washington, D.C.: The Brookings Institution.

Surrey, S. S. 1973. *Pathways to tax reform: The concept of tax expenditures.* Cambridge, Mass.: Harvard University Press.

Tajfel, H. 1969. Experiments in intergroup discrimination. *Scientific American, 223,* 96–102.

Teichler, U. 1978. *Admission to higher education in the United States: A German critique.* New York: International Council for Educational Development.

Thurow, L. C. 1977. Government expenditures: Cash or in-kind aid? In G. Dworkin, G. Bermant, and P. Brown (eds.), *Markets and morals.* New York: John Wiley and Sons.

Titmuss, R. M. 1959. *Essays on the welfare state.* New Haven: Yale University Press.

———. 1968. *Commitment to welfare.* London: Allen and Unwin.

Tobin, J. 1966. The case for an income guarantee. *Public Interest,* No. 4 (Summer), pp. 31–41.

Tobin, J., Pechman, J. A., and Mieszkowski, P. 1967. Is a negative income tax practical? *Yale Law Journal, 77,* 1–27.

Tullock, G. 1971. The charity of the uncharitable. *Western Economic Journal, 9*, 379–392.

U.S. Commissioner of Internal Revenue. 1978. *Annual report, 1977.* Department of the Treasury, Internal Revenue Service. Washington, D.C.: U.S. Government Printing Office.

U.S. Comptroller General. 1979. *Who's not filing income tax returns?* Washington, D.C.: U.S. General Accounting Office.

U.S. Congress, Joint Economic Committee (Subcommittee on Fiscal Policy). 1972–1974. *Problems in administration of public welfare programs.* (Papers 7 and 15 particularly.) Washington, D.C.: U.S. Government Printing Office.

_____. 1974. *Income security for Americans: Recommendations of the public welfare study,* 93rd Congress, 2nd session. Washington, D.C.: U.S. Government Printing Office.

U.S. Congressional Budget Office. 1979. *Controlling rising hospital costs.* Washington, D.C.: U.S. Government Printing Office.

_____. 1980. *Reducing the federal budget: Strategies and examples.* Background paper. Washington, D.C.: U.S. Government Printing Office.

U.S. Department of Commerce (Bureau of the Census). 1973. *Current population reports,* Series P-60, No. 91. Washington, D.C.: U.S. Government Printing Office.

_____. 1976. *The statistical history of the United States.* Washington, D.C.: U.S. Government Printing Office.

_____. 1979. *1977 Census of governments.* Washington, D.C.: U.S. Government Printing Office.

U.S. Department of Health, Education, and Welfare (Social Security Administration). 1974. Estimating the number of people eligible for Supplemental Security Income program. Staff study.

_____. 1978a. Lead agency memorandum on a national health program. Mimeo, April 3.

_____. 1978b. Unpublished statistical study, April 12.

_____. 1978c. Double-decker models. Staff paper prepared for 1979 Advisory Council on Social Security. Nov.

_____. 1978d. *Social security programs throughout the world, 1977.* Washington, D.C.: U.S. Government Printing Office.

_____. 1979. *Social security and the changing roles of men and women.* Washington, D.C.: U.S. Government Printing Office.

_____. n.d. Overview of NHI issues. Mimeo.

U.S. Department of the Treasury (Internal Revenue Service). 1974. *Statistics of income, 1972: Individual income tax returns.* Washington, D.C.: U.S. Government Printing Office.

_____. 1977a. *Statistics of income 1974, individual income tax returns.* Washington, D.C.: U.S. Government Printing Office.

_____. 1977b. *Blueprints for basic tax reform.* Washington, D.C.: U.S. Government Printing Office.

_____. 1979. *Estimates of income unreported on individual income tax returns.* Washington, D.C.: U.S. Government Printing Office.

U.S. Executive Office of the President of the United States. 1979. *Special analyses; budget of the United States government, fiscal year 1979.* Washington, D.C.: U.S. Government Printing Office.

U.S. Government Accounting Office. 1978. *The well-being of older people in Cleveland, Ohio.* Washington, D.C.: U.S. Government Printing Office.

U.S. President's Commission on Income Maintenance Programs. 1969. *Report: Poverty amid plenty: The American paradox.* Washington, D.C.: U.S. Government Printing Office.

U.S. Senate. 1979a. Health care for all Americans Act. S.1720. 96th Congress, 1st Session, Sept. 6.

———. 1979b. National health plan act. S.1812. 96th Congress, 1st Session, Sept. 12.

Vadakin, J. C. 1958. *Family allowances: An analysis of their development and implications.* Coral Gables, Florida: University of Miami Press.

———. 1968. A critique of the guaranteed annual income. *Public Interest,* No. 11 (Spring), pp. 53–66.

Vickrey, W. 1947. *Agenda for progressive taxation.* New York: Ronald Press.

Waldman, S. 1976. *National health insurance proposals: Provisions of bills introduced in the 94th Congress as of February 1976.* Department of Health, Education, and Welfare No. (SSA)76-11920. Washington, D.C.: U.S. Government Printing Office.

Warlick, J. L. 1979. An empirical analysis of participation in the Supplemental Security Income program among aged, eligible persons. Ph.D. dissertation, University of Wisconsin, Madison.

Watts, H. W. 1972. Income redistribution: How it is and how it can be. Testimony for the Democratic Platform Hearings, St. Louis, Missouri. Processed.

Watts, H. W., Jakubson, G., and Skidmore, F. 1979. Single-parent households under alternate tax and transfer systems: Detailed simulations and policy conclusions. Institute for Research on Poverty Discussion Paper No. 549-79, University of Wisconsin, Madison.

Watts, H. W., and Peck, J. K. 1975. On the comparison of income redistribution plans. In J. D. Smith (ed.), *The personal distribution of income and wealth.* New York: National Bureau of Economic Research.

Weaver, C. 1977. The emergence, growth, and redirection of social security: An interpretive history from a public choice perspective. Ph.D. dissertation, Virginia Polytechnic Institute and State University, Blacksburg, Va.

Weisbrod, B. A. 1969. Collective action and the distribution of income: A conceptual approach. In *The analysis and evaluation of public expenditures: The PPB system.* Vol. 1. Washington, D.C.: U.S. Government Printing Office.

Weiss, R. 1979. *Going it alone: The family life and social situation of the single parent.* New York: Basic Books.

Welter, R. 1962. *Popular education and democratic thought in America.* New York: Columbia University Press.

Wetzler, J. W. 1977. Capital gains and losses. In J. A. Pechman (ed.), *Comprehensive income taxation.* Washington, D.C.: The Brookings Institution.

Wicker, A. W. 1969. Attitudes versus actions: The relationship of verbal and overt behavioral responses to attitude objects. *Journal of Social Issues, 25,* 41–78.

Wildavsky, A. 1977. Doing better and feeling worse: The political pathology of health policy. *Daedalus, 106* (Winter), 105–124.

Wilensky, H. L. 1975. *The welfare state and equality: Structural and ideological roots of public expenditures.* Berkeley: The University of California Press.

———. 1976. *The "new corporatism," centralization, and the welfare state.* Contemporary Political Sociology Series/06/020. London and Beverly Hills: Sage Publications.

———. 1978. The political economy of income distribution: Issues in the analysis of government approaches to the reduction of inequality. In J. M. Yinger and S. J. Cutler (eds.), *Major social issues: A multidisciplinary view.* New York: Free Press–Macmillan.

Wilensky, H. L., and Lawrence, A. T. 1979. Job assignment in modern societies: A reexamination of the ascription–achievement hypothesis. In A. H. Hawley (ed.), *Societal growth: Processes and implications.* New York: Free Press–Macmillan.

Willis, A. B., ed. 1969. *Studies in substantive tax reform.* Chicago: American Bar Foundation and Southern Methodist University.

Wiseman, J. n.d. The economics of subsidies: Some taxonomic and analytic problems. Institute for Social and Economic Research, University of York, reprint series, no. 256.

Witte, E. E. 1973. *The development of the Social Security Act.* Madison: University of Wisconsin Press.

Yokelson, D., ed. 1975. *Collected papers on poverty issues. Vol. III, Public attitudes towards poverty and the characteristics of the poor and near-poor.* Croton-on-Hudson, N.Y.: Hudson Institute.

Young, M., and Willmott, P. 1962. *Family and kinship in East London.* Baltimore: Penguin Books.

Zook, C. J., Moore, F. D., and Zeckhauser, R. I. 1980. Catastrophic health insurance—A misguided prescription? *Public Interest,* No. 62 (Winter), pp. 66–81.

Author Index

Subject Index

Institute for Research on Poverty
Monograph Series

Published

Irwin Garfinkel, Editor, *Income-Tested Transfer Programs: The Case For and Against*. 1982

Richard V. Burkhauser and Karen C. Holden, Editors, *A Challenge to Social Security: The Changing Roles of Women and Men in American Society*. 1982

Jeffrey G. Williamson and Peter H. Lindert, *American Inequality: A Macroeconomic History*. 1980

Robert H. Haveman and Kevin Hollenbeck, Editors, *Microeconomic Simulation Models for Public Policy Analysis, Volume 1: Distributional Impacts, Volume 2: Sectoral, Regional, and General Equilibrium Models*. 1980

Peter K. Eisinger, *The Politics of Displacement: Racial and Ethnic Transition in Three American Cities*. 1980

Erik Olin Wright, *Class Structure and Income Determination*. 1979

Joel F. Handler, *Social Movements and the Legal System: A Theory of Law Reform and Social Change*. 1979

Duane E. Leigh, *An Analysis of the Determinants of Occupational Upgrading*. 1978

Stanley H. Masters and Irwin Garfinkel, *Estimating the Labor Supply Effects of Income Maintenance Alternatives*. 1978

Irwin Garfinkel and Robert H. Haveman, with the assistance of David Betson, *Earnings Capacity, Poverty, and Inequality*. 1977

Harold W. Watts and Albert Rees, Editors, *The New Jersey Income— Maintenance Experiment, Volume III: Expenditures, Health, and Social Behavior; and the Quality of the Evidence*. 1977

Murray Edelman, *Political Language: Words That Succeed and Policies That Fail*. 1977

Marilyn Moon and Eugene Smolensky, Editors, *Improving Measures of Economic Well-Being*. 1977

Harold W. Watts and Albert Rees, Editors, *The New Jersey Income— Maintenance Experiment, Volume II: Labor-Supply Responses*. 1977

Marilyn Moon, *The Measurement of Economic Welfare: Its Application to the Aged Poor.* 1977

Morgan Reynolds and Eugene Smolensky, *Public Expenditures, Taxes, and the Distribution of Income: The United States, 1950, 1961, 1970.* 1977

Fredrick L. Golladay and Robert H. Haveman, with the assistance of Kevin Hollenbeck, *The Economic Impacts of Tax—Transfer Policy: Regional and Distributional Effects.* 1977

David Kershaw and Jerilyn Fair, *The New Jersey Income-Maintenance Experiment, Volume I: Operations, Surveys, and Administration.* 1976

Peter K. Eisinger, *Patterns of Interracial Politics: Conflict and Cooperation in the City.* 1976

Irene Lurie, Editor, *Integrating Income Maintenance Programs.* 1975

Stanley H. Masters, *Black—White Income Differentials: Empirical Studies and Policy Implications.* 1975

Larry L. Orr, *Income, Employment, and Urban Residential Location.* 1975

Joel F. Handler, *The Coercive Social Worker: British Lessons for American Social Services.* 1973

Glen G. Cain and Harold W. Watts, Editors, *Income Maintenance and Labor Supply: Econometric Studies.* 1973

Charles E. Metcalf, *An Econometric Model of Income Distribution.* 1972

Larry L. Orr, Robinson G. Hollister, and Myron J. Lefcowitz, Editors, with the assistance of Karen Hester, *Income Maintenance: Interdisciplinary Approaches to Research.* 1971

Robert J. Lampman, *Ends and Means of Reducing Income Poverty.* 1971

Joel F. Handler and Ellen Jane Hollingsworth, *"The Deserving Poor": A Study of Welfare Administration.* 1971

Murray Edelman, *Politics as Symbolic Action: Mass Arousal and Quiescence.* 1971

Frederick Williams, Editor, *Language and Poverty: Perspectives on a Theme.* 1970

Vernon L. Allen, Editor, *Psychological Factors in Poverty.* 1970